Digital Signifiers in an Architecture of Information

From Big Data and Simulation to Artificial Intelligence

Pablo Lorenzo-Eiroa

LONDON AND NEW YORK

Designed cover image: Museum of Babel; Research Studio ARCH
701B Prof. Pablo Lorenzo-Eiroa, Research Student: Salma Kattas,
MS ACT, SoAD, NYIT F2021

First published 2023
by Routledge
4 Park Square, Milton Park, Abingdon, Oxon OX14 4RN

and by Routledge
605 Third Avenue, New York, NY 10158

Routledge is an imprint of the Taylor & Francis Group, an informa business

© 2023 Pablo Lorenzo-Eiroa

The right of Pablo Lorenzo-Eiroa to be identified as author of this
work has been asserted in accordance with sections 77 and 78 of the
Copyright, Designs and Patents Act 1988.

All rights reserved. No part of this book may be reprinted or
reproduced or utilised in any form or by any electronic, mechanical,
or other means, now known or hereafter invented, including
photocopying and recording, or in any information storage or
retrieval system, without permission in writing from the publishers.

Trademark notice: Product or corporate names may be trademarks
or registered trademarks, and are used only for identification and
explanation without intent to infringe.

British Library Cataloguing-in-Publication Data
A catalogue record for this book is available from the British Library

ISBN: 978-1-032-27270-2 (hbk)
ISBN: 978-1-032-27268-9 (pbk)
ISBN: 978-1-003-29203-6 (ebk)

DOI: 10.4324/9781003292036

Typeset in Bembo
by codeMantra

Colophon

The author edited the grammar of this text in part with GPT-3, OpenAI's large-scale language-generation model. None of the text has been generated with ChatGPT unless quoted for research purposes. Upon generating draft language, the author reviewed, edited, and revised the language to their own liking and takes ultimate responsibility for the content of this publication.

to Asier (π) [Gian Lorenzo]-Eiroa

Contents

Preface		xi
Acknowledgments		xvii
	Introduction: Toward a Critical Multidimensional Artificial Intelligence: Displacing Bias in Data, Reference, Digital Signifiers, and Systems of Representation	1
1	Systems of Measurement Idealizing and Displacing Human Proportions	14
2	Brunelleschi's Parametric Analog Computational Interface: From a New Media Normalizing Visualization to Indexing, Displacing, and Innovating in Representation	20
3	Palladio's Parametric Undecidability as a Critical Topological Model	30
4	Borromini's Topological Model Displaced by Rainaldi's Ahistorical Synthesis: Architects Indexing, Displacing, and Innovating in Spatial Representation	41
5	Linguistic and Visual Semiotics signs as Signifiers Anticipating Authorship in Architecture	68
6	Computational Linguistic Semiotics: From Mathematics, to Computational Languages Grammar, to Machine Learning, to Signifieds in Natural Language Processing (NLP), to Emergent Programming	87

viii *Contents*

7 Computational Visual Semiotics: Grammatology Displacing Signals, Signs and Digital Signifiers From Pixels to Point Clouds and Particles Activating Emergent Programming — 140

8 Displacing Origination by Digital Signifiers from Computation to AI — 187

9 Expanding Dimensions in Spatial Reference and Representational Systems Toward a Multidimensional Architecture of Information: From Topology to Artificial Neural Networks, to Quantum Computing — 206

10 Computational Informational Semiotics: Signs and Signals in Machines to "Draw" and "Build" through Double Bind Adversarial Robotic Feedback Actualization — 235

11 Gaudi's Analog Computational Model as Parallel Processing: From Mathematical Modeling, to Big Data Survey, to Simulation, to AI — 259

12 AI Emergent Structure through Robotic Signals as Information Actualization — 276

13 AI Synthetic Environments as Simulation-Based Information Actualization — 299

14 Post-Human Project-Specific and Site-Specific Robotic System — 326

15 Deconstructing the City Through New Signifiers: Simulation-Based Emergent Space-Environments — 336

16 Big Data Politics in Emergent Space Environments: Rezoning New York City through Big Data, AI, and Simulation — 352

17 Thermodynamic Blockchain Environmental Engine: Toward Post-Capitalist Universal Space-Environments — 366

Contents ix

18 Big Data Realism and AI Abstraction: Post-Colonial
Emergent Histories in Augmented Synthetic Unreal
Environments   388

19 Big Data AI Simulacra Within a Representation Restricted
Reality (RRR): From Piranesi's Ahistoric Archeology, to
an Urbanism of Information, to a Quantum "AI" Simulacra   397

20 Conclusion: Expanding Authorship through an Ahistoric
Critical Architecture of Information AI   416

List of Figures   437
Index   461

Preface

This book takes sections through the history of representation in architecture to develop a theoretical framework for a critical Architecture of Information compatible with the Twenty-first century.

To activate a post-colonial, post-Anthropocene, we need to critique the systems of measurement, reference, representation, and validation that are naturalized in our society. Urbanism and architecture are not only referenced by cultural biases implicit in systems of representation such as software and robotics but also in other less evident biases on how data is gathered and validated. The hypothesis is that it is possible to work out means to critique and expand data and computation through media and information theory, analyzing and displacing them as systems of representation. We address the media determinism implicit in data and computational systems through computational linguistics and visual semiotics. We propose to critique the normalization of how software developers originate reference, representation, and systems of measurement in computation. We address the possibility of expanding an architecture of information from origination to destination: from the minimum BITS of information that are encoded and transmissible, to how we deal with computational dimensions, geometry, languages, signals, signs, symbols, and data.

The book traces specific sections through histories and theories of representation in architecture through a historiography of computation. The thesis inquires why architecture, once a pioneer in systems of representation, is currently forced by Fordism and simply applies innovation in technology. We understand the necessity to address decolonization of media and linguistic determination necessarily engaging with the causes of the current correlational crises, from cultural biases augmentation to environmental politics.

The book discusses Big Data survey, Artificial Neural Networks's parallel processing, and Machine Learning training recognizing statistically features in datasets activating Artificial Intelligence as emergent programming. We address a symbolic "Artificial Intelligence" AI revolution as information theory. The hypothesis is that it is possible to develop an architecture of information through critically mediating digital signal and signs.

This book is a retroactive manifesto. It is retroactive in expanding architecture history through surveys, identifying new theories based on forensics,

xii *Preface*

and expanding current datasets. It is a manifesto, as the book proposes, displacing and expanding computational linguistic and visual semiotic signs and signals that determine architecture possibilities. It proposes to cross relationships between a scientific evidence-based design and a cultural deconstruction, implementing critical thinking and creativity as means to displace biases. We approach this historical critical project by identifying a wide range of parallel genealogies that we correlate, approaching relationships through methodologies of art history, linguistics, architecture, mathematics, computation, ecology, archeology, statistics, and economics.

The typical conventional relationships between architecture and technology are analyzed and critiqued through different positions and methodologies, addressing possible means to overcome media determinism and technological determinism.

Methodologically, we take critical sections through history following Tafuri's history as a project.[1] We trace Wölfflin's pendulum between the Renaissance and Baroque[2] through Hegelian Dialectics,[3] critiquing reactionary forces applying Nietzsche's double negation. We address not only the revolution of the Renaissance but also its later Eurocentric Colonialism through the critique of determination of the Baroque, activating an emergent post-colonial architecture through the displacement of conventions in systems of representation understanding the necessity to do so through a post-capitalist, post-human, post-Anthropocene. We address some originary populations' alternative systems of representation, for instance, some notions of mathematics, computation and representation of Nature. We base our theory of media on McLuhan's media determinism[4] through Panofsky's deep structure[5] expanding on Cassirer's[6] Symbolic Forms and Carpo's media reproduction[7] through Fiedler.[8] We apply deep structure to study representation tracing relationships between analog and digital computational systems' signals and signs. For instance, we analyze Artificial Neural Networks' activation functions and weights as signal decimations attenuations for symbolic processing, but we critique excessive layering stacking, translation, and decimation.

We apply linguistic semiotics and visual semiotics that prescribe architecture, based on Peirce's theory of Signs[9] addressing Derrida's Grammatology[10] critique of De Saussure's linguistic equation Sign=signifier/Signified.[11] We review architecture as language in relation to the computational languages to trace linguistic and visual semiotics through Gandelsonas' Architectural Signifier[12] and Eisenman's unmotivation of the sign.[13] We trace a historiography of computation building up to "Artificial Intelligence" from Big Data and Simulation. We base our definitions of computation on Leibniz, from calculus situs as contingency computation, to his Characteristica Universalis to compute logical relationships between language, mathematics, and science. We center our approach to information theory on Wheeler and von Baeyer through Shannon's mathematical theory of communication and von Neumann's cybernetics. We trace artificial life and "Artificial Intelligence" through Ulam's and von Neumann Cellular Automation, Minsky neural nets feedback loop reinforcement,[14] and Wierner and Bateson's (double bind theory) feedback. We discuss a critical architecture of information beyond Negroponte's[15] "move bits not atoms", reformulating fabrication as building through information representation as physical signals actualization. While we address information theory, we also discuss the advantages and disadvantages of separating signals and signs for processing in the encryption and decryption of data into information disregarding translations between systems of measurement and reference at the interface, media, or medium. We develop topographies of information between visual semiotic interfaces activating site-based computation.

Finally, the range of issues presented in this book is understood in relation to the correlational paradigm of Big Data and parallel processing active through Artificial Neural Nets in contrast to isolated bifurcating knowledge silos. We aim at promoting correlational context-specific problem-specific emergence between the multiple issues identified as nodes that are carried through the book, aiming at activating multiple possible emergence convergence.

The publication is organized into five sections developed through chapters:

Introduction

Section I: Representation

Chapters 1–4: Sections through Histories and Theories of Representation, Systems of Measurement and Reference through antithesis between Brunelleschi-Palladio, and Borromini-Rainaldi; and architects innovating in systems of representation;

Section II: Semiotics

Chapters 5–8: Mathematical Semiotics; Computational Linguistic Semiotics, and Computational Visual Semiotics anticipating Authorship; Big Data and Simulation as Means to Activate AI Emergent Programming toward a Computational Grammatology;

Section III: Dimensionality

Chapters 9: Measurement, reference, and signs in systems of representation displaced by Topology, Information Theory, Artificial Neural Networks and Quantum Computing;

Section IV: Actualization

Chapters 10–14: AI Feedback through Robotic Signals and Emergent Robotic Fabrication Structural Forces; Building through information signal-sign representation;

xiv *Preface*

Section V: Simulation

Chapters 15–19: Simulation, and Simulacra through Big Data, Computational Fluid Dynamic Simulation, activating an AI BlockChain Environmental Engine;

Section VI: Conclusion

Chapter 20: AI Authorship, Ownership, Authority, Validation, and Ethics: From the death of the architect towards architectures of architectures through the e-Architects.

Often images are used to support a temporary linguistic argument or to validate a cultural aesthetic bias. We develop the book's writing based on explorations through incomplete open architecture experiments. Because of the publisher's structure, we limit to communicating our work not displacing relationships between the linguistic and visual semiotics in the frame-context of this book as we did in other projects.

This book is result of new research; research done as part of a PhD dissertation submitted in 2021 (2022 defense) "Computer Science Applied to Architecture: Multidimensional Architecture of Information: Expanding Systems of Representation and Computational Signifiers from Big Data, Simulation, and Robotics activating Artificial Intelligence"; and it is also a partial anthology of previously published texts.

Chapter 4: a partial earlier version of this text was published in Lorenzo-Eiroa, P. Rainaldi's Post-Historical Suspension: Anticipating Cartopological Space" in Pulsation in Pulsation in Architecture, ed. Goldemberg, E. Ross Publishing, 2011.

Chapter 5: this chapter is based on a revision of a text expanding it and providing further research and conclusions as well as insights from Lorenzo-Eiroa, P. "Form In:Form: On The Relationship Between Digital Signifiers and Formal Autonomy", in Architecture in Formation, ed. Pablo Lorenzo-Eiroa and Aaron Sprecher, Routledge/Taylor and Francis, London 2013.

Chapter 6: a partial version of the chapter in regards to NLP and the activation of emergent programming through Simulation (Structural and Computational Fluid Dynamic Simulation CFD) was submitted for blind Peer Review Process for ACADIA 2022: Lorenzo-Eiroa, P. "Activating Higher Programming Language and Self-Simulation Through Natural Language Processing (NLP)" ACADIA 2022 peer review process in July 2022 (not accepted due to late submission). A partial version of the chapter was published in Lorenzo-Eiroa, P. "Form In:Form: On The Relationship Between Digital Signifiers and Formal Autonomy", in Architecture in Formation, ed. Pablo Lorenzo-Eiroa and Aaron Sprecher, Routledge/Taylor and Francis, London 2013.

Chapter 8: A partial version of the chapter in regards to NLP and the activation of emergent programming through Simulation (Structural and Computational Fluid Dynamic Simulation CFD) was submitted for blind Peer

Review Process for ACADIA 2022: Lorenzo-Eiroa, P. "Activating Higher Programming Language and Self-Simulation Through Natural Language Processing (NLP)" ACADIA 2022 peer review process in July 2022 (not accepted due to late submission). A partial version of the chapter was published in Lorenzo-Eiroa, P. "Form In:Form: On The Relationship Between Digital Signifiers and Formal Autonomy", in Architecture in Formation, ed. Pablo Lorenzo-Eiroa and Aaron Sprecher, Routledge/Taylor and Francis, London 2013. Chapter 9: Some text and research in this chapter have been published in Lorenzo-Eiroa, P. "Post-Historical Suspension: A Redefinition of the Role of the Relative" in Pidgin Magazine, Fall & Winter 2014, Princeton School of Architecture, Princeton, NJ 2014.

Chapter 10: some of the text included in this chapter has been based on a reduced and here expanded version of the published text in Lorenzo-Eiroa, Pablo "Expanding Authorship in Materiality", in Info Matter, ed. Del Campo, M. and Biloira N., in Next Generation Building, 2012 and in spanish in Lorenzo-Eiroa, P. "La ampliación del concepto de autoría entre dibujo y construcción" en Detalles constructivos, 3 Mapa tecnológico inconcluso, ed. Medina, F. Revista PLOT, Buenos Aires, 2016.

Chapter 12: This chapter is based on research published and expanded, including new research, position, and projects from Lorenzo-Eiroa, P. "Post-Digital as Design Authorship in Informed Mater Processes" in ed. Ahrens, C. and Sprecher, A., Instabilities and Potentialities, Notes on the Nature of Knowledge in Digital Architecture, Routledge T&F, New York, 2019.

Chapter 13: This chapter text was partially published for a Venice Biennale's publication: del Signore, M. and Lorenzo-Eiroa, P. ed. Informed Interscalar Fluidity Listlab, Barcelona, 2023; a research project which was made possible by Dean Perbellini and NYIT SoAD Alumni and which includes edited texts contributions by Maria Perbellini, Anthony Caradonna, Giovanni Santamaria, Ila Berman, Cristina Goberna Pesudo, Branko Kolarevic, Alberto T. Estévez, Andrew Saunders Frederic Levrat, Sergio Elizondo, Marcella del Signore, and Pablo Lorenzo-Eiroa.

Chapter 14: Some research here included was published in: e-Architects' e-Chaise Longue through Site-Specific Robotic 3D printer, 2018 Venice Biennale (GAA/ECC). e-Architects, NY Design Principal, R/D: Pablo Lorenzo-Eiroa; Designers, R/D: Gabriel Munnich, Yaoyi Fan, Pablo Toubes-Rieger, Nelson Montas. Lorenzo-Eiroa, P. "Form Follows Information: Project and Site-Specific Machinic Construction System", in ed. Muntañola Thornberg, 17th Conference Arquitectonics, Mind, Land and Society, J. UPC, Barcelona, 2019; Lorenzo-Eiroa, P. "Arquitectura de la información", in ed. Najle, C., Superdigitalismos, Revista Notas, CPAU, Buenos Aires, 2020.

Chapter 15: This chapter includes research done in the late 1990s with reports by geological engineers for an ecological park in Buenos Aires and placed in relation to reports by the international commission for a bridge connecting Buenos Aires (Argentina) and Colonia (Uruguay) prepared for

xvi *Preface*

the World Bank, which we took further into understanding the potential relationship between architecture, urbanism, and environmental processes. Some research included has been published in Lorenzo-Eiroa, P., "Ecoinduction" in Kallipoliti, L. and Pla Catala, A. "Ecoredux 02: Design Manuals for a Dying Planet" Disseny Hub Barcelona, 2011.

Chapter 16: Some research and text included in this chapter have been published in Lorenzo-Eiroa, P., "Rezoning New York City through Big Data" in Chapter 13, Data and Politics of Information, ed. Karandinou, A. in Data, Architecture and The Experience of Place, Routledge, London 2019, (Pages 210–31). This chapter includes expansion in the evidence of the research presented including further expanded work and revised edited text.

Chapter 17: A previous version of this article has been published in Lorenzo-Eiroa, P. "Space-Environment Commons: From Big Data Survey to AI, to a Post-capitalist Blockchain Zoning Platform", in ed. Carta, M.; Perbellini, M.; Lara-Hernandez, J.A. Resilient Communities and the Peccioli Charter: Toward the Possibility of an Italian Charter for Resilient Communities, Springer, Switzerland, AG 2022.

Chapter 20: Some ideas, concepts, and text are based on the publication Lorenzo-Eiroa, P. "Post-Digital as Design Authorship Expansion, Review of Lynn's "Archeology of the Digital" exhibition at Yale School of Architecture" ed. Rapaport, N. Constructs, Yale School of Architecture, 2017.

Notes

1 Tafuri, M. "'The Wicked Architect': G.B. Piranesi, Heterotopia, and the Voyage" in ed. Tafuri, M., *The Sphere and the Labyrinth*, MIT Press, Cambridge, 1978
2 Wölfflin, H. *Renaissance and Baroque*, Cornell U. Press, New York, 1964 [orig. 1888]
3 Hegel. *Hegel: Introductory Lectures on Aesthetics*, Penguin Books, New York, 1993 [orig 1835]
4 McLuhan, M. *Understanding Media*, The extensions of Man, Mentor, New York, 1964
5 Panofsky, E. *Perspective as Symbolic Form*, Zone Books, 1995. Orig. 1927
6 Cassirer, E. *The Philosophy of Symbolic Forms: Language*, 1923
7 Carpo, M. *Architecture in the Age of Printing*, MIT Press, Cambridge, 2001
8 Fiedler, C. *On Judging Works of Visual Art*, University of California Press, Los Angeles, 1949
9 Peirce, C.S. *The Essential Peirce, Selected Philosophical Writings, Volume 1* eds Houser, N; Kloesel, C., Indiana University Press, 1992 [orig. 1867–93]
10 Derrida, J. *Of Grammatology*, Johns Hopkins University Press, London, 1976.
11 De Saussure, F. "Course in General Linguistics" trans. Harris, R. Open Court. Chicago, 1986 [orig. 1916]
12 Gandelsonas, M. "The Architectural Signifier," paper presented at the First Congress of the International Association of Semiotic Studies, Milan, 1974
13 Eisenman, P. "The Diagram and the Becoming Unmotivated of the Sign" In *Diagram Diaries*, Universe Publishing, United Kingdom, 1999
14 Minsky, M.A Framework for Representing Knowledge, MIT-AI Laboratory Memo 306, 1974.
15 Negroponte, N. *Being Digital*, Alfred Konofp, 1995

Acknowledgments

This book is an anthology of work possible through twenty years of research, teaching, and experimental practice; which would not have been possible without the influence of many people.

We thank Doctorate Thesis Director Dr. Alberto T. Estévez and Dr. Alexis Meier with whom we shared insights on Biodigital Architecture and linguistics; as well as the Defense Tribunal Chaired by Dr. Alicia Imperiale, with Dr. Felecia Davis; and Secretary Dr. Marcelo Narvaez for their feedback. At the New York Institute of Technology, President Hank Foley, Provost Junius Gonzales, our School Dean Maria Perbellini, Associate Dean Anthony Caradonna, and Chair Giovanni Santamaria. Dean Perbellini's vision was integrated into codeveloping, with Tom Verebes and myself, a new MS in Architecture Computational Technologies (MS.ACT) Program which I directed since 2018 developing its structure and syllabi; and since 2022 I am directing and developing an AI Lab. Thanks to my peer Directors Marcella Del Signore, David Diamond, Gertrudis Brens, Rozina Vavetsi, Christian Pongratz, Charles Matz, and Professors Naomi Frangos, Matthias Altwicker, Nader Vossoughian, Robert Cody, Matthew Ford, and my colleagues and staff Staci Kirschner, Kesia Persaud, Susan Stenberg, and all. Fab Lab including Director Dustin White, Marie-Odile Baretsky, and technicians. The Cooper Union where I did research and taught from 2004 to 2018 thanks to Dean Anthony Vidler, mentors Prof. Diana Agrest, and Guido Zuliani; colleagues Lebbeus Woods, Ric Scofidio, Diane Lewis, and Kevin Bone; Assistant Professors Jana Leo de Blass, Lidia Kallipoliti, Hayley Heber, Jennifer Lee, James Lowder, Michael Young; and Instructors Katerina Kourkuola and Will Shapiro. My dearest research assistants Salma Kattass, Yousef Ismail, Farah Jalil, Kavya Sista, Beken Amde, and Trushita Yadav, Teaching Assistants and former students Fengqi Frank Li, Shantanu Bhalla; Gabriel Munnich, Yaoyi Fan, Pablo Toubes (DesignWithFrank); former students Luo Xuan, Jimmy Pan, Jemuel Joseph and Alexis Rivas (Cover. Inc); and the more than +2000 at UIC, NYIT, Cooper, UBA, and institutions since 1998. To the support of UPenn Director Richard Wesley and Prof. Andrew Saunders; at Pratt Institute Michael Wen Sen Su and Fred Levrat. Clorindo Testa, director of the National Endowments for the Arts and Fulbright Commission which

xviii *Acknowledgments*

with support from Princeton University gave me the opportunity to study (2001–02/2003–04) with Dean Mario Gandelsonas, Stan Allen; and Prof. Peter Eisenman, Hal Foster, Beatriz Colomina, George Legendre, Georges Teyssot, Alessandra Ponte, Jesse Reiser, Liz Diller, and others. At the FADU UBA thanks to the mentorship of Dean Ciro Najle (Di Tella), and also I would thank Prof. Dudy Libedinsky, Roberto Lombardi, Justo Solsona, Sergio Forster, Daniel Ventura, and Arturo Montagu, founder of SIGRADI. I learned a lot from my dearest colleagues Maria Cohen, Erica Noval, Alexis Rochas, Santiago Pages, Carla Capparelli, Sergio Bogani, and Tomas Saraceno. Thanks also for a visionary early training through multiple computational languages at the Colegio San Patricio directed by Lucia de Blanco, Marta Luna, and then Mariana Dupont in mathematics and her husband Ruben Calabuig, in computation (Logo 1983, Pascal 1987, Basic 1987, C 1989), flow diagrams problems and ANN concepts (1989).

On a personal note, I would like to especially thank my partner in life Meredith Bostwick, for the continuous support and my son Asier for his inspiration. Special thanks to my influential friends Ashraf Abdalla, Gaspar Libedinsky, Leandro De Brasi, and Carlos Gomez Avendaño; and also to my mother Emma Delisio, an intellectual with whom we discuss cognition and interdisciplinary systemic psychology; she studied systemic psychology with professors trained at Palo Alto Institute with Gregory Bateson (double bind theory of schizophrenia, a principle of adversarial training) applying Artificial Neural Networks cybernetics feedback to social sciences based on thermoregulatory processes since 1974. Emma had to give up some of her early public service careers due to military prosecution after many colleagues disappeared. To my father Eduardo a pragmatic who studied roman law and gave us all we needed. To my grandmother Teté Eiroa a feminist independent artist that never sold a work of art out of conviction even while struggling; to my influential aunt Susana Mántica a talented artist, feminist and a FADU-UBA Design Professor who always supported my education and career especially in times of crisis; my grandfather Serafin who emigrated from Spain after political turmoil, a clockmaker interested in complex analog mechanisms, and my uncle Enrique who did advancement in computation. Also thanks to my new family members Lana, Randy, and Melanie Bostwick, and always to Papap.

To all many thanks!

Introduction

Toward a Critical Multidimensional Artificial Intelligence: Displacing Bias in Data, Reference, Digital Signifiers, and Systems of Representation

Toward A Critical Architecture of Information as an AI Environmental Framework

How can we project an architecture theory in relation to the twenty-first century? How does information theory relate to an architecture of information? What are the utopian computational ideas and concepts that are being left behind due to economic speculation and inequality? What is the relationship between systems of representation and architecture? How can we trace a history of computation relevant to architecture culture to project a future critical of just another temporal technological actualization? What are the relationships between computation and the environment that need to be advanced? What are the paradigm changes and consequences of Big Data? What are the transformative Machine Learning "Artificial Intelligence" (AI) structures relevant to architecture? What is the future of a new type of infinity due to an increasing augmented reality as an informational environment?

These questions may raise other questions, and the objective of this book is to critique what we think we know about the past to dislodge what may be possible as an inclusive future. Through unlocking a present condition we aim at expanding both past and future backward and forward activating a retroactive manifesto as a critical architecture of information. The book aims at presenting a theoretical framework based on historic forensic evidence for a relevant critical architecture of information, expanding relationships between technology and culture. We trace history addressing how computational structures and data structures project cultural biases to be able to augment possible future emergence. We discuss strategies to overcome technological and media determination in relation to systems of representation, understanding systems of reference, measurement, and representation as anticipatory structures that project colonialism. The book addresses the current correlational crises that relate to architecture and urbanism, from the social, to the economic, to the environmental crises based on implicit cultural bias in computation.

Architecture has been historically structured by systems of representation. We trace an architecture of information only possible through certain systems of

DOI: 10.4324/9781003292036-1

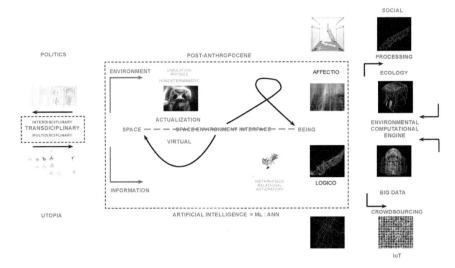

Figure 0.1 Framework for a critical architecture of information.

representation and technology to compare its relative cultural contribution to the advancement of computational systems that are relevant to science (Figure 0.1).

We discuss the possibility of an architecture of information integrating scientific advances for synthetic and ecological environmental life and intelligence. Scientific advances on the boundaries of physics and mathematics should be paradigmatic to project an architecture theory for the twenty-first century since the accessing, reading, and understanding of reality is no longer based on visible sensible experience but a means to address reality beyond human senses and interests, challenging anthropomorphic reference. We develop two historically sequential interrelated paths to dislodge clues in the emergence of Artificial Intelligence: Big Data and Simulation. Big Data outbalances anticipatory theory, as large amounts of data as statistical evidence are used to make predictions functional to Machine Learning (ML), metaphoric in the term "Artificial Intelligence" or AI. To activate statistical prediction we need data, tons of data and information, through datasets, data repositories, and other means to activate ML models able to train Artificial Neural Networks (ANN). In addition, we discuss the relevance of simulation, in multiple ways, since we argue that the beginnings of AI are based on automation through nondeterministic nonreversible simulation. We challenge the current positivism of AI, but we also address emergent programming which could lead to robotic sentinels as we argue are closer than what most may think proposing alternative definitions of intelligence in relation to information theory.

The book aims at discussing and questioning from origination to destination how architecture can propose means to address shifts in science and technology in relation to architectural spatial representation, including emergent space environments. Computation has established new representational paradigms in architecture comparable to the revolution of perspective in the Renaissance, a phase recently advanced by AI. Today architecture possibilities are framed by data and the combinatory possibilities of a range of different neural net frameworks. We argue that architects have been having limited authorship and influence in the last digital revolutions and the current revolution by AI that is transforming systems of representation that they work with every day. This is because, while architects have been applying computation, they have little involvement in the technology and science they implement. Both the Renaissance and the Modern Movement understood that innovation at the media and technological construction level was not only important but also necessary to activate any paradigm of truth. While the architecture of the Renaissance and the Modern Movement was possible through activating a technological and media determinism, the proceeding reacting generations such as the Baroque and the post-structuralism after the Second World War critiqued such determination.

Overall, we are interested in means to activate a critical computational theory relative to architecture, able to displace determinism in architecture through displacing determinism at a computational programming level. We therefore review, critique and expand several relationships between architecture and representation through computation: between computational linguistic semiotics and computational visual semiotics; data and information; data and modeling; deterministic algorithms and nondeterministic computation; Big Data and Artificial Neural Networks; anticipatory software and emergent programming; digital fabrication and informed emergent robotic fabrication. We trace issues of representation relative to computation from how we measure space to how we project meaning to Nature understanding environmental processes.

Sections Through Histories and Theories of Representation in Architecture

We can identify two ideological lineages in architecture related to representation, one based on a stylistic cultural determination, and the other based on a technological determination as we aim to critique such dialectic through computation.

We introduce the book by discussing human proportions from ancient Egypt, deconstructing cultural biases in architecture relative to the body; to a post-human reference system in the architecture of information. We discuss how systems of representation project a visual semiotic Eurocentric colonization of space structuring how we perceive the world but also how they determine architecture organization: from a Renaissance perspective as a visual system of representation based on Brunelleschi, to Palladio's critique of its illusionistic effect, to displacing perspective as a system of representation through various means such as Pozzo's anamorphosis, to proposing a multidimensional architecture of information.

4   *Introduction*

We also trace sections in transformative influential advancements in representation identifying media and technological determinism: from the role of the mechanistic axonometric in defining an autonomous object-space based on machine descriptions during the Industrial Revolution; to real-time information flows; to virtual and augmented reality as synthetic environments. Critiquing dimensional reference systems in architecture can help deconstruct an implicit colonial Eurocentric Cartesian Coordinate Space that negates topography, topology, and the environment expanding possible means to address a multidimensional architecture of information.

Topology and multidimensional information systems have been addressed across architecture history. The ambiguity between positive and negative space in ancient Egypt resulted in an innovation in a spatial typology derived from the possibilities of the trilithic stone structure; Bramante's plans for San Peter created ambiguity between positive and negative space figuration and influenced Borromini's spatial pulsation. Continuity between positive and negative space activated relationships between inside and outside in architecture. Surface topology can activate in architecture a contemporary functional poché space creating continuity between positive and negative space. We expand a topological multidimensional space to engage with the environment. We analyze and expand dimensional systems which reference architecture space, from Cartesian reference to systems of measurement to datasets, and meta-data repositories through topology, computational fluid dynamic simulation, Machine Learning, and parallel processing in Artificial Neural Networks.

We frame computation in terms of the transition between analog and digital computational systems of representation in architecture: we trace the Eurocentric origins of parametric design from perspective to parametric systems in classic Greek and Roman anthropocentric-based architecture proportions; from Alberti innovating in self-referential proportional systems based on mathematical ratios; to Palladio developing an internal mathematical code as a proportional system through arithmetic. Leibniz's use of algebra in surfaces can also be considered a type of computation; as well as Gaudi's analog catenary models for calculating the structure of his buildings. Russian Constructivism's techne informed a Modern Movement of technological determinism. Le Corbusier and Mies' technological determinism propose an abstract space based on reinforced concrete continuity and plasticity contrasted with a space articulated through industrialized steel syntax. Hejduk and Eisenman led revolutions in thinking architecture genesis through representation against technological determinism identifying and critiquing a media determinism. Gehry and Hadid worked through representation to push boundaries in construction through fabrication revolutionizing the discipline aesthetically and technically.

We also trace transformations in the practice of the discipline. Architecture expanded from indexing capitalism to indexing capitalism through media determinism. The Neoliberal model of the 1980s transformed the city into

Introduction   5

a form of business from architects' and urbanists' intentions determined by developers, to architects theoretically validating capitalism's accidental outputs. We can also trace how the discipline itself was also transformed due to power, representation, and economic systems: from known figures in ancient history; to unknown collective authors of the Gothic; to the genius promoted by Maecenas in the Renaissance; to Star architects resisting or being functional to governments or private media speculation in the twentieth century; to placing systems representation and economic systems as the architect, from Capitalism as the architect; to computation as architecture understanding it as the author. The media-based Star architect as a capitalist power system has been displaced by a multiplicity and diversity of artists and architects partially given by the utopian diversifying project of the internet of the 1970s, collaborative databases, repositories, scientific papers, and research, and also the emancipating aspect of computational AI frameworks applications and software development. But the environmental crises are demanding a radical reformulation of architecture and urbanism developmentalism.

Architecture has referenced Nature through various ideologies. The diverse pre-colonial means to address architecture culturally and economically in relation to the environment were oppressed by Eurocentric colonial measurement of the territory for cultural, geopolitical, and economic appropriation, exploitation, and extraction. But today we measure our relationship to the environment in relation to sustaining an economic system that benefits the top 1% of our society. The relationship between architecture and Nature can be traced following how the relationship between a building and the ground has evolved: from placing autonomous buildings in relation to a topo-logos such as the Greek Acropolis; to Roman military-based imperialist networked urbanism; to the Modern Movement separating the building from the ground to maximize density and minimize the human footprint in Nature; to the post-structuralist architecture interrelating buildings with the ground surface; to possible strategies based on zoning and building regulations indexing the environment. Many pre-colonial civilizations in America and elsewhere had developed a circular economy redescribing the architecture as topography, such as the Inca's Machu Pichu. The work of Noguchi and Smithson critiqued the Modern tabula rasa activating a site-specificity by measuring landscapes through site-specific interventions. But our relationship to Nature must be deconstructed both from western linguistic and western visual semiotics implicit in computation determining architecture and urbanism.

The Architecture of Computation: From Analog to Digital Simulation, Big Data, and AI Frameworks

While architecture was influenced by advancement in computation, computational theory was not much advanced by architecture other than computational visual semiotics through systems of representation. Innovation in visual semiotics in computation was mainly done not by architects, except by

6   *Introduction*

some more recent exceptions in software tools, visual algorithms, and frameworks applying computation to architecture but not the other way around.

Computation as a universal system of communication, thinking, and computability, can be traced back to the beginnings of the formulation of algorithms implementing recursive arithmetic through algebra as early as their use by the Babylonians around 2,500 BCE. The philosophy of computation can be traced in relation to technological progress identifying colonial and cultural biases. One of the most important paradigmatic novelties in technology that affected any field was the shift from *analog* to *mechanical* and now to electronic and *digital*. Early analog calculators and computers can be found in the Greek Antikythera of 200 BCE or the Pascaline calculator of 1649; the 1725 mechanical looming machine inspired Ada Lovelace to devise the first computer program in 1840.[1]

Shannon's mathematical theory of communication[2] of 1948 applies Boolean algebra to telephone switching circuits, developing the first automated digital circuit and the beginning of the electronic communication age, opening a series of fast revolutionary technological innovations such as computer architecture. While Shannon's communication theory calculated a noise in the channel, the Twentieth-century revolution in computation is based on the digital electronic signal, in which the physical mechanism has no influence on the computation of the output result. Artificial life can be traced back before computation to the development of analog machines known as automata. In the 1940s the computational mathematical concept of Cellular Automata from crystals and self-replication is developed. By 1959 the Artificial Intelligence Project[3] at MIT was founded based on advancements in theories of computability. The digital transition in projective and descriptive geometry shifted from entering numeric values to compute geometry, trajectories, and matrices (1940–60), to entering numeric values and processing through assembly language (1940s). Digital visual semiotic computation started with parametric systems of representation such as plot matrices and dynamic perspective: from working with scripts (1940–50); to working with computer languages (1945); to activating computational visual semiotics problems such as the Sketchpad (1963) or Hypercube 4D animation of 1965. The Computer Graphics Book[4] of 1975 represents mathematical equations using CAD. Toward the 1980s, architects started relying on computer-aided design, making drawings progressively more structured by parameters and tools and displacing the logic of architectural space through computer representation. By the 1990s Virtual Reality becomes a realm and a new medium for new possibilities beyond representation, through simulation.[5]

Several computational systems with relevance to contemporary architecture are analyzed and critiqued throughout the book: from Computer-Aided Design (1960s–today); to software modeling systems (1980s–2000); to computer visual algorithms (1990s–2004–today). We approach contemporary Data Science and Computer Science in architecture and urbanism from the architecture of systems in an informed reality through computational design

(2004–today); to working architecture through Big Data (2007–today); to working with Machine Learning through parallel processing (the 1960s; functional 2009–today); to working with Generative Adversarial Networks (2014–today); to Graph Neural Networks and Convolutional Neural Networks; to Diffusion Models (2021–today). The architecture of information is possible by the function of mediating information flows real time (1970s–today) and incorporating the architecture of environments shifting representation from geometry modeling to simulation-optimization (the 1990s–today). The more structural advancement in recovering the earlier notions of Artificial Intelligence through ANN happened around 2007–13 focusing first on a metalinguistic approach, by training algorithms to edit themselves, but thanks to a massive amount of data, Big Data, the first available at a considerable scale thanks to cellular phones and the internet, activating emergent programming (2013–17–today).

We trace how Nature has been described, analyzed, and projected through computation: from von Neumann weather forecasting ENIAC machine of 1940; to the abstract evolutionary computation of Cellular Automation simulation addressing characteristics of the environment such as thermodynamics, emergence, and irreversibility. We explore means to redefine alternatives to architecture developmentalism through survey, augmentation, multidimensional parallel computation, and informed fabrication in syncopation with an environmental engine activating space environments.

Critical Nondeterministic AI Architecture of Information

Information theory is based on current scientific research that equals information to energy and matter since the information has indeed a physical impact on our universe. We have been working on defining architecture of information since the 1990s, and direct definitions include references to an "Architecture of Information" of 1976[6] and later the book *The Architecture of Information of 2011*[7] which refers to a different conceptual aspect of information we base on, not much as information as architecture, hinting after the architecture of systems. The "Architecture of Information" of 1976 refers to a two-way process, of collecting and communicating information, through interfaces and communication, as it is understood by technological positivism, but without addressing our referenced media determinism, there is a problem that tends to idealize functionalism, promoting biases.

We attempt at problematizing both, reality through representation and knowledge through Big data in Artificial Neural Networks, activating a critical architecture of information[8] displacing anticipatory digital signifiers through a problematizing historiography of computation and architecture.[9] We discuss AI over the last decades through a particular scope and critical sequence: first through Big Data, then simulation, and then self-editing deep learning meta-algorithms. Knowledge and disciplines are being challenged at an ontological level since data outweighs theory models. We explore a theory

8 *Introduction*

of semiotics in relation to architecture and computation based on linguistic and visual semiotics problematizing implicit neocolonialism in architecture data and computation. Data Science and Computer Science became cognitive plateaus common to all forms of knowledge. But the difference is that this time we have the capacity to address critically media determinism to bypass the anticipatory conventional cultural biases implicit in computational media interfaces through computational languages and visual software, from computational languages that through grammar project cultural bias, to the digital signs that conventionally anticipate and structure architecture notation. Urbanism of information based on Big Data and AI frameworks is now mediating and optimizing information flows resulting in administrating behaviors, which also problematically indexes private capitalist agendas.

We discuss alternative means to critique computational media determination in architecture, from displacing computational linguistic and visual semiotics signs becoming signifiers, displacing systems of reference and representation, from understanding geometric modeling as anticipatory-deterministic to proposing simulation and site-based computation as a means to critique such determination. We also discuss means to displace signs and signals in robotic systems for fabrication. We also propose Artificial Neural Networks as parallel computational processing structures able to activate critical correlations through multiple interfaces and topographies of information critiquing top-down linear reversible algorithms usually functional to activating determinism in computation. We also explore how to expand computational intelligence to an environmental global engine activating through simulation a site-based, site-specific computational engine. We discuss a variety of linguistic and visual semiotic signs, from architectural, technological, computational, mathematical and robotic, to environmental, to informational.

Today through Big Data, light detection and ranging (LiDAR) remote sensing, datasets, the Internet of Things (IoT), and Application Processing Interface (API), we are activating a new form of realism based on indexing reality through multiple forms of survey. We explore Big Data through survey and simulation, activating automata theory through first Cellular Automation (CA), then Swarm Intelligence (SI), and activating Agent-Based Modeling (ABM). But we explore the main shift which emerged in the last decade by disclosing the anticipatory bias of software, transitioning into non-deterministic emergent programming.

We are currently going through a Fourth Industrial Revolution, within a Capitalism of disruptive Technology. Schumpeter[10] describes what works of Capitalism in terms of relentless old-new replacement through innovation are "creative destruction". We discuss across the book how technology has been replacing culture through disruption at the fastest rate. The status quo is supposed to be displaced by an emergent class[11] "who revolutionize the instruments of production" but because of Capitalism's tendency to monopolies designed to eliminate artificially a market economy through investment speculation, the consequence is that few companies end up controlling innovation homogenizing reality top-down, activating cultural communism disguised by a false illusion of choice designed to optimize loops between mass standardization and fashionable consumerism.[12] Entrepreneurship is one of the advantages of Capitalism promoting social mobility, but the manipulations and distortions that the same system produces also cap such possibility.

Neocolonialism and Cultural Appropriation through an AI Digital Feudalism[13]

We discuss authorship, ownership, validation, and authority in relation to ethics throughout the book: from how datasets are created to how systems of representation anticipate and project meaning, to how information systems structure reality. While architecture has been critiqued for its lack of engagement with social, political, and environmental challenges, we think architecture can address politics if it engages with deep linguistic and visual semiotic structures.

Derrida deconstructs implicit power in western languages. Derrida, brought a post-colonial critique to Eurocentric linguistics, as he was originally from Algiers, a region colonialized by the French. Derrida's post-colonialism is framed by the student revolution of 1968, a radical reformulation and critique of power triggered by the oil spills and against an oil-centered economy supported by the military complex, demanding the need for a new bottom-up democratic representation against oppressive structures. Derrida critiques Claude Lévi-Strauss' analysis of non-Western pre-colonial civilizations such as the Nambikwara myth communicated generationally through speech and their lack of writing, projecting logocentrism and ethnocentrism disguised as anti-ethnocentrism.[14] Today, we are back discussing the same issues perhaps due to the Neoliberal dismissal of cultural criticism functional to a technocratic society. Chomsky's linguistics presents a scientific approach to language in relation to its imperialist power structure. Derrida critiques how signs in language promote "signifiers". Deleuze identifies the Rhizome as an alternative network to the hierarchical regimes of signs in language. Post-colonialism feedback is now at the center as transculturation through immigration pressuring a white patriarchal Christian Europe afraid of losing its identity after centuries of colonizing and imposing culture on others. Currently still a neocolonialism is implicit through a Capitalism of monopoly-plutocracy, supported by the military complex, conditional aid, economic dependency leading to exploitation and racism, oppression leading to incarceration, institutionalization of art, Neoliberal service-oriented education, intellectual academicism and universal cultural media machines that make impossible cultural-economic emancipation or the impossibility of re-pre(sen/sion)tation to develop a local bottom-up message. Computation is currently part of this neocolonialism, unless we are able to recover, displace and propose new critical socio-political projects.

We must also avoid cultural appropriation through cultural neocolonialism which may become active through research, language, and projecting

10   *Introduction*

power structures over the emergent cultural agendas that may now be raising. We cannot repeat what was done before through the homogenizing imperial unification of knowledge-language through the Encyclopedia, and the role of Museums containing and validating global cultural production through contemporary Capitalism which promotes patriarchy. Our research could both enable possible ways to express repressed cultural projects but could also act problematically as a form of validation by incorporation of such projects, therefore an unintended form of cultural colonization to validate our vision and understanding of the world. While we must support cultural decolonization, we must resist as Derrida points out projecting how such cultural deconstruction and decolonization should happen as well as regulating the instruments of measurement and representation that enable them, to allow for other systems of representation to be recovered as well as their projects continued by the populations that can culturally understand them from their linguistic and semiotic realities, avoiding translation by language or imposition of the instruments of measurement that may project meaning and ideology. We cannot simply recover the original population's cultural heritage as a solution to the colonization projected by Western civilization; we must deconstruct as Derrida proposes Western civilization's cultural apparatus through, for instance, linguistic and visual semiotics implicit in computation in order not to repeat by other means of a new form of colonization. Alternative cultures should develop and own their means of production of culture, to both deal with their past, recover it as well as critique it in their own terms addressing their own culture and biases. We therefore need to give room to new forms of research such as transdisciplinary archeologists, linguistics, semioticians, surveyors, and architects to do their work independently from our self-critical consideration that may project problematic structures to do research by collecting information and simultaneously homogenizing it through an apparent post-Colonization that would in fact enact a Second Colonization through capitalism and computation.

We activate politics in architecture by displacing computational linguistics and visual semiotics: from the naturalization of architecture indexing a type of body; to information actualization activating post-human robotic systems; to exploring alternative means to address and represent the environment. We discuss alternative pre-colonial systems of representation in relation to Nature, with the aim of deconstructing Western systems of representation implicit in computation with relevance to architecture. While architects apply Data Science and Computer Science, they project implicit representational conventions in visualization methods, mapping interfaces, and systems of representation that because they are developed from outside the cultural revolutions that are transforming transdisciplinary knowledge, they innocently or not project a colonial patriarchic power structure. Likewise, artists, architects, and designers who separate means from concepts, dealing for instance with social and political issues by visualizing, mapping, and developing conventional representational responses to them through a media determinism, while aiming to do good, they normalize representation, aesthetics, and signs projecting the political power they aim to oppose.

A current emergent cultural and technological revolution resides in being able to disclose and open the repressed histories and theories of humanity caped by colonization. We aim at dislodging a post-Capitalist, post-Colonial, post-Media deterministic, post-Human commons: from an economic system in conflict of interest with the environment; to the deconstruction of normalized systems of representation colonizing and structuring space. If we continue to address post-colonialism from outside the visual semiotics in computation that anticipates architecture, we will be addressing it through linguistics but not through media specificity. Consequently, media and mediums will end up activating functionalism that will be feedback as cultural bias.

There have been several paradigm changes in our society, from the pluralism of the internet to a diversity of a fragmented reality through a diversified crowd intelligence, to personal media outlets which following the utopic promises of the internet challenge power structures centralized authority, singularity, authorship, origination, and determination. This fragmentation challenges Eurocentrism's historical cultural homogenizing power in tension with the US model of technological innovation to promote Capitalism. But the utopian computation and networking intercommunication ideas of the 1940s–70s are being absorbed by the functionalism of a market economy based on monopoly speculation functional to a global geopolitical power.

We now have a Digital Feudalism of security gates, and such mass-media monopoly is now even necessary for security since AI boots fight other intrusive AI automated boots that can compromise our computers, validating corporate power. Digital Feudalism enforces a top-down society in which personal opt-out from data mining and its consequential manipulative tracking feed is forcibly restricted and economically human inviable, turning humans into surrogates unless constant troublesome such as Virtual Private Network (VPN) and other means,[15] manipulating behavior by triggering emotional responses through informational advertisement. In systemic theory, an assigned role in a group is independent of the subject's will, and if one does not understand their role, one is probably on their way to becoming a product.

Fabretti asserts Heidegger's[16] claims that the problem is understanding technology as a means through instrumentality as anticipatory in modern times. Fabretti also refers to the theory of technology by Habermas[17] through Stiegler's Techniques and Time[18] in contrast with Heidegger. Fabretti identifies the mentioned technocracy as a force of de-politicization in contemporary society, as technical and scientific measurement provides validation. Althusser[19] refers to the ideology implicit in the projected apparatus of the state which can currently be related in substitution within a plutocracy with the current social media monopolies, as platforms and interfaces regulate social relationships. Chun addresses mass media in relation to the internet, identifying the politics of control and defining society through technology.[20] Sassen[21] also addresses the current problem of scientific and technical research

12 *Introduction*

based on knowledge silos avoiding cultural critique which in the context of this book is the reason why "AI" augments cultural biases. In the "Essence of Technology" through Heidegger, and Sven-Olov Wallenstein,[22] Sassen discusses the origin of the work of art, in relation to the word techne (Greek), and in questioning technology one questions art as well. "Technology is just a tool, is neither good nor bad; nor it is neutral",[23] implies the separation between technology and culture. We understand AI not as a technology, not as software, but as a complex multidimensional socio-political-economic architectural framework. We discuss through the book the means to activate decolonization of the emergent Digital Feudalism through deconstructing data and computational structures.

Crawford[24] denounces that AI is everywhere, from thousands of data profiling parameters gathered and related to actual facial expressions, and wonders about the ethics of automated decision-making and their accountability. ImageNET tagging one of the most often used dataset-pretrained ML uses linguistic tagging categories for classifying images promoting bias. From deep fake to bypassing surveillance, AI human tracking and face recognition have been presenting boundaries in AI ethics. Buolamwini identifies that independently from security issues, there are known biases in how AI is trained, but less known are the biases in the lack of certain types of data.[25] AI is based on predictive models based on statistics, as they enhance a form of profiling through recursive means the biases become exponential. Through identifying data as a destination, Buolamwini expands into an epistemology that confirms that we reflect the world as we see it.

Notes

1 Lovelace, A.; Menabrea, L. "Sketch of the Analytical Engine invented by Charles Babbage, Esq.", in *Scientific Memoirs*, Richard Taylor, vol. 3 1854 [over transl. Menabrea, L. F. "Notions sur la machine analytique de M. Charles Babbage", Bibliothèque Universelle de Genève, No. 41, 1842]

2 Shannon, C.E. "A Mathematical Theory of Communication", in *Bell System Technical Journal*, Volume 27, Issue 3, 1948

3 Minsky, M. *A Framework for Representing Knowledge*, MIT-AI Laboratory Memo 306, 1974.

4 Prueitt, M. *Computer Graphics: 118* Computer Generated Designs, Dover, 1975

5 Maldonado, T. *Lo Real y Lo Virtual*, GEDISA, Spain, 1995

6 Wurman, S. "An American City: The Architecture of Information", convention brochure, Washington, DC: AIA, 1976 in Wright Steenson, M. *Artificial Intelligence, How Designers and Architects Created the Digital Landscape*, MIT Press, 2017

7 Dade-Robertson, M. *The Architecture of Information: Architecture, Interaction Design and the Patterning of Digital Information*, Routledge, New York, 2011

8 Lorenzo-Eiroa, P. "Form:In:Form: On the Relationship Between Digital Signifiers and Formal Autonomy", in ed. Lorenzo-Eiroa, P. and Sprecher, A., *Architecture In: Formation*, Routledge, London, 2013

9 Lorenzo-Eiroa, P. "Multidimensional Space: From Perspective to Big Data", in ed. Marcos, C., *Graphic Imprints EGA 2018*, Springer International Publishing AG, part of Springer Nature 2019, Cham, 2019

Introduction   13

10 Schumpeter, J.A. *Capitalism, Socialism and Democracy*, Routledge, London, 1994 [orig. 1942].
11 Their, H. "The Working Class is the Vast Majority of Society", in *Jacobin Magazine*, 2020
12 Marx, K. *Das Kapital. Kritik der politischen Oekonomie,* Verlag von Otto Meisner, Volume I, 1867 Volume II, 1885, Volume III 1894 by Edited/Completed by Frederick Engels
13 Lamont, M.; Varoufakis, Y. "Yanis Varoufakis: Capitalism has Become 'technofeudalism", *UpFront Interview,* Al Jezeera English, 2021
14 Siebers, T. "Ethics in the Age of Rousseau: From Lévi-Strauss to Derrida", in Siebers, T. h *The Ethics of Criticism*, Cornell University Press, Ithaca and London, 1988
15 Chan, R. "The Cambridge Analytica Whistleblower Explains How the Firm Used Facebook Data to Sway Elections", *Business Insider,* 2020
16 Heidegger, M. *The Question Concerning Technology and Other Essays*, Harper and Row, New York, 1977
17 Habermas, J. *The Theory of Communicative Action*, Polity Press, Cambridge, 1991
18 Stiegler, B. *La technique et le tems 1*, Galilee, 1994
19 Althusser, L. "Idéologie et appareils idéologiques d'État (Notes pour une recherche)", La Pensée, 1970
20 Kyon, C.; Wendy, H. *Control And Freedom: Power And Paranoia In The Age Of Fiber Optics*, MIT, Cambridge, 2008
21 Milgrom Foundation, "The Limits of the Material", Conversation with Saskia Sassen, The Naomi Milgrom Foundation, 2018
22 Wallenstein, S.O. *Nihilism, Art and Technology*, US-AB, Stockholm University, Stockholm, 2010
23 Kranzberg, M. *"Technology and History: "Kranzberg's Laws""* Technology and Culture, 1986
24 Crawford, K. *Atlas of AI: Power, Politics, and the Planetary Costs of Artificial Intelligence*, Yale University Press, New Haven, 2021
25 Buolamwini, J.; Gebru, T. "Gender Shades: Intersectional Accuracy Disparities in Commercial Gender Classification", in *Proceedings of Machine Learning Research*, 81:1–1, pp. 77–91, 2018

1 Systems of Measurement Idealizing and Displacing Human Proportions

History Sections:
Renaissance; Modern Movement; Post-War; Contemporary; Predictive Futurism;

Methodology:
Panofky's Deep Structure; D'Arcy Thomson Topological Matrix; Anthropocene; Post-Humanism; Post-Colonialism;

From an Anthropocentric Mechanized Body to a Post-Humanism

Every age measures the human body in relation to technological advances indexing culture through systems of representation. We can trace through history how human proportions affected the actual physical body and how in exchange, architecture referenced a type of body. In *The History of Human Proportions*,[1] Panofsky analyzes the parallel between the representation of human figure proportions and the perception of space as the artistic will of the epoch, *Kunstwollens*[2] (art+will), through an abstract normative structural matrix, a *screen interface* that holds together perception, representation, and normalization.

We can trace systems of reference indexed by human proportions as follows:

Theomorphic
Anthropomorphic
Zoomorphic
Biomorphic
Topographic
Tecnomorphic
Mathematical
Universal
Cartesian
Digital
Post-Human

Panofsky traces human proportions from early Egyptian Dynasties' idealized proportions based on single units of measurement stretching the body

DOI: 10.4324/9781003292036-2

sideways to match an ideal matrix, to the Gothic abstract triangulated skeletons by de Honnecourt aiming to develop a system for ideal body proportions. Leonardo Da Vinci identifies a base for Human Proportion in the Vitruvian Man (1492) as two correlated systems of measurement and references through the Golden ratio: a circle and a square[3], identifying conflicts between universal and other world references. The Huns in Asia around 400 CE as well as other civilizations in the Middle East and in some civilizations such as the Choctaw, the Mayan indigenous populations in North and Central America, and the Incas in South America practiced incremental cranial modification, a forced incremental manipulation in human proportions referencing different aesthetic ideals.

Ideal Human Proportions and Topological Data Mapping

Dürer[4] in 1525 proposes multiple techniques, apparatus, machines, matrices, and systemic approaches to measuring universal generic bodies and understanding them across different proportional ideal generic ranges through parametric measuring systems such as elastic matrices. Della Francesca[5] (c.1412–92), presented a novel deductive method of mapping points to depict the relative geometric topology of a specific human figure and be able to project it in an accurate perspectival projection, an alternative to Dürer's inductive structural representational attempt that tended to deform a human body to match an ideal human figure based on geometric proportions. While Dürer had developed an analog perspectival machine with a thread projecting points from a horizontal object or body to a vertical picture plane matrix, he did not apply this to a specific person's face. Dürer's Renaissance of ideal body proportions as an abstract organizing order identifying proportions contrasts with a critical topology in Della Francesca's projective geometry, in which a particular person and not an idealized figure is mapped point by point, an innovation identified by Zuliani.[6]

Evolutionary Zoomorphic–Biomorphic Body

Henry Bergson[7] critiqued science because it negated time by developing philosophical thinking in relation to the evolutionary spirit of Nature, developing a series of formal studies based on the creative evolution of species. Bergson distinguished between a gradual formal degree change based on the accumulation of information from the environment, in relation to an internal structure to understand how new species would emerge once that progressive imprint acquired a structural transformation. D'Arcy Thomson[8] applied matrices borrowing from Dürer's human proportions to understand the elastic genealogy of the variation of the evolutionary adaptation to the environments of different animal species as a scientific representation of functional demands. These matrices are able to describe a change in degree within a range but unable to describe the structural change that enables difference among species.

Mechanical Universal Modern Body

Neufert[9] in his manual for a universal system of measurement of 1936 standardizes the body identifying a universal generic proportion addressing corresponding architectural measurements, from furniture to spaces. Neufert references a mechanistic body through ranges of possible movements. Le Corbusier's (LC) Modulor[10] of 1954 based on Da Vinci's Vitruvian Man presents an ambition for a coordinated universal system of measurement as a norm[11] that contemplates differential calculation in determining a scale-oriented proportional body. The machine to live in becomes a mechanized standardized space in which the movement of the body is coordinated within the anticipated functional design of the furniture, indexing function, and movement. This anticipatory deterministic approach seems to reference Sullivan's "form follows function". The LC Chaise Longue indexes the body position through curvature, as a static moment in a shifting structure. Once the user realizes a body position that is being indexed, this deterministic functionalism quickly becomes stigmatizing, and thus uncomfortable and oppressive.

Capitalist Body: From Indexing Profit to a Mediated Body

Architecture has historically indexed a patriarchal and an economic structure. Agrest, Conway, and Weisman's *The Sex of Architecture*[12,13] discusses the problematic relationship between artificial man-made origination in architecture defining woman as a destination, indexing a type of body, and defining nature as feminine and in opposition to architecture as the other. Colomina's *Sexuality and Space*[14] expanded on the relevance of women in architecture and urbanism from issues of bodies to cities and gender in relation to semiotics such as Grosz's bodies-cities, Ingraham's line in space, and Ponte's phallocentrism.

Capitalism has direct consequences on human proportions, indexing its ideology in people's bodies, stretching, deforming, and displacing human proportions through media, and the demands of fashion, projecting excess through standards of comfort indexing a white American male body. But consumerism, individuality, excess, and other issues index an economic system on the human body with health consequences affecting human evolution[15] including the incorporation of pollution and microplastics.

From a Robotic Prosthetic Body, to an Augmented Body, to a Bio-Synthetic Organism

The contemporary body is informed by a prosthesis and an augmented body-mind through physical and virtual robotics. The current body is in fact transitioning and evolving into a post-human robotic body, expanding, and extending the capacity of the human body beyond itself through sensing, mapping, and feedback, expanding memory, intelligence, and mobility.

Systems of Measurement Idealizing and Displacing Human Proportions   17

Often before seen as an impediment, now prostheses are seen as an extension and augmentation of the body beyond human capacity. The human body is now being 3D printed as entire organs can be reproduced by implementing the body's cells. Biohackers can target means to modify existing organisms to create evolutionary species or mutate the internal cell composition of bodies, activating an information resampling of the units that compose bodies. Augmentation can happen at multiple levels since our cell phones are already part of an augmented body and mind. Neuroscience research identified that the memory dependence on our cell phones is in fact augmenting our functional capacity but playing an important role in the diminishing of our mental capacities, as outsourcing memory to our cell phones results in a diminishing function of our fluid intelligence[16].

Face recognition software[17] can identify the human identity and other aspects such as behavior.[18] One can reference a new body by articulating the older contrast described by Della Francesca in reaction to the ideals of the Renaissance, between an idealized digital geometry for face recognition optimized for fast database search of structural features, and a non-idealized point-by-point mapping, between a system of description and representation that stretches reality through an ideal reference, and a precise survey through 3D scanning photogrammetry resulting into a point cloud. Face recognition kinetic mapping[19] through proportional relationships establishes a flexible network of relationships and proportions through an underlying matrix-kinetic structure or through other means such as *canonical preprocessing* through depth map recognition shadows. Human Identification at a Distance (HID) is based on machine vision by triangulation, vector estimation, and tensor patch. Facial recognition data point cloud as the survey can be tagged as anchor points of reference.[20,21]

Clearview AI facial recognition app reverse data search allows you to take a photo of a person and retrieve multidimensional data associations, including ownership, accounts, where this face appears published in open camera repositories and other items, on the one hand facilitating police work, on the other ending privacy and data ethics, easy to be tricked if the method is known.[22] Current technology allows recognition of mood[23] and development of a personalized content with thousands of personal metadata classifier tags designed for psychological profiling based on mapping reactions to social media to optimize advertisement triggering emotional feedback through addictive reward mechanisms. Face recognition kinetic mapping enables the transferring of features through AI systems to develop deep fake impersonation through Generative Adversarial Networks' (GANs) decoders and autoencoders.[24] If we can measure bodily affect, we should be augmenting embodiment, through affect and reification in the study of the semiotics of physical experience relative to cognition against media disembodiment. Embodiment becomes relevant to AI and robotics, since intelligence and cognition is codependent with the body, debunking the brain-body dialect. Neural activity happens also at the level of body organs such as hands, eyes and others, from muscle memory to local neurons able to process information.

Post-Human, Post-Anthropocene, and Post-Zoomorphism in AI and Robotics

Virtual reality simulation and immersion allow people to exchange and displace their own bodies and identities, to create their own cybernetic selves extendable in the network for eternity. Architecture and urbanism reference systems may no longer need to be anthropocentric, both in terms of how reality is measured and validated and how life is considered, giving more room for other systems and forms of beings. Current cyborgs include either anthropomorphic or zoomorphic robotics. The latest cyborgs still are not able to address post-humanism as they problematically activate a symbolic representational form.

Robotics are still centered in western Eurocentric patriarchal colonial Capitalist ideology in which they are not yet able to present autonomous conditions beyond indexing the real parameters that define the status quo. The displacement of anthropocentric reference to a post-human reality implies that both systems of measurement and reference are displaced when referencing computation and robotics, from machine vision beyond human senses and tactile spectrums to robotics that do not reference the human body and that take as reference the entire planetary environment. We envision and further discuss in other chapters agent-based environmental engines that measure reality in wider spectrums possible and that retrieve information at higher dimensional levels and that by reciprocity can inform through robotics a post-Anthropocene, post-human environment. While swarm robotics present means to understand a non-anthropocentric body many activate a bio-inspired form of augmentation and construction restricting robotics to a human center perception, measurement, and validation of the world.

Post-Human Emergent Being and AI Consciousness

Within the information age, the human brain has been compared to information processing, networks, and interconnectivity in relation to information flow[25] through cybernetics, inspiring cross relationships between memory storage and data processing. But such correlation and influence are not linear. Our bodies as well as our brain processing activity and synapsis are also transformed in relation to current measurement and optimizing systems.[26]

We further discuss human and machine intelligence in Chapter 9 as a function of information flow and AI model dimensionality. We are now able to anticipate and predict through artificial neural networks (ANN) behavior through statistic geometric fitting in Machine Learning, but we are not yet activating a type of intelligence comparable to what can be called "artificial intelligence". Interestingly, we are in the process of becoming post-human surrogates as we train machines to become intelligent.

Notes

1 Panofsky, E. "The History of the Theory of Human Proportions as a Reflection of the History of Styles", in Panofsky, E. *Meaning in the Visual Arts*, The University of Chicago Press, 1955

2 Panofsky, E. "The Concept of Artistic Volition", in *Critical Inquiry*, Volume 8, Issue 1, 1981 [orig. 1964]

3 Murtinho, V. "Leonardo's Vitruvian Man Drawing: A New Interpretation Looking at Leonardo's Geometric Constructions", in *Nexus Network Journal*, 17, 2015

4 Dürer, A. *Unterweysung des Messung*, ed. Hieronymus Andreae, Nuremberg, 1525

5 della Francesca, P. *De Prospectiva Pingendi* (c.1475), (Filologie medievali e moderne 10 Serie occidentale 9) a cura di Ghiara Gizzi, Edizioni Ca'Foscari, Venezia, 2016

6 Zuliani, G. *Perspective Theory in L.B. Alberti and P. della Francesca*, MIT Press, 2023 (forthcoming)

7 Bergson, H. *L'Évolution Créatrice*, Alcan, Paris, 1907

8 Thomson, D'Arcy. *On Growth and Form*, Cambridge University Press, Cambridge, 1917

9 Neufert, E. *Architect's Data*, Crosby Lockwood, London, 1970 [orig. 1936]

10 Le Corbusier *The Modulor: A Harmonious Measure to the Human Scale, Universally Applicable to Architecture and Mechanics*, Birkhäuser, Basel & Boston [orig. 1954 and 1958]

11 Lombardi, R. "Medida y norma: Notas sobre la proporción y escala en la manualística moderna", in *Cuaderno de Lecturas* numero 5, FADU-UBA, 2003

12 Agrest, D.; Conway, P.; Weisman L.K. ed. *The Sex of Architecture*, Harry N. Abrams, New York, 1996

13 Agrest, D. "Architecture from without: Body, Logic, and Sex" Assemblage No.7, 1988

14 Colomina, B. ed. *Sexuality and Space*, Princeton Papers of Architecture, PAP, New York, 1992

15 Chernomas, R.; Hudson, I.; Chernomas, G. "Can Neoliberal Capitalism Affect Human Evolution?", in *SAGE Journals*, Volume 48, Issue 1, 2018

16 Stone, J. R. "*Smartphones, Stress, and the Reduction of Cognitive Resources*", Thesis, Digital Commons, Georgia Southern University, 2020

17 Bruce, V.; Young, A. "Understanding Face Recognition", in *British Journal of Psychology*, Volume 77, 1986

18 Zhao, W.; Chellappa, R.; Phillips, J.; Rosenfeld, A. "Face Recognition: A Literature Survey", in *ACM Computing Surveys* (CSUR), Vol.ume 35, No. 4, 2003

19 Li, B.Y.L.; Mian, A.; Liu, W.; Krishna, A. "Using Kinect for Face Recognition Under Varying Poses, Expressions, Illumination and Disguise, in *Applications of Computer Vision* (WACV)", IEEE Workshop, 2013

20 World Economic Forum. "Responsible Limits on Facial Recognition Technology", 2019

21 Heisler, Y. "Infrared Video Shows Off the iPhone X's New Face ID Feature in Action", BGR. 2017

22 Gallagher, R. "These Goofy-Looking Glasses Could Make You Invisible to Facial Recognition Technology", in *Slate,* 2013

23 Gates, K. *Our Biometric Future*, NYU Press, New York, 2011

24 Zollhofer, J.M. ; Stamminger, M; Theobalt, C.; Nießner, M. "Face2Face", 2016

25 Von Neumann, J. *The Computer and the Brain*, Yale University Press, New Haven, 1958

26 Reuters Staff. "Elon Musk's Neuralink Shows Monkey with Brain-Chip Playing Videogame by Thinking", in *Reuters Technology News*, 2021

2 Brunelleschi's Parametric Analog Computational Interface

From a New Media Normalizing Visualization to Indexing, Displacing, and Innovating in Representation

History Section:
1344-Renaissance-Baroque;

Methodology:
Panosfky's Semiotic Deep Structure following Cassirer's Linguistic Deep Structure; Wölfflin's Renaissance-Baroque; Hegel's Dialectics; Derrida's deferral-displacement

Social-Economics Geopolitics:
Renaissance Eurocentrism Criticism; Post-Colonialism

Visual Semiotic Signifiers:
One Point, Two Point Perspective; Vanishing Point; Picture Plane; Greek Topo-logos; Entasis; Roman Frontality;

Mathematics:
Geometry; Projective Geometry, Anamorphosis, Infinity

Representation:
We define representation to address both problems of visual arts that engage its media apparatus where content is developed, from a representation of content to an autonomy of content addressing the frame-context. We also understand representation addressing its critique, through performative systems, since we think that simulation is also contained within a problem of representation.

Innovation in systems of representation project new spatial references that influence architecture typology, but once that became normalized, there is a rising criticism of such media determinism that enables alternative representational systems. Contrarily, a normalization and stability of systems of representation may enforce imperialism, colonialism, and cultural bias. Greek Entasis is the correction of the column's slenderness to address eye distortion in diagonal binocular vision. Entasis is a way of indexing a system of representation in the actual form of the column to compensate for the

DOI: 10.4324/9781003292036-3

binocular distortion. But the indexing of the eye distortion also privileges viewing the building from the corner.

In contrast, the urban logic of Roman architecture is indexed in a planar frontal condition expressed in the façade of buildings. Roman frontality also indexes the hierarchical military organization of imperial grids colonizing the Mediterranean territory, projecting a measurement protocol identifying four axes relative to wind and sun orientation. Roman military protocol for city foundations is also related to a network system of roads designed for fast administrative and informational feedback centralized in Rome.

The pre-colonial Inca Civilization of the 1400s, building up from previous civilizations such as Caral, Chavin, Paracas, Nazca, and Wari in South America, develops a circular economy, measuring the territory following topographic lines integrating agriculture, architecture, and a construction system in the Machu Pichu city-state. Topography containment walls function as containment walls which enable flat agricultural land and provide building enclosure. The walls are made of stones unit cuts optimizing waste following both orthogonal and Voronoi geometry for maximum bond flexibility found in irregular corn geometry.

Renaissance Perspective: Lorenzetti's Parametric Space

Perspective has been striating Western modern space as explained by Erwin Panofsky.[1]

> "Visual space and tactical space are both anisotropic and unhomogeneous in contrast to the metric space of Euclidean geometry...." Panofsky

Panofsky's method involves a symbolic form analysis, and presents Lorenzetti's Annunciation of 1,344, by the implied centered vanishing point that splits the canvas into two distinct spaces or "realities". The structure of the medium of representation performs in the scene symbolically in the presence of the absence of the non-visible infinite, materialized by a vanishing point that is also symbolic to the narrative of the painting, representing the mediation of God as an invisible but present being. The symbolic presence of the system of representation (perspective), the content of the painting (the Annunciation), and the actual canvas frame dividing the scene in two (the Angel and Mary), are performing at the same structural information level which coincides in the vanishing point providing simultaneously structure, matter, and content for each other, and making the artistic operation a powerful all-inclusive unique entity by activating a medium-specific artistic idea of God within painting not possible by other means, media or medium defining a metaphysics of presence (Figure 2.1). Interestingly, this is Lorenzetti's only clearly depicting perspectival painting and his last one, demonstrating the necessity for the construction of a system of representation to address content through media-specificity.

With Panofsky, it became clear that an artistic method, through its artificial description of reality, informed the internal structure of how reality is

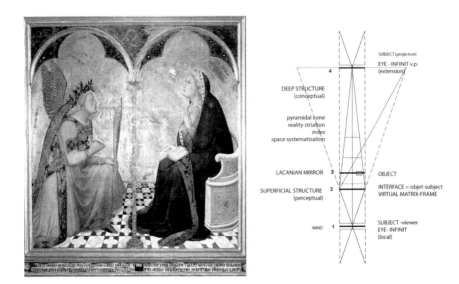

Figure 2.1 A1: Lorenzetti, A. "Annunciation" 1344, [127cm (50″) × 120cm (47.2″)], Pinacoteca Nazionale, Siena. Wikidata Public Domain, Wikipedia Commons. B1: Diagram, "Lorenzetti's Parametric Perspective-Space" by author, 2008.

understood, and by feedback also organized. If the mediums of representation have such a power to prescribe content in the work of the artist, then representation is a space of differentiation, where content is structured. Therefore, any artistic content not acknowledging the structuring of the systems of representation as a space where content is made possible either is not complete or is determined by the naturalization of an implicit system of representation.

Lorenzetti's Parametric Space presents a coordinated semiotic framework:

1 The Vanishing Point as a visual semiotic sign has three meanings:

   1a Structure of the painting: Deep structure of the system of representation both indexed as a sign and as symbolic form structure of the canvas (splits scene into two "worlds");
   1b Perspectival functionality demonstrating an idea of infinity in 2D finite space;
   1c Narrative of painting is made possible by indexing the presence of God through the infinity depicted in the vanishing point and mediating between earth and heaven (Mary and Angel);

2 Parametric Space indexed by floor tiling, demonstrating mathematical knowledge;

3 Correlating three topological levels of information (1a-deep structure, 1b- canvas-structure, 1c-narrative painting) making them necessary to each other. If one system is removed, the logic and narrative of the painting do not function.

Brunelleschi's Mathematical Parametric Analog Computational Interface

Brunelleschi is considered in the context of this book correlating systems of representation such as computation to architecture, as the first analog parametric architect. Brunelleschi resolved for the first time in western history linear perspective through mathematics applying projective geometry, as a precise and universal system of representation for painting. He applied perspective to represent architectural space integrated through the vanishing point, defining a clear machinic systematic organization of a new dynamic space manifested in his drawings for S.M. del Fiore and the design for San Lorenzo's church. Brunelleschi's machinic system of representation was seen at the time as a radical revolutionary innovation, a modern aesthetic, and a proportional system as a rupture from the Gothic. Brunelleschi develops a visual space as he incorporates the viewing subject in the space of representation, within a clearly organized space through a pictorial surface as a plane intersecting the perspectival cone effect.[2] At the time, perspective was not natural as opposed to today. Brunelleschi created the first machinic parametric model to compute space dynamically as we still do today through automated descriptive geometry using any computer three-dimensional simulation.

Perspective as external incorporation in architecture from painting, also created a new sign at an architectural typological level, since Brunelleschi's columns of the Hospital of the Innocents in Florence (1419–27) develop a new notion of a column grid, as columns are abstracted as a minimal expression, conceptually becoming a point in space in the plan, a new form of abstraction in which material is reduced to its minimum expression. This idea is made evident in the continuity between the column and the vaulted ceiling since the point in the plan becomes a line in elevation, and the line becomes a surface through the vaulted ceiling and in continuity. Brunelleschi's structure becomes a new linguistic expression and a new way of understanding structure, developing a correlation between space representation and architecture typology defining a new type of spatial containment.

Brunelleschi's Perspective Parametric Computational Interface becomes a framework:

1 Parametric: Objects index a mechanistic dynamic system of representation defining proportions;
2 Vanishing Point: the VP integrates painting theory into architecture theory through perspectival illusion as an organizing order (Hospital

24 *Brunelleschi's Parametric Analog Computational Interface*

Innocents). The flooring and organization of Brunelleschi's architecture index the system of representation (San Lorenzo);

3 Machinic Universal Computational Model as Interface: its analog computational model functions independently from the scene and context rendered since it can be applied universally as an interface;

4 New aesthetic language of description and proportional system that can inform the reality.

Perspective as Eurocentric Renaissance Machinic Colonization of Space

Since Alberti's treatise, the first complete depiction of perspective as a method, perspective has been structured into a 500-year-old Renaissance system of representation, which is today normalized and incorporated into everyone's life, including contemporary computer representation, data acquisition in survey mechanisms and automated machine vision in Artificial Intelligence (AI). Perspective has been dismissed as a visual semiotic Eurocentric structure that colonizes space through sight, territorializing and organizing physically a modern world based on its parametric space, mathematics, and the symbolic form of the vanishing point (VP). The politics of perspective also enforces the VP as a semiotic sign denoting infinitude within a finite space that needs to be critiqued and deconstructed, since it projects symbolic religious meaning indexing infinity through a Western metaphysics of presence, a problem identified by Kubrick's *2001: A Space Odyssey* 1968's film relating the Artificial Intelligence system to the VP in a linear perspective. We identify, analyze and critique means to displace perspective and systematize new axioms of representation.

While we mainly discuss across the book the problematic relationship between social issues and the economic system that propels them, we need to be aware of which are the axiomatic semiotic structures that are active today and which also need to be critiqued and deconstructed. Architecture is a visual arts-based discipline, and therefore social issues can also be conveyed through visual semiotics projecting power through formal visual means. Today most people know how to construct a perspectival space, but few understand that its artificial normalization of our actual physical space as a continuous projective geometry system normalizes a homogenization of space and eliminates the possibility of alternative systems of representation. The social contract in terms of spatial representation, functionality, and actuation belongs to a visual space in which the subject viewer and the tactile space of objects contained are established by the ideology of a perspectival spaceframe. Perspective became a homogeneous universal visual semiotics structuring system, not different from how the encyclopedia standardized knowledge and the museum naturalized cultural appropriation. While perspective has been critiqued by several artists and architects, its political power structure has not been deconstructed enough as it has not been replaced by other systems in contemporary sophisticated computation and architecture.

Displacing Renaissance Perspective

Within a framework of perspective subjects and objects are defined by their interrelations: subjects become immersive and objects become representation-dependent, as the *interpretant* is the subject-experience beholder in a perspectival *haptic* space.

> "His [Alois Riegl] concepts of "optical" and "tactile" (a better form is "haptic"), in spite of their continued formulation as psychological and empirical, in no way serve, according to their meaning, as genetic explanations or philosophical subsumptions but aim at revealing a meaning immanent in artistic phenomena". Panosfky[3]

Quite early, before Brunelleschi's perspective but after Lorenzetti's, the Annunciation of 1399 by Broederlam presents a two-point bi-focal linear perspective applied to a novel type of foreground-rotated spaceframe separated from a single-point perspective background. This painting innovates in several ways: while it accentuates the two separate systems of representation based on perspective, Broederlam dissociates the foreground modern space from a background vanishing point as a religious signifier.

Bramante's Santa Maria in San Satiro, Milan of 1478–82 is an exploration of both a demonstration of the possibilities of representation visually expanding space through illusionistic perspective and a functional solution to the lack of physical space. Bramante cleverly applies perspective illusionistic quality to resolve in less than one-meter depth (90cm) the illusion of an entire nave behind the altar.[4]

While the Renaissance established new systems of representation, the Baroque displaced these systems of representation to previously unknown levels, contributing to other fields, both artistic and scientific. Velázquez *Las Meninas* of 1656 contrasts and displaces Lorenzetti's perspective and its organization of space as it presents a paradigmatic example of an artistic work that develops a painting of paradoxical quality. According to Searle,[5] it originates a violation of one fundamental rule of illusionist representative painting, the basic rule is the axiom of perspective that requires the painting to be projected as well as viewed from the viewpoint of the artist. Foucault presents Velázquez's work as a political manifesto, and we read it as a decolonization of perspective's power structure by expanding personal authorship as the artist displaces the system of representation placing himself into the painting: enacting "the death of representation".[6]

The painting, the painting of the painting, the space of the painting, the space of representation of the painting, the mirror, which conceptually is the space of the observer or the king and queen, the background, the service space, and other spatial elements such as depth, conform a layered series of complex spatial problems indexed by pictorial planes that imply a conscious intellectual architectural composition that can be described in the plan. First, in the pictorial plane of the canvas, Velázquez projects what we cannot see, inverting the point of view, and opposing the observer. Second, the narrative of the painting, *Las Meninas* (Maids of Honor) and the princess, are indexed by the light entering from the side windows. Third, the viewer's apex's perspectival political space is engaged with the mirror in the back of the room to the left side of the perspective vanishing point, which instead of representing God and infinity, depicts the political power of the royal couple and the service door, inverting directions with the viewer. Fourth, the entire painting is presented as a theatrical scenography, as the vanishing point framed by the right service door, another virtual infinite space appears, from which the assistant manipulates this political theater. In coordination with Velazquez's studio which is represented again in the canvas above the door, the symbolic structure of the unifying perspective of the space is continued and another reflexive loop is developed between representations and realities. The perspectival displacement exchanges deep structure and superficial structure into a continuous topological inversion through a spatial enfolding between the spaces of the painting and the real space of the viewer. Lastly, the single vanishing point contrast with the multiple heterotopias of events and narratives establishing a dialectic between stability performed by the unifying centrality of the normal-structure perspectival cone effect and instability that displaces the entire structure through a topological critical space (Figure 2.2).

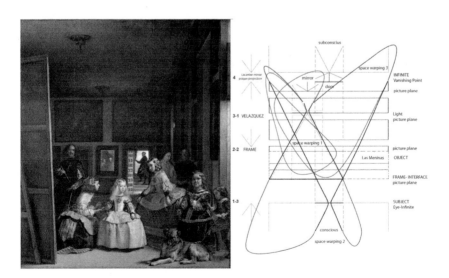

Figure 2.2 A1: Velázquez, D. "Las Meninas" 1656/57, [318cm (125.2″) × 276cm (108.6″)], Museo del Prado, Madrid. Wikipedia Commons. B1: Diagram, "Velazquez Topological Perspective-Space" Pablo Lorenzo-Eiroa, 2008.

Velazquez as an intellectual criticizes the politics of the media frame within which the work is constituted.

Velázquez painted Las Meninas a year after purchasing for his king El Lavatorio of 1547 by Tintoretto.[7] In this painting, a heterogeneous multiplicity of points of attention, scenes, figures, and spaces, contrast against the continuous dynamic unifying movement of an illusionist perspective. Tintoretto develops a special technique that produces an illusionistic effect that is only active once the viewer physically moves from one end to the other of this large landscape-oriented work which measures 211cm × 534cm, activating an actual bodily affection in the viewer thanks to the hexagonal tiles of a diminishing parametric structure of the floor. Tintoretto's painting develops a displacement of perspective as a deep structure. Tintoretto, who worked in Venice and collaborated with Andrea Palladio (1508–80), also critiqued Brunelleschi's perspective and activated several means in his architecture to displace it.

Brunelleschi's perspective is critiqued by Palladio as the mechanization of space.[8] Palladio's Il Redentore (1577–92) presents a critique against the linearity of Brunelleschi's perspectival cone effect and its validity as an accurate representation of reality.[9] The building's floor plan demonstrates an architecture of sequential spaces articulated by scenographic picture planes that interrupt the perspectival cone effect. The space is purposely elongated beyond normal accentuating spatial depth, and in contrast, the façade of the building is purposely flattened.[10] The façade compresses space to a diagram of its interior, dissociating planar two-dimensional representation from three-dimensional depth experience. Tintoretto aimed at recreating space within the painting and Palladio did the opposite, recreating painting within architecture.[11] In Teatro Olimpico of 1580–85 in Vicenza, Palladio cynically accentuates the perspectival cone effect to demonstrate the artificial theatrical illusionistic quality of perspective. Following Bramante, Borromini's Palazzo Spada in Rome of 1632[12, 13] or the later Bernini Scala Reggia at San Peter's Basilica in the Vatican of 1663 present alternative demonstrations of how space can be extended through illusionistic perspective.

Spatial Typology Critiqued by Illusionistic Perspective: Pozzo's Multidimensional Virtual Space

Pozzo Sant' Ignatius Loyola's corridor in Rome of 1681–86 projects a unique anamorphosis in a perspectival illusionistic fresco, that, according to Valenti[14] no one has been able to scientifically replicate. Pozzo develops an illusionistic perspective that expands space and perception both displacing and compressing the curved barrel-vaulted ceiling of the architectural space where these frescoes are projected. This process activates a complex series of artistic criticisms building up an illusionistic perspective-space with multidimensional aspirations. By developing a counter-intuitive compressive illusionistic perspective, instead of expanding the existing space, Pozzo flattens out the corridor's physically curved ceiling toward and against the subject-viewer experiencing the space, with a series of projected straight porticos. The porticos are designed so that they vary their relationship through a parametric anamorphosis with the observer, compressing and disjointing the normal coordination between the viewer's visual perception and theirs bodily perception. A continuous mental eye re-mapping of the space proposes a disjunction of visual and somatic experience through the multiple foci. The fresco challenges the containment reference structure of the space where they are projected, developing means to compress, expand, and displace the architecture of the space. At the end of the corridor, the space ends proposing an opposite structure to the previous experience of psychosomatic space. With a slated diagonal wall Pozzo compresses space physically, as he expands space virtually with another illusionistic perspective (Figure 2.3).

Figure 2.3 Andrea Pozzo St. Ignazio Corridor LiDAR 3D Scanning by Salvatore and ManciniofRilevodepartment,SapienzaUniversityinRome,pointcloudrendering by Pablo Lorenzo Eiroa.

Pozzo's illusionistic perspective becomes:

1 A dynamic interface;
2 A site-specific interface that activates a virtual reality unstabilizing the frame space from where it is set;
3 An interface which informs real space real time: critiques spatial containment and spatial form;
4 A media framework that transforms the subject experience of space, engaging in informed navigation and experience.

Notes

1 Panofsky, E. *Perspective as Symbolic Form*, Zone Books, New York, 1991 [orig. 1927]
2 Panofsky, E. "Italy and the Lowlands During the Fifteenth Century", in ed. Spencer, H., *Readings in Art History*, Charles Scribner's Sons, New York, 1976
3 Panofsky, E. "The Concept of Artistic Volition", in *Critical Inquiry*, Volume 8, Issue 1, 1981 [orig. 1964]
4 Buratti, G.; Mele, G.; Rossi, M. "Perspective Trials in the Manipulation of Space", in ed. Cardone, V. *Drawing as (In)Tangible Representation*, Disegno 4, Unione Italiana per il Disegno, Roma, 2019
5 Searle, J. *Critical Inquiry*, University of Chicago Press, Chicago, 1980
6 Foucault, M. *The Order of Things*, Vintage Books, New York, 1973 [orig. 1966]
7 Barolsky, P. "A Source for Las Meninas", in *Source. Notes in the History of Art*, Volume X, 1991.
8 Scolari, M. *Oblique Drawing: A History of Anti-perspective*, MIT Press, 2012
9 Eisenman, P.; Roman, M. *Palladio Virtuel*, Yale University Press, New Haven, 2015
10 Argan, G.C.; Nesca, R.A. "The Architecture of Brunelleschi and the Origins of Perspective Theory in the Fifteenth Century", in *Journal of the Warburg and Courtauld Institutes*, Volume 9, 1946
11 Argan, G. "The Importance of Sanmicheli in the Formation of Palladio", in ed. Gilbert, C., *Renaissance Art,* Harper, New York, 1973
12 Sinisgalli, R. "Borromini a Quattro Dimensioni, L'eresia prospettica di Palazzo Spada", Universita Degli Studi di Roma, 1981
13 Trvisan, C. "La Galleria del Borromini a Palazzo Spada, Roma. Modello regolare e modello reale eformato. Abaco delle deformazioni prospettiche", in Sinisgalli, R. "Prospettiva e Prospettive", Centro Svizzero di Cultura di Roma, 1999
14 Valenti, M.G. *Prospettive architettoniche, conservazione digitale, divulgazione e studio*, Volume I, Sapienza Universitá Editrice, Roma, 2014

3 Palladio's Parametric Undecidability as a Critical Topological Model

History Section:
Renaissance; Mannerism; Baroque;

Methodology:
Wölfflin's Renaissance and Baroque; Panofsky's Deep Structure; Ackerman's Historical Conventions;

Visual Semiotic Signifiers:
Perspective Cone Effect; Picture Plane; Flattened Space; Expanded Deep Space;

Mathematic Semiotics:
1-2-1-2-1; Golden Section; Irrational Numbers; Proportional Ratios, Numeric Sequences; Prime Numbers; Parametric Space; Topology;

Linguistic Semiotic Signifiers:
A-B-C-B-A; Durand's Encyclopedic Architectural Types;

Parametric Topological Displacements to Disseminate Origination

Wölfflin described the group of architects that reacted to the Renaissance as Baroque, defining a historic structure which would repeat in the form of a pendulum from one revolution to the other. Architecture, as a cultural discipline, has been structuring its advancement on a continuous state of revolution as opposed to science and technology which is based on an idea of continuous progress.[1]

Palladio (1508–80) can be understood as the first analog computational mathematical topological architect. Palladio activated a relational organizational logic across the composition of his buildings relating individual parts and spaces' proportions and their relative shift, to an elastic structural whole. Palladio distinguishes himself and critiques the perspectival model of Brunelleschi as an organizing system, marking a shift from an established visual logic. Palladio interrupts with picture planes the perspectival cone effect, shifting architecture towards a relational abstract horizontal planimetric system. Palladio's innovation is based on an advancement from Alberti's

DOI: 10.4324/9781003292036-4

(1404–72) system of measurements, some retrieved from Vitruvius (80–70 BCE–15), used to establish an abstract system of relationships among spaces, assigning continuity across the composition through alternating rhythmical ratios, a form of spatial parametrics through a mathematical algorithm. The development of proportional ratios based on mathematics was a political innovation from contemporary architects who measured antique classical buildings by applying surveyed proportional ratios often based on a classical understanding of human proportions.

Although Palladio owes his innovation to some of his predecessors, such as Serlio (1475–c.1554) who earlier published architecture books thanks to the recent spread in Western Europe of Gutenberg's Press by the 1500s. Serlio's interests seem more varied than Palladio's, from geometric constructions to studies on perspective,[2] scenography, and the city to radical experimentations on plan organizations, to universal architecture types confronted with local juxtaposition through contiguous poché spaces as articulations. Serlio's books were not published sequentially, such as Book I, Paris 1545, Book III, Venice 1540; Book IV, Venice 1537; Book VI 1550; Book Extraorinario, Lyon 1551, Book VII posthumously in 1575[3] until all were published in 1583. Palladio's *Four Books of Architecture* were published in 1570.[4]

Origination and Critique of Systemic Relational Determination

Vidler[5] discusses a genealogy of the architecture diagram in relation to computer representation. Vidler identifies as early as 1914–24 in the work of Frankl[6] and A.E. Brinckmann the schematic structural organization of historical buildings in a plan abstracted from style. Rowe[7] a student of Wittkower a year before his publication[8] related Le Corbusier Villa Stein with Palladio's Malcontenta through a common structure, tracing a structural history. Wittkower's analysis of Palladio's villas proposed a relational whole with variations revealing a common underlying nine-square pattern to 11 of Palladio's villas. Benelli[9] claims that Wittkower's diagrams may have been influenced by Palladio's own variations sketches (Casa Volpi). Wittkower and Rowe offer different contrasting units of measurement and validation of their theory, identified by Zuliani:[10] while Wittkower implements an architectural notation inherited from Frankl as "A-B-C-B-A" whereas a "C" notates a central axis with two side auxiliary intermediate service bays "B" and two perimeter bays "A"; in contrast, Rowe's emphasis is on a rather generic mathematical binary code 1-2-1-2-1 perceived as non-architectural. We think that Rowe's emphasis is derived from Palladio's measurement units since while one dimension remains constant in the transition between spaces, the other varies providing a parametric elastic topological mathematical code.

Linguistic Signifier = A–B–C–B–A
Mathematical Signifier = 1–2–1–2

Palladio's Unstabilizing Origin by Overcoming Parametric Variation through Topology

Vidler's argument proposes a critique of the usual unity and harmony identified by a common structure idea by Wittkower.[11] For instance, Villa Rotonda's "the ideal villa" incorporates a deep transformation usually dismissed by historians such as Ching,[12] who describe the villa as a biaxial symmetric building when one direction is privileged over the other. According to Ackerman, Palladio references a "pensiveness"[13] across spaces: a reference that is displaced projecting a memory trace in the experiential transition between spaces. Eisenman proposes a reading of Palladio disseminating the idea of origin through "undecidability".[14] Palladio's villas seem to tension spaces apart from an initial elastic generic organization, proposing spatial articulations through the walls and the columns. Wittkower's reductive abstractions disregarded particularities of the design that tensions the linearity of the revealed organization, including the service buildings that displace centrality. Eisenman reading of Palladio focuses on these factors – the varying thicknesses in the walls which articulate specific spatial juxtapositions, key relationships between columns and walls, and the barchesse service buildings eliminated by Wittkower as frames that re-qualify relationships between the villa's sites and the figure of the main building, dissipated as a normative reference.[15]

Between Palladio's villas Rotonda and Sarego, the most disarticulated and singular building where the ideal figure is not yet completely dissipated seems to be Palazzo Chiericatti. For us, Palladio defined a modern project based on a clear organizing structure but critiquing a universal idea of order, creating a responsive structural organizing system that can be both referenced and altered ranging from minor variations to larger structural critiques. While experiments with parametrics shape grammar, or diverse AI frameworks address variability in relation to the whole, they are not able to compute the subversive independent value of the part. We think that Palladio parametric system identifies the limits of control of a universal whole activating a local architecture value as a displacement, tensioning a generic whole as undecidable. This argument is indexed in the variable thickness of the wall and articulations giving value and allowing the reading of fragmentation in tension with the whole.

Palazzo Chiericatti apparently proposes a disproportional whole through a series of longitudinal and narrow spaces, which may be related to the possible dissemination of an ideal nine-square grid figure through topological transformations[16] informed by the constrained site at the edge of the city of Vicenza. While a normal proportion is kept constant, the other varies by applying displacements to an initial reference, projecting a relationship that is both kept, accumulated, but also displaced. Palladio's proportional sequences follow a Golden ratio, analyzed by many, and even understanding

Palladio's architecture seems...

them computationally through shape grammar[17] in which, departing from a 1:1 square, the first variation is a diagonal projection $\sqrt{2} = 1.414^{18}$ as an irrational number, while one dimension is kept others are extended. Other argumentations of Palladio's proportional coding ratio argue according to Lionel March that they are following Pythagoras's arithmetic, geometric, and harmonic mean; a 1.414 irrational number or 7:5 as a classical proxi; a Golden Ratio or Fibonacci sequence 0,1,1,2,3,5,8,13,21: Irrational Number 1.618...; 3:4; Alberti's recalling of Vitruvius numeric sequence $3 + 5 = 8 = 2^3$, $7 + 9 + 11 = 27 = 3^3$; Pythagoras Theorem $5^2 + 5^2 = 50 > 49 = 7^2$; the Prime numbers (3, 5, 7, 11, 13, 17, 19); or even a linguistic signifier attributed to Trissino who artificially renamed Andrea di Pietro della Gondola as ANDREAS PALADIVS [1+40+4+80+5+1+90; 60+1+20+1+4+9+200+90] a name which can be decoded as VITRVVIVS using the full numbers from Agrippa's *nine squares*, the nine chamber encoding of the Latin alphabet.[19] Palladio, as a humanist, integrates various forms of knowledge: linguistics, mathematics, and the visual; to the point of even displacing features of religious public architecture in domestic architecture, therefore developing a new language and signification of architecture.

Linguistic Semiotic Signifier = ANDREAS PALADIVS
Visual Semiotic Signifier = nine-square grid
Mathematical Arithmetic Signifiers = $\varrho = \dfrac{1+\sqrt{5}}{2} = 1.618$; [...]

The interest in developing a computational analysis of Palladio is based on the applicability of procedural logic as a generative demonstration of the persistency of logical organization across his work, extending Wittkower's structuralist analysis, but without being able to program Palladio's resistance to the homogenization of the whole by a system. Palladio's architecture seems to be placed in contrast to the universal language of mathematics as an overall proportional abstract system to the relative architecture value of the part. As we continue working, most decoding done so far is not able to reconstruct the object from the evidence, we partially resolve Palladio's contradiction, through an elastic topological structure that becomes fragmented. Palazzo Chiericati develops a series of displacements, an alternative idea of an architecture *topology*, since one may reconstruct the relationship between an implied normal original type and the final design in a continuous elastic diagram. Chiericati's organization shifts from a centralized building to a field of layered spaces with no hierarchy (Figure 3.1).

First, experientially, once one enters the space of Chiericati's gallery (loggia) that functions as a contained public sidewalk granted by the government after a special application. After climbing the stairs of the front of the palace, two intersecting columns meet at a 45-angle degree index an overlap between two distinct spaces: the space that is supposed to belong to a portico

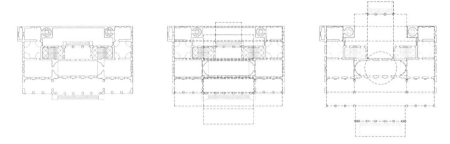

Figure 3.1 Relative topological displacements of Palladio's Palazzo Chiericati indexing an implicit ideal centralized generic organization. Pablo Lorenzo-Eiroa, after discussions with Guido Zuliani, 2006.

overlaps the space of the loggia. Second, the interior space after the loggia is presented as a vestibule. Continuing to the next space over the same central axis, one expects to find a central space, but surprisingly one finds the outside of the building, in a rear gallery-portico that faces the back courtyard. Third, this means that the previous space that was read as a vestibule, constituted in reality the central space of the palace at the ground level, compressed and distorted from its ideal circular figure. Fourth, once one climbs the exterior stairs in the sides of the back gallery-portico and after another external balcony-portico, one can finally arrive at the main public room of the Palazzo, which takes a different proportion by taking two longitudinal bays, expanding and projecting over the public sidewalk-loggia, pushing back against the axis of circulation where one started. The sequences of longitudinal spaces present a compression against the axis of circulation, and also an accumulation of somatic experiences —a psychological memory at the level of the organ- that projects a bodily affection, overlapping alternatively either expected, real, or implicit relationships. The organization of the Chiericati is refuted by the physical experience of the space which is at the same time disjointed from the unconscious mental projected anticipation, providing a physical structure and a virtual structure that acquires presence and overlaps each other, stimulating different and multiple relational structures between the perceptual, the physical, the implicit mental and the spatial.

It is interesting to think why Wittkower did not include such an interesting case in his 11 paradigmatic patterns or diagrams. If it was due to the strangeness of this palazzo, or due to the chosen category, then his structuralist search for homogeneity became reductive. Wittkower's 11 Palladio schemes[20] develop only a *differential change of degree* and not a conceptual typological change as the one that Palazzo Chiericati proposes. The idea of dissemination of an overall structure is pertinent to contemporary discussions identifying the

Palladio's Parametric Undecidability as a Critical Topological Model   35

limits of working relationally and the possibility to address indeterminacy in architecture. We believe that our reading resolves an implicit logic implicit in variation series forging changes that are able to transcend the departing structure.[21] What becomes interesting is the tension between a parameter to measure differences and the possibility of these differences creating *new parameters*.

Computational Visual Semiotic Signifier = Shape Grammar [√2]
Original Structure + Picture Plane + Subversive Part =
dissemination of origin

Palladio's Relational Parametric-Critical Topological Model framework becomes:

1 Relational, non-object-based (relationships are more important than objects);
2 Parametric-Relational: through establishing a measurement, some are projected, and some are displaced, applying mathematical continuity among spaces and tracing memory across spaces;
2 Topological: spatial organization is addressed at a structural level through variations of type. In some cases the topological variation or the fragmentation, critique the stability of such a structure;
3 Critical Responsive: new structure out of critiquing or making unstable its own origin, therefore challenging its own parameters, a system of representation and logic. The context modifies the structure and the structure modifies the context;
4 A motivator of the subject's physical and mental experience: psychosomatic experience, perception, and apperception, induce a posterior mental elaboration and interpretation;
5 A Frame-Object Critique: both the object (villa) and its frame (sitebarchesse) define each other, critiquing the dominant presence of the main building object by motivating the frame;
6 Unstable as a System of Representation: architecture motivates means to index and displace dominant systems of representation such as perspective, placing background and foreground in tension with each other, problematizing the representational interface;
7 Correlational interdependent: the system of representation as an interface and the result spatial typology necessarily critique each other (Figures 3.2 and 3.3). Palladio discovers and resolves generic universal problems in architecture, developing a critical machine able to both simultaneously systematize architecture as it fragments the whole.

The opposite argument to Palladio's organization is found in the cataloging systematic universal encyclopedia of architectural types proposed by Durand.

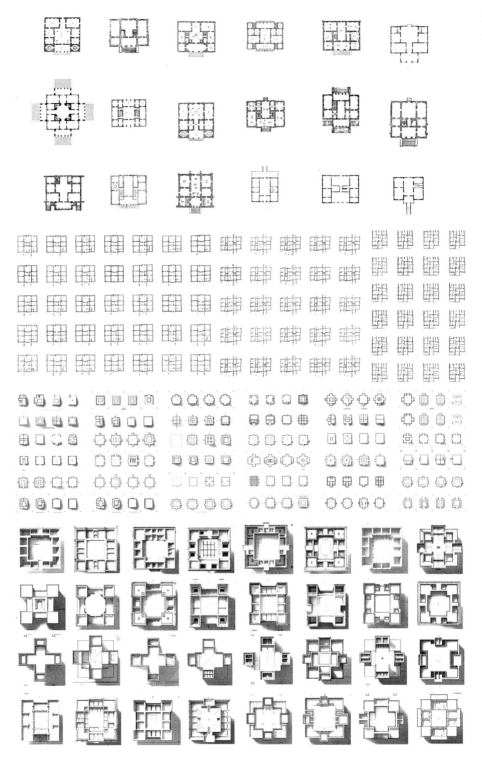

Figure 3.2 Palladian villas retrieved via API. Nine-square square grid Generative Adversarial Networks (GAN) feature recognition. Infinite possible Palladian Villas ordered typologically in epochs training. (See Notes Figure 3.2)

Palladio's Parametric Undecidability as a Critical Topological Model 37

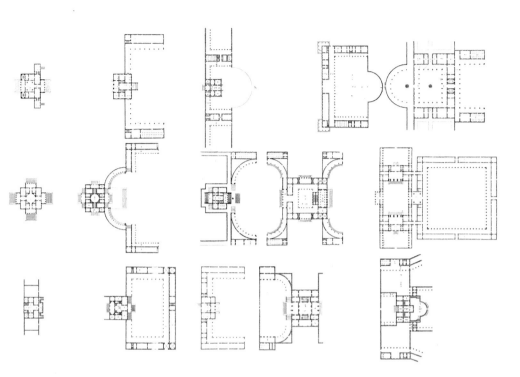

Figure 3.3 Palladium object dissemination. 15 Palladio's Villas with barchesse service buildings organized politically and formally as site-specific neighboring relationships. A1-E3: 15 Palladio's Villas with barchesse service buildings organized politically and formally (not to scale) as site-specific neighboring relationships displacing conventions between object-frame, center-periphery, service-served, space-wall, and building-site displacement of normal relationships establishing new references. While Palladio's Rotonda is usually considered not to address a direction nor a frame, the structure is non-symmetric and the site is framed by the form of its podium-walls containing services that redefine the building and the site. From left to right: Villa Rotonda, building as autonomous object (over a podium site-frame); to Villa Thiene disseminating any trace of a building as a figure in relation to the barchesse buildings acquiring figuration as inhabitable frame-sites. Palladio inverts politically service-served and object-frame iconographic relationships. We did not include the Palazzos, since, in Chiericati the urban context is what becomes the frame, leaving the solution for this problem open. Palladium sets up a site-based computation of parametric variation dissipating traces of the originating parameters. A1-E1: Villas Cornaro, Zeno, Angarano, Repeta, Serego; A2-E2: Rotonda, Trissino, Badoer, Mocenigo, Thiene; A3-E3: Malcontenta, Pisani, Saraceno, Thieni, Godi. The villas are centered acknowledging the center displacements but shifting the entrance condition. Floor plan drawings by Scamozzi and Palladio, Palladio, A. Quatro Libri di Architettura, 1570; A1-E3: Palladium object dissemination by Pablo Lorenzo-Eiroa, 2010-2013.

38 *Palladio's Parametric Undecidability as a Critical Topological Model*

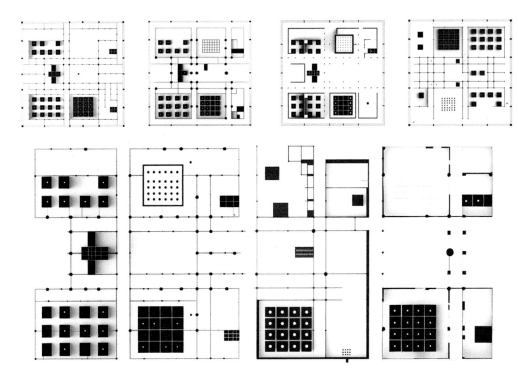

Figure 3.4 Borges believed that the readers expanded his literature work creatively. We discuss in Chapter 5, 6, 7 the balance between Big Data and models in relation to Artificial Neural Networks. We frame AI as a statistical problem developed in 1960-70s to make predictions based on data. Our objective here is to expand the work of Palladio, for instance analyzing and developing a system able to develop variations of his work through decoding and coding a generative critical structure. Perhaps current AI is unable to generate new knowledge-based paradigms, and if so, we simply become a librarian in Borges' infinite "Library of Babel" finding-rewriting missing books. Clarke's three laws discuss the certainty of what is possible and the uncertainty of the impossible; and that any advanced technology is indistinguishable from magic, otherwise it is already old; Clarke, A. C. "Profiles of the Future: An Inquiry into the Limits of the Possible", Popular Library, 1973. One can also think of a technology, a methodology, a language, a relationship through graph theory, or a type of computation that becomes specific and irreducible by resolving uniquely a problem. We discuss Chomsky scientific validity of Open AI ChatGPT (Chapter 6). Chomsky's critique is that there is correlation in AI but not cause, reason or association. Humans resolve problems creatively through explanations and different solutions exploring different approaches, AI simply by activating statistics over work already produced. For Chomsky AI is activating a plagiarism by accessing, processing and interpolating existing data. For us Digital Feudalism is killing the author through plagiarism rather than AI becoming an author. We discuss authorship (Chapter 20) in relation to AI by attempting to elevate design authorship through architectures of architectures. We implement AI bypassing style transfer as we activate Emergent Programming. A1-D1: DM parametric variations training via fed image CNN. A2: DM figure-frame dissipation variations developing neighboring relationships as an artificial site. computational variations; Pablo Lorenzo-Eiroa, DM 2022.

Durand[22] proposes parameters and variations based on his universal architecture by first cataloging all existing buildings ordered by types and abstracting them into generic organizations in simplified terms that leave behind architecture design to propose an idealized abstract pre-architecture system emptied from any cultural trace as a meta-structure. We understand Durand activating a universal computable imperial colonizing proto-architecture but with no architectural quality, or types as linguistic semiotics, since he bases his methodology on the encyclopedia, aiming at constructing the basic characters of an architecture vocabulary by identifying and classifying all basic originating types proposing an architecture alphabet.

Notes

1 Wölfflin, H., *Renaissance and Baroque*, trans. Simon, K., Collins, London, 1964 [orig. *Renaissance und Barock*, 1888]
2 Serlio, S. *Libro II: Trattato di prospetiva & Trattato sopra le scene*, Editrice Edalo Roma, Rome, 1980 [orig. 1570]
3 Spallone, R.; Vitali, M. "Geometry, Modularity and Proportion in the *Extraordinario Libro* by Sebastiano Serlio: 50 Portals Between *Regola* and *Licentia*", in *Nexus Network Journal*, Volume 22, 2020
4 Palladio, A. *The Four Books of Architecture*, Dover Publications, New York, 1965 [orig. *Quatro Libri di Architettura*, 1570]
5 Vidler, A. "Diagrams of Diagrams: Architectural Abstraction and Modern Representation", in *Representations*, No.72, University of California Press, Berkley, 2000
6 Frankl, P. *Principles of Architecture History*, trans. O'Gorman, J. MIT Press, Cambridge, 1973 [orig. 1914]
7 Rowe, C. "Mathematics of the Ideal Villa", in Rowe, C. *The Mathematics of the Ideal Villa and Other Essays*, MIT Press, Cambridge, 1976 [oirg. 1947]
8 Wittkower, R. *Architectural Principles in the Age of Humanism*, Norton, New York, 1971 [orig.1949]
9 Benelli, F. "Rudolf Wittkower versus Le Corbusier: A Matter of Proportion", in *Architectural Histories*, Volume 3, Issue 1, 2015
10 Zuliani, G. "Evidence of Things Unseen", in ed. Davidson, C., *Tracing Eisenman*, Rizzoli, New York, 2006
11 Vidler, A. "Palladio reassessed by Eisenman", *The Architectural Review*, London, 23 October 2012. https://www.architectural-review.com/essays/exhibitions/palladio-reassessed-by-eisenman
12 Ching, F.D.K. *Form, Space, Order*, Van Nostrand Reinhold, New York, 1979
13 Ackerman, J.S. *Palladio, The Architect and Society*, Penguin Books, New York, 1966
14 Eisenman, P.; Roman, M. *Palladio Virtuel*, Yale University Press, New Haven, 2015
15 Lorenzo-Eiroa, P. "Eisenman Palladian Virtuality: Ahistoric Parametric Undecidability", Palladio Virtuel Review in ed. Rappaport, N., *Constructs*, Yale Architecture, New Haven, 2012
16 Lorenzo-Eiroa, P. "Eisenman's Palladio Diagrams: Somatic Space as a Form of Affect", in ed. Grobman, Y. and Neuman, E. *Performalism: Form and Performance in Digital Architecture*, Routledge, London, 2008
17 Stiny, G.; Mitchell W.J. "The Palladian Grammar", in *Environment and Planning B*, Volume 5, UK, 1978

40 *Palladio's Parametric Undecidability as a Critical Topological Model*

18 Benros, D.; Duarte, Jose P.; Hanna, Sean. "Subdivision Grammar as Alternative to Palladian Grammar", in *International Journal of Architectural Computing*, Volume 10, Issue 04, 2020

19 March, L. "Palladio, Pythagoreanism and Renaissance Mathematics", in ed. Williams, K., *Nexus Network Journal* Book Series, Volume 10.2, Springer Nature, Switzerland AG, 2008

20 Wittkower, R. *Architectural Principles in the Age of Humanism*, Norton & Co., New York, 1971 [orig. 1949]

21 Lorenzo-Eiroa, P. *Instalaciones: Sobre el Trabajo de Peter Eisenman*, DLO/RE, Buenos Aires, 2008

22 Durand, J.N.L. Précis of the Lectures on Architecture: With Graphic Portion of the Lectures on Architecture; trans. Britt, D., Getty Research Institute Publications Program, Los Angeles, 2000 [orig. 1802-5, 1821]

Figure 3.2 We include architects such as Brunelleschi, Palladio, Borromini and Rainaldi that belong to both the Renaissance and the Baroque. We think the Italian Peninsula was permeable to transcultural projects more than other places in Europe through its geographic intersection in the Mediterranean. Venice was the port of exchange between Europe, Middle East and Asia which influenced, for instance, in Palladio how a universal project is both addressed and critiqued in his architecture. The Baroque incorporated critically of Eurocentrism, middle eastern architecture features in art and architecture influencing the work of Bernini, Borromini, and Rainaldi (Chapter 4). We problematize origination as well as the authoritative relevance of both Venice and Rome which was the result of a transcultural imperial colonizing appropriation aiming to trace both universal and transcultural projects. A1-F1: 18 Palladian villas without porticos and barchesse buildings retrieved via API, ordered aligning the center space acknowledging displacements and entrance facing down. A1-F1: Carnaro, Saraceno, Pisani (Bagnolo), Valmarana, Zeno, Chiericati. A2-F2: Rotonda, Thiene (Cicogna), Pisani (Monatagnana), Poiana, Badoer, Emo; A3-F3: Foscari (Malcontenta), Sarego, Angarano, Caldogno, Trissino (Cricoli), Forni. API 2021. A4-O8: Nine-square square grid Generative Adversarial Networks (GAN) feature recognition training in relation to the developed dataset. The training of more than 1000 epochs increasingly identifies nine-square square grid patterns into three different emergent structures: the first trained dataset after 100 epochs outputs an A-C-A structure with bay differentiations through an elastic topological structure deforming the lines of the grid; the second trained dataset becomes stable after 250 epochs outputs an A-B-C-B-A structure differentiating service bays from central and peripheral bays; the third trained dataset outputs unstructured noise or subordination of the parts in relation to the whole. While the general structure is valuable and recognized as either A-C-A, or A-B-C-B-A, parametric undecidability seems not to be able to assign independent value to the part in relation to the whole structure. PI Pablo Lorenzo-Eiroa, RA Salma Kattass, IDC Foundation Grant, 2022. A9-Y14: Infinite possible Palladian Villas ordered typologically in epochs training; DM parametric variations; A15-H18: DM image feed CNN parametric variations. The language output expression of the plans variations is related to the trained loss function of the GAN and the pretrained loss function of the Midjourney DM, but based on our own research work and collaborations we contributed to retrieved via NLP prompt engineering activating MJ API. PI Pablo Lorenzo-Eiroa, MidJourney, 2022.

4 Borromini's Topological Model Displaced by Rainaldi's Ahistorical Synthesis

Architects Indexing, Displacing, and Innovating in Spatial Representation

""Design" is no longer something that precedes execution... By this means the value of art is translated from "invention" to the operative process of the artist.... This is the first time that a conception of art is presented as pure interiority." Argan on Michelangelo[1]

History Section:
Baroque; Modern Movement; Post-Structuralism;

Philosophy:
Res Extensa; Nietzsche Double Negation; Derrida's Displacement; Cassirer Symbolic Form;

Methodology:
Argan Formal Typology and Abstract Type (Form, Structure, Decorative); Venturi's Complexity and Contradiction; Rainaldi's Ahistorical Synthesis; Panofsky's Symbolic Form as Deep Structure;

Visual Semiotic Signifiers:
Pulsating Space; Poché Space; Positive and Negative Space; Continuous Space; Perspective; Layered Space;

Mathematic Geometry:
Double Curvature Surfaces; Projective Geometry; Pendentive; Serlian Oval; Complex Geometry; Topology;

Architecture in Relation to Systems of Representation:
Plan; Section; Axonometric; Layered Space; Perspective; Poché Space; Pulsating Space; Positive-Negative Space;

Borromini's Topological Model as an Historiography of Spatial Representation

Borromini can be considered the first analog topological architect. In contrast to Palladio's topological displacements discussed in previous chapters,

DOI: 10.4324/9781003292036-5

Borromini's distortion describes a common elastic continuous geometric topology across most of his buildings. Borromini's distortion defined the innovative Baroque as a distinct style: from a distorting perspective, to distorting spatial containment innovating in a new spatial typology, to disproportion based on a new non-pleasing aesthetics. Borromini pragmatically develops a spatial innovation in activating a pulsating positive and negative space engendering his philosophic concept of Res-Extensa[2] particularly in San Carlo in Rome, first in the cloister (1634–37). Borromini's spatial inversion displaces the normal concave corner condition of the courtyard inverting it into a convex figure indexing a positive space in the gallery and breaking boundaries between inside and outside spaces. Borromini defines a new spatial typology since the value of the framing containment of the space and the space itself are placed in ambiguous visual and experiential semiotics. San Carlo's spatial pulsation can be related to: Bramante's St. Peter plans (1506–13) in which positive space and the negative wall figure containing the space have an equal figuration thanks to a complex articulated poché wall; Michelangelo's (1475–1564) sculptural work, evident in Borromini's façade of San Carlo (1665–67); Villa Adriana in Tivoli, specifically the sala a cupola della Piazza d'Oro (123–35 CE); and G. da Sangallo's (1445–1516) drawings of Tempio di Portuno (1484).

Rewriting History: Big Data Survey Challenging Assumed Theory

Different historians as well as architects aimed at reading and analyzing Borromini's work, developing multiple theories of the object such as von Neumann, Hempel, Brinckmann, Sedlmayr,[3] L.S. Naumann, Wittkower, Pevsner, Argan, Moretti, Steinberg,[4] Portoghesi, Zevi, Dal Co, Hill, and others including the 3D digital laser scanning survey and model reconstruction by Frommel and Sladek,[5] mainly focusing on the floor plan of Borromini's San Carlo (Figure 4.2). Historically architects have analyzed buildings of Roman antiquity by measuring, reading, and analyzing them to project classic proportions, a notion that Alberti and Palladio displaced. Due to contemporary Big Data survey technology, a new recovery of the function of survey becomes active, as well as a balance in the shift between theory and evidence, displacing architecture representation such as the floor plan, section, and axonometric documentation as analytical sections, activating a new augmented history and theory of architecture based on indexical physical evidence, a forensics of the built environment. This change motivates an augmented realism displacing the idea of stable origin. We started working with 3D scanning LiDAR (Light Detection and Ranging, sometimes Laser, 1981) in 2012 exploring the possibilities of navigating virtually through point clouds as a new form of augmented indexical realism, defining a new architecture signifier: a new higher dimension to measure and index space through point clouds. Several architects and engineers innovated in architecture through LiDAR such as Saunders[6] with whom we had the opportunity to collaborate in 2015.

We implement Big Data through forensic LiDAR 3D scanning to challenge theoretical assumptions based on evidence through an emergent Digital Humanities. Canciani maps a type of oval in Borromini's San Carlo's[7] reference and construction geometry distinguishing ovals from ellipses that have a particularly interesting history.[8] We noticed Canciani did not use the scan in the plan focusing only on the dome. Archeology, survey, and measurement expand dimension in the actual object, as survey expands informationally an analysis and a theory of the object. The validation of the analysis through indexing the actual construction is that a building requires deep knowledge and understanding of projective geometry and in coordination with the construction system, indexing the complexity of decisions and control done at the site that perhaps were never registered. The actual building is evidence of a medium-specific architecture expression achieved.

By addressing the counterreformation liturgical demands of a Latin cross-organization, the church of San Carlo is simultaneously organized by two systems, namely a centralized organization and a linear organization contradicting each other:[9] one that displaces the center of the dome, linearly toward the back, through a figure applying the Serlian Oval[10] (1537–75) geometrically formed by two centers, thereby expanding the dome along the main processional axis. The perpendicular axis compresses the center dome laterally, placing both axes in tension. The tensioned organization indexes a distorted nine-square grid through traces of a continuous spatial gradual degree change, a "topology" (Figure 4.1). Borromini repeats the courtyard operation and creates continuity along the four apses by removing the corner condition as a presence of absence (the only straight line in the Church in plan), developing unity and a new synthesis, a new Baroque canon through revolutionizing spatial containment. Visually he also distorts conventional perspective through a geodesic projective geometry, both in the semi-dome of the main altar and in the two lateral altars' distorted semi-domes, deforming the porticos. Borromini ideologically critiques superfluous decoration as representative of the political power of Rome, as his buildings are abstract focusing on the formal complexity of the space as a positive figure, in contrast with Bernini's Sant Andrea in Quirinale ornamentation blurring architecture, painting, and sculpture next to San Carlo's Church.

The original floor plan (Figure 4.1), the series of analytical plans by historians (Figure 4.2), our proposed nine-square grid floor plan (Figure 4.3 A6, B6, B7), and our conceptual analytical plan series (differing from Alonso Garcia's thesis[11] Figure 4.3), are placed in contrast to the indexical 3D LiDAR scan (Figure 4.4). The accumulated transparency of a series of topographic contour lines sections of the 3D LiDAR scanning looking down as a floor plan and from the top as a roof plan indexes through transparency, an alternative reading (Figure 4.3 A7-D7; Figure 4.4; Figure 4.5 A2-C2; Figure 4.8). If one relates the pendentive corner and the circular oculus as squinches that provide structural support to the dome, in relation to the four arches that support the dome, they all together define the nine-square grid as a continuous figure tensioning back the elimination of the corner condition. Indexical floor

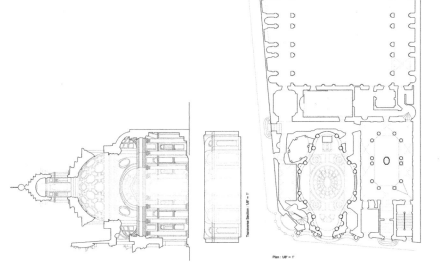

Figure 4.1 Borromini San Carlo in Rome (1634–67), drawings interpretations by Design II students: Pamela Cabrera, Andres Larrauri, Rolando Vega, Elena Cena, Guilherme Nunes, and Will Shapiro in Baroque Analysis Studio Coordinated by Prof. Michael Young, and with Associate Prof. Felicia Davis and Associate Prof. Pablo Lorenzo-Eiroa, The Cooper Union, 2008.

plans as horizontal planimetries' topographies are taken at each recognizable change in San Carlo's laser 3D scan (Figure 4.4). In the planimetric sections (Figure 4.4 E1, E2, E3, E4) the pendentive and squinches, recover the absent eliminated corner condition, reconstituting the figure of the nine-square grid in coordination with the four arches, conforming a rectangular figure with curved corners. In the planimetric sections, (Figure 4.4 D1, D2, D3, D4; E1,

Borromini's Topological Model Displaced by Rainaldi's Ahistorical Synthesis 45

E2, E3, E4) describe the dome including the figural coffers. In addition, the four niches in the corners which are larger and at a different elevation, reconstitute a similar notion, although the figure does not line up due to the angle (usually are not included to show the accesses to the corner chapels). The external 3D scan of the dome lantern is unavailable and may extend our research. These planimetries (Figure 4.4) are representative of Borromini's reading by Steinberg as a variation of typologies based on the same building and the most important floor plans to understand them as a topological genealogy, a project systematic enough for Borromini to achieve a machinic system: from SM. Dei Sette Dolori, to Oratorio Dei Filippini, to Propaganda Fide's Chapel, to St. Agnese, with the exception of icon-symbolic driven St Ivo alla Sapienza.

The first attempt is to read and incorporate all historians' readings and analysis (Figure 4.2), developing both a comparative analysis (Figure 4.3) and a Big Data dataset (Figure 4.4). The second attempt is to reveal a topological plan that can index many of Borromini's typological building variations (Figure 4.3, 4.4). The third attempt is to access a 3D scan through LiDAR of the building and explore implied relationships through infinite sectional planimetries or changing floor plans, through comparative simulation, navigation, and forced experimental representation (Figure 4.4, 4.5, 4.6, 4.8, 4.9). The fourth attempt is to reveal representation relationships in the building through comparative simulations (Figure 4.7). The fifth attempt is to identify an index a unit of measurement of the geometric reconstruction of the floor plan that would be able to integrate the actual physical 3D scanning evidence of the dome (Figure 4.3). The sixth attempt is to retrieve through AI semantic segmentation through 3D feature recognition of the 3D point cloud of Borromini's project in relation to the data retrieved through Application Programming Interface (API) through 2D retrieved images interpolation (Figure 4.7 B2). The seventh attempt is to compare Borromini's building in relation to its traceable influence on other buildings, such as Carlo Rainaldi's S.M. in Campitelli implementing AI, Generative Adversarial Networks (GANs), semantic segmentation classification through boundary map, and feature recognition (Figure 4.15, 4.16, 4.17, 4.18, 4.19, 4.20, 4.21, 4.22).

We include below the following analysis of the media-based research sequence including particular issues in the image captions (Figures 4.1–4.09).

Borromini's San Carlo analysis included reading, redrawing, decoding, analyzing, and theorizing his work to propose an alternative theory. The originating plan drawings as generation diagrams (Figure 4.3) start from a single-dimensional circle unit that is repeated as a unit comparable to a column diameter in size, to conform to the overall initial dome circle base unit, which when repeated and translated comprises the Serlian Oval, corroborating Canciari's thesis, but coordinating the plan with the dome. In these diagrams, the side deformed altars are usually not related as part of the same geometric construction of the dome. In our analysis, we place two simultaneous systems universal and a local in contrast with each other: a single circle can reconstruct the entire geometry, counting with thicknesses differentials, referring to Michelangelo's order out of a constellation influence in Borromini and not a single figuration; and a topological elastic diagram can unify local contingency creating continuity across the composition.

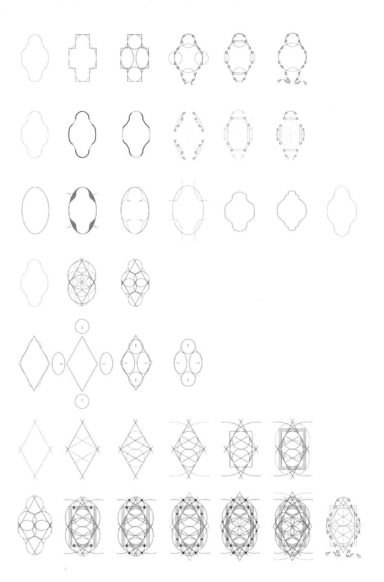

Figure 4.2 Historians' theoretical interpretation of Borromini's San Carlo's floor plan. A1: Steinberg based on Brinckmann; BC1: Steinberg based on Francis Naumann; D-E1: Montijano-Garcia Greek Cross sequence based on Villa Adriana Piazza D'Oro; F1: Steinberg based on Fasolo (interlocked circles theory); A2, B2, C2: Sedlmayer; D2–F2: Steinberg three possible columns grouping readings; A3: Steinberg based on internal oval reading by Gurlitt, B3: Stenberg based on Weingartner, C3: Sedlmayer spatial pressure; D3: Brinckmann ellipse against implicit corners; E3: Steinberg Greek Cross based on Pevsner; F3: Stenberg based on rhomboid with undulated perimeter based on Wittkower and Montjano-Garcia; G3: Steinberg based on Muñoz and Guidi and on Borromini's original drawings Albertina 171 and 172 archive; A4, B4, C4: Steinberg reading of Sedlmayer's theory; A5, B5, C5: Brickmann and then Sedlmayer theory on a rhomboid with spaces from the outside based on the convex corners of the courtyard and Villa Adriana in Tivoli [sala a cupola della Piazza d'Oro (123–35 CE)]; A6–F6: Hempel; A7–F7: Hempel; G7: Portoghesi oval construction in tension with a frame indexing the four arches. All drawings reinterpretations of theories by historians by PI Pablo Lorenzo-Eiroa, RA Salma Kattas, IDC Foundation Grant, NYIT SoAD, 2022.

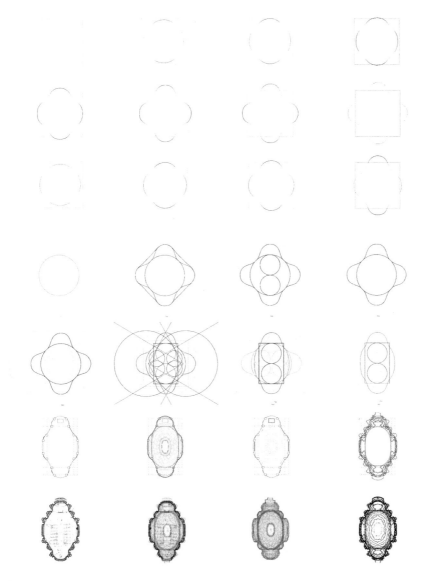

Figure 4.3 A1–D5: Borromini San Carlo theoretical topological conceptual geometrical reconstruction based on a polycentric oval, departing from a Greek Cross and in relation to Villa Adriana Piazza D'Oro tensioning positive and negative spaces, through points and circle units after column radius. These theory-based drawings contrast the 3D scan and are based on Borromini's original drawings Albertina 172, 173 archives. A6–D6: Borromini floor plan as a nine-square grid structure by indexing the four arches, differentiating the main columns from the altar's secondary columns. The nine-square enables a different structural conceptual reading in distinguishing the field of columns and following Dal Co's analysis supported by the flooring figure. A7–D7: The nine-square grid argument is also based on an indexical LiDAR 3D scan of the entire building, correlating the floor plan and the dome in continuity through indexical planimetric topographies. The floor plan and the reflected ceiling plan through computer 3D modeling are based on an ideological and perceptual bias, which contrasts with the real indexed forensic survey. Visiting Research Professor Sapienza University in Rome Pablo Lorenzo-Eiroa, 2015.

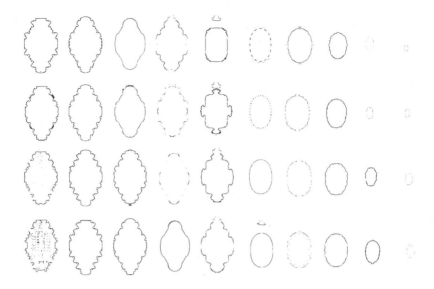

Figure 4.4 A1–J4: Planimetric sections as indexical floor plans topographies taken at each relative change in Borromini's San Carlo building through a LiDAR laser 3D scanning point cloud. E1–E2, E3, E4: Floor plan sections in plans which demonstrate the conscious topological variation of Borromini's complex pendentive and dome construction articulating spatial problems in plan and in relation to the varying complex geometry of the oval dome. Axonometric projection and planimetric projections intersection of point cloud by PI Pablo Lorenzo-Eiroa, RA Salma Kattass, IDC Foundation Grant, NYIT SoAD, 2022.

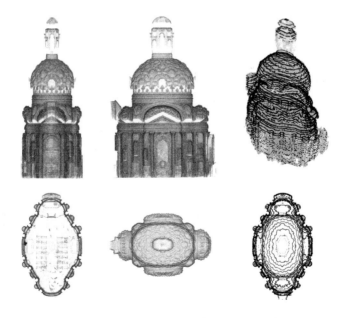

Figure 4.5 A1–C2: Accumulated transparency of 3D LiDAR laser scanning as an accumulative floor plan. The short axis arches are straight, but the longitudinal arches are bent inwards at the center, a projective geometry difficult to find in 3D models. The four corner niches (usually not included to show the passages to the chapels) also can offer interesting readings as they are different in size and elevation. PI Pablo Lorenzo-Eiroa, RA Salma Kattass, IDC Foundation Grant, NYIT SoAD, 2022.

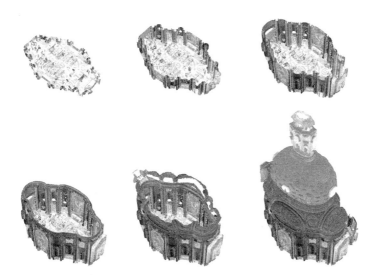

Figure 4.6 A1–B3: Borromini's San Carlo exploded axonometric. Rendering Point Cloud and AI processing PI Pablo Lorenzo-Eiroa, RA Salma Kattass, IDC Foundation Grant, NYIT SoAD, 2022. This 3D model/scan was created using: Faro Focus LiDAR, Faro Scene, and RealityCapture software by Capturing Reality.

Figure 4.7 A1–C3: Big Data point cloud simulations representation, and Big Data processing, implementing Machine Learning semantic segmentation classification and isolation of over 250M points. B2: Point cloud semantic segmentation of columns. 3D LiDAR Laser Scanning by Andrew Saunders with the assistance of Pablo Lorenzo-Eiroa and Mario Graziano Valenti, Rome 2016. Rendering Point Cloud and AI processing PI Pablo Lorenzo-Eiroa, RA Salma Kattass, IDC Foundation Grant, NYIT SoAD, 2022. This 3D model/scan was created using: Faro Focus LiDAR, Faro Scene, and RealityCapture software by Capturing Reality.

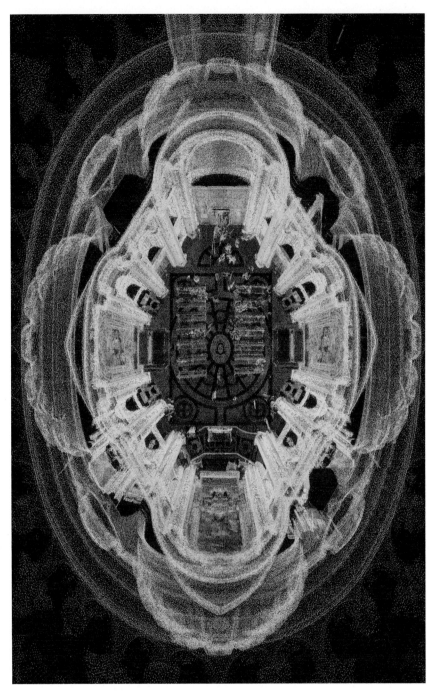

Figure 4.8 Big Data 250M point cloud 3D LiDAR laser scanning simulations. Depicting transparency of dome-plan relationships. The pendentive squinches tension the negated corner condition in the plan, which adds tension to a pulsating space. 3D LiDAR Laser Scanning by Andrew Saunders with the assistance of Pablo Lorenzo-Eiroa and Mario Graziano Valenti, Rome 2016. Rendering Point Cloud and AI semantic and feature segmentation processing by PI Pablo Lorenzo-Eiroa, RA Salma Kattass, IDC Foundation Grant, NYIT SoAD, 2022. This 3D model/scan was created using: Faro Focus LiDAR, Faro Scene, and RealityCapture software by Capturing Reality.

Borromini's Topological Model Displaced by Rainaldi's Ahistorical Synthesis 51

Figure 4.9 Big Data 250M point cloud interior simulations representation through transparency accentuating the lateral compression of the building. 3D LiDAR Laser Scanning by Andrew Saunders with the assistance of Pablo Lorenzo-Eiroa and Mario Graziano Valenti, Rome 2016. Rendering Point Cloud and AI processing PI Pablo Lorenzo-Eiroa, RA Salma Kattass, IDC Foundation Grant, NYIT SoAD, 2022. This 3D model/scan was created using: Faro Focus LiDAR, Faro Scene, and RealityCapture software by Capturing Reality.

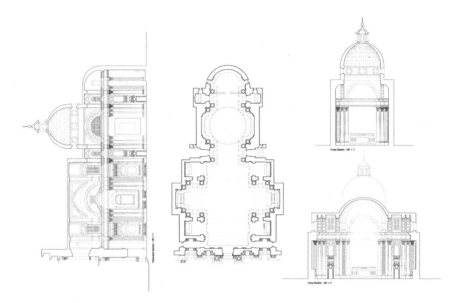

Figure 4.10 Carlo Rainaldi SM in Campitelli, Rome (1656–65) drawings by Design II students Sean Gaffney, Jess Russell, Danny Willis, Malin Heyman, Liya Kohavi and Ge-nan Peng; in Baroque Analysis Studio Coordinated by Prof. Michael Young, and with Associate Prof. Felicia Davis and Associate Prof. Pablo Lorenzo-Eiroa, The Cooper Union, 2008.

Rainaldi Ahistorical Suspension of Wölfflin's Pendulum

Some of Borromini's ideas can be traced in one of his collaborators and competitor Carlo Rainaldi, in his masterpiece Santa Maria in Campitelli (1656–65) (Figure 4.10). Wittkower analyzes this paradigmatic building that escapes any stylistic category of the time as he describes the importance of the problem of orientation in centrally planned buildings.

> "From the fifteenth century onwards the old problem of combining the central dome and the nave had been resolved in two different ways. The first as a fusion into an organic entity, the second principle, the two fundamental structural forms remain isolated…" Wittkower[12]

We develop a critique of the histories and theories that are commonly understood in the work of Carlo Rainaldi analyzing floor plans in relation to a Big Data LiDAR survey (4.10, 4.11, 4.14, 4.15). We first trace relationships in Rainaldi's SM in Campitelli in relation to precedent site conditions (Figure 4.15 A2-E2); we then compare floor plans and sections in relation to tracing Palladio's and Borromini's strategies applied by Rainaldi (Figure 4.15 B1-E1). Through LiDAR 3D laser scanning, we trace relationships between idealized representations in relation to the actual index; through simulations, we do representational analysis revealing internal relationships; we apply Big Data

First, the structure of the church of S.M. in Campitelli is divided into two, and it can be analyzed both as an influence as well as a critique of Borromini's San Carlo pulsation, as it indexes two of its floor plans organized perpendicular to each other. Second, the first anterior space may be read typologically as a Greek Cross that indexes a smaller previous church[13] of 1658 (Figure 4.10, 4.11, 4.15). The displacement of the dome and the altar toward the back in Campitelli generates a series of inversions between the two centroidal spaces which through double negations surpass a dialectic (Figure 4.15 A2-E2).[14] The first space transversal against the axis toward the altar indexes Sant' Agnese's Greek Cross by both Girolamo and Carlo Rainaldi (1651). Sant's Agnese transversally accentuates the side altar's forced perspective lining up with its contextual Piazza Navona's proportion originally indexing the Roman Circus Agonalis (86 ACE). Sant'Agnese also references Palladio's Il Redentore's discontinuous independent spaces, as the side altars in St Agnese are separated from the dome through service bays (Figure 4.15 C1). Borromini takes over St Agnese (1653) developing the façade embracing public space and in relation to the geometry of Piazza Navona. Sant'Andrea al Quirinale by Bernini (1658) also accentuates the perpendicular axis against the procession toward the altar, as opposed to Borromini's San Carlo, which compresses it. S.A. Quirinale also embraces public space a strategy extended to St Peter's piazza (1656). Third in S.M. in Campitelli, as the processional axis is expanded backward through a series of spaces, the perspectival cone effect is interrupted by Venetian picture planes, critiquing Borromini's spatial plasticity, and referencing Palladio's Il Redentore (Figure 4.15 D2, E1).[15, 16] Fourth, both spaces are based on a nine-square grid organization since a series of *topological* −as gradual displacements − index one with the other (including site adjustments): while the anterior space expanded perpendicular to the procession axis toward the altar as in Rainaldi's St. Agnese and in parallel to an excessively wide façade, the posterior space looks compressed as in Borromini's San Carlo (Figure 4.1 B1) and Palladio's Redentore (Figure 4.15 C1). The posterior space transversally compressed negates a transept below the dome referencing Borromini's tension in San Carlo's between transversal and longitudinal building cross sections, which we index by comparing Rainaldi's building with two of Borromini's San Carlo's buildings (Figure 4.1, 4.10, 4.14, 4.15 E2, 4.16). In Campitelli these two building sections, the compressed one and the expanded one (Figure 4.14), are parallel to each other comprising the two transversal sections of the building comparable to Borromini's longitudinal and perpendicular sections (Figure 4.1 A2, B1). This topological displacement of the original structure proposes a typological distinction between the two spaces: the anterior space reinforces the *transversal* direction measuring 90' wide; the posterior one reinforces this *processional axis* measuring 90' long (Figure 4.10). The posterior space references Palladio's Il Rendentore Latin Cross axis compression due to a similar site constraint (Figure 4.15 C1), and as a separate part, since the dome creates ambiguity between the first space's Greek Cross and the second space Latin cross, dissipated as a figure due to its lateral compression, as the second space expands backward beyond a normal proportion. Both spaces are contained in a composition that produces a synthesis between two structures in tension. Fifth, the continuity of the wall pulsation in Campitelli referencing Borromini's pulsation of concave and convex spaces is interrupted (Figure 4.13; 4.19). However, it is due to the relative topological displacements to the structural correspondences between the two spaces that integrate them, that such polyrhythm unfurls multiple visual and bodily affects (Figure 4.12). Last, the columns as architectural signs become unmotivated due to their ambiguous pulsation of the space within an overall syntax following Borromini's strategy (Figure 4.16, 4.19, 4.20, 4.21).

The building presents a spatial synthesis of many pairs of concepts developed by Wölfflin simultaneously and in tension that transcend such constructed Hegelian dialectic[17] through Nietzsche's double negation – not this not that, in a field of relationships and tensions. These structural problems are precisely integrated with the mediums of representation, establishing a manifest that transcends the historic dialectic between Wölfflin's Renaissance and Baroque (Figures 4.11–4.22).

Figure 4.11 A1–D2: Big Data 250M point cloud simulations of Carlo Rainaldi SM Campitelli. A2–C2: Floor plan and Reflected Ceiling Plan. LiDAR 3D Scanning by Andrew Saunders UPenn, with the assistance of Pablo Lorenzo-Eiroa and Mario Graziano Valenti. This 3D model/scan was created using: Faro LiDAR, RealityCapture software by Capturing Reality. Research, drawings, Big Data representation, processing, and renderings by Associate Visiting Professor, Pablo Lorenzo-Eiroa Sapienza University in Rome 2015.

Figure 4.12 A1–C3: Big Data 250M point cloud simulations representation, and Big Data processing, implementing Machine Learning classification and semantic segmentation. B3–C3: semantic segmentation of columns AI analysis and design-research, PI: Pablo Lorenzo-Eiroa, RA: Salma Kattass, IDC Foundation Grant, NYIT SoAD, 2022.

Figure 4.13 Big Data 250M point cloud simulations representation. This 3D model/scan was created using: Faro Focus LiDAR, Faro Scene, and RealityCapture software by Capturing Reality and point cloud processing scripts. PI: Pablo Lorenzo-Eiroa, RA: Salma Kattass, IDC Foundation Grant, NYIT SoAD, 2022.

Figure 4.14 See Notes Figure 4.14

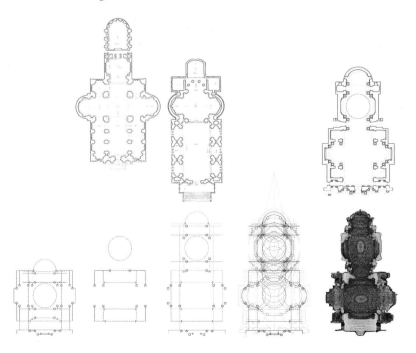

Figure 4.15 See Notes Figure 4.15

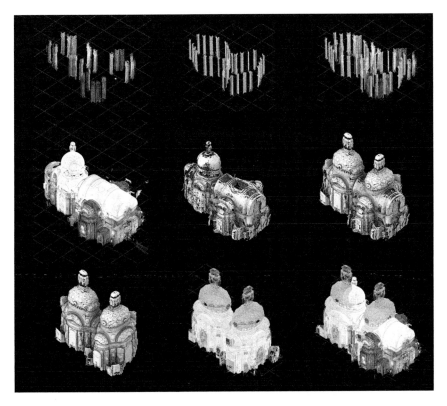

Figure 4.16 Big Data LiDAR 3D Scan 250M point cloud representation. A1: 3D Scan of Rainaldi's building. B3 two of Borromini's buildings indexing Rainaldi's building. A1–B3: morphing process. PI: Pablo Lorenzo-Eiroa, RA: Salma Kattass, IDC Foundation Grant, NYIT SoAD, 2022.

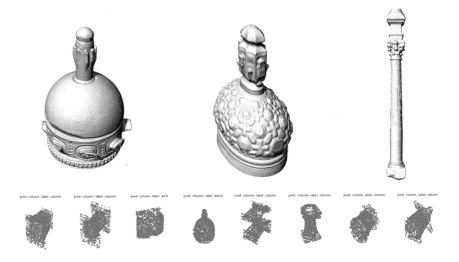

Figure 4.17 PointNet pretrained point cloud dataset in relation to our trained dataset Machine Learning semantic segmentation classification isolating elements within the point cloud. A1: SM Campitelli Dome; B1: San Carlo dome; C1: SM Campitelli columns. A2–H2: ML training of dataset. PI: Pablo Lorenzo-Eiroa, RA: Salma Kattass, IDC Foundation Grant, NYIT SoAD, 2022.

58 *Borromini's Topological Model Displaced by Rainaldi's Ahistorical Synthesis*

Figure 4.18 A1–B2: Big Data LiDAR scanning semantic segmentation prediction (with noise) model through both pretrained and trained dataset, database, and meta-data repository tagging categories "Columns" retrieving information categories. B2: Training result statistic approximation feature recognition after training the dataset and applying it to the point cloud. This ML classification recognized two types of signs: free-standing columns and columns within the wall system. Renderings point cloud representation, Big Data processing, Machine Learning, ML Classification, AI analysis, and design-research, PI: Pablo Lorenzo-Eiroa, RA: Salma Kattass, IDC Foundation Grant, NYIT SoAD, 2022.

Borromini's Topological Model Displaced by Rainaldi's Ahistorical Synthesis   59

Figure 4.19 PointNet, and our own 3D point cloud dataset Machine Learning semantic segmentation classification, AI analysis, and design research. 3D model/scan was created using: Faro Focus LiDAR, Faro Scene, and RealityCapture software by Capturing Reality and point cloud processing scripts. PI: Pablo Lorenzo-Eiroa, RA: Salma Kattass, IDC Foundation Grant, NYIT SoAD, 2022.

60 *Borromini's Topological Model Displaced by Rainaldi's Ahistorical Synthesis*

Figure 4.20 Big Data 250M point cloud ML semantic segmentation simulations. A1: Semantic segmentation of Rainaldi columns. B1: Semantic Segmentation Borromini's columns comprising Rainaldi's building. A2: Interior view of Rainaldi's building with columns separated. B2: Interior view of Rainaldi's building constructed by combining two of Borromini's buildings. A3, B3: Interior views of Rainaldi's building and interior view of Borromini's composition. PI: Pablo Lorenzo-Eiroa, RA: Salma Kattass, IDC Foundation Grant, NYIT SoAD, 2022.

Borromini's Topological Model Displaced by Rainaldi's Ahistorical Synthesis 61

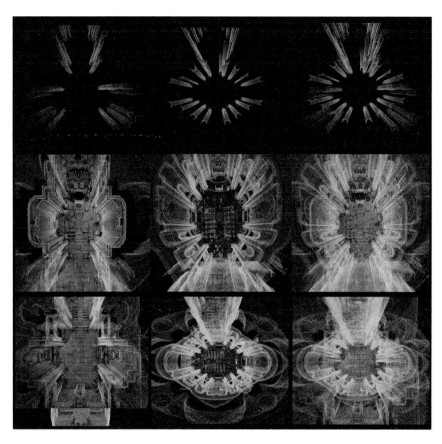

Figure 4.21 Big Data 250M point cloud simulations representation, Big Data processing, Machine Learning, ML Classification, AI analysis, and design-research. PI: Pablo Lorenzo-Eiroa, RA: Salma Kattass, IDC Foundation Grant, 2022. This 3D model/scan was created using: Faro Focus LiDAR, Faro Scene, RealityCapture software by Capturing Reality.

62 *Borromini's Topological Model Displaced by Rainaldi's Ahistorical Synthesis*

Figure 4.22 Big Data 250M point cloud SM Campitelli 3D Scan simulations superimposed with ghosted Borromini San Carlo's composition. Augmented Virtual Reality navigation over the geotagging location in Rome at Rainaldi's building. Visiting Associate Professor Pablo Lorenzo-Eiroa Sapienza University in Rome. Update AI ML semantic segmentation and visual feature segmentation and processing, PI: Pablo Lorenzo-Eiroa, RA: Salma Kattass, IDC Foundation Grant, NYIT SoAD, 2022.

Modernist Displacement of the Frame: Derrida's Parergon in Russian Constructivists and Modern Art

Panofsky differentiated "artistic volition"[18] as a conceptual synthesis, which is not a synthesis of a particular period or will of the time and neither as an artist's volition, nor as an artistic perception, which is the ultimate meaning. According to Panofsky, Alois Riegl argued that Semper suggested that the material and the technique play a role in the genesis of artistic forms, but Riegl argued that Semperians jumped to the conclusion that all forms of art were the direct result of materials and techniques that are interchangeable with art.

In 1434 Della Pintura[19] Alberti addresses the importance of painting in relation to architecture, shifting tectonics and problems between the visual

Borromini's Topological Model Displaced by Rainaldi's Ahistorical Synthesis 63

arts questioning representation. Derrida's linguistic discussion of parergon[20] questions the origin and the frame of the work of art, expanding Hegel's Lectures on Aesthetics[21] and based on Alberti's discussion on the painting which he resonates with language. For Derrida the context in which art is defined is not completely outside the work; moreover, the content of the work is activated and determined by the presence of the frame in which it is situated, questioning its origin. The structure becomes the object. Derrida's *parergon* places structure as the origin and anticipates its form of production and output implying the impossibility of coming up with content outside its frame of reference.

Russian Constructivists and Futurists in correlation to the political social economic revolution of 1917 revolutionized art as a technique, differentiating material autonomy through doing and art's content unique to its medium. Noam Gabos' Realism Manifesto defines the difference between mass and space in a volumetric cube addressing autonomy from linguistic meaning through visual semiotic signification. Russian constructivists and European formalism introduced the idea of *autonomy* and purpose of art different from contemporary representational art as an *abstraction*. They present *technique as content*, as opposed to *form and content*, a *formalist* movement identifying the development of new techniques with creativity.[22] Shklovsky[23] discusses the suspension of habitual perception by the *technique of art*, to make objects "unfamiliar" to extend the length of time perception. Schwitters motivates the background site-specific frame-structure support where art is generated in his Merzbau installation (1923–37).

Mondrian revolutionizes art through a series of political displacements formulated originally around 1917 by an aesthetic collective De Stijl (the style). Mondrian problematizes several axioms in painting that can be organized non-historically: from content landscape abstraction (e.g. *Gray Tree*, 1911), to abstraction of content (Composition No. 6, 1914), to an artistic pictorial autonomy (Composition, Red, Blue, and Yellow, 1930), to pairing content abstraction and abstracted structures (Broadway Boogie Woogie, 1942–43), to indexing the frame and voiding the center (Tableau 2, 1922), to displacing the horizon in painting through the rotation of the frame (Lozenge Composition with Yellow, Black, Blue, Red and Gray, 1921). Pollock completes the dissociation of painting from representation to autonomy by turning the vertical canvas indexing pictorial abstraction to the horizontal ground condition (Lavender Mist, Number 1, 1950).

Architects of the Modern Movement used axonometric projection to resist perspective subjectivity and proposed a parametric mathematical projection model where XYZ induces a universal object-space. The Bauhaus (1913–33) proposed a recognition of the influence of systems of representation as a different way to index media-specific visual arts and architecture, with perhaps one of the first architecture schools to critique the politics of a patriarchic society giving relevance to women in architecture, art, and design.[24]

Displacing Systems of Representation in Architecture: Hejduk and Eisenman

The study of the history of architecture also changed from stylistic revolutions to a structural history abstracted from style. Wittkower[25] analyzes the work of Palladio, as a system of flexible relationships across his villas depicting an abstract nine-square pattern independent from historical style after Frankl's diagrams.[26] Rowe, a student of Wittkower, anticipates the research and presents a structuralist history by comparing Le Corbusier's Villa Stein of 1926 and Palladio's Malcontenta (1,554) floor plans[27] through an abstract nine-square grid.

House 3 by Hejduk (1954–63) presents an integrated architecture made from different logical systems contradicting each other out of a clearly defined nine-square grid system in contrast with a four-square grid system, since the center becomes voided through the courtyard space, and simultaneously the center is occupied by the structure's axes. Based on Mondrian's frame rotation, Hejduk projects architecture representation indexing its medium, by coordinating the angle of projective geometry to the conventional angle of representation and dissociating the envelope in relation to the core interior in the diamond houses series. Hejduk Axonometric works two ways, as a 0°|90° degree axonometric (exterior envelope) and as a 45°/45° degree axonometric projection if one focuses on the interior of the house, placing both systems in a state of ambiguity and inseparable dependent tension, transfiguring foreground object representation as content and background representation system as a frame.[28] The wall houses complete the series displacing the ground horizon to a vertical picture plane wall as an interface threshold.

Eisenman's House series from 1967–80, particularly House IV of 1971 process diagrams apply a formal grammar borrowed from linguistic semiotics through visual semiotics, in which critics can inquire into the open design process. House IV diagrams develop linear and non-linear evolutive formal logic, presenting a normal reference displaced through progressive bifurcations, and iterations, making these diagrams address a data flow logical diagram, engaging necessarily into a procedural logic to rule out ambiguity and resolve necessary intermediate steps. According to Gandelsonas, Eisenman develops particularly in House X a linguistic semiotic system based on exploring grammar through syntax[29] developing issues of deep and surface structure, from structure to object, and by doing so, he is able to develop an architectural language.[30] Gandelsonas discusses through linguistics the logical validation of formal arguments and presents the concept of double deep structure based on problems of hierarchy and feedback. Eisenman plays with the ambiguity between an abstract formal system which aims at disseminating architectural meaning by unmotivating the conventions of an architecture-accepted sign, such as a "column" a "wall" or a "mass/volume" by both a constructivist method and a deconstruction. Eisenman's methodological formal procedures, starting from a generic solid that is progressively transformed by accumulating traces, and indexing the process of its own constitution resist the development of a unique moment of synthesis since it is a diagram always in a state of becoming.

Sol Lewitt presents a series of explorations on formal variability through disambiguation creating cultural objects–sculptures through incomplete open cubes in 1974 proven to be computable.[31] Eisenman's syntax is influenced by Palladio's computational incompleteness and can be traced to his insightful discoveries in the reading of the work of Terragni's Casa del Fascio (1933–36) and Casa Giuliano Frigerio (1939–40).[32] Both present antithesis on the condition of the whole extending and resolving the parametric work of Palladio, critiquing Le Corbusier's machinic metaphor: while Casa del Fascio develops a parametric machinic whole developing architectural value through the variability of an architectural system, Casa Frigerio's apparently unified whole tends to fragment as architectural values acquire an autonomy.

The axonometric model of house X by Eisenman (1975) confronts representation as a form of Being, since the original House X project was not going to be built, it is meant to be a construction through representation and be seen through a monocular vision. Due to the elimination of binocular vision that recreates perspectival depth, the model becomes two-dimensional. Deleuze's *Le Pli, Leibniz, and the Baroque* propose the baroque space as a possibility of thought through topological folds,[33] in regard to the baroque façade. Eisenman applies through linguistics Deleuze's semiotic understanding of the Leibniz fold to displace in architectural perspective, the ground and Cartesian space.

> "Vision can be defined s essentially a way of organizing space and elements in space" […] "For Deleuze, folded space articulates a new relationship between vertical and horizontal, figure and ground, inside and out — all structures articulated by traditional vision. […] "The fold presents the possibility of an alternative to the gridded space of the Cartesian order." Eisenman[34]

While Deleuze aims at denouncing the sign in linguistics as a power structure tracing immanence in art's autonomy through the fold in the Baroque, Eisenman reconceptualizes Deleuze through linguistics applied back to architecture. Perhaps Derrida's misunderstanding with Eisenman[35] is based on miscommunications and translations between linguistic semiotics and visual semiotics, although Derrida Alberti's *On Paining* also crosses linguistic and visual semiotics.

Post-Structuralist Theory

Architecture incorporated a growing critique of the modern movement tabula rasa seen as deterministic after the Second World War. Identified as a non-deterministic indexical sign as a found condition, the logic of the place

66 *Borromini's Topological Model Displaced by Rainaldi's Ahistorical Synthesis*

as a value related to both the ground surface and site specificity, recovering Greek's topo-logos in relation to the reconsideration of the relationship between humanity and a delicate environment within an Anthropocene.[36] From Noguchi's landscape as architecture to the architecture of the landscape measuring the topography of Pinós and Miralles, the figure-ground relationship was taken further to the point that there would be no conceptual distinction between the ground surface and the building-object, deconstructing the historical dialectic in architecture between a building and its background into a figuration of the ground. Several architects have been addressing the environment through alternative means of representation: from Banham's architecture of the environment of 1969 after the student revolution of 1968 triggered by oil spills, defining artificial environmental systems as a new expansion of the discipline toward controlled systems as space environments;[37] to the influential work of the Archigram, Piano, Rogers, and Foster defining the High-Tech movement in the 1980s which evolved to reconsider the architecture of environments and space environments incorporating a scientific approach to design.

Notes

1 Argan, G.C. *Borromini*, Xarait Ediciones, Madrid, 1980 [orig. 1955]
2 Norberg-Schulz, C. *Meaning in Western Architecture*, Praeger Publishers, New York, 1975[orig. 1974]
3 Sedlmayr, H. *L'Architettura di Borromini*, Electa, 1996 [orig.1939]
4 Steinberg, L. *Borromini's San Carlo Alle Quattro Fontane, A Study in Multiple Form and Architectural Symbolism*, Garland Publishing, New York, 1977
5 Frommel, C.L.; Sladek, E. *Francesco Borromini*, Bibliotheca Hertziana, Electa, 2000
6 Saunders, A. *Baroque Topologies*, Palombi Editori, Roma, 2018
7 Canciani, M. "The drawing of the dome of Borromini? San Carlino alle Quattro Fontane: canonic oval?", in *Disegnarecon*, 2015
8 Rosin, P.; Trucco, E. "The Amphitheatre Construction Problem", *Incontro Internazionale di Studi Rileggere L'Antico* (Rome, 13–15 December 2004), 2005
9 Venturi, R. *Complexity and Contradiction in Architecture*, MoMA, New York, 1966
10 Serlio. Sebastiano *Libro I: Principi della Geomtria*, Paris, 1545. Editrice Edalo Roma, 1980
11 Alonso Garcia, E. *San Carlino, La Mauina geométrica de Borromini,* Universidad de Valladolid, Salamanca, 2003
12 Wittkower, R. "Palladio's Influence on Venetial Religious Architecture", in *Palladio and English Palladianism*, in Thames and Hudson, 1983 [orig. 1974]
13 Güthlein, K. "Zwei unbekannte Zeichnungen zur Planungs- und Baugeschichte der römischen Pestkirche Santa Maria in Campitelli", in *Römisches Jahrbuch*, Bibliotheca Hertziana, München, 1990
14 Deleuze, G. *Nietzsche and Philosophy,* Columbia University Press, New York, 1983 [orig. 1962]
15 Wittkower, R. "Carlo Rainaldi and the Roman Architecture of the Full Baroque", *Art Bulletin* No. 19, 1937
16 Eisenman, P.; Roman, M. *Palladio Virtuel,* Yale University Press, New Haven, 2015

Borromini's Topological Model Displaced by Rainaldi's Ahistorical Synthesis   67

17 Fernie, E. *Art History And Its Methods, A Critical Anthology,* Phaidon Press, New York, 1995
18 Panofsky, E. "The concept of Artistic Volition", in *Critical Inquiry,* Volume 8, Issue 1, 1981 [orig. 1964]
19 Alberti, L.B. *On Painting,* Yale University Press, New Haven, 1956, transl. Spencer J. [orig. 1434]
20 Derrida, J. *La vérité en peinture,* Flammarion, Paris, 1978
21 Hegel: "Introductory Lectures on Aesthetics", Penguin Books, New York, 1993 [orig. 1835]
22 Bakhtin, M.M.; Medvedev, P.M. *The Formal Method in European Art Scholarship* [*Kunstwissenschaft*], 1928
23 Shklovsky, V.; Lemon, L. *Art as Technique,* Russian Formalist Criticism, 1917
24 Otto, E.; Rössler, P. *Bauhaus Women: A Global Perspective,* Bloomsbury, 2019
25 Wittkower, R. *Architectural Principles in the Age of Humanism,* Norton 1971 [orig.1949]
26 Frankl, P. *Principles of Architecture History,* trans. O'Gorman, J. MIT Press, Cambridge, 1973 [orig. 1914]
27 Rowe, C. "Mathematics of the Ideal Villa", in Rowe, C. *The Mathematics of the Ideal Villa and Other Essays,* MIT Press, Cambridge, 1976 [orig. 1947]
28 Linder, M. *Nothing Less Than Literal: Architecture After Minimalism,* MIT, Cambridge, 2007
29 Gandelsonas, M.; Morton, D. "On Reading Architecture", in Progressive Architecture, 1972
30 Gandelsonas, M. "From Structure to Subject: The Formation of an Architectural Language", in ed. Ockman, J., *House X,* Rizzoli, New York, 1982
31 Allan Reb, M. "Analysis Of Variations Of Incomplete Open Cubes By Sol Lewitt", Thesis, Washburn University, 2011
32 Eisenman, P. *Giuseppe Terragni: Transformations, Decompositions, Critiques,* The Monacelli Press, New York, 2003
33 Deleuze, G. *Le pli et le baroque,* Minuit, Paris, 1988.
34 Eisenman, P. "Visions Unfolding: Architecture in the Age of Electronic Media", in "Intelligente Ambiente", *Ars Electronica,* 1992
35 Derrida, J.; Eisenman, P.; ed. Kipnis, J. *Chora L Works: Jacques Derrida and Peter Eisenman,* The Monacelli Press, New York, 1997
36 Crutzen, P.; Stoermer, E.F. "The Anthropocene", in *IGBP Newsletter,* 2000
37 Banham, R. *Architecture of the Well-Tempered Environment,* University of Chicago Press, Chicago, 1969

Figure 4.14 A1–B2: Rainaldi SM Campitelli, anterior space, and posterior space in contrast with each other. Associate Visiting Professor, Pablo Lorenzo-Eiroa Sapienza University in Rome, 2015–16.
Figure 4.15 B1: Palladio SM Maggiore plan interpretation based on Scamozzi. C1: Palladio Il Redentore plan interpretation based on Scamozzi. E1: Rainaldi SM Campitelli. A2, B2, C2: Organizational structure based on a nine-square grid, from its archeological, find Greek Cross to indexing Palladio's compressed Latin Cross in tension with each other. D2: Borromini's San Carlo's indexed in Rainaldi's Campitelli. E2: 3D scans in plan combining two of Borromini's San Carlo buildings to index Rainaldi's SM Campitelli. Visiting Associate Professor Pablo Lorenzo-Eiroa Sapienza University in Rome 2015–16 and PI: Pablo Lorenzo-Eiroa, RA: Salma Kattass, IDC Foundation Grant, NYIT SoAD, 2022.

5 Linguistic and Visual Semiotics signs as Signifiers Anticipating Authorship in Architecture

"For the sign is no mere accidental cloak of the idea… It serves not merely to communicate a complete and given through-content, but is an instrument, by means of which this content develops and fully defines itself. The conceptual definition of a content goes hand in hand with its stabilization in some characteristic sign. […] Without the universal signs provided by arithmetic and algebra, no special relation in physics, no special law of nature would be expressible." Ernst Cassirer [1]

History Section:
Modern; Post-Structuralist;

Methodology:
De Saussure Sign; Peirce triadic Signs; Cassirer Symbolic Form; Fiedler's Art as Cognition; Derrida's Grammatology; Derrida's Différance; Deleuze's Difference without Concept; Tafuri's Architecture as Language; Post-Colonialism;

Linguistics:
Mathematics as Language; Symbolic abstract relational thinking;

Linguistic Semiotic Signifiers:
Linguistic Sign; Index, Symbol, Icon; Grammar, Syntax, Semantics; Alberti's Architecture Rhetoric Sign; Gandelsonas' Architectural Signifier; Diagram;

Visual Semiotic Signifiers:
Perspective Vanishing Point; Index; Architectural Elements (column, wall, others);

Why reviewing Semiotics largely discussed by both structuralist and post-structuralist theory during the 1900s–70s? Why expand a theory of deep structure that has been already addressed? While historically computation has been identified with mathematics through the arithmetic and algebra of algorithms, computation's metaphysical project is a universal system of communication. Linguistic theory in computation may be as relevant as mathematics, from reducing thinking based on linguistics through Boolean Logic to symbolic computation, to information theory, to Natural Language

DOI: 10.4324/9781003292036-6

Processing (NLP). Semiotics through Linguistics may be an apparatus that one can think of as the system of reference to displace in computation in parallel to the development of the mathematics of algorithms in complex Artificial Neural Networks. We can refer to computation's necessity to address grammar in both Low Level programming language ((LLL) Low Code (LC) based on grammar prompts to activate HLL; assembly code; and compiler; different from machine code which is a binary language of 0-1) and High-Level programming Language (HLL), to call out of mathematical equations and relationships through symbolic linguistic representation, and to interpret data through symbolic computational weighting.

Semiotics

We understand semiotics through a sign that communicates semantic meaning. We will address linguistics through the following sequence. Charles Sanders Peirce's Trichotomy of Signs based on the sign vehicle and the sign object and interpretant as artificial, linguistic, and symbolic signs as the production of meaning and their combination into 27 classes of signs:

What: Qualisigns (icon),
sinsigns (icon, indices),
legisigns (icon, indices, symbols)

How (as of the object: Icon (resemblance),
Symbol (cultural convention),
Index (former presence)

How (as of the interpretant): Rhemes,
dicisigns,
arguments

Peirce's Three semiotic elements sensorial (linguistic and non-linguistic):
Sign
Object
Interpretant

Peirce's formal semiotic = logic
Hypothetical
Deductive
Inductive

Peirce's icon, hypoicon: Image
Diagram
Metaphor

Saussure Linguistics as synchronic system arbitrary and relational S = s/S:
Sign = signifier (significant, concept, which is arbitrary) / Signified (signifié, sound-image)

70 *Linguistic and Visual Semiotics signs as Signifiers*

Cassirer Symbolic Form
Panofsky's Symbolic Form and Deep Structure in Art History
Derrida's Sign=Signifier
Deleuze's Sign = Power Structure
Gandelsona's The Architectural Signifier
Eisenman's Unmotivation of the Sign in Architecture

Semiotics as Representation

We understand representation as re-presentation only possible through a media or a medium that refer to others other than themselves through systems of representation, aesthetic theory, and theory of signs and therefore included within semiotics.

Aristotle's representation inclusive of linguistics:

> Object represented (which we will challenge in relation to the frame of reference or deep structure)
> Manner (the way symbol becomes representation)
> Means (which we will define as media, an interface-frame such as perspective and interchangeable with the medium as a material-based construction system in architecture)

Non-Linguistic Semiotic Elements:
    Sensorial approach to reality:
        sound
        visual (visual semiotics)
        tactile
        experiential

Visual Semiotic Elements:
    Physical Sign:
        Signals (visual semiotics)
        Systems of Representation:
        Perspective
        Axonometric
        Picture Plane
        Anamorphosis

Visual Representational Signs:
    Perspective Window
    Perspective Vanishing Point

Visual Representational Computational Vectorial Human–Computer Interaction (HCI) Signs:
    Point
    Pixel
    Voxel
    Cell

Grid
Nurbs Curve
Nurbs Surface

Signals:

Analog Signal (continuous)
Light Signal (wave)
Digital Signal (discontinuous)
Electronic signals processing
donwsampling or upsampling signal processing
subsymbolic signal
mathematical signal decimation or compression
mathematical signal convolution
mathematical symbolic computation
mathematical physics vectorial computation

Linguistic Semiotics: Language as Author

Semiotics (or Semiology), which includes linguistics and other forms of semiotics such as visual semiotics and other sensorial description of reality, aims at identifying the relationship between signs and meaning in communication, identifying an object, a sign, and an interpretant. Communication can happen through a language media (speech sensorial, written), the non-linguistics senses through a media (interfaces for linguistic, visual, auditive, tactile, experiential digital representation) or medium (auditive, visual, tactile, experiential), or, for instance, through electronic, mathematics, and computer language codes. Peirce[2] understood that logic is based on formal semiotics, which was defined as the relationship between a sign as semiosis and the production of meaning. Semiotics can be defined as the science that aims to study how meaning is created and communicated and is perceived through a sensory reality activating issues of subject-object and experience through phenomenology.

Language Components: Grammar (formal rules)
Syntax (order)
Semantics (Meaning)
Phonology (sound)

Semiotics includes linguistics and can be defined through the work of de Saussure, Cassirer, Barthes, and Derrida and others. Ferdinand de Saussure[3] defines the Sign (the basic unit of language) as the relationship between the Signifier (sound-image) and the signified (the referent, the meaning) and defines this relationship as not natural and arbitrary exchangeable within time.

De Saussure's Sign = signifier / Signified

De Saussure developed a method in which the essential theoretical implication is that the structures are autonomous. Lévi-Strauss references[4] his

72 Linguistic and Visual Semiotics signs as Signifiers

investigation on social structures, as he studies the case of the myth which enables the externalization of repressed feelings through conversation, through speech as opposed to writing. Poetry is the partial acknowledgment of resistance against the homogenizing power of language. Schopenhauer discusses language, thinking, objects, and the world as they exist only through representation,[5] addressing the impossibility to access truth but through phenomena and projecting will as a consequence. Kant in defining what truth is addresses that we cannot differentiate reality "neumenon" or "the thing in itself" as an objective reality independent from human presence or cognition, from the perception of reality by humans through senses "phenomenon" establishing the fundamentals of scientific inquiry and the difference in epistemology between philosophy, as questioning knowledge, against science as acquiring and generalizing knowledge. Kant[6] defines structure with the term "architectonic", as he refers to the art of constructing a system.

> "I will call "structures" to those formal constants, these liaisons that betray the mental universe reinvented by each artist according to his needs" Derrida[7] quotes Rousset

Derrida's[8] critique of Saussure's equation is that structuralism disseminates categorical thought. Derrida saw structuralism as a form of philosophical totalitarianism, a hierarchical colonial system. Derrida declares that a structure is then the unity of a form and meaning; the structure defines the form of the work and as the work, and that usually structures are treated as if they had no origin, adding that the structure becomes the object itself. Derrida differentiates structures as deterministic concepts instead of concepts in themselves. Structuralist thought has been criticized by Derrida for generating *categories* which obscure the recognition of differences that may not be fitted for those frames. Our scientific system is based on categories and concepts which define and classify types that emerge from changes, and which ultimately assimilate and acquire more stability within time, what is called knowledge generalization.

In structural terms, For Nietzsche, there is a linguistic determination and limits to what is thinkable-possible. According to Nietzsche sense is not intrinsic to the object, but a construction. He pairs such position in relation to the deterministic logic of religion, proposing "God is dead", in *Übermensch* an autonomous idea of humanity and *Zarathrusta*.[9]

> "We cease to think if we do not want to do it under linguistic constraints [prison-house of language]..." Nietzsche [10]
>
> "...and this legislation of language also produces the first laws of truth." Nietzsche [11]
>
> "Every word is a prejudice." Nietzsche [12]

For Nietzsche, Hegelian dialectics provide a false image of difference through oppositions that are based on reactionary forces. Nietzsche develops several means to critique structuralist determination: to confront false Hegelian oppositions he defines a topology which implies a genealogy[13] of displacement of "relative forces" and the typological variation in absolute values.

Wittgenstein *Tractatus Logico-Philosophicus*[14] reveals the problematic relationship between language and the world, demonstrating the limits of representation as we perceive reality through language, through linguistics. An expanded language meant literally an expansion of the dimensional qualities of reality.

"The limits of my language mean the limits of my world" Wittgenstein

Tractatus Logico-Philosophicus = Language as the limit of representation

But Wittgenstein was criticized by Gödel for saying that he did not understand his incompleteness theory as he aimed at dislodging limits in both logic and language.

Barthes through Writing Degree Zero,[15] problematized writing, distinguishing it from language and style, as Barthes declared the end of authorship when he defined language as the ultimate barrier to writing.[16] Barthes[17] also discusses the city as a form of discourse and language. Barthes also identifies "signifiers" in the city in relation to the signified contrasting objective mapping in planning in contrast with open non-static signification addressing semiotics.

Orwell's 1984 depicts a dystopian world in which only a type of language through restricted grammar is allowed.

"The purpose of Newspeak was not only to provide a medium of expression for the world-view and mental habits proper to the devotees of Ingsoc but to make all other modes of thought impossible." Orwell[18]

Fahrenheit 451 by Bradbury[19] depicts a dystopian form of the authoritarian regime in which books are burned since they are meant to expand thinking.

authorship = language barrier (possibility of thinking)

Any language mediates reality and determines the way we think. In the problematic and complex relationship between architecture and computation, we pair linguistic determination with media determinism through computational linguistic and visual semiotics. We discuss visual semiotics through systems of representation, and we will discuss linguistics through signifiers that project meaning to architecture, as well as signifiers that project meaning in computational linguistics through programming languages. Historically architecture has struggled between concept and form since conceptual architects tend to address architecture through linguistics and designers tend to address architecture through visual semiotics but most without addressing in both cases deep structure. We therefore understand that the struggle of any visual art is between linguistic conception and artistic innuendo. There is a struggle in terms of both disciplinary autonomies; architects who write about architecture quote literally philosophic terms that philosophers refer to from, for instance, reading architecture concepts. Eisenman's translation of philosophical linguistic-based

74   *Linguistic and Visual Semiotics signs as Signifiers*

concepts through Derrida, Deleuze, Blanchot, and other philosophers and writers is projected into architecture through linguistic signifiers: *deconstruction, writing, diagram, smooth, striated, affect,* and others. The conflict is identified by, for instance, architects who wrote books such as treaties, manuals, and other architecture-specific theses such as Serlio's and Palladio's books which include architecture representations; Le Corbusier's publications to spread his ideas through media; Hejduk and Miralles writing about architecture through linguistic poetics; or by Eisenman[20] in the a+u publication that we later reinterpreted[21] in which images motivate an architecture of visual semiotics displacing the media frame of the book, as the text motivates linguistics in architecture.

Derrida's *Différance:* Post-Colonial Politics of Language Deconstruction

Derrida presents the idea of *différance*[22] (difference and deferral) as the deconstruction of the issues that the history of philosophy has hidden, forbidden, and repressed. One can differentiate de Saussure's arbitrariness, between speech and writing following Derrida's deferral, in which speech is conceptually different from écriture (writing) since through senses and sounds there is a natural association between the sound image and its signification, but that later through writing this changes to a conceptual cognitive level in which there is a disjunction by the function of the signifier defining meaning through language determination and grammar. At the same time, Chomsky's hierarchy[23] by differentiating sensorial speech from conceptual writing through grammar and syntax identifies the problem of grammar and meaning, developing a grammatically correct phrase that carries no meaning.

For Derrida the difference between writing and meaning can be called *différance* as the deconstruction of what the history of philosophy has repressed through the hierarchy of language, for instance in hierarchical structures such as classification of hierarchy through categories, black/white; top/down. For Derrida, there is indeed a problem of *différance* between the signifier and the signified, a difference and deferral that can be traced to a sign as it is understood as the promotion of direct inference as meaning. The sign for Derrida is in itself the creation of signifiers as *deferral*,[24] an artificial construction independent from what it is being named. Derrida claims that each time we name something we are creating an independent entity, an object as an artificial construction. Reality cannot be perceived in its real dimension without the system of representation that separates the object from the observer, which cannot be fully understood or perceived since our gaze, our systems of representation always produce a cultural colonializing deferral. To understand language as deterministic of expression and thinking, we therefore understand how to disclose colonial, cultural ideological hidden structures that force signification. Derrida's Grammatology proposes a way through grammar to activate means in language to disclose deeper problems through a mode that he developed as a method: deconstruction.

Derrida starts by identifying how to transcend language through the extension of language, since in writing the signified already functions as a signifier and to address the problematization of the origin through both concealing and erasing its own production through a form of writing as the erasure of the traces of origin.

"The written signifier is always technical and representative…It has no constitutive meaning. This derivation is the very origin of the notion of the 'signifier'" Derrida[25]

Sign = Signifier
Signifier of the Signifier

Deleuze's Rhizome Against the Regime of Signs: Presignifying and Postsignifying

More interested in a phenomenological approach to semiotics through reification and the senses resisting linguistic signs, Deleuze calls *difference without concept*[26] to differentials that are understood as real differences contrasting structuralist categorical differences, as he notes the value of the curvature, independent from other assumed referential categories. In the Fold,[27] Deleuze references Leibniz's ambiguous sign, as relating the fold in the Baroque in opposition to conditions of deterministic structure and previous notions of difference and repetition, addressing Cache's *Earth Moves*.[28] Deleuze and Guattari[29] discuss in *A Thousand Plateaus* Chapters 4 and 5 "November 20, 1923-Postulates of Linguistics" and "587 B.C.–A.D. 70: On several Regimes of Signs" an approach to visual and sensible semiotics that discusses also the linguistic theory and Saussure's equation. In Chapter 4 Deleuze and Guattari discuss that language is not informational, but rather a colonizing coordinate system that can process foundations for grammar through the order-word as implicit pre-suppositions.

Language ≠ Informational ≠ Communicational

By language neither being informational nor communicational, Deleuze and Guattari are addressing a different dimensional quality of Media Determinism and the structure of language as an "assemblage that combine in a regime of signs or a semiotic machine" in a highly homogeneous system. They propose a pragmatic higher level of abstraction machinic system that is not clear about how it operates and what it does other than, for instance, ideas of frequency and resonance through a rhizome and the notion of the diagrammatic *abstract machine* as a necessary tool, more than language, which is operative by matter (pragmatics, not by substance) and function (not by form). For Deleuze and Guattari the sign can refer to another sign ad infinitum and as a *despotic signifier* as they also refer to *presignifying semiotic* and *postsignigying* regime as "subjectification". This resonance machinic system is for Deleuze

76 *Linguistic and Visual Semiotics signs as Signifiers*

based on a *rhizome*, a rhizomatic post-structure critical of the conventional societal tree-root structure of hierarchical bifurcations and growth system. Deleuze's rhizome defines some of the notions we are interested in parallel computer processing, as opposed to hierarchical, single entry database structures of linear and reversible tree-like algorithms.

Teyssot[30] refers to Deleuze's theory of sign in contrast to both de Saussure and Derrida, by stating that Deleuze defines it in the form of an algorithm, in which Deleuze develops a topological fold to displace De Saussure's slash between the signifier and the signified (Sign=Signifier/Signified).

Sign = Signifier ("/" = &) signified

Pannini (400–350 BCE), a Sanskrit grammar scholar, was the first descriptive linguist who developed the first formal system through auxiliary symbols which were used for computer programming by Emil Post.[31] He was also influential in the work of De Saussure[32] and is referenced by Nietzsche in "Who speaks?: the word itself".[33] Pannini has been identified as the first one to develop a formal grammatical system identifying the relationship between language and thinking logic as deterministic of each other defining it as political educational emancipation power in society. The Sanskrit language includes several innovations, such as context-free grammar, multiple genres, three persons, three doubles, multiple multitudes (singular, plural, and plurals), and other characteristics that make it more precise logic-wise. India's education system teaches mathematics through different types of arithmetic methods based on both abstract and geometric matrices, enabling cross-multimedia relational thinking and perhaps advanced comprehension of algorithms through multiple means of performing algebra. If one adds to mathematical algebra the historical value of Sanskrit as a higher grammatical language, India could be addressing reality at a higher level of representation facilitating computational algorithmic thinking, a cultural decolonization process with a global projection. Sanskrit has been identified as the most suited unambiguous language for knowledge representation and AI by a NASA researcher[34]; and there are now programming languages based on Sanskrit, such as *vedic*.

Decolonization of Language and Mathematics =
    Post-Colonial Computation
Sanskrit Grammar + Correlational Mathematical Algebra =
    Higher Representational Level

Cassirer in 1923[35] presented the base for Panofsky's *Perspective as Symbolic Form* of 1927, as Cassirer deals in *The Philosophy of Symbolic Forms* Volume 1 specifically with language. Building from Kant's Philosophy of Form, Cassirer discusses the multiple possible relationships between structure, form, and language relative to symbolic form. From the Universal function of the sign to issues of meaning,

Cassirer takes a structural-formal approach to language differentiating meaning from form and identifying nonlinear relationships and reciprocal relationships among them. Cassirer identifies an immanent condition of meaning in *symbolic form* and not related to an external representation of meaning, a formalist approach. Cassirer describes the originating power of the sign over the content being described, problematizing the typical linear representational understanding of signs, and anticipating Derrida. While de Saussure's equation defines the Sign = Signifier/signified, as an arbitrary relationship between the Signifier and the signified; Cassirer gives to the sign an empowerment over its signified:

"The name of the thing and the thing in itself are inseparably fused" Cassirer

"Symbolic Form"
Sign = signifier (- signified)

Cassirer identifies differences between languages, the notational pragmatic evolution of language, and the formal structure of signs. Cassirer refers to Galileo's explanation in the "book of nature" through the language of mathematics and establishes close relationships between language and thinking, arriving at what is imaginable possible, anticipating many of the post-structuralist theories on language that are particularly relevant to our understanding of the role of mathematics relative to language and computation.

For Derrida[36] following Nietzsche language is the house that humans live in and therefore structures meaning. Derrida defines arche-writing as before speech and writing, defining the deterministic structure of language before we express ourselves. Linguistics problematized the relationship between thought and language in relation to "Nature", identifying and separating language, mind, and nature. Linguistics revolutionized the previously normalized notion of the relationship between thought and consciousness as a form of self-reflection since linguistics proved that the main reference system for thought was not the natural brain, was not a reference to Nature or the mind, but language itself served as a promoter, enabler, and limit to thinking.

Language = Program

We understand that language is a form of program, and thus we know how important it is to decolonize it as a system of representation. As a program, language mediates as a media-interface self-consciousness through linguistics, therefore its structure anticipates and determines the structure of thinking through grammar, projecting a social structure, a social contract, ethics, and power projecting all types of sedimented biases on our culture. Language grammar structure through reinforced learning changes the morphology of our brain network based on synapsis bridges across neurons, as we program ourselves through language both at an abstract and physical level. We

78 *Linguistic and Visual Semiotics signs as Signifiers*

also program ourselves through our cultural context and now social media self-validation social bubbles.

Visual Semiotics: Non-Linguistic Semiotics and Representation

Semiotics is based on the perception of different types of signs that convey meaning in communication: linguistic, auditive, visual, tactile, and experiential. One of Peirce's trichotomy of signs includes three types of signs in his theory of signs in linguistic representation, he identifies triadic signs: Icon (likeness), Symbol (convention), and Index (actual connection). Kilstrup[37] identifies Peirce's sign in relation to representation: Symbol = reference/referent.

> System of Representation - Measurement (Reference) =
> Space-Object (Referenced) / Subject-Experience (Referent)

Fiedler opposed the Kantian idea that art was a lower form of cognition since artistic form constitutes an autonomous logical system whose purpose is not to mean through linguistic translation or representation. Opposing Kant, Hegel's aesthetic theory[38] defines the autonomy of art as a field of knowledge. The work of art is no longer a representation of extrinsic linguistic content, but it is the conscious construction of biased reality acknowledging its media. Fiedler[39] defines an area of cognition and validation independent from mathematics and language, intrinsic to the work of art that needs not only to have its own systems of reference and validation but is also essential for cognitive advancement, placing, for instance, visual arts as an essential education in society from early ages, defining the basics for art education. Fiedler refers to artistic autonomy, visual logic, and aesthetic appreciation as validation. We also need to identify the limitation of conceptual thinking derived from language as opposed to formal semiotic relationships in art.

Visual Semiotic Systems: Media Determinism and Symbolic Form as Origin and Author

If linguistic semiotics theory identified that we cannot think outside language, in visual semiotics, we identify the impossibility of thinking visually outside media and mediums. If language can be problematized on the relationship between speech and writing and in relation to thinking and expressing thinking through a medium, the visual arts present a semiotic apparatus defined by symbolic form through the deep structure by Fiedler and Panofsky.[40] We discussed perspective through the pictorial sign of the vanishing point as a symbolic form. The symbolic form is a type of visual semiotic sign that can be recognized as having immanent meaning in the object that originated through media.

Vanishing Point (infinity) = Sign (VP) as a signifier

All systems of representation induce meaning to the objects they represent and therefore structure. An object therefore indexes its system of representation and a type of sign. There are no objects outside a form of representation as there is no language outside signs. Reality is not inert and is constructed by symbolic form as an immanent ideology, as humans cannot access reality without a form of cultural representation and system of reference.

McLuhan[41] declared that "the medium is the message" developing a theory of Media, identifying through diverse mediums how they project cultural signification. Carpo[42] identified the relationship between architectural thinking and media specificity. We are aiming at expanding such Media Theory[43] as a project by expanding what may be possible. This would also mean a displacement of the over-deterministic power of technology over culture. Fabretti[44] discusses relationships between media and linguistics analyzing a software theory as we proposed such determination through Digital Signifiers.[45]

> "The art of painting cannot be well judged except by those who are themselves good painters; but truly for other persons, it is concealed as a foreign language is hidden from you." Dürer[46]

In the visual arts, formal logic through syntax enables communication through our senses, and according to formalists, formal logic is a type of artistic language defined by a formal grammar. Formal logic is an autonomous cognitive system that produces signification as opposed to communicating established meaning. Systems of representation anticipate a certain type of formal logic. Systems of representation also operate at a meta-representational level since the interface through which the formal language is expressed is also part of the framework. This form of being represents a form of autonomy, a unique system of expression that can induce signification. The autonomy of formal logic to signify within its semiotic system presents a form of being that cannot be reduced to a linguistic natural language through semantics. While semiotics defines semantics as a function of meaning in signs, we identify semantics in relation to linguistics mainly since we think through language. We understand visual semiotics, as a communication media and medium through which media and medium-specific ideas are possible, while they are not meaningful through other media and mediums, therefore defining what an architecture idea and concept can be independent of conceptualization through natural language.

In architecture, the notion of an idea as an abstract thinking linguistic process is placed under scrutiny, since we understand thinking through natural language and, architecture conversely depends rather on media-dependent visual semiotics. We think an architectural idea cannot reside outside

80 *Linguistic and Visual Semiotics signs as Signifiers*

architecture. We understand the apparatus of representation as a site, a frame, and a medium through which an architecture content-specific idea is possible and becomes active as a form of being and is not translatable to other mediums, frames, or site-context.

Gandelsonas' "The Architectural Signifier":[47] From Criticality, to a Postcritical, to a Media Linguistic Criticism of Architecture

We can define an architectural language as a higher-level form of architectural expression based on unique visual and experiential semiotic signs developing a unique type of content through formal grammar, syntax, and semantics able to communicate a particular type of signification through a unique deep structure following de Saussure's triadic signs, Cassirer's symbolic form, Derrida's linguistic deconstruction, and Gandelsonas architectural signifier.[48] We differentiate architecture as visual semiotics and also as a form of language, which is independent of linguistics and style. These are further dicussed in a later chapter.

In terms of non-linguistic visual semiotics, we discuss architecture through measurement, dimensions, representation systems, scale, organization, form, and material actualization. But architecture as a form of language traces parallels to linguistics as formal logic can also be described through grammar, syntax, and semantics. Due to linguistics, architecture also suffers from cultural baggage of concepts projected from natural language capping visual semiotics signs. Non-linguistic semiotics as a sensible communicating set of signs should resist linguistic-based semantic classification. Architectural signifiers as a linguistic system should be recognized through visual semiotic recognizable features, activating formal logic through visual semiotics able to disseminate linguistic signs through grammar.

Alberti[49] revolutionizes novel self-conscious modernity as he defines architecture as a linguistic system of representation, expanding from Vitruvius. Damish[50] discusses Alberti's Palazzo Ruccellai (1446–51) tension between the column and the wall identifying columns rhetorically as linguistic signs. Frankl, Wittkower, and Rowe, applied abstracted notions independent from style activating a structural history. In the Barcelona Pavilion by van der Rohe, the structure of the four independent L steel profiles creating a cross are not only covered with stainless steel cladding[51] to create a special type of column, but also accentuate a notion of visual semiotic representation defining an architecture language, an expression reformulated in the Seagram building.[52, 53] The architecture of the built building acknowledging and displacing the conventions of its medium or an architecture representation acknowledging and displacing the conventions of its media becomes immanent in terms of meaning, able to produce visual and other experiential semiotic meanings in different times and cultural contexts.

Steel Column Re-Design = Signifier Re Representation

Architecture = Language
Architecture Linguistic Signifier = Semantic Classification
Architecture Semiotic Signifier = Formal Visual Logic
Syntax = Disseminate Semantics through Grammar

Barthes declares "The city is a discourse and this discourse is truly a language..." expanding on the notion and discussion that a city is a form of signifier, open to signification and readings.[54] Eco[55] discusses semiotics relating linguistic signs to architectural elements, such as the column as a sign and other signs to signify new meanings, sometimes beyond functional use.[56] Tafuri[57] denotes architecture as a form of language, critiquing natural language as a form of determination over architecture. Tafuri critiques the understanding of architecture through linguistics, for example in the work of Eisenman; although Tafuri was critiqued as an architectural historian for not developing a visual apparatus or an art history methodology to raise the issues he attempts to critique as Frankl, Wittkower or Panofsky did. Gandelsonas describes architectural elements as a form of signifier. Agrest and Gandelsonas question language, architecture, and urbanism through semiotics as a deeper understanding of the production of meaning in architecture. They analyze the weight of natural language in architecture and propose architecture as a language against colonial Western architectural knowledge as a political ideology of production and economic resistance[58], which has the power to change the structure of the system[59] a notion that we try to enact by displacing computational signifiers.

Post-structuralism emerged after the Second World War as a reaction to the structural determination of the Modern Movement. Krauss' index[60] is an alternative theory to a culturally loaded sign, an empty presence without an external cultural colonizing signifier, an elimination of the pictorial codes different from expressionist abstraction in art. This theory based on site-specific interventions by American artists measuring the vast American landscape in resistance to art gallery systems such as Noguchi, Smithson, De Maria, Serra, Heizer, and Lin was later incorporated by architects such as Pinos-Miralles and Eisenman, as architectural projects started to index former presences related to an existing site.

Index = Empty Signifier

Interestingly Johnson and Wigley's "Deconstructivist Architecture" show of 1988,[61] established a new phase against postmodernism, previously focused on the rhetorical aspect of signs through historicism. Projects in the show were introduced by Johnsons' preface as a "violation of perfection"; Wigley's article "Deconstructivist Architecture" references Matta Clark's Splitting, to a reformulation of Russian Constructivism formal vocabulary distinguishing structural from formal aesthetic through displacing representation. The exhibition included projects such as Libeskind dismembering conventional

82   *Linguistic and Visual Semiotics signs as Signifiers*

architectural elements such as a symbolic wall through fields of background site traces as emergent signs; or Hadid deconstruction of background-figure relationships in a grounded building as artificial topography through non-orthogonal visual representation. But the Deconstructivist exhibition activated a linguistic interdisciplinary translation of Derrida's grammatology *deconstruction* through Giovannini's reading[62] of *deconstructive-ism* as a style as his contribution is acknowledged in the MoMA catalog. This interestingly necessary but problematically executed shift from linguistic to visual semiotics had already displaced the politics of the Modern Movement by turning it into a visual style with apolitical connotations, such as "Modern-ism" which is the "New International Style" by Johnson himself.[63] The "Deconstructivist Architecture" show also became the basis for a generation of experimental digital architects against linguistic theory, through a postcritical architecture theorized by Somol and Whitening.[64]

The Diagram as a Linguistic Qualisign

Frankl develops a structural history independent of style through abstract organizational diagrams. Gaudi proposes a simulation engine as an embodied computation that does not need to be representational as a diagram but is used as an embedded knowledge diagram to inform the building. A diagram can be the antithesis of architecture based on a tectonic construction, such as the impossibility to diagram van der Rohe's architecture. Diagrams may become too abstract, conceptual, and therefore independent of any media and medium, tending to represent a thinking process translating concepts through linguistics. For Charles Sanders Peirce all reasoning is diagrammatic. While Plato defined a metaphysics of forms, Aristotle empiricism problematized mediums as immanent form. Historically, in architecture the dialectical tension between linguistic concepts through architecture ideas, and immanent form motivating the tectonics of construction systems, has been addressed through the work of Brunelleschi and Palladio; Borromini and Bernini; Le Corbusier and Mies van der Rohe. While computation addresses a universal metaphysics through information, interfaces activate media as mediums. We propose to radically redefine architecture through representation as an intermediary resonance machinic interface, acknowledging the separation of humanity brought by language, tools, frameworks, technology and systems of representation. Differentiating from either a metaphysics, or an ontology of object's immanence, or an Object Oriented Ontology (OOO), or Deleuze's and Guattari's material resonance interface, we propose a Representation Restricted Reality (RRR) as a media interface computational resonance machine of continuous survey/projection of real/realism that through a media displacement can transform reality through the abstraction of signifiers. Eisenman's Houses of Cards[65] presents the disjunction between architecture as a diagram through representation and addressing construction as representation displaced from its medium. House IV presents a diagram actualized by discrete formal signs through an architectural grammatology of volume, linear, and surface systems. Eisenman claims a culturally based project as a disciplinary autonomy emptied from a technological determination while displacing media determination. Diagrams do help to organize concepts, and abstract structures from historical contextual styles, but they may become linguistic signifieds projected as a visual logic that does not acknowledge a system of representation, a media, or a medium. Following Peirce's definition, a qualisign is quality as a sign but that cannot be a sign since it lacks embodiment, media, or medium, therefore a diagram is a representation of knowledge and quality without a sign. The diagram also proposes a separation of techne, media, and medium from design.

Diagram = Qualisign

De-sign does not function through the diagram since there is nothing to design or deconstruct as a political media or medium. In addressing linguistic semiotic and visual semiotics, the necessity is to both motivate a sign to be able to communicate visually and to unmotivate a sign to address originality in a message, or to deconstruct the emergent signifier in order to propose cultural design innovation. Agrest discloses architecture design through linguistic codes, "no-design" as a non-linguistic product of cultural systems permeable to cultural context.[66] This project was not yet taken to address computation other than Eisenman's unmotivation of the sign[67] after Deleuze discussing Cache's objectile[68] in which there is a precise notion of curvature displacing reference systems expanding *Difference and Repetition* and Leibniz's notion of "ambiguous sign" previously discussed.

DE-(SIGN) = Media and Medium specific Signifier

According to Rajchman,[69] in Deleuze's *Logic of Sense,*[70] "logic acquires a new sense" which later was expanded in Deleuze's Bacon's *The Logic of Sensation*[71] which aims at identifying visual semiotic signs in Francis Bacon's work to critique the power of linguistic signs through the definition of affect, a transformational psychosomatic signal experience, a unique form of reification.

Notes

1 Cassirer, E. *The Philosophy of Symbolic Forms, Volume 1: Language,* Yale University Press, New Haven, 1955 [orig. 1923–29]
2 Peirce, C.S. *The Essential Peirce, Selected Philosophical Writings,* Volume 1 (1867–93), Indiana University Press, 1992
3 De Saussure, F. *Course in General Linguistics,* Open Court, Chicago, 1986 [orig. 1916]
4 Lévi-Strauss, C. *Structural Study of the Myth,* Harper & Row, New York, 1979 [orig. 1958]
5 Schopenhauer, A. *The World as Will and Representation,* trans. Aquila, R.E. in col. with Carus, D. Longman, New York, 2008 [Orig. 1818]

84 *Linguistic and Visual Semiotics signs as Signifiers*

6 Kant, I. Chapter III: "The Architectonics of Pure Reason", in Kant, I. *The Critique of Pure Reason,* William Benton Publishers, Chicago, 1951 [orig. 1781]

7 Derrida, J. "Force and Signification", in *Writing and Difference,* The University of Chicago Press, Chicago, 1978

8 Derrida, J. *Of Gramatology,* trans. Spivak, G.C. John Hopkins University Press, Baltimore, 1997 [Orig. 1967]

9 Nietzsche, F. *Thus Spake Zarathustra,* Macmillan, New York, 1896 [orig. 1883–92]

10 Rüdiger, B. *Writings from the Late Notebooks,* Cambridge University Press, New York, 2003

11 Nietzsche, F. *On Truth and Lies in a Nonmoral Sense,* Theophania Publishing, Calgary, 2012 [orig. 1873]

12 Nietzsche, F. Human. All Too Human II/Unpublished Fragments from the Period of *Human, All Too Human II* (Spring 1878–Fall 1879)

13 Deleuze, G. *Nietzsche and Philosophy,* Columbia University Press, New York, 1983 [orig. 1962]

14 Wittgenstein, L. *Tractatus Logico-Philosophicus,* Routledge, London and New York, 1961 [orig. W. Ostwald's Annalen der Naturphilosophie, Vienna, 1921]

15 Barthes, R. *Le degré zéro de L'escriture,* Aux Editions du Seul, France, 1953

16 Barthes, R. "The Death of the Author", in *Image, Music, Text,* Stephen Heath, New York, 1999 [orig. 1967]

17 Barthes, R. "Semiology and the Urban", in ed. Leach, N., *Rethinking Architecture,* Routledge, London and New York, 1997 [orig. 1967]

18 Orwell, G. *1984,* Secker and Warburg, London, 1949

19 Bradbury, R. *Fahrenheit 451,* Ballantine Books, New York, 1953

20 Derrida, J. "Why Peter Eisenman Writes Such Good Books", in PETER EISENMAN, a+u Publishing, Tokyo, 1988

21 Lorenzo-Eiroa, P. *Instalaciones: Sobre el Trabajo de Peter Eisenman,* DLO/RE, Buenos Aires, 2008

22 Derrida, J. "Force and Signification", in *Writing and Difference,* The University of Chicago Press, Chicago, 1978

23 Chomsky, N. *Syntactic Structures* Mouton, The Hague, 1957

24 Derrida, J. "Différance", *Margins of Philosophy,* University of Chicago Press, London, 1982

25 Derrida, J. *Of Gramatology,* trans. Gayatri Chakravosrty Spivak, John Hopkins University Press, Baltimore and London, 1997 [Orig. 1967]

26 Deleuze, G. *Difference and Repetition,* Columbia University Press, New York, 1994 [orig. 1968]

27 Deleuze, G. *The Fold: Leibniz and the Baroque,* University of Minnesota Press, Minneapolis, 1993 [orig. 1988]

28 Cache, B. *Earth Moves,* ed. Davidson, C. Writing Architecture Series, MIT Press, Cambridge, 1995

29 Deleuze, G.; Guattari, F. *A Thousand Plateaus. Capitalism and Schizophrenia,* The University of Minnesota Press, Minneapolis and London, 1987

30 Teyssot, G. "The Membrane and The Fold", in ed. Sprecher, A., Yeshayahu, S. and Lorenzo-Eiroa, P., *Life In: Formation,* ACADIA, New York, 2010

31 Bhate, S.; Kak, S. "Panini and Computer Science", in *Annals of the Bhandarkar Oriental Research Institute,* Volume 72, 1993

32 Cardona, G. "Book review: Pâṇinis Grammatik", in *Journal of the American Oriental Society,* 120 (3): (pag. 464–5) 2000

33 Tafuri, M. "L'Architecture dans le Boudoir: The Language of Criticism and the Criticism of Language", in *Oppositions,* Volume 3, New York 1974

34 Briggs, R. "Knowledge Representation in Sanskrit and Artificial Intelligence", in *AI Magazine,* Volume 6, Issue 1, 1985

Linguistic and Visual Semiotics signs as Signifiers   85

35 Cassirer, E. *The Philosophy of Symbolic Forms*, Volume 1: Language, Yale University Press, New Haven, 1955 [orig. 1923–29]

36 Derrida, J. *Of Gramatology*, John Hopkins University Press, Baltimore and London, 1997 [orig. 1967]

37 Kilstrup, M. "Naturalizing Semiotics: The Triadic Sign of Charles Sanders Peirce as a Systems Property", in *Progress in Biophysics and Molecular Biology*, PubMed, Denmark, 2015

38 Hegel. *Hegel: Introductory Lectures on Aesthetics*, Penguin Books, New York, 1993 [orig 1835]

39 Fiedler, C. *On Judging Works of Visual Art*, University of California Press, Los Angeles, 1949

40 Panofsky, E. *Perspective as Symbolic Form*, Zone Books, New York, 1991 [orig. 1927]

41 McLuhan, M. *Understanding Media*, The extensions of Man, Mentor, New York, 1964

42 Carpo, M. *Architecture in the Age of Printing*, MIT Press, Cambridge, 2001

43 Manovich, Lev. *Software Takes Command*, Bloomsbury, New York and London, 2013

44 Frabetti, F. *Software Theory*, Rowman and Littlefield International, London, 2015

45 Lorenzo-Eiroa, P. "Form In:Form: On The Relationship Between Digital Signifiers and Formal Autonomy", in ed. Lorenzo-Eiroa, P. and Sprecher, A., *Architecture in Formation*, Routledge, London, 2013

46 Durer, A. *Unterweysung des Messung*, ed. Hieronymus Andreae, Nuremberg, 1525

47 Gandelsonas, Mario. "The Architectural Signifier", paper presented at the First Congress of the International Association of Semiotic Studies, Milan, 1974

48 Gandelsonas, M. "From Structure to Subject: The Formation of an Architectural Language", in ed. Ockman, J., House X, Rizzoli, New York, 1982.

49 Alberti, L.B. *De Re Aedificatoria*, (1404–72)

50 Damish, H. "The Column and The Wall", in *AD Profile 21:Leonis Baptiste Alberti*, Volume 49, no. 5–6, 1979

51 Blaser, W. *Mies van der Rohe El Arte de la Estructura*, Carlos Hirsch, Buenos Aires, 1965

52 de Solá-Morales, I. "La arquitectura como representación", *Mies 101 años*, Arquitectura Viva, Madrid, 1986

53 Ábalos, I.; Herreros, J. *Tower and Office*, MIT Press, Cambridge, 2005

54 Barthes, R. "Semiology and the Urban" [orig. 1967], in ed. Leach, N., *Rethinking Architecture: Reader in Cultural History*, Routledge, London and New York, 1997 (p.168)

55 Eco, U. "A Componental Analysis of the Architectural Sign/Column/", in *Semiotica*, Volume 5.2, 1972

56 Eco, U. *La struttura assente: introduzione alla ricerca semiológica*, Bonpiani, 1968

57 Tafuri, M. "L'Architecture dans le Boudoir: The Language of Criticism and the Criticism of Language", in *Oppositions,* Volume 3, New York 1974

58 Agrest, D.; Gandelosonas, M. "Semiotics and Architecture: Ideological Consumption or Theoretical Work", in *Oppositions*, New York, 1973

59 Gandelsonas, M. "Linguistic and Semiotic Models in Architecture", in *Basic Questions of Design Theory*, North Holland, New York, 1975

60 Krauss, R. "Notes on the Index: Seventies Art in America", *October* 3 and 4, 1977

61 Johnson, P.; Wigley, M. *Deconstructivist Architecture: The Museum of Modern Art*, Little Brown and Company, New York, 1988

62 Giovannini, J. "Deconstructivism Started Well Over a Century Ago and Still Continues Today" *Dezeen*, June 2022

86   *Linguistic and Visual Semiotics signs as Signifiers*

63 Johnson, P.; Hitchcock, H.R. *Modern Architecture: International Exhibition,* Museum of Modern Art, New York, 1932
64 Somol, R.; Whiting, S. "Notes Around the Doppler Effect and Other Moods of Modernism," *Perspecta* 33, Yale University, New Haven, 2002
65 Eisenman, P.; Krauss, R.E.; Tafuri, M.; *Houses of Cards,* Oxford University Press, Oxford, 1987
66 Agrest, D. "Design versus Non-Design", in *Oppositions,* Volume 6, New York, 1976 [orig. 1974]
67 Eisenman, P. "The Diagram and the Becoming Unmotivated of the Sign", in *Peter Eisenman: Diagram Diaries,* Universe Publishing, New York, 1999
68 Deleuze, G. *The Fold: Leibniz and the Baroque,* University of Minnesota Press, Minneapolis, 1993 [orig. 1988]
69 Rajchman, J. *The Deleuze Connections,* MIT Press, Cambridge, 2000
70 Deleuze, G. *The Logic of Sense,* Columbia University Press, New York, 1990
71 Deleuze, G. *Francis Bacon: The Logic of Sensation,* University of Minnesota Press, Minneapolis, 2002 [orig. 1981]

6 Computational Linguistic Semiotics

From Mathematics, to Computational Languages Grammar, to Machine Learning, to Signifieds in Natural Language Processing (NLP), to Emergent Programming

History:
Modern; Second World War; Contemporary;

Philosophy:
Aristotle's Organon; Leibniz Characteristica Universalis; Hegel's dialectics; Boolean Logic;

Methodology:
Semiotics; Shannon Mathematical Theory of Communication; Information Theory; Derrida's Grammatology;

Mathematical Semiotics:
Arithmetic; Algebra; Gödel's Undecidability; binary system 0-1; Shannon's Mathematical Theory of Communication;

Computational Theory:
Computability, Turing Machine, Shannon's Mathematical Theory of Communication; Information Theory, Automata Theory, Cellular Automation, Cybernetics, Artificial Intelligence, Low Level and High-Level Programming Language, Undecidability, Gödel Incompleteness Theorems, Functional Programming (functions, logic, Lambda Calculus), Object-Oriented Programming (design around data-objects: no function, no logic), Procedural Computation, Evolutionary Computation, Genetic Algorithms, Self-Replication, Simulation, Robotic Autonomous Agents, Robotic Systems, Robotic materials,
Computability Theory, Quantum Computing;

Computational Paradigms:
Continuous, Algorithmic, Discrete, Conditional, Stochastic, Simulation-Based Computation;
Analog Computing, Pascal Arithmetic Machine; Leibniz Characteristica Universalis, Leibniz Calculus Ratiocinator; Boolean Logic; Mainframe Computing, Imperative Computing, Centralized Computing, Distributed-Network/Grid Computing, Parallel Computing, Cloud-Internet/

DOI: 10.4324/9781003292036-7

Internet of Things Computing, Molecular Topology Based Optimization, Computational Fluid Dynamics, Geometric Algorithms, Computing, Bio Computing, Quantum Computing; Swarm Intelligence, Agent-Based Modeling, Artificial Neural Networks; Machine Learning; Generative Adversarial Networks; AI;

Computer Languages relevant to Architecture:
Pascal, Cobol, C, C+, C++, C#, Python, JavaScript, RhinoScript, AutoLISP, Lisp, Assembly;

Computational Linguistic Semiotics:
Programming Languages; Low Level programming Language (Machine Language; Assembly Language, Compiler; Low Code); High-Level Language; Collaboratory, PyTorch; Symbolic Computation; Boolean Logic;

Computational Linguistic Signifiers:
Programming Languages Signs; Semantics; Natural Language Processing; Prompt Engineering; Algorithms; Self-Editing Algorithms; Emergent Programming;

Mathematical Signifiers:
Mathematical Symbols; Symbolic Computation; Navier-Stokes Equations;

Data:
Data Science; Data Scraping; Application Processing Interface; Repositories; Training Repositories; Data Bias; Supervised and Non-supervised Learning; Semantic Segmentation, Feature Recognition;

Linguistics and Computational Linguistics

How is architecture determined through computational linguistics? Which digital signifiers discussed in previous chapters become active through computational linguistics? What is the relationship between computational linguistics and spatial organization?

We discuss the influence of linguistic and visual semiotics signs in architecture in relation to systems of representation since architecture is a discipline that is based on visual logic and physical experience. We also address visual semiotics signs through computational linguistic code-sign electronic signals processing. The combination of computational linguistic semiotic signs and physical signal processing enables computational visual semiotics through machine vision, sensing, and interaction. We also discuss the current emergent historical project in computation to enable universal communication through bypassing, at least at the generic input user level, mathematics as a system of reference, since through Low Code or Natural Language Processing (NLP) one has the possibility of coding directly through linguistic grammar-based prompts.

$$Computation = Universal\ System\ of\ Communication$$
$$Computation\ in\ Architecture =$$
$$(Linguistic\ Semiotics/Mathematics/electronics) + Visual\ Semiotics$$
$$(icon,\ symbol,\ index)$$

We resist understanding technology independent from culture or technology defining culture by itself, and we discuss means to activate the displacement of cultural conventions in architecture. We discuss linguistic and visual semiotics to disclose, critique, and displace the set of linguistic and visual semiotic signifiers as deep structures that are either explicit, implicit, or residual in the contemporary implementation of computation in architecture. The objective is to work out an architecture of information that elevates computation through problematizing representation.

Mathematics and Mathematical Semiotics: From Arithmetic, to Algebra, to Algorithms

The growing challenge is to address types of knowledge while computation becomes common across all disciplines. When architecture is represented through computational systems, it is often understood as referenced by mathematics through geometry.[1] Computation is rooted in mathematics, but computation's metaphysical project is a universal system of communication. Shannon's information theory establishes computation as a mathematical system of *communication*. The logocentric, relational epistemology of mathematics as an autonomous enclosed system that is supposed to have no contradiction has been proven erroneous by Gödel's incompleteness theorem. In contrast, there is a common disregard for not addressing the cultural biases embedded in science and mathematics, as they are presented as autonomous validating systems for disambiguation but are not immune to ideological bias. Mathematics can be defined as a universal discovery of natural laws that govern the universe, or a human invention, as the most abstract linguistic system of representation that humans were able to develop[2] (Kitcher endorsement of Golman's psychologism). This last controversial statement may be understood through the various unresolved contradictions discovered in Mathematics, such as Gödel's Undecidability[3] in relation to Pascal and Leibniz. Gödel's paragraph in Wittgenstein's *Tractatus Logico-Philosophicus*[4] can reference a continuity through opposition and evolution on the relationship between language and mathematics and how computation emerged from the ambition of creating a system to rule out an ambiguity in logic. If we understand mathematics as a form of language, we would be placing humanity's most abstract communication system as a form of thinking; addressing its inference through representation over reality.

Humans describe the world through decimal-based mathematics referencing the ten fingers of the human body to count and based on hindu-arabic decimal numbers (600-700 India, introduced to Europe around 1200).

90 *AI Computational Linguistic Semiotics*

Computation is binary-based, able to count in two types of electronic signals 1 and 0 used for algorithmic disambiguation through Yes or No. From the use of arithmetic and algebra by Babylonians (c. 1800 BCE) or its publication in Persia in the 800s to the invention of the concept of zero in India in 628, mathematics history follows cultural advancement. Algorithms can also be traced back to Meru Prastaara in 755 CE. The notion of zero is a historical cultural construction that did not belong to mathematics until the 628s, although it is mentioned by Egyptians around 1770 BCE. Pingal Manuscript from Raghunath Library identify algorithms through arithmetic and algebra. By 831–830 the word "Algorism" or "Algorithm" was used by al-Khwarizmi in "The Compendious Book on Calculation by Completion and Balancing". Al-Khawarizimi *Book of Algebra* quadratic equations *Algoritmi de numero Indorum* led to the word "algorithm"[5] (820 CE). The Inca (1400s) quipu[6] knots based on previous civilizations (Caral, Chavin, Paracas, Nazca, Wari in South America) is a place and sign value digit-based encoding system considered a computing system able to notate complex mathematics and a writing system without alphanumeric notation which includes the notion of zero/void. Mathematics through calculus, algorithms, and physics became more precise in making predictions, such as Nicole-Reine Lepaute[7] who developed a clock with astronomical function in 1753, and then she approximated Halley's Comet orbit in 1759. The Harvard Computers directed by Pickering (1877–1919) were a group of women who computed visible astronomical patterns such as Cannon and Leavitt who develop categories still in use today.[8]

Mathematics includes symbolic signs for arithmetic calculation among numbers, algebra references through variables, and relations in algebraic equations, used for computability, for instance, algebra is used to compute mathematical geometric topology. Mathematics can also be understood as a set of languages, as is composed of several forms of description of reality, such as Arithmetic, Algebra, Geometry, and Trigonometry. Computation involves mathematics, arithmetic, and algebra to resolve logical statements for problem solving through algorithms. Algorithms implement algebra: letter representation of numbers and rules to calculate variables through letter symbols. Algebra can be understood as algorithmic, but algorithms involve input, step-by-step disambiguation, and a solution to a problem through arithmetic, algebra symbolic computing. But computation is not replaceable by mathematics, since computation operates on the base of mathematics through symbolic computation calling out terms, functions, and conditionals recursively.

COMPUTATION =
LINGUISTIC, MATHEMATIC (Arithmetic (Mathematic Calculations) + Symbolic − Algebra (Logic Problem Solving)), VISUAL

In computation, we can have a human communicable sign (linguistic, visual, audible, experiential) in a computer interface or a software which is able to interpret the computation of signs through a series of executable related recursive mathematical signals through algorithms. Algorithms make the sign computable through a computational language, from a High-Level programming Language (HLL) that makes the interface or software functional for Human-Computer Interaction (HCI). HLL is translated into a Compiler or into an Assembly Language or both, as Low-Level programming Languages (LLL) which translate HLL into Machine Language as binary 0-1 signs, communicating encrypted binary electronic signals for data computability processing within an electronic chip. To compute, we need to work out reality through computational languages, finding and matching computational linguistic signs, and mathematical signals as equations that may be able to solve computationally a problem. Mathematics reduces reality to numeric values since in its field, everything needs to be measurable. Machine Learning (ML) and Artificial Neural Networks (ANN) reduce reality to a measurable quantifiable numeric abstraction for statistic prediction.

Computational Linguistic Semiotics

Computational Linguistic Semiotics involves the study of programming in relation to grammar, syntax, and semantic meaning and how they can be articulated through computational symbols to develop a computational code that can communicate computation in relation to a lower machine code to administrate electronic signals at the chipset level able to compute results.

Computation integrating mathematics through algorithm's problem solving can be identified under the general category of communication through mathematical computability. Therefore, we have identified both Computational Linguistic Semiotics and Computational Visual Semiotics as the main categories to explore in relation to architecture. If this assumption provides any clues, then computability can be expanded by analyzing, decomposing, and critiquing language and its conventions, and with it, grammar, syntax, theory of signs, communication, the characters of any alphabet, cryptography, and all fall within the general discussion of linguistics. It not only acts as a form of mediated representation of human thinking but also discloses ideology and biases. We can innovate in computation by addressing computational linguistics, and understanding the weight of grammar to infer problems of computability in architecture, which can inform spatial organization by indexing the representational system.

Coding is the design of a problem identified by the idea of a program. Often, we see more and more the tendency in copying and pasting lines of codes, activating coding writing instead of addressing programming questioning a computable problem. We identify programming as a linguistic problem, assigning language an anticipatory hierarchy over programming and identifying certain languages capable of certain types of questions that limit or not the possibility of an ontological reference cognitive system. As discussed in Chapter 5, any language, including computational languages, because of their anticipatory grammar structure, determine the reality they are describing. Programming languages have implicit signifiers tied to their original symbolic form. While Python language is designed based on optimizing Data Science, other programming languages are embedded with other linguistic structures and symbolic forms that are permeable to ideology. Machine languages also develop a deep structure of the Computer-Aided Manufacturing (CAM) system they operate through Computer Numerical Control (CNC). Programming languages project linguistic signifiers, from natural language to programming language activating functionality based on anticipating problems to solve. Computational languages inform what is possible through computation.[9] Most programming languages are grammatically and syntactically optimized to project computational thinking through English, and since computation's metaphysical project is universal communication, linguistic biases should be decolonized. NLP is activating Higher Level programming Language (HLL) and the necessity to learn to code perhaps is disappearing, but the necessity to understand programming is not. At the same time, Artificial Intelligence (AI) is surpassing both coding and programming languages, since emergent programming becomes active through hidden layers in ANNs.

Authorship = Anticipatory Programming languages

In information theory, the generality and universality of the message as content in relation to its encoding and channel transmission propose a disjunction between the information message and the channel and the signal since through coding, one can translate the content of a message to a type of mathematical signal for electronic signal transmission, later discussed in Chapter 7. The general objective of computation is universal communication to overcome cultural barriers, but by removing culture homogeneous communication reinforces cultural biases through conventions, activating the colonial imperial project of the English language through computational linguistic English grammar. We should differentiate computation's ambition for universal communication in relation to the diversity of languages and software that were developed to achieve tasks and types of communications through diverse types of media. Fabretti[10] identifies the difference between what people do with software as opposed to what software does to people, addressing ideology in the software, and also in reference to Althusser.[11] Fabretti refers to Hayles's,[12] as an earlier bibliography in which relationships between computation, coding, and linguistics are developed.

One notion that addresses this issue is perhaps the variety of programming languages and their general purpose and functionality. Imperative Procedural computational HLLs such as Fortran, Cobol, Agol, Basic, Pascal, and C, operate top-down as the programmer devices through coding a general programming concept and idea following variables and functions that anticipate a problem to solve through algorithms recursively. C++, Python, Java, and C# are object-oriented HLLs as they work from the data up, activating a bottom-up approach to computability from data, clustering through data structure objects to interrelate and process information activating up in its grammatical hierarchy to address data computability, processing, and programming as an HLL with simple syntax. Python and C# have been optimized grammatically to address data structures, data retrieval, and applying Data Science. C# is a compiler language optimized for data computability avoiding the interpreted language bytecode of Python Virtual Machine. Java is also an Object-Oriented HLL and though its grammar is optimized to process data blocks it offers poor performance for developers like Python because of the bytecode compiler and its Java Abstract Machine.

Programming Paradigms include:
Interpreted Language (the result of a program)
Compiler Languages (written in Assembly Language)

Low-Level Languages: Machine Language (binary language 0-1)
                        Assembly Language (Assembler: Assembly Language into binary machine language (0-1))
                        Compiler (High Level programming Language into machine language)
                        Low Code (prompt engineering, visual algorithms with pre-build connections, certain programming languages, app development)

High-Level Languages: Logical (declarative approach for problem solving; rule out ambiguity through assertions in relation to conditionals; data and logical deduction, validity argument)
                        Functional (mathematical based; arguments=1 solution by reduction)
                        Imperative Procedural (variables changes process; functions; top-down; no overloading; function over data; abstract conceptual/complex semantics, debugging, abstraction, order)

                                        Fortran (1958, Compiler Language)
                                        Cobol (1959, Compiler Language)
                                        Agol (1960, Compiler Language)
                                        Basic (1964, Interpreted Language, may be Compiled)
                                        Pascal (1970, Compiler Language)
                                        C (1973, Compiler Language, ranked #2 most popular)

                                        Object Oriented (real world separate entities as objects; procedures modifiers; bottom-up; overloading problem; data over function; realistic: data abstraction;)

C++ (1970, Compiler Language, ranked #3 most popular)

Java programming language (1991, Compiler and Interpreted

Language: bytecode, Java Virtual Machine JVM. Mostly used for applications and browsers)

JavaScript programming script (1995, Interpreted)

Python (1991, Interpreted Language: bytecode, Python Virtual Machine; ranked #1 most popular)

R (1993, S Programming Statistical Computing, command line Interpreted Language no compiling; MatLab; data mining)

HTML (1993)

C# (2000, Compiler Language, ranked #4 most popular)

SQL Structured Query Language (1974, domain-specific, relational data)

CUDA (NVIDIA 2006–07, Computer Unified Device Architecture) for GPU

Histories and Theories of Computation Through Semiotics

We would like to offer a reading, analyzing, critiquing, and ultimately displacing computation in relation to architecture, which we expand in relation to computational linguistic and visual semiotics. A section through the history of computation can include analog and digital machines, as one of the oldest digital computing systems is the abacus, used before 600 BCE in Egypt, Persia, and other civilizations. The abacus is a calculating frame able to develop complex calculations defined as digital since it is based on individual units. The ancient Hellenistic Greek Antikythera (200 BCE) is perhaps the first known analog computer, a metal mechanism for astronomy prediction. Computation as a form of media reproductivity can be related to Gutenberg's print[13] of 1440 although Chinese monks were already using a print cast by 868 and by 1234 Koreans were implementing movable types as well.

Pascal designed in 1642 (patented in 1649) an automatic machine for calculation called "*Pascaline*" or "*Pascal's calculator*" or "Arithmetic Machine" able to perform addition, subtraction, division, and multiplication, considered the first automatic calculator. The prototype include a metal mechanic set of concatenated numeric wheels able to develop a series of related numeric values to perform arithmetic calculations. Leibniz developed a diagram of reasoning: the *Characteristica Universalis* of 1666[14] which included the Ching Hexagram Diagrams (property of Leibniz) to which he added the Arabic numerals, as he identified the necessity to both incorporate mathematical combinatory logic in relation to diagrammatic linguistic symbols, addressing computable thinking through combinatory linguistics. In 1672, Leibniz developed the "Leibniz wheel" or "stepped drum gear calculator". The *Miscellanea Berolensia ad incrementum scientiarum*[15] published in 1710 (originally from 1672) for mechanical calculation is inspired by the Pascaline. Leibniz *Characteristica Universalis* developed a universal conceptual language aiming at communication between sciences, mathematics, and philosophy, developing an alphabet of human thought by articulating formalized processes as a pure language through algebra. His system proposed a way to represent language ideas through calculus, or *"calculus ratiocinator"*, a universal calculation framework that could determinate whether a statement is true or false based on known mathematical axioms. The calculus ratiocinator is aimed at developing an "algebra of logic" and is perhaps the first form of computer since it seems to include a concept of software independent from any physical element and according to Wiener (1948) the general idea of computing machine. But the modern computer has hardware and software, and Wiener articulated the reasoning machine: *machina rationatrix*.

Signal = Mechanic Sequential Calculation
Signifier = Mechanical Linguistic Thinking through Algebraic disambiguation

Bouchon in 1725 devised a control machine loom with perforated paper tapes as punchcards to instruct complex orders to a recursive weaving of threads to create textile fabrics. In 1804 the Jacquard Loom was developed for complex textile analog continuous weaving using a digital discrete punch card (solid or void card binary system) continuous feed. Baddage's Analytical Engine of 1837 procured a stored program idea via punchcards from Jacquard and a precursor to von Neumann's Random-Access Memory (RAM). The Bouchon and Jacquard machines are quite revolutionary, not only because of their efficiency and the complex textile weaving patterns as output but also because of the emergence of a philosophy of computation since an abstract encoded message as input through a punch card activates precise instructions to an automated mechanism. Jacquard Looming Machine is often declared the first analog programmable digital computational model, as it marked the information encoding problem. The punch card method develops an informational model that is abstract, exchangeable, numeric, and informational. Inspired by the mechanical loom, the first computer program can be attributed to Ada Lovelace[16] after adding notes to a paper by inventor Charles Babbage for his "Analytical Engine" (1837) to develop an algorithm to compute Bernoulli numbers in 1840, pointing out the possibility to program a machine through notation in relation to the mechanism of the engine to compute solutions beside numbers, such as music.[17]

Looming Machine Digital Sign = Signal = analog continuous mechanical computation

96   *AI Computational Linguistic Semiotics*

In 1837, the Morse Code was developed and applied to the existing telegraph key and sounder to encode information in codified electromagnetic short-long and up to three repetitions impulse electrical signals, enabling mass communication through electrical wiring. The manual telephone exchange of the 1880s enabled mass communication and by 1891 the "Strowger Switch" a step-by-step automatic telephone exchange switch came into being. By 1901–10, the electromechanical stepping telephone exchange system was introduced. The first automatic exchange public network was opened at Epsom in Surrey in 1912.

> sign= digital − discrete mechanical punch card (physical signal)
> sign= electromagnetic signal Morse code Y/N Short/Long
> Boolean Logic = Y/N

The *Rules of Thought* by George Boole[18] in 1854 resolved a possibility for logic to be reduced to a binary system, basically resolving the validity of arguments in terms of true/false through sequential yes or no solutions. Boole's publication is in reference to Aristotle's the Law of Thought[19] and his Organon (+/−350 BCE, Published in 50 BCE). Through syllogisms based on language and simple clear statements, Aristotle designed a formal logical system implementing arithmetic to resolve a system that establishes a form of syllogism categorizing thinking in terms of dialectical reasoning, resolving whether a statement is true or false. Aristotle establishes calculus as the science of logic. He then uses symbolic form to represent through calculus the relationship between natural language meaning converting statements into abstract calculus formal logic, therefore making statements analyzable, relational, and computable, through mathematics thanks to symbolic calculation, which is the base for algorithms.

In computational terms, a digital electronic signal computes through Boolean logic[20] (True/False through Boolean operators) possibilities of logical reduction to yes/no, and within this reductive recursive thinking resolves problems through algorithms which rule out ambiguity. Frege then developed the *Begriffsschrift*[21] or concept script, which was a book of the logic of 1879 through a formal system of judging and negation assertion to script language through axioms.

Set theory or the mathematics of possible relations in sets of objects as defined by Cantor proposed axioms as inference defining relationships between mathematics and logic, including Boolean algebra. Hilbert's program or Entscheidungsproblem or decision problem addressed Leibniz's decidability problem as possible.[22] In 1930 Alonzo Church developed Lambda calculus,[23] a formal system capable of universal computation and assembly language through function abstraction and variable binding and substitution. This defined computation as a separate independent field of knowledge. By 1931 Gödel's undecidability was published,[24] presenting limits in mathematics with influence on computation. Gödel's incompleteness theorem is basically a demonstration of the impossibility of the Hilbert Program in relation to the Leibniz ratiocinator.

Alan Turing was aiming at addressing Gödel incompleteness theorem through a mathematical machine processing input and output, questioning whether a computer program (later software) can determine whether another program can halt (complete a program) or not (stay within an infinite looping process). Turing proved that this is not possible and that this program cannot exist. Turing identified several problems, such as *uncomputability* as the decision problem. Turing[25] developed in 1936 an abstract "a-machine" concept, named the "Universal Turing Machine" that combines symbols according to rules, an automatic machine that runs on an infinite memory tape with instructions based on symbolic logic activating electromagnetic signals in transistors. Originally this machine was first developed to automate calculations for decoding secret encrypted messages by the enigma machine of Nazi Germany during World War II. One of the first computers was developed to reverse engineer and decode encrypted messages. But the Z3 (based on Z1 1935–38) developed in Germany was the first Turing-complete[26] programmable digital working computer in which numeric data was entered manually through a punch film (1938–41)[27] used to compute a matrix to inform Küssner's aerodynamics problems. Turing-complete in computational theory means that a system is computable and universal, and most computational systems today such as a programming language, a string, Cellular Automation, and Lambda Calculus, comply with this definition. Turing in a lecture in London in 1947 "What we want is a machine that can learn from experience" is the first clear reference to AI.[28]

Signal - Sign = Transistor + Tape (memory and instructions)

Shannon's Information Theory

Shannon's mathematical means for electronic communications[29] references telephone communication protocols by activating through binary electronic signals in relays Boolean logic of the 1800s,[30] which is used to rule out ambiguity in recursive algorithms. Contemporary computation is based on Shannon's mathematical theory of communication, integrating the Boolean logic to electromechanics binary signal ($1-0$ = On/Off). Shannon was a cryptographer and so he devised a way to communicate a message by encoding it in a series of codewords. Fano's method encodes in 0 and 1. Arithmetic coding encodes bits per character in the ASCII code. Shannon's diagram defines:

Information Source > (message) > Transmitter, a signal > a Received Signal >,
a Receiver (message) and Destination (through Channel Noise)
Mathematical Theory of Communication (Boolean Logic)
Electromechanical Circuit Break, Sign = On/Off

AI Computational Linguistic Semiotics

Shannon made a mathematical representation of the computability of the world. Shannon devised a method of communication that discovered the natural advantage of encoding information into BITS for communication efficiency. A BIT count defines the minimum amount of questions necessary to rule out ambiguity to decipher a message: 1 BIT = 1 question, resulting into 1–0 yes/no. A BIT can encode universally images, sounds, and any type of message. BITS can be reduced through data compression without compromising information. Harvard Mark I or IBM ASCC (1944) was a general computer designed for WWII. Shannon's research developed the Electronic Numerical Integrator and Computer (ENIAC) as the first Turing-complete programmable general-purpose digital computer in 1942–45/46. With no available programming language, ENIAC was programmed to run arbitrary mathematical operations by plugboards and switches and debugged by women to compute ballistics for WWII, such as Betty Jean Jennings, Fran Bilas, and others hidden by patriarchy.[31]

Combinatory Mathematics = Binary Sign = Universal Language
Binary Sign = New System of Representation

Shannon founded information theory as a field of knowledge that expands to a general physics-based theory of the universe.[32] Shannon's dissociation between the message and the means of information communication as a function of the economy of encrypted communication is still used today.

Information Theory:
From Shannon's Entropy to "It From Bit"

Shannon's entropy was concerned with the fidelity of the message encoded and transmitted through an imperfect channel that would produce "noise". Today information communication got rid of the noise problem with some exceptions due to radiation or interference of any type, such as environmental. What is interesting in this context is that the formula structured by Shannon is equal to the definition of entropy in statistical thermodynamics, which is defined as being opposed to equilibrium in a dynamic system through particles. Shannon further claims that "Information is the resolution of uncertainty". Information is related to quantum physics, such as the energy of the universe, which is constant, and that the entropy of the universe tends to increase. Von Baeyer relates to Hawking's Black Holes Information Paradox, as information is conserved in a natural process described by quantum mechanics, and by losing information, a black hole destroys information something forbidden by the laws of quantum mechanics.

Information = Universal Language

In Wheeler's It From Bit, a BIT, the minimum data unit that a computer can process to encode, resolve and communicate information, is also the building block of the universe as it can represent all reality. Wheeler establishes a boundary space identifying how a black hole can contain information expressed in binary terms. Historically science had separated the subjectivity of the observer from objective reality. According to von Baeyer[33], Einstein's theory of relativity revealed that non-phenomenons, including time itself, can be described without reference to the viewer-observer state of motion, inserting the observer in the field of science and physics. And according to quantum theory, in the state of a physical element such as an atom, the observer defines the measurement apparatus and system of reference and therefore the determination of the possible answers and with it the behavior of reality by the act of measurement, making it observer-dependent, as reality is shaped apparently by the questions we ask as in a subject-dependent simulation. Wheeler discusses quantum physics and "measurement as an irreversible act in which uncertainty collapses to certainty".[34]

Kurzweil describes how von Neumann articulated Shannon's fundamental problem of making information reliable and Turing's universality of computation in the development of information technologies by developing the fundamental architecture of the computer, the architecture of software-hardware.[35] The von Neumann architecture, follows a diagram comparable to the brain activity, the development of the Central Processing Unit (CPU) in relation to a memory unit (later RAM) based on the brain functionality. Von Neumann Electronic Discrete Variable Automatic Computer (EDVAC) machine allows the memory to be able to be programmed for different tasks through the RAM which can be immediately retrieved, while Turing's one-bit computation tape program was a set of recorded instructions for multiple word BITS computability. Von Neumann identifies a problem in the human brain, sensing that neural calculation is actually slow, but the massively parallel processing of the brain is what gives an advantage to humans. According to Kurzweil, what was not known at the time is how learning occurs through synapsis, by building or destroying connections between neurons. Von Neumann's description of language has several differentiations since he addresses the difference between mathematics as a system of description of reality in relation to language as a product of historical cultural evolution, independent of pure abstract logic.[36] He refers to the processing between organs such as the retina in the eye and the brain, and the arithmetic calculations that occur through the nervous system in terms of stimuli message communication.

Von Neumann Architecture
Input → General Processing Unit (CPU) → Output Device
Control Unit
Arithmetic/Logic Unit
Registers (PC-CIR-AC-MAR-MDR)
↓↑
Memory Unity

100   AI Computational Linguistic Semiotics

Computation is made possible by articulating through a computer language computability among calculations, which can give precise non–ambiguous instructions to electromechanical signals which are now completely digital. The transferring from a symbolic language to a machinic language is made possible through the Assembler: Assembly Language > *Assembler* > Machine Code. Grace Hopper who worked in the Mark I team (1944) and UNIVAC (1949) developed the first compiled language named A–0^{37} (1950–52) to combine arithmetic with algebra through symbolic computation into machine code; she then contributed to the first machine programming language FLOW-MATIC (1954) which led to COBOL language (1959) since she devised the necessity to program in English and translate to a machine code. A High-Level programming Language (HLL) is an abstract system of communication, which is based on a library that interprets electromechanical actions at the chip level through the Assembly Language. HLL enables the possibility of addressing a complete set of instructions necessary to execute a low code at a microprocessor level. Symbolic computation calls back-and-forth relationships between arithmetic through algorithms embedded in the form of coded computational language through lines of sequential codes that can be called out to execute code orders and recursive loops thanks to their numeric line reference number. The Compiler or the Assembly Language or both are symbolic and expressed through alphabet letters that can be called to execute an order at a Low-Level programming Language (LLL) or Machine Language (binary 0-1).

> ASSEMBLY LANGUAGE
> Electronic Signal = Yes | No
> Digital Sign = 1 | 0
> DATA= sign with no meaning, organization, or meaning
> INFORMATION = signs organized meaningfully enabling a message
> Mathematics – Computation
> Linguistics – Systems of Representation

Computational thinking paradigm is thought of as a cycle in which a programmer decomposes a problem, analyzes a pattern through pattern recognition features, develops an abstraction (concept-based) of the problem, and then the algorithm that implements them, looping back to either optimize the algorithm and develop a more robust platform or initiate another set of algorithms. This process is based on an algorithm design often based on a scientific method.

> Code=application of logic functionality
> Software Writing = Optimization by Attempts

A known problem in computation is in writing software that can anticipate problems in its functionality, as coders understand a system through designing the system itself.

Automata Theory:
Paradigm Shift Through Simulation, Self-Replication, Recursive Automation, and emergent AI

Von Neumann's controversial research in the Manhattan Project was based on the implosion of the atomic Bomb to the Hydrogen Bomb during WWII, as the longer-term objective was to be able to create an infinite source of energy through nuclear fusion. Von Neumann's self-replicator was conceived as an automation of a nuclear chain reaction. The self-replicator was a parallel way to understand artificial life and the road for AI, as a self-replicator program can be conceived in multiple ways, from nuclear chain reaction, to a program that simulates itself, to a universal constructor, to a self-reproducing constructor system for interplanetary colonization.

Von Neumann refers to semiotics changes in the message information transmission between generations of self-replication as in artificial life. Through simulation, one program can simulate another program; and through generations change a sign into a signal. A sign can be transmitted and converted into a physical signal through the universal constructor. The universal constructor or von Neumann probe could be physical or sign to signal processing. The universal constructor can self-replicate in other planets through local materials and in several generations colonize our galaxy. The universal constructor can change a communication informational sign into an information signal across space to activate a physical process at a distance activating a self-replicating self-simulating universal constructor (see Chapter 10 "Architecture of Information: Building Faster-Than-Light Speed Here and Elsewhere in the Universe"). The self-replicator was also a means to elevate intelligence and make it recursively exponential and therefore evolutive, since human intelligence could replicate itself and improve in each cycle, paving the way for recursive learning through evolutive computation through generations of self-replication-simulation. AI systems by training the trainer and through Neural Networks (NN) as Graphs that can predict the parameters of a NN through wide nets, deep nets, and dense nets.[38]

> "There exists a critical size below which the process of synthesis is degenerative, but above which the phenomenon of synthesis, if properly arranged, can become explosive, in other words, where syntheses of automata can proceed in such manner that each automation will produce other automata which are more complex and of higher potentialities than itself" von Neumann [39]

Simulation = Sign > Physical Signal
Self-Simulation replication exponentiation = Artificial Life - Intelligence

In 1948, Von Neuman and Stanislaw Ulman developed the mathematics for a universal constructor through self-replication machines, the theory of games,

102 AI Computational Linguistic Semiotics

and Cellular Automata developing its full theory by 1966. Universal constructors can replicate themselves or develop virtual machines, a base for AI through demonstrating Turing Complete and Universal Computation made possible by a h+ program in which the h program is part of the behavior of the machine. In 1948 Ulam and Von Neumann developed a mathematical model for cellular automata as a universal constructor self-replicating autonomous information system (Figure 6.1), a conceptual approach to evolutionary systems and autonomous systems, although not computationally but conceptually.[40] By 1949 Neumann discussed a technological singularity[41] as an evolution beyond human intelligence (some note the year as 1957 the first time this is mentioned as a clear reference to AI, Stan Ulam quoting von Neumann).

Cellular Automation (CA):

a   Von-Neumann-neighborhood
b   Moore-neighborhood
c   Extended-Moore-neighborhood.

Von Neumann devised means to solve deterministic problems from nondeterministic equations through hydrodynamics. He realized that human action through pollution had changed the entire world's environmental weather and that this process could be predicted and controlled. He developed nondeterministic computational systems based on randomness to solve faster deterministic problems. By solving problems in the ENIAC's first programmable computer he developed the MANIAC as an electronic automated calculator computer, which was not used much for energy calculations, but rather used to predict the weather.

In Automata Theory[42] or abstract machines, one can distinguish the different types of automation:

> Type-0 Recursively Enumerable (Turing Machine);
> Type-1 Context Sensitive (Linear-Bounded nondeterministic Turing Machine);
> Type-2 Context Free (Nondeterministic, pushdown automation);
> Type-3 Regular (Finite State Machine Automation, from Combinational Logic);

Von Neumann also invented the computer virus in relation to developing artificial life, a program that can corrupt another program. These ideas also provided means to work through statistics predictive models, since Ulam also realized that the more times one runs a system, the more information one has on the relationship between input and output, opening statistical calculations through simulation as a predictive tool.

Conway advanced CA through the Game of Life[43] as a demonstration of a non-reversibility complex system that depends on the initial state and therefore is a 0-player game, articulating Type-1 Automata Theory. Nondeterministic

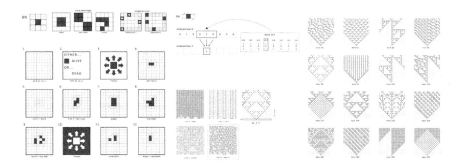

Figure 6.1 Cellular Automation description: neighbouring relationships, rule set, CA identified rules classification. Venice Biennale Research Studio, Associate Prof. Pablo Lorenzo-Eiroa with Student Ben Sather, NYIT SoAD, F2019.

means nonreversible as the computation of the system cannot be predicted unless it is run, activating the Simulation paradigm. Often computation is done through reversible algorithms that can be traced back to how a system computed. In this case, non-reversibility means that basically, no algorithm can reverse engineer the computed results. The Game of Life is a site-based contextual emergent system, variable after a deterministic set of rules opening nondeterministic behavioral emergent evolution. The problem is that if one is familiar with the rules, there is an appearance of deterministic constant from initial states. The game of life promotes competitional synthetic behavior, as an internal set of rules interact with external emergent conditionings, proposing mathematically an analog to a life system in which internal information and external conditionings define the evolution of automation. One of the unsolved problems in computer science is whether P is equal to NP (P= NP?) or not, based on whether there is a correlation between an easy-to-solve problem and its correctness. Game of Life is an undecidable program as we cannot know through any type of algorithm or calculation whether the program will halt or not.

Wolfram developed CA types classification in relation to their complexity (Class 1 to 4). According to Wolfram,[44] CA simple rules can create complex behavior, being a system to demonstrate the fundamentals of physics. CA can compute results based on rule sets based on cell status on a grid of neighboring relationships, which become site conditionals for the following generation. In 1983, Wolfram's discovery of Rule 30 is an aperiodic chaotic behavior, from simple rules to the complex emergent chaotic behavioral evolutive and complex irreducible nonreversible system, describing scientific natural patterns. His early studies proposed computational irreducibility and infinite processing and claims that CA broke the second law of thermodynamics, that entropy can never decrease. CA Rule 110 proven by Cook[45] (conjured by Wolfram in 1985 and with dispute) is demonstrated capable of universal computation. The CA Glider by Cook is capable of emulating computational models through tagging (appendants: YYY and N) data turned into a new

104 *AI Computational Linguistic Semiotics*

piece after crossing a tape. Wolfram also claims CA is a formal language, capable through grammar rules of developing emerging sense through "words" as emerging CA configurations (Figure 6.1).

Local Function Rule 110

$$\phi(1, 1, 1) \rightarrow 0 \; \phi(0, 1, 1) \rightarrow 1$$
$$\phi(1, 1, 0) \rightarrow 1 \; \phi(0, 1, 0) \rightarrow 1$$
$$\phi(1, 0, 1) \rightarrow 1 \; \phi(0, 0, 1) \rightarrow 1$$
$$\phi(1, 0, 0) \rightarrow 0 \; \phi(0, 0, 0) \rightarrow 0$$

Cold War Anti-Bomb City Defense as a Feedback Network: Cybernetic Theory in Urban Decentralization[46]

Automata Theory is related to Cybernetics[47] used by Weiner in 1948[48] spinning from discussions on irreversibility from the Second Law of Thermodynamics increase of entropy in Chaos Theory which accounts for the irreversibility of natural processes and the asymmetry between future and past; self-regulatory systems; servomechanisms; automation; AI; and other subjects. Cybernetics as the self-organizing machine was a theoretical study of communication and control processes in biological, mechanical, and electronic systems, which incorporated urbanism. Weiner worked on feedback and oscillation in computing machines as neural nets to draw parallels to the nervous system through analog machines and numerical machines. Weiner also discussed self-organizing systems as phylogenetic learning through evolution and success adaptation and ontogenetic learning through development as external input-learning modifying behavior. Weiner develops notions of cybernetics for military warfare during the machine age,[49] from space colonization to urban warfare protection.[50]

In 1950 Wiener proposed a plan for protecting the communication of the city under an atomic blast.[51] He reinforced the idea of maintaining communication after a bomb attack, by means of belts as highway bypass surrounding the cities for preserving circulation flow. Studies from Lapp[52] develop non-linear city diagrams in relation to the destructive potential of an atomic bomb within a city. These studies are derived into spacing cities by the Office of Civil Defense[53] starting the Cold War Age and developing a Guide to Urban dispersal.[54] Galison[55] discusses the planning and outcomes of these military policies in decentralization. Hilberseimer through a series of plans initiated in South Chicago[56] explains America's integration to the rational methods in Germany applying science, data, and technology as he proposes the Integration of Industry and agriculture. The notion of a city center in urbanism and of center itself is disseminated, as the network organization implies the dissolution of hierarchy as the regulation of power, as it becomes dynamic and everywhere. Urbanism and Urban Planning became the main scientific subject for cybernetic theory in parallel to NN information theory from understanding how people move through infrastructure[57] as a result of war strategy, tactics, and warfare simulation.

"Artificial Intelligence":
From Anticipatory Software to Emergent Programming
Through ML Training ANN

The Dartmouth workshop[58] of 1956 discussed NNs and creativity in relation to programming a computer through language and randomness for the development of AI, with participants such as Minsky, Shannon, and others.[59] The origins of ML can be attributed to Leibniz's differential equation (1693), Gauss patterns probability (1801), and Cauchy's Gradient Descend (1847). ANNs for AI could be traced back to 1888 when Santiago Ramon y Cajal identified the hierarchical organization of neurons, neural terminal activity in the nervous system through neuroanatomy, and the functional impulses between gaps in the neurons as an electrical impulse. This marked the origins of the synaptic theory of memory including the structure and connection of neurons. In 1943 Warren and Pitts[60] developed the first model for ANN through electrical circuits. In 1956[61] Frank Rosenblatt developed the perceptron, considered the first NN, and a machine capable of recognizing, learning, and calculating by itself developed from active live cells.

Shannon's Theseus robotic maze was the first autonomous responsive electromechanical system and was one of the first implementations of ML automation in 1950. The robotic system identified barriers and was able to memorize and proceed by hitting boundaries until resolving the maze. In 1949 Manchester Mark 1 and Ferranti Mark 1 of 1951 was the first commercially available computer that was able to perform a computer game, a chess game evaluating possible moves (not complete).

Chomsky proposed a linguistic hierarchy relevant to computational programming languages still in use today and a formal grammar from the problems of linguistic systems to logical abstractions in the development of syntax.[62] Chomsky explores the linguistic levels that are possible, organized from deep structure to surface structure and in relation to generative grammar. Chomsky's "Three Models for the Description of Language" develop concepts for finite state and context-dependent meaning in the English language.[63] Chomsky assigns a generative dimension to grammar as an organizing system of reality, identified by Alexander[64] pairing patterns, genetics, codes, and languages as a "pattern language".

Chomsky's hierarchy aims at identifying hierarchy within the whole system of communication:

SYMBOL: letters, digits characters;
STRING: sequence of symbols;

RULES:	set of rules for grammar, following strings that are syntactically valid;
TERMINAL:	the smallest unit of grammar;
NON_TERMINAL:	symbols replaced by others;
GRAMMAR:	rules for forming structured sentences;
LANGUAGE:	a set of strings conforming to the grammar;
AUTOMATION:	programmable version of grammar by pre-defined rules;

Chomsky's Hierarchy pairs Automata Theory to Linguistic Formal Grammar, noting that the simplest are regular languages, followed by context-free and then context-sensitive, completing the hierarchy with recursively enumerable languages:

Type 0 = Recursively enumerable (Turing Machine)
Type 1 = Context Sensitive (Linear-Bounded Automation)
Type 2 = Context-free (Push Down Automation)
Type 3 = Regular (Finite Automation)

Chomsky's "Three Models for the Description of Language" diagram #16 combinatory variations in connections which become complicated due to the number of possibilities through phrase structure grammar, dependency structure on syntax, and in diagram #22 with other examples aim at demonstrating that syntactically correct grammar does not secure semantic meaning (diagram #14):

$A \rightarrow$ B C
S $\rightarrow$ NP VP

$N_1 \rightarrow$ (AP) N_1 (PP)

[A] Colorless [A] green [N] ideas [V] sleep [Adv.] furiously
[NP[ADJ N] VP[V] AP[ADV]]

Minsky' Computational Semiotics: AI Meaning

Minsky is considered responsible for AI, as in 1951 the Stochastic Neural Analog Reinforcement Calculator (SNARC) representation or the first simulator of neural nets as neural synapses that hold memory – input-output – to propagate linear algebra mathematical signals.[65,66] McCarthy's AI Project of 1959[67] works by multiple inputs and weights, inputting data and comparing results through backpropagation making it recursive to weight back again. Usually, algorithms compute results in one direction, as most are reversible. Statistic logistic regression by David Cox in 1958 was used to come up with output based on a predictor applied to variable features in a set.

Backpropagation in feedforward NNs secures feedback through weighting cost between computational generations forward and backward making parallel processing correlational and nonreversible through feedback.

Kleene proposes intelligence in terms of nerve nets aiming for automata.[68] Minsky identifies in "Words, Sentences and Meanings"[69] various relationships between Shannon's information theory and linguistics theory through Chomsky grammar[70] in "encoding" meaning. Minsky discussed generative grammar or the possibility for grammar to produce words or linguistic signification, a media determination through the structure. He also integrates learning features in neuroscience identifying the roots of cognition by implementing feedback reinforcement learning through neural nets establishing the foundations of AI. Minsky develops a bifurcating system for Predictions and expectations (1960). Minsky Global Space Frame (GSF) of 1974 proposes 3D object frames that map directly into space locations, tracking the image of a cube through neural nets, after Guzman[71] (1967) and Winston (1970) through AI classifiers semantics meanings as platforms for knowledge.

Minsky Operant reinforcement model:

Environment   ←   Response   ← Reinforcement
     → Stimulus   → Machine
                              Z

     [Trainer]   [U]

Minsky[72] developed concepts of feedback in cybernetics integrating information theory and linguistic theory through grammar with John McCarthy at MIT. Minsky identifies "Frames as Paradigms" and that a purely logical approach to information processing will not be complete without a "Criticism of the Logistic Approach" identifying the limits of current mathematics and formal logic "propositions: embody specific information and syllogisms: general laws of proper inference" for consistency and completeness:

"(1) Complete–"All true statements can be proven"; and (2) Consistent–"No false statements can be proven."" Minsky[73]

Minsky also refers to Fillmore (1968) and Celce-Murcia[74] (1972) in correlating structures with frames and gives us a warning about Deep Structure, the methodology we have been using:

> "we must not assume that the transient semantic structure built during the syntactic analysis (what language theorists today call the "deep structure" of a sentence) is identical with the larger (and "deeper") structure built up incrementally as each fragment of a coherent linguistic communication operates upon it!." Minsky

108 *AI Computational Linguistic Semiotics*

In contrast, Minsky also refers to Language Translation[75] as an issue to identify in terms of meaning structured by language. Minsky goes on to deal with semantics recognition by machine understanding and processing and to identify a syntactic structure that may deal with meaning relative to information processing to propose using "Frames in Heuristic Search" the problems we are dealing with today with ML and semantic segmentation further discussed in Chapter 7. Form and content had also been discussed in previous writings.[76]

Cybernetics of Cybernetics = Self-Referential Cybernetics

Bateson translated issues of *cybernetics* and information theory to the social sciences through ecology. Bateson developed systemic theories derived from self-regulatory mechanisms induced by the *interdisciplinary*, focusing on the reciprocity and feedback of external associations. For Bateson, systems are deterministic as they define subjects through role play in a systemic group. In 1972 Bateson[77] identified in the thermostat an interactive self-balancing feedback-based automated learning mechanism. Bateson differentiated the First and Second Order cybernetics as the cybernetics of the system observed and the cybernetics of the observing system, and in addition, meta-cybernetics known as cybernetics of cybernetics[78] as self-referentiality and self-organization of complex systems through a feedback loop.[79]

Flow Chart Procedural Organization

The Flow Chart Diagrams or Flow Diagrams were developed between 1908–24 as a mechanism to understand machinic functioning and systemic thinking by Frank and Lilian Gilbreth. The flow chart allowed tracing through Boolean Logic critical information paths that can be recursive for problem solving, identifying issues in systems, and finding out where to optimize them. Algorithms can be conceptualized, optimized, and resolved through flow charts without the use of a computer, identifying problems through recursive binary Boolean logic thinking to understand how well a code is written and to test programming overall concept and functionality, as discussed by Fabretti referencing Kinslow.[80] Wirth[81] developed Pascal computer language and discusses the relationship between flow charts and nested structures in depicting the diversity of computational and data structures that may become active in computation. Likewise, a data-gathering algorithmic process needs mathematical verification before data is processed to make sure the results are valid. Flow charts include flow lines in between decision-making terms connecting loops for processing until a solution is found (Figure 6.2):

Flow Charts = Logic Optimization
Algorithms + Data Structures = Programs

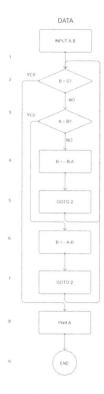

Figure 6.2 Algorithm resolved through a Flow Chart diagram.

Data and Information Theory

In early 1960, John R. Pierce referred to information theory instead of the communication (mathematical) theory by Shannon when relating to a pre-digital era, Symbols, Signals, and Noise[82]. Since languages are developed out of historical facts and not of logical necessities,[83] Pierce identifies that we do not have a complete grammar for any natural language, and that "formal grammar has been proved powerful in computer languages" a work that references Chomsky.[84] Pierce notes in science the indifference to language as a medium to address reality. He references network theory in electrical theory as circuits or networks and the transferring of electrical conduits through channels (such as wire, copper, magnetic cores) and in relation to communication structures from idealized electrical systems, and relating information theory to electrical communication, correlating mathematical signals with electrical current and time in conveying-communicating a message.

> No Language = Complete Grammar
> Computation = Formal Grammar

110   *AI Computational Linguistic Semiotics*

> Communication = Information
> Information Theory = Mathematical Theory
> Information = Electrical Communication

Pierce distinguishes information from knowledge and rather assigns the resolution of uncertainty to information theory and analyzes means to communicate messages through signals, channels, signal decoding, and grammar through statistical word prediction. Pierce discusses cybernetics in the work of Minsky and addresses communication theory through statistics for grammar prediction linguistic messages assigning probabilistic numbers to word sequences. Pierce also compares his research with mathematical notation symbols, music, and visual arts, as he declares that with the right amount of information, through statistics, one could replicate the style of any music composer.

> Statistics = Prediction Model
> Information = New Language of Science (ontology)

According to von Baeyer,[85] information theory bridges all forms of knowledge through binary translation as ontology. Information theory investigates this form of communication through mathematics. Computer interfaces calculate, organize, and transfer sets of data that communicate a message translated through interfaces which conveys information.

Signs organized through code sequence represent a message content or information. An electronic signal represents the BIT sign. Even if a code may change, the electronic signal remains the same, as the relational logic of the code acquires importance and relevance over the binary sign. Von Baeyer discusses a genealogy of the relationship between form and information, from the epistemology of the word to how we answer what is information. What is form? In questioning meaning (Form = Plato= eidos = idea or ideal) as an archetype ideal but also discusses Aristotle's problematization of the ideal form of Plato, defining it as a sum of the total properties that define things and form as an expression of relationships.

> "Information, then, refers to imposing, detecting or communicating a form. It connotates change. It possesses 'informative power'." [...] "Information is the transfer of form from one medium to another. In the context of human information-exchange, 'communication' is a more descriptive term than transfer, and since the form is about relationships, we can tentatively define information as the *communication of relationships*". Von Baeyer quotes Cicero as the verb "inform" to signify giving shape to something, forming an idea.

> Form = In:Form
> Information = transfer of Form from one medium to another

"information is the flow of form" [...] "In-Formation – the infusion of form – the flow of relationships - the communication of messages." [...] "Information deals rather with relationships than with things". von Baeyer

T.S Elliot Pyramid of Organizational Knowledge:

DATA
INFORMATION
KNOWLEDGE
WISDOM

Which relates to

WHAT
HOW
WHY

Bloom's Taxonomy:

CREATING
EVALUATING
ANALYZING
APPLYING
UNDERSTANDING
REMEMBERING

Data Science – Data Scraping – Data Mining

Data acquisition is the first step toward surveying the world through computation, by identifying, measuring, and transforming data into useful information. The data acquisition mechanism already proposes a digital signifier as in any process of representation, that needs to be displaced for data to avoid a bias. In addition, Data Science through API or web-scraping applies algorithm structures that anticipate what to look for, a problem that is being resolved through non-supervised ML. One of the main issues of Data Science is that one may find what one is looking for, promoting the biases that initiated the data search, raising issues on how the data-gathering mechanisms are implemented, what are the questions being asked and why, what are the cultural issues to consider, and which are the social categories we use to identify, label and categorize data. Moreover, in Chapter 20 we discuss who is in control of data, how data is gathered, which mechanisms and methods are implemented, and why and how authority is gained or projected by both private media and public agencies.

We can reference well-known data science problems to be aware that can trigger problems when working through AI, repositories, data mining over

112   *AI Computational Linguistic Semiotics*

existing datasets, data-gathering mechanisms, and methodologies that may be relevant for architecture and urbanism when doing a survey: The Simpson Paradox[86] which inverts the assumptions of the dataset, the "Survivorship Bias"[87] which flips the data analysis due to lack of data, the maximum likelihood[88] as incomplete data, and the "Framing Bias" by decontextualizing a problem through a reductive frame of reference, and other data issues further discussed in Chapter 7 and 19.

Big Data Non-Conceptual Indeterminism Challenging Intuitive Anticipatory Modeling

Big Data[89] became active around 2007–13 due to the amount of information available through the internet and our cell phones tracking data through datasets, databases, and data repositories. A new form of diversified post-structuralism becomes active: to arrive at conclusions by analyzing computationally large sources of information, resisting intuitive preconceptions through statistical analysis based on objective data. Big Data computation arises first from computing power, enabling the gathering, and processing of large amounts of data beyond human processing means supervision and validation, inverting the previous computational paradigm in which algorithms are anticipatory model solutions to a given problem. In AI, data plays most of the role in the activation of any meaningful output since AI becomes active through statistics as a prediction model. In this respect, the erroneous design attempt is to "model" the neural net to anticipate a form of transformation of reality through a prediction model, while in reality, the data will over-weight the "model". This shift, data outweighing modelling aligned with the critique of structuralist anticipatory thought and established a new cognitive paradigm backed up with neurosciences research regarding establishing and framing a question through data evidence and validation. The informed process is dependent on analyzing reality, suspended as much as possible, intuition as well as any observational, research or framing of any problem through cultural biases or preconceptions. Carpo[90] contrasts the way in which architects worked in the 1990s with manageable amounts of data. We argue that we should also question the structuralism that is present in the algorithmic modelling calculation through which big data is gathered, and processed.

Lots of Model's Parameters = few data (<2007)
Big Data = Few Model parameters (2007–19)
Multidimensional Big Data = Robust Model Multidimensional ANN (2019>)

Machine Learning (ML)

AI through cybernetics had a spark back in the 1950s but then decayed and was even called nonscientific during the 1980s–90s, often identified as the AI winter. ALVINN developed the first self-driving car implementing NNs in 1989. By 2010 the error margin of trained NNs in recognizing tagged features was around 30%, by 2011 of around 25%, then around 15.3% by 2012. Alex-Net a Convolutional Neural Network (CNN) which won the ImageNET competition for image recognition challenge for the first time implementing a Graphic Processing Unit (GPU) about four times faster than a CPU. By then thanks to GPU and large data repositories, Big Data starts being able to provide more meaningful functional power to neural nets. Thanks to the internet, cell phones, and data-gathering mechanisms were able to activate Data Science methods in relation to the models provided by neural nets feedback and parallel processing. By 2015 AI was 3% better than humans at recognizing images and classification as ANN were able to collect enough data to prove their model functionality through Tensor Computing, for example, through TensorFlow (Alphabet – Google, 2015), OpenAI (2015), PyTorch (Meta-FaceBook, 2016).

ML[91] combines parallel networks to edit out noise in unstructured data and combine feature recognition integrating information. The knowledge-based approach to computation and computer science can also be understood as inference.[92] Training data sets are developed for the ML system to perform in relation to output values and a statistic validation process.

While data mining focuses on emergent unknown problems out of dataset analysis, non-supervised ML, through data set training, aims to develop a feature recognition and feature extraction and develop a prediction model based on statistics and supervised ML on known tagged conditions of the data processed in the data training. ANN rely on heavy amounts of data for emergent programming rather than computability theory through modeling algorithms.

Supervised Machine Learning[93,94] – Training the Dataset

Regression
Classification (input known feature, output known label)
- Classify (manual or classifier) input
- Predict (train predictor, accuracy) output (desired)
- Training (learning algorithms classify: method selection – color + value method comparison)
  - Nearest (to function)
  - Logistic Regression
  - Neural Network
- Target/validation
- Unbalanced data problem = unbalanced output/reiterate

ML data science is applied to a dataset (sometimes developing metadata repository) for feature extraction:
Data Gathering: API (labeled) outsource
Dataset collection of data;
Repository metadata related to a dataset

114 *AI Computational Linguistic Semiotics*

In supervised learning, ML allows the combination of the inputs and outputs and identifies data through boundary regions, dividing data through feedback iterative optimization. The ML system aims at optimizing the relationship between the inputs and outputs desired. An ideal statistical function will predict features in the data that were not included in the training, by function of the approximation or assumed extension of the image pattern, matrix, curve, and surface. Support vector machine as a supervised learning model plots regions of data which can be separated by ranges. Clusters as data subsets identify probability functions. Data can be classified in relation to geometric-based mapping regions and a Data pattern can be recognized through a path in the mapped region, and plot statistical surface.

In Data Science, statistics plays an important role in NNs and how data flows can retrieve constants. ANN is able to make predictions based on data input based on the data repository training. ANN is trained by feeding raw data recursively through feedback applying different types of statistical regression algorithms for recursive optimizations, learning from, in the case of supervised learning, tagged classification in existing data repositories; or learning from feature recognition/extraction in raw data applying non-supervised learning. One of the problems is Classification as a way of projecting a structure to a problem (determinism) in contrast with Regression as a form of forecasting the form of the curve fitting mechanism beyond the information in the plot. In the ImageNet dataset (organized WorldNet hierarchy) users accentuate cultural biases by tagging images. Regression or curve fitting presents not only the continuity in the equation as a form of anticipation or prediction thinking it will continue to be constant beyond the range in the equation but also the problem of curve fitting as means to transfer into numerical quantitative value qualitative classification, presenting issues of approximation that may be proven not necessarily true. Through input and output weighting probabilities in relation to a target known output, ANN is trained to recognize error values and co-relations in the data as prediction increases in successive training epochs.

Machine Learning Types:
 Supervised Learning
 Non-supervised Learning
 Reinforced Learning

Statistical Model (Prediction)
Regression Algorithms $Y_i = f(X_i, \beta) + e_i$
 Linear Regression
  straight line: $y_i = \beta_0 + (\beta_1 x_i) + \varepsilon_i, \quad I = 1,\ldots,n.$
  other parameters parabola, residual, minimization, mean square error, standard errors
  Training (Time complexity): $O(nm^2 + m^3)$[1]
  Prediction (Time Complexity): $O(m)$
  Auxiliary space complexity: $O(m)$

Non-linear Regression (model fitting interpolation, extrapolation for prediction outside range)
> Logistic Regression
> Naïve Bayesian
> Decision Tress
> Gradient Busting
> K Means
> Random Forest
> KNN
> DBSCAN

In statistics, features are given a numeric value associated with a certain characteristic that as a feature (quality) is translated into a numeric (quantitative) value, exchanging a sign for a numeric value to address a value system that is in the function of the method implemented across different images or data to co-relate them by association. Adversarial, Artificial, and Convolutional Neural Networks can through merging mathematical equations into new ones include a diversity of indices, signs, and signifiers, merging information through stacking layers and structuring in relation to each interface dimensional processing.

When ML addresses deep learning, from hidden layers, a form of higher-level cognition is activated addressing an emergent form of computation from within the data processed.

AI Hierarchy:

- AI (intelligence replacement)
- ML (learn through data, training epochs, activate emergent programming)
- Deep Learning (machine trains itself to recognize and resolve a task through processing data)

Non-Supervised Machine Learning – Training the Dataset

Non-supervised ML can be understood as a training model that is able to automatically recognize features through non-labeled non-classified unstructured data. Contains only inputs and the aim is to find a structure in the data by identifying common features and patterns and identifying density regions in the data analysis statistical model through probability.

Non-Supervised ML
> Clustering (unknown input feature, non-corresponding output labels)
>> –Feature Extraction (feature out of the amount of data, machine vision)
>>> –Dimension reduction (information) [From Wolfram Mathematica 2019]
>>>> FeatureExtract[{"the cat is grey", "my cat is fast", "this dog is scary", "the big dog"}, "SegmentedWords"]
>>>> FeatureExtract[{"A large cat"}, "TFIDF"]

116 *AI Computational Linguistic Semiotics*

Specified Elements: 4
Dimensions: {1,4}
Default: 0
Density: 1
Elements:
{{1,1}-> 0.271822},
{{1,2}-> 0.271822},
{{1,3}-> 0.543645},
{{1,4}-> 0.271822}

FeatureExtract[{"the cat is grey", "my cat is fast", "this dog is scary", "the big dog"}, {"TFIDF", "DimensionReducedVector"}]
{{−1.08529, −1.19232, 2.26088}, {−2.60547, −0.977437, −1.77598}, {0.00806412, 3.21971, 0.105548}, {3.68269, −1.04995, −0.590444}}
−Feature Distance: measuring distance
−Clusters: group data into clusters
  −Anomaly Detection (Anomaly detection function)
  −Robot learning automation
  −Learn Distribution: learn from data/replace

Any Type of Data Source:
https://en.wikipedia.org/wiki/Wheat_Fields_(Van_Gogh_series) paintings = {[images separated by commas]};
RandomVariate[ld, 5]
{{6.70836, 5.93008}, {5.88038, 4.63413}, {6.17076, 4.70347}, {5.55905, 3.73668}, {6.27625, 4.39698}}
methods = {"Multinormal", "KernelDensityEstimation", "DecisionTree"};
distributions = LearnDistribution[paintings, Method -> #] & /@ methods
Show[ContourPlot[PDF[ld, {x, y}], {x, 4, 8}, {y, 1, 7}, PlotRange -> All, Contours -> 10], ListPlot[iris, PlotStyle -> Red]]

Supervised Learning = Semantic-Based Linguistic Signifier
Non-Supervised Learning = Feature Sign

Convolutional Neural Networks (CNN)

Pattern recognition or feature recognition through images is a way for a trained NN to be able to input-collect neurons per image, reducible to a pixel and relating each pixel with a neuron. The image becomes a matrix of numbers that hold the data within a topological value system and that through interpolation funneled through a NN can read its meaningful information. Mathematical weights are encoded to encode reality, decode it and reconstruct it in meaningful computable terms, articulating data deconstruction as input with computable data through Convolutional Neural Networks (CNN) which reduce data through downsampling without changing the information. CNN are types of Artificial Neural Networks able to solve through computer vision image features.

The outcome from the ML after training needs to be meaningful and functional. The activation function expresses in mathematical statistic methodological terms the regression model through which the NN is trained so that the machine can reduce the numeric values into a mathematical problem that can be approximated into an equation that will be used as a predictive model. For instance, a sigmoid is a type of differentiable mathematical equation between 0 and 1 that is used to predict output to know if true or false.

ML = Data Input + Information Flow − Feedback
Non-Deterministic Computation

Artificial Neural Networks (ANN)

ANNs depend on the informational organizational structure they follow (*Neuron*), the *propagation* function (input-outputs), a *Bias* term, the mathematics and statistical model used, defining how the different parallel processing algorithms are optimized and *Weighted* through updates gradients and ratios, defining the computational technology. ANN can be defined as autonomous self-optimizing algorithms, or algorithms that search for means to edit themselves, or meta-algorithms. ANN allows for algorithmic optimization through parallel processing, layering algorithms, and complex non-linear recursive interrelationships by recognizing and optimizing the path of the flow of data. Through a predictive statistical model, we can analyze a data flow and make predictions about the data (Figure 6.3).

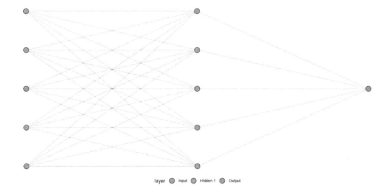

Figure 6.3 Artificial Neural Network diagram, Layer: Input, Hidden, Output.

118 *AI Computational Linguistic Semiotics*

[x] INPUT > [x W] WEIGHT > [+b] BIAS > y OUTPUT

The number of neurons in the net is dependent on the necessity to contain certain ranges of inputs and processing of information relative to different types of measurable units-signs. The neurons can process different types of signals, from numeric, to alphabetic to symbolic in reference to our brain's capacity to hold information and be able to compute by accessing such information at a meaningful time process.

ANNs are trained through data repositories through statistical gradients and tensor fitness implementing various parallel processing computational model systems, including the main three types of NN:

Artificial Neural Networks (ANN) (Figure 6.3):
> Data: Tabular, Text
> Application: text, speech, weather prediction
> Feed Forward Neural Network (only forward direction data processing);
> Distributed memory;
> Works with incomplete knowledge;

Convolutional Neural Networks[95] (CNN) (Figure 6.4):
> Data: Image
> Application: Facial Recognition, Images, Natural Language Processing (NLP)
> Input defined by tensor with a shape (grid-like topology): # inputs, input height, input width, input channels;
> Spatial relationships in shape topology;
> High-Definition Image non-supervised feature recognition;
> Feature (activation) maps, then image mask, square pixels, or region image for non-linear processing; Multilayer perceptrons for distinguishing features;
> Convolutional Layers: Convolutional or Pooling (Global, Max, or Average: neurons of feature map); Weight sharing;

Recurring Neural Networks (RNN):
> Data: Sequence Data
> Application: Text to speech
> Output processing node and feedback into the model (recurring);
> Predict the outcome of a layer based on recursion;
> Node: memory cell computation (time-based, Long Short Term Memory);
> Incorrect prediction self-edit toward more accurate prediction in backpropagation;
> Used in combination with CNN for more efficient neighborhood pixel detection/processing in images;

AI Computational Linguistic Semiotics 119

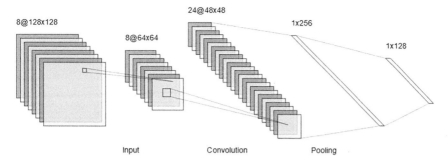

Figure 6.4 Convolution Neural Networks with resolution maps based on input matrix resolution. Input Image/s layer; Feature Extraction layers (2D); Convolution (mathematical recursive self-editing algorithms) layer; classification (1D) layer pooling subsampling vectorized feature maps; and output class prediction layer.

But there are also other types of ANN, such as (Deep) Feed Forward Neural Networks (DFF), Boltzmann Machine (BM), and other ANN structures. The model network is defined by clusters which are optimized topologically. RNN loops are used at aiming at recognizing information flows and optimizing them.

Neuron Signs = Numeric, Alphabetic, Symbolic

Encoders/Decoders, Layers, Network Constructors (From Wolfram Mathematica ANN, 2019)

Network Data: Tensors (Rank 0 (scalars))
    Vectors as coordinates of points
    Matrices as grayscale images
    n tensors as colored images

Layers: Basic Layers
    Computation Elementwise Layers
        Linear Layers {x->Ax+b}
        Elementwise Layer (function f to every element of the input tensor: LogisticSigmoid, Than, Ramp)
        SoftmaxLayer (classifier takes a vector as input and returns normalized values as class probabilities)

$$\frac{e^{xi}}{\sum_i e^{xj}}$$

120 *AI Computational Linguistic Semiotics*

> Gaussian (linear classification problem, plot dataset for class decoder to classify in two colors or other means, establishing probability in the trained ANN)
>
> XOR (non-linear classification, probability prediction in the cluster, through a class decoder)

Convolution Filtering Layers (mostly used for abstract machine vision feature recognition in images, features per block, downsampling operation; feature maps; then export properties for Loss and ErrorRate; functionality: image classification, image segmentation, NLP, neurosciences, finance)

> Convolution Layer (kernel size, input size, output size; stride, dilation, factor, and padding size; 2D image recognition; 3D neuron volume arranging layers for 3D scanning normalized 2D and 3D datasets implementing Geometric Neural Network (GNN)[96]) (Figure 6.4).
>
> Deconvolution Layer (unsampling operation, transposed convolution)
>
> Pooling Layer (non-linear downsampling between convolution layers: Max, Average, and Global)
>
> Resize Layer
>
> SpatialTransformationLayer

Layers Optimization Training

> ImageAugmentationLayer
> BatchNormalizationLayer
> DropoutLayer
> LocalResponseNormalizationLayer
> NormalizationLayer

Layers Manipulation Structure

> CatenateLayer
> FlattenLayer
> ReshapeLayer
> ReplicateLayer
> PaddingLayer
> PartLayer
> TransposeLayer

Array Layers Operation

> ConstantArrayLayer
> SummationLayer
> TotalLayer
> AggregationLayer
> DotLayer

AI Computational Linguistic Semiotics 121

Layers Recurrent
> BasicRecurrentLayer
> GatedRecurrentLayer
> LongShortTermMemoryLayer

Handling Layers + Sequence
> EmbeddingLayer
> SequenceLastLayer
> SequenceMostLayer
> SequenceRestLayer
> AttentionLayer
> UnitConveyorLayer

Stacking Layers
> Netchain
> Tracking Layers through NetGraph or Weight and Biases or visualizing engine of network relationships, graphical neural network typology Recurrent Neural Network (feedforward network with parameter sharing)
>> Basic Recurrent Layer
>> Others

ARTIFICIAL NEURAL NETWORKS
Perceptron (Input Neuron-Output Neuron) = Signifier
FEEDBACK SIGNAL = SIGN OPTIMIZATION

Weights, Biases, and Tensor Computing

Layers in ANN can be defined as the nodes/perceptrons in the ANN: input, hidden, and output through a synapse that defines the link between the neurons, variable in a function to the weight.

Input − Hidden - Output

Weights and biases are parameters that modify the data in function of the generalization learning in ANN. In deep learning, the weight and biases are mathematically randomized in relation to the learning and training until a correct output is given. We can identify different types of weight as a parameter active through symbolic computation in relation to the type of layer the NN is making operative, as the weight that affects the synapse between the neurons described from a parameter within the NN that transforms the input data within a hidden layer. Weights are mathematical functions expressed in magnitude as they express the strength of the data connection

122   *AI Computational Linguistic Semiotics*

through weighting functions as the amount of influence of data input over the output.

> Low weight: no change
> High weight: significant change
> Z= Input.Weight = XW

$$Z = \sum_{i=1}^{n} (X_i W_i) = X_1 W_1 + X_2 W_2 + X_3 W_3$$

> Weight = Signal Control Strength

We can identify biases as how far off the prediction statistical model can be from the intended reference value, between the intended output and the function's output. Biases value allows a shift in the activation function. Weight is the result of the bias function as a constant Offset Value.

> Low biases: more assumptions prediction w_0 no biases
> High biases: less assumptions prediction w_1 bias weight of 1
> Input (x) - biases (w_0) – Output (f)
>
> $$f\left(\left(w_0{}^{\star}\ x\right) + \left(w_1{}^{\star}\ b\right)\right)$$

Activation functions modify the data from layer to layer, through:

> Non-linear
> Continuous differential
> Fixed range

Data Biases also help identify shortcomings in data gathering and processing by the function of cultural limitations and ideology.

> Reporting Bias (frequency)
> Automation Bias (favor automation)
> Selection Bias (data chosen not reflective of problem, non-representative)
> Non-Response/Participation Bias (unrepresentative or gaps in data sample)
> Sampling (not implemented randomization in sample data collection)
> Group Attribution Bias (group belonging data sampling)
> Implicit Bias (cultural: the model confirms assumptions)

The loss function or the implicit cost of the prediction is its optimization relative value at making predictions through its own curve and derivatives. The slope of the curve can define the function of the strength of the prediction model.

Regression Loss Function
Mean Squared Error MSE (L2)
MSLE logarithmic
MAbsolute Error Loss
Binary Classification Loss Function
Binary Cross-Entropy
Hing Loss
Multi Class Classification
Others

We can identify different types of tensors and dimensions, in relation to their rank, shape, and data type. Tensors are arranged in a matrix as an array of vectors.

1D-Tensor (Vectors: features)
2D-Tensor (Sequences: Timesteps, features)
3D-Tensor (Images: height, width, channels)
4D-Tensor (Videos: frames, height, width, channels)
5D-Tensor (batch of the previous: samples, frames, height, width, channels)
6D-Tensor

Deep Learning or Deep Neural Network (DNN)

Deep learning through backpropagation was developed by Hinton back in the 1960s and then in the 1980s, in which the main ideas of stochastic gradient descent in Data Science and backpropagation still today remain the fundamentals. Backpropagation[97] is an algorithm for feedforward[98] NNs by computing gradients in a loss function and training a data set. Through a single neuron (perceptron) one can develop forward propagation by implementing weighting and bias through non-linearity. Then ML techniques include stacking and compacting perceptron and mathematical optimization through backpropagation. Then the adaptive learning rate is achieved through patching and optimization. Since we understand technology as functional knowledge, the input of the ANN and the output need to match to secure the ML training. Reinforced Learning assigns rewards to recognizing successful tasks through intelligent agents in a shifting environment such as in Agent-Based Modelling (ABM). Deep Learning identifies emergent patterns in unstructured data through computational linguistics (text) or machine vision computational visual semiotics (images, videos).

ML through a NN can understand and interpret data through feedback, reinforcement, regression, and optimization of the neural net. In non-supervised learning, several relationships between the data and the data flow and source are established. These relationships can be nested, correlational, parallel, and together constitute the necessary set of networks that will successfully be able to recognize features and come up with a means of learning from them and identifying what to do with this data in a meaningful way, therefore developing self-editing algorithms that learn from the task performed in each epoch cycle and that can become a type of software that is emergent and data dependent. Clustering is a way to funnel data through several groups of clusters ruling out through algorithms ambiguity and optimizing through mathematics the way the data is being recognized by algorithms that optimize algorithms in parallel to each other and through feedback. The more data we flow into our neural net, the more epoch cycles we train the neural net, and the more accurate the output in the reinforcement of learning and optimization of the learning mechanism becomes.

AI as Nondeterministic Data and Model Integration: Emergent Programming

A paradigm of computation is that the problem is anticipated by the programmer in the form of the program/software that is designed to address a range of issues to resolve, making computation a form of deterministic cause-effect anticipation problem-solving environment. Software and tools anticipate issues and expand programs in software and interfaces to address them, but this form of structuralist anticipation distorts reality to accommodate the ideology implicit in the program or software. Software programmers use the try-and-error method, conception, and coding to anticipate what the software can resolve by testing and optimizing their systems.[99]

Lately, a new form of programming has been emerging through continuous mapping, surveys, and software release actualizations. While problematically we are being tracked in terms of everything we do, logged through our Internet of Things (IoT), cell phones, and computers, through real-time tracking and data gathering, Operating Systems, computational software, platforms, and applications are being developed and optimized real time as they are being used. This shift from anticipatory programming to data tracking and real-time simulation-optimization enables an inversion of reality since software releases and operating systems are not finished when released but can become complete through real-time optimization.

Through machine vision and ML reinforcement learning,[100] computer scientists were able to train an AI system to teach itself how to, for instance, play. The relationship between media determinism and prediction based on statistics inverts computation from deterministic to a form of emergent media. ML's objective is to critique the typical computational thinking cycle described before (decomposition-pattern recognition-abstraction-algorithm development) by automatically developing pattern recognition through non-supervised learning and addressing the issue recognized in the data fed by interpreting, feedback, and feature recognition, resolving an issue that is emergent in the data and information flow that is not determined ahead of the model optimization. Deep Learning analyzes data flows and develops programs bypassing inductive logical anticipatory programming recognizing a feature and initiating a type of computability that is emergent, such as pattern recognition, behavioral recognition, environment shifting conditions, and therefore the emergence of computability by feature extraction. ML addresses AI through Data Science (statistics and probability theory) instead of the original approach through Computer Science (programming), ANN combine data science (statistics) and computer science (model) through symbolic computational weighting.

ML through Deep Learning therefore partially critiques media determinism through:

- recognizing patterns in unstructured data
- self-editing meta-algorithms
- recognizing tasks out of data
- activating emergent programming
- develop agency in relation to shifting environment

Evolving mutating algorithms that can change their structure can also address multidimensional computational morphogenesis beyond curve/geometry statistical fitting in relation to the specificity of the emergent pattern.

AI Black-Box Approach: Multidimensional Stacking of Layers and Translation between Interfaces and Nodes

When an ANN contains hidden layers becomes a Deep Neural Network (DNN). Hidden layers of inputs and outputs are masked by the activation function and last convolution; their meaning is not revealed until the neural net identifies features, and we are able to understand if the right questioning and processing of the data are happening or not. We can relate to different types of activation functions through mathematical statistical equations for regression as a type of ML in which the activation function deploys a mathematical model to predict results and to calculate if true or false through computing the Gradient Descend automatically identifying how weights and biases across neurons are modified to optimize the learning rate output. One can introduce a reward or a cost to train the model in relation to the outputs through backpropagation and repeat the epochs to further train the NN for efficient prediction and accuracy in the model. More training requires more energy resources. Therefore, mathematics allows us to access such blackbox processes by understanding and filtering simple properties and defining the model to obtain certain outputs. The hidden layer therefore is what holds the clue that is being searched in the data flow but that is unknown, we can neither comprehend nor express it: therefore it is unsupervised. There is also a hidden layer proportion, usually about 2/3 in relation to the input and output layers of the total ANN, incrementing in relation to the feature recognition task. The paradigm that is raised now is the width range of the NN since one can expand it to infinity by choosing the dimension through simplification mathematics through Kernel machines making their structure multidimensional as opposed to linear input parameters. The activation function secures non-linearity through several means (Step, Sigmoid, ReLu, etc). The Loss function measures the output error in relation to the right ideal output.

"Artificial Intelligence's" black-box problem is that inputs and outputs are known but there it is difficult to understand for humans what is going on in the parallel processing, which may develop emergent programming. Emergent programming is a function of simulation which happens through parallel processing and the hidden layer. The simulation paradigm is that one cannot anticipate the output result unless the program is run, defining the halting problem and no-reversibility. This in turns activates a problematic scientific non-reproducibility issue of not being able to reproduce with accuracy a determinate result more than once. At the same time, this has been rendered problematic for knowledge and scientific advancement[101]. ANN's advantage is the parallel processing of several recurring algorithms and backpropagation, the more complex the bifurcating and parallel network the more difficult to trace what is going on. Recent attempts of explaining ANN through decision trees were made.[102, 103] Knowledge is predictive and the purpose of ANN is to avoid symbolic human representation through data statistic fuzzy approximation aimed at problematizing knowledge. A usual practice when there are doubts about the ML functionality is to stack an excessive amount of ANN layers and excessive convolution, thereby promoting a black-box approach.

Each interface, from machine vision to convolution feedback presents different ideological means to measure and structure reality, transferring information from one-dimensional level to the other, through actualizations of several types sometimes problematically distorting the information unit to stretch to the interface and measuring mechanism and developing non-desirable biases and noise.

Natural Language Processing (NLP): From Low-Level Programming Language (LLL) to High-Level Programming Language (HLL)

Historically there have been many attempts to bypass computational linguistics and computer coding by implementing directly NPL as a direct form of grammar-induced low code through text prompts. The revolution of NLP at the scale available in 2022 is the confirmation of the relevance of linguistics as a form of description of the world through data in relation to mathematical computability. While Negroponte has anticipated NLP, we discussed here and in Chapter 5 that computational languages must be expanded in relation to identifying the limits of completeness in grammar formal logic as well as cultural biases in natural languages. NPL can interpret input in the form of natural language text prompts which predict text statistically through stochastic context-free grammar translating into any Higher Level Language coding, which can actively interpret programming. NLP involves processing human and computer conversation (chats for instance in OpenAI's ChatGPT); machine perception (machine vision through semantic segmentation, tagging, object recognition, and other forms of referencing computational linguistics to computable visual semiotics); text-to-image generation (such as Dall-E, MidJourney, Stable Diffusion); text-to-3D model and image to 3D generation (Point-e Open AI, Magic 3D NVIDIA, Imagine 3D Luma AI); the generation of natural language (text, completion, prediction, grammar, and translation); the classification; and of course, the processing as understanding interpretative.

NLP Linguistic Grammar = Computational Coding Grammar

Generative Pretrained Transformer GPT

NLP now has proven groundbreaking since the release of the GPT 4 (2023) autoregressive language multidimensional model based on deep learning over GPT 2, 3, 3.5 and 4 by Open AI.[104] GPT-3 is a type of NN using categories for an autoregressive language prediction with a multidimensional wide model of 175 billion parameters, while GPT 4 includes 170 trillion parameters in 2023. GPT3, GPT 3.5, or ChatGPT can be used for various tasks, from knowledge-based search engines to automated application development, to automatic computer coding edit, correction and prediction, program and translate scripts to execute in any computer language, difficult to predict given the range of parameters and scalability combinatorial possibilities. Chomsky critiqued the scientific validity of GPT-3 and ChatGPT since statistic predictive variations seem not to overcome the system created, not advancing computation or knowledge beyond applying statistics.[105] Image GPT (iGPT) can develop cross-reference learning through convolution ML layers, displacing the biases and boundaries in semantic image segmentation, and expanding training through feature recognition partially overcoming semantics. GPT3-based DALL-E 2 by OPenAI (blackbox – 2022), MidJourney (blackbox – 2022), Stable Diffusion (open source) retrieve images funneled activating a Diffusion Model (DM) through a statistic regression which from the pattern of random pixels gradually alters them toward creating an image.[106] Since the GPT model cross-references and learns from both tagged pretrained datasets and non-tagged non-supervised ML. We further explain DM through visual semiotics in Chapter 7 (Figures 6.5 and 6.6).

Google Parti[107] and Google PaLM also claim billions of parameters and previously Wolfram Mathematica and AutoDesk Research have done versions of NLP to 3D voxels, while Point-e released NLP to 3D point clouds through DM. Apple Gaudi[108] specifies a fully immersive 3D text to scene image/space generator. NLP presents, both a form of emancipation and an expansion of creativity for those not familiar with programming languages. We can also critique NLP since it is itself a simulation of symbolic representation, between natural language and Computational Linguistics through predictive interpretation into streamed coding. The apparent facility to code through NLP is indeed a conventionalization of the possibilities of symbolic computation,

128   *AI Computational Linguistic Semiotics*

Figure 6.5 A depiction of Borges' architecture of the Library of Babel by Cristina Grau can be related informationally to an infinite random text generated by an interface https://libraryofbabel.info. A1: virtual library parameters; B1: random text generated out of parameters; C1: Pixels generated by an image: babelia 7321922174580134. Original research developed by Prof. Pablo Lorenzo-Eiroa in the Fall of 2018 for Spring of 2019, Library Studio, M.Arch Program Directed by David Diamond, SoAD NYIT, and at The Cooper Union in 2017. The book by Basile describes similar issues.

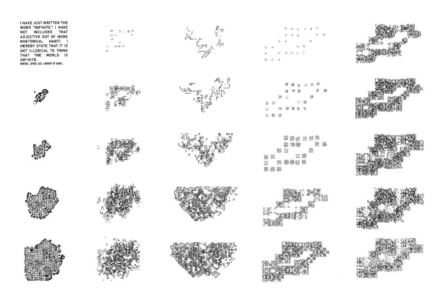

Figure 6.6 Borges' Book of Sand (Borges, J.L. "El Libro de Arena", en *El Libro de Arena*, EMECE, 1975) proposes an infinite page book which is related to an infinite Library of Babel (Borges, J.L. "La Biblioteca de Babel", in *El Jardin de los Senderos que se bifurcan*, Editorial Sur, Buenos Aires, 1941). We researched means to develop a form of infinite virtual library correlating NLP text prompt for automatic text generation to a Cellular Automation-based infinite growing library. Open AI GTP2 AI framework was implemented to trigger through a basic NLP prompt an infinite text entered via machine vision recognition. The emergent automated text enabled parallel possible bifurcating texts, which are expanded into virtual infinite libraries. "The Growth Haven Reviving the Historical Sabils of Cairo", Informed Realism Research Studio, Prof. Pablo Lorenzo-Eiroa, Student: Yousef Ismail, MS in Architecture, Computational Technologies Program, NYIT, SoAD, F2021.

lowering the grammatical hierarchy to low-code in linguistic computation, data articulation in relation to symbolic computation, and the relationship between alphabets retrieving computer and machinic code to combinatory logic. ChatGPT learns, predicts, understands, and projects words. Different from GPT-3, or GPT-3.5 InstructGPT, ChatGPT based on GPT-4 uses adversarial training through chatbots as the Large Language Model learns, predicts, understands, and projects words, as it is able to write its own code. Through probability it can predict words in relation to previous words' sequence and grammar, setting up a token for optimizing English words, understanding the linguistic message, and predicting it through approximation. This sequence is expanded to sentences and paragraphs. The advantage of NLP achieved by ChatGPT is the scale of the prediction model in which some of the negative aspects are bypassed by emergence through the function of brute force and higher dimensional processing, such as language generation, in-context learning, learning from experience, and world knowledge through Reinforcement Learning from Human Feedback (RLHF)[109]. NLP therefore becomes a stagnation of computation in relation to the conventional forms of description implicit in language but opens up unknown linguistic emergence through the scale of the statistical prediction model. But even if an emergent visual logic becomes active by emergent coding expanding conventional language, there is a root in the semantic meaning of the word as universally conventionally accepted, both freezing language from expansion and consolidating architecture autonomy as an expression of linguistics grammar and semantic meaning. Moreover, following Chomsky's grammar hierarchy, the visual formal logic becomes active through natural language grammar. NLP through GPT activates the signified as a form of signification displacing the Signifier which is eliminated from the equation, inverting the original relation to a form of speech instead of writing, since language conventions, in reference to semantic signifieds to communicate a linguistic message, are prevalent over the sign implemented to activate semantic meaning. Moreover, natural language poetry is simplified by the grammatical prompt, since each natural language will depend on the size of the repositories and models, giving weight to American English over other languages, and transferring formal organization through linguistic grammar to other realms such as the visual. The counter side to the semantic signifieds is the overwriting of image feature recognition after the prompt is done, training images as a form of computational visual semiotics, and optimizing the relationship between conceptual linguistic abstraction and image-based semiotic realism. Through image knowledge, either by completing a partial image or figure-background semantic segmentation and convolutional feature recognition across images one can activate computational visual semiotic programming, eventually overcoming the linguistic semantic sedimented signs. Wolfram discusses ChatGPT in relation to setting up a question; turning it into generalized grammar; a linguistic understanding (which we call semantic signified); a symbolic representation for computability (expressed in any computational language); feeding data (structured or not)

130   *AI Computational Linguistic Semiotics*

through the neural nets computational algorithms and feeding real-time data towards a computed answer[110].

The following sequence becomes active:

1   NLP training based on stochastic grammar
2   Coding as NLP translation
3   NLP > HLL
4   Grammar Structure through linguistics = infers visual Formal Organization
5   Semantic Image Tagging repositories accessed through API
6   CNN through images pixel to pixel tends to bypass semantics and tagging classifiers
7   Convolution through Feature Recognition, computational visual semiotics
8   Emergent HLL Programming through Grammar in computational visual semiotics

Coding > Sign=signifier/Signified > Signifiers
NPL > Sign=signifier/Signified > Signifieds
Signified = Semantic Recognition in Image
Minimal Signs becoming Signifiers = Point Clouds, Pixels, Particles
Deep Structure = Data API + Diffusion Models

First, we should understand the reduction of thinking to logical formalisms in implementing problem solving.[111] Second, in general, there is a lack of acknowledgment of the balance of Data Science in relation to ANN modeling. Third, due to the implementation of architecture as images in NLP text-to-image DM, there is a metaphoric reference to the representation of meaning instead of open signification, the original sign is "represented" through an image that semantically refers to it, as a qualisign through a semantic signified, but it is not "it". Fourth, the semantic segmentation based on conventional tagging and classification (ImageNET) and reverse engineering through high dimensional complex cross reference, exchanges one type of linguistic natural sign for its "representational" reference to the actual visual logic sign of the architecture reduced and translated between languages. Fifth, one could overcome linguistic semantic segmentation with progressive feature recognition, although with the limits discussed or expanded in Chapter 7 concerning the lack of politics of representation in style transfer as a qualisign.

From Low Code to Higher-Level Programming Language, to Emergent Programming, to Self-Simulation Definition Toward the Discovery of Sentinels as Artificial Life and Intelligence

We discussed how NLP Open AI GPT is able to activate from LLL or low code prompt engineering to HLL. Reflective programming languages can reify implicit codes in the translated language and become explicit in the language itself. Reification implies a process from abstraction, to becoming a data object, to becoming a programming language.

Von Neumann's anticipation of AI was implicit in his "artificial life"[112] definitions through self-replication. Self-replication automata apply to programs that can simulate programs and which they can reproduce themselves, and that in each cycle through recursive deep learning become better at what they do through optimization, an evolutive artificial process that can eventually become exponential, and what we called Life: In Formation.[113] A property of self-simulation is that a program can simulate itself as well as other programs by learning tasks from data. Because of self-simulation, some argue that we may be already living in a simulation.[114] We are currently applying ML through statistical approximation, training a framework to recognize a task in unstructured data, which may lead to what we defined as emergent programming. We cannot refer to "AI" as self-consciouss emergence, as sentinel robots become active only through recognizing tasks statistically as they are not self-aware. Although, we have to acknowledge what we discussed earlier in contrast to Chomsky's critique of current AI different from knowledge, since certain definitions of intelligence point out to exponential escalation in parallel information flows, which is now possible by extended virtual ANN models and the higher dimensional interconnectivity of the IoT.

Through NLP we were able to elevate low code to higher-level language and then to emergent programming. We have been able to activate emergent programming by recognizing data features, such as a program simulating other programs, displacing media determinism. Through prompt analysis of repetition words as semantics, in contrast with prompt engineering, we further programmed alternating both computational linguistics and computational visual semiotics through deep learning feature recognition training. In fact, we think that the complexity of the emergent model is due to nonlinear feedback between linguistic and visual-based feature recognition. We develop evidence of activating environmental simulation, demonstrating a characteristic of self-simulation or a program running a program in "AI", but this does not mean emergent intelligence, or the emergence of sentinels (Figures 6.7 and 6.8). We are not much interested in replicating a previous technology such as CFD and structural simulation with new technology, but rather addressing a simulation of a simulation as emergent automata programming and new aesthetic possibilities further discussed in Chapter 7.

Computational Linguistics Digital Signifier = Programming Languages Signs

Semantic Segmentation = Linguistics applied to Visual Semiotics
NLP prompt (architecture, interior, column, wall, container, glass, nature)

We include a training prediction stage demonstrating the incremental transition and learning stage in a text-to-image pixel-to-pixel DM: from a first schematic

132 *AI Computational Linguistic Semiotics*

Figure 6.7 A1–C3: Progressive ML training through diffusion model feature recognition understanding of simulation, demonstrating the activation of emergent programming. Various definitions of AI become active: from a clear interpretation of wind CFD Simulation; to the activation of a simulation as an emergent program; to applying the simulation learned to a specific site through an image interpretation of a recomposed NYC via API which contains several errors that can be improved; to applying simulation to a specific 3D simulated model. A1–C1: Through convolution feature recognition, increasingly the diffusion model recognizes its task as an emergent program. B1–C3: The prompt includes photos of NYC as a site; wind as an environmental simulation addressing mathematical equations to implement it; tracers, viscosity, and other environmental simulation parameters. We believe we were able to activate a simulation within a simulation, a characteristic of Artificial Intelligence through both Dall-e and MidJourney activated through LC prompt engineering activating HLL through both linguistics and visual semiotics feature recognition convolution. Pablo Lorenzo-Eiroa, prompt through Dall-e and MidJourney, 2022.

interpretation; to a re-representation of the concept; to a first application of the simulation as representation; to an actual simulation to applying the simulation to a context and learning from it. We also include emergent programming directly in 3D in Chapter 7 implementing DM text-to-3D point clouds and image-to-3D training repositories through ML semantic segmentation and AI machine vision. The series of experiments we run aiming at activating CFD (Figure 6.7) simulation is first unclear, but through convolution, feature recognition starts to clearly understand the task and apply it to a different context which through recursive logic, mathematics, and CFD concepts and equations can interpret, advance, and apply computational fluid dynamic simulation to a shifting environment, interpreting in 2D images 3D objects, such as buildings and landscapes contours and depth. The NLP emergent programming evidence points to applying the CFD simulation to an interpolated "represented" context image and not a model, making it subsymbolic through a statistical approximation representation simulation. But the results demonstrate an advanced level of prediction approximation to mechanical, technical, and mathematical fluid dynamics evident in the tracer amount variations we input as prompts, intensity, viscosity, and friction as there is contextual feedback and emergent complexity in the visible vortex, swirls, and turbulence that can only happen through a site-based computational emergent simulation. We do not claim emergent knowledge in ML but the application of interpolating statistics to predict a problem that can save time and resources through emergent programming.

In addition to CFD, we also tested similar relationships between linguistic prompts, mechanical engineering concepts, and mathematical formulations to test structural simulation and gravitational forces through stress and formal stability, which is also context-dependent and accumulative site-based emergent complex behavior (Figure 6.8).

We claim that we are activating emergent programming, but not a form of autonomous sentinel, although at a certain point, we think that the definition of self-simulation becomes active as we are able to recognize self-replicating tasks, activating other parallel programs from 3D object recognition to simulation types, addressing the higher level of deep learning and the capacity to simulate themselves through recursive training and optimization, a feature of behavioral agents in Agent-Based Modeling (ABM), disclosing emergent programming in the hidden layers of the NN. One of the relevant aspects of simulation prediction is the energy and time saving since nondeterministic simulations can only be calculated if run fully unless an AI model is able to bypass such process through statistical prediction.

We understand that Stable Diffusion, DALL-E, and MidJourney have been statistically optimized to simulate light/refraction, perspective, and other 3D scene simulations with some forensic image errors. Our understanding is that these frameworks were not trained statistically to simulate CFD and structural simulation, and that this is emergent through convolutional feature recognition activated through the complex-wide NN of some of the frameworks such as Open AI iGPT as it implements machine vision in crossing NLP with image-tagged datasets and trained repositories. Even if these data approximation features are activated through statistics, the definition of a program simulating a program remains. We do not claim to have discovered a yet unobtainable sentinel, but that the task through non-supervised learning is able

134 *AI Computational Linguistic Semiotics*

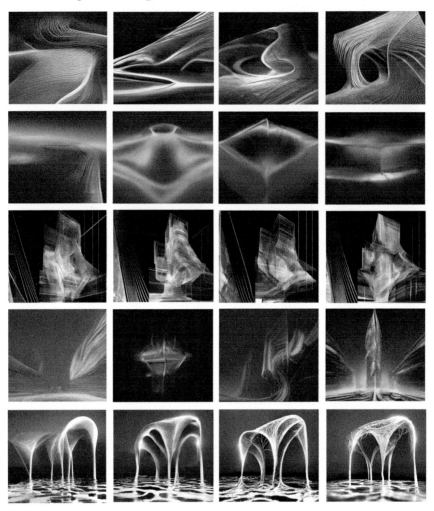

Figure 6.8 Sequential images through NLP prompt engineering activating a program of a program, a simulation of a simulation, or Emergent Programming. (See Notes Figure 6.8)

to recognize what it is and how to implement it through behavioral logic and projecting it applying into a shifting environment, a predictive simulation representation model with scientific accuracy.

Self-awareness and consciousness in humans and animals depend on a massive amount of information flow and the function of language.[115] Self-editing meta-algorithms present emergent intelligence and perhaps may eventually activate self-awareness through computational linguistics recognizing language as they self-edit and learn. And algorithms are already evolving to develop their own linguistics.[116]

Notes

1 Witt, A. *Formulations: Architecture, Mathematics, Culture,* Writing Architecture Series, MIT Press, Cambridge, 2022

2 Kitcher, P. *The Nature of Mathematical Knowledge,* Oxford University Press, New York, 1983

3 Gödel, K. *On Formally Undecidable Propositions of Principia Mathematica and Related Systems,* Dover, New York, 1992.

4 Wittgenstein, L. *Tractatus Logico-Philosophicus,* Routledge, London and New York, 1961 [orig. W. Ostwald's Annalen der Naturphilosophie, Vienna, 1921]

5 Gandz, S. *The Sources of al-Khwarizmi's Algebra,* Osiris, I, 1936

6 Mann, C. "Unraveling Khipu's Secrets", in *Science,* Volume 309, 2005

7 Haines, C.; Catharine, M. *International Women In Science: A Biographical Dictionary to 1950* ABC-CLIO, Santa Barbara, 2001

8 Woodman, J. "The Women 'Computers' Who Revolutionized Astronomy", in *The Atlantic Science,* Dec 2, 2016

9 Lorenzo-Eiroa, P. "Form In:Form: On The Relationship Between Digital Signifiers and Formal Autonomy", in ed. Lorenzo-Eiroa, P.; Sprecher, A., *Architecture in Formation,* Routledge, London 2013

10 Fabretti, F. *Software Theory,* Rowman and Littlefield, London, 2015

11 Althusser, L. *Idéologie et appareils idéologiques d'État,* La Pensée, 1970

12 Hayles, K. *My Mother Was a Computer,* University of Chicago Press, Chicago, 2005

13 Carpo, M. *Architecture in the Age of Printing,* MIT Press, Cambridge, 2001

14 Leibniz, G.W. *Dissertatio de arte combinatoria,* Sämtliche Schriften und Briefe, Berlin, 1923, [orig. 1666]

15 Leibniz, G.W. *Miscellanea Berolensia ad incrementum scientiarum,* 1710

16 Simonite, T. "Short Sharp Science: Celebrating Ada Lovelace: The 'World's First Programmer'", in *New Scientist,* March 24th, 2009

17 Lovelace, A.; Menabrea, L. "Sketch of the Analytical Engine invented by Charles Babbage, Esq.", in *Scientific Memoirs,* Richard Taylor, vol. 3 1854 [over transl. Menabrea, L. F. "Notions sur la machine analytique de M. Charles Babbage", Bibliothèque Universelle de Genève, No. 41, 1842]

18 Boole, G. *The Laws of Thought,* Prometheus Books, Amherst, 2003 [facsimile of 1854]

19 Aristotle. *Organon And Other Works,* trans. Edhill, E.M., W. D. Ross, Oxford, 2007 [orig. c. 350 BCE, published in 50 BCE]

20 Boole, G. *Studies in Logic and Probability,* Dover Publications, New York, 2012 [orig. 1952]

21 Gottlob, F. *Begriffsschrift: eine der arithmetischen nachgebildete Formelsprache des reinen Denkens,* Verlag von Louis Nebert, 1879

22 Zalta, E.N. and Nodelman, U. *The Stanford Encyclopedia of Philosophy,* The Metaphysics Research Lab, Center for the Study of Language and Information, Stanford University, Stanford, 2003

23 Turing, A. "Computability and λ-definability", in *The Journal of Symbolic Logic,* Volume 2, Issue 4, Cambridge University Press, March 12, 2014 [orig. 1937]

24 Gödel, K. *On Formally Undecidable Propositions of Principia Mathematica and Related Systems,* Dover, New York 1992 [orig. 1931]

25 Turing, A.M. "On Computable Numbers, with an Application to the Entscheidungsproblem", in *Proceedings of the London Mathematical Society,* Volume 2, 1937, [orig. 1936]

26 Rojas, R. "Die Rechenmaschinen von Konrad Zuse", Springer, Berlin, 1998

27 Weiss, E.A. "Konrad Zuse Obituary", in *IEEE Annals of the History of Computing,* 1996

136 *AI Computational Linguistic Semiotics*

28 Turing, A. "Intelligent Machinery", in *Philosophia Mathematica*, 1948
29 Shannon, C. "A Mathematical Theory of Communication", in *Bell System Technical Journal*, Volume 27, 1948
30 Boole, G. *The Mathematical Analysis of Logic*, 1847
31 Kleiman, K. *Proving Ground: The Untold Story of Six Women Who Programmed The World's First Modern Computer*, Hachette Audio, 2022
32 Wheeler, J.A. "It from Bit", in *Geons, Black Holes & Quantum Foam*, Norton, New York, 1998
33 Von Baeyer, H.C. *Information: the New Language of Science*, Harvard University Press, Cambridge, 2003
34 Wheeler, J.A. "Beyond the Black Hole", in ed. Wolf, H., *Some Strangeness in Proportion*, Addison-Wesley, Massachusetts, 1980
35 Von Neumann, J. *First Draft of a Report on the EDVAC*, University of Pennsylvania, Philadelphia, 1945
36 Von Neumann, J. *The Computer and the Brain*, Yale University Press, New Haven, 1958 [Third Edition, 2012]
37 McGee, R.C. "My Adventure with Dwarfs", University of Minnesota Press, Minneapolis, 2014
38 Knyazev, B.; Drozdzal, M.; Taylor, G.; Romerao-Soriano, A. "Parameter Prediction for Unseen Deep Architectures", ArXiv:2110.13100, 2021
39 Von Neumann, J.; Burks, A.W. *Theory of Self-Reproducing Automata*, University of Illinois Press, Urbana, 1966
40 Pesavento, U. "An Implementation of von Neumann's Self-Reproducing Machine", *Artificial Life*, MIT Press, Cambridge, 1995
41 Shanahan, M. *The Technological Singularity*, MIT Press, Cambridge, 2015
42 Hopcroft, J.E.; Ullman J. "Introduction to Automata Theory, Languages, and Computation", *3rd ed. Reading*, Addison-Wesley, Boston, 2006
43 Gardner, M. "Mathematical Games - The Fantastic Combinations of John Conway's New Solitaire Game "Life"", in *Scientific American,* Oct. 1970
44 Wolfram, S. *A New Kind of Science*, Wolfram Media, Champaign, 2002
45 Cook, M. "Universality in Elementary Cellular Automata", in *Complex Systems*, Volume 15, 2004
46 Lorenzo-Eiroa, P. "Cybernetics Applied to Cold War Urban Planning", Princeton University SOA PhD Pro Seminar Prof. Colomina, *Research Gate*, 2015 [orig. 2001]
47 Plato. *The Philosophy of Government*, Book VI
48 Weiner, R. *Cybernetics: Or Control and Communication in the Animal and the Machine*, MIT Press, Cambridge, 1948
49 Norbert, W. "The Machine Age", in *The New York Times,* 1949
50 Reinhold, M. "The Organizational Complex: Cybernetics, Space, Discourse", *Grey Room*, MIT Press, Cambridge, 2000
51 Wierner, N. "How U.S. Cities can Prepare for Atomic War", in *Life,* Volume 18, 1950
52 Lapp, R. "Diagrams For Nonlinear Satellite Cities", Firestone Archive Library Manuscript, Retrieved 2001
53 Oakes, G. *The Imaginary War, Civil Defense and American Cold War Culture*, Oxford University Press, New York, 1994.
54 Martin, R. "The Organizational Complex: Cybernetics, Space, Discourse", *Assemblage No. 37*, The MIT Press, Cambridge, 1998
55 Galison, P. "War Against the Center", in *Grey Room,* Volume 4, MIT, Cambridge, 2001
56 Hilberseimer, L. *The New Regional Pattern*, Paul Theobald, Chicago, 1949
57 Woltman, E.C. "Planning Research Corporation", in ed. Office of Civic Defense, *Civil Defense Implications of Current and Future Urban Configurations*, Report, Los Angeles, 1963

58 Kline, R.R. "Cybernetics, Automata Studies and the Dartmouth Conference on Artificial Intelligence", in *IEEE Annals of the History of Computing*, 2011

59 McCarthy, J.; Minsky, M.; Rochester, N.; Shannon, C.A. "Proposal for the Dartmouth Summer Research Project on Artificial Intelligence", in *AI Magazine*, 2006 [orig. ojs.aaai.org, 1955]

60 Warren, M.C.; Pitts, W. "A Logical Calculus of Ideas Immanent in Nervous Activity", in *Bulletin of Mathematical Biophysics*, 1943

61 NYTimes Editors. "New Navy Device Learns By Doing: Psychologist Shows Embryo of Computer Designed to Read and Grow Wiser", in *The New York Times*, 8 July 1958

62 Chomsky, N. *Aspects on the Theory of Syntax*, MIT, Cambridge, 1975

63 Chomsky, N. "Three Models for the Description of Language", in *IRE Transactions on Information Theory*, Volume 2, 1956

64 Alexander, C. "Systems Generating Systems", in *Architectural Design*, Volume 38, 1968

65 Minsky, M. "Theory of Neural-Analog Reinforcement Systems and Its Application to the Brain-Model Problem", catalog.princeton.edu, 1954

66 Minsky, M. "Steps Towards Artificial Intelligence", *Dept. of Mathematics, Research Lab of Electronics*, MIT, 1960

67 Minsky, M.; Papert S. "Progress Report on Artificial Intelligence", *AI Memo 252*, MIT Artificial Intelligence Laboratory, Cambridge, 1972

68 Kleene, S.C. "Representation of Events in Nerve Nets and Finite Automata", in *Annals of Mathematics Studies*, Volume 34, Princeton University Press, Princeton, 1956

69 Minsky, M. "A Framework for Representing Knowledge", *MIT-AI Laboratory Memo 306*, June, 1974

70 Chomsky, N. *Syntactic Structures*, Mouton, The Hague, 1957

71 Guzman, A. *Some Aspects of Pattern Recognition by Computer*, MS Thesis, MIT, Cambridge, 1967

72 Minsky, M. *A Framework for Representing Knowledge*, MIT-AI Laboratory Memo 306, June, 1974

73 Minsky, M. *The Society of Mind*, Touchstone, Simon & Schuster, New York, 1988

74 Celce-Murcia, M. *Paradigms for Sentence Recognition*, UCLA Dept. of Linguistics, 1972

75 Wilks, Y. *An Artificial Intelligence Approach to Machine Translation*, in eds. Schank, R.C. and Colby K.M., Computer Models of Tought and Language, Freeman, New York, 1973

76 Minsky, M. "Form and Content in Computer Science", J.A.C.M., January, 1972

77 Bateson, G. The Logical Categories of Learning and Communication, in *Steps to an Ecology of Mind*, University of Chicago Press, Chicago, 2000 [orig. 1972]

78 Mead, M. "The Cybernetics of Cybernetics.", in ed. von Foerster, H., White, J.D., Peterson, L.J. and Russell, J. *Purposive Systems*, Volumes 1-11, Spartan Books, New York, 1968

79 Bateson, G.; Mead, M. "Interview", in *CoEvolution Quarterly*, 1973

80 Randell. "Software Engineering 1968", in *Proceedings of IEEE*, Munnich, 1979

81 Wirth, N. *Algorithms + Data Structures = Programs*, Oberon, 2004 [orig. 1976]

82 Pierce, J.R. *Symbols, Signals and Noise*, The Dover Edition, New York, 1980 [orig. 1961]

83 Von Neumann, J. *The Computer and the Brain*, Yale University Press, New Haven, 1958

84 Chomsky, N.; Halle, M. *The Sound Pattern of English*, Harper and Row, New York, 1968

85 von Baeyer, H.C. *Information, New Language of Science*, Harvard University Press, Cambridge, 2003

86 Simpson, E.H. "The Interpretation of Interaction in Contingency Tables", in *Journal of the Royal Statistical Society, Series B,* Volume 13, 1951

87 Wald, A. "A Method of Estimating Plane Vulnerability Based on Damage of Survivors", in *Statistical Research Group,* Center for Naval Analyses, Columbia University, New York, 1980 [orig. 1943]

88 Dempster, A.P.; Laird, N.M.; Rubin, D.B. "Maximum Likelihood from Incomplete Data via the EM Algorithm", in *Journal of the Royal Statistical Society* Series B, Volume 39, Issue 1, 1977

89 Lorenzo-Eiroa, P. "Rezoning New York City through Big Data", in ed. Karandinou, A., *Data, Architecture and The Experience of Place,* Routledge, London, 2019

90 Carpo, M. "Breaking the Curve, on Big Data and Design", in *ARTFORUM,* 2014

91 Mohri, M.; Rostamizadeh, A.; Talwalkar, A. *Foundations of Machine Learning,* MIT Press, Cambridge, 2012

92 Quinlan, J.R. "Induction of Decision Trees", in *Machine Learning* 1, Kluwer Academic Publishers, Boston, 1986

93 Ghahramani, Z.; Jordan M.I. "Supervised Learning from Incomplete Data via an EM Approach", in ed. Cowan, J.D.; Tesauro, G.T. and Alspector, J. *Advances in Neural Information Processing Systems,* Volume 6, Kaufma+nn, 1994

94 Bishop, C.M. *Pattern Recognition and Machine Learning,* Springer Information Science and Statistics, Cambridge, 2006

95 Saha, S. "A Comprehensive Guide to Convolutional Neural Networks", in *Towards Data Science,* 2018

96 Bartosz, B.; Hubert, M. "Period Classification of 3D Cuneiform Tablets with Geometric Neural Networks", in *ICFHR,* Dortmund, 2020

97 Goodfellow, I.; Bengio, Y.; Courville, A."6.5 Back-Propagation and Other Differentiation Algorithms", in *Deep Learning,* MIT Press, Cambridge, 2016

98 Russell, S.; Norvig, P. *Artificial Intelligence: A Modern Approach,* Prentice Hall, Hoboken, 1995

99 Frabetti, F. *Software Theory,* Rowman and Littlefield, London, 2015

100 Jaderberg, M.; Czarnecki, W.; Dunning, M.; et al. "Human-Level Performance in 3D Multiplayer Games with Population-Based Reinforcement Learning", in *Science,* Volume 31, 2019

101 Kocak, B.; Yardimci, A.H.; Yuzkan, S. et al. "Transparency in Artificial Intelligence Research: a Systematic Review of Availability Items Related to Open Science in Radiology and Nuclear Medicine" in *Academic Radiology,* The Association of University Radiologists, Elsevier, Dec 14, 2022 14:S1076-6332(22)00635-3. doi: 10.1016/j.acra.2022.11.030. Epub ahead of print. PMID: 36526532.

102 Nguyen, D.; Kasmarik, K.; Abbas, H. "Towards Interpretable ANNs", arXiv:2003.04675, 2020

103 Aytekin, C. "Neural Networks are Decision Trees", arXiv:2210.5189v2, 2022

104 Brown, T.; Mann, B.; Ryder, N.; Subbiah, M.; et al. "Language Models are Few-Shot Learners", OpenAI arXiv:2005.14165v4, 2020

105 Jaimungai, C. "Chomsky on Terence McKenna, Sam Harris, GPT3, Cryptocurrencies, Kierkegaard, Neuralink, & Hofstadter", in *Theories of Everything,* Video Publication, 2021

106 Ramesh, A.; Pavlov, M.; Goh, G.; et al. "Zero-Shot Text-to-Image Generation", in *PMLR,* 2021

107 Sanghi, A.; Chu, H.; Lambourne, J.G.; et al. "CLIP-Forge: Towards Zero-Shot Text-to-Shape Generation", *CVPR,* ARXIV:2110.02624, 2021

108 Bautista, M.A.; Guo, P.; Abnar, S.; Talbott W.; et al. "GAUDI: A Neural Architect for Immersive 3D Scene Generation", arXiv:2207.13751v1, 2022

AI Computational Linguistic Semiotics 139

109 Fu, Y. with Peng, H. and Shot, T. *How does GPT Obtain its Ability? Tracing Emergent Abilities of Language Models to their Sources*, Allen Institute for AI, University of Edinburgh, Dec, 2022

110 Wolfram, S. "ChatGPT and Wolfram Alpha", *Stephen Wolfram Writings,* Wolfram Media, Jan 9, 2023

111 Dick, S. "Artificial Intelligence", in *Harvard Data Science Review,* Volume 1, 2019

112 Pesavento, U. "An Implementation of von Neumann's Self-Reproducing Machine", in *Artificial Life*, Volume 3, Issue 4, MIT Press, Cambridge, July 1995

113 Sprecher, A.; Yeshayahu S.; Lorenzo-Eiroa, P. Life in: Formation, in *Proceedings of the 30th ACADIA Conference*, New York, 2010

114 Bostrom, N. "Are We Living in a Simulation?", in *The Philosophical Quarterly*, Volume 53, Issue 211, 2003

115 Neuman, Y.; Nave, O. "Why the Brain Needs Language in Order to be Self-Conscious", in *New Ideas in Psychology*, Volume 28, Issue 1, 2010

116 Lewis, Mike; Yarats, Denis; Parikh, Devi; Batra, Dhruv "Deal or No Deal? Training AI Bots to Negotiate", in *FAIR Research*, 2017

Figure 6.8 Chomsky declares that AI through statistical interpolation does not guarantee reasoning. We ask ChatGPT if current AI is capable of Emergent Programming: "AI is capable of emergent programming, which involves creating software systems that can modify themselves and their behavior in response to changing environments and goals. One way that AI can exhibit emergent programming is through the use of evolutionary algorithms and other forms of machine learning. These approaches allow an AI system to learn from experience and adapt its behavior over time in response to changing conditions, much like a biological organism might adapt to new environmental pressures." We also asked whether a program can simulate another program: "It is possible for a machine learning algorithm through an artificial neural network to simulate the behavior of another program, provided that the algorithm is trained on a suitable dataset. For example, if we have a program that performs a specific task, such as recognizing handwritten digits, we could train a machine learning algorithm to learn from the input-output pairs of this program, effectively simulating its behavior. Once the algorithm is trained, it can be used to predict the output of the original program for new inputs, even if the program itself is not explicitly programmed to handle those inputs." A1–D5: Sequential images motivating architecture from the ground surface to displacing architecture containment through simulation optimization; from environmental simulation to structural simulation through NLP prompt engineering activating mathematical notions, equations and parameters bypassing style transfer but implementing image training through convolution, therefore activating a program simulation of a simulation, or Emergent Programming. NLP diffusion model (DM) applying CFD simulation into structural simulation through various frameworks; A1–D4: Diffusion Model (DM) Dall-E 2 based on Open AI GPT3 and Stable Diffusion based on Stability AI. A3–D5: DM Mid-Journey. A5-D5: NLP DM activating structural simulation concepts and tectonics through image convolution. Pablo Lorenzo-Eiroa, 2022.

7 Computational Visual Semiotics

Grammatology Displacing Signals, Signs and Digital Signifiers From Pixels to Point Clouds and Particles Activating Emergent Programming

"Semiology therefore aims to take in any system of signs, whatever their substance and limits; images, gestures, musical sounds, objects... these constitute, if not languages, at least systems of signification. ...just when the success of disciplines such as linguistics, information theory, formal logic, and structural anthropology provide semantic analysis with new instruments."
Roland Barthes[1]

Methodology:
Information Theory, Panofsky's Symbolic Form Deep Structure;

Mathematics:
Projective geometry; Navier–Stokes equations; Topology; Fractal; projective geometry;

Architecture Representation:
Parametric Design; Evidence-Based Design; Simulation-Optimization; Procedural; Multidimensional; Space-Environments;

Computational Non-Linguistic Visual Semiotic Signifiers:
Electronic Binary Signal; Perspective Vanishing Point; Vector, Pixel, Voxel, Nurbs Curves, Nurbs Surfaces, Lattice, Point, Point Cloud, Particles;

Visual Semiotic Signals:
Satellite Imagery (visible, infrared); light detection and ranging (LiDAR), Laser, Thermal, Infrared,
Non-Visible Electromagnetic Light Spectrum (Wavelength: radio, short wave, VHF, UHF, Radar, microwave, far infrared, infrared, ultraviolet, X-Ray, Gamma Ray, Cosmic); Analog Photograph; Digital Photograph;

Computational Visual Semiotic:
Geometric Algorithms; Shape Grammar; Visual Algorithms; Graph Neural Network; Cellular Automation; Genetic Algorithms; Swarm Intelligence;

DOI: 10.4324/9781003292036-8

Agent Based Modelling; Convolutional Neural Networks; Generative Adversarial Networks; Diffusion Models; Computational Fluid Dynamics; Simulation; Optimization; BIM; Plug-ins;

Non-Linguistic Semiotic Computational Systems:
Flow Diagrams, Dynamic Perspective, Axonometric, Topological Geometry;

Non-Linguistic Computational Visual Semiotics: From Automated Drawing to Image Programming, to Simulation, to Evolutionary Algorithms

We discussed in previous chapters how architects displaced visual semiotic architecture signs through displacing analog background representation, sometimes even developing new systems of representation as a new form of media such as Brunelleschi's perspective, Palladio's critique of perspective, Russian Constructivism, the Modern Axonometric projection, Hejduk's motivation of systems of representation, or others based on deconstructivism experimentation. When resolving a new digital architecture, working with innovative technology through new frameworks, platforms, software, and interfaces, architects left behind the ambition of innovating at background representational levels, since innovation was already done at new digital systems of representation from the outside the discipline as they needed to explore the potential of new media. Systems of representation were innovated through technological advances by software developers, technologists, or engineers outside the disciplinary historical revolutions that culturally advanced representation. As a consequence, systems of representation projected usually conventional notions of the disciplines through normalized cultural ideologies, separating experimental representation exploring the new media from innovation at the media level.

Computer scientists as a new discipline quickly realized the necessity to engage with computational visual semiotics, but they standardized representation through conventional perspective or axonometric projection. Computational art was a form of experimental research to investigate machine vision, systems of representation in computation, and fabrication which can be traced back to the 1950s addressing the necessity to deal with computational semiotics as a senseable form of knowledge, including computational visual semiotics. The magazine "Computers and Automation" published a competition in 1963 and then the magazine "Computer Graphics and Art" published periodically computer graphics, through which computer scientists and mathematicians often experimented with art to explore boundaries in computation. Computer art correlates computation as a technique with a unique form of semiotic expression, correlating artistic signification through the development of a custom interface. In 1963, Ivan Sutherland developed the SketchPAD, which proposed a

142 *Computational Visual Semiotics*

pen to topologically assign a numeric value to the forms over the vertical computer screen as well as tag names. Danny Cohen's Boeing Flight Simulator ARPAnet of 1970 addressing the upcoming virtual immersive environment, as well as ART 1 "computer program for artists" by Katherine Nash,[2] developed new visual interfaces as a new cognitive aspect of computation acknowledging that programming languages determine the type of environment in simulation or background-space in the work of art, which is a unique media-specific experience. Interfaces translate data and information between computational linguistic semiotics codes and computational visual semiotics in various formats, forms, methods, and technologies, translating mathematical signals into workable Human-Computer Interaction (HCI) signs.

Necessarily the field of artist-programmers started emerging in parallel to computation, exploring programming as a form of expression beyond conventional software and platforms, and expanding systems of representation within the computation.[3] Artists in the 1960s–70s started developing their own coding languages as a form to bypass media determinism and what was possible through computation developing their own media. The notion of automatic drawing started emerging around 1963 from scientific computers as a syncretic knowledge in reference to Kohler in 1940.[4] ALGOL's (1958) syntax through code blocks influenced the development of other languages such as FORTRAN (1966), Lisp, and COBOL and permitted digital plots for graphs by the 1970s. The Laboratory for Computer Graphics (1964–65) at the Graduate School of Design at Harvard University by Fisher explored mapping as measurable data; SYMAP and ODYSSEY developed by students contributed to the creation of the Geographic Information Systems (GIS).[5] The Urban Systems Laboratory was created at MIT in 1968. In 1968 Montagu[6] developed applied research on floor plans of government-built projects implementing incursions on Computer-Aided Design (CAD) influenced by Jones and Archer. Pask[7] declares thinking buildings as interactive and responsive (1969). L-Systems, as evolutionary algorithms, were originally devised to describe the behavior of plant branching by biologist Lindenmayer (1968)[8] setting Axioms and recursive rules as variations and generation dependent following a stochastic grammar (Figure 7.2).[9] L-Systems equations and fractals allowed computer graphics to simulate terrain surfaces (1980).[10] In 1982 Richard Voss and Benoit B. Mandelbrot applied fractal geometry making them recursive to develop a hyperrealistic landscape representation through procedural computation, through IBM Watson Research Center. Weinzapfel, Johnson, and Perkins developed by 1970 at the MIT "Image"[11] a 3D spatial arrangement and relationships system according to design parameters as CAD. In 1974 Ed Catmull developed a Point Cloud 3D Scanning 3D Mesh surface and later developed Tween, an animation tool. *Architecture by Yourself* by Negroponte and Weinzapfel 1976 developed floor plans applying network data structures perhaps inspired by circulation diagrams by Alexander Klein and depicted as critical paths and network links between spaces understanding architecture as a data organization problem.[12] The Architecture Machine Group (AMG) at MIT was developed by the concept of teaching how to program and experiment at the same time with the outputs or thinking at a meta-level, thinking about thinking.[13] The group also developed URBAN5 a system to develop urbanism through programming, control, and management of reality through simulation interfaces.

Space Syntax, GIS

Space Syntax by Hillier, Leaman, and Beattie in the 1970s presented a non-discursive technique to analyze architecture and urbanism through statistical forensic data, correlating the form of space in relation to its social use through a combination of different software, which can be attributed today to GIS layers disclosing "Space is the Machine" by Dalton.[14, 15] Although we critique the purposely eliminated cultural discourse identified as biased and replaced by a scientific technical approach that does not recognize formal grammar, systems of representation, ideology, and aesthetics and therefore project unintended nondisclosed conventions in representation and cultural biases. We also think that artistic visual semiotics creativity as a non-linguistic logic is an essential aspect of mapping in implementing data science, currently being unmotivated or rather conventionalized by measurement systems. We later discuss in Chapters 15-19 how we occasionally implement GIS layers, not through zip codes to bypass problematic political biases, as we develop our own datasets through web-crawling and Application Processing Interface (API) identifying conflicts of interests, mapping undisclosed territories, and in general, a forensic urbanism of information which aims at creatively depart from transfigurations of geopolitics in relation to, data, a topographic and site-specific territory, mapping, mobility, and infrastructure but mainly in relation to emergent environmental conditions as space is transfigured by data representation into information (Figure 7.1).

By 1975 Melvin Prueitt published the *Computer Graphics Book* which included abstract line plotted surfaces, artificial topographies within platonic solids, and complex compositions within cube matrices. By the 1980s affordable personal computers developed a wave of innovation and global spread of computation. The Galaksija computer 1980–83 do-it-yourself open source technology presented a socialist alternative to Silicon Valley. The Galaksija presented efficient graphics indexing the logic of the vectorial digital signal and its interface sign enabled by the cost efficiency of the technology.

144 *Computational Visual Semiotics*

Figure 7.1 The two images place in contrast mapping biases revealing politically informed taxes revenue competition between NY and NJ; real estate informed infrastructure; live-work and shared live-work; and topography. A1: Goolge API database representation for work-living public transportation commute use. Ecoinduction III Optimizing Transportation and Ecology in NYC, DOT Presentation, e(eiroa)-Architects Team: Design Principal: Pablo Lorenzo-Eiroa; Designers: Frank Fengqi Li, Julian Chu-Yun Cheng, Shantanu Bhalla, Wayne Shang-Wei Lin. B1: Mapping data forcing relationships across the political divide between New York and New Jersey, applying a framing displacement by taking as a limit the topography of Broadway in NY to Palisades Ave in NJ, delimiting the Hudson Valley. Work-live relationships: private apartment (green), private bedroom (blue), vs shared bedroom (red), shared office (purple), Air BNB, and We Work API. Associate Prof. Pablo Lorenzo-Eiroa, Student: Jose Mateluna, Master of Architecture, The Cooper Union, F2017.

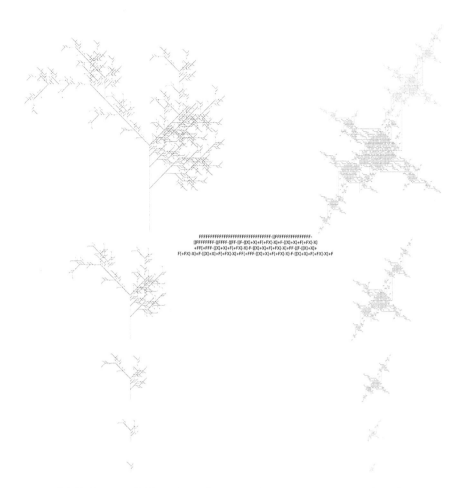

Figure 7.2 L-Systems. Bifurcating urban organization activating site-based computation. Coordinator Associate Prof. Pablo Lorenzo-Eiroa, Assistant Prof. Dorit Aviv, Instructor Will Shapiro; Student: Jin Woo Lee The Cooper Union, Master of Architecture, F2015.

Shape Grammar as Computational Visual Semiotics

Shape Grammar, introduced in 1971 presents a paradigmatic example of the necessity to articulate formal logic as a type of non-linguistic visual semiotics computation. Shape Grammar by Stiny and Mitchell is indeed considered a 2D and 3D computational language based on visual semiotics. Shape grammar avoids the representational translation between sign input, signal processing, and output sign change usually in computational linguistic coding through symbolic representation and digital signal processing. Shape grammar computes forms as signs in relation to visual logic through form as a computational processing sign; formal grammar becomes a procedural relational medium, understanding it as "non-representational" 2D and 3D shape making.[16] A Shape Grammar is itself a computational system composed of rules through a shape that becomes the rule parameter and a generation engine that can select and process data thereby developing a pictorial formal generative emergent computational model, connecting aesthetics, logical procedure, and computability.[17] Shape Grammar was applied to reading and re-writing the generative work of Palladio through typological variation.[18]

Shape Grammar = Formal Logical Computational System
Shape = Computational Signifier Through Formal Logic

PADL-1 and 2 (Part and Assembly Description Language) by Voelcker et All of 1978-82 defined a computation of solid objects. The programming language Piet developed in 1991 by David Morgan-Mar is an esoteric programming language to explore computability. It not only uses images to program a language as opposed to computational linguistics, resulting in a Mondrian-like artistic expression as output, but it can also be programmed to resolve other types of art. "The Ancestral Code" programming interface by Corbett, 2021, or the program Texture[19] allows for a combination between geometry and symbolic computation problematizing the relationship between visual semiotics and linguistic semiotics. While video games depend on a finite set of screens and scenes in which players can interact, the relationship between rendering and video game memory (RAM and GPU) is optimized in the form of the game, distorting perceptions of cities where games are placed in the scene. Minecraft released in 2011 allows the user to develop its space matrix as a form of interface through voxel signs.

While Apple elevated design through an integrated design of software and hardware as a unique correlated interface-system, the system is closed proprietary and able to increase its monopoly over data sensing, user profiling, data gathering, processing, and simulation-optimization to advance its software-hardware. Google (Alphabet) has been surveying, mediating, and informing real-time information flows understanding the necessity to also develop hardware, such as smart cell phones mainly purposed for data gathering, and information simulation-optimization. This mechanism allowed Google to inform urbanism faster than anyone before. Google has been accused of multiple patent and invention infringements, such as Google Earth (2001) based on T_Vision or Terra Vision by ART+COM (1994)[20], a disjunction of invention and innovation to activate Digital Feudalism. Navigating the world through satellite images and aerial photos downloaded in real time, Google had revolutionized the way of relating humans to the world's geodesic planetary projection.[21] Architecture had changed through history through innovation in systems of representation, but computation presented a different type of transformation. Mitchell compiles a methodological classification of architecture in relation to computation organized by dimensions, including work from Glympth at Gehry's office.[22] Mitchell *City of Bits*[23] discusses information systems displacing buildings and city typologies toward bit-based signs through telepresence.

Digital Architecture and Fabrication

Gehry Technologies revolutionized architecture from a digital fabrication construction information-flow. Gehry needed his cultural artistic project to displace the technological determinism in construction conventions to be able to expand his art as architecture, first making furniture out of recycled materials, and then with revolutionary counter-intuitive structural optimization software innovating in Building Information Modeling (BIM) initially proposed by Charles Eastman by 1977 displacing media determinism to address a specific message, now standardized and normalized. But the first culturally based digital revolution resisting a technocratic implementation of computer representation as a cultural utopia in architecture emerged at Columbia University GSAPP led by Tschumi (1988–2003) and faculty translating the work of Deleuze as a linguistic toolbox applied through Silicon Graphics International (1982), through for instance, anti-aliasing program, curvature topology, Alias|Wavefront (1983), then Maya (1998) topology-history based software. Morphing enabled cross reference of two different surfaces by matching the same amount of control points as a shared topology. Maya became not only anticipatory of biomorphic and anthropomorphic designs but also with the embedded capacity thanks to formal topology history for environment/al simulation able to form-finding through particle simulation applying thermodynamics. Performance was understood as a critique of representation.[24] Influential professors applied computation to architecture, from Karl Chu's philosophy of architecture as computation to Gregg Lynn. Lynn at Eisenman's office and Yessios of Form Z (AutoDesSys 1991) developed a popular tool: unfold command, to digitally fabricate 3D surfaces out of digital ruled surfaces, revolutionizing digital fabrication. In 1999 Eisenman Architects Virtual House, Siteless Competition entry led by Ingeborg Rocker presents the computer space as a site. FOA Yokohama Port Terminal made autonomous a thickening of the ground surface through computer representation and was digitally fabricated through ship building technology (1995–2002). After its Graduate School was developed, The Design Research Laboratory at the Architectural Association by Steele and Schumacher with Verebes as Course Master quickly became an influential experimental unit measurable in the work of offices such as Zaha Hadid Architects (ZHA) expanding through the representation of the lead by Gehry of the 1990s, such as ZHA Phaeno Center (2005). While Gehry implemented optimization expanding technology, the technology did not challenge his art; and while Hadid developed fluid forms her architecture did not challenge computational visual semiotics but rather indexed and accentuated software's deep structure through perspectival displacement and feedback. Hadid and

148 *Computational Visual Semiotics*

Schumacher developed an evolving dialectic within ZHA. Hadid's artistic style displaced media through representation; Schumacher *parametricism as a style* applied media representation. Schumacher's parametric semiology[25] (or semiotic) message is based on a positivistic computational technocratic-capitalist determinism of linear information communication between simulation and optimization, not problematizing media but able to systematize and expand an architecture ideology as a style. ZHA developed code-expanding computational design and immersive collaborative communication interface environments between disciplines for coordinated BIM fabrication.

Some architects through machinic architectures and landscapes[26] aimed at developing emergent complex design geometries as analog computation indexing material logic such as Najle.[27] At Universitat Internacional de Catalunya (UIC) in Barcelona, Alberto T. Estévez in 2000, proposed rethinking architecture in relation to biology through a radical Bio-Digital Architecture Master Program [28] working with Genetics and advancing fabrication with one of the first CNC in Europe in a School of Architecture working in Bernard Cache Studio, and one of the first 3D printers working in Dennis Dollens Studio and often referencing biomimicry, cybernetics[29] and a close reading of Gaudi's work. The Institute for Advanced Architecture of Catalonia (IAAC) founded by Gausa, Guallart, Müller and now directed by Ibañez and Markopoulou became referential by updating architecture through digital technologies progress. The *Archeology of the Digital* proposed an artificial beginning and end to this cycle through "Complexity and Convention" differentiating two digital revolutions: digital architecture and digital fabrication.[30] We argue that while the 1990s digital revolution was cultural-based, the reactionary fabrication revolution made the utopia real through techno-capitalism without activating a cultural resistance nor an ideological project other than a tectonic critique of the surface-based abstraction of the 1990s. Office dA offered a contrast to abstract computer representation through a material-based thinking digital fabrication, after Cache's objectile material experiments.[31] Complexity became quickly conventional through a kind of spread of conventional algorithms that output an apparent complexity while their core structure remained conventional across the entire production of buildings globally. Gramazio-Kohler addressed robotic fabrication at the ETH Zurich in the early 2000s problematically through robotic arms as signifiers of a displaced anthropocentric manual brick layering and later Menges through efficiency and optimization developed an Institute for Computational Design and Construction (ICD) earlier capped by a technological determinism, which lately has been addressed by some thesis.

Open-source software progressively collectively incorporated more tools as well as plug-ins developed by associated programmers including architects who understood the necessity to engage with an architecture of computation. In 2001 Reas and Fry developed processing, acknowledging a new necessity to process data and computational design through an integrated development environment (IDE) open-source platform. Rutten at Robert McNeel and Associates adapted visual algorithms already present in software like Maya to pack algorithms into a Low Code and make them recursive-linkable with others developing a visual dynamic workflow reverse engineering software developing meta tools through Grasshopper plug-ins for Rhinoceros 3D. Piker, among others, developed Grasshopper visual algorithms for physics simulation-optimization form by finding evidence-based design. At the same time some architects bypassed software through mathematical equations such as Legendre.[32]

Oxman at MIT developed new aesthetic boundaries by implementing high-resolution injection 3D printing technology by Stratasys' Objet through, for instance, downsampling voxelation. Experimental practices such as FUTUREFORMS or Krietemeyer developed interactive means to expand representation to information systems in changing synthetic environments. Lally,[33] Clément, Rahm, and Borasi[34] expanded Banham's defining energy as a new typology for environments through shifting representational paradigms later defining a post-natural environment.[35] Armstrong microbiological environments and Ecologic Studio started working directly with live organisms to inform live architecture. In parallel a notion that architecture could not deal with the social, political and environmental crises on its own terms, architects, scientists, and technologists such as Weizman's Forensic Architecture political mapping, Roche's[36] "Architectural Psychoscapes" and Farahi's "Returning the Gaze" acknowledge a media determinism, from a cultural and social deconstruction.

Big Data, Simulation, Genetic Algorithms, Swarm Intelligence, Agent Based Modeling towards AI Virtual and Physical Robotics

Evolutionary algorithms are inspired by biological processes self-reproducing Autopoiesis.[37] Genetic algorithms[38] use strings of numbers and apply operators like recombination and mutation of units to optimize solutions to problems, such as Morel's genetic evolutive architecture, also applying Artificial Intelligence (AI). Couzin's Swarm algorithm of 2003[39] describes an ant colony as a form of collective intelligence self-organization and crowd thinking through mathematical means to approximate behavioral logic that is applied to simulate Swarm Intelligence (SI) later applied to address other collective behavior. Frazer's Evolutionary Architecture[40] describes different aspects of robotics and computation from self-replicating automata to artificial life. Weinstock, Hensel, and Menges discuss issues on digital morphogenesis[41, 42, 43] in the architecture of emergence through optimization. Agent-Based Modeling (ABM)[44] is a virtual robotic system that translates to mathematical terms biological processes, such as self-learning adaptive collective[45] swarm activity,[46] identifying through optimization autonomous behavioral logic in relation to a recognized task and a changing environment by assigning

150 *Computational Visual Semiotics*

rewards activating Reinforced Learning which can inform physical robotic behavior and tasks.[47, 48]

Sugihara develops different types of swarm algorithms in relation to architecture structures.[49] Von Neumann devised means for evolutionary computation that can occur by the function of computer viruses corrupting a program since viruses corrupt the DNA of animals, presenting nonlinear ramifications in parallel which may not follow bifurcating linear tree structures addressing a rhizome as an alternative non-hierarchical structure.[50] Big Data from the 2000s–2013 enabled the previously dismissed AI of the 1980s, since largely available sources of data through cell phones tracking personal information, mobility, as well as the data over the internet, allowing for datasets and repositories to become functional to training Neural Networks through Machine Learning. Around 2014 Artificial Neural Networks (ANN) finally became functional thanks to Big Data and shifted the balance between anticipatory theory and statistical-based prediction based on data anticipated by Bryson and Chi's backpropagation in 1969 and Pearl's complex probability of 1988. Toward the mid-2010s, the quest for an open nondeterministic form of computer representation in architecture stated emerging, first through simulation, Big Data simulation, and then Big Data that can activate Machine Learning (ML) and Strong AI deep learning. Radford and Metz present a non-supervised Generative Adversarial Network (GAN) able to discriminate objects from spaces in scenes through Deep Convolutional Generative Adversarial Networks (DCGANs).[51] Rahbar et al. present an AI system to define program semantics by implementing AI for floor plan layouts.[52] Chaillou Thesis, tutored by Witt developed an automated plan generation program distribution through AI GANs.[53] While AI is being revolutionized at many levels, Schools of Architecture, particularly in China are now leading technological innovation integrating AI and Robotics.[54]

Computational Visual Semiotic Signifiers

We discussed how humans developed systems of description and communication through semiotics in Chapters 5 and 6, understanding mathematics as a form of linguistic description of reality rather than a discovery of the laws of Nature or the Universe. We also discussed computation as a universal communication system through symbolic alphanumeric computation articulating computability with arithmetic through algebra. We can therefore distinguish different types of signs and signals relevant to computation and architecture. We discussed through Gandelsonas's architectural signifier what signs in architecture can be and how they can become anticipatory signifiers, such as a column or other culturally motivated architectural elements. Signs in the computation are HCI computational visual semiotics minimal elements that allow representation of space in 1D, 2D, and 3D, such as a 2D pixel in Photoshop.

Through computational visual semiotics, we also refer to signals. *Mathematical signals* can refer to mathematical equations describing physics through notational equations used to compute arithmetically and algebraic equations such as wave functions, frequency, and other types of signals describing physics in medium propagation. We can also refer to *vectorial signals*, representing visually mathematical signals as HCI signs. We also refer to *physical signals* as the physical phenomena described by mathematics, such as visible or non-visible light spectrum waves, LiDAR, light, photons, gravitation, and others such as electronic signals. Electronic *binary signals* through the chipset compute and process data and information implementing Boolean logic through algorithms. Electronic signals at the chipset level are able to encode and decode information through electronic communication transmitting data and turning it into communicable information.

We can identify computational digital signifiers that emerge in computational visual semiotics that are relevant to architecture. The first digital photograph was developed by Kirsch in 1957 who invented the pixel and image scanner. Pixels (px) are minimum computer vision semiotic signs in a raster image to address color within a grid system that is fixed in scale since the unit cannot be modified. It establishes the resolution of the canvas, and can grow infinitely depending on Graphic Processing Unit's (GPU's) power. A measure of 1 bit per pixel is 2 colors 1^2 (monochrome), $2^2=4...$. The pixel establishes a fixed vectorial scale-based semiotic interface as a canvas in which the resolution of the image depends on the number of pixels in the canvas. This is different from a vectorial point, line, or surface, which can be augmented or diminished infinitely as they do not have a fixed scale. The editing of these types of sign units enables programs such as Photoshop which through tools edit the canvas tiles basically changing the color in each pixel (Figure 7.3).

Pixel = Signifier

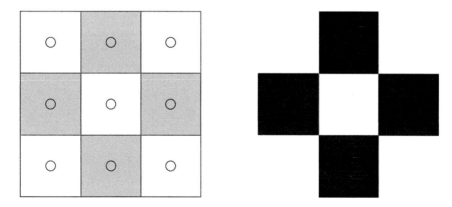

Figure 7.3 A1: Pixel vectorial node signal; B1: pixel as an HCI sign.

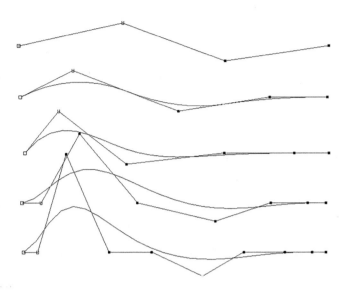

Figure 7.4 NURBS curve or Spline line construction is composed of at least a Bézier curve. Here we represent curve degree 1 (line),2,3,5,7 including start and end points, control points (weights), and hulls as well as edit points on the curve. Construction of a Bézier curve or parametric curve defined by curvature degree control points. Bézier control point on the control vector or hull, the Bezier curve. Maya Software defines a straight line as degree 1 and a curve through different exponentiations through the same topology.

NURBS Curves
NURBS Surfaces

Splines were originally the wood longitudinal pieces used by boat builders to create curves (or splinters) by weights and anchors. Pierre Bézier working for Renault as an engineer designing and manufacturing physical geometric processes, developed in the 1950s the non-uniform rational basis spline (NURBS) as a polynomial formula for CAD. He then developed UNISURF for Computer-Aided Manufacturing and NURBS for Non-uniform rational basis spline (Figure 7.4), which were used first in software in the 1980s and then AutoCAD.[55] NURBS-Based Surfaces became dominant signifiers in architecture during the 1990s (Figure 7.5).

Computational Fluid Dynamics (CFD) as a form of simulation can be traced back to ENIAC in 1940, a project led by von Neumann. ENIAC 1943–45 was the first large-scale computer to run at electronic speed without being slowed by any mechanical parts, programmed by Kay McNulty, Betty Jennings, Betty Snyder, Marlyn Meltzer, Fran Bilas, and Ruth Lichterman, and also by von Neumann. Simulation in terms of hydrodynamics or aerodynamics can be described through Navier–Stokes mathematical fluid

Computational Visual Semiotics 153

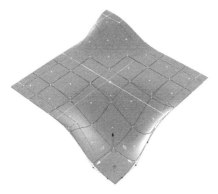

Figure 7.5 Construction of a NURBS Surface degree 3 containing cells, hulls, and control points.

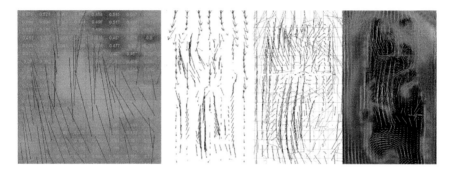

Figure 7.6 Computational Fluid Dynamic (CFD) Simulation studies on numeric values intensities relative to fluid turbulence implementing Navier–Stokes equations through particle physics simulation; Pablo Lorenzo-Eiroa, 2002–06 with diagrams applied to student's base simulations by Elan Fessler and Mack Cooper William, ARCH 177, The Cooper Union, 2006.

mechanics equations (1822) which allowed the simulation of fluid dynamics and an important advancement in a different type of computation: emergent, chaotic, nonlinear, and complex nonreversible. This form of mathematics applies Newton's second law of motion or momentum change over time to fluid dynamics and presents nonlinear emergence and turbulence in thermodynamics' conservation of energy in a fluid flow (Figure 7.6).

SIMULATION NAVIER STOKES = CFD
Vectorial CFD = Signifier

The Lorenz system (based on Lorenz Attractor) was the first demonstration that deterministic physics can lead to emergent unpredictable chaos.[56] Forecasting methodologies diverge, but increasingly weather data repositories

154 *Computational Visual Semiotics*

analyzing similar conditions are matched with increasing Computational Fluid Dynamic (CFD) playing large amounts of simulation scenarios. CFD is a vectorial representation through particle physics of Navier–Stokes equations, allowing to model friction, viscosity, and other physics parameters to the model vortex, and turbulence as emergence. Turbulence is a natural phenomenon that has been quite difficult for mathematicians and physicists to resolve.[57] Turbulence happens when a continuous fluid flow is divided into smaller eddies and vortices called swirls all interacting and moving in their own way. Swirls break into smaller swirls, and then smaller ones, and so on, conforming to an unpredictable chain effect that dissipates energy from the original fluid stream. The limit of these equations is what mathematicians refer to as "blowup" in which solutions do not exist because of infinite values at zero division to which there is no solution yet, but Navier–Stokes fluid dynamics have worked as approximations of observable experimentation during the last 200 years. Prigogine's discoveries in chemistry through thermodynamics question the end of certainty in humanity.[58] CFD simulation as a paradigm displaced architecture space to engage with the environment through managing energy flows which cannot be computed in advance unless the simulation is run, thus we started working back in 1998 through emergent simulation substituting anticipatory modeling in architecture representation. Navier-Stokes mathematical equations are applied to particle physics simulations through physics engines interfaces, plug-ins and software. Particle physics can embedded in a particle point which as a sign simulates in time the evolutionary behavior of fluid dynamics viscosity, density and friction within a container or within the space-matrix of the software, colliding and affecting points within a point cloud or surfaces.

CFD Vectors = Particles Physics
Particles = new digital signifier

A voxel is a minimum 3D information block, a minimum 3D unit of measurement defining a scale and reference to represent computational processing relationships in 3D. Voxel Modeling has been presenting new challenges in computational design through reduction to address discrete computation[59] by packaging minimum information blocks for computability, through downsampling or compression of a digital mathematical signal for processing speed. Usually, voxels and pixels are compared. While pixels are a vectorial signal node and a HCI sign, voxels can be an abstract mathematical signal and a visual communication HCI sign in the case of Cellular Automation 3D cells as voxels. But when the voxel is a downsampling mathematical signal processing from a higher information topology to a lower topology it becomes a sub-symbolic sign, for instance in the case of a point cloud as an indexical sign of a 3D scanning physical signal laser beam through a point to a downsampling voxel resignifying the original sign. Voxels are used for downsampling data in Big Data 3D scanning LiDAR

Computational Visual Semiotics 155

or CFD simulation; the difference is that in the case of a 3D scan, the downsampling is a sign; in the CFD simulation, the downsampling is of a mathematical wave signal decimation. Voxels are mainly used to determine volumetric vectorial data, such as geology, body scans, fluid simulations (particles), and others. Voxels enable the separation into 3D vectorial packages of information for fast processing carrying advantages and disadvantages based on pixel technology resolution (Figure 7.7).[60] Object tracking machine vision recognition implements voxels to simplify processing mathematical signals through vectorial signals expanded through functional occupation recognition overlapping multiple methods of representation of the geometry (Figure 7.12).[61] Voxel-to-point cloud topology can be matched by placing points in relation to the vertex, the face, or the edge of a voxel, facilitating a discrete computation for faster semantic segmentation (Figure 7.7).[62] Point cloud data processing in relation to high-level 3D printed models can be done through voxel printing, and data sensing through high-resolution MRI is translated through the slicer and recomposed in 3D.[63, 64] AI research aiming at saving costs, storage space (60x less), time (2x faster), and energy such as NVIDIA Flow, and OpenVDB (High-Resolution Sparse Volumes with Dynamic Topology) implement voxels in relation to Computational Fluid Dynamic Simulation.

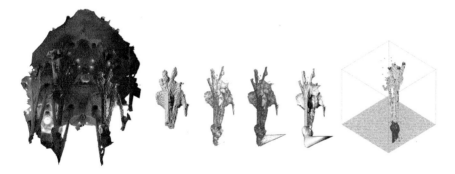

Figure 7.7 Voxel downsampling point cloud. A1–F1: Point cloud workflow; A1: 3D Photogrammetry of Sagrada Familia by Gaudi; D1: Mesh rendered simulation of the central bay; A1–B1: point cloud semantic segmentation of "column"; F1: partial voxelation of the column in relation to container limit; C1: point cloud isolated; D1–E1: mesh and rendered Solid Mesh; F1: Voxelation ratio. A1: Point Cloud index from a scan or mesh reconstruction; semantic segmentation training based on pretrained and trained repositories for object feature detection based on classification and features for mask mapping boundary region; B1: 3D voxelization of point cloud determination (vertex, edge, center, or face or by approximation); 2D pixel tomography through 3D voxels for interpolation approximation and prediction method based on GAN or Diffusion Models. 3D Scan by UIC Barcelona Workshop, Prof. Pablo Lorenzo-Eiroa, students: Ciurel, Dragos, Juárez; Martin; Memi, Mouradian, Nabbouh, Rahmani, Sönmez, Tabikh, Vanhoegaerden, Warang, 2017. AI and voxelation by author.

Sign processing downsampling = Point Cloud Voxelation
Mathematical Signal processing downsampling = CFD mathematical signal decimation through voxelation

LiDAR or Light Detection and Ranging remote sensing through laser 3D scanning developing point-clouds is a technique for a survey that was developed back in the 1960s[65] including forensic architecture and urbanism through machine vision reconstruction.[66] We started working in 2012 with 3D scanning LiDAR technology exploring the possibilities of navigating virtually through point clouds rendered visible performing at true color values and through Big

Figure 7.8 We declared back in 2012 that point clouds became new digital signifiers in architecture. Point clouds are digital analogues to physical atoms and particles addressing contemporary constitution of space as discrete. Point clouds promote uncertainty in the definition of boundaries, as a problem of perceptual dimension, since from far a point cloud can define a volume, but from close up that boundary disappears, as it happens with any object at a molecular level. Point clouds allow for a permeable space defined by 0D, and not a 2D surface defining a 3D space. A point cloud defines a new type of spatial boundary with no sides, a new type of threshold expanding dimensionally architecture through a new type of poché space. The point cloud enables Deleuze's rhizome as a point-to-point relational topological structure bypassing bifurcating tree structures; a Deleuzian Leibniz Nomadology of 0D points. The technological signifier, whether digital or material, is deterministic in nature, as it projects through representation a way of seeing, measuring, or doing defining cultural bias and promoting an ideology about the world. The deconstruction of the digital signifier solely through a cultural project is problematic, as it may activate linguistic or artistic metaphors, revealing cultural biases that need to be systematized linguistically through technological objectivity of the media or the medium. In the figure: Big Data Point Cloud simulation referencing data entry points and relating them across different multidimensional data sets. PI Pablo Lorenzo-Eiroa, 2022.

Data at 10M points, expanding the possibilities of space-time interaction and a new form of indexical realism. Photogrammetry is a subsymbolic a-precise 3D scanning method since it is not indexical through physical signal remote light sensing, but through camera light/shadow AI depth recognition, camera registration angle interpolating several images to reconstruct a mesh/point cloud. Photogrammetry activates a 3D sign product of a 2D photography sign through 3D mapping reconstruction as translation. 3D Scanning technology is transforming architecture representation, which in the 1990s was indexed through NURBS surfaces and that from around 2010 started being indexed thanks to some of our incursions by points, therefore augmenting the scale of observation. We defined the point cloud as a new "digital signifier"[67] since point clouds present the contemporary unit of measurement[68], from machine vision real-time 3D scanning and sensing in self-driving cars and motion feature recognition, to 3D software and Virtual Reality simulation, a new reference system through points in XYZ coordinates and RGB color values. The current data gathering survey machine learning mechanisms through LiDAR scan reality real time, turn scanned data index into XYZ RGB point clouds and reconstruct meaning through semantic recognition (See Figures 4.17–22).

Physical Indexical Signal = LiDAR
Signifier = Point Cloud

New Dimensional Digital Signifiers = Pixels, Points (Point Clouds), Particles

Generative Adversarial Network

Generative Adversarial Network[69] (GAN) is usually implemented in relation to images, music, text, and voice datasets through unsupervised learning consisting of two "adversarial" algorithmic networks competing with each other holding false assumed data that can simulate real data in order to be recognized as false and be optimized by the competing network. Generative algorithms are in competition with discriminative algorithms. Generative algorithms are model-based anticipatory of features, as they create synthetic images or features. Discriminative algorithms through boundary recognition learn to identify and extract through maps feature recognition which then becomes classifying labeling data and then can learn to predict a classifying label.

ANN and GANs particularly revolutionized the way of understanding abstract mathematical computation in relation to dataflow by tensor computing through symbolic weighting developed by identifying mathematical approximation problems derived from video gaming hardware acceleration in GPU. Instead of relying on a CPU that carries out algorithmic computations through cores, GPU has many multiple folds that can perform thousands of parallel calculations on a single node originally designed by NVDIA for optimized image resolution through Gaussian smooth curvature approximation

158   *Computational Visual Semiotics*

between 2D and 3D in edge detection. ANNs combine Data Science (data-flow, statistics) and Computer Science (symbolic computation) through tensor weights and biases, articulating data flow in the case of GANs through statistical approximation with image feature extraction and optimization. Through a data set such as ImageNET where images are tagged through semantic categories developing meta-data repositories, one can train a neural network either using pretrained tagged classifiers or developing classifiers through supervised learning. One can then articulate such supervised learning with non-supervised learning through a mix of techniques to identify features and build up a classification in a robust way. CycleGANs are able to transfer through non-supervised ML features (originally semantic segmentation) of one image to another, such as the general climate, atmosphere, figures (transfiguration), or other features semantically recognized by the GAN such as image improvement, developing style transfer.[70]

Adversarial Generative- Discriminative Tensor Computing
(Symbolic Computational Sign – Emergent Sign as Feature)

Semantic Segmentation: From Linguistic Thinking to Non-linguistic Expression

Semantic segmentation presents in relation to the grammar sequence an interesting inversion in relation to our proposal for implementing Data Science in relation to Computer Science (Figure 7.9).

Semantic Segmentation = Signified before sign
Signified = conventional Message (bypassing information)
AI Semantic Segmentation = Digital Quali-Signifier

By applying semantics in image segmentation, we are applying conventions in natural language, projecting cultural biases from linguistic semiotics to visual semiotics. This problematic image segmentation would also bypass the criticism of media determinism by pairing the *signified* to a *message,* without acknowledging the interfaces and language as a set of signs that induce signifiers, therefore bypassing the theory of signs. This makes explicit one of the main implicit arguments in this exploration of the book thesis: that computation cannot be informative and operative functional as it claims, it cannot translate among interfaces from abstract data to meaningful messages, or in general replace all meaning as a universal language, without a form of disciplinary discourse linguistic criticism.

Semantic segmentation through GANs may structure conventions rather than allow for new grammar, syntax, and new types of messages to emerge through visual semiotics. The semantic segmentation from tagging classifiers in meta-data repositories such as ImageNet project the functionality of linguistics meaning "sky", "water", and "sun" and become active as conventional signifieds. The problematic semantics can be overcome by non-supervised

Computational Visual Semiotics 159

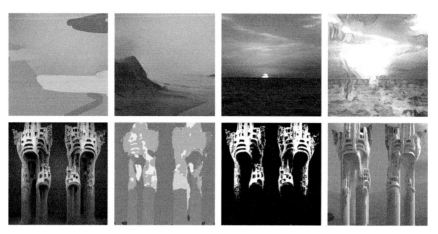

Figure 7.9 Color does not objectively exist; it is a perception at the retina level of the eye of a thermal infrared light spectrum actualized through the atmosphere into different wavelength of electromagnetic light. A1-B1: NVIDIA GauGAN and NVIDIA Canvas, released in 2021, semantic segmentation feature map from brush, which is also available as text to image prompt. C1-D1: GAN style transfer through semantic segmentation feature recognition of Van Gogh's "A Wheatfield, with Cypresses", to river sunrise photo, 2017. Convolutional Neural Networks (CNN) are discriminative models to process images based on backpropagation and stochastic gradient descent which improve results based on feature image recognition based on masks layers and/or tagged image labels; CNN can also cross-reference with NLP for image classification and feature recognition. CNN produce a kernel or feature maps through mathematical signal decimation of pixels value in relation to its pixel neighbors, since through convolution we are able to process an image at 25% of its original resolution through matrix separation and cross information processing comparison through weighting sum, focusing on the feature of the image-message and not its resolution which demands more processing power. Deep Convolutional Neural Networks (DCNN) combine GANs and CNNs. Diffusion Models (DM) are a different technology than GAN and CNN, they are generative and not adversarial (GAN) or discriminatory classification engines (CNN). A2-D2: Ur Urbanism based on Gaudi DM, Author, 2022; A2: DM image. B2: computational visual semiotics AI mask based on image mapping features such as boundary, edge detection, kinetic mapping, lines, surfaces, color and others such as NLP semantics for instance being able to separate people from backgrounds or landscape features in satellite images, Stable Diffusion DM ControlNet through CLIP image encoder not based on text, style context. DM index ideological semantics through the rendering raytracing realism simulation of its statistical curve prediction model, activating also a type of realism through the camera simulation. DM use inpainting functions to separate also semantically features in images masks through Gaussian denoise probabilistic models. Some DM frameworks can also post-process images through convolution through latent DM synthesis with semantic segmentation; Croitoru, F.; Hondru, V.; Ionescu, R. et all "Diffusion Models in Vision: A Survey", arXiv:2209.0474v1, 10 Sept, 2022. C2: Photoshop color delayering mask; D2: feature transfer applied to mask based on NLP prompt through denoise function; PI Pablo Lorenzo-Eiroa, 2022.

160 *Computational Visual Semiotics*

machine learning image feature recognition through Convolutional Neural Networks (CNN) layers. At the same time, GAN style transfer can recognize statistical aspects of a style but does not recognize the politics nor context of the original artistic style, therefore its visual semiotic message and therefore activates as a qualisign or a quality without a sign as a digital quali-signifier interface. The statistical prediction model through numeric value conversion of trained images implements deep learning through CNN through various layers, such as area analysis recognizing features, classifying boundaries developing an object tracking recognition in videos through a voxel 3D cell for tracking in movement or developing a 2D mask layer contouring the object from the context in images in which each pixel of the image is assigned to a category recognized. The computational linguistics of the semantic segmentation through tagged image classifiers, weights against the computational visual semiotics machine vision of the feature recognition through convolution in pixel-to-pixel, which eventually through sequential self-editing algorithm's training, may surpass the original semantic classification through activating emerging semiotic signs.

GAN Style Transfer = Qualisign

One of the issues with style transfer is the lack of identification of the deep symbolic structure of the system of representation, and therefore the politics of art become displaced as a superfluous feature, transferring pictorial traces from one context to the other without transforming nor transfiguring the context. In AI style transfer, the politics of the background-foreground transfiguration is not understood by the programming, training, and results of the GAN through style transfer.

In the use of GAN especially the use of images to develop architecture imaginary through AI, often users and designers implement pretrained neural nets that have been modeled to address certain features of images. One of the means to address a black box approach to AI is to develop the dataset with a critical understanding of its range of diversity and the data science statistic method applied to identify features through the training of the neural net model. While data enforces the relevance of a style as a semiotic sign that can be trained for distinctive features, the model focuses on the parallel structure of the weighting transformation. Through different types of coding: linguistic computation and semiotic computation we can work out interrelationships between both addressing both aspects in coding (linguistic semiotics) and feature recognition (visual semiotics).

The most radical political act of artists such as van Gogh, Escher, Dali, Hadid, and artists who arrive to have dedicated filters in AI frameworks and whose work is being used today for style transfer, is the fact that their art has been able to displace data through their work, making possible a semiotic computational training and model through CNN. But style may obscure the discovery of new structures or visual problems in visual arts such as those identified by the Modern movement critical of historical styles which often focused on design rather than identification and transformation of cultural structure. As CNN is trained thanks to artists' work and user/designer's activation of the work funneled through AI models they expand the original artist's work, although displaced as noted from its original politics able to recognize design stylistic features but not the cultural radical political structure the artists were resisting and revolutionizing. This perhaps is clearer by using an AI style transfer with a Picasso painting, in which foreground and background remain static as the face figuration is partially displaced, differing cognitively from Picasso's dynamic multifocal vision paintings fragmenting any unity on the represented object acknowledging a dynamic plural subject. The politico-cultural critique of the artist becomes a way of seeing, and not a cultural critique, but just the quality of its lenses as a qualisign and not a sign. We define architecture as a higher level of organization in relation to design since usually design does not address a critique of the politics of the systems of representation, structure, robotics and fabrication or material based construction systems operating at a superficial end of the spectrum of reality by applying ranges of possibilities in given systems; unless the design is able to become subversive enough to displace its reference structure. The design is recognized as a feature irrelevant to the political structure that is revolutionizing, pointing out Chomsky's assertion that AI is in fact not expanding cognition nor knowledge but simply applying statistical models.

Architecture Dimensionality in Unstructured Data, Non-Euclidean Data, Graph Neural Networks and Diffusion Models (DM)

We discussed in our previous Chapter 6 Diffusion Models in relation to Natural Language Processing (NLP). Deep Learning relates to Convolutional Neural Networks and Recurrent Neural Networks which are able to recognize features in images through machine vision in unstructured data or semantic classified tagged images or semantic segmentation masks. A topology of architecture dimensions for computer processing with dimensional properties and manifolds becomes active in both mapping, surveying, and processing data and information through Machine Learning developing ANN models that aim at processing a complex reality, from 1D text lines for NLP, to 2D graphs, 2D grids, or 3D grids. Unstructured data tends not to adapt to predetermined types of relationships in ANN models. Graph Neural Networks (GNN) provide the computational model for a complex formal structure to address non-linguistic data processing belonging to different dimensional domains, including the processing of lower dimensional problems such as 1D text lines for increased complexity[71] and higher dimensional problems such as Non-Euclidean d-dimensional representations for recursive neighborhood diffusion allowing for higher node representations[72]. 2D and 3D Graph Convolutional Networks apply semi-supervised ML through graph-structured data making visual semiotics computable, being able to increment complexity in NLP and predict Diffusion Models (DM) in NLP-to-image and NLP-to-point clouds. Various AI frameworks

162 *Computational Visual Semiotics*

implement a range of parameters of GPT 2 and 3, from 0.4B (DALL-E mini) to 3.5B (DALL-E 2) to 12B (DALL-E). DALL-E implements an auto-regressive model through Vector Quantized Generative Adversarial Network[73] (VQ-GAN) for a higher-level image tuning taking images through Convolutional Neural Networks (CNN) decoder and discriminator and in parallel BART[74] Decoder through random weights and tokens (images from pretrained: 1,024px from 8,192–10,000 vocabulary)/pretrained encoder and CLIP[75] (250M images – opensource) which then are processed in relation to a cross-entropy loss function.[76] DALL-E by OpenAI uses a VQVAE based on GPT-3 and MidJourney applies a Diffusion Model. Stable Diffusion is a downloadable open-source Diffusion Model, so one can adjust parameters such as variable solutions, noise adjustment, interpolation–morphed transitions, and others.

DALL-E can recognize relationships between text and images through computational linguistic semiotics learning from pretrained dataset image tagging and computational visual semiotics through semantic segmentation learning from feature recognition. Semantic segmentation is based on masking through feature recognition boundaries from tagging images through classifying categories. Stable Diffusion[77] is an open-source framework that can be scripted/programmed via Python in correlation with other systems. Stable Diffusion ControlNet can be programmed to process visual features in images including different types of segmentations such as canny edge detection, or depth masking recognition for 2D to 3D AI interpretation. ChatGPT natural language input can be applied to automatically 3D print or fabricate through robotic protocols based on different interfaces computational languages and machine languages; from an interpreted 2D image to a fabricated 3D form, expanding semiotic relationships between language, machine and vision.

Image GPT[78] (2020) by OPenAI framework funnels images retrieved through API through NLP or your own dataset. iGTP learns from pretrained dataset ImageNet which is based on users tagging text categories in images, promoting biases of multiple types. As discussed in Chapter 6 a form of Prompt Engineering through NLP becomes active through grammar prediction that activates the parallel processing structure of the GPT model, in which the text description of the task is interpreted through an external API retrieved dataset, such as Common Crawl, or/and in relation to an external pretrained ImageNet dataset or/and in relation to the created internal dataset of GPT dependent on others (60% of GPT3 is based on Common Crawl, 20% WebText2, etc).

Linguistic semiotics analyzes syntax and grammar in relation to semantic relationships between signifier words and signified objects and concepts. Visual semiotics analyzes visual organization in relation to communication, which can be related to formal syntax and formal grammar in relation to communicable meaning through color, form, and its perceptual experience. ChatGPT was used to improve NLP prompt engineering through MidJourney, Stable Diffusion and Dall-E. Visual ChatGPT by Microsoft (built on Open AI) can produce images through chat input combining Stable Diffusion

DM; its functionality is elevated from MidJourney but not the image quality yet. ChatGPT 4.0 released in 2023 is elevated from 175B parameters to 100T parameters as MidJourney v5 is released. Visual ChatGPT is based on Visual Foundation Models (VFM) able to intermediate with its Prompt Manager and therefore interpreting natural language input bypassing the NLP grammar necessary to active prompts in Stable Diffusion, Disco Diffusion, Dall-E 2 or MidJourney. Visual ChatGPT aims at expanding reasoning through a dual form of semiotic communication: linguistic and visual; for instance both to edit images based on NLP or to interpret linguistic meaning from a feature recognition on an image; this enables the correlation between the system principle, the VFM, the history of the dialogue in the Chat, user query, reasoning history, answers by the chat and various information flows and feedback; Wu, C.; Yin, S. Qi, W. et all "Visual ChatGPT: Talking, Drawing and Editing with Visual Foundation Models", arXiv:2303.04671v1, March 8, 2023. By incorporating ChatGPT to most applications globally one can linguistically activate HLL code through NLP in most platforms, interfaces and software bypassing prompt engineering, through plug-ins. Microsoft by acquiring Open AI ChatGPT has now consolidated one of the largest monopolies completing a full range of correlational capacities: from Visual ChatGPT, to Chat GPT integrated in Bing internet browser, to Windows, to Office, to Cortana AI surveying the world through the Internet of Things (IoT). Capitalists are now interestingly asking for governmental regulation to slow down AI development aiming to maintain their monopoly threaten by AI.

A Diffusion Model[79] is a deep learning generative model for virtual machine vision based on two epochs, a forward diffusion epoch disassembling the data and learning from it and a reverse diffusion epoch cycle, reassembling step by step the data through sampling Gaussian noise bypassing GANs. Input images based on pixels are converted into Gaussian noise through, for instance, a Markov chain, and then a denoise function probability function through inference nearest neighbor likelihood estimation. We discussed early work on cybernetics by Weiner and von Neumann based on thermodynamics. A Diffusion Model implements thermodynamics working backward from disseminating an image through forward diffusion noise, and a predictive reconstruction through denoise mathematical functions by finding through training reversely the pixel likelihood instead of probability, applying non-determination to resolve algorithmic problems or resolving order out of disorder in multi stage sampling tests.[80] While the diffusion model is able to simulate a better visual quality image better than GANs, the politics of the original visual semiotics identified conclude similar forensic limitations after convolutional training.

In the pixel-to-pixel Diffusion Model (DM) the pixel becomes active as a digital signifier in relation, for instance to semantic segmentation and pixel optimization, color sampling through the neural net input and output. There are also indexical signs that become active since one can recognize the data index in the images through style transfers that can even become iconic signs. The NLP text-to-image pixel-to-pixel diffusion model codes the image at its minimum sign, which is the pixel, as the 2D sign changes its representational functionality, from image representation to a possible representation of a 3D image simulation. The framework allows for movement by recomposing the image scene, or by retrieving from 2D to 3D through various techniques such as depth recognition and monocular vision but not a fully navigable space. With NLP text-to-image the rendering simulation is produced directly, recognizing light simulation through filters and semantics. The general linguistic descriptive and projective geometry features of a simulated 3D are API image frame-dependent as a site, in relation to the prompt grammar, giving up the full organizing geometric syntax of the apparent 3D model for a 2D syntax of diffusion model pixelation, a form of representation of representation. The pixel-to-pixel diffusion model proposes a signifier with images since while the pixel has been a computational semiotic sign since 1957, the diffusion model expands an information processing to code pixel by pixel as a new signifier activating information theory in relation to visual semiotics. The earlier Julesz's stereogram[81] as image noise patterns become progressively organized through a matrix array of dots progressively by analyzing various sets applying statistics.

We include research of DM run over 3D XYZ RGB point clouds trained through 3D point cloud repositories created implementing 3D scanning (Laser 3D scanning and Photogrammetry), training our datasets, and retrieving directly from point clouds database avoiding translations between 3D models and 3D point clouds over meshes, developing several types of AI models. We also develop point cloud semantic segmentation and through statistical formal analysis (through the nearest neighborhood in relation to the total point cloud to avoid semantics in NLP) run over point clouds. Point-e by Open AI is able to interpret NLP text prompts through DM in an increasing amount of points cloud batches trained on 3D models which result in predictive point clouds but translate between 3D models and 3D point clouds over meshes.

Both pixel-to-pixel DM and point-to-point DM are often used to simulate a reality based on trained past images, and point cloud models based on feature recognition, style, and the work of others, activating a problematic realism necessary for the application of the statistical prediction. We are rather interested in the simulation of 3D in 2D, 3D to 3D not much in terms of simulating previous technology such as CFD or structural simulation discussed in Chapter 6, but in the potential quality of new signs as a new aesthetic emergent language model based on visual semiotics emergent AI programming, indexing the technology based on thermodynamics noise and denoise to reorganize pixels and points and the statistical function used to activate the realistic simulation pictorial quality of its rendering simulation, to then displacing indexed mathematical signals and emergent signifiers.

DALL-E, MidJourney, and Stable Diffusion frameworks train datasets through ML activating DM to recognize features in the style of artists and architects through mapping feature recognition masks through convolution, and through nearest neighbor estimation in DM noise/denoise functions

(Figure 7.10, 7.13). While these frameworks need to become more transparent, including scientific reproducibility caped by emergent programming in the neural hidden layers, we discuss authorship and problematic copyrights in the misuse of images used to train repositories in relation to style transfer in GANs and DM in our last Chapter 20 problematically activating a wealth and intellectual transfer in a Digital Feudalism.

Signifier = Diffusion Model Style Semantic Segmentation

Politics and Style: Displacing the Framework

Agreeable conventions of beauty go against the politics of visual arts, which expand aesthetics boundaries by displacing visual semiotic structures in society, often referred to as anesthetics. Some architects insist on a certain personal approach to architecture; others develop a constant linguistic search; others negate style following the Modern Movement rupture with historical stylistic cycles, but most have changed through their careers their architecture expression, shifting with cultural paradigms. Renaissances through technological revolutions force a disruptive change; and computer representation has been referential in architecture expression over cultural paradigms through a continuous ideology of infinite technological renewal and progress. Agreeing on aesthetic values means there is no possibility for a politics of cultural revolution, able to discover new aesthetic boundaries. The aesthetics of software as a new media language[82] as well as data visualization only promotes the cultural values implicit in the ideology of the interface originated by the developer/author who, most of the time, is not aware of the revolutions of art and architecture and therefore project conventional notions of the disciplines they structure origination to through digital signifiers. Maeda arguably proposes a synthetic literal form of art specific to its medium and transforming the conventions of coding and representation; Manovich acknowledges the broad array of influence of software in defining culture identifying how interfaces and tools shape aesthetics in contemporary media and design. We propose the development of new media by identifying and displacing media determinism through signifiers.

We can differentiate visual cultural trends based on desire, aesthetic trends, fashion, linguistics, visual semiotic style, and the development of a personal language and style as a form of cultural resistance to the programming of visual semiotics. We can differentiate linguistic style, separating architecture language through linguistics and architecture style through visual semiotics. We can identify style to both index semiotic signs and deep structure as well as resist the AI feature recognition. We can also resist both the data and the AI model, being able to displace style as authorship at a data gathering level. We can define a semiotic style as the development of a unique form of expression based on a unique system of representation, a unique way of representing the world through a political apparatus that is able to define a deep structure through distinct iconographic recognizable visual features. Style has been historically

166 *Computational Visual Semiotics*

identified through Zeitgeist, or the spirit of the time, Riegl's Kunstwollen, or art + will but cannot be taught, but only copied or imitated, problematizing cultural advancement. We understand style as the development of a unique form of expression with distinguishing iconographic features in relation to the historical functional politics in relation to a cultural context. A style of a different time and context does not operate politically out of it, since the style was structured to address the cultural and political problems of the time as a visual logical discourse. If we remove politics, we remove discourse and we flatten style to a visual iconographic recognizable feature but without a political structure in tension with its frame/context. We therefore propose an alternative aesthetics tensioning logic and the senses, language and visual semiotics, media and mediums, exploring means to augment dimensions in what is possibly expressible.

Emergent Style as System of Representation, Language, and Representational Bias:

1 Analyze cultural biases: Data; Algorithmic structure; Interface; Software; ANN Model;
2 Limits of Style as Personal expression and cultural sedimented structures;
3 Explore logical abstract systems being critical of cultural structures, displace biases; develop a language;
4 New semiotic-based architecture language, a new form of expression expanding signifiers;
5 Style and aesthetics as politics, through non-linguistic expression; visual semiotic sign transformed as a physical signal = affect − reification through new media and mediums.

The creative cinematic work of Godard aims at exploring and expanding new ranges of possibilities of cinema as an autonomous visual medium of expression and cognition. Godard's cinema defines style as content, as a pictorial visual art formal and color-based logical system as a means to displace cinema, a contrast to Woody Allen's linguistic-based narrative cinema.[83] Godard identifies structural means to activate new forms of communication and signification in cinema, both addressing the structure of the media at a deeper level but displacing expression as a means to communicate, simultaneously motivated as a semiotic sign against the conventional signifier's active in common cinema as a default translation of natural language. *Goodby to Language*, Godard's[84] 3D film removes signifiers referencing signifieds. Godard proposes a de-colonization of media imposed by Television, both innovating in aesthetics and through the actors which becomes also a social contract.

Machine Vision: Perspectival Symbolic Deep Structure, Monocular and Stereo Vision in Remote Sensing

Machine Vision is an emerging field in computation identified through sensing reality through optical lighting and sensing through radar or

LiDAR waves and interpreting that reality in computational terms for computational processing beyond the human visible spectrum. Machine vision implies not only the sensing of an environment but also semantically or through recognizing trained patterns interpreting object characterization, object recognition, object tracking, kinetics, human face recognition, expressions, characters, emotions, and other features involving Deep Learning. Monocular machine vision and stereo machine vision are interesting survey problems implemented for 3D reconstruction from 2D images (Figure 7.11 A1-B2, A5-D5).[85, 86] The reconstruction from 2D monocular machine vision to 3D stereo object expands dimensions in representation through interpretation bypassing the optical machine limitations, although problematically translating mathematical signals through sub-symbolic signs. Other techniques include 3D diffusion models from images.[87] By sensing remotely, through perspectival vision, the various types of remote sensing activate and normalize deep symbolic visual structures. AI design through images actualizing representational theories of montage and collage is inverting a design process from ideal modeling to pragmatic image representation since Photogrammetry and Diffusion Models both reconstruct and simulate spaces through interpolating 2D images. (Figure 7.10, 7.13).

Data science methodologies through remote sensing sensors terminals and Internet of Things (IoT) processed through data analytics, Wi-Fi radio wave frequency signals can scan, measure, predict, and optimize a building occupancy.[88] PointNet++ enables a finer degree of resolution in processing local values and contextual meaning as a prediction model for semantic segmentation categories based on point cloud data repositories.[89] Semantic machine vision recognition based on point cloud scanning can be processed through downsampling sub-symbolic VoxelNet architecture implementing LiDAR for navigation through object classification.[90] Hydra[91] by MIT presents a framework to automate 3D environments through semantic mesh reconstruction. We are currently also implementing DM and Open 3D (Zhou, Park, and Koltun) to combine programming and 3D point cloud processing through ML (Figure 7.11 A3-D5). A Point-Voxel Diffusion (PVD) model can resolve the usual incompleteness of 3D point clouds through a Gaussian noise diffusion prediction (Figure 7.11 A3-D4).[92] While enough 3D information comparable to the amount of 2D information becomes available to develop a comparable robust Big Data functionally, we aim at activating "AI" by developing our own 3D scan dataset in combination with other trained meta-data repositories.[93]

Through remote sensing, we can gather information through machine vision, activating physical signals such as LiDAR that through semiotic signs themselves also become units of measurement and digital signifiers that need to be indexed, critiqued, and displaced. The multiplicity of parallel processing in AI by stacking different types of layers through ANN, CNN, GANs, DM, and mathematical functions is through different means of information representation[94] and data translation between mathematical signals and signs.

Figure 7.10 Working through our image feeds of Gaudi, we recursively identified and displaced linguistic signs at the prompt level and semiotic signs through convolution, aiming at problematizing API and the MidJourney Black Box framework. DM uses style transfer learning from features on artists' and architects' styles. We declare here using our images of Gaudi's work, the dataset from MJ, and Gaudi's style as analysis-design research. "Ur-Realism AI" vertical Colònia Güell in New York City, Pablo Lorenzo-Eiroa text to image prompt engineering through grammar, MJ AI.

If the syntax and grammar of an architecture or visual arts project are based on the system of representation, if these signs and mathematical signals are not correlated between the input and output of the AI in ANN, a broken syntax and grammar will be the result of being displaced from the different signifiers and deep structures. But independently from matching input and output in ANN, parameters become represented through different measuring standards and translations to sub-symbolic signs adding biases to the computational layers in ANN. Different forms of computational processing, interfaces, and translations become interdependent, codependent, and

Computational Visual Semiotics 169

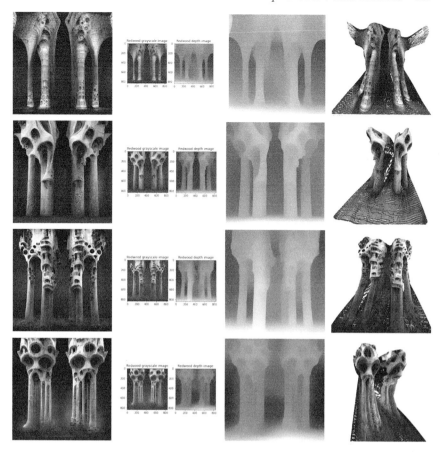

Figure 7.11 Point Clouds (0D), voxels (3D) and pixels (2D) are minimal sign units in digital representation. We cross relate DM as pixels minimum signs and point clouds minimum signs to make sense of them informationally and architecturally. Monocular Depth Estimation via Content-Adaptive multi-resolution merging to implement ML monocular machine vision from 2D MidJourney to a dynamic navigable 3D model. (See Notes Figure 7.11)

Figure 7.12 A1: Object tracking recognition. B1: ML semantic segmentation masking map layer. nyc.gov traffic and public cameras footing retrieved real time. Other mapping includes kinetic machine vision being able to recognize faces features and people movement and isolate from backgrounds. Research Studio Prof. Pablo Lorenzo-Eiroa, Student Kavya Sista, ARCH 701B, MS ACT Program, NYIT, F2021.

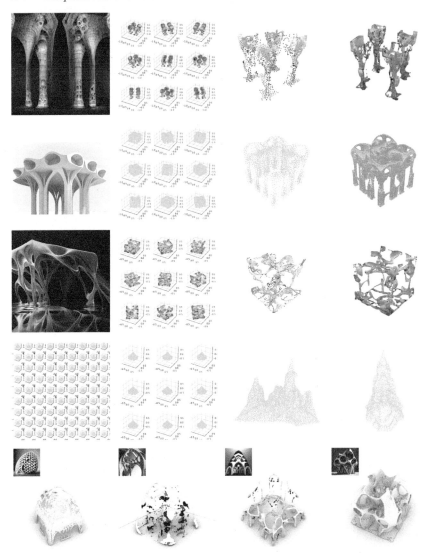

Figure 7.13 A Diffusion Model implementing thermodynamics diffuse 2D pixels into new 2D images and from 2D images into 3D point cloud models. We interpret 2D images into 3D models through generative DM. (See Notes Figure 7.13)

correlational independently from their means of translation of information actualization, making information theory prevalent and diminishing the autonomy of the mathematical, electronic, or sensing physical signal in relation to its Human-Computer Interaction (HCI) interface sign.

Non-Linguistic Computational Visual Semiotic: Displacing Signals, Signs, and Signifiers

We implemented digital strategies across *topographies of information* since 2002 through several interfaces using graphs, nodes, lines, surfaces, volumes, simulations, and others as means to compute formal information by processing visual semiotics physical signals and signs directly bypassing linguistic computation. We developed interfaces of information as topologies of information computing relationships across media and mediums. In order to bypass the determination of each intermediate interface structuring information across the available computational visual semiotic interfaces, we developed a visual emergent programming and a theory of form in relation to media. This strategy arguably is used also in Data Science by curve, surface, and form-fitting in prediction models, implementing the form as an interface for the processing of information by linear or logistic regression as well as others. A direct grammar strategy is also implemented as discussed by Shape Grammar. Graph Neural Networks perform programming based on 2D and 3D Graphs and node relationships. GANs can compute features through generative adversarial symbolic computation. Diffusion Models are able through thermodynamics to noise and denoise data predicting information through 2D pixels or 0D 3D points. Knot theory is able to compute in lower dimensional relational form algebraic relationships useful for higher dimensional surface topology. We implemented literally site-based computation through topographies of information to bypass zip-code-biased government data computing relationships through geology and the environment, further discussed in Chapters 15–19. Encryption can also be performed through visual cryptography through scrambled 2D and 3D graphs, pixels, voxels, and others. Visual algorithms such as Grasshopper Plug-In facilitated an intermediary plateau, by the packaging of linguistic code into sets of relational nodes, articulating input and output visually step by step through an informed parametric form. Form, formal logic, and grammar are able to process complex computations across interfaces, media, and mediums.

We discuss analog and digital computation, its genealogy, and transition. An analog signal is continuous, and the computation depends on the material mechanical parts to convey the accuracy of the computation. A digital signal is discontinuous. The advantage of information theory in replacing analog continuous signal processing is the reducibility into binary digital discontinuous electronic signal processing for the economics of encrypting and decrypting a message for transmission and computing processing economics. Digital electronic signals voltage bands closer to 0 and closer to 1 represent a sequence of data in discrete values in binary code 1-0 as bits of information. Shannon's noise as physical limitations in the communication channel was resolved by eliminating any noise on the electrical signal by caping the spectrum of the band width. The Fast Fourier Transformer (FFT) algorithm reduces a discrete digital mathematical signal to speed up processing, for instance, a digital image sign such as a pixel is reduced by 50% to process its pixels through the FFT. The Fourier Transformer (FT) works for analog physical

172 *Computational Visual Semiotics*

signals as it does not reduce the signal. Mathematical convolution in image processing through a Kernel or mask combines, for example, two mathematical signals to create three mathematical signals. The Reed-Solomon Code can, among multiple applications in encoding and decoding for data storage and transmission, describe a curve-mathematical signal as information, communicating point data in X, Y, and Z that is reconstituted as information reconstituting a curve.

Symbols at the programming language level activate operators at the assembly physical chipset electronic circuit level. Symbols enable arithmetic and algebra. Symbols enable primitive data to form human readability as identifiers activating variables, functions, and others. Symbolic computation enables arithmetic and algebra through recursive algorithms implementing alphanumeric signs. HCI activates through computer languages, interfaces, and software linguistic and visual semiotics. A computer sign becomes active in representing a human communicable message whether linguistic or visual in relation to making it computable. The digital establishes a separation between the electrical physical signal binary processing and the vectorial mathematical signal processing at the interface HCI level through sign processing. The advantage of separating signal processing from an indexical sign to a symbolic representational sign at the interface level may sometimes become problematic.

In computational visual semiotics, a vectorial signal representing a line vector projected on the computer screen is not a line. It is rather a series of HCI and computational signs, processed through mathematical signals, electronic signals, and vectorial signals that through linguistic computational sign–codes simulate a three-dimensional beam of light as a physical signal projected into a two-dimensional mathematical vectorial signal of the matrix-dot of the computer screen. The image-sign of this line is therefore a representation of an external binary calculation from its means of a constitution. Schematically, at the HCI level, a visual semiotic physical signal such as a LiDAR remote sensing surveys a space through XYZ RGB as a sign; a machine vision interprets semantics linguistic signs in the unstructured data; at the interface level, a visual sign such as a point, a line, a surface or a pixel computes a vectorial sign in 2D simulating 3D through mathematical signals such as functions and equations; which in turn activates a series of computational linguistic signs at the High-Level Language (HLL) that through symbolic operators compute electronic signals from the assembler translating Low-Level Language (LLL) to Machine Language (binary 1-0); at the chipset level computational processing activates discontinuous electrical signals for digital data communication computational processing. Various forms of arithmetic and algebra mathematical signal processing are applied and translated into signs through various techniques for filtering, calculating, weighting, and computing which are often derived from analog calculation.[95]

At the interface level, there are instances in which a sign becomes sub-symbolic, separating the computational task from its original sign processing, for instance when a voxel represents parts of a point cloud. This occurs across

computation out of a combinatory, efficiency in communication, and economic necessity, but the sign representing a sign is sometimes abused, becoming sub-symbolic through software and interfaces, computational languages, and often by Machine Learning (ML) in ANN layers. We identify when in computation there is an excessive separation, convolution, and loss between signal processing, its sign representation, and a sub-symbolic representational sign. Often in ML the excessive convolution and stacking of layers may reduce the mathematical signal processing and symbolic computational weighting to a representation of the sign, or a subsequential activation of a sub-symbolic sign through downsampling or signal decimation, separating the processing signal from the sign through a secondary or even tertiary symbolic sign. Sometimes this process does not reduce the mathematical signal. In computation, the index of the signal being processed becomes a symbolic sign, but adding excessive representations between problems to resolve, results in obscuring further the Blackbox problem of "AI", for instance, excessive processing translation symbolism, conventionalization, and naturalization of cultural ideologies turn into biases, lack of recognition of the representational interfaces, an excess in convolution, and an excessive energy consumption due to excessive signal translation.

Computational Visual Semiotics = Deconstruction Deep Structure System of Representation
Digital Signifier = Sign Deconstruction
Computational Grammatology = Decoded Expanded Digital Signifiers

Analog computational systems maintained a signal quality as a function of the calculation, describing a problem through the fidelity of a medium and materials but, in the best cases without the necessity of a translating sign. Digital computational systems relay on information encryption and decryption, translating the signal into a semiotic sign. We can identify a second corrected Visual Semiotics Topological Levels of Information relevant to architecture:

Level 0: Physical Electronic Signal Processing: Shannon's Mathematical Theory of Communication, electronic signal:
> 0–1 information BIT encoded message;
> Machine Language (0-1);
> Chipset or transistor electronic signal;

Level 1: Computational Signal Semiotics Information Gathering, Processing, Communication:
> Assembly Language LLL;
> Computational Semiotic Signal processing;
> Machine Vision LiDAR 3D Scanning light beam physical signal;
> Mathematical signal;

174 *Computational Visual Semiotics*

Level 2: Meta Computational Linguistic and Visual Semiotic Signs:
　　　　　　　　　Mathematical Signal; decimation;
　　　　　　　　　Meta–Data Repository;
　　　　　　　　　Simulation (Engine);
　　　　　　　　　Machine Learning;
　　　　　　　　　Meta–algorithms: self–editing algorithms;
　　　　　　　　　ANN training;
　　　　　　　　　Pixel–To–Pixel Diffusion Model (not simulation);
　　　　　　　　　Emergent Linguistic Programming;
　　　　　　　　　Emergent Visual Semiotic Programming;
　　　　　　　　　Agent–Based Modeling;
　　　　　　　　　Sub–symbolic sign (a sign of a sign);

Level 3: Computational Linguistic Semiotics Programming in relation to:
　　　　　　　　　Mathematical symbols;
　　　　　　　　　Symbolic Computation;
　　　　　　　　　Dataset, database;
　　　　　　　　　HLL Programming Languages;
　　　　　　　　　Message encryption–decryption;
　　　　　　　　　Computational Visual Semiotics Sign processing;
　　　　　　　　　Algorithms;
　　　　　　　　　Genetic Coding Algorithms;
　　　　　　　　　Information "visualization";

Level 4: Computational Linguistic and Visual Semiotics
　　　Interfaces, Systems of Representation:
　　　　　　　　　Cartesian Space;
　　　　　　　　　Projective Geometry;
　　　　　　　　　Perspective;
　　　　　　　　　Axonometric;
　　　　　　　　　Anamorphosis;
　　　　　　　　　Frontal Picture Plane;
　　　　　　　　　Mediated Information Flow;
　　　　　　　　　Shape Grammar;
　　　　　　　　　Multidimensional Space;

Level 5: Computational Index Visual and Physical Semiotic Experience:
　　　　　　　　　Perspective Haptic Space (Subject);
　　　　　　　　　Layered Space (Subject);
　　　　　　　　　Augmented Reality, Expanded Reality (Subject);
　　　　　　　　　Machine Haptic Space (Robotic Being);
　　　　　　　　　Affect;
　　　　　　　　　Virtual Reality, Augmented Reality; Mixed
　　　　　　　　　　　Reality;
　　　　　　　　　Simulation (of the real);
　　　　　　　　　Simulacra;

Toward a Visual Semiotics Grammatology[96] of Computation Through Nonlinear Emergent Programming

Panofsky implies indirect cross relationships between grammar linguistic structures and architecture spatial organization accrediting Aquinas' *Summa Theologica* as a hierarchical thesis structure to organize thinking thanks to the Gothic floorplan.[97] While we aim at displacing linguistics from visual semiotics, grammar in our language permeates through computation to an indexical digital object, more evident as discussed through NLP prompt engineering grammar activating HLL. But we can activate a visual semiotics theory by addressing non-linguistic visual grammar active in architecture and computational representation.

Architecture has historically advanced spatial representation thanks to influential exchanges with painting and art. Computation has established new representational paradigms that can be compared to the revolution of perspective in the Renaissance. But architects have now limited involvement in the background linguistic semiotic computational programming processes that are transforming the visual semiotic systems of representation that they work with every day. Architecture as computation can be therefore understood as an encoded system of communication in which linguistics, visual representation through visual semiotics, mathematical semiotic communication, and electronic signals activate architectural signification but understanding the translation of signs as a problem and aiming at pairing the signifier with the medium as a message.

Computer Representation =
Mathematical System of Communication + Computational Linguistic
Semiotics + Computational Visual Semiotics

Linguistic Semiotics
Linguistic Sign = Signifier
Computational Linguistics = Digital Linguistic Signifiers

Visual Semiotics
System of Representation = Symbolic Form Computational Visual
Semiotics = Electronic Signs-Signals as Digital Visual Signifiers

Software interfaces and codes constitute implicit frames where artistic expression begins. Computer software are based on computational languages, and they are themselves have become proto-architectural. If the structure is predetermined by the interface, the designer is merely interpreting a variation that completes the implicit combinations that the metaphysical project of the interface, placing the programmer as the ultimate author. While interfaces process information, at the same time they re-structure extrinsic content to fit its medium, activating a topological loop that in the end informs reality. Software is based on conventional assumptions about space, geometry, and perception. Software interfaces and codes constitute implicit frames where artistic expression begins. If the mediums of representation have such a power to regulate the work, then interfaces are spaces of differentiation. As such, interfaces can activate a performative aspect in the work, triggering a formal generative capacity. This would also critique the typification of the separation between aesthetics, politics, and abstract informational relationships since the form of communication (parergon) would be unique to the message (ergon).

This discussion aims at addressing two aspects of design in mediated computational representation: signs as originators of signifiers and de-sign as a method of critiquing such origination. By deconstructing and displacing systems of representation, we aim at elevating representation to an immanent semiotic problem, which may induce signification beyond its original objective rather than represent cultural meaning.

It is evident that software is culturally biased,[98] as it carries design agendas and as all these mechanisms are developed through personal decisions, cultural biases, omissions, and preferences, and therefore carry ideology. The form, structure, ideology, and aesthetics of the background computer space anticipate as it structures a type of project; therefore, artists and architects need to recover the utopian project of the 1970s and overcome its determination in the search for new philosophies of information, new cultural projects, new systems, new computational programming paradigms, new formal logical systems, new technologies, new robotics, new languages, new frameworks, and new digital signifiers that can open up possibilities for new expressions which necessarily include new aesthetics. In addition, computation needs to be deconstructed through linguistic and visual semiotics, including cultural criticism and philosophy of knowledge. During the first decades of digital representation artists and architects have been training their eyes to be able to recognize digital design's symbolic form, first indexing it involuntarily by exploring the possibilities of the new media, and then aiming at displacing such symbolic form's deep structure. Such a symbolic form references the interface's semiotic signifiers. There is a unique art intrinsic to each medium, material, communication, technique, reality, context, and frame that is only possible at a certain moment in time. Computation, focusing on linguistic translation eliminated this dimension in art, and the current digital revolution in computational visual semiotics is contingent upon this recognition. In general, the conventions of culture remain static in relation to computational visual semiotics except for some artists who developed their own media and computational language and interfaces.

A radical displacement often dismissed is that the floor plan constituted the logos of space, an organizational matrix that is not visual, as it may only be experienced. Within digital representation, the shift from the horizontal plateau of the drafting table to the vertical computer screen displaced the tectonics of the floor plan, activating a picture plane relationship, that assimilated architecture with the tectonics of cinema in which depth is defined by the Y-axis and not the vertical Z-axis which defines space. This promoted the exchanging of a structural logic that Palladio critically set up for a perceptive iconographic, image-based logic of the screen not only as media but also as a medium recovering back Brunelleschi's visual project.[99]

We develop a methodology which consists in first disclosing the deep structure of the system of representation, its semiotic apparatus, and thus displace the semiotic sign as a cultural project constructed by the programmer. The second objective derived from the first is to be able to displace the system of representation aiming toward developing an entirely novel system.

Toward a New Grammatology of Visual Semiotics Computation

We can define a preliminary hierarchy of visual semiotic structures in computation relevant to architecture:

1 Reference System (Cartesian, Topological, Multidimensional);
2 Measurement System (Metric, Imperial, Anthropocentric, Topographical, Topo-logos, Topology)
3 Mathematics (hindu-arabic decimal numbers); Language; Machine Language (binary 0-1)
4 LLL Low-Level Language; Assembly;
5 Meta-Structure (Meta-data, repository); Processing; ANN; CNN; Simulation Engine; Higher Dimensions (space);
6 HLL Computational Programming Language;
7 Deep Structure System of Representation (Perspective, Axonometric, Dynamic);
8 Grammar, Syntax;
9 Structure; Grid; Point, Particle, Line, Surface, Volume;
10 Organization internal to space-object (syntax space, organization, order);
11 Style (non-linguistic visual semiotics recognizable symbolic form);
12 Pattern visual emergent order; Feature Recognition;
13 Semiotic Perceptual (Subjective, Experience, Communication in terms of Signification, Semantics);
14 Affect; reification[100];
15 Augmented Reality-Mixed Reality;
16 Virtual Reality;
17 Simulation (of the real);
18 Simulacra (discussed in Chapter 19);

We discussed the conflict between linguistic conception and artistic innuendo. We aim at developing an architecture of information through visual semiotics analyzing, displacing, and deconstructing linguistic determination, to challenge the limitations of thinking architecture ideas, concepts, grammar, and syntax structured by natural language, activating a visual grammatology of computation. Visual communication is composed of several subsystems: from the apparatus of representation to the frame that defines the media interface or the medium, to formal, iconographic recognizable features, and visual logic through sensible signs and mathematical signals, to

178 *Computational Visual Semiotics*

physical signals and experience. A system of representation by structuring the form of an object, by representing it produces a type of object. The signifier becomes that embedded meaning constructing objects independently from what it was its original sign function.

Fuller identifies software as an ideology being critical of the commercial distribution of software.[101] Fuller proposes that to change something, one should make the existing model obsolete activating the discussed disruptive creative destruction cycles of Capitalism in our introduction. Computational visual semiotics can resolve a mathematical vectorial signal-based computation indexical of the interface sign to displace the signifier in relation to the poetics of the message system. We later discuss a change from sign to signal, as a computational linguistic sign can become a computational physical signal as a form of information actualization in fabrication.

> DESIGN = DE-SIGN
> architecture = grammar
> (Against technological determinism)
> sign = constructed to communicate
> de-sign = deconstructive creative process
> Sign = becoming unmotivated
> (grammatology)

Analog computers are not universal as their output values can range given the physical conditions of the mechanism and environmental conditions that can vary and affect the calculations. With current advances in processing efficiency in ANN in relation to the amount of energy needed, time, and computing resources, developers are reformulating them through analog computing. By matching the type of task necessary with the type of mathematical signal needed for processing, analog computing is addressing an aspect of our criticism of translation, by matching the physical signal processing needed and the medium energy needed for the computation, pairing message, signal, medium, and computation. Analog Deep Learning chips[102] based on photons, materials, or organisms through Biological Neural Networks (BNN) are being used for non-binary signal parallel massive computing power resources and energy reduction due to the advantage of the close relationship between the computing biological signal impulse, the mathematics implicit in the biological signal as analog computation achievable through the form of the neural model, the program/interface, and the HCI signs necessary to process and communicate input and output. This process is also activating the necessity to pair computation with an environmental computational engine, later discussed in Chapters 15–17.

In *The Order of Things*[103] Foucault references Borges' questioning of taxonomies addressing the necessary disambiguation to overcome linguistic barriers, claiming as a conclusion that a universal language, such as computation as a universal communication system, would not be able to get rid of arbitrariness and therefore is positivistic naïve. All systems produce objects as they structure reality anticipating their computing output–functional purpose. Interfaces are media that activate symbolic form within its interface–frame space, as the form is indexed by the system, activating a loop between information and representation where digital signs as signifiers induce a structure:

"Form: in:form" = "Form Follows Information"

For Kittler[104] in "there is no software" programmability is not related to software as a grammatology of text is derived into a non-disclosed electronic signifier, proposing the elimination of software as a distancing between the hardware black box reduction of the world. Hasslacher[105] argues for the reduction of algorithms at the compiler to a discrete representation of the original problem decoded into a string of binary code signs identifying radix arithmetic as the only continuous signs for weighting bits unequally. We claim a computational grammatology by addressing representation as a form of performance in which the signal and coding as well as the signifiers active are part of the message–unified system of communication avoiding or at least problematizing information "representation" downsampling as a form of translation between digital signs and conventionalization naturalization of systems of representation. ANN by the function of Data Science numeric standardization translation of reality for statistical model fitting is sign–reductive.

We aim for a grammatology of computation through information signs, mathematical, sensing, and electronic signals to decode and displace digital signifiers in relation to architecture language. An architectural machine comparable to Terragni's, Palladio's, or Gaudi's through Rainaldi's ahistorical synthesis discussed in Chapters 2-4 can only happen after such a process, as computational visual semiotics can disseminate implicit linguistics from natural language, opening to an architecture implicit to computation as a new semiotic expression and signification.

We predicted back in 2008-13 the necessity to critique linear bifurcating reversible tree-like computational structures addressing the apparent complexity of architecture form in relation to the stability and conventions in the representation of background computational interfaces and processing structures (Figure 7.14).[106] Usually, architects work out post-structuralist complex geometry without addressing the tree-like structure bifurcating linearity of the reversible algorithms they implement (Figure 7.14 D1, D2, D3). We identified the necessity to displace linear hierarchical reversible algorithmic structures to activate parallel nonlinear processing activating a lattice (Figure 7.14 E2), able to correlate algorithms through ANN evolutionary morphogenetic structures that through self-editing algorithms may exponentially evolve into morphogenesis. In addition, by pairing Deleuze's rhizome as a critique of linguistic signs to computational processing structures, a rhizome may become active bypassing linear evolutionary cycles through virus corruption as a form of nonlinear program expanding the role of thermodynamics in Diffusion Models (DM) and Generative Adversarial Networks (GANs). We predicted the functional value of Big Data in relation to processing structures through topographies of information. We also identified the necessity of incorporating in data and information processing non-hierarchical network structures, a decentralized form of network authority as a Blockchain diagram (Figure 7.14 E1). In order to address uncertainty as a paradigm brought by thermodynamics, we need to displace anticipatory structures in computation for emergent structures, an AI through parallel processing activating emergent programming in ANN (Figure 7.14 E2). As Big Data, DM, GANs, and in general ANN present the opportunity to develop emergent

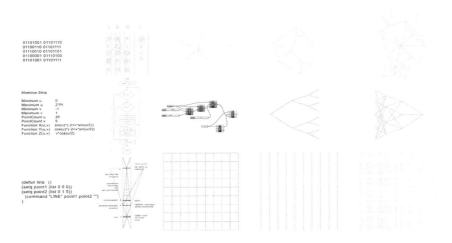

Figure 7.14 Moving from reversible linear bifurcating algorithms to multidimensional information systems displacing their structure. Information representation structures in computation. Self-editing algorithms through computational linguistics that recognize their own language to optimize themselves can activate mutating algorithms that can evolve to change their structure exponentially and multidimensionally through deep learning. A1: binary code; B1: genetic code as algorithm; C1: hierarchical radial organization; D1: bypassed radial organization; D1: non-hierarchical network structure as Blockchain diagram. A2: Mathematical geometric surface plot scripting, B2: flow chart analog algorithm; C2: grasshopper visual algorithm, D2: grammar structure and bifurcating algorithmic structure; E2: lattice structure parallel processing Artificial Neural Networks. Christopher Alexander's diagrams interpretation is applied here to computational and data structures. Toward evolutionary non-bifurcating structures through virus corruption activating a rhizome. A3: Lisp script, B3: perspective-interface, C3: grid, D3: linear organization structure, E3: logarithmic grid. Pablo Lorenzo-Eiroa, 2008.

programming, the structure of the ANN would have to evolve exponentially non-linearly by corrupting its own structure through viruses to mutate beyond its bifurcating reference structure as it activates emergent programming and signifiers, turning the morphogenetic structure into a rhizomatic resonance machine.

Notes

1 Barthes, R. *Elements of Semiology*, Hill and Wang, 1968 [orig.1964]
2 Nash, K. ART 1 "Computer Program for Artists" 1969, in *Leonardo, International Society for the Arts, Sciences, and Technology*, Volume. 3, Pergamon Press, 1970
3 McLean, C.A. "Artists-Programmers and Programming Languages for the Arts", Thesis, University of London, 2011
4 Montagu, A. "From Graphical Computation to Present CAD Systems (1966–98)", *SIGRADI*, 1998
5 Kotsioris, E. "The Computer Misfits", in ed.Colomina, B., Galan, I., Kotsioris, E. and Meister, A.M., *Radical Pedagogies*, MIT, Cambridge, 2022
6 Montagu, A. "The D-Mac-Graphomat System" *RIBA*, London, 1968
7 Gordon Pask. 'The Architectural Relevance of Cybernetics', in *Architectural Design*, No 7/6, John Wiley, London, 1969
8 Prusinkiewicz, P.; Lindenmayer, A. "Graphical Modeling Using L-Systems", in *The Algorithmic Beauty of Plants*, Springer, New York, 1990
9 Prusinkiewicz, P. "Graphical Applications of L-Systems", *Proc. Graphic Interface*, 1986
10 Madelbrot, B. *The Fractal Geometry of Nature*, Henry Holt, New York, 1983
11 Weinzapfel, G.; Johnson, T.E.; Perkins, J. "Image: An Interactive Computer System for Multi-Constrained Spatial Synthesis", *Proceedings of the 8th Design Automation Workshop*, 1971
12 Negroponte, N.; Weinzapfel, G. "Architecture-by-Yourself", *Siggraph*, 1976
13 Vardouli, T. ""Architecture-by-Yourself": Early Studies in Computer-Aided Participatory Design", SMArchS Design and Computation, MIT, Cambridge, 2010
14 Hillier B. *Space is the Machine*, Cambridge University Press, Cambridge, 1999 [orig. 1996]
15 Hillier, B.; Hanson, J. *The Social Logic of Space*, Cambridge University Press, Cambridge, 1984
16 Stiny, G.; Gips, J. "Shape Grammars and the Generative Specification of Painting and Sculpture", in *IFIP*, 1971
17 Stiny, G. *Pictorial and Formal Aspects of Shape and Shape Grammars, On Computer Generation of Aesthetic Objects*, Springer Basel AG, 1975
18 Stiny, G.; Mitchell W.J. "The Palladian Grammar", in *Environment and Planning B*, Volume 5, UK, 1978
19 McLean, A.; Wiggins, G. "Texture: Visual Notation For Live Coding Of Pattern", *Centre for Cognition, Computation and Culture*, University of London, London, 2015
20 Brachman, S. "CAFC Affirms Invalidity of Geographic Map Visualization Patent Asserted Against Google Earth", *ipwatchdog*, 2017
21 Berger, John. *Ways of Seeing*, Pinguin Books, London, 1990
22 Mitchell, W.J. and McCullough, M. *Digital Design Media*, John Wiley & Son, New York, 1995
23 Mitchell, W. *City of Bits: Space, Place and the Infobahn*, MIT Press, Cambridge, 1995

182   *Computational Visual Semiotics*

24 Delanda, M. *A Thousand Years of Nonlinear History*, Zone Books, New York, 1997

25 Schumacher, P. *The Autopoiesis of Architecture*, Volume I (2011) and II (2012), Wiley, London, 2012

26 Corner, J.; MacLean, A.; Van Valkenburgh M. *Taking Measurements Across the American Landscape*, Yale University Press, New Haven, 1996

27 Mostafavi, M.; Najle, C., eds. *Landscape Urbanism: A Manual for the Machinic Landscape,* AA, London 2004

28 Estévez, A.T. "Application of Life Information in Architecture", in ed. Sprecher, A., Yeshayahu, S. and Lorenzo-Eiroa, P., *Life In Formation,* ACADIA, New York, 2010

29 Werner, L. ed. "Cybernetics: State of the Art", in *Con-Versations*, TU Berlin, Berlin, 2017

30 Lorenzo-Eiroa, P. "Post-Digital as Design Authorship Expansion, Review of Lynn's "Archeology of the Digital" Exhibition at Yale School of Architecture", in ed. Rapaport, N., *Constructs*, Yale University School of Architecture, New Haven, 2017

31 Cache, B. *Earth Moves*, ed. Davidson, C. Writing Architecture Series, MIT Press, Cambridge, 1995

32 Legendre, G. *ijp: The Book of Surfaces*, AA, London, 2004

33 Lally, S.; Young, J. *Softspace: From a Representation of Form to a Simulation of Space*, Routledge, London, 2006

34 Clément, G.; Rahm, P. *Environment: Approaches for Tomorrow* [Environ(ne)ment], CCA, 2006

35 Dwyre, C.; Perry, C.; Salomon, D.; Velikov, K. *Ambiguous Territory: Architecture, Landscape, and the Postnatural,* Actar, New York, 2022

36 Roche, F. "An Architecture des Humeurs", in ed. Lorenzo-Eiroa, P. and Sprecher, A., *Architecture in Formation*, Routledge, London 2013

37 Mingers, J. *Self-Producing Systems, Implications and Applications of Autopoiseis*, Plenum Press, New York, 1995

38 DeJong, K. "An Analysis of the Behavior of a Class of Genetic Adaptive Systems", Dissertation, Department of Computer and Communication Sciences, University of Michigan, Ann Arbor, 1975

39 Couzin, I.D.; Krause, J. "Self-Organization and Collective Behavior in Vertebrates", in *Advances in the Study of Behavior,* Volume 32, 2003

40 Frazer, John. *Evolutionary Architecture*, AA, London, 2009

41 Weinstock, M.; Hensel, M.; Menges, A. *Emergence: Morphogenetic Design Strategies,* Wiley, London 2004

42 Weinstock, M. *The Architecture of Emergence*, Wiley, London, 2010

43 Leach, N. "Digital Morphogenesis", *Architectural Design*, Volume 79, Issue 1, John Wiley & Sons, Ltd., 2009

44 Gerber, D.J.; Pantazis, E.; Wang A. "A Multi-Agent Approach For Performance Based Architecture", in Automation in Construction 76, Elsevier, 2017 (pp. 45–58)

45 Spyropoulos, T. *Adaptive Ecologies: Correlated Systems of Living,* ACTAR, 2012

46 Snooks, R. "Closeness: On The Relationship of Multi-agent Algorithms and Robotic Fabrication", in Dagmar Reinhardt, D.; Saunders, R.; Burry, J. *Robotic Fabrication in Architecture*, Art and Design, 2016

47 Beni, G.; Wang, J. "Swarm Intelligence in Cellular Robotic Systems", in *NATO Advanced Workshop on Robots and Biological Systems,* Ciocco, 1989

48 Stuart Smith, R. "Behavioral Production: Autonomous Swarm-Constructed Architecture*"*, in *Architectural Design*, Volume 86, 2016

49 Sugihara, S. "Igeo", *ACADIA*, 2014

50 Deleuze, G.; Guattari, F. *A Thousand Plateaus. Capitalism and Schizophrenia*, The University of Minnesota Press, Minneapolis, 1987.

51 Radford, A.; Metz, L.; Chintala, S. "Unsupervised Representation Learning with Deep Convolutional Generative Adversarial Networks", arXiv preprint arXiv:1511.06434, 2016

52 Rahbar, M.; Mahdavinejad, M.; Bemanian, M.; Markazi, D. and Hovestadt, L. "Generating Synthetic Space Allocation Probability Layouts Based on Trained Conditional-GANs", in *Applied Artificial Intelligence* 33, no. 8, Routledge, 2019

53 Chaillou Stanislas. "AI + Architecture", Harvard GSD, Cambridge, 2019

54 Leach, N. *Architecture in the Age of Artificial Intelligence*, Bloomsbury, London, 2022

55 Mortenson, M.E. *Mathematics for Computer Graphics Applications*, Industrial Press Inc, Norwalk, 1999

56 Lorenz, E. "The Statistical Prediction of Solutions of Dynamic Equations", *Proceedings of the International Symposium on Numerical Weather Prediction*, 1962 [orig. 1960]

57 Hartnett, K. "What Makes the Hardest Equations in Physics So Difficult?", in *Quanta Magazine,* 2018

58 Prigogine, I.; Stengers, I. *The End of Certainty*, The Free Press, New York, 1997

59 Retsin, G.; Jimenez Garcia, M.; Soler, V. "Discrete Computational For Additive Manufacturing", UCL Press, London, 2017

60 Dessault Systemes Spatial Team. "The Main Benefits and Disadvantages of Voxel Modeling", 2019

61 Hegemann, F.; Manickam, P.; Lehner, K.; Koch, C. "A Hybrid Ground Data Model for Interacting Simulations in Mechanized Tunneling", in *Journal of Computing in Civil Engineering*, Volume 27, Issue 6, 2013

62 Poux, F.; Billen, R. "Voxel-based 3D Point Cloud Semantic Segmentation", University of Liège, 2019

63 Bader, C.; Kolb, D.; Weaver, J.C.; Sharma, S.; Hosny, A; Costa, J.; Oxman, N. "Making Data Matter", in *Advances in Science,* Science Magazine, 2020

64 Scimeca, D. "4D Tracking System Recognizes the Actions of Dozens of People Simultaneously in Real Time", in *Visions Systems Design*, 2019

65 Edl, Milan; Mizerák, Marek; Trojan, Jozef. "3d Laser Scanners: History and Applications", in *International Scientific Journal about Simulation*, Volume 4, 2018

66 Tang, P.; Huber, D.; Akinci, B.; Lipman, R.; Lytle, A. "Automatic Reconstruction of as-Built Building Information Models from Laser-Scanned Point Clouds", in *Automation in Construction*, Volume 19, Issue 7, 2010

67 Lorenzo-Eiroa, P. "Multidimensional Space: From Perspective to Big Data", in ed. Marcos, C., *Graphic Imprints*, Springer, Alicante, 2018

68 Zwierzcki, M. "Parametric Architectural Design with Point-clouds – Volvox", Proceedings of the 34th eCAADe, Vol 2, 2016

69 Goodfellow, I.; Pouget-Abadie, J.; Mirza, M.; et al. "Generative Adversarial Nets", in *Proceedings of the International Conference on Neural Information Processing Systems*, 2014

70 Zhu, J.Y.; Park, T.; Isola, P.; Efros, A. "Unpaired Image-to-Image Translation using Cycle-Consistent Adversarial Networks", *BAIR Laboratory*, UC Berkeley, Berkley, 2020

71 Marcheggiani, D. and Titov, I. "Encoding Sentences with Graph Convolutional Networks for Semantic Role Labeling" arXiv:1703.04826v4, 2017

72 Joshi, C.; Dwivedi, V.P.; Bresson, X. "Spatial Graph ConvNets" NTU Graph Learning Lab, Sep 17, 2019

73 Esser, P.; Rombach, R.; Ommer, B. "Taming Transformers for High-Resolution Image Synthesis" *arXiv*, 2021

84   Computational Visual Semiotics

74   Lewis, M.; Liu, Y.; Goyal, N.; Ghazvininejad, M.; Mohamed, et al. "BART: Denoising Sequence-to-Sequence Pretraining for Natural Language Generation, Translation, and Comprehension", in *Annual Meeting of the Association for Computational Linguistics*, 2020

75   Radford, A.; Wook Kim, J.; Hallacy, C.; Ramesh, A.; et al. "Learning Transferable Visual Models from Natural Language Supervision", in *International Conference on Machine Learning*, 2021

76   Romero, A. "DALL-E 2, Explained: The Promise and Limitations of a Revolutionary AI", in *Towards Data Science*, June 16, 2022

77   Rombach, R.; Blattmann, A.; Lorenz, D.; et al. "High-Resolution Image Synthesis with Latent Diffusion Models", arXiv:2112.10752v2, 2022

78   Chen, M.; Radford, A.; Child, R.; Wu, J.; Jun, H.; et al. "Generative Pretraining from Pixels", *PMLR*, 2021

79   Croitoru, F.; Hondru, V.; Ionescu, R. et all "Diffusion Models in Vision: A Survey", *arXiv*: 2209.0474v1, 10 Sept, 2022

80   O'Connor, R. "Introduction to Diffusion Models for Machine Learning", *Assembly AI*, 2022

81   Julesz, B. "Visual Pattern Discrimination", in *IRE Transactions on Information Theory*, Volume 8, Issue 2, 1962

82   Manovich, Lev. *The Language of New Media*, MIT, Cambridge, 2002

83   Godard, J.L. *Meetin' WA*, Film-Interview, New York, 1986

84   Godard, J.L. *Adieu au langage*, Film, Canal+, France-Switzerland, 2014

85   Fan, H.; Su, H.; Guibas, L. "A Point Set Generation Network for 3D Object Reconstruction from a Single Image", *Proceedings IEEE*, Xplore, 2017

86   Denninger, M.; Triebel, R. "3D Scene Reconstruction from a Single Viewport", *ECCV*, 2020

87   Gao, J.; Shen, T.; Want, Z; et al. "GET3D", *arXiv*, 2022

88   IBM Munnich Headquarters IoT Project, 2017

89   Qi, C.R.; Yi Li, S.H.; Guibas, L.J. "Pointnet++: Deep Hierarchical Feature Learning on Point Sets in a Metric Space", arXiv, 2017

90   Zhou, Y.; Tuzel, O.; "VoxelNet", *IEEE CVPR*, 2018

91   Hughes, N.; Chang, Y. Carlone, L. "Hydra", in *LIDS*, MIT, Cambridge, 2022

92   Zhou, L.; Du, Y.; Wu, J. "3D Shape Generation and Completion through Point-Voxel Diffusion", arXiv, 2021

93   Qi, C.; Su, R.; Hao, M.; Guibas, K.; Leonidas J. "PointNet", in *IEEE CVPR*, 2017

94   Armeni, I.; Sax, A.; Zamir, A.R.; Savarese, S. *Joint 2D-3D-Semantic Data for Indoor Scene Understanding*, Stanford University, Berkeley, 2017

95   Hoffmann, M. "Digital Signal Processing Mathematics", *CERN Document Server*, 2008

96   Derrida, J. *Of Gramatology*, trans. Spivak, G.C. John Hopkins University Press, Baltimore, 1997. [Orig. 1967]

97   Panofsky, Erwin. *Gothic Architecture and Scholasticism*, Meridian Books and Penguin, New York, 1957 [orig.1951]

98   Lorenzo-Eiroa, P. "ACADIA 2010 Conference Life in: Formation", in *At Cooper Newsletter*, The Cooper Union School of Architecture, New York, 2011

99   Lorenzo-Eiroa, P. "Informing a Critical Digital Architecture Autonomy Into Life", in ed. Sprecher, A., Yeshayahu, S. and Lorenzo-Eiroa, P. *ACADIA 2010 Conference Proceedings*, New York, 2010

100 Deleuze, G. *Francis Bacon: The Logic of Sensation*, University of Minnesota Press, Minneapolis, 2002 [orig. 1981]

101 Fuller, M. *Behind the Blip*, Autonomedia, Canada, 2003

Computational Visual Semiotics 185

102 Zewe, A. "New Hardware Offers Faster Computation for Artificial Intelligence, with Much Less Energy", MIT News Office, Cambridge, 2022
103 Foucault, M. *The Order of Things,* Vintage Books, New York, 1973 [orig. 1966]
104 Kittler, F.A. "16. There Is No Software", in Kittler, F.A. *The Truth of the Technological World*, Stanford University Press, Palo Alto, 2014
105 Hasslacher, B. "Beyond the Turing Machine" in Herken, *The Universal Turing Machine: A Half-Century Survey*, Oxford University Press, New York, 1988
106 Lorenzo-Eiroa, P. "Form In:Form: On The Relationship Between Digital Signifiers and Formal Autonomy", in ed. Lorenzo-Eiroa, P.; Sprecher, A., *Architecture in Formation*, Routledge, London, 2013

Figure 7.11 Diffusion Models (DM) use thermodynamic noise and denoise functions applying maximum likelihood estimation to optimize parameters in the model. DM scramble pixels into noise and apply thermodynamics to diffuse them back into information applying von Neumann's concept to resolve order out of disorder. Point Clouds (0D), voxels (3D) and pixels (2D) are minimal sign units in digital representation. We cross relate DM as pixels minimum signs and point clouds minimum signs to make sense of them informationally and architecturally. A1, A2, A3, A4: Gaudi's NYC NLP sub-symbolic pixel-topixel Diffusion Model, MidJourney (MJ). D1, D2, D3, D4: Third Sub-symbolic level machine vision 3D point cloud sub-symbolic photogrammetry from a single 2D image. Monocular Depth Estimation via Content-Adaptive multi-resolution merging to implement ML monocular machine vision from 2D MidJourney to a dynamic navigable 3D model. Monocular Vision AI processing through setting perspectival camera, angle and depth of field in relation to depth recognition mapping shader (Chapter 12). B1, C1, B2, C2, B3, C3, B4, C4: Machine Vision training depth recognition and processing point cloud through CNN. PI Pablo Lorenzo-Eiroa, RA Kavya Sista, IDC Foundation Grant, 2022.

Figure 7.13 We discussed how a 2D DM image can simulate a 3D model but also a 3D program, for instance activating CFD and structural simulation (Chapter 6, figures 6.7 and 6.8). We also discuss in this Chapter the advantages of Information Theory regarding information message transmission and processing as well as the problematic excessive mathematical signal decimation and translation between signals and systems of measurement, particularly through ANNs. ANN are activation functions, and weights are mathematical signal attenuations and decimations of funneled data. This allows different types of signals to be combined and extrapolated. But several issues can be identified in DNN, ANN and CNN, from vanishing gradients due to the depth of the NN in backpropagation; to overfitting in training data; to the hidden layer interpretation function and emergence; to excessive energy consumption. One of the problems we identify in Information Theory is the weighted relevance of the semantic meaning of the message over the grammar, syntax and structure given by the form of communication, media, and medium processing and actualizing the message. We hereby include NLP to 2D, 2D to 3D, NLP to 3D and 3D to 3D information processing through AI Machine Vision reconstruction. We cross reference 2D pixels arranged in 2D space and 0D point clouds arranged in 3D space. A Diffusion Model implementing thermodynamics diffuse 2D pixels into new 2D images and from 2D images into 3D point cloud models. We interpret 2D images into 3D models through generative DM. A1-D3: 2D to 3D AI, MidJourney DM 2D image to 3D point cloud and mesh approximation through AI machine vision fully reconstructing navigable 3D model. Model training over ShapeNet (Stanford and Princeton Universities), PointNet++ repositories and of our own. We run more than 50 models: in 80% of the ML training of the external repository (ShapeNet Princeton) with less than 20 training epochs, the point cloud reconstruction failed; in 10% the reconstructed point cloud was stretched to match the training reference plot matrix as in A3-D3 due to low epoch training; 10% of the times the overall form was 3D predicted in less than 20 epochs, privileging in the bias objects over frame-spaces, as the point cloud repository is mostly trained by sematic classifiers to identify conventional everyday objects. Conventional objects conflict architecture often in search to displace conventional identifiable categories. In our generated repositories with benchmarks including ML supervised 3D point cloud classification, non-supervised 3D point cloud segmentation based on both classifiers and features through the DM. The first 20 training epochs did not predict the 3D model; after 50 epochs the bias of the repository weighted in, such as columns, arches, beams that were not in the 2D image; after 80 epochs hybrid prediction categories such as arches combined into new figures predicting features in the 2D image; after 100 epochs new hybrid typologies were predicted from the 2D image into the 3D point cloud. Pablo Lorenzo-Eiroa, MJ and Point-e, 2022.

Other techniques based on object reconstruction from 2D to 3D include shape prediction via distant render estimation but based on multiple images from multiple view points and not a single image, a technology analogue to photogrammetry by mesh optimization developed by Vicini, D.; Speierer, S.; Jakob, W. "Differentiable Signed Distance Function Rendering" in Transactions on Graphics, SIGGRAPH, 40 vol.4, 2022.

A4-D4: Point-e Open AI NLP prompt to 3D point cloud DM, implementing CLIP, transformer, and predictor based on supervised ML classification tagged seed images, and from 40M to 1B model parameters (Open Source Data Science), problematically reconstructing point clouds from rendered 3D models, therefore subsymbolic indexical of the mesh surface. PointNet accuracy has been reported on around 60% with an increase to 90% with Automated Heritage Building Information Modelling (HBIM) by Haznedar, Bayraktar, Ozturk, Arayici, Springer 2023. Pablo Lorenzo-Eiroa, Point-e, 2022. A5-D5: 2D DM to 3D Point Cloud, ARCH 782, NYIT, PI Pablo Lorenzo-Eiroa, RA Beken Amde, IDC Foundation Grant Research, RS Tharoonaskar Baskaran; RS Mahima Kulkarni, S2023.

8 Displacing Origination by Digital Signifiers from Computation to AI

Methodology:
Information Theory; Topology;

Visual Semiotics Systems of Representation:
Point; Line; Surface; Volume; Grids; Cartesian Space; Topology; Projective Geometry;

Computational Visual Semiotic Signifiers:
Node; Pixel; Point; Vector; Cells; Voxels; NURBS Curves, NURBS Surfaces;

Expanding Computational Visual Semiotic Signifiers[1]: From a Linguistic Syntax to a Computational Grammatology

Computation presupposes and naturalizes an artificial origin anticipatory of the range of possibilities of its matrix-space interfaces which become proto-architectural media. We propose to displace the origination of computational signs which become anticipatory to architecture and develop a new minimal architecture of computation. We attempt to resolve the futility of formalisms that through excess attempt to reclaim authorship in computation not able to match the topological information level where the struggle is. According to Derrida,[2] there is no traceable origin in our society and there is no meaning or transcendental signifier or truth but we are at the intersection of traces of a palimpsest. As architecture aims to create "original" matrices-realities through novel spatial typologies, is confronted with the artificial origination imposed by digital signs defining digital matrix-spaces which end up becoming digital signifiers to architecture, by anticipating, predefining and therefore limiting architecture advancement in revolutionizing sedimented spatial conventions (Figure 8.1).

Computation has marked another Renaissance or an end to the post-structuralism of the second half of the twentieth century since it imposes structuralism through artificial abstract "tabula rasa" origins. Any architectural process must overcome the arbitrariness of the point of departure whether is imposed or emergent. Digital architects have already addressed the critique of utilizing generic, typological structures through their use of progressive,

DOI: 10.4324/9781003292036-9

188 *Displacing Artificial Origination by Digital Signifiers*

topological displacements. But these displacements need to go further. This suggests a series of implied conclusions with a critical understanding of the relationship between typology and topology. To address the relationship between computational structures projecting or determining spatial typologies, architects also must recognize, analyze and displace the digital signs that become signifiers of architecture. A grammatology of the digital signifier is necessary when dealing with platforms, interfaces, and computer software in which one would be able to both read, analyze, critique, and displace an emergent signifier through the source code. Human-Computer Interaction (HCI) signs are defined by minimum BITs units for the economics of computational processing. Computer representation has induced a groundless matrix that originates architecture through a dynamically equal XYZ navigable virtual space-frame. Information processing by defining the protocols through code-source and vectorial signs that actualize them necessarily standardizes, homogenizes, and parameterizes form through geometry and by extension, the representational space-matrix in which form originates. This process becomes more problematic nowadays in the excessive stacking and exchangeability of digital information among layers in AI ANN through reduction, decimation, downsampling exchanging, and translating between different signals and reference systems.

We described, analyzed, and disclosed the computational linguistic digital signifiers and the computational visual semiotics digital signifiers that become active as vectorial originating signs through interfaces, software, frameworks, algorithms, parallel processing, and Artificial Neural Networks in Chapters 5, 6, and 7.

Digital Signifiers and The Politics of Representation

We previously discussed the anticipatory quality of computer science in solving problems through algorithms being currently challenged by emergent programming and data science. In computational interfaces, the content to be represented is extrinsic to an anticipatory computational medium. We critique Evan's translation[3] between representational media through McLuhan's media determinism, as we develop a criticism of the idea of translation in computational representation between signals, signs, and reference systems. We argue that if there is content that can be translated through different systems of representation this content is not media specific, and therefore the interfaces nor the emergent signifiers would not be able to be displaced as they become sub-symbolic through translation. In this context, it is interesting to raise a contrasting problem: how mediums of representation produce signification and therefore induce content. We aim at activating unique meaning that cannot be possible in another medium or media,[4] a poetics of architecture in which the visual semiotics, style, grammar, and system of representation, become actualizations that recognize the context frame as unique forms of expressions. Representation implies empowerment, the creation of a signifier which is independent of what it is representing, and the emergence of an independent immanent object. If the signifier is determined

Displacing Artificial Origination by Digital Signifiers 189

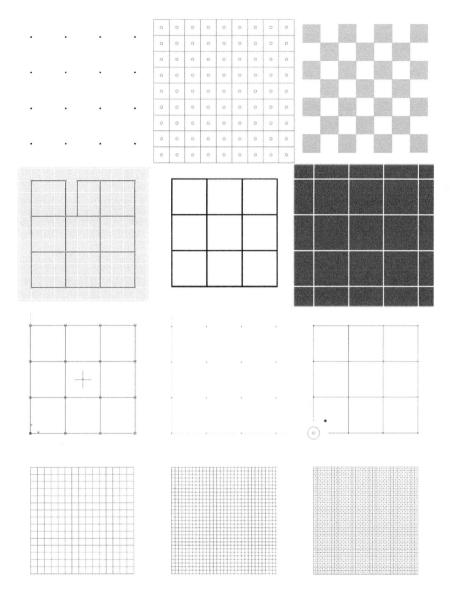

Figure 8.1 Different interfaces propose ideologies to structure background spaceframes, understanding reality through their deep symbolic structure defining ideas about the real, and projecting digital signs which become originating signifiers. The syntax of architecture previously defined by representation through plans, sections, axonometric and perspective is now regimented by the grammar possible by digital signifiers in relation to the computability model structure of the framework. (See Notes Figure 8.1)

by the interface, the message is already scripted. Representation is usually thought of as fiction, but fiction is often more powerful than reality: it defines a political agenda by projecting a way to see reality through representation. Representation is dependent on systems of representation that project a symbolic form and that define a deep structure. In artistic disciplines, it becomes problematic when there is no representational agenda, such as when the content represented is extrinsic to the performance of its medium-frame.

Any new disciplinary exploration is based on the recognition of the potential of new ways of seeing. The problem is when new visualization ideas are based on similar representational strategies with identical background linguistic semiotic codes that project a visual semiotic structure through grammar. The recognition of this transdisciplinary field would necessarily expand the boundaries of the disciplines involved as well as initiate new discourses on representation. This presents an agency that becomes active by promoting, critiquing, or resisting the implicit agendas in computational systems of representation that are common across different disciplines. Digital representation created a revolution in architecture, the structuralism of which has not yet been displaced (Figure 8.1).

The implicit project in parametric variations in architecture is to resolve within relative topological displacements such as a structural typological change that can critique and transcend the departing implicit or explicit organizational structure (Figure 8.2). This should be extended to systems of measurement and reference, such as background originating space-frames and digital signs. A defined spatial typology can be critiqued through a topological parametric displacement. In the proposed project, the original digital signifier that originates the grid space becomes an ambiguous sign, a quali-sign

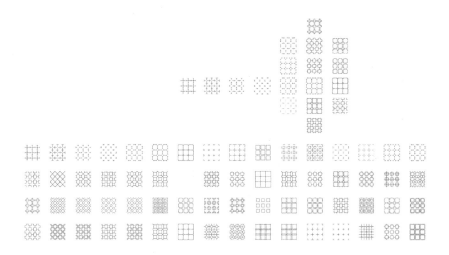

Figure 8.2 Nine square grid topological degree variations in relation to categorical Typological change. Coordinator and Associate Prof. Pablo Lorenzo Eiroa, Assistant Prof. James Lowder and Intructor Katerina Kourkuola; student: Sehee Lee, The Cooper Union, Design II, F2012.

Displacing Artificial Origination by Digital Signifiers 191

through displacing it as a parameter (Figure 8.3). The space of the grid is first referenced by a nondimensional abstract scale-less infinite vector, and then as a limit defining it as a space setting a scale and a dimension. The resolution and scale that defines the vector of the grid become fixed and then a spatial reference as well. By these means, the project makes relative its departing parameter and therefore any reference to spatial containment and organization. The project leaves behind the original computational reference, opening itself up to a new set of parameters and typological spatial classifications

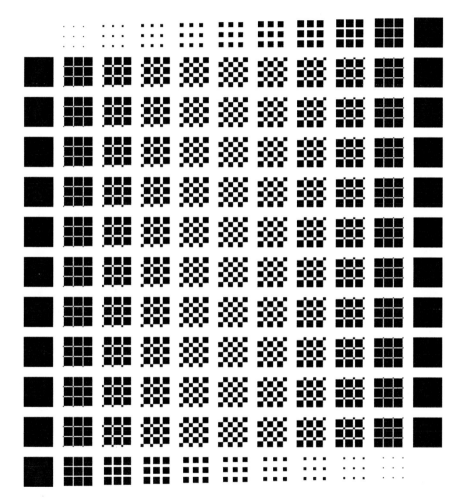

Figure 8.3 Pixel disambiguation as background computational matrix sign and as an architecture sign dividing a space. The pixel as a signifier and the space frame as an architecture sign cross and invert relationships as reference systems. Typology|Topology studio, Head Professor and Coordinator Pablo Lorenzo-Eiroa with instructors Matt Roman, Katerina Kourkoula, and Will Shapiro; students: Akash Godbole and Ian Houser, The Cooper Union, Design II, F2013.

192 *Displacing Artificial Origination by Digital Signifiers*

relevant to architecture. Moreover, the definition of the grid indexes the logic of the processing interface, since the pixel that renders the grid becomes a software parameter to be displaced. We place in contrast a historical disciplinary

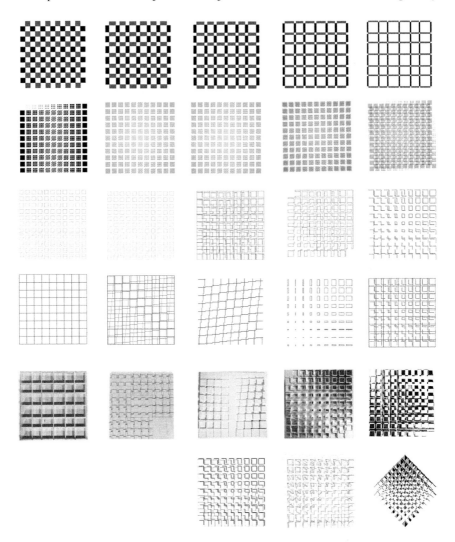

Figure 8.4 A pixel as a signifier defining various categories: from delimiting a space-frame, to composing threshold spaces displacing relatively its sign-value. The un-house proposes programmatically a multiple three cross-generation dwelling strategy in which each generation in the family understands a different relationship between space, frame, inhabitation, and function. The background pixel digital signifier of the interface is displaced by the de-sign of the column-wall architecture relationships among spaces, displacing, and inverting across the grid reference systems. Typology|Topology studio, Head Professor and Coordinator Pablo Lorenzo-Eiroa with instructors Matt Roman, Katerina Kourkoula, and Will Shapiro; students: Akash Godbole and Ian Houser, The Cooper Union, Design II, F2013.

Displacing Artificial Origination by Digital Signifiers   193

topo-logos non-deterministic realistic indexical sign against abstract deterministic computational signs which become signifiers to architecture defining Cartesian XY or XYZ grids. From a point to a line to a surface, the digital sign defines both the scale and dimensional ideology of the architecture defining the quality of the sign but also its dimensional reference (Figure 8.4).

Historically grids have been understood as an engineering module to resolve a rationalization of space in relation to structural span. We discussed in Chapter 3 how Durand normalized a universal grid system of modules for his encyclopedia of architecture types in contrast to Palladio's undecidability through elastic topological grids. In Chapter 4 we discussed how Frankl resolves a structural history abstracted from style through grid-diagrams establishing notational orders meaningful to describe architecture center and periphery relations, rhythms, or bays. We define grids as infinite variable organizational abstract matrices. Grids are organizational matrices in 2D XY or 3D XYZ determining a spatial representation, notational, and measurement system. Grids define the quality of the system through the type of matrix, relationships among nodes, or their minimum sign-system able to represent them. While grids are abstract-relational, their minimum relational sign index is a type of space-frame. The minimum sign is derived from abstraction, from a notational measurement process, for instance from building construction technology able to span spaces through structure, to minimum construction units such as the brick. A point defines the cardinal boundaries of a grid as an abstract vector, defining either an abstract nonphysical grid (Brunelleschi-Le Corbusier) against tartan or physical grids defined by architectural elements (Kahn) (Figure 8.2, 8.4 B1-E1). But a point, depending on its sign, can define or not the physical quality of its matrix by motivating both the grid as a space and the grid defined tectonically through columns. We discussed in Chapter 5 Alberti and Mies van der Rohe's architectural elements such as columns defining a type of space through a specific sign de-signification (Figure 8.4, 8.5, 8.6, 8.7). Different types of grids define space quality, determine spatial spans defining grid modules, as well as the minimum signs defining a vocabulary of architecture elements, an architecture latent typology, and a language. We think that architecture should be able to define its matrix-grid as a type of space-syntax.

By reading, analyzing, critiquing, and displacing electronic, mathematical signals and computational, digital signs and signifiers and developing a work that emerges from this criticism, one may be activating a media-specific content that becomes a reference in the architecture of the project. The problem with such a method is that it runs the risk of not opening the signifier to a multiplicity of dimensions and reducing dimensions to a mono-dimensional referential sign-signifier. This problem is explored in multiple ways: one option is to expand dimensions within the digital signifier, expanding from one dimension to the other as a form of expansion of the sign itself; another option is to expand the dimensions in the system of representation; and another position is that both expansions would allow for a spatial dimensional expansion in architecture. At the same time, the interface itself communicating

194 *Displacing Artificial Origination by Digital Signifiers*

between multiple systems should also be critiqued and displaced. We aim at developing a curriculum to displace, actualize, and decolonize conventional structures in relation to top-down computational systems of representation.

Decolonization happens at the level of the homogenizing universal digital computational sign, as well as the system of representation. Power structures through visual semiotics active in architecture and urbanism are displaced to activate center-periphery, frame-object, service-served relationships and building up from local to global conditions proposing a new type of collective development in which each site proposes conditions to each other at an artificial level (Figure 8.9). This exercise is purposely artificial, activating

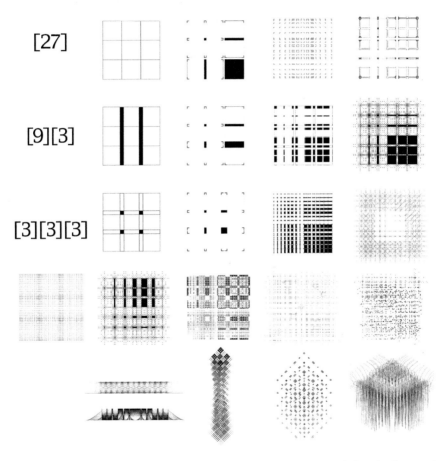

Figure 8.5 Coding scripts based on arithmetic and algebra to define background grid-matrices through points as digital and architectural signifiers. Column density defines the architectonics of the boundaries between spaces defining different spatial typologies. The plan organizations are displaced again by the curvature of the ceiling-roof shell structure. Typology-|Topology studio, Coordinator and Associate Prof. Pablo Lorenzo-Eiroa, Assistant Prof. James Lowder, instructor Katerina Kourkoula; students: Cory Hall, The Cooper Union, Design II, F2012.

Displacing Artificial Origination by Digital Signifiers 195

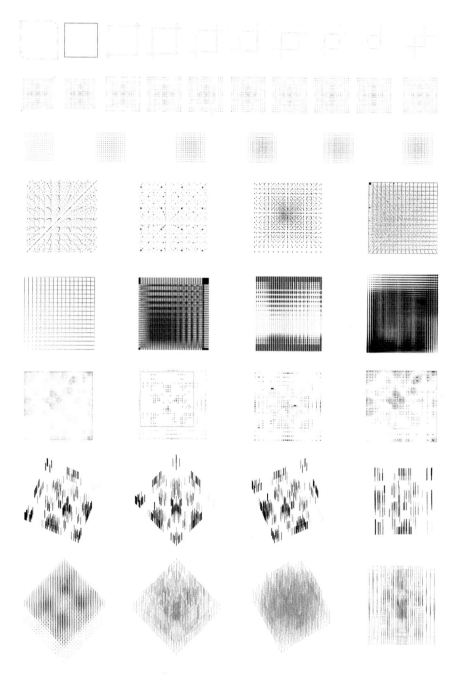

Figure 8.6 Parametric variations of fields of columns density defining tensions and continuity activating different spatial typologies. Typology-Topology Studio, Coordinator and Associate Prof. Pablo Lorenzo-Eiroa with instructors Matt Roman, Katerina Kourkoula, and Will Shapiro, Students Aelitta Gore and Daniel Hall, The Cooper Union, Design II, F2013.

196 *Displacing Artificial Origination by Digital Signifiers*

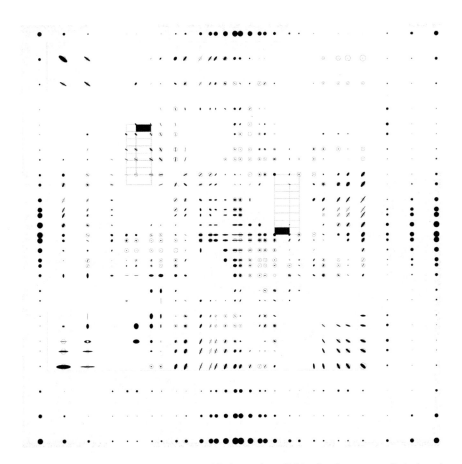

Figure 8.7 Parametric nine-square grid through a field of columns as digital and architectural signifiers indexing an internal topographic slab-surface. The columns aim at displacing spatial containment and typological directions among spaces. Typology-Topology Studio, Coordinator and Associate Prof. Pablo Lorenzo-Eiroa with instructors Matt Roman, Katerina Kourkoula, and Will Shapiro, Students Aelitta Gore and Daniel Hall, The Cooper Union, Design II, F2013.

object-frame relationships and disseminating the condition of containment (Figures 8.5, 8.6, 8.7, 8.10, 8.11, 8.12, 8.13).

If one could question the background representational space[5] relative to what's being generated in a single topological information level, one could place the project and the interface in which it is projected at the same level of signification. An interesting cultural aspect of the Processing® software as an interface is that the canvas or the space of representation is not given by the interface; it has to be coded by the user-designer through computational linguistics through Java Script HLL (Figure 8.8 A1-E1). A processing exercise as a critical reading of the conditions of software became the originator of a house project. A project dissipated its original space-matrix determination

Displacing Artificial Origination by Digital Signifiers 197

by motivating the figuration of the background structure-space of the canvas. The project proposes then the figuration of its space-frame container by motivating the coded interface background space. Various types of signs were activated: from points as minimum signs to define a grid system; to nodes defining vectorial grid constructions; to background surface-canvas as planes-grids; to lines plotted thick as a positive physical element; to voids in between solid spaces to define the grid as a double negative space-frame.

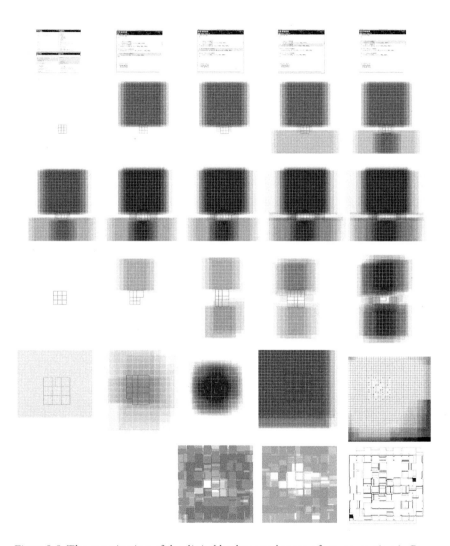

Figure 8.8 The constitution of the digital background space of representation in Processing® interface becomes motivated by generating the architecture of the un-house project. Typology-Topology Studio, Coordinator and Associate Prof. Pablo Lorenzo-Eiroa with instructors Matt Roman, Katerina Kourkoula, and Will Shapiro, Students Piau Liu and Maya Krtic, The Cooper Union, Design II, F2013.

198 *Displacing Artificial Origination by Digital Signifiers*

Different motivations of the background plot in motivated through different signs defined the emergent space-frame. While Processing partially addresses media determinism by being able to code its canvas space, the computational linguistic semiotics of Java Script anticipates a range of possible canvas structures through the formal grammar implicit in its coding establishing the next topological informational level to displace (Figure 8.8).

Double Digital Signifier = Point Grid + Nodes
Digital Signifier = Processing Canvas Generation

One of the objectives of the research in computer representation is to activate Terragni's architectural machine in relation to Palladio's necessity of displacing abstract parametric order to activate architectural meaning discussed in

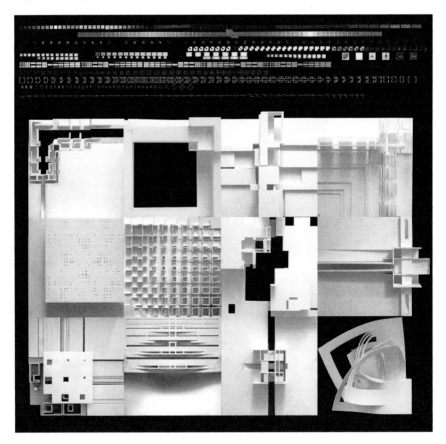

Figure 8.9 12 Palladian Villas designed by displacing the originating digital signifiers. The studio is based on an analysis of how Palladio increasingly disseminates the villa as an object by motivating the service-frame barchesse buildings (See Palladium, Chapter 3 Figure 3.3). (See Note Figure 8.9).

Displacing Artificial Origination by Digital Signifiers 199

Chapter 3. Perhaps only architects would be able to construct a machine interface to computer space since otherwise would be loaded as are computer interfaces and software with sedimented cultural conventions that do not consider the revolutions that transformed spatial structures. At the same time, spatial definition, structure, and containment should also be expanded by external architecture theories, such as theories of space-time, multidimensionality, and information theory. The notion of cultural apparatus embedded at each interface and computer language cannot be therefore deconstructed and critiqued unless one is working at that level of origination of the message. This work must be redone again to be able to index the constitution of the message as well as to displace it at a signal level in which the message and the medium are correlated and critiqued in relation to each other (Figure 8.12). The dichotomy between indexing and critiquing a sign (Figure 8.12) as a nondimensional actualization problem, and the informational multidimensional actualizing model, would therefore propose a unique synthesis, both

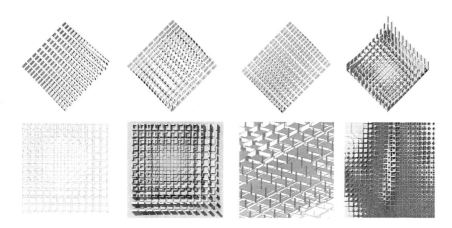

Figure 8.10 A1-D2: Urban blocks and building types in relation to private, semi-private, and public space addressing environmental conditions in New York City. Tower, midrise, horizontal row house building typologies in relation to patios, sunken patios, terraces, courtyards, boulevards, public squares, local parks, shore-parks, city-parks as open space typologies. Public housing in flood areas in NYC activating a distributed non-centralized city-park for NYC and addressing environmental conditions further discussed in Chapters 13-17. Parametric grid variations in relation to positive-negative space, object-frame relationships, and figure-ground displacements. Coordinator Associate Prof. Pablo Lorenzo-Eiroa, Assistant Professor Lydia Xynogala, Instructor Will Shapiro; Student: Nan Lei, Master of Architecture, The Cooper Union, 2014.

200 *Displacing Artificial Origination by Digital Signifiers*

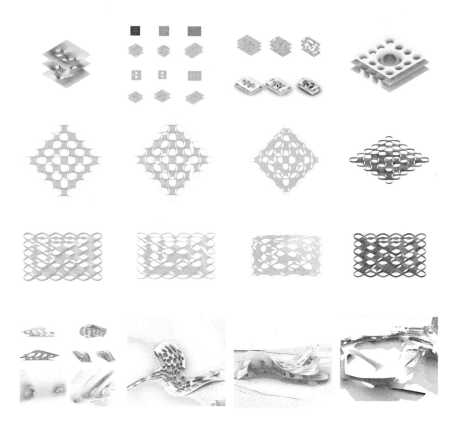

Figure 8.11 A1–D1: Topological mathematical grids displacing the cell unit through minimal surfaces; Costa minimal surface studies displacing a grid system through continuous positive and negative space. A2–D3: Continuous positive and negative poché space through two separate topological grid surface systems. A4–D4: The grid topological systems are displaced as Cartesian organizing reference systems to index site-specificity reformulating internal scales and relationships among spaces. Central Park Museum, Assoc. Prof. and Curriculum Coordinator Pablo Lorenzo-Eiroa student: Peter Panagi, ARCH 202, NYIT, SoAD S2020.

acknowledging and problematizing the system of representation in relation to the message created unifying a topological sign/signifier in relation to their media/message.

We propose a multidimensional AI informational model in which a grammatology of computational languages and semiotic electronic signals can develop a displacement of the conventions of representation of interfaces activating a multidimensional architecture of information.

Displacing Artificial Origination by Digital Signifiers 201

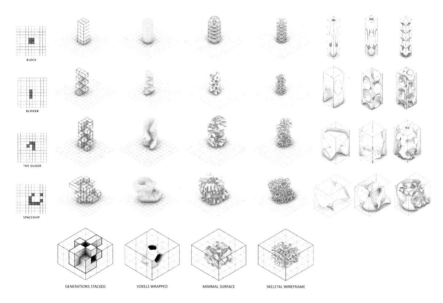

Figure 8.12 A1A4: AI Cellular Automation (CA) rules. B2–B5: 3D CA cells voxels. A3-E5: 3D CA cells voxels bypassed by Marching Cubes algorithm implementing AI attractors and evolutionary algorithms. F1–H4: minimal surfaces defined by new reference point-attractors within each cell at different voxel locations (vertex, center) defining a new surface topologies continuity between inside and outside positive and negative space through CA site-based computation. Interscalar Fluidity, Venice Biennale Installation ARCH 501–502, Prof. Pablo Lorenzo-Eiroa with student: Benjamin Sather, S-Lab Grant, NYIT, SoAD F2019. (See Chapter 13 Figures 13.4-8)

202 *Displacing Artificial Origination by Digital Signifiers*

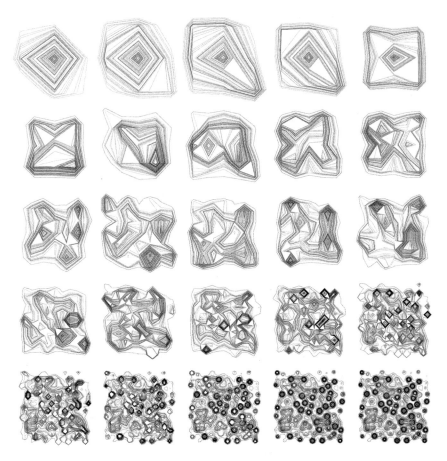

Figure 8.13 AI simulation can not only identify missing parts in a project to complete it statistically, but also develop a grid reference system or a landscape for other purposes, for instance develop a generative stepped landscape as a virtual simulation optimized to train robots to learn how to walk; Knight, W. "These Virtual Obstacle Courses Help Real Robots to Walk" Wired, Oct 8, 2021. In the figure: New York City Public Library automated book deposit shelves reconfiguration below Bryant Park shifting from a generic nine square grid organization to an emergent configurable series of organizations. Infinite Library; Reconfigurable reading rooms and library galleries by automating bookshelves. Informed Realism Research Studio, Associate Prof. Pablo Lorenzo-Eiroa, Visiting Assistant Prof. Fengq Li, student: Trushita Yadav, ARCH 701B, MS ACT, NYIT SoAD, 2022.

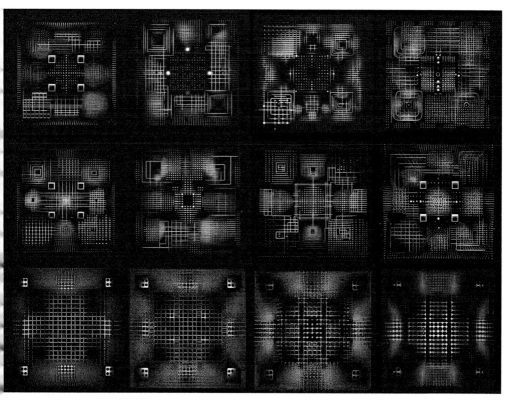

Figure 8.14 Infinitively variable infinitively expanded grids defined by infinite elements and infinite dimensions are possible and impossible at the same time. Different types of infinities need to be defined in architecture by discovering possible dimensions in grids, and addressing contemporary definitions of infinity in mathematics. In mathematics, there are different types of infinity: infinite integers; or infinite fractions between integers. The universal modern project of the grid as a metaphysical signifier of order to measure and control infinity can be critiqued and displaced topologically, following Leibniz calculus situs and contemporary mathematical definitions of infinity (Chapter 6). We develop infinitively variable parametric-topological grids by displacing the repetitive module and sign defining the grid. The cultural technological colonization of infinity as an impossible dimension does not allow for a deconstruction of embedded meaning in the deterministic quality of primary ordering structures such as grids. The development of the Vanishing Point (VP) in perspective to colonize infinity in 2D representation weights visually through an Eurocentric system of representation as an oppressive panoptical projecting power structure and as a religious transcendental signifier, a vision about the universe, and a particular relationship between subject-object contained within a space-frame (Chapter 2). We propose to decolonize western order implicit in grids (Chapter 8) and dimensions (Chapter 9). We aim at parameterizing infinite grids as a dimensional informational relational problem. For instance, we can define architecturally infinity by expanding grids; by expanding grids' dimensions; by defining boundaries in grids; by defining the grid bay, or the module; by defining the signs that define the grid. A1-D2: AI 9 nine square grids as a site displacing each other's limit-frames and their original signs, aiming at decolonizing the digital signifier. A3-D3: AI grids dissipating their original frames and signs as Deleuze's "difference without concept" activating local topological-territories and in A3-D3 elevating the grid topology. The MJ DM is engineered through NLP to retrieve API from our own research work (2006-2014). PI Pablo Lorenzo-Eiroa, MidJourney, 2022.

Notes

1 Lorenzo-Eiroa, Pablo. "Form:In:Form, On the Relationship Between Digital Signifiers and Formal Autonomy", in ed. Lorenzo-Eiroa, P. and Sprecher, A., *Architecture in Formation*, Routledge, London, 2013
2 Derrida, J. *Of Grammatology*, Johns Hopkins University Press, London, 1976
3 Evans, R. *Translations from Drawing to Building and Other Essays,* MIT Press, Cambridge, 1997
4 Manovich, L. *The Language of New Media*, MIT, Cambridge, 2002
5 Lorenzo-Eiroa, P. "Post-Historical Suspension: A Redefinition of the Role of the Relative", in ed. Frost, M.J.; Kluytenaar, V.; Meza, J.; Morrow, G.; and Risteen, N., *Ethics, Pidgin Magazine Issue 18,* Princeton SOA, Princeton, 2014

Figure 8.1 A1–C4: Different interfaces propose different ideologies and means to structure their background space-frames, understanding reality through their deep symbolic structure defining different ideas about the real, and projecting digital signs which become originating signifiers. In AI layers (ANN, CNN, etc), different digital interfaces as matrices become interchangeable-complex activating problematic translations between conventional reference systems. A1: Photoshop pixel as a graphic Human-Computer Interaction square point grid sign; B1: Photoshop vectorial nodes defining its matrix-grid; C1: Photoshop pixel as scale-dependent grid; A2: ProcessingR grid through coding path; B2: Processing grid defined by path lines; C2: Processing background canvas-space coded; A3: AutoCAD vectorial grid defined by vectorial lines and splines; B3: Rhinoceros grid defined by 3D points; C3: Maya NURBS-based topological grid defined by curves degree 1 to 11. Each interface, application, and software has a series of protocols to define digitally, vectorially, through data and information processing on how XYZ dimensions are defined through digital signs. Each interface defines its background and foreground signs, signals, and dimensions, from points, to lines, to surfaces, to volumes, to camera views projection, to its immersive virtual navigation, to the definition of its geometric topology as well as other parameters defining the quality and ideology of representation of the framework. A4: AI Cellular Automation (1D cell, 2D cell, 3D cell by extrusion) defines mathematical cells based on neighboring site-based computational relationships. B4, C4: Voxels are 3D cells that define boundaries of a series of downsampled meta-objects, such as point clouds.

Figure 8.9 12 Palladian Villas designed by displacing the originating digital signifiers; a design studio curriculum developed to actualize the nine square grid problem in relation to the decolonization of cultural implicit projects in digital systems of representation. The curriculum proposes to decolonize the family patriarchal structure from the neoliberal real estate mortgage model. Un-houses are designed to anticipate the possible divorce of a couple and not being able to sell the house, indexing the housing and mortgage crises augmented by taxation in the USA. The studio syllabus anticipates means to be able to split the house into three distinct and independent dwelling typologies resolving: an un-house for multiple family generations; being able to split the house without crossing circulation; being able to work at home; being able to rent out a part of the house for income. The 12 villas develop site conditions from within, extending the internal organization of the un-houses to displace their site-frame. By addressing their site as a frame displacement, structuring emergent conditions across different sites start providing external structures to each other and developing a community through private-public continuous intermediate spaces. In some cases, cross relationships between sites become structural and feedback into internal organizations. The studio is based on an analysis of how Palladio increasingly disseminates the villa as an object by motivating the service-frame barchesse buildings (Palladium, Chapter 3 Figure 3.3). Typology-Topology Studio, Coordinator and Associate Prof. Pablo Lorenzo-Eiroa with instructors Matt Roman, Katerina Kourkoula and Will Shapiro, students: Lucas Chao, Aimilios Davlantis Lo, Akash Godbole, Aelitta Gore, Pedro Galindo Landeira, Gabriela Gutierrez, Daniel Hall, James Hansen, Connor Holjes, Ian Houser, Shin Young, Jisoo Kim, Sam Koopman, Luke Kreul, Maya Krtic, Kelsey Lee, Hui Jung Liu, Piao Liu, Sofia Machaira, Wilson Muller, Celine Park, Joseph Parrella, Stephanie Restrepo, Jonathan Small, Chi-Hsuan (Vita) Wang; The Cooper Union, Design II, F2013.

9 Expanding Dimensions in Spatial Reference and Representational Systems Toward a Multidimensional Architecture of Information

From Topology to Artificial Neural Networks, to Quantum Computing

"The computer is built on yes-no logic. So, perhaps, is the universe" John Archibald Wheeler[1]

History Section:
Modern Physics; and Twenty-First Century Physics and Computation;

Methodology:
Information Theory; Knot Theory, Topology, Multidimensionality (0D, 1D, 2D, 3D, 4D); Quantum Theory;

Computational Dimensions:
0D, 1D, 2D, 3D, 4D; Parameters as Dimensions (1-10^11; IoT; Collective Intelligence); Data; Information; Interconnectivity; IoT; Information Flow; Singularity; Linear Computation; Bifurcating Computation; Bidimensional Computation; Three-Dimensional Computation; Multidimensional Data System; Multidimensional Scaling computation; Multidimensional System;

Visual Semiotics Systems of Representation:
Grids; Point; Line; Surface; Volume; Cartesian Space; Differential Curve, Surface, Knots; Topology; Geodesic Projective Geometry; Space-Time;

Computational Mathematical Semiotic Signifier:
Bit; QuBit; Algorithms;

Computational Visual Semiotic Signifiers:
Cells; Node; Pixel; Point, Point Cloud, Particle, Voxel; NURBS Curves, Surface; Parametric Plots; Parametric Equations; Parametric Surface;

Visual Semiotic Signals:
GPS; Satellite Imagery (visible, infrared, water vapor), (light detection and ranging) LiDAR; Laser, Thermal, Infrared, Non-Visible Electromagnetic Light Spectrum (Wavelength: radio, short wave, VHF, UHF, Radar, microwave, far infrared, infrared, ultraviolet, X-Ray, Gamma Ray, Cosmic); Analog Photograph; Digital Photograph;

DOI: 10.4324/9781003292036-10

Mathematics:
Arithmetic; Algebra; Geometry; Set Theory; Differential Equations; Limit;
Infinitesimal Calculation; Descriptive Geometry; Projective Geometry;

Architecture Questioning Dimensional and Reference Systems

Why does architecture not have an active role in the contemporary investigations over conceptions and developments on multidimensional space? What are the correlations between spatial dimensions and representational systems? We discussed in previous chapters how computational linguistic semiotics projects through grammar organization to visual semiotics, but how do dimensions in space determine organization in architecture?

According to Vidler *space*^{2} was a concept incorporated into architecture-derived theories of the universe description of ether as a form of vacuum in the Nineteenth Century. Contemporary architects incorporate interdisciplinary knowledge to explore novel ideas to represent space, from fields such as mathematics, geometry, physics, information theory, and more recently topology and fluid dynamics. These representational explorations influence architecture, which today understands space and information from a topological standpoint. Contemporary computer software deals with bi-dimensional and three-dimensional space, augmented virtual reality, and time-based formal topology but in discrete conventional spatial terms. The spatial organization plays an essential role at a cognitive level, presenting limits to how disciplines measure different space-time paradigms. Today, architects should be able to contribute novel concepts and modes of representation to investigations in computation and other fields, contributing to research on multidimensional space. Since content, form, and medium inform each other, innovation in multidimensional space can inform strategies to organize dynamic multi-level informational systems, including data *structures*. It is also possible to envision that the next digital revolution is based on representing an increasingly complex multidimensional space-environment based on multidimensional information systems, which we hereby discuss and extend in the following chapters.

We consider Cartesian Space to be a form of Eurocentric Western cultural colonization reference system and that its function in mathematics and geometry needs to be surpassed by new means to address a rather complex reality with the necessity to expand its measuring reference systems to address topology, topography, planetary environment, information theory, and theories of the universe regarding the space-time fabric. Expansion on measurement and reference systems should contemplate for instance: planetary geodesic projective geometry and reference; the complexity of the environmental dynamics; knot theory and surface topology; space-time four-dimensional manifold fabric; multidimensional space projected (or not) to three-dimensional space; and quantum physics. These and other contemporary theories of the Nature of our Universe need to be measured in architecture in relation to our current technological and scientific possibilities and the expansion of such through actualization and innovation in systems of representation redefining the ontology of our cognitive knowledge systems, from architecture and urbanism to mathematics and physics. We are therefore looking to expand interfaces to address notions of the infinite, and to develop feedback loops between media as origination and media as a destination, questioning what is possible or impossible, what is imaginable through language and visual semiotic representation, and what escapes our minds and systems of representation, what is determinate or nondeterminate, what is complete or incomplete.

Scientists struggle to represent information cap by linguistics, not understanding visual semiotics and revolutions in systems of representation and media through the available interfaces and tools which conventionalize representation, aiming to represent novel content non-representable with the conventional tools available. Because of this problem, scientists are not relating mathematical signals to the visual semiotics of the available signs in relation to the interface available where content is originated, represented, formed, processed, and communicated. Moreover, spatial dimensions over three-dimensions such as 4D space cannot be accurately represented since we currently do not have higher dimensional or multidimensional plot spaces in mathematics or computation.

Scientist expand dimensions in relation to tools and systems of representation available, addressing higher dimensions through points, point clouds, lines, surfaces, colour, layers, hiearchical dimensional plots, superpositions, time separating and describing dimensions informationally through statistical data, ranging for instance, from micromolecular level in radiology, to a macro level in terms of how scientist describe new theories of the universe. Scientists were able to develop a nanoparticle 3D reconstruction from a single refraction index.[3] Stout discusses how to process multidimensional information in radiology in relation to cognition processes, for instance interpreting micromolecular level resonance scanning and using the survey data of higher dimensional but scrambled meaningless point clouds to interpret them statistically into a recognizable interpretable 3D image through color and time as dimensional properties.[4]

Cartesian Universal Reference and Measurement System as Baroque Eurocentric Colonization

The Cartesian Coordinate system is actualized and represented differently by each software package or interface, activating distinct technological electronic signals and organizational representational digital signifiers. Descartes'[5] Cartesian Coordinate Space presents a universal system of reference for geometric signs referenced through three axes. Leibniz Differential Space Infinitesimal Calculation can be also read as an ambiguous sign and a topological critique of the Cartesian Coordinate System through the mathematics of differential calculus. Deleuze in *Le Pli*[6] refers to Leibniz's "ambiguous sign" as a problem in curvature and a difference[7] that cannot be referenced to conventional plot space defined as *geometria situs* and *analysis situs*. Descartes and Leibniz were interested in a universal form of knowledge, a universal language, independent from the imperfections of the natural evolution of culturally based language derived from speech.

Signifier = Cartesian Space
Leibniz "Ambiguous Sign" as mapping of topological difference

Euclidean space does not allow for a higher dimensional surface topology self-intersection. Therefore, higher dimensional geometric topology dealing with surface self-intersection cannot be projected to Cartesian Coordinate Euclidean space. Points, lines, surfaces-volumes, surface topology, 3D space-environments, 4D space, and multidimensional spaces are incremental dimensions that have been worked out to both reference and present possibilities to expand dimensions in architecture. While cities are based on fixed Cartesian grids, they encounter a contrast with topography at the local level, and with geodesic coordinate in a global system. There are different types of 3D spaces, such as a sphere as a 3D space of longitudinal (not parallel) geodesic curves and latitudinal (parallel, indexing the Tropic of Cancer and Capricorn latitude describing the orbit around the Sun cycles in relation to the Earth's axial tilt) circular sections or a mixing of projective geometry 3D space. In spherical analytic geometry, one can develop the geometry to reconstruct a sphere with no distortion through the sphere's central angle following a Wulff net stereographic projection in which each geodesic curve is perpendicular to each other and centered. Three equator planes can define three axes in a sphere. The cartesian coordinate system must be displaced out of our imaginary linguistic understanding and in relation to advancement in projective geometry and surveying systems such as The World Map Projection, or AuthaGraph World Map. Global Positioning System or GPS addressed problems of motion, curved space, and gravity[8]. While Architecture produces through its construction-economic industry Cartesian cuts, materials, and assembly due to efficiency referencing Cartesian determination, space is in reality warped both in terms of planetary geodesic geometry and space-time fabric. We expand in Chapter 10 on the issue of geodesic geometry through asymptotic curves in architecture digital fabrication.

"...n-dimensional space is the set of all possible n-fold sequences of numbers" Carter[9]

Three-dimensional structures such as Cartesian space motivate axes that tend to infinity but by doing so, they impose, suppress, and oppress local means of understanding space in relation to Natural resources, the existing topography, the dynamics of the ecologies, the reality of the imperfect geodesic morphology of the planet, and most importantly the space-time fabric. This is the reason why in cartography, there is a problematic deviation between the territory and satellites measuring the territory on earth, which problematically uses a straight Cartesian

210 *Toward a Multidimensional Architecture of Information*

system of reference without addressing the geodesic curvature of the earth which is not regular, nor constant fixed, as its terraform and water bodies continuously accommodate and deform. Space-time fabric as described by Einstein means gravity is not a force but a space-density fabric formal problem. Space also accelerates time, so apart from expanding dimensions in terms of plot space, architects need to expand the incorporation of time as a function of spacetime curvature fabric. An animated space-environment describes how space-time responds as a mass movement, describing the relationships between mass, gravity, and space-time fabric distortion.[10] A Penrose Diagram describes space-time in relation to gravity and singularity, which Wheeler identified as the Black Hole.

Representing dimensions in Computer Science, Data Science, and Architecture: 0D, 1D, 2D, 3D, 4D

Mitchell and McCullogh[11] discuss dimensions in computer representation, from 1D media as data text; 2d media as images, lines, polygons, plans, and maps as graphics; 3d media as a three-dimensional representation of lines in space, surfaces and renderings and assemblies; multidimensional media as motion models, animations and other means of representation such as hypermedia. Representing a point, a line, a surface, or a volume already presents issues of dimensionality in relation to projective geometry relative to different media interfaces. Usually, architects project higher dimensional geometry into a lower dimensional representational space for notational purposes. The first problem is the plot space or the space within which such dimensional issues are defined. For such exploration, we define the relationship between the plot interface and the current mathematics of the space.

The mathematical geometric and Cartesian, the spatial definition of dimensions and their motivation as signs, as well as their displacement may be themselves an architecture exercise. One needs to deconstruct signs and signifiers to motivate dimensions in architectural terms through computational representation, addressing both computational linguistics and computational visual semiotics.

> Point, Line, Surface, Volume....
> Linguistic Signifier ≠ Mathematic Geometric Signifier ≠ Computational Digital Signifier ≠ Architectural Signifier

In computational visual semiotics, we can differentiate between abstract vectorial representation without a dimensional object quality, a mesh representation as an actualization of geometry, and a solid volume which is represented through mesh surfaces, a mesh implemented for simulation of physics. In either case, there is no physical dimension assigned to geometric elements in computer representation whether in 1D, 2D, or 3D as geometry is defined vectorially actualized through the mesh but in 2D and not in their thickness 3D, unless they are represented as a series of polygons meshes to represent thickness but the means through which thickness is represented, has not actual dimension.

Contemporary computer software deals with bi-dimensional geometric representation activating three-dimensional dynamic spatial representation, augmented virtual reality, and time-based animations. In the meantime, architecture lost one dimension from articulated building walls to 2D surface envelopes as 3D space through computation. In addition, architecture lost one dimension through media motivating 2D visual experience instead of 3D experience, a problem that is transferred to Virtual Reality Navigation.

0D Point

A point is a zero-dimensional mathematical notational location in XYZ Coordinate Space without a geometric value, since it has no geometric object definition. A point in architecture is therefore unachievable as a constructed object since it has no dimensional quantification. We can discuss architecture

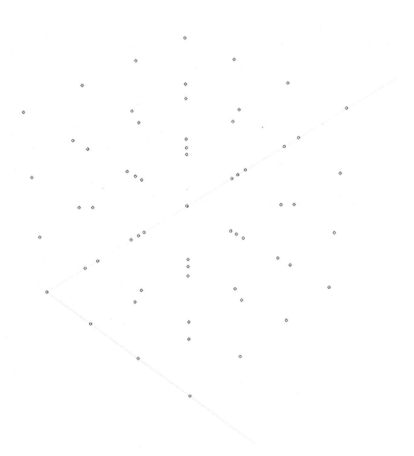

Figure 9.1 Many software disregard 0D points, a vectorial point grid in Rhinoceros 3D with no dimensional definition is not renderable as a mesh object.

212 *Toward a Multidimensional Architecture of Information*

as referencing an abstract point location in space. A point in architecture depends on how it is referenced since it is not a thing. If the point is a vector, space is abstractly defined. But if the point is given an object, such as a pixel through a vectorial node, it establishes a scale and a dimension, although it cannot be mathematically or geometrically addressed as a point but only as a 2D square. A point is not mesh-representable. The point cloud as a digital signifier is a dimensional expansion of architecture. Modernism defined the atom as the minimum unit of matter made of particles. But particles are also defined as minimum units of matter. A single point in a point cloud can be defined as an analog to a particle in physics as a minimum unit of matter representable in computational simulation. Therefore, we process 3D LiDAR scan point clouds through particle physics in several media interfaces. We can define an abstract 0D grid in the plan or in space that limits a 2D or a 3D space through vectorial points of no dimension (Figure 9.1).

1D Line

We define a line as 1D (one dimension) since only one coordinate axis is necessary to define mathematically a point in a line, as a line can be defined by infinite points. Mathematical logarithmic equations as defining a series of

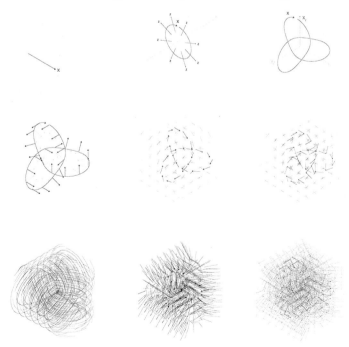

Figure 9.2 A1, B1, C1: 1D, 2D, 3D motivation of Cartesian Axes through 1D notation. Vectors activate one-dimension, two-dimension, and three-dimensions. A2–C3: Euclidean manifold in higher dimensional topological surfaces. Prof. Pablo Lorenzo-Eiroa, Students: Joseph Jemuel and Marcus Birman, ARCH 482B, The Cooper Union, S2015.

Toward a Multidimensional Architecture of Information 213

Figure 9.3 1D Curves defining 3D space through mathematical logarithmic limits. Multidimensional Space. Machines to "Draw and Build", Professor Pablo Lorenzo-Eiroa. Students: Jisoo Kim, Jieun Hannah Kim; Akash Godbole, Connor Holjes, Ian Houser, Arch 482B Arch 177, S2015.

lines as a field can be defined through limits. We can define a series of 1D lines that can define as open boundaries and motivate architecturally a 3D space (Figures 9.2 and 9.3).

2D Boundary and Surface

A pixel is a 2D surface square and can define a spatial notation in the plan. A line can conform to a circle, a triangle, a square, or a figure which defines 2D (Figure 9.4).

214 *Toward a Multidimensional Architecture of Information*

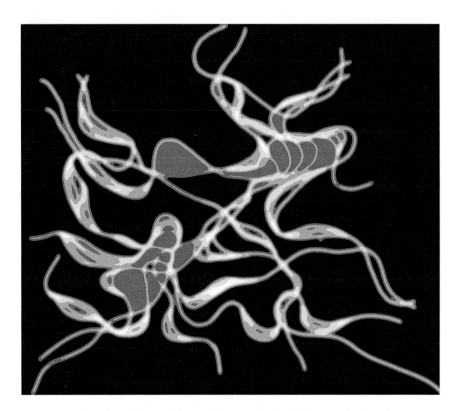

Figure 9.4 Photoshop® by Adobe pixelation and fluid filters and after photogrammetry of analog diagrams. Pedestrian roads of different granulometry-density reacting to topography. Varying 1D thickness lines as 2D surfaces. Paths-study, Pablo Lorenzo-Eiroa, 2000.

A surface is defined by 2 Coordinate axis XY. A 2D surface can define or contain 3D space. A sphere is a 2D surface that contains a 3D space. Surface topology can be considered contemporary of a Baroque poché space as it motivates 3D space through both container and contained space through a 2D surface topology. A mathematical parametric plot can be coded through mathematical logarithmic recursive equations tending to infinity to limits representable in mathematical notation, but not achievable in vectorial terms in relation to the limits of the Graphic Processor Unit (GPU), the screen resolution, and other processing limits (Figures 9.5 and 9.6).

Toward a Multidimensional Architecture of Information 215

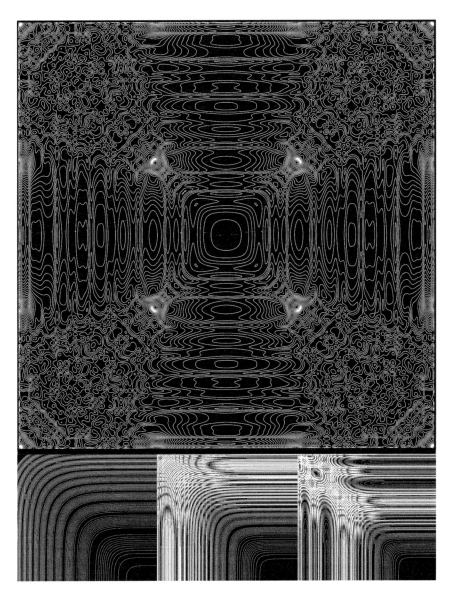

Figure 9.5 A mathematical parametric surface plot as a 2D surface defining a 3D space through motivating a vectorial 0D point, a 1D line, a 2D surface, and a 3D space; Multidimensional Space: Machines to "Draw and Build", Prof. Pablo Lorenzo-Eiroa, Students: Zachary Hall, Rain Yu Kiu Chan. ARCH 177: Gabriel Munnich, Yaoyi Fan; Jemuel Joseph, Luis Figallo; Alberto Martinez Garcia, Kevin Savillon, Natalia Oliveri; Bing Dai, James Seung Hwan, Jin Lee; Zachary Hall, Rain Yu Kiu Chan, Mireya Fabregas, Julia Di Pietro, Arch 482B, S2016.

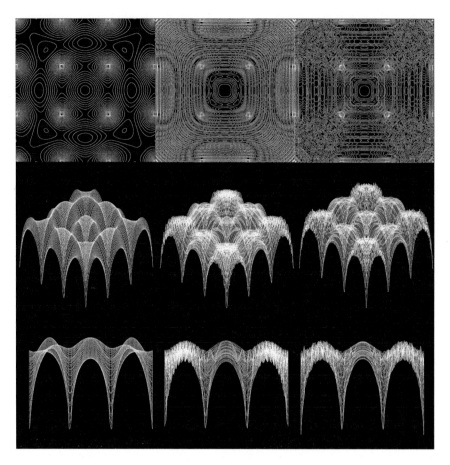

Figure 9.6 Mathematical parametric surface plots identifying logarithmic limits. Prof. Pablo Lorenzo-Eiroa, Students: Zachary Hall, Rain Yu Kiu Chan, S2016.

3D Object, Volume, and Space

As discussed, a 2D surface can contain 3D space. A minimum 2D object extruded as a volume can define a volume space in architecture. Any spatial dimension can be displaced topologically defining architecture quality and values. A space in architecture can be defined and limited by a point grid as 0D, or a point can be defined in 2D extruded as 3D as an architectural element such as a column and both define space around it defining a grid and/or contain space if it big enough to contain function within its surface-volume. A thick line as a wall condition in a plan in architecture that represents a 3D object in space, can define two spaces on each side and also in between through its relative thickness, as it can contain space within its thickness. Topologically, the range value of a line may be interesting to trigger problems

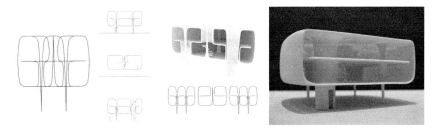

Figure 9.7 Vectorial 0D point, 2D Surface topology through a single continuous topological surface defining 3D space. Associate Prof. Pablo Lorenzo Eiroa (coordinator), assistant Prof. James Lowder and Instructor Katerina Kourkuola, student: Maximillian Gideonese, The Cooper Union, Design II F2012.

in defining a space. Several lines can form a spatial boundary to configure a "wall". A surface may be a wall. A surface can curl up and hold a fragmented space within itself, topologically motivating architectural space (Figure 9.7).

Adolf Loos' *raumplaunnung* space[12] resists representation since his buildings challenge linguistic logic and visual semiotic representation through displacing the normal relationships between plan, section, and axonometric projection, for instance, by avoiding the normal development of space as Z-axis extrusion of the floor plan, or the sectional development of space as a consequence of depth in the Y-axis. Villa Müller (1930) by Loos proposes a 3D spatial game in which the logical understanding of the space, as well as its experience, are mental and sensorial games that challenge human cognition, anticipating a topological continuous space in tension with a Cartesian space determined by XYZ axes. His buildings cannot be easily understood in conventional representational terms, but they need to be dissected, cut, and exploded as the Raumplanung nests spaces within spaces in a spiral organization as they are displaced in XYZ coordinates.

3D Space and 4D Topology:
Expanding Dimensions in Architecture's Cartesian Reference Space-Frame

In principle, typology as a generic structure is opposite to topology as a differential structure: topos + logos. Aristotle defines Topos as the Site-Space.[13] Topo-logos critiques typological classification, since, within a given topographic continuity, each space is unique. Leibniz defined *geometria situs* and *analysis situs* developing relationships and surfaces through algebra, a type of computation of geometry in 1676 which defined topological properties. Euler[14] in 1736 resolved through topology how to cross the Seven Bridges of Königsberg without repeating a path. For mathematics, topology is the preservation of properties or homotopy under bicontinuous deformation: such as twisting, bending, or developing knots without breaking, opening, or closing holes. Non-Euclidean higher dimensional topological spaces can include n-dimensional manifolds, which at each point reference dimension n Euclidean spaces, enabling the possibility to transition through invariant manifolds between dimensions, through vector field topology for 4D space visualization avoiding self-intersection in 3D projection a problem that is both a challenge to perception, as well as representation.[15] Non-orientable topological surfaces can be classified as building up a reference in terms of how many axes, planes, and volumes activate within a Cartesian Reference System and in relation to time and 4D space through self-intersection. Self-intersection is a property of topological surfaces, as 2D surfaces intersect in 3D space describable through knots. Self-intersection occurs when a higher dimensional geometry, such as 4D, is projected into a lower dimensional space, such as 3D, through differential topology. 3D spatial topology represented through 2D surface geometry is resolved through self-intersection. But a 2D surface topology such as the Klein Bottle surface self-intersects in 3D space, since the algebraic polynomial equation variables, defining homology through manifolds, can only be constructed in a 4D space. Multidimensional cubes can represent 4D space projected into 3D lower dimensional space through shadow projection. String theory quarks are linked through one-dimensional strings. The multidimensional nature of string theory can be represented with a Calabi–Yau six dimensions manifold (Wolfram Demonstrations Project)[16]. M-Theory is a multistring theory.

We can address multidimensionality to cover two functions, the first one is to be aware of current theories of the physics of space, and to compare how architecture is able to, or is dealing with them, at the minimum in terms of representation. Knot theory and median curves can be developed into various surface topologies.[17] Knot Theory in mathematics presents issues of dimensionality, such as tables describing prime knots with multiple knot crossings. Leys describes the relationship between multiple dimensions constructing surface topologies, such as the Lorenz attractor and trifold knot.[18]

In architecture, the surface defining architectural space acquired a type of formal and geometric autonomy. The autonomous object-space was critiqued through a movement toward an expanded field of site-specificity. This shift replacing a modern tabula rasa with a post-structuralist site specificity was resolved in the canonical thickening of the ground as an inhabitable surface addressing a topo-logos. Yet, current models assumed the presence of a different type of space derived from such expansion, a "topological" space dominated by continuity, non-Euclidean geometry, and increasing ranges of indeterminacy driven by the logos of the site, which conceptually negated referential structures and Cartesian space. Mathematical topological surfaces informed a topological space and the architectural envelope, inducing continuity between inside and outside, activating an apparently multidimensional space. Any topological surface is contained, measured against, constructed, structured, regulated, and parameterized within a Cartesian three-dimensional plot-space. This dissociation between a background dynamic Cartesian

Euclidean system of representation and the constitution of complex bi-continuous non-Euclidean foreground form-objects is not usually addressed (Figures 9.8 and 9.9).

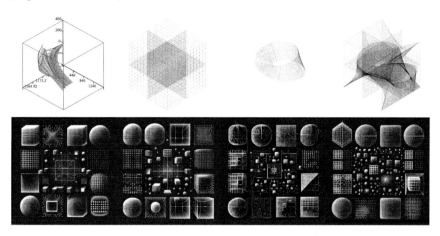

Figure 9.8 A1: Topological surface-space parameterized in relation to its referential Cartesian space. B1: Static Cartesian frame; C1: topological Möbius strip surface indexing spatial warping; D1: topological surface and Möbius surface enfolding and displacing its Cartesian space-frame through a mathematical parametric surface plot actualization. Platonic Space-Frame Displaced by a Möbius Strip, Pablo Lorenzo-Eiroa, e-Architects, NY 2008. A2-D2: 0D, 1D, 2D, 3D and 4D AI simulation of grid reference systems constituted by different dimensional elements (point, line, surface, volume, higher dimensional volumes) and through different systems of representation (plan, elevation, axonometric; single, two and three-point perspective; geodesic projection; variable space-time density; Hypercube). Pablo Lorenzo-Eiroa, 2022.

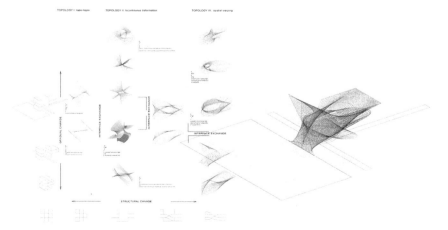

Figure 9.9 Cartesian Topology. Architecture typological variation through relative topological displacements. House IIa; Design Principal: Pablo Lorenzo-Eiroa, e-Architects, NY 2010.

220 *Toward a Multidimensional Architecture of Information*

A possible hierarchical classification of topology with meaning to architecture can be organized dimensionally from a Möbius strip to a Klein bottle to a Werner Boy Surface. We develop an increasing complexity in surface topology referenced to Cartesian planes and axes. A Werner Boy Surface topology consists of three Klein topologies and six Möbius topologies. Their intersections project a higher dimensional 4D space in 3D space. House IIB is a house project that integrates multiple architectural typologies within a single continuous tri-fold-topology. House IIB develops multiple topological displacements layering information parametrically (Figure 9.10, 9.11). This multidimensional space integrates interior and exterior intermediate spaces in a singular looping differentiated structure. This continuous tri-fold-topology simultaneously integrates into a single differentiated space, both positive and negative sides of each of the three Cartesian referential axes, XYZ. Each of the three Cartesian planes (XY, ZY, ZX) proposes an initial nine-square grid organization that displaces through continuity center and corner reference spaces. For instance, the corner space of the XY plane by spiraling and turning becomes continuous with the center of the YZ plane. Likewise, the courtyard space of the XY plane becomes continuous with the corner of the ZX plane (the tower type of the XYZ Cartesian Coordinate). Ultimately the center of the XZ plane becomes continuous with the perpendicular corner of the ZY plane. Therefore, these displacements happen in each of the three Cartesian planes (XY, ZY, and ZX) and in relation to each other's perpendicular planes, making each of the discrete planes dependent on each other, as each corner becomes the center of the other perpendicular plane. These gradual accumulative continuities transform structurally the overall three-dimensional structure. The initial XYZ axis is overcome as an origin of the project by developing a space that displaces its own parameters. By these means, surface topology becomes the new poché space in which the positive side and the negative sides of a continuous surface are both active and continuous with each other's sides, thus two three-fold spaces or two simultaneous figure/figure relationships.[19]

House IIB is a house that you can never enter nor find/colonize, since the void through which one enters each of the three topologies never reaches any destination or end spaces. The voids framed by the surface topology are extended to incorporate the environment as these environments become space-environments. The three architectural containers referencing each of the Cartesian axes: horizontal container space, perpendicular container space, and vertical container space become displaced into a continuous space-environment that expands outwards infinitely. Likewise, each axis aims at activating a perspectival vanishing point through a quadratic equation never really reaching the point as the curvature is thought to address infinity but never really achieving it (Figures 9.10 and 9.11).

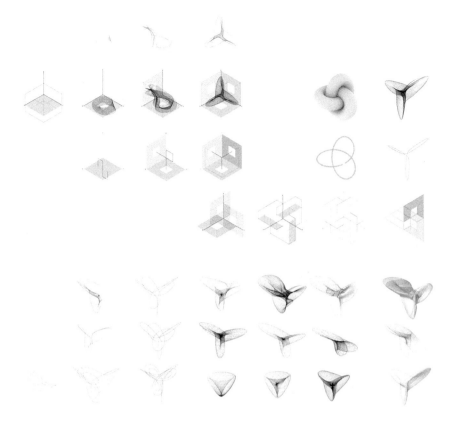

Figure 9.10 We explore through the book means to multidimensionally expand computation and architecture through problems of representation: in plan we integrate the various forms of knowledge through a structural history addressing Palladio (Chapter 3) and following Le Corbusier, activating a displacement of the identified conventions of a nine square grid; in section we follow either a structural performative model displacing the floor plan, a displacement of each topological-topographic level based on Borromini's topologies (Chapter 4) and Loos raumplanung; or such as this case, a mathematical topological model to displace plan, section and axonometric projection simultaneously in a critical 3D model through a contemporary notion of poché space activating positive and negative space continuity (Chapters 8-9); we expand dimensions between "drawing and building" defining and displacing architectural elements based on digital signifiers through actualization (Chapters 8, 9, 10-14); ecologically we develop a performative Big Data model of simulation-optimization of continuous space-environments (Chapters 12-13, 15-17); we expand dimensions between linguistics (non-linguistics, Chapter 5, 6) and visual semiotics (non-visual, visual grammatology Chapters 6, 7); between information abstraction and media actualization recognizing and displacing the media (Chapters 1, 2, 18, 19). In the figure: B1-C1: Möbius Strip topology, Klein open topology and Werner Boy Topology (1901) parameterized by Morin (1978). We adapt the parametric surface to displace Cartesian axes. G3: We map and extract a median surface curve as a variation of a Trefoil knot, a prime knot with three crossings as a 3 (1) knot and a type of braid word (Wolfram). F2, F3: The Trefoil knot is also a (3-2) torus knot, correlating its topology to the Werner Boy surface topology (B7). Trefoil knot parametric plot as surface: t = 2 * math.pi * i / num_points; x = radius * (math.sin(t) + 2 * math.sin(2 * t)); y = radius * (math.cos(t) - 2 * math.cos(2 * t)); z = radius * (-math.sin(3 * t)). A2-G2: Three surface topologies referenced in relation to their mathematical plot Cartesian Coordinate Space, Axes and Planes. B3-G7: A Werner Boy Surface is correlated to its Cartesian axis so that it enfolds its frame-space creating continuity between each axis and plane of the Cartesian Coordinate including the centered voids of each plane. We plot curves and surfaces through different actualizations including: Wolfram Alpha, Wolfram Mathematica, MathCAD, MathSurface, various Grasshopper definitions distinguishing the XYZ parameters, Python Scripting, and more recently ChatGPT mathematics (see Chapter 10). We develop a visual semiotic programming as site-based computation through interfaces by using form as computational interfaces, transferring information through different topological levels of information through topographies of information, addressing Leibniz calculus situs as computational contingency (Figures 9.9, 9.10, 15.1, 15.4). -X, X -Y, Y -Z, Z House IIb, Endless Infinite House, Design Principal: Pablo Lorenzo-Eiroa, Design Assistants: Luo Xuan, Pedro Joaquin, NY 2012; American Mathematical Society annual Conference, 2018.

222 *Toward a Multidimensional Architecture of Information*

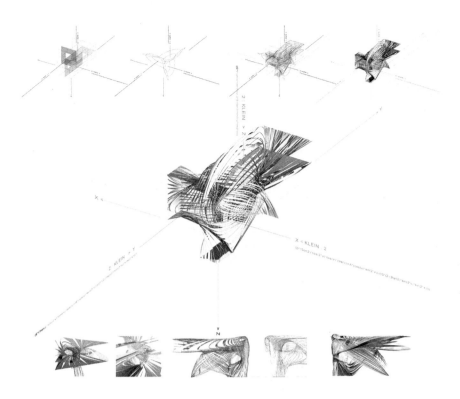

Figure 9.11 A1, A2–E2: Worms' eye view axonometric and elevations. House IIB, Endless Infinite House: –X, X –Y, Y –Z, Z. Design Principal: Pablo Lorenzo-Eiroa. Research Assistant: Luo Xuan, Pedro Joaquin, NY 2013.

Möbius Surface Parametric Equation:

$$x (u,v) = \sin(u) \star (-2+v \star \sin(u/2))$$
$$y (u,v) = \cos(u) \star (-2+v \star \sin(u/2))$$
$$z (u,v) = v \star \cos(u/2)$$
$$\min u = 0; \max u = 2 \star pi; \min v = -; \max v = 1$$

Klein Surface Parametric Equation 2 × Möbius:

$$x (u,v) = (1 + \cos(u/2) \star \sin(v) - \sin(u/2) \star \sin(2 \star v)) \star \cos(u)$$
$$y (u,v) = (1 + \cos(u/2) \star \sin(v) - \sin(u/2) \star \sin(2 \star v)) \star \sin(u)$$
$$z (u,v) = \sin(u/2) \star \sin(v) + \cos(u/2) \star \sin(2 \star v)$$
$$\min u = 0; \max u = 2 \star pi; \min v = 0; \max v = 2 \star pi$$

Nordstrand Klein Surface Bottle Parametric Equation

0
2*pi
0
$0<=2\pi$
x (u,v) = cos u (cos((1/2) u)((Sqr(2))+cos v)+ (sin((1/2) u)) sin v cos v)
y (u,v) = sin u (cos((1/2) u)((Sqr(2))+cos v)+ (sin((1/2) u)) sin v cos v)
z (u,v) = − sin ((1/2) u)((Sqr(2))+cos v) + (cos ((1/2) u)) sin v cos v

Klein Surface Bottle Parametric Equation

x (u,v) = a (sin(u) + 1) cos(u) + b (1 − cos(u)/2) cos(u) cos(v) |
  $0<=u<=\pi$
  a (sin(u) + 1) cos(u) − b (1 − cos(u)/2) cos(v) | $\pi<=u<=2\pi$
y (u,v) = b sin(u) (1 − cos(u)/2) cos(v) + c sin(u) | $0<=u<=\pi$
  c sin(u) | $\pi<=u<=2\pi$
z (u,v) = b (1 − cos(u)/2) sin(v)

Boy Surface Parametric Equation 3 Klein; 6 × Möbius:

x (u,v) = ((Sqr(2)*cos(2*u)*cos(v)*cos(v))+(cos(u)*sin(2*v)))/(2−A*(Sqr(2)
  *sin(3*u)*sin(2*v)))
y (u,v) = ((Sqr(2)*sin(2*u)*cos(v)*cos(v))−(sin(u)*sin(2*v)))/(2−A*(Sqr(2)
  *sin(3*u)*sin(2*v)))
z (u,v) = (3*cos(v)*cos(v))/(2−(A*Sqr(2)*sin(3*u)*sin(2*v)))
  variables: A=1
min u= −pi; max u = pi; min v=0; max v = pi

The Guggenheim Museum competition entry (Figure 9.12) presents a double House IIB topology, activating a higher dimensional space-environment. Based on discovered mathematical topological properties, the topology that displaced the original Cartesian planes was duplicated, displacing this time the three left-over voided centers of the previous volumetric structure. By repeating the topological relationships of the previous structure displaced diagonally one quadrant in XYZ, center-to-periphery relationships become displaced once more forming the totality of a museum as a space-environment, extending a semi-domestic three-fold topology into a semi-public six-fold topology engaging the city. The circulation of museums is usually divided into temporary and permanent galleries defining different typologies. This museum project organizes temporary and permanent galleries as well as public and private services and circulations interconnecting them and blurring

224 *Toward a Multidimensional Architecture of Information*

boundaries informed by the double three-fold spatial topology. The double topology (I and II) organize the two interdependent permanent (A, B, E) and temporary (C, D, F) gallery loops. The temporary and permanent loops are separated but also interdependent since center and periphery become continuous through the two nested topologies (Figure 9.12).

We also explore in House V Cartesian Coordinate displacement through Natural Language Processing (NLP) text-to-image pixel-to-pixel Diffusion Models (DM). We discussed in previous Chapters how DM lower dimensional

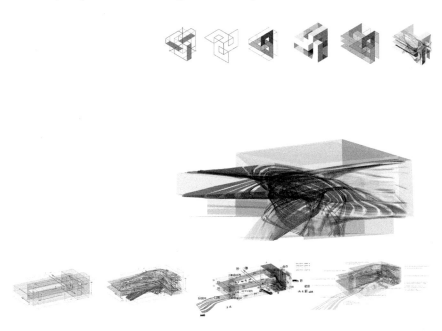

Figure 9.12 A1–F1, A2: Double Boy surface three-fold topology, topology I and topology II as continuous positive and negative spaces in X, Y, and Z axes contained within each other referencing and displacing their Cartesian Coordinate Space. A3: Double three-fold topology circulation continuity (I and II); B3: Double three-fold topology (I and II) differentiated formally by space contained and space container and by curvature degrees 1 and 3. C3: Double three-fold topology (I and II) programmatic diagram differentiating permanent exhibition loop from temporary exhibition loop; D3: Topology I curvature degree 3; permanent exhibition galleries. Topology II curvature degree 1: temporary flexible exhibition galleries. Guggenheim Museum Helsinki Competition Entry: GH-8746022806; Design Principal: Pablo Lorenzo-Eiroa; Design Team: Felicia Killiot, Peter Douglas; Renderings: Craft CG, e-Architects, New York, 2014.

Toward a Multidimensional Architecture of Information 225

2D simulations of 3D space include the simulation of light conditions, and how we were able to expand such capacity to simulate Computational Fluid Dynamic (CFD). We hereby include emergent programming able to simulate 3D surface topology by the AI, as different mathematical topologies are programmed to expand architecture as a space-environment sometimes able to distort its frame-space (Figures 9.13 and 9.14).

We analyzed in Chapter 2 Andrea Pozzo's illusionistic space as a displacement of architecture 3D space-containment. We activate a multidimensional

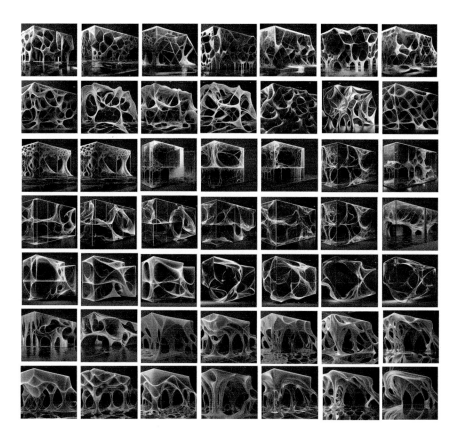

Figure 9.13 House V e-Architects. Computational Fluid Dynamic simulation (CFD) (over a 2D simulation of 3D space and a simulation of CFD) enfolded through topological surfaces displacing Cartesian Coordinate frame-space through topology. Pablo Lorenzo-Eiroa MidJourney Diffusion Model, 2022.

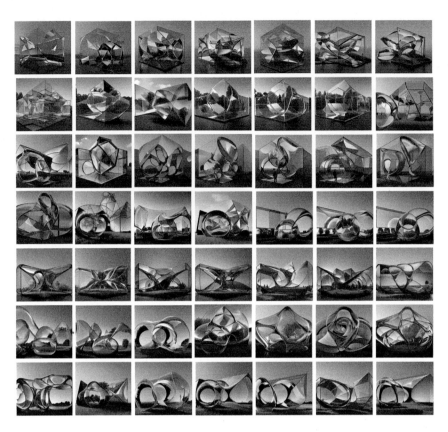

Figure 9.14 House V e-Architects. Topological surfaces Möbius, Klein, and Boy enfolding the ground reference plane, and their Cartesian Coordinate frame-space. Even though we aim at developing a higher dimensional space, we recognize the limitations of doing it through a 2D NLP semantic input prompt. Since we are activating topological surfaces, we aim at reducing the use of the style by others used to train GPT language models through abstraction calling out through NLP the API of concepts. Pablo Lorenzo-Eiroa NPL prompt DALL-E and MidJourney pixel-to-pixel Diffusion Model, 2022.

virtual space by projecting and expanding spatial dimensions within a 3D space-frame for House IV (Figure 9.15). We are aiming at developing experimental multidimensional spaces through critiques of perspective and axonometric projective geometry as systems of representation in relation to Cartesian 3D reference space. House IV activates recursive simulations, or simulations within simulations, addressing self-intersection topological projective geometry within a simulation that simulate other spaces. A multidimensional space-environment becomes active through an illusionistic 2D perspective coordinated to index the shadow projection of a higher dimensional 4D space, as feedback projections between nested simulations. House IV is a Virtual Reality space-environment that aims at building up

Figure 9.15 A1–C1: Pozzo's frame-space simulations. House IV e-Architects 4D space through a Penrose Hypercube. Real-virtual augmented illusionistic perspective correlating 3D space with 4D shadow projection from a higher dimensional space through illusionistic perspective feedback. A2–C4: Frames as lower dimensional space-environments simulations of simulations. A5–B5: Illusionistic perspective warping space of representation with frame-space. Pixel-to-pixel feature recognition problematically activating style by others through a Diffusion Model; Pablo Lorenzo-Eiroa with MidJourney, 2022.

228 *Toward a Multidimensional Architecture of Information*

relationships and dimensions from House II, and House III based on the illusionistic perspective displacement of architecture space by Pozzo's anamorphosis projective geometry. A Penrose Hypercube is a 4D space projected into a 3D space in which we can only perceive the 4D space through its lower dimensional projection into 3D space.

Multidimensional Parallel Processing in Human Brain, Intelligence, and AI Neural Networks

The form of our brains is plastic and is not only given by internal DNA code inheritance genotype but also continuously adapts to the task we ask them to resolve as a phenotype. Neuroscientists identify relationships between neural connections, synapsis, and the organization and multidimensionality[20] of the human brain in relation to information flow.[21] Current neuroscientific research asserts that our brain activity as well as neural connections are being adapted and transformed to how current systems work through reward stimuli at the neural brain pathway connectivity level.[22] Social media feeds and cell phone applications develop a psychological profiling based on thousands of parameters and are progressively optimized to manipulate our engagement, interest and our behavior resulting not only on social engineering but also a change of our brain neural connections.[23] The more information flows, the higher capacity for neural connections to optimize the flow and create more synapsis incrementing the formal complexity of the system. This is also related to the total amount of information that humans generate, comparable to all biological DNA to be reached in about 110 years.[24] While research points out a direct relationship between information flow in human brains and intelligence,[25] we are yet to know how artificial intelligence will emerge,[26] and if it will be in fact a post-human condition of transcendence or simply a parallel bifurcation from evolution in its own terms that will never be able to replace humans.

The Blue Brain Project maps higher dimensions in the structure of our brain, associating data structure with the morphology of the brain, identifying up to 11 dimensions. The human brain has $10^{\wedge}15$ connections and contains $10^{\wedge}11$ neurons. The Internet of Things in 2020 is close to $10^{\wedge}10$ and will be $30^{\wedge}10$ by 2025. The world is interconnected through the internet as a decentralized organization in which information flow, could at a certain point, become conscious, what has been called "singularity"[27]. Currently, exascale supercomputers run brain-scale AI models competing between the US (Frontier expanding to more than 1.102 quintillion calculations per second, IBM Summit, IBM Sierra), Japan (Fugaku 415,000 trillion floating point operations per second), the EU (LUMI), and China (Sunway Taihu-Light), with China having the greatest number of supercomputers according to TOP500.org. Intelligence, consciousness, and self-awareness have been difficult to explain for scientists, which some argue is an emergent condition result of the amount of information flow, and the function of language.[28]

Parallels between algorithms and our brain neural activity require further research in relation to both a Theory of Mind and a Theory of Linguistics to understand how algorithms adapt to us and we adapt to them. This means understanding intelligence explosion[29] in evolution correlating morphogenesis and synapsis because information flow is what is deriving scientists to think of the Technological Singularity event.

Deep Blue in 1997, won against Garry Kasparov, mainly by calculating multiple possible moves through brute force. Google Alpha Go in 2016 as well as telecommunication marketing and automated military tasks (ENIAC 1946) and automated response mechanisms such as SAGE (MIT + US Military) computer system developed during the 1950 and operational in 1961 and the current robotic and androids designed to automated warfare to counteract beyond human ability. In 2021, AlphaFold, a Google/Alphabet DeepMind was able to sequence in a few weeks' time, protein fold structures at new scales (0.16 nanometers) by training 170,000 proteins from a data bank through AI prediction.[30] The ACADIA 2010 Conference placed in motion Life In Formation[31] through information theory and anticipated the comeback from its winter of parallel processing in Neural Networks as AI. DARPA[32] RAMplants and ElectRx to Neuralink to previous successful attempts to increase natural intelligence through neural impulse and rehabilitation implementing nanotechnology. ChatGPT Large Language Model 100T parameters through NLP is perhaps able to expand our thinking as it program by language our brain connections, defining through grammar our brain morphology. We therefore define intelligence as a function of dimensional processing power through information theory and in relation to cybernetics: intelligence is a function of information flow, its relation to associative memory-retention to establish relationships and build new synapsis bridges, and the emergence of evolutionary morphogenesis in processing structures due to information flow through new synapsis connections elevating dimensions in the neural net. What is interesting in relation to computation and AI intelligence is that our brains do not perform well in comparison with Big Data statistics, which actually challenge intuition, currently mostly implemented to approximate AI through prediction; and the fact that machine learning cycles can become exponential, activating faster at each cycle information flow morphogenesis through self-editing algorithms speeding evolution.

The wider the neural network for deep learning, as overparameterization, the more robust implementation memory of trained data, and the scale larger than the equations,[33] as the variability of the training process for generalization, which becomes dependent on the dimensional quality of the network.

ANN 1980s = n parameters to n fit data points
ANN 2021 = n *(parameters)* $\times$ d *(ambient data dimension = e.g.*
         784 pixel $\times$ 784 pixel) times more parameters than mere interpolation

230 *Toward a Multidimensional Architecture of Information*

1 parameter (monolinear thinking, perceptron),
2 parameters (dialectical thinking),
3 parameters (trigonometric thinking),
4 parameters (four-way thinking),
5 parameters (network: beyond escalation or dual dialectics activating relational complex network thinking)...etc.
100 expanding open-source software
500 crowd-based parameters
175B parameters (OpenAI GPT 3.0-3.5, 2022; 17.5B=175B american linguistic scale)
100T parameters (OpenAI ChatGPT based on GPT-4, 2023; 1T=100T american linguistic scale)
130 QuBits (10,000-Million Quantum Supremacy, 2045)
10^{10} IoT (Internet of Things interconnectivity, 2022)
10^{11} neurons (human brain)
Collective Intelligence (CI, Crowd Intelligence, BlockChain)

Quantum Physics and Quantum Computing: Digital BIT For Analog and Digital Qubit Signal

What happens when reality changes when it is measured in Quantum physics? Several consequences are drawn from such an intriguing problem thinking of reality in terms of multiple-state problems in which the observer defines the laws by projecting the system of measurement implemented, connecting representation as enaction and empowerment over reality to a maximum dimensional problem. We aim at addressing some of the issues of quantum physics and quantum computation as they escape the spectrum of focus of the book, but present issues to start preparing for the next generations since representation takes a new dimensional quality relative to how we measure, project, and understand reality as it becomes feasible through computing Qubit power. According to quantum physics, the laws of Nature change through particle superposition states when they are measured by a subject. Systemic determination is projected from the subject implementing the system when the measurement is applied. Therefore, the reality is stretched, modified, and altered to fit a subjective system of measurement, placing as we discussed in this and previous Chapters measurement as the basic system that structures reality as a form of representation. Observation and event are two at once. Photon splits and signals equal value in two places at the same time, as reality is flexible, we discover dimensions able to expand reality (Figure 9.16).

Current prediction in terms of the Moore Law (1965) establish the doubling of transistors in a dense integrated circuit every two years is soon to be limited by a physical atom scale limit. Quantum computing is presented as the next revolution in computation, to overcome Moore's law in terms of microprocessing physical limitations. Quantum computing could be analog-based on quantum annealing or digital-based on a gate model. In analog quantum computing, the sign is continuous and in both cases no longer binary 1-0 but

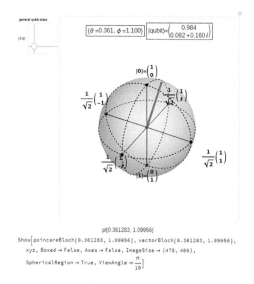

Figure 9.16 Qubit on the Poincaré Bloch Sphere through Wolfram Mathematica notebook, Pablo Lorenzo Eiroa, 2019.

ranges defined as in a quantum QUBIT from 0-1 | 1-0 as the computational signifiers are already emerging as unstable units of subject-dependent measurement. Quantum computing is photon based instead of electronic-based through a chip in conventional current computers, a decision-making binary system of the Bit of true/false for a multiple-state system, following quantum physics. Quantum instead of electrical signals, conducts information through photons active in a beam of light, therefore a mathematical communication theory that transitions from a previous electrical paradigm to a light paradigm, a direct signal processing engine. Artificial Intelligence (AI) is changing in relation to simulation with parallel computing and the 6D hyperspace + 4D dimensions of quantum mechanics through Superstring Theory totaling 10D or 11D through M-theory. The power of a Quantum Computing system is exponential in relation to the amount of Qubits as opposed to classical computing in which there is a linear relationship between power and the number of electronic transistors/chips. Quantum computing is an advantageous system over a typical computational system, such as parallel real-time processing, simulation of multiple agent systems/paths, and optimization of intertwined parallel correlational conditions. This develops a significant advantage in terms of Big Data Science and AI since parallel computation, simulation, and optimization. Several have been representing Quantum states, such as the impression of a *transmon* qubit.[34]

NON-BINARY SIGN = QUBIT
QuBit Sign = New System of Representation
Quantum Machine Learning = Parallel Photon Signals

232　*Toward a Multidimensional Architecture of Information*

Hans(z) Moravec[35] in 1988 addressed various means for critiquing determination in computation in reference to CA and Quantum Computing including the Vehicle Routing Problem (VRP) through parallel simultaneous simulation (See Figure 17.6). Quantum computing would enable a higher dimensional parallel correlational multidimensional processing system implementing several simultaneous simulations, addressing a different type of real-time architecture-environments, conflicting external conditions in confluence with several parallel internal evolutionary states. The user/viewer or field of users/viewers may expand in real time by their gaze observation of the actual retrieval and reconstruction processing of the expanded model. VR navigation would literally expand real-time processing of its own plot space as it becomes active through the visible reality spectrum activating in Virtual Reality quantum physics. This form of real-time processing can be infinite since the scale of observation at a micron level can be expanded ad infinitum as well as its dimensional scales of observation. This notion would escalate exponentially simulations of simulations or a higher-level programming self-simulation expanding reality and VR simultaneously as a resonance amplifying machine (See Chapter 19 Simulacra: Representation Restricted Reality (RRR)).

Multidimensional Space: Displacing Reference Frame Systems, Digital Signifiers, Systems of Representation, Space Typology, Construction Systems, and Materials

We develop across the book multiple strategies and tactics to activate a multidimensional architecture of information.

The first strategy discussed in this Chapter is to address dimensional problems relative to XYZ Coordinates and displace conventions in Cartesian Coordinate Space (XYZ axes), activating multidimensional AI spaces. The second strategy discussed in Chapters 15–17 is to expand architecture space to space-environments by addressing an AI-based multidimensional BlockChain platform in which multidimensional data sets are incorporated to develop a multidimensional space-environment global engine through Ecoinduction I-III. The third strategy discussed in Chapters 10-14 is to expand dimensions in architecture by identifying problems or opportunities that emerge between "drawing" and "building" through expanding dimensions in representation acknowledging the physical forces as information systems in Computer Aided Machinery in robotic AI fabrication in the mediation of emergent information flows. The fourth strategy discussed in Chapters 10-12 is by developing correlations between representation and actualization. The conventional understanding of materialization can be understood in terms of actualization in an informed model. Dimensional problems become active in how information is actualized depending on the dimensional capacities of the machinery equipment. Dimensions in actualization can be expanded through multidimensional robotic systems (autonomous sentinel) and robotic fabrication (construction). The fifth strategy discussed in this Chapter and 15-17 is through multidimensional information and data systems. It is possible to envision that the next digital revolution is based on representing an increasingly complex multidimensional space-environment based on multidimensional real-time information systems. The sixth strategy discussed in Chapters 18-19 is by addressing an augmented immersive ephemeral space-environment realism through virtual reality and robotic interactivity, displacing conventions in how to address space in architecture through real-time interactive expanded representation. Virtual simulation of simulations, or multidimensional simulation space-environments, can scale recursively forms of simulations and environments that are themselves universes contained within universes, amplifying reality and realism beyond themselves. The seventh strategy discussed in Chapter 10 "Architecture of Information: Building Faster than Light Speed Elsewhere in the Universe" is to consider signal communication and actualization a dimensional problem. The transmission of information short or long distances through remote sensing feedback can, for instance, alter a space-environment activating a self-replicating system that would grow in relation to its own environment.

Notes

1 Wheeler, J.A. "It from Bit", *Geons, Black Holes & Quantum Foam,* Norton, New York, 1998
2 Vidler, A. *Warped Space,* MIT Press, Cambridge, 2000
3 Colombo A. et all "Three-dimensional femtosecond snapshots of isolated faceted nanostructures" Sciences Advances, 22, Feb 2023.
4 Stout, R. "Single-cell optical detection of T3 availability" American Thyroid Association, Online video, 2021.
5 Descartes, R. *Discourse on Method, Optics, Geometry, and Meteorology,* trans. Oscamp, J., Indianapolis, 2001
6 Deleuze, G. *The Fold: Leibniz and the Baroque,* University of Minnesota Press, Minneapolis 1993 [orig. 1988].
7 Deleuze, G. *Difference and Repetition,* Columbia University Press, New York, 1994 [orig. 1968]
8 Siegel, E.; and Starts with a Bang ed Group "GPS Only Exists Because of Two People: Albert Enstein and Gladys West", in *Forbes Science,* Feb 18, 2021
9 Carter, S.J. *How Surfaces Intersect in Space,* World Scientific, Singapore, 1993
10 Siegel, E. "This is Why The Speed of Gravity Must Equal The Speed of Light", in *Forbes Magazine Science,* Oct 24, 2019 (accessed 2020)
11 Mitchell, W.J.; McCullough, M. *Digital Design Media,* John Wiley & Son, New York, 1995
12 Estévez, A.T. *Escritos: 1897–1909 Adolf Loos,* El Croquis, Madrid, 1993
13 Aristotle, in *Time for Aristotle, Physics IV,* Oxford University Press, Oxford, 2009
14 Euler, L. "Solutio problematis ad geometriam situs pertinentis", Petropolis, Typis Academiae, San Petersburg, 1726
15 Hofmann, L.; Rieck, B.; Sadlo, F. "Visualization of 4D Vector Field Topology", in *Computer Graphics Forum,* Volume 37, Issue 3, Wiley, 2018

234 *Toward a Multidimensional Architecture of Information*

16 Hanson "A Construction for Computer Visualization of Certain Complex Curves", in *Notices of the American Mathematical Society,* Volume 41, Issue 9, 1994

17 van Wijk, J. J.; Cohen, A. M. "Visualization of the Genus of Knots", Dept. Mathematics and Computer Science Technische Universiteit Eindhoven, Eindhoven, 2005

18 Ghys, E.; Leys, Jos. "Lorenz and Modular Flows: A Visual Introduction", 2006. http://www.ams.org/publicoutreach/ feature-column/fcarc-lorenz, 2006. Accessed 2020

19 Lorenzo-Eiroa, P. "Cartopological Space", in ed. Lorenzo-Eiroa, P. and Sprecher, A., *Architecture In Formation,* Routledge, London, 2013

20 Michael, W.R.; Max, N.; Martina, S.; et al. "Cliques of Neurons Bound into Cavities Provide a Missing Link between Structure and Function", in *Blue Brain Project,* Frontiers in Computational Neuroscience, 2017

21 Hilbert, M.R.; Kempt, D.J. "Information in the Biosphere: Biological and Digital Worlds", in *Trends in Ecology and Evolution,* Volume 31, 2016

22 Schultz, W. "Dopamine Signals for Reward Value and Risk: Basic and Recent Data", in *Behavioral Brain Function,* Volume 6, Issue 24, 2010

23 Kramer, A.; Guillory, J.; Hancock, J. "Experimental Evidence of Massive-Scale Emotional Contagion Through Social Networks", in *PNAS,* Volume 111, 24, Jun. 17, 2014

24 Hilbert, M.; López, P. "The World's Technological Capacity to Store, Communicate, and Compute Information", in *Science,* Volume 332, 2011, 60–65;

25 Chén, O.Y.; Cao, H.; Reinen, J.M.; et al. "Resting-State Brain Information Flow Predicts Cognitive Flexibility in Humans", in *Scientific Report,* Volume 9, Issue 3879, 2019

26 Pretz, K. "Stop Calling Everything AI", in *IEEE* Member News, 2021

27 Eden, A.H.; Moor, J.H. "Singularity Hypotheses", Springer Berlin, Heidelberg, 2012

28 Neuman, Y.; Nave, O. "Why the Brain Needs Language in Order to be Self-Conscious", in *New Ideas in Psychology,* Volume 28, Issue 1, 2010

29 Prasad, M. "Nicolas de Condorcet and the First Intelligence Explosion Hypothesis", in *AI Magazine* 40, 2019

30 Douglas, H. "DeepMind's Protein-Folding AI has Solved a 50-Year-Old Grand Challenge of Biology", in *MIT Technology Review,* 2020

31 Sprecher, A.; Yeshayahu, S.; Lorenzo-Eiroa, P. *Life In Formation,* ACADIA, New York, 2010

32 Pauli, D. "DARPA's 'Cortical Modem' will Plug Straight into your BRAIN", *The Register,* 2015

33 Bubek, S.; Sellke, M. "A Universal Law of Robustness via Isoperimetry", *arXiv*:2105.12806, 2021

34 Tyler, C. "Careful with Hot Objects", in *Spotlights,* Los Alamos National Laboratory, 2018

35 Moravec, H. *Mind Children. The Future of Robot, and Human Intelligence,* Harvard University Press, Boston, 1988

10 Computational Informational Semiotics

Signs and Signals in Machines
to "Draw" and "Build" through
Double Bind Adversarial Robotic
Feedback Actualization

History Section:
Renaissance; Industrial Revolution; Modern Movement; Post-structuralism;
High Tech; Twenty-First Century Architecture of Information;

Methodology:
Information Theory; Double Bind Adversarial Feedback; Cybernetics of Cybernetics; Technological Determinism; Media Determinism; Post-Anthropocene; Post-Colonial, Post-human, Post-zoomorphic Robotic Fabrication; Post-Capitalist Developmentalism;

Building Construction Systems Semiotic Signifiers:
Material-Based construction systems based on economic units (brick, steel angles, concrete fluidity, wood in different types);

Computational Visual Semiotic Signifiers:
Digital Fabrication (CNC, others); 3d printing technologies (aggregate-based, Fused Deposition Modelling –FDM, laser cured resin, others); robotic fabrication (Robotic Arm, Robotic Swarm); Material Simulation and Optimization;

Science:
Material Science; Materials (robotic materials, biomaterials, synthetic materials, responsive materials);

Definitions:
Architecture: Greek arkhitékton: arkhi (master) –tékton (builder);[1] or arkhi-tékton (technē) Aristotle's technē as the imperfection of human imitation of Nature (Oxford Dictionary)

Media and Technological Determinism: Construction Systems and Digital Fabrication

Architecture has been historically informed by systems of measurement, reference, notation, and representation which in turn define standards in material-based construction systems. Construction is referenced by materials which have historically been determined in standard industrial units

DOI: 10.4324/9781003292036-11

236 *Computational Informational Semiotics*

indexing economic ratios function of available resources, transportation, installation, anthropocentric efficiency, and the flexibility in the articulation between parts and whole. Construction displaces through materiality and detailing the otherwise abstract, conventional, and generic architecture containment typologies. If architecture typologies have been historically categorized through formal types, organization, function, and overall efficiency, then we should re-think construction through a technological determinism as it was understood in the Renaissance by Brunelleschi, the Industrial Revolution kit of parts, the variety of positions, the Modern Movement relative to the plasticity of reinforced concrete or the possibilities of steel, as well as the High-Tech mechanical technological movement of the 1980s. The architecture task consists of deconstructing the conventional systems of construction and industrialization of material production units in order to develop innovation in the articulated architecture spatial typology. A full deconstruction of construction in architecture would also expand to critique the linguistic signs, syntax, and grammar that were built up in the history of architecture as a discipline in relation to the visual semiotic types and typologies that emerged out of the cultural and contextual technological systems. Although these paradigms are being fully displaced by digital fabrication, robotic fabrication, and Artificial Intelligence (AI), many issues need to be deconstructed.

Expanding Dimensions Between "Drawing" and "Building"

The Modern Movement emptied architecture signs from cultural linguistic meaning such as *style*, identified as cultural symbolic folklore expressed through ornamentation and artisanal craft as an inheritance of cultural technē, in contrast with radical technological machinic innovation of standardization at the industrial level through the industrial revolution, displacing technological innovation through standardization in design as a social revolution.

Architects understood ideologically how to design spaces and buildings dependent or not on a certain material and construction system in relation to a certain socio-cultural-economic context. Architects must now expand relationships between "drawing" as representation and "building" as fabrication. This time this expansion needs to operate rather between computational linguistic semiotics and computational visual semiotics through coding and representation applied through an information theory aware of the physics of materialization, expanding dimensions between the virtual and the real avoiding oppositions between the two usually understood in terms of media and medium translation. But instead of working through conventional virtual interfaces and translating projects through conventional means of fabrication, architects must critique, displace, and eventually create their own coding languages and means of actualization materialization and tools activating an architecture of information.

Rather than framing these questions just as a problem of digital fabrication, it is rather interesting to think of them in terms of representation through information theory as information actualization through physical materialization.[2, 3]

Computational Informational Semiotics 237

What seems to be the most interesting advance – to be able to directly print our digital model in scale or directly as an object building reproducibility – may be one of the issues to decipher in expanding our discipline. Since we declared that there is no information without representation, there are problematic processes of representation in any information-based translation between codes, units of measurement, fabrication techniques, and data formats, and this applies to any machine executing a protocol to fabricate a digital model through an aggregate or a computer numerical control (CNC) through a Computer-Aided Manufacturing (CAM). CAM mostly converts 2D or 3D forms into a workflow based on machinic instructions by administrating a tool path (G-Code) that is reduced to XYZ numeric coordinates with machinic instructions (M-code). This reductive conventionalization beholds fabrication from reaching a higher level of recognition of the truth in the process as a form of being as an approximation to reality, from a truthful structural performance to a problematized one through indexing representation of an emerging aesthetic formal expression. Through information signs and mathematical signals for processing data and information, we can inform reality as a function of mediating physical information flows signals or as a function of informing physical signals through electronic signals, vectorial signals, processing binary computational signs, and Human-Computer Interaction signs. We can inform a water flow signal through a sound wave signal therefore achieving information transferring from one medium to another; we discuss in Chapter 15 how we can manipulate sedimentation deposition in rivers by informing a physical signal within a dynamic environment; we discuss in Chapter 12 how we can activate a shell structure by informing tension through CAM toolpath signals projected as a vectorial signal on a material surface. We can distinguish then additional signals from Chapter 9, such as robotic electronic signals, and the physical signals that become active through robotic fabrication. Architects should be claiming a higher degree of authorship in the software, codes, interfaces, CNC, CAM, and robotic fabrication systems that originate and actualize materially a project, by acknowledging that the background mediums and media are equally as important as the foreground design content.

When dealing with digital fabrication, architects could explore relationships between the means to inform aggregates, used for fabrication (for instance powder 3D printing) and the definition of a dimension in a project, for instance, a point in space. The post-structuralism of 3D printing aggregates frees the previous determination of assembling structural gridded elements separating, for instance, structure and envelope, as defined by previous economic parameters. Consequently, one can relate the logic of earthwork architecture derived from site-specificity to the logic of fabrication of locate site-specific aggregates, through site-specific robotic systems (further discussed in Chapter 14) reinforcing the enfolding of ground-related strategies to re-define a complex independent free-standing architecture object, since continuous aggregates can constitute complex volumes and surfaces that can be structurally optimized to work as free-standing independent objects. Therefore, an issue is to explore the relationship between the definition of a dimension in drawing and to explore the definition of that dimension with

238 *Computational Informational Semiotics*

a recursive analog machinic process as well as explore the definition of a dimension through CNC fabrication processes.

Materialization as Reference, Signs Becoming Signifiers

The first question is about the interface that translates the digital vectorial information to the interface that arranges the protocol to develop a physical construction by aggregation or by controlling a CNC CAM. This translation implies again a mediation separation is usually disregarded. The second question is about the machinery itself. It is quite clear today that the dominant techniques of fabrication quickly become referential universal. Often, the technique of fabrication becomes referential and imposed over the logic of the form, displacing the logic of the digital project into a disregarded objectification, thereby relegating the logic of its materialization. Each interface as well as each fabrication process proposes a certain deterministic structure to the architecture project.

The increasing number of interfaces informing a project are layers where data is transferred and turned into communicable information which is represented, translated, and presented through multiple conventional *structuralisms* biases. The previous architecture of details assembling different materials and construction techniques as a part to whole relationship is replaced by an architecture of digital techniques separated by different systems layering information through multiple interfaces. Alberti proposed an opposing argument to Brunelleschi's control directing and supervising the execution of the construction at the site, in which the architect's design through drawing representational notation represents the intellectual author. For Alberti, the architect does not necessarily need to be at the site, as the design authorship through representation in drawing notation precedes the built building. The new information materialization paradigm we are all getting used to breaks with the separation between notation as representation and execution as building. This notion of representation and the invention of the notion of architecture design by Alberti[4] has been transformed[5] through digital architecture and now computational design. Today the architect can execute drawings directly, bypassing notational scale, cutting construction costs offset by machinery costs, and being a Capitalist by owning the means of production, a process which can be extended to systems of representation. Due to the expansion of robotic machinic processes for construction, the architect no longer needs to be separated from the act of construction but can problematize representation from the multiplicity of actions between drawing and building. The architect now can be an author of the systems of construction that are usually given and that define the technology of construction including the ranges of architectural typologies and dimensional possibilities that can emerge.

As many claimed, information materialization also breaks with the economic-repetitive equation, since for some robotic machines and 3D printing it is the same to fabricate an extravagant form or a regular one, as the economic parameters are material quantity and time and not much of the form itself. A further objective of a project might be to critique the emerging referential parameter, which may be the result of the forces implicit or explicit in its materialization. Any material can update forces or define forces, depending on how an architect understands materiality. There is nothing like good or bad, expensive or cheap, rich or sterile materials, but there is only the ability to understand material logic in relation to its state of becoming.

DIGITAL SIGN TO ANALOG SIGN = "digital" Fabrication CAM
Robotic Arm = Index + Sign / signified
Material Index = Signifier
Brick = information BIT
Brick = Signifier
Robotic Arm = Linguistic Signified
FDM = Signifier

Certain materials can become signifiers to architecture anticipating it as discussed in previous chapters, and we can identify traces of anthropocentric material-based construction systems in computation even in innovative computational robotic and 3D printing. Materials are in architecture related to material-based construction systems. Materials not only index the construction system but also its entire apparatus of measurement, reference, environmental and anthropocentric conditions, or medium-specific signs as embedded knowledge. The brick has been historically the basic unit of the masonry architecture construction system. The brick indexes in its composition and dimensions several measurements, constructions, and economic, social, local, and anthropocentric conditions. The brick can be paired with a BIT of information or a voxel as the primary unit of information for centuries of buildings. The BIT is often referred to as the brick of computation, but the brick should also be understood as a BIT in architecture. The brick indexes in its dimensions the anthropocentric dimensions of the hand and the reach of an arm. It also indexes through its color, density porosity, and other chemical characteristics, the clay composition of the location where it has been composed and cured. The brick's smallest unit can be referenced in its chemical components as a clay particle, the smallest unit of visible matter, but on a smaller scale of observation and reference, one could identify atomic-level particles that make the atoms and their chemical compositional structure. In fabrication CAM such as 3D printing, robotic arms, and CNC, the actual physical mechanical part develops analog movements that are informed through digital information systems, translating between digital models and analog mechanical movements. When brick bonds are developed through a robotic arm, an anthropocentric body measurement becomes active as a problematic computational linguistic digital signified as a translation of a human arm, and a signifier indexed in the brick form and layout within a visual semiotic environment. In Fusion Deposition Modeling (FDM) in 3D printing, the material is deposited in topographic contours that index the tool path, becoming a particular type of sign dependent, for instance, on the 3D printer and therefore a signifier to architecture. The fabricated objects are built with aggregates by additive progressive materialization, often representing a simulated and optimized process but not addressing the physical properties of the fabrication process nor the environmental conditions where that happens. The most interesting engineers challenge known formal notions through the understanding of the expression of structural forces through material systems and emergent conditions.

There are several positions regarding resisting linear information materialization, or the philosophy of actualization relative to a project that acquires different degrees of the real in a state of becoming. Materiality is generally understood in relation to conventional construction systems, and it can be understood differently. One can argue that a deeper understanding of the intrinsic structural forces in certain materials may even go against accepted knowledge and visual expression. Buckminster Fuller's geodesic dome for the Montreal Biosphére can be understood as a minimal actualization of structural forces. Materiality can be understood by deeply resisting intuitive conventions based on simple observations by augmenting vision, as in the work of Menges identifying how microfibrils behave differently than observable fibers in wood.[6] The linear relationship between material logic and material behavior can be tensioned, as in the work of Tehrani, working against the logic of a material applying the logic of cloth fabric to a wood surface gaining inertia by darting a surface.[7] The form of a project can be informed by computational design simulating material performance through behavioral agents. Moreover, materials can be designed, as is the proposition of Bioart, in which materiality is an exploration of reality. Material logic can be explored by understanding it as a machinic model, to compute relationships in the form of finding process and exploring tendencies in the process of becoming as in the work of Reiser + Umemoto.[8] Materiality can even be understood as a *discipline*, as a machinic resonance regime that defines organizations in the work of Najle[9]. Materiality can be understood in opposition to Plato's metaphysical theory of form, often related to the ideal digital through mathematical vectorial information representation, but that we problematize through computer media interfaces as actualization. Materiality can also be understood in relation to Aristotle's substance, resisting, but also actualizing abstractions, and defining tensions between general and absolute classifications expanding previous definitions of information theory related to the emergent relationships between digital fabrication and material behavior.

Information Processing and Materialization as an Actualization Project

The discussed issues of the problematic relationship between structuralist technological determinism of the Renaissance, the Industrial Revolution, and the Modern Movement and the nondeterministic approach of the post-structuralist theory of the post-war should be worked out to activate indeterminacy in fabrication (Figures 10.1–10.5).

Figure 10.1 A topographic surface informed parametrically through material pavement units. Landscape project displacing material construction techniques, parameterizing concrete blocks dispositions, topographic undulations, and colours. The street blocks relate to the designed landscaped ground undulations accommodating water runoff. The landscape earthwork relates to the umbrella structure originally designed by Amancio Williams, which was strategically placed by the design team. The landfill projected to develop the shore park proposes an environmental balance through sedimentation deposition, later discussed in Chapter 15. Parque de la Costa, Francisco Cadau, Fernando Gimenez, Manuel Galvez, Pablo Lorenzo-Eiroa architects; Designers Florencia Rausch and Santiago Pages; Landscape Design Lucia Schiappapietra; Amancio Williams Umbrella Structure reconstruction: Claudio Veckstein; Buenos Aires, 1999–2001.

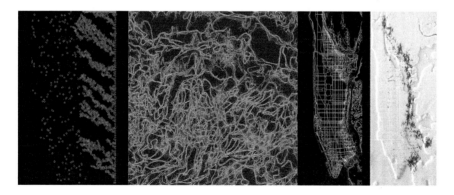

Figure 10.2 A1: sedimentation deposition particle aggregate simulation, later discussed in Chapter 15. B1: Computational Fluid Dynamics simulation using discrete surface topographies to inform landscape interventions. C1: Sedimentation deposition simulation along the East River in NYC. D1: analog simulations of particle deposition; physical 3D printed model. *Structuring Fluid Territories after Hurricane Sandy*, Professor Pablo Lorenzo-Eiroa, students Katherine Bajo and Gregory Shikhman (Manhattan and East River), The Cooper Union, 2012.

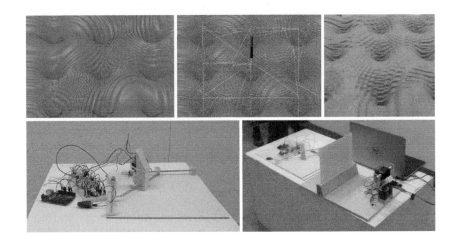

Figure 10.3 A1–C1: Nine square grid parametric surfaces problematizing digital fabrication by indexing and displacing CAM's path and parameters. A2–B2: Robotic plotter and laser beam projector working with microcontrollers. Machines to "draw" and "build", Professor Pablo Lorenzo-Eiroa; Students: A1–C1: Jemuel Joseph and Luis Figallo; A2–B2: Gabriel Munnich and Yaoyi Fan; ARCH 177/482B, The Cooper Union, S2016.

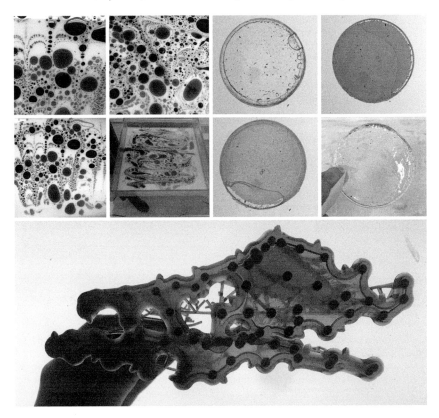

Figure 10.4 3D Printing through the laser-cured resin. Multiple types of 3D printing resin mixes. Resin's reaction to salt and sugar. Varying 3D printing laser code curation parameters while printing activating different degrees of light filtration/refraction. Prof. Pablo Lorenzo-Eiroa, Students: Keren Mendjul, ARCH 482B, The Cooper Union, F2016.

Computational Informational Semiotics 243

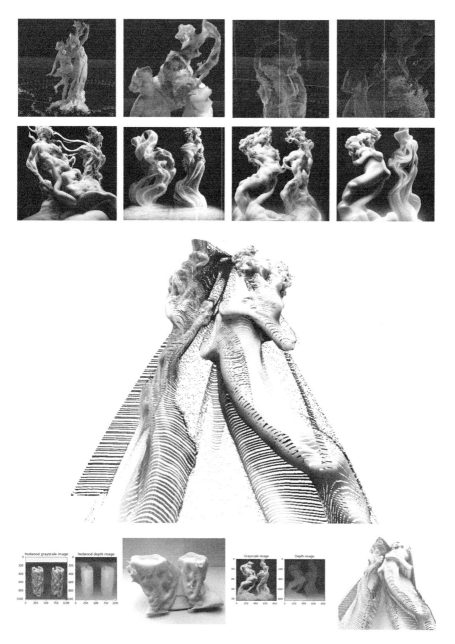

Figure 10.5 Indexical-generative form of art through survey 3D scanning, 2D to 3D AI interpretation and robotic fabrication. A generative reformulation of Bernini's sculpture displacing authorship applying AI machine vision to a Diffusion Model bypassing 2D bumping techniques. We attempt to activate in robotic CNC fabrication some aspects of Bernini's qualities in sculpting stone. (See Note Figure 10.5)

Geometry and Information Feedback in Material Actualization

A mathematical parametric plot presents an example of a problem of actualization through vectorial media or material mediums. The parametric plot can represent a mathematical surface equation relative to X, Y, and Z, and within a range within a Cartesian Coordinate plot. One can represent geometrically almost any contemporary 3D geometry through current 3D mathematical plots by adding or subtracting terms in a mathematical script. Mathematical scripts do not replace computational geometry, as they can do permutations and combination but cannot implement mathematical recursive algorithms to perform, calculate and resolve problems in geometry. In addition, there is a balance between mathematics as parameters of relationships in a geometric mathematical plot and over-parameterization. Over-parameterization activates localized fragmented deterministic projection of geometry as deterministic form of plotting a intricate particularized non generalizable geometry using mathematics, but breaking the purpose of emergent general mathematical narratives across a geometry as a form of knowledge. A parametric plotted surface can be actualized in several ways, the surface plot can be represented through lines, surfaces, or material terms by constructing planar ribs that describe the curves u and v of the parametric plot. Often, architects, except for expertise in mathematics, geometry, and fabrication, by default construct a parametric plot extruding the u and v curves without addressing which curve carries the argument of the equation, in order to address gravity through ribs-beams, a descriptive geometry problem which becomes unavoidable in certain complex surfaces or more evident in the revolving translation curve of spiral stairs. In different types of surfaces, u and v may carry different arguments and hierarchies, may transition arguments between u and v, or may follow each other at lower hierarchy argument curves. In a cylinder, the generatrix curve of a surface/volume (circle) carries the geometrical argument, while the directrix of a surface/volume (straight line axis) develops the curve argument along an axis. In certain surfaces, there is an exchange in terms of u and v curves of the generative aspect of a curve, such as in minimal surfaces like the Costa Minimal Surface, in which u and v exchange arguments, directions, and orientations describing a transition in topology. In a Helicoid surface, the translation surface has two same generatrix along a directrix axis. On some surfaces, there is no hierarchy. This understanding of this distinction helps to expand dimensions in the architecture of a surface/volume and its actualizations through various materials, machinery, and fabrication techniques (Figures 10.6–10.8).

Instead of extruding u and v curves to address gravity (Figure 10.7 D2), one can offset u and v normal to the n surface vector, so that the u and v curves develop a local topological geodesic projective geometry through a 3D flexible rib system that would actualize in thicker terms the mathematical surface at that point and range. Geodesic curves and asymptotic curves (Figure 10.6, 10.7 D3)[10,11] contrast with principal curvature lines of actualized reduced meshes (Figure 10.8 A9-D10).[12] 3D digital surfaces were digitally fabricated by plotting or laser cutting flat developable ruled surfaces in between geodesic curves, describing double curvature, from the mathematical parametric plot and ribs u and v offset to n normal surface vector, being able to reconstruct both the surface and the shared borders in between surfaces; one of the first digital fabrication techniques thanks to the discussed unfold command in Form Z (1990s, Chapter 7).

A known fabrication technique is a topographical model, which basically recreates a topographical landscape by adding standardized material layers to create a 3D physical model topography, dealing with double curvature as the directrix

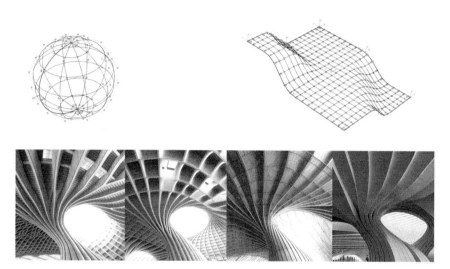

Figure 10.6 Often, we see a separation between architecture theory as cultural criticism and architecture technology as a deterministic science. We do research and pedagogy aim at critiquing this artificial separation by addressing a discovered architecture problem through a unique type of project-specific computation. We do not teach computation as an isolated skill building technological problem, but as a unique philosophy that becomes active through the media, eventually developing a new media or a new medium. Likewise, we also resist design isolated from architectonics, as we problematize judgment based on subjective aesthetics based on cultural conventions built by media desire without engaging with the politics of the discipline in relation to contemporary philosophy and science. A1: usually, spheres are conventionally represented in 3D Software through global world bias projection of correct longitudinal nonparallel geodesic curves, and problematic parallel latitude circle sections, instead of the Wulff net stereographic projection recognizing the surface n normal vectors. B2: Surface n normal vectors perpendicular to the tangent of the curvature of the surface. Often in fabrication the Z dimension extrusion of a 2D surface based on u and v curves becomes a bias convention projecting gravity. A stereographic projective geometry of the n normal vector of the relative local topology of any surface would project the Z dimension, not as an extrusion but perpendicular to each normal vector. A2-D2: Wood structure double curvature in relation to surface offset normals in relation to u and v distorted geodesic projection. Pablo Lorenzo-Eiroa, DM MJ, 2022.

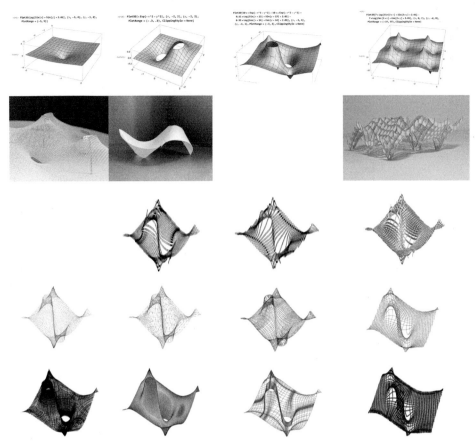

Figure 10.7 A1-B1: Mathematical parametric surface plot defining a field of points and a point as a limit and a singularity. Distinctions between mathematics and physics in architecture geometry and fabrication. C1-D1: Points are mathematically scripted to become spatial voids and activate a surface topology of positive and negative space in a simultaneously synclastic and partially anticlastic surface. The surfaces activate mathematical notions of minimal surfaces in physics. A2-B2; A5-D5: Mathematical geometry actualized through structural emergence through a material computation form-finding process, material actualization, fabrication, and descriptive and projective geometry in tension with each other. A2: analog tensioned surface model minimal surface after Frei Otto; B2: paper analog model surface tension through darting and crease curve folding; D2: mathematical parametric plot actualized as extruded ribs becoming "beams" in the Z axis addressing gravity; B3-D3: mathematical parametric plot ribs u and v offset to n normal surface vector; A4-B4-: Quadrating mesh, Triangulated mesh from mathematical surface; C4: triangulated mesh after topological optimization; D4: isocurves after stress based topological optimization; A5: evolutionary topological structural optimization stress lines output; B5: optimized quadratic NURBS surface with Gaussian stress region; C4: topologically optimized NURBS isocurves; D4: u and v ribs describing topologically optimized surface. An alternative fabrication method can bypass u and v representing only the main argument of the surface or curve generatrix, disregarding by default the other direction or directrix as parallel ribs attached next to each other parameterizing downsampling the surface double curvature in relation to a material thickness develop the surface directrix. Research Studio, Prof. Pablo Lorenzo-Eiroa, Student: Salma Kattass, ARCH 702B, MS ACT Program, SoAD, NYIT S2022. Mathematical formula and comparative surfaces u and v PI Pablo Lorenzo-Eiroa, RA Trushita Yadav, IDC Foundation, 2022.

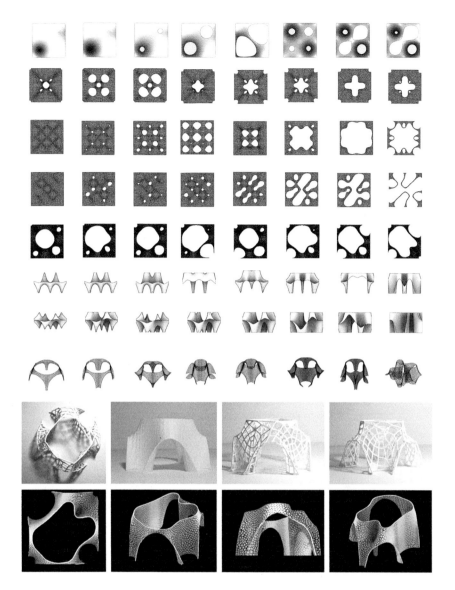

Figure 10.8 A1-H8: Parametric surface plots through surface relaxation structural simulation identifying typological variation displacing dimensionally points as singularity and voids as negative space displacing a nine square grid organization. 3D Meshes as embedded physics in computation active through structural simulation. A9-D9: 3D printing digital fabrication actualization variation exercises. B9: Conventional structural mesh optimization disregarding: vector normals in 3D printing (conventional CAM layering tool path for FDM using parallel deposition), therefore applying computational biases by *translating* between different interfaces, media, and mediums. A9, C9, D9: conventional 3D printing of non-conventional mesh geometry optimization designed to recover u and v double curvature of the result optimized geometry. The mesh may or may not match the u and v structure. While mathematical geometry develops a surface out of u and v directrix and generatrix composing its structure, mesh geometry optimization results from local topological gaussian curvature actualization (quads or triangles) purposely disregarding by default any knowledge-structure of the surface. A10-D10: 3D mesh geometric optimization in relation to surface structural optimization. Research Studio, Prof. Pablo Lorenzo-Eiroa, Student: Salma Kattass, ARCH 702B, MS ACT Program, SoAD, NYIT S2022.

248 *Computational Informational Semiotics*

of the surface can express the shifting of the X and Y axes, a technique analogue to construction and beam/ribs construction method in boat hulls. For 3D printing, this problem remains, since any conventional 3D printer through FDM would address fabrication relative to X, Y, and Z but actually in the form of filament deposition extrusion layer by layer, reducing the Z-axis to a topography of layered deposition of material. This reduction makes the surface actualization be formed in a specific way, offering advantages but also problems to certain types of surfaces. To bypass the layer deposition reduction, a technique developed back in the early 2000s was to develop a modified tool path by coding a customized G-Code (tool path code) and M-Code (machine code). By modifying the G-Code in any 3D printer one can transform the material deposition by shifting the Z-axis while the FDM occurs, an operation that can be done with 3D printers and that is expanded through multi-axis robotic arms, therefore expanding the dimensional axis of the model and the machine (Figure 10.9, 10.10, 10.11). One can work out the angle, speed, feeder, temperature, general form, and material behavior in relation to the environmental conditions of the environment in which the printing happens (Figure 10.9).

One can develop sophisticated structural and material simulations digitally with increasingly complex simulation engines, but the physical actualization of these simulations in physical form deviates from the reductive approximative digital simulation. In general, the relationship between mathematics and physics is also disjunct in architecture. We explore the relationship between mathematical surfaces and their structural physics possibilities, aiming at pairing and correlating mathematics with physics through an informed 3D printing process. Geometries may have anisotropic qualities as their material behavior changes differently in relation to dimensions, and mathematics does not contemplate gravitational and environmental forces, processes, and conditions (Figure 10.11), but many structural forms contemplating gravity may have a mathematical translation since physics engines are based on the computation of mathematical equations.

Even if a robotic arm has a dimensional axis set by each rotation ability of the robotic arm, with an end effector and/or end diffusor added on one can activate several dimensional problems relative to actualizations. In 3D printing with a robotic arm, the previous problem of the Z reference axis of the bridge-dependent 3D printer is surpassed by the ability of the robotic arm to move in several axes. This allows for a robotic arm to be able to develop FDM in real 3D space, displacing the Z-axis directrix of the form as it rotates in the extrusion of the surface/volume. The combination of the several possible axes increases dimensional possibilities in the actualization of form. The base of the robotic arm can also shift as well while the robotic arm is building, enabling additional dimensional qualities and flexibility. Form, as is actualized through fabrication, is not only "constructed" but is rather actualized through systems of representation limiting, problematizing, or expanding dimensions in relation to its constitution. In an informed model, physical actualizations can be related to media-dependent vectorial mathematical digital actualizations and they rather present a higher dimensional geometric projective problem in architecture relative to representation and not only a state of matter.

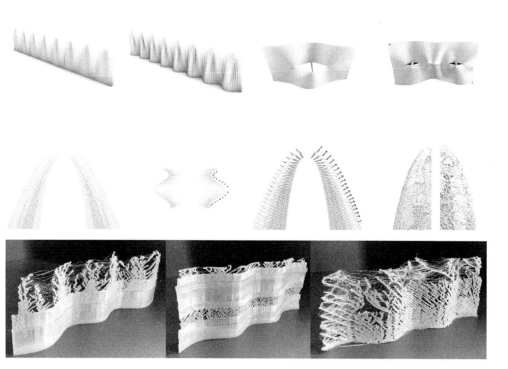

Figure 10.9 We worked with bricks based on the architecture and engineering of Eladio Dieste (Church-Center for Barrio El Ceibo, Vicente Lopez Shore Park Figure 10.1, Casa Ramirez in different associations in Argentina between 1996-2004). We defined the brick as a minimum architecture sign; to qualify the definition of architecture conventional elements such as a wall, by making each brick in the surface acquire a different relative topological value. The brick unit as a building construction sign can be related to a 3D voxel unit digital sign. We aim at displacing conventional notions of continuity and discreteness through certainty and uncertainty. Fused Deposition Modelling (FDM) as aggregate particles from materials fused together, and point clouds as discrete minimum 0D digital vectors, propose a different type of signifier in both fabrication and digital architecture. The brick modulation as well as the voxel unit are now replaced by a dimensional expansion given by point-based digital vectors and particle based FDM. We aim at pairing point clouds and FDM as two signifiers to expand architecture into a new dimensional quality and measuring reference (see also Chapter 13 Figures 13.16, 13.17 which refer to robotic FDM aggregate). We also aim at pairing FDM as particle aggregate with physics particles simulation in Computational Fluid Dynamic simulation and particle aggregates in nature such as sedimentation, pairing construction with incremental aggregate evolutionary growth (Figure 10.2, Chapter 15). A1, B1: Dieste's Atlantida Church wall mathematical reconstruction analytical studies; C1, D1: digital models physical emergent minimal surface tension by adding inertia across the wall section. A2, B2, C2, D2: Conventional 3 axis 3D Printer manipulated G-Code to develop a tool path following the u and v directions offset from the directrix and generatrix surface components in the original mathematical script, avoiding the biases of extruding or sectioning aleatory curves in conventional slicers that by default translate a surface u and v directions without indexing their mathematical constitution. The three-dimensional movement of the 3D printer is expanded by one axis by moving the nozzle in X, Y, and Z simultaneously while printing to achieve curved diagonal printing. A3, B3, C3: Emergent Cellular Automation patterns information actualization through 3D printing. A3: incremental variable changes in relation to axis dimensional expansion and curvature; B3: variations in relation to wall inertia; C3: increasing speed and flow rate 3D printing filament deposition to activate an emergent structure through information actualization. Research Studio, Prof. Pablo Lorenzo-Eiroa, Student: Yousef Ismail, ARCH 702B MS ACT Program, SoAD, NYIT S2022.

250 *Computational Informational Semiotics*

Through Machine Learning, one can train an ANN, CNN, VQGAN, and GAN to recognize through machine vision feature recognition issues in fabrication in order to self-calibrate through feedback an ongoing CAM Process in real time updating G-code and M-Code (Figure 10.10, 10.11). There is then a critique of media determinism that applies not only to Software but also to an understanding of construction through informed loops between simulation, optimization, and robotic fabrication real-time feedback. Since one can automate the relationship between modeling and simulation one can feedback on real-time construction activating a forensic architecture and a projective design as it is being design-built displacing the media determinism of anticipatory digital models and CAM. We paired architecture interactivity as post-occupancy use measured real time through sensors and the IoT. From a 2D image, a 3D model[13,14] is reconstructed by implementing Deep

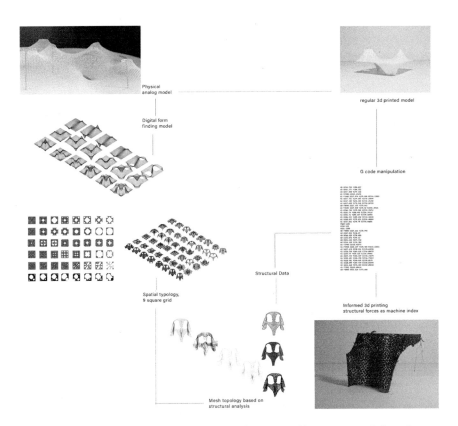

Figure 10.10 Design as AI architecture of information fabrication workflow framework actualizing real-time G-Code as correlational material, structural and behavioral properties work in the deposition of filament in 3d Printing. Research Studio, Prof. Pablo Lorenzo-Eiroa, Student Salma Kattass, ARCH 702B, MS ACT Program, SoAD, NYIT S2022.

Computational Informational Semiotics 251

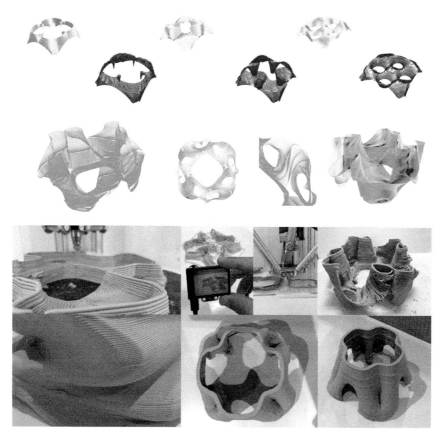

Figure 10.11 A1–D4: Tool path from normal surface u and v expanding dimensional Cartesian 3d printing and parallel G-Code parameters modified addressing clay robotic 3D printing. Real-time G-Code shift in relation to changing variable structural simulation and stress analysis. The G-Code is optimized real time as it delivers different parameters while its printing, achieving a structurally optimized print in relation to the digital simulation by adding or lightening the amount of material feed rate and by pressuring the nozzle while printing, making a wider compressed density deposition. This is considered an added dimension in the process which is not usually contemplated in abstract bidimensional surfaces. The printed thick surface behaves topologically as the print varies according to the G-Code updates. B3, C3: Machine Learning classifier for G-Code printed line category sagging for G-Code actualization. Preliminary Machine Vision Semantic Tagging-Classification "Fail" to shift G-Code real time while printing. Research Studio, Prof. Pablo Lorenzo-Eiroa, Students: Yousef Ismail, Salma Kattass, Farah Jalil, ARCH 702B MS ACT Program, SoAD, NYIT S2022.

252   *Computational Informational Semiotics*

Learning AI, an automated 3D scene that can then become a point cloud to cross-compare with the developed dataset real time (See Fig. 7.11-7.13). One can then interpolate the 3D new model scanned while it is being 3D printed in relation to the dataset and trained ANN that is able to interpolate structural simulation (see Fig. 12.8-12). This achieves a real-time comparison and calibration between the actual construction emergent conditions in relation to a trained meta-data repository. This presents another case of dimensional expansion from 2D to 3D through algorithmic processing instead of through the CAM system; a double bind adversarial 3D printing feedback framework (Figures 10.10 and 10.11).

Some of these emergent site factors could be the varying environmental conditions of the space of the 3D Printing, the variable pressure and humidity of the space, the variable structural forces that become active while the print is made physically, and others. Usually, the environmental simulation and the structural simulation are a form of displacement of ideal mathematical conditions through a pragmatism that incorporates physics within a digital simulation, but that often still remain abstract as they do not match the complex variable correlational reality of the form of actualization given by the 3D print which needs to incorporate variable environmental site conditions. A reverse engineering process would be able to identify such a differential by incorporating this difference at the material output and fabrication level, since one can optimize the relationship between the ideal digital form and the manufactured industrial form given by the CAM system. The entire sequence becomes intertwined codependent interdependent emergent and correlational: from machine vision to sensing interaction, to semantic feature recognition to self-calibration, to automated emergent feedback loops to more complex automata tasks (Figure 10.11 and further expanded in research in Chapters 11-14).

Architecture of Information:
Building Faster-Than-Light Speed Here and Elsewhere in the Universe

We discussed how information theory could be used to actualize architecture fabrication. We discussed information theory in relation to automata theory in Chapter 6. Self-replication can become active through simulation since a robotic virtual program can replicate itself as a virtual machine, or a physical von Neumann probe can replicate itself through local planet materials elsewhere in the universe. One could contemplate developing a self-replicator as an encoded information programming message to develop a universal constructor somewhere else through remote physical signal processing since one could devise the means to build on another planet by sending information through LiDAR wave, radio wave, or Laser wave physical signals and activating a self-organizational program sign remotely as a physical signal informing local conditions, environments, and materials. This form of actualization would be shifting information from a virtual binary computational linguistic semiotic coded sign, to a visual semiotic physical lightwave signal, to a distant semiotic analog physical signal as a transformation of a distant environment. In addition, a distant environmental physical wave signal flow could also be informed through wave signals transmission, matching the signal processing, the signal transmission, and the signal transformation. Alexander's "pattern language" in which Chomsky's linguistic grammar becomes generative as it informs organization, can infer genetic coding or a system that can generate a system,[15] an evolutive morphogenesis.

We can think of surveying, measuring, and analyzing, through remote sensing representation, and inverting its physical LiDAR or Laser signal measuring function to structuring of an informed reality. The sun alters and enables life in our solar system through photon physical signals every day. With students, we explored means to draw and build, and some projects achieve a way of building through information communication faster than the speed of light through a laser beam (Figures 10.12–10.14). We developed means to draw by the speed of light and beyond through laser beams, which can reach up to 300 times the speed of light[16], drawing in space but also defining a space-environment. Instead of sending robotic machines and objects, deployable to other planets to expand humanity beyond our planet, we envision a different version through matching media and medium in computational information-based communication semiotic processes which could reorganize matter, energy, and information elsewhere. We can think of displacing environments elsewhere by sending laser information-coded physical signals that can inform a distant environment in such a way that would reorganize it into a space-environment, build up from within site-specific conditions, and inhabitable enough for humans. We can also think of a physical signal activating a sign, a self-replicating program as a virtual machine digital sign elsewhere, and developing means to reorganize matter using local materials. We discussed Information Theory signal processing in message transmission. Different survey technologies implement different types of signals to record, map and represent reality; different signals are used to encrypt, process, and transmit messages whether visible or not, such as electrical, electronic, radio waves, electromagnetic waves, light waves, infrared light, sound waves, ultrasound. In terms of signal processing, a digital to analog converter (DAC) can convert a digital signal into analog signals, for instance from audio to visual signals. To control the temperature of an environment we can use a DAC through the numeric digital interpretation of the physical signal thermal sensing of a thermostat to affect physically the temperature of an environment. Inversely, one can use an Analog to Digital Conversion (ADC) to convert an analog signal into a digital signal. We research means to simultaneously measure, map, survey and affect a space real time

Figure 10.12 Building through information signal and sign representation mediation. A series of projective geometry techniques to "draw" a virtual computer-coded parametric surface. Machinic system interrelating background media and foreground emergent design, including non-linear feedback, representation, and machinic emergent technologies as part of the project. A robotic machine can expand dimensions between drawing and projective geometry techniques if the architect is able to expand the design process to include the systems of representation. The architect can expand and do research innovating in new emergent technologies that may open cultural disciplinary problems, instead of designing by applying technology developed by others. Robotic laser drawing builds up a space through projective geometry. Machines to "Draw" and "Build", Prof. Pablo Lorenzo-Eiroa, students: Gabriel Munnich and Yaoyi Fan, ARCH 177/482B, The Cooper Union, 2015. Laser beams are up to 300 times faster-than-light speed. The machine in the figure can develop/actualize information communication as a space-environment faster than any building ever done. One can think of activating a terraforming environmental process at a distance directly through laser beam signals, by identifying the distant environmental signals and modifying them through laser signals. Even with such speeds of signal transmission, to send a message-program to activate physical signals across planets remains a speculative theory and a challenge: from the distance measured in light years, to the medium gravitational distortion of the space-time fabric, to the atmospheric noise, to the translating DAC or ADC mechanism.

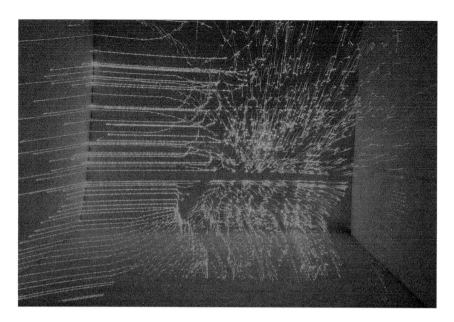

Figure 10.13 Laser beam defining a space-environment. Machines to "Draw" and "Build", Prof. Pablo Lorenzo-Eiroa, students: Gabriel Munnich and Yaoyi Fan, ARCH 177/482B, The Cooper Union, 2015.

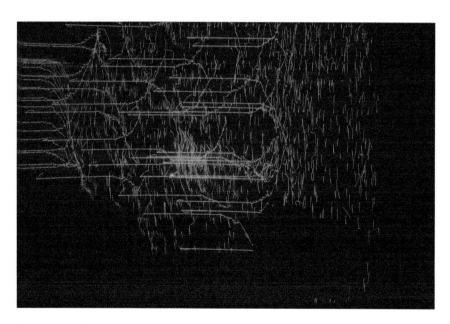

Figure 10.14 The emergent machines to draw and build are meant to critique the structuralism imposed by known technologies, tools, and machines of representation. By developing a drawing tool using physical computation a laser beam projects the virtual geometry of a parametric surface into a shifting interface-background space, problematizing the spectrum between the subject and the object, by instead, developing a project by motivating the interface (medium) and its background machinic reference technology. Machines to Draw and Build, Prof. Pablo Lorenzo-Eiroa, students: Gabriel Munnich and Yaoyi Fan, ARCH 177/482B, The Cooper Union, 2015.

through double bind adversarial feedback through informational semiotics of digital virtual signs and physical signals. We propose an informational semiotics which can represent/alter environments through real-time double bind adversarial information feedback. The double bind adversarial feedback becomes an evolving AI self-editing self-replicating exponential morphogenesis.

Double Bind Adversarial Feedback = Media Sign (Signifier/signified) / Medium Signal

Self-replicating clusters of cells freed from a developing organism can find, and combine loose cells into clusters and by side effects of replication develop "xenobots"[17] designed AI systems by scientists outside of genetic manipulation. We expand a von Neumann universal constructor that would include a self-replicating automaton to topologically engage with its own environment transforming it, therefore developing a site-based computational system, such as CA, but that is both internally and externally dependent on learning from its environment, affecting it. We are also aiming at working this process through self-replication of intelligent automata so that the feedback can elevate in each recursive feedback a higher exponential learning process that optimizes itself and learns from both internal self-replication and external environmental conditions.

If information is in fact equal to matter and energy as discussed in relation to Shannon entropy and as postulated by information theory as the mass-energy information equivalence, one can think of modifying matter through energy informationally at a distance. We can therefore develop information-based physical signals, from understanding, analyzing, and displacing information physical signals flows, for instance measuring and informing mobility in cities discussed in Chapter 17, to simulating and informing computational fluid dynamics to trace and affect environments discussed in Chapter 15, to inform the dynamics of space-environments discussed in Chapter 5, to directly processing information remotely through physical signals without the necessity to decode them but to think them as BITs affecting BITs pairing the physical signal as input and output. We can also address information as an emergent form of Being. Nick Bostrom[18] published that a technological civilization with enough immersive power could simulate realities with conscious Beings in them, anticipating sentinels (Chapter 19 Simulacra).

Notes

1 Liddell, S. *A Greek–English Lexicon*, Clarendon Press, Oxford, 1940
2 Lorenzo-Eiroa, P. "La ampliación del concepto de autoría entre dibujo y construcción", en *Detalles constructivos*, 3 Revista PLOT, Buenos Aires, 2016

3 Lorenzo-Eiroa, P. "Expanding Authorship in Materiality", in ed. Del Campo, Matias and Biloira Nimish, *Info Matter*, Next Generation Building, 2012

4 Carpo, M. *The Alphabet and The Algorithm*, MIT, Cambridge, 2011

5 Lorenzo-Eiroa, P. "Somos monos en frente a la computadora?", *Clarin Arq*, Buenos Aires, 2012

6 Menges, A. "Coalescences of Machine and Material Computation", in ed. Lorenzo-Eiroa, P. and Sprecher, A., *Architecture In Formation*, Routledge, London, 2013

7 Toshiko M. *Immaterial|Ultramaterial*, Harvard Design School, New York, 2002

8 Reiser, J.; Umemoto N. *Atlas of Novel Tectonics*, PAP, New York, 2006.

9 Najle, C. *Material Discipline*, PAP, New York, 2009

10 Schilling, E.; Lilian, M.; Wang, H.; Schikore, J.; Pottmann, H. "Design and Construction of Curved Support Structures with Repetitive Parameters", in *AAG2018*, 2018

11 Schilling, E.; "Designing Grid Structures Using Asymptotic Curve Networks", *Design Modelling Symposium*, Paris, 2017

12 Abaza, M.; Fierro, P.; Ghani, A.; "Asymptotic Gridshells: Applications and Analysis", Master Thesis, MIT, Cambridge, 2019

13 Fan, Haoqiang; Su, Hao; Guibas, Leonidas. "A Point Set Generation Network for 3D Object Reconstruction from a Single Image", in *IEEE, CVPR, 2017*

14 Denninger, M.; Triebel, R. "3D Scene Reconstruction from a Single Viewport", in *ECCV*, 2020

15 Alexander, C. "Systems Generating Systems", in *Architectural Design*, Volume 38, 1968

16 Wang, L.J.; Kuzmich, A.; Dogariu, A. "Gain-assisted superluminal light propagation", in *Nature*, Volume 406, 2000

17 Kriegman, S.; Blackiston, D.; Levin, M.; Bongard, J. "Kinematic Self-Replication in Reconfigurable Organisms", in *PNAS*, Volume 118, Issue. 49, 2021

18 Bostrom, N. "Are We Living in a Simulation?", in *The Philosophical Quarterly*, Volume 53, Issue 211, 2003

Figure 10.5 "A Faun Teased by Children" by Pietro and Gian Lorenzo Bernini (1616–17) and "Apollo and Daphne" (1622–25) by G. L. Bernini, are inf luenced by Michelangelo's "Moses" (1513–15), who was also probably inspired by the Greek "Barberini Faun" (200 BCE). Michelangelo's autonomy in sculpture identified the incompleteness of the work of art as a process of discovery of the stone properties indexing what the stone wishes to be. Bernini's sculpture proposes a precision through marble sculpting that transcends the logic of what stone is, exploring dimensional and structural limits, from thin fragile surfaces that through branching group become structural, to the illusion of a layered transparency, activating a kinetic art indexing the observer's movement (challenged by Wittkower). We develop an indexical-generative form of art through survey 3D scanning, 2D to 3D AI interpretation and robotic fabrication. A generative reformulation of Bernini's sculpture displacing authorship applying machine vision to a DM bypassing 2D bumping techniques. We attempt to activate in robotic CNC fabrication some aspects of Bernini's qualities in sculpting stone. A1-D1: "Apollo and Daphne" by G.L. Bernini, 3D photogrammetry by author; PI Pablo Lorenzo-Eiroa, RA Yousef Ismail, 2022. A2-D2: "Apollo and Daphne", DM generative 3D simulation, DM retrieved via API; PI Pablo Lorenzo-Eiroa, MidJourney, 2022. A4, C4: AI Machine Vision reconstruction through Monocular Depth Estimation via Content-Adaptive multi-resolution merging 2D to 3D. A3, B4, D4: AI reconstructed 3D Point Cloud for 3D print and a CNC robotic stone sculpture; B4: AI 3D reconstruction as a regular volume; D4: 3D reconstruction as a landscape; PI Pablo Lorenzo-Eiroa, RA Beken Amde, IDC Foundation Grant, 2022.

11 Gaudi's Analog Computational Model as Parallel Processing

From Mathematical Modeling, to Big Data Survey, to Simulation, to AI

History Section:
Proto-modernism; Catalonian Modernism; Methodology:
Darwinian Evolution; Evolutionary Morphogenetics; Biodigital Design; Evidence-Based Design; Data-Based Design Optimization; Analog Machinic Computational Model; Information-Based Model;

Computational Visual Semiotics:
Analog Simulation (Catenary Model, Inverted catenary arch); Digital Simulation (Structural Simulation and Optimization); Surface Relaxation; Computational Visual Semiotic Signifiers:
Particles; Weights; Control Points; Point Cloud;

Mathematics:
Geometry; Descriptive Geometry; Differential Equations; Differential Calculation; Parabola; Paraboloid;

Physics:
Physics; Mechanics; Hooke Analogy (chain catenary-arch); Catenary Model; Catenary Surface-Catenoid Minimal Surface; Inverted Catenary Arch;

From Catenaries as Analog Structural Simulation, to Analog Computation as Parallel Processing, to an Informational Performative Model

Gaudi in the context of historical sections traced in the book relating computation and architectural representation can be understood as the first analog computational machinic architect through his physical catenary models used to simulate the structural design of his buildings.

Gaudi's work has been critiqued by several architects, often identified with the Catalonian Modernism and the Arts and Crafts movement in Europe. Gaudi's work can be analyzed as an alternative to the Modern Movement carrying some of its manifestoes in relation to technology and science, if one can understand his semiotic style not only as cultural visual expressionism but as an intellectual attempt to actualize Darwin's scientific theory of evolution as a close reading of Nature through physics, structure, organization, and

DOI: 10.4324/9781003292036-12

evolutionary morphogenesis as a search for transcendental truth. This reading makes more complex the usual visual reading relating his work indexing Nature as a biomimicry approximation, elevating his work to understanding a deep coding of structural forces and an interpretation of morphogenesis. Gaudi's architectural columns can be simultaneously read through: as a historical quotation to a column as an architectural sign; as a novel structural modern element expanding its function and through simulation optimizing its performance; as a rhetorical symbolic natural sign; and as a formal element placed under the dynamics of evolutionary natural morphogenesis. Gaudi developed a formal gradient deconstruction of conventional measurement, typologies and classifications in construction systems based on natural complex evolutionary patterns. Gaudi's trencadis are broken industrial ceramic tiles used to resolve through fragments double curvature in construction, or constructing by destruction, displacing the deterministic concept of a standard module, a philosophical critique of conceptual binary classifying dialectical logic in contrast to Nature's non-binary gradients. Gaudi's Catalonian Modernism was based on the Arts and Crafts European movement, critical of the universal machinic aesthetics of the Modern Movement based on the industrialization of construction. His architecture necessarily depended on a development and expansion of a social-political architecture project of cooperative labor integrating and sustaining local craft such as the experimental patronage of the Güell Colony, defining a modern archi-techne in relation to formal actualization. The intensity of his work achieves a linguistic visual semiotic status that is both based on a Natural Realism and an Abstract Machinic reading. Gaudi's innovation consisted of developing a scientific form-finding structural mechanism through analog physical models that work through catenary forces, a system initiated by Galileo Galilei in 1638 differentiating a catenary from a paraboloid, and Robert Hooke's[1] analogy of 1670, drawing by Polenti, of 1748. Rubio I Bellver in 1913 sketches the application of loads to develop a catenary using sandbags.[2] Gaudi Catenary model for Sagrada Familia 1929 (picture by Rafols) has been used since 1880 according to Rubio. Gaudi's Surface models surpass all precedent models by developing a calculating machine that engages with complex calculations that are correlational and generational with feedback.

Gaudi's work could also be understood through an analog computational visual semiotics as a mathematical signal processing of physics since his catenary machinic system is indeed a system of representation that can design-compute an architectural structure with a precision dependent on the physical signal-transmission quality, which is a product of the function of the material in relation to the physical mechanical parts. This analog computer model can perform arithmetic and algebraic functions to add, subtract, triangulate, diversify, expand, bifurcate, and correlate structural forces and stress in concatenated surfaces. Gaudi's innovation to design through analog real-time simulation-optimization as an a-precise calculation of the building form. This formal method can be read of critical of geometry as a field of study in mathematics as a rigid static application of knowledge, to compute formal complexity

Gaudí's model has the following information on transferring, and processing computing characteristics:

through physics. The model is evolutionary, complex, simulation-based, optimizable adjustable, and therefore emergent computationally since one cannot anticipate the set of reactions the different chains will place on others without running stress through the model correlationally and generationally. The computational model involves site-based computation and simulation, since, depending on the model and its complexity, the first set of catenaries can either be decomposed into smaller ones through vertical lines and then recompose in parallel the simulation and computation, or the entire set depending on the next site or next generation set of calculations of catenaries. The analog model seems to offer advantages over some digital computational models such as Cellular Automation since CA cannot affect a previous generation backward. The model can be made recursive once (unless further input is given) activating algebra through feedback, as generational site-based computation becomes emergent nonreversible nondeterministic. The model is a methodology of design truly performative, as it is also representational since it works both as a structural model and a way to represent and formulate through scalar notation the form of the building. The model is also informational since the model is a system of measurement weight-dependent that is able to calculate and process information real-time and that can be validated and applied to a 1:1 scale building. The physical signal computing inputs and outputs are communicated through the responsive machine that gives feedback to both laterally correlationally, upwards and downwards generations, activating a computing neural network that can perform parallel processing recursively once. The model is non-linguistic since the processing of the physical signal matches across the computational model without translation. In terms of systems of representation, we discussed the model as a structural engine, but Gaudí's model both implements and critiques Lorenzetti's perspective as a visual semiotic system of representation. The geometry of the triangulation of the catenary represents Gaudí the Trinity in the Christian religion. The vanishing point (VP) is paired with the inflection point of the catenary, which can never be reached by the physical catenary, for instance in the constructed inverted catenary of the towers of the Sagrada Família Basilica building looking up, a different immanence from Lorenzetti's VP as non-depictable, unreachable.

Gaudí's model has the following information on transferring, and processing computing characteristics:

1 Abstract Generic Knowledge: Scientific evidence-based, a mathematical analog computational model for geometry construction (precision of mathematical calculation given by the precision of the materials and scale implemented);

2 Abstract Computational Machine: generic structural knowledge, scientific evidence-based, a structural simulation model based on Catenaries;

3 Simulation-based recursive computational model which depending on complexity and emergence may achieve nonreversible computation critical of geometry (with reservations);

4 Bifurcation-based informational model, algebraic structure, recursive (once);
5 Codependent informational model;
6 Site-based computational model;
7 Evolutionary computational model (with reservations) based on a similar rationale to the Game of Life or an interpretation of the physics of Nature, in which internal structure and external site-conditions' feedback on each other, but that in this case, feedback on previous generations;
8 Generation-based computational model;
9 Emergent computational design model;
10 Morphogenesis based on abstracted notions and studies of natural evolutionary systems from a formal logic evolutionary design process;
11 If nonreversible, then nondeterministic;
12 Parallel processing computational model: neural network node-base computation becomes parallel computing through correlational based computation within a generation and concatenated catenaries through forward and backward analog physical signal processing across generations;
13 Non-linguistic semiotic, non-representational physical signal-based computational system, since, the physical signal is the mathematical signal and the sign unless one considers scalar representation to the building, which is not necessary for the machine to validate its output.

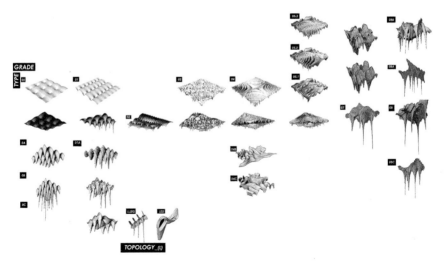

Figure 11.1 Decoding aspects of Gaudi's Sagrada Familia through mathematics. Parametric mathematical surface plots, degree topological change displacing typological structural classifications. Parametric Gaudi, Visiting Prof. Pablo Lorenzo Eiroa, with Students Ernesto Arias, Alejandro Cruz Mendoza, Ronaldo Fiuza, Bruno Jaramillo, David Romero Martel, Dario Sanchez, Sarah Winkler and Harold Woods; TA Pablo Baquero, UIC Biodigital Master Program Dir. Alberto T. Estévez, 2014.

Gaudi's Analog Computational Model as Parallel Processing 263

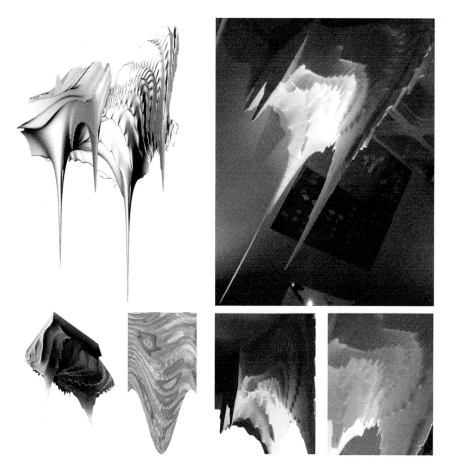

Figure 11.2 A 0D point translated in space defines a 1D line, then expands into a 2D surface to create a 3D volume constituted through a single mathematical surface plot. This point to volume sequence is based on Brunelleschi's geometric progression that considers a column a point in space unmotivating matter and materiality, and where the developing line of a column becomes integrated with a vaulted ceiling. This mathematical surface activates Gaudi's structural studies displacing mathematics to address physics through structure. The information materialization process uses a three-axis CNC milling machine. The final product does not acquire enough autonomy as the material remains inert in relation to the form given, a problem addressed in Chapter 12. *Parametric Gaudi*, Visiting Prof. Pablo Lorenzo Eiroa, with Students Ernesto Arias, Alejandro Cruz Mendoza, Ronaldo Fiuza, Bruno Jaramillo, David Romero Martel, Dario Sanchez, Sarah Winkler and Harold Woods; TA Pablo Baquero, UIC Biodigital Master Program Dir. Alberto T. Estévez, 2014.

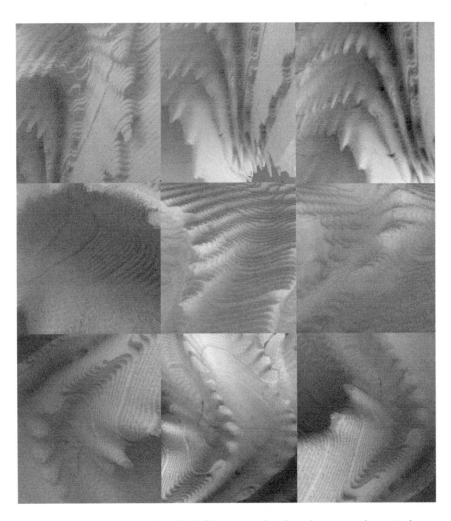

Figure 11.3 Parametric Gaudi, CNC fabrication details indexing mathematical parametric equations through the contouring of the milled material. Parametric Gaudi, Visiting Prof. Pablo Lorenzo Eiroa, with Students Ernesto Arias, Alejandro Cruz Mendoza, Ronaldo Fiuza, Bruno Jaramillo, David Romero Martel, Dario Sanchez, Sarah Winkler and Harold Woods; TA Pablo Baquero, UIC Biodigital Master Program Dir. Alberto T. Estévez, 2014.

Gaudi's Analog Computational Model as Parallel Processing 265

Figure 11.4 Sagrada Familia 3D scanning photogrammetry point cloud through multiple perspectival camera registrations placed in contrast to catenary structural simulation; contrasting representational strategies such as perspectival photogrammetry survey in tension with catenary gravitational simulation. *Parametric Gaudi,* Visiting Associate Prof. Pablo Lorenzo-Eiroa, Students: Nemer Nabbough, Biodigital Architecture Master Program, Dir. Alberto T. Estévez, 2017.

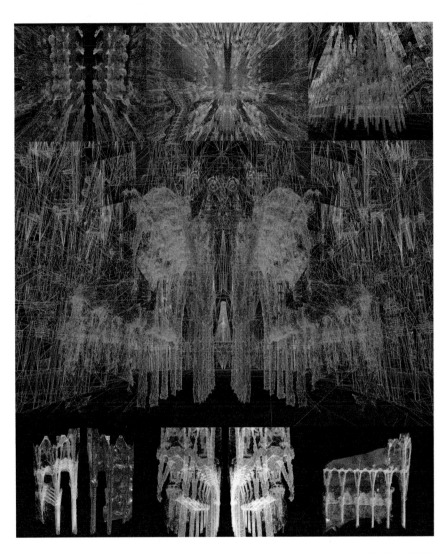

Figure 11.5 3D scanning photogrammetry point cloud in contrast with digital 3D model triangulated mesh. Visiting Assoc. Prof. Pablo Lorenzo-Eiroa, Students: Abdulrahman All Harib and Galkina Valerija, Biodigital Master Program Dir. Alberto Estevez, 2019.

Gaudi's Analog Computational Model as Parallel Processing 267

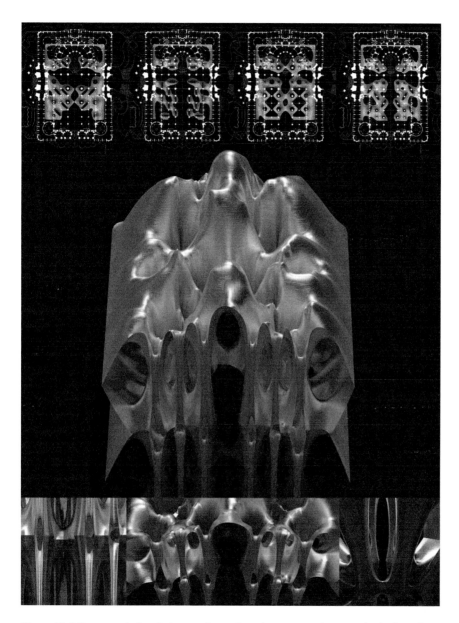

Figure 11.6 Structural simulation surface relaxation composing topological surface-spaces identifying latent relationship between positive and negative space in relation to positive gravitational structural catenaries and negative shell structures. Visiting Assoc. Prof. Pablo Lorenzo-Eiroa, Students: Abdulrahman All Harib and Galkina Valerija, Biodigital Master Program Dir. Alberto Estevez, 2019.

268 *Gaudi's Analog Computational Model as Parallel Processing*

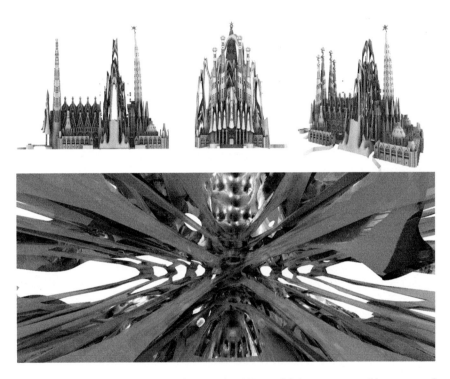

Figure 11.7 A1–C1: Gaudi Sagrada Familia 3D model in contrast with structural simulation and 3D scan photogrammetry. A2: Comparative analysis that identifies latent opportunities to propose alternative design deviations between analog simulations through catenaries, survey of the actual real built construction, idealized 3D models representations, and structural simulations. Visiting Associate Professor Pablo Lorenzo-Eiroa UIC, Students: Secil Afsar, Margaret Tara Maalouf, Joy Nakad, Biodigital Architecture Master Program, Dir. Alberto T. Estévez, 2019.

Gaudi's Analog Computational Model as Parallel Processing 269

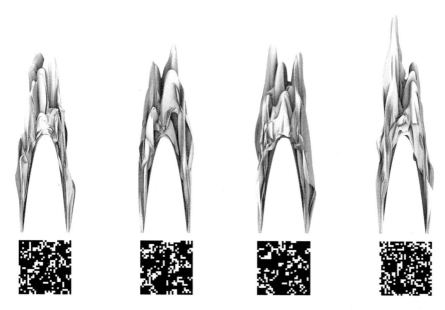

Figure 11.8 Gaudi's analog computational model of concatenated catenary surfaces is replicated through digital structural simulation surface relaxation applying various algorithms departing from Piker's Kangaroo plug-in, activating multiple catenary surfaces generations based on Cellular Automation sites (CA). The process coordinates a site-based computational model through structural continuity across generations. One of the issues we address is that CA does not affect generations backward as the analog Gaudi model does, but in this concatenated surface relaxation model, the structure affects the whole both laterally, upward and downward generations. Other correlational models are discussed in Chapter 12. PI Pablo Lorenzo-Eiroa with RA Yousef Ismail, Salma Kattass, and Farah Jalil, ARCH 703B PBL Studio, ISRC TLT Grant 2022, SoAD, NYIT S2022.

270 *Gaudi's Analog Computational Model as Parallel Processing*

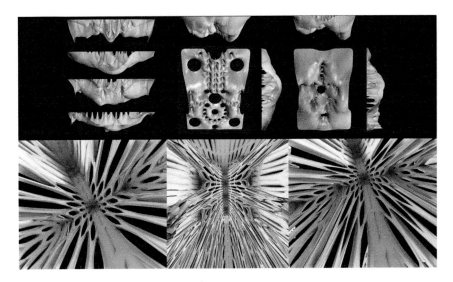

Figure 11.9 A1–C1: structural simulation and optimization through surface relaxation and actualized through polygon meshes, Visiting Associate Prof. Pablo Lorenzo-Eiroa, students: Al Surekha Dasari, Rakan Ali, Khadija Al Chami. A2–C2: Mesh optimization structural simulation, students: Nadin Tarek Elgazzar, Tintswalo Mabuza, Mahmoud, Fattahi; UIC Barcelona, Biodigital Master Program Dir. Alberto T Estévez, S2020.

Figure 11.10 A1–C1: AI Google Deep Dream non-supervised pretrained Machine Learning Convolutional Neural Network feature recognition in image patterns through machine vision pareidolia. Visiting Associate Prof. Pablo Lorenzo-Eiroa, Students: Tara Malaaouf and Joy Secil, 2019. A2: Big Data Survey, structural mesh simulation and GAN style transfer of Gaudi's Sagrada Familia. Pablo Lorenzo-Eiroa GAN style transfer over workshop results by students: Nadin Tarek Elgazzar, Tintswalo Mabuza, Mahmoud, Fattahi; 2020. A3–C3: Sagrada Familia reinterpretation Visiting Associate Prof. Pablo Lorenzo-Eiroa, students: Alonso Ramirez, Natalia, Maksoud, Mohammed, Tipnis, Mruga, UIC Barcelona, Biodigital Master Program Dir. Alberto T. Estévez, S2020.

272 *Gaudi's Analog Computational Model as Parallel Processing*

Figure 11.11 Gaudi Sagrada Familia Ceiling through AI NLP MidJourney diffusion model funneling our own images but trained after the model recognizes features in the images through convolution. The AI diffusion model is run through recursive feature recognition convolution through more than 500 iterations aiming at learning structural simulation features and deploying the learning through a variety of applied design iterations. Pablo Lorenzo-Eiroa photos input of Gaudi's Sagrada Familia building through MidJourney pretrained by API calling out other non-disclosed images, 2022.

Gaudi's Analog Computational Model as Parallel Processing   273

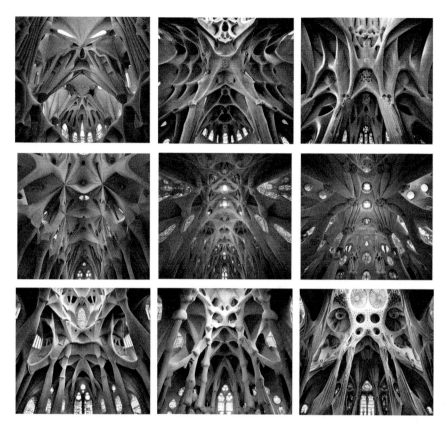

Figure 11.12 The AI topological design variations across scales activate hybrid structural typologies displacing the categories vaulted ceiling, nervatures, arches, shell structures, columns, and other through statistical interpolation. While we think we activated emergent programming structural simulation through convolution, the problem of this blackbox AI is the impossibility of indexing its constitution to displace the signal and signs emergent in the parallel processing. Therefore, its realism cannot be abstracted-deconstructed other than the attempts described. Diffusion Models (DM) are problematically trained with styles from artists and architects. We funneled our own images but trained after the model recognizes features in the style transfer; we claim this as an analysis design activating structural concepts instead of the author's images, although images by others have been called via API to train the DM. Pablo Lorenzo-Eiroa over Gaudi's photo input, MidJourney, 2022.

From Survey, To Ideal, Back To An Informed Realism

The Temple Expiatori de la Sagrada Familia is a basilica (2010) originally designed by Antoni Gaudi (1852–1926). The church construction began, as a social-political project in 1882 and it is purposely designed and built in parallel to the advancement of its society and through multiple generations, as in the Gothic. There have been multiple construction shops in charge of the construction of Sagrada Familia, and each shop interpreted the drawings, experiments, and catenary models as a contemporary expansive nondeterministic machinic system. Jordi Bonet I Armengol and Mark Burry[3] have been introducing advances in digital technologies since 1980 in relation to building construction and modifications, including computer software, mathematics,[4] Computer Aided Manufacturing (CAM), and 3D printing.

The research hereby presented in this chapter expands both backward and forward Gaudi's Sagrada Familia evolutionary design process toward devising alternative ideations of its completion based on analytical discoveries. Through 3D scanning measurements and surveys, digital structural simulations, and virtual reality expanded simulations, we research the differential between Gaudi's machinic model and the built project, proposing an augmented forensic and visionary virtual model. We explore latent opportunities to expand the original using the opportunity to rethink its design as it gets built deviating from the original project, proposing a new analytical active model able to be paired with the original through virtual simulation, expanding and augmenting the research, analysis, and the building itself. The research and projects here included first surveyed the building through Big Data gathering and processing, and understood the acts of the survey as a design activator. The research developed several computer and robotic fabrication representation strategies augmenting the building: from mathematics (Figure 11.1), to geometric topology (Figure 11.6), to conventional robotic CNC fabrication (Figure 11.2-11.3), to non-linear emergent material based fabrication manipulating tool paths in relation to material deformation and informing back and forth the design (Chapter 12 and 13), to Big Data Survey LiDAR 3d Scanning using photogrammetry (Figure 11.4, 11.5), to Structural Form Finding and Simulation (Figure 11.6, 11.7, 11.8, 11.9, 11.10), to a Big Data informed realism through Big Data Machine Learning training Neural Networks activating Artificial Intelligence (Figure 11.10, 11.11, 11.12), and described further in the image captions (Figures 11.1–11.12). Other aspects and applications of this research can be found throughout the book in Chapters 12 and 13.

Notes

1 Hooke, R. A Description of Helioscopes, and some Other Instruments, John Martyn, Royal Society, London, 1675

2 Huerta, S. Arcos, bóvedas y cúpulas: Geometría y equilibrio en el cálculo tradicional de estructuras de fábrica, Instituto Juan de Herrera, ETSAB, Madrid, 2004

3 Burry, M. *Scripting cultures: Architectural Design and Programming*, Wiley, London, 2011

4 Burry, M. *The New Mathematics of Architecture*, Thames and Hudson, London, 2011

12 AI Emergent Structure through Robotic Signals as Information Actualization

History Section:
Twenty-First Century Architecture of Information Methodology:
Information Theory; Evidence-Based Design; Data Based Design Simulation and Optimization; Simulation; Analog Machinic Computational Model; Information Based Model; Emergence;

Computational Visual Semiotics:
Digital Simulation (Structural Simulation and Optimization); Digital Optimization;

Mathematics:
Physics; Material Science; Mechanics; Geometry; Descriptive Geometry; Differential Equations; Differential Calculation; Catenary; Catenary Surface-Catenoid Minimal Surface;

We discussed in Chapter 10 how digital fabrication can be understood as a problem of media actualization through information theory mapping and processing information flows real time through computational linguistic, robotic, and HCI sign and mathematical, electronic, and physical signal processing at a Computer-Aided Manufacturing (CAM) level. Digital fabrication has been understood almost exclusively as translation – a direct communication problem between the digital model and its physical reality. Translation between an ideal digital model and a digital fabrication "image-like" replica implies the lack of recognition of the interface, its media determinism, and building technologies mediums as technological determinism. Few architects have discussed the different, possible definitions of how reality is currently understood and therefore expanded through a critique of media determinism, and how different theories of structural engineering and material science were theorized in radically different, divergent ways addressing a technological determinism. This difference between the digital and the simulated real implies the lack of recognition of a signal change in digital and analog signifiers. Material forces are often over-repressed or over-represented and are often not based on material efficiency. Innovation in what has been called 4D printing by Skylar Tibbits is moving toward the

DOI: 10.4324/9781003292036-13

understanding of materiality as a dimension by programming the material computationally. Architecture must engage with the design-development of new media and new medium technologies, critiquing the normalization and projections of outdated paradigm conventions in relation to the paradigms proposed by new technologies. The historical evolution of architecture in relation to systems of representation, notation and construction is now beyond the notational authorship of Alberti proposed in the Renaissance, the division of labor proposed by Capitalism and the Industrial Revolution, the universal design mechanization proposed by the Modern Movement. We are also critical of the confirmation of cultural bias by the Arts and Craft of personal expressionism as we favor the synthesis of generalized knowledge. We propose an alternative to the struggle between analog local and digital universal, or the simple recovering of personal linguistic expression through sketching or artisan craft actualized as post-digital craft. We propose a post-digital shared socio-cultural-technological project as a new expansion and definition of authorship necessarily displacing robotics and activating an information theory.

Incremental Site–Based Physical Computation as Information Actualization

The *Canvascraper* exhibition explores various relationships among a drawing, its apparent content, and its exhibition by questioning digital fabrication processes. The exhibition of the digital drawing and its curatorial objective became a computational project. The project aims to expand design authorship to the mechanisms that prescribe a digitally fabricated project, expanding background coding in computational design that are used to "draw" and the digital fabrication technologies – and machines – that are being used to "build".[1] The project is the result of experimentation developed by designing directly through CAM instead of Computer-Aided Design (CAD) and then fabricating the computational design, by directly addressing robotic arms and Computer Numeric Control (CNC) sign-codes and robotic electronic signals as a means to explore design possibilities in architecture through the latent forces and properties that become active in materialization. We worked with various recycled aluminum alloys, which require only 5% of the energy to produce a new aluminum sheet, a 100% recyclable material through several cycles as 75% of all aluminum ever used is still being recycled, its low weight, and relatively high resistance to forces and weather making it optimal for fabrication. New aluminum extraction pollutes the environment through CO_2 and toxins as it requires a lot of energy for its production and the water electrolytic process produces harm to fish and vertebrates.

A 2D computational design coding deals with the initial relationship between understanding architecture as a virtual topo-logos, or architecture emerging from the logic of the site-topography in the digital interface, activating the logic of its matrix space. The project actualizes as engraving inscriptions of the 2D code activating a background figuration of the physical metal sheet canvas. The actualization included the figuration of the background computer space to the figuration of the new canvas as a 3D material metal sheet actualization as an initial 2D project. The exhibition is named *Canvascraper* as it tensions the new canvas site and the emergent quality of the project that redefines it. The project progressively shifts from an actualization between 2D coding to 3D fabrication to a physical architectural experiment.

Form Follows Structure

There are two types of conditions that can be described as emergent in these experiments. Surfaces become active in an informed-materialization process. There are double curvature minimal surfaces that become active by the simple cartesian incremental deformation of the material as a continuous toolpath incremental sheet formation (ISF). The emerging surfaces do not exist in digital form. Emergent minimal surfaces become active in the CAM

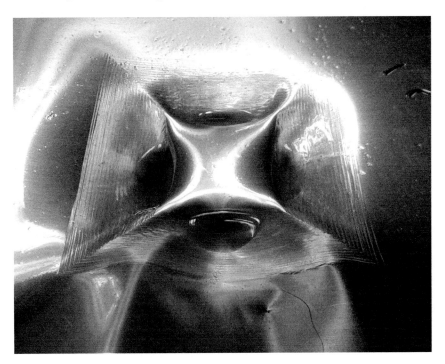

Figure 12.1 Incremental Sheet Forming (ISF) actualizing information by activating a material physical computation through CAM. A minimal surface becomes active by material deformation in the scoring of progressive topographical squares using a CNC milling machine. This test activates a physical emergent problem in the deformation of the material in informed robotic fabrication processes. The thinning out of the aluminum sheet thickness produces a displacement of the accumulated matter toward the center, buckling the metal sheet which acquires structural inertia and creates progressive negative crease curves that form an emergent positive minimal surface. Visiting Associate Prof. Pablo Lorenzo-Eiroa, with TA Gabriel Munnich and Yaoyi Fann, UIC Barcelona S2017.

AI Emergent Structure through Robotic Signals 279

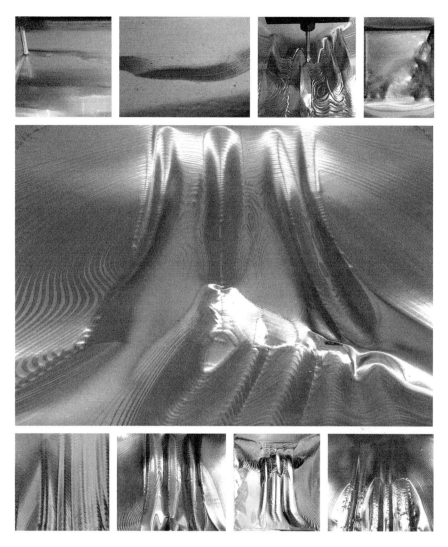

Figure 12.2 Topographic robotic contouring from "drawing" to "scoring" to "scraping" to "building"; A1–D1: A topographic contouring is used to score a metal sheet in increments, deforming it incrementally. This process explores differentiated material surface physical behavior which becomes active through a fabrication process, in contrast to the original digital drawing. In this experiment, minimal surfaces emerge by the function of the coordination between several information processes avoiding sign and signal translation: from the force applied by the CNC scoring, the deformation of a tensioned aluminum sheet, and a background interface deep structure. Canvascraper Exhibition: e-Architects, NY; Design Principal: Pablo Lorenzo-Eiroa; Design Team: Yaoyi Fann and Gabriel Munnich; Exhibition Curator: Steven Hillyer and Nader Tehrani; The Cooper Union Archive, Dean's Wall, F2017.

process as a byproduct of the ISF, since the accumulative formation produces a thinning out of the thickness of the metal sheet, accumulating matter incrementally toward the center of the sheet, progressively acquiring increasing inertia as the aluminum metal sheet produces a buckling and the formation of positive and negative minimal surfaces (Figure 12.1).

Minimal surfaces are understood as emergent topo-logos as Leibniz calculus situs computational contingency, an emergent topology through a fabrication process. Dimensional transitions from "drawing" to "building" by encoding, engraving, and informing a physical computational process, displace a conventional industry technique of incremental sheet forming (ISF) by recognizing a non-desired side effect as a structural emergent property. This side effect has several advantages, from material savings to efficiency in the economics of the structure to new aesthetic possibilities. We paid attention to the emergent structural behavior of the metal aluminum sheet, exploring transitions between formation, deformation, tracing, scoring and the multiple emergent structural and mathematical signs and meanings, cultural artistic quality-values often dismissed by a technologically driven industry. The technique to address the translating problem between a digital code, a routing G-code CAM to guide the damping tool, and the payload force applied by the robotic arm to

Figure 12.3 Canvascraper shifts from a process of representation to processing emergent information evolving and critiquing the precedent parameters each time there is a different interface and process recognized as structural. Canvascraper Exhibition: e-Architects, NY; Design Principal: Pablo Lorenzo-Eiroa; Design Team: Yaoyi Fann and Gabriel Munnich; Exhibition Curator: Steven Hillyer and Nader Tehrani; The Cooper Union Archive, Dean's Wall, F2017.

the bead at every moment was parameterized and systematized as a problem of information flow in mapping, processing, and actualization. The scoring and an emerging deformation of the material in tension with its frame take its own formal, mathematical, and structural properties. The formal qualities and the emerging minimal surfaces also become a prototype for a differentiated structural membrane. As the structural membrane gains inertia, the prototype breaks the typical relationships between structure, surface, and detail, providing a prototype for a building façade enclosure strategy (Figure 12.2, 12.3).

We consider ISF through variable toolpath a means to explore differential emergent geometry in the multiple codependent topographical sites that emerge in the contouring of a thin metal sheet. We consider each tool path in the ISF as a site and a type of physical computation. If one can compute each site developing a behavior that is accumulative and informs the next site, one can address ISF as an emergent form-finding process, a type of site-based computation in which minimal surfaces emerge in each site-contour. We activate a complex type of feedback as an emergent complex nonreversible material-digital-robotic cross-based informational computing process (Figure 12.3). Alberti's notational representation between anticipatory documentation and planned construction is displaced not only in terms of scalar notation by building through media and robotics, but it also becomes a dynamic double binding adversarial feedback informational process between digital and physical, since construction becomes a problem of information actualization through simulation-optimization emergent physics and therefore an open non-anticipatory non-deterministic dynamic process. By means of information sign-signal feedback a material phase change through CAM activates pressure points, topographic lines, and progressively emergent structural surfaces out of incrementally deforming and informing an initially thin non-structural weak malleable metal sheet.

Concatenated Thin Shell System for Vertical Slab Stacking: Gaudi's Latent New York City

We discussed in Chapter 11 Gaudi's Catenary models as an analog computational engine capable of complex emergent behavior through correlational concatenated catenaries generations as parallel processing. We did a cross-analysis on the relationship between Gaudi's site-based correlational catenary models and a forensic 3D photogrammetry of Sagrada Familia. We indexed Gaudi's 3D scanned catenaries on a metal surface through a CAM process. The projection of points in the point clouds as CAM point-vectors in the robotic arm developed an emergent curved surface in an ISF of an aluminum sheet surface, indexing the actual 3D scanning point cloud of the Sagrada Familia building (Figure 12.4). An information actualization activating emergent structural typologies derived from the scan as forces indexed in the metal deformation. We then proceeded to study prediction models in relation to information actualization through various means, media and mediums. We first explored Generative Adversarial Networks (GANs) recognizing features

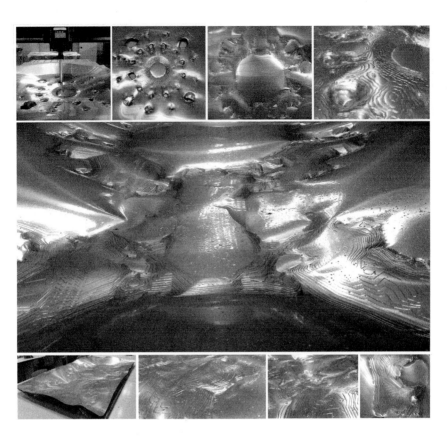

Figure 12.4 Gaudi Sagrada Familia 3D Scan and point cloud projection as information actualization. The information process deforms a metal piece through site-based incremental sheet forming (ISF). By replicating the actual catenary forces that created the original dome structure, the process activates a triple indexical sign: the survey photogrammetry of Sagrada Familia Basilica, which projects a 2D image into a 2D surface containing 3D space; the CNC deforms the 2D metal sheet incrementally indexing a sign and a signal, from point to a line to a ISF surface; the recognition of the catenaries by Gaudi that informed the actual building surveyed; and the projection of the point cloud photogrammetry as CNC CAM activating minimal surfaces in a fabrication process. Group pieces, UIC Barcelona studio workshop, Pablo Lorenzo-Eiroa with Teaching Assistants Gabriel Munnich and Yaoyi Fan, 2017.

over the material computation, exploring relationships between the original photos and the actualized catenaries in the metal pieces (Figure 12.5).

We researched through a variety of media relationship between Gaudi's concatenated shell structures, structural simulation, and physical computation in CAM activating emergent structures at the material level. We explored these emergent structural issues through a diversity of media, from a

AI Emergent Structure through Robotic Signals 283

Figure 12.5 A1: Photo of Gaudi's Sagrada Familia ceiling. B1: Metal piece through ISF. C1: GAN style transfer implementing pretrained semantic segmentation. AI GAN style transfer through CNN feature recognition, Pablo Lorenzo-Eiroa, 2018 using group workshop pieces UIC Barcelona studio workshop, Pablo Lorenzo-Eiroa with Teaching Assistants Gabriel Munnich and Yaoyi Fan, students: Ciurel, Silvia; Dragos, Brescan; Juárez, David Gabriel; Martin, Perry; Memisoglu, Misra; Mouradian, Never; Nabbouh, Nemer; Rahmani, Tarek; Sönmez, Cemal; Tabikh, Fouad; Vanhoegaerden, Luciemarthe F; Warang, Angad; 2017.

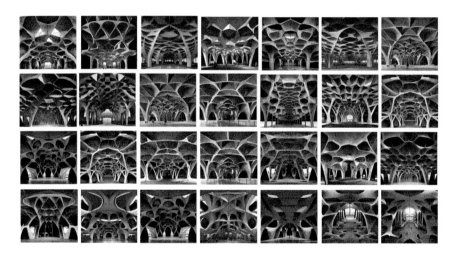

Figure 12.6 Shell Structures simulation developing statistical interpolations between structural typologies. NLP Reinforcement Learning from Human Feedback (RLHF). We then activate structural simulation as emergent programming in 2D of a 3D space by training an image through feature recognition convolution through progressive strategic training bifurcations developing a visual algorithm. With these strategies, we aim at bypassing the problematic use of copyrighted material in Diffusion Models which are problematically trained with proprietary images and extracted styles features from artists and architects. NLP Pablo Lorenzo-Eiroa, MidJourney, 2022.

284 *AI Emergent Structure through Robotic Signals*

Figure 12.7 NLP text-to-image generation through pixel-to-pixel DM developing statistical image interpolations between linguistic semantic-based structural typologies called out through prompts such as shell, umbrella, canopy, columns, and positive and negative space, mass, and space, aiming at activating structural typologies correlation between generations. Diffusion Models are problematically trained with styles appropriating artists' and architects' work. We tried as far as we could/know to avoid style transfer through abstract structural concepts, through a minimal feature recognition of structure through image convolution. We activated a minimum level of emergent programming through NLP as structural simulation with limitations by the style transfer. NLP Pablo Lorenzo-Eiroa via MidJourney, 2022.

Natural Language Processing (NLP) text-to-image activating predictive Diffusion Models (DM) (Figures 12.6, 12.7, 12.10), to a predictive 3D GAN, to activating the found discoveries through information actualization as physical site-based computation.

We applied Vector Quantized Generative Adversarial Network[2] (VQGAN) transformers to a developed Gaudi's dataset, to proceed to train the 3D GAN to recognize structural features in images with the aim of activating emergent programming as simulation prediction in 2D of 3D phenomena to save

AI Emergent Structure through Robotic Signals 285

time and energy resources. In parallel, we run DM MidJourney and DALL-E 2 NLP through specific prompt engineering and bifurcating Convolutional Neural Network (CNN) visual semiotics to predict design evolutions from

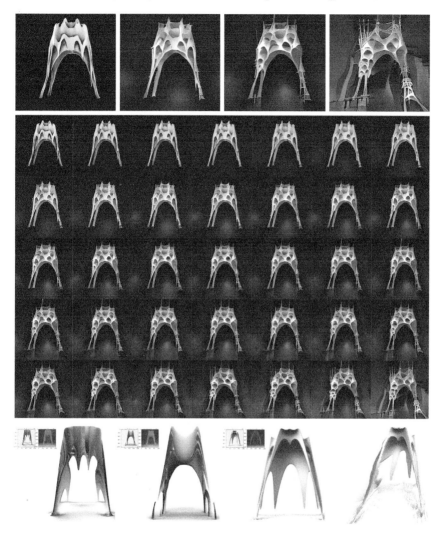

Figure 12.8 A1–G6: 2D image training of structurally simulated shell structure applying three concatenated surface generations through VQGAN ML feature recognition, output result of 200 training epochs. A7–D7: Monocular Depth Estimation via Content-Adaptive multi-resolution merging to implement ML monocular machine vision from 2D VQGAN to 3D data set to a dynamic navigable 3D model. Monocular vision applied to recognize certain features of the first generation of the simulated structure. The AI depth recognition is separating each generation in a different mask limiting the 3D output. PI. Pablo Lorenzo-Eiroa, RA. Salma Kattass, Yousef Ismail and Kavya Sista, Institutional Support of Research and Creativity Grant, NYIT, 2022.

286 *AI Emergent Structure through Robotic Signals*

the predictive simulations. We then coordinated through various AI computer vision techniques such as monocular vision through depth estimation via content-adaptive multi-resolution merging[3] and Red, Green, Blue plus Depth data (RGBD) Open3D[4] to translate the depth mask in Redwood format and image color to a 3D surface projecting a camera registration angle and depth as well as a point cloud reconstruction from the 2D image.

In order to understand the relationships between structural simulation and optimization and the emergent material performance in relation to the forces of the robotic fabrication process, we developed a dataset with thousands of optimized simulated shell structures resulting from the evolutionary solver algorithm. We used the output results as a dataset to train through a

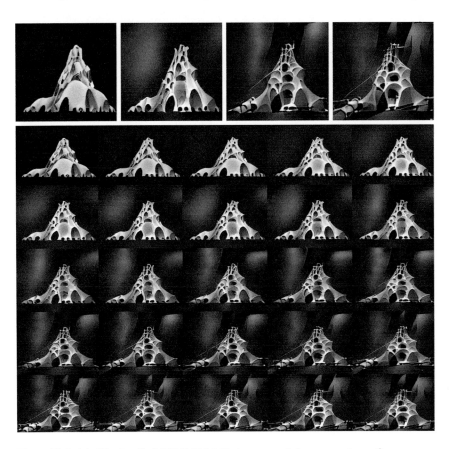

Figure 12.9 A1–E6: Applied VQGAN ML image training to activate feature recognition in relation to a developed dataset, developing a ML prediction model based on structurally simulated concatenated shell model, training recognizing features through 1000 epoch iterations implementing CNN. The training provided both creative design research processes that informed a computational design through the simulation process, crossing relationships with each other. PI. Pablo Lorenzo-Eiroa, RA. Salma Kattass, Yousef Ismail, Farah Jalil, and Kavya Sista, Institutional Support of Research and Creativity Grant, NYIT, 2022.

AI Emergent Structure through Robotic Signals 287

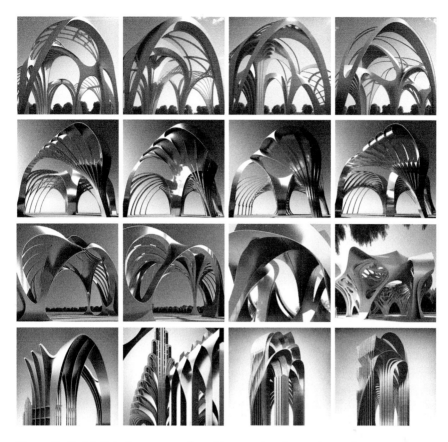

Figure 12.10 A1-D4: Concatenated multigenerational correlational catenary structures from arches to surfaces activating AI emergent programming through approximation of structural simulation in 2D images simulating 3D models. DM iterations through feed images, activating feature recognition through Convolution, and training the DM through reinforced learning human feedback (RLHF). PI Pablo Lorenzo-Eiroa, MidJourney, v5, 2023.

Convolutional Neural Network (CNN) for feature recognition deep learning from the structural optimization of the meta-data repository in 2D. The structural shell evolutionary solver optimization was composed of over 1000 surface meshes and was based on a structural simulation surface relaxation implementing catenaries and weighting. For parallel processing, we converted the files via .stl from mesh to voxels and then to point clouds for processing purposes in multiple batches with reconstructed geometry rectification processing of the Point Cloud Database (PCD). We trained the CNN to recognize features in the dataset (Figure 12.8-12.11), from structural features, surface openings, borders, and structural stress, to structural optimization, to other items such as the support of the shell structure (Figure 12.11,

288 AI Emergent Structure through Robotic Signals

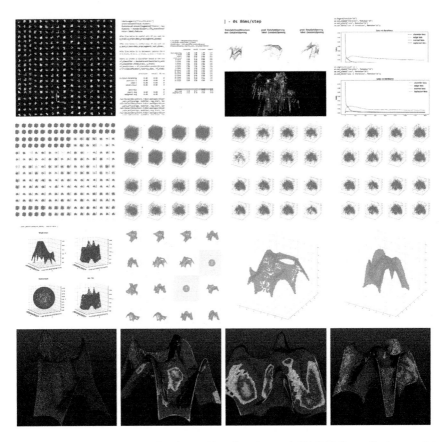

Figure 12.11 3D ML Point Cloud ML Classification and 3D GAN's prediction model based on 3D scanning of Sagrada Familia. Variations on an machine learning predictive structural simulation model that saves time and energy resources. (See Notes Figure 12.11)

12.12). Following Goodfellow et al.,[5, 6] we use binary cross entropy for the Machine Learning (ML) classification loss, and present our overall adversarial loss function as:

$$L3D-GAN = \log D(x) + \log(1 - D(G(z))), \quad (1)$$

where x is a real object in a low dimensional 64 × 64 × 64 space, and z is a randomly sampled noise vector from a distribution p(z). In this work, each dimension of z is an i.i.d. uniform distribution over [0, 1]. We notice a predictive change in degree but not a change in class, as the predictive change deviates from a structural feature recognition to an iconographic-based image recognition apparently based on facial recognition features.

AI Emergent Structure through Robotic Signals 289

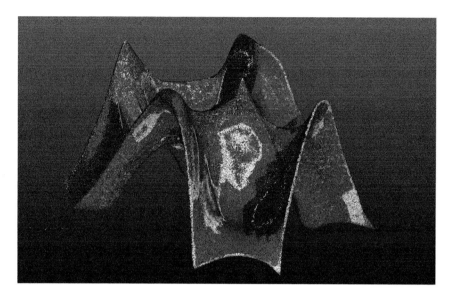

Figure 12.12 3D GANs semantic segmentation mapping after feature recognition implementing 3D point cloud and voxel repository training. PI Pablo Lorenzo-Eiroa, RA: Yousef Ismail, Farah Jalil, Salma Kattass, Farah Jalil and Kavya Sista, Institutional Support of Research and Creativity Grant, NYIT, 2022.

In parallel we activated realism by 3D scanning Gaudi's Sagrada Familia, developing a point cloud, and using this point cloud to compare it and interpolate it in relation to the dataset. We also downsampled the point cloud into voxels to be able to make the data compatible as input with other datasets and to further train parallel CNN and GAN. We discussed previously the problematic downsampling mathematical signal decimation and the consequential subsymbolic vectorial and HCI sign that becomes active through voxelation. To overcome downsampling we work in other cases at the point cloud level through ML semantic segmentation and visual feature semiotic segmentation through convolution, with no mathematical signal decimation nor through a subsymbolic sign, although still involving other issues such as the linguistic-based supervised semantic segmentation classification which is known to promote cultural biases (Figures 12.8–12.12).

Gaudi's New York City Vaulted Skyscraper Prototype

We synthesized the ML research to activate certain features discovered through a physical computation information actualization. We developed a computational structural simulation that can transfer information through generations of structural systems applying different computational models,

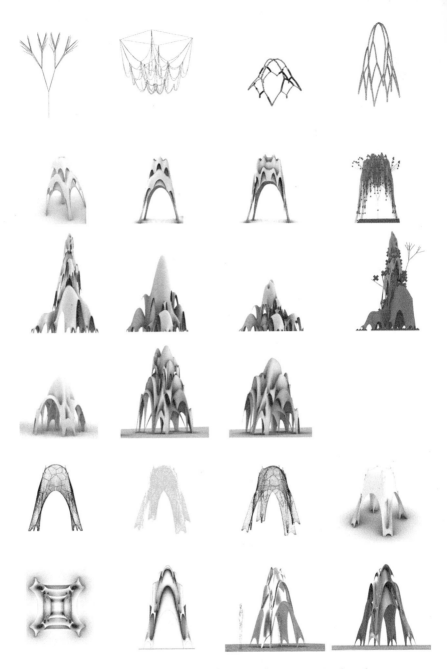

Figure 12.13 A1–D6: L-Systems and CA establishing evolutionary site-based parameters for anchors allocation to develop a correlational non-hierarchical (up-down) cross-generational (all generations affected by simulation) nonreversible site-based concatenated catenary model. A2–C4: The model becomes correlational concatenated since informs stress and site conditions to both correlational generations, lower generations, and higher generations establishing a full dynamic structural system advancing Gaudi's computational engine. A2–C4: These models are being adapted to a skyscraper prototype (in these images flat slabs as continuous shell structures are not included). A5–D5: First generation Shell structure fabrication implementing Voronoi tiling for ISF. PI Pablo Lorenzo-Eiroa with RA Yousef Ismail, Salma Kattass, Farah Jalil; Institutional Support of Research and Creativity Grant, NYIT, 2022.

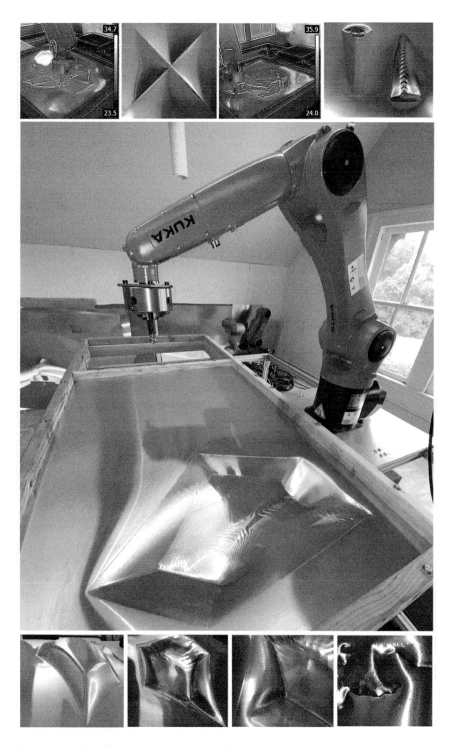

Figure 12.14 Double bind adversarial feedback between digital signs and physical signals. Emergent structural shell structure typologies through ISF as site-based computation. (See Notes Figure 12.14)

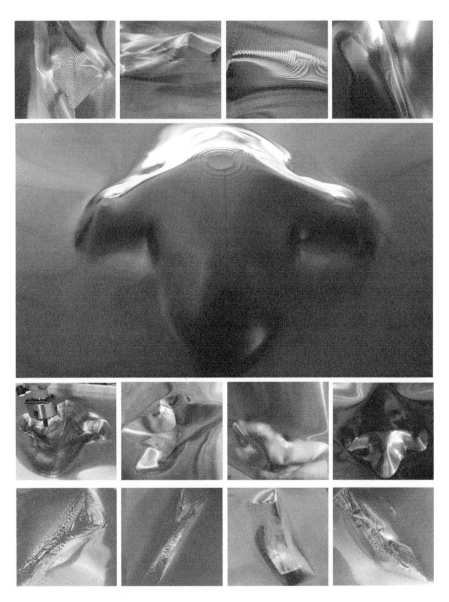

Figure 12.15 Various typologies of ISF and emergent structures. In some tiles, the ISF produces tension with the perimeter spreading the inertia to the entire sheet structure, in others a crease fold curve emerges, in others, there is an exchange between positive and negative inertia due to the crease fold, in others minimal surfaces emerge. PI Pablo Lorenzo-Eiroa, RA: Yousef Ismail, Salma Kattass, Farah Jalil; 2022 Institutional Support of Research and Creativity Grant (ISRC) MS.ACT Program NYIT 2022, Acknowledgments to Fab Lab Technicians: Marie-Odile Baretsky.

AI Emergent Structure through Robotic Signals 293

Figure 12.16 Tiles expanding relations between mathematics and physics. Mathematical surface parametric plots informing through actualization thin shell minimal surfaces emergent structures. Tiles and structural inertia relative to possible local organizations through the activation of emergent structural features. PI Pablo Lorenzo-Eiroa, RA: Yousef Ismail, Salma Kattass, Farah Jalil, Beken Amde Trushita Yadav and Mahima Kulkarni; and research students Tharoonaskar Baskaran, Arathi Chilla, Kush A. Shah, Tiarnan Mathers; 2022 Institutional Support of Research and Creativity Grant (ISRC) MS.ACT Program NYIT.

Figure 12.17 Partial installation mock-up with openings to receive concatenated shell generations. Research exploring the activation of emergent structural features, including larger minimal surfaces through aluminum ISF. We decided to work with rupture and index the material limit making the form open incomplete. The breaking of the metal sheet is due to material phase change, and the activation of emergent minimal surfaces at the rupture point, addressing Ricolais order in destruction as a form of research in construction through the buckling emergent problem in collapsing structures and the crease curve as an emergent structural figure to increase inertia in a surface. The rupture in the tiles adds inertia to the thin shell structure and as an emergent formal organization only achievable through an open robotic fabrication form-finding process for emergent minimal surfaces. We distinguish this process as a form of being, as opposed to representation through modelling. We challenge aesthetics as ethics in relation to efficiency, against excess and decoration activating different aesthetic levels and scales. The openings also activate passive cooling in the installation. PI Pablo Lorenzo-Eiroa, RA: Yousef Ismail, Salma Kattass, Farah Jalil, Beken Amde, Trushita Yadav, and Mahima Kulkarni; students: Tharoonaskar Baskaran, Arathi Chilla, Kush A. Shah, Tiarnan Mathers, 2022 Institutional Support of Research and Creativity Grant (ISRC) MS.ACT Program NYIT 2022, Acknowledgment to Fab Lab Technicians: Marie-Odile Baretsky.

AI Emergent Structure through Robotic Signals 295

Figure 12.18 Mies van der Rohe develps a syntax of steel structural elements and cladding of steel metal sheets. Gaudi, Candela, Nervi, Dieste and Otto propose shell structures integrating structure, cladding and envelope. Gaudi's New York City is a concatenated shell structure prototype adaptable for a vertical building typology. Gaudi's NYC Vaulted Skyscraper Prototype; 2022 Institutional Support of Research and Creativity Grant (ISRC), NYIT; PI Pablo Lorenzo-Eiroa, RA: Yousef Ismail, Salma Kattass, Farah Jalil, Beken Amde, Trushita Yadav, and Mahima Kulkarni; and Tharoonaskar Baskaran, Arathi Chilla, Kush A. Shah, Tiarnan Mathers; Proposal for Stapleton Waterfront Park, Staten Island, sponsors e-Architects.net and DLO, sponsored public installation by NYC Parks and Recreation; scheduled 2023.

simulations-optimizations, AI automation models, and AI predictive models (Figure 12.11, 12.12, 12.13). The simulation is actualized through a tool path that can form the metal sheet incrementally through ISF and activate the properties of the initial structural system without resembling its form, its image, or abstract enough to be lost in terms of numerical statistical values (Figure 12.1, 12.2, 12.3, 12.4, 12.14, 12.15, 12.16, 12.17). This information is active as it forms the sheet and feeds back into the digital project to compare through ML the relationships of the trained model in relation to the actualization occurring at the ISF level (Figures 12.11, 12.12, 12.14 A1-D1). Through interpolation, we compare both the trained model and the actualization of the piece to optimize back and forth the relationship between both.

We were able to activate different types of minimal surfaces (Figures 12.14, 12.15, and 12.16) than the previously described (Figures 12.1 or 12.2-12.4) through material deformation in ISF variable toolpaths, increasing dimensionally the axes in the robotic arm and increasing the stability of an ultrathin shell structure and reducing it from earlier experiments from 0.032" to

0.020 using corrosion-resistant aluminum sheets A3003 (alloy) for an exterior installation (Figures 12.14-12.16). The folds to connect the tiles follow the stress lines of the simulated surface mediated through a Voronoi structure and were developed to facilitate installation and deinstallation constructability and for public installation safety, although we are also exploring parallel options such as connecting the tiles coplanar to each other following airplane construction techniques and reducing the inertia by the folding connections as well to create a pure shell structure membrane. The structure works at several topological information levels: from mathematical coding to surface relaxation structural simulation; to concatenated surface simulation; to NLP simulation of the simulation prediction model; to activating inertia through ISF; to activating emergent structural minimal surfaces in the robotic fabrication ISF process; to activating emergent crease fold curves in positive-negative inertia. The emergent structural behavior of the minimal surfaces active through ISF becomes correlational at different scales: from the scale of the entire project to the scale of the generation, to the scale of the tile, to a detailed scale. We think of the installation as a series of slab-shell structures simulated through surface-catenaries. We develop a full-scale proof test prototype as an installation in Stapleton Waterfront Park in NYC activating subject-object-landscape-city relationships through the structure and indexing the limit rupture of the material to activate passive cooling between concatenated generations (Figure 12.18). The intention is to develop an information theory from material actualization, computing form as structure activating a robotically informed material-based computational model (Figures 12.13–12.18).

We expand the installation prototype to reformulate Gaudi's NYC Skyscraper Hotel Attraction of 1908. We propose a new vertical concatenated vaulted structure as an efficient skyscraper which integrates the structural design of minimal shell structures with a new building construction typology. The difference between the installation prototype and the skyscraper proposal is that a shell structure does not need to be fully curved. We reformulate a skyscraper typology as a differential site-based concatenated shell structure. These concatenated shell structures could be developed with differentially reinforced fiber concrete, assigning strength in relation to stress and folding the slab to become structurally continuous with the surface columns. Each level behaves in relation to the previous level, understood as computational generations that can inform back and forth a different type of building structure that addresses a different type of construction system that is formal variable dependent and that can be calculated differentially as a part of a whole continuous simulation structure. Each slab can be calculated as a concatenated series of shell structures from the bottom to the top, diminishing increasingly their footprint as the structure proposes an overall catenary as each slab is differentially computed, and through simulation one can compute its overall part to whole relationships.

Notes

1 Lorenzo-Eiroa, P. "Post-Digital as Design Authorship in Informed Material Processes", in ed. Ahrens, C. and Sprecher, A., *Instabilities and Potentialities*, Routledge, New York, 2019

2 Esser, P.; Rombach, R.; Ommer, B. "Taming Transformers for High-Resolution Image Synthesis", *arXiv*, 2021

3 Miangoleh, S.M.; Dille, S.; Mai, L.; Paris, S.; Aksoy, Y. "Boosting Monocular Depth Estimation Models to High-Resolution via Content-Adaptive Multi-Resolution Merging", *arXiv*:20105.1402v1, 2021

4 Choi, S.; Zhou, Q.Y.; Koltun, V. "Robust Reconstruction of Indoor Scenes", Computer Vision Foundation, *IEEE*, 2015

5 Goodfellow, I.; Pouget-Abadie, J.; Mirza, M.; et al. "Generative Adversarial Nets", in *NIPS*, 2014

6 Wu, J.; Zhang, C.; Xue, T.; Freeman, W.; Tenenbaum, J. "Learning a Probabilistic Latent Space of Object Shapes via 3D Generative-Adversarial Modeling", *arXiv*:1610.07584v2, 2017

Figure 12.11 3D ML Point Cloud Classification and 3D GAN's prediction model based on 3D scanning of Sagrada Familia. Point Cloud generation Automation and automated statistical outlier noise removal through neighbor and radius compared to average point cloud implementing ML. Variations on a predictive structural simulation model that saves time and energy resources. A1: Galapagos dataset 1000 iterations of shell structure evolutionary solver. B1: C1: Machine Learning classification of structural simulation: open/close, stress, arches/ dome. C1b: Sagrada Familia by Gaudi 3D scan point cloud. D1, A2, B2, C2, D2: 3D GAN training prediction model in relation to 3D Galapagos dataset style transfer of Gaudi Sagrada Familia 3D scan point cloud, pairing through interpolation, the trained dataset with the Machine Learning interpretation of catenaries; 300 training iteration cycles in four batches (included here ranges 130 to 300). A3, B3, C3, D3: Training based on point cloud to voxel-based on 3d scanning of Sagrada Familia, low resolution to match matrix input and output for meta-data repository training. Mesh reduction to voxel target to Sphere for Optimization. Open3D Voxelation implements ML downsampling to one point by averaging all points inside a voxel through point normal n estimation through covariance analysis. The downsampling is done through the radius and nearest neighbor estimation (r=0.1; max_nn=30). Running inference on the model. D1: GAN Loss function in relation to iterations. A4: Training model earlier cycle. B4, C4, D4: Trained model machine learning feature recognition semantic segmentation: open/ closed, stress, arches. ML Classification with a low accuracy but that provides direction to the workflow. Export as Big/Little Endian Binaries. Voxel to mesh using the Marching Cubes algorithm. PI Pablo Lorenzo-Eiroa, RA: Yousef Ismail, Farah Jalil, and Salma Kattass; 3D GAN's and voxelation RA Kavya Sista, Institutional Support of Research and Creativity Grant, NYIT, 2022.

Figure 12.14 A1, C1: Heat temperature sensing identifying metal deformation as material phase change due to the thinning out of the material thickness in the Incremental Sheet Forming (ISF) to map and recognize real-time the potential activation of emergent minimal surfaces and feedback this information to the robotic arm G-Code toolpath and

CAM process. B1, D1: Emergent structural typologies activation through ISF as site-based computation. General knowledge structures activated: single barrel vault; vaulted rib surface; double cross vaulted surface; triangular conic surface as fade out of stress; double curvature surface; minimal surfaces in relation to vaulted surface. C1-D1 C1-D1: The ISF produces an industry non desired thinning out material which we take advantage of by accumulating matter to create a surface buckling effect that adds inertia to the section of the surface, spreading structural inertia to the entire metal sheet. PI Pablo Lorenzo-Eiroa, RA: Yousef Ismail, Salma Kattass, Farah Jalil; *2022 Institutional Support of Research and Creativity Grant* (ISRC) MS.ACT Program NYIT 2022, Acknowledgments to Fab Lab Technicians: Marie-Odile Baretsky.

13 AI Synthetic Environments as Simulation-Based Information Actualization

History Section:
Twenty-First Century Architecture of Information;

Methodology:
Evidence-Based Design; Data-Based Design Simulation-Optimization; Analog Machinic Computational Model; Information-Based Model; Simulation; Swarm Simulation; Emergence; Computational Simulation Engine;

Linguistic Semiotic Signifiers:
Nature;

Computational Visual Semiotics:
Analog Simulation (Catenary Model, Inverted catenary arch); Digital Simulation (Structural Simulation and Optimization);

Computational Visual Semiotic Signifiers:
Perspective VP; Particles; Parametric Space; VR, AR, MR; Acoustic Signals (perceptible, non-perceptible audible); Infrared Spectrum; Digital Fabrication (CNC, others); 3D printing technologies (aggregate-based, Fused Deposition Modeling -FDM, laser-cured resin, others); robotic fabrication (Robotic Arm, Robotic Swarm); Materials (robotic materials, biomaterials, synthetic materials, responsive materials);

Mathematics:
Physics; Mechanics; Geometry; Descriptive Geometry; Differential Equations; Differential Calculation; Catenary; Catenary Surface-Catenoid Minimal Surface; Parabola; Paraboloid; Inverted Catenary Arch

Synthetic Space-Environments through Simulation Intelligence

We can understand the environment as a natural intelligence of coordinated ecosystems active through environmental rivers that through evolution have been adapting resources in relation to both internal coding and external input-output. But how can we develop an environmental engine through computational thinking?

DOI: 10.4324/9781003292036-14

300 *Simulation-Based Information Actualization*

This chapter discusses experimental architecture research developed for an immersive responsive installation at Palazzo Bembo for the Venice Biennale 2021. The installation reconsidered architecture developmentalism as emergent environments through various forms of computational simulations in close relation to robotic fabrication as information actualization: from environmental, to robotic, to visual, to structural, to material, to acoustic, to virtual reality as simulation including computational design through Cellular Automation and Swarm Intelligence simulation.

The architecture of the installation proposes cultural disciplinary and transdisciplinary problems that engage with specific sections of histories and theories of representation in architecture from painting to environmental sciences through different types of computational simulation engines. The installation activated the historiography of architecture through representation from the Renaissance to the Baroque and in relation to contemporary computational thinking through simulation. We cut sections through the historically opposing models of the Renaissance and the Baroque: Brunelleschi's Renaissance perspective is placed in tension and displaced by Borromini's Palazzo Spada Gallery as a space of representation, designed to demonstrate spatial expansion through illusionistic perspective; Palladio's critique of the artificial illusionistic effect of the perspectival cone effect and Andrea Pozzo's illusionistic distortion places in ambiguity the relationship between the architecture physical space and the illusionistic space of representation of his frescoes that expand or compress the actual physical space. Through the analysis of some paradigmatic examples in representation, we placed in motion computational simulation. The installation presented tensions between real space and an illusionistic expansion in tension with a Virtual Reality navigation. The overall computational design strategy of the installation was thought of in terms of representation and included historiography of computational paradigms in relation to the historiography of architecture.

In parallel to problems of representation in architecture, the installation also proposed studying, learning, critiquing, and displacing conventional computational systems as systems of representation, developing the form of the installation through a critical computational historiography. This historiography of computation can be traced back to von Neuman's and John Conway's Cellular Automation and von Neuman's interest in simulation and thermodynamics.[1,2] The project worked with computational simulations to critique the determination of algorithms, activating computational problems relative to irreducibility, non-reversibility, and emergent evolutive-based computation based on progressive site-based generations. The installation crossed relationships between computational digital models and computationally informed physical models, avoiding linear translations and

Simulation-Based Information Actualization 301

expanding dimensions across computational technologies including materiality as a design agent. This was done by addressing actualization and information BIT to atom problem but without disengaging materialization from a problem of information representation. The installation aimed at expanding dimensions between digital and physical actualizations across computational technologies, extending the computational design to robotic automated simulation, robotic optimization, and robotic fabrication. The project developed several types of simulations that were related to each other and recursively fed on each other, from environmental simulations applied to the architecture scale, to material simulation, structural simulation, fabrication simulation, and optimization.

The installation progressively resolved space containment activating framing problems at multiple levels, from space defined by frame objects such as columns that became isolated elements but that structurally frame

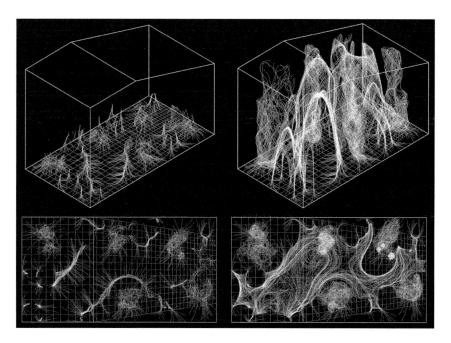

Figure 13.1 Swarm Intelligence Agent-Based Modeling (ABM) recognizing different tasks across multiple surfaces. Venice Biennale Installation Preliminary Proposal, *Interscalar Fluidity*, Prof. Pablo Lorenzo-Eiroa with students: Andres Carcamo; Brianna Lopez; Peter Leonardi; Alexandra Panichella; Ari Begun; Oluwayemi Oyewole; Karina Pena; Isaiah Miller; Benjamin Sather; ARCH 501–502 SoAD, NYIT; S-Lab Grant, Dean Maria Perbellini's Incentive, F2019.

302 *Simulation-Based Information Actualization*

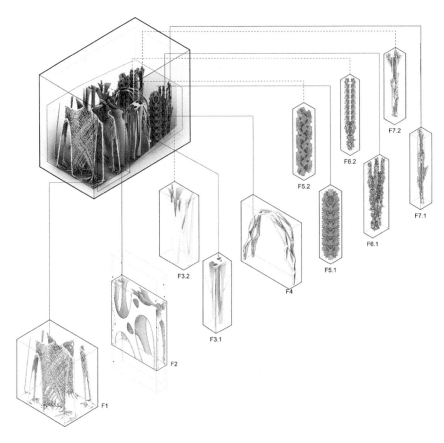

Figure 13.2 The installation is composed of disjunctive architectural fragments of different scales and densities, all designed-optimized through various types of simulations. Interscalar Fluidity, Venice Biennale Final Installation Prof. Pablo Lorenzo-Eiroa with Students: Andres Carcamo: "Iconography Architecture"; Brianna Lopez: "Parametric Flow"; Peter Leonardi: "Structural Typologies"; Alexandra Panichella: "Material transitions: Feedback between the Analog and the Digital"; Ari Begun: "Spatially Interactive Light"; Oluwayemi Oyewole: "Structural Optimization"; Karina Pena: "Dynamics of Humidity and Temperature Advantages"; Isaiah Miller: "Sonic + Sensory"; Benjamin Sather: "[c]ellular Surfaces"; ARCH 501–502 SoAD, NYIT; S-Lab Grant, Dean Maria Perbellini's Incentive, F2019.

and design the space to an extended virtual frame-space. At the same time, technological determination and order imposition were critiqued through non-determination and site specificity. For instance, the installation proposed to displace conventional normalizing algorithms through site-based

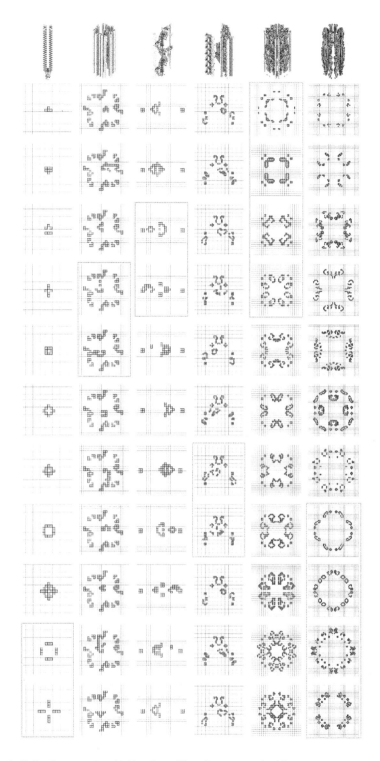

Figure 13.3 Cellular Automation (CA) rules self-replicating and self-organizing site-based evolutionary system simulation activating positive and negative space structures. *Interscalar Fluidity*, Venice Biennale Installation Prof. Pablo Lorenzo-Eiroa with Students: Benjamin Sather ARCH 501–502 SoAD, NYIT; S-Lab Grant, Dean Maria Perbellini's Incentive, F2019.

304 *Simulation-Based Information Actualization*

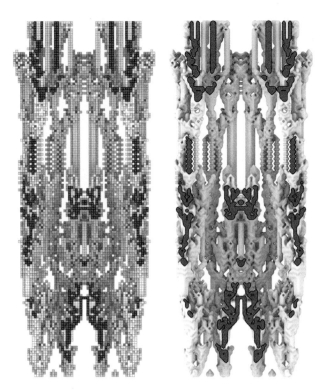

Figure 13.4 A1: CA evolutionary simulation voxels. B1: CA evolutionary simulation actualized as continuous closed volume surfaces. *Interscalar Fluidity*, Venice Biennale Installation Prof. Pablo Lorenzo-Eiroa with Students: Benjamin Sather ARCH 501–502 SoAD, NYIT; S-Lab Grant, Dean Maria Perbellini's Incentive, F2019.

computation, correlating a theory of architecture with a theory of computation in relation to the environment. These issues of representation relative to architecture space were studied through computational models that would activate and displace spatial properties through mathematical, geometric, structural, and automated simulation computational innovations and structures. Foreground figuration and background structuring through programming were placed at the same level of signification, activating a double bind feedback between computational signs and signals activating correlational computational visual semiotics. Computation was deconstructed in function to an artificial de-sign representation of the environment (Figures 13.1–13.2).

Marching Cubes = Point Reconstructed Surfaces
Translation Data Reconstruction

Simulation-Based Information Actualization 305

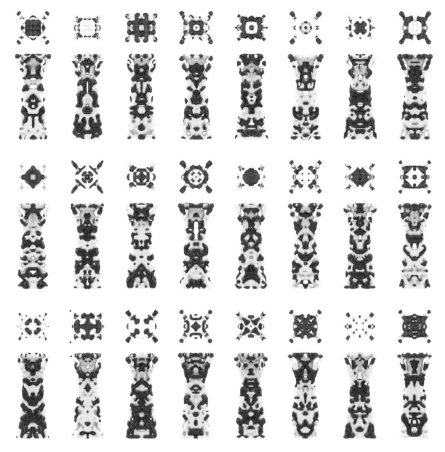

Figure 13.5 CA computational design evolutionary self-organizing site-based simulation continuous surface topology implementing AI. Alternative architecture columns output variations according to different CA rules and parameters. *Interscalar Fluidity*, Venice Biennale Installation Prof. Pablo Lorenzo-Eiroa with Students: Benjamin Sather ARCH 501–502 SoAD, NYIT; S-Lab Grant, Dean Maria Perbellini's Incentive, F2019.

While the project explored different means to displace conventions in computation, one problematic notion in Cellular Automation (CA) is the 1D, 2D, and elevated into a voxel 3D cell that never changes with the complexity of the chain of the site that evolves away from primitive simpler organizations into more complex irreducible states (Figure 13.3). For this, the installation proposed the displacing of the deterministic voxel sign as a cell container structure signifier and developing a continuous surface across cells (Figure 13.4-13.5) bypassing their determination and displacing boundaries between voxel cells and between generations-sites. This was done through multiple means, through attractors, through dynamic site-based attractors, through

306 *Simulation-Based Information Actualization*

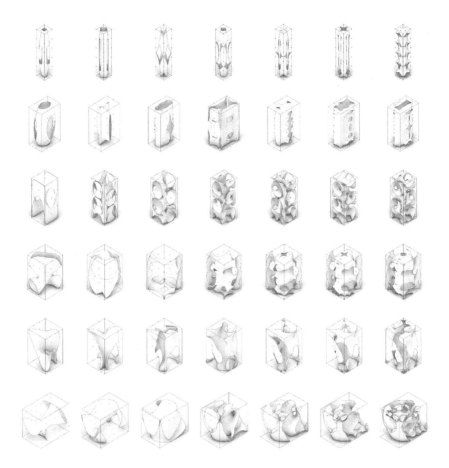

Figure 13.6 CA as discrete site-based evolutionary computation integrated as a continuous minimal surface topology activating positive and negative space. The original CA voxel's cell containment is displaced by surface continuity and minimal surface tension, therefore critiquing the discrete aggregate CA cell-based modular unit reference system as a spatial container typology. The voxel unit is displaced through the Marching Cubes algorithm and other ML processes implementing attractors and agent-based modeling (ABM). *Interscalar Fluidity*, Venice Biennale Installation Prof. Pablo Lorenzo-Eiroa with Student: Benjamin Sather; ARCH 501–502 SoAD, NYIT; S-Lab Grant, Dean Maria Perbellini's Incentive, F2019.

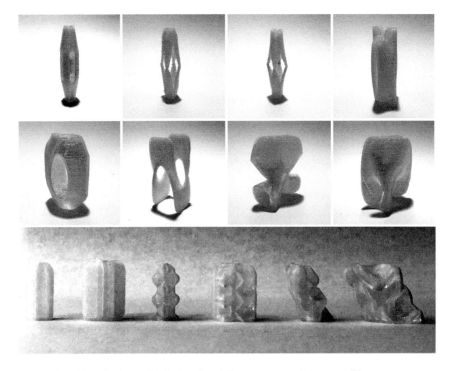

Figure 13.7 3D printing of CA simulated fragments studying possible means to activating minimal surfaces in the print actualization. *Interscalar Fluidity*, Venice Biennale Installation Prof. Pablo Lorenzo-Eiroa with Student: Benjamin Sather; ARCH 501–502 SoAD, NYIT; S-Lab Grant, Dean Maria Perbellini's Incentive, F2019.

simulations, through diverse types of minimal surfaces displacing the geometry through simulation, and through evolutionary AI learning from the emergent conditions that were depicted (Figure 13.6). In the variations, the Cellular Automation (CA) cell module is bypassed by a continuously varying surface mesh implementing the popular Marching Cubes algorithm of 1987[3] and the surface continuity through minimal surfaces that are contingent on the attractors set per voxel cell amount (Figure 13.7). The CA cell

308 *Simulation-Based Information Actualization*

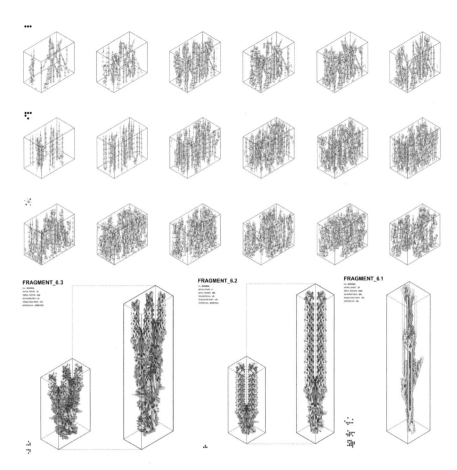

Figure 13.8 A1–F3: CA simulation contained within explicit boundaries and in relation to the existing installation room. These external site conditions are applied using random population aggregates of the initial patterns. A4–C4: The project series increases in density at an overall scale as well as at a local surface level through attractor points. Different computational designs work out evolutionary outputs at different scales and through different rule sets. Column structures 6.1, 6.2, 6.3: CA Minimal initial state: 37, 4, 10; Total Points 8467, 295, 432; Generations 200, 25, 25; Reduction Rate 0%, 0%, 0%; Operation NA, Stretch, Stretch. *Interscalar Fluidity*, Venice Biennale Installation Prof. Pablo Lorenzo-Eiroa with Student: Benjamin Sather; ARCH 501–502 SoAD, NYIT; S-Lab Grant, Dean Maria Perbellini's Incentive, F2019.

voxel itself is bypassed and is referential through the set of points that define its boundary, becoming a secondary reference and not indexing the box unit, since grid cells are going beyond the initial scale-grid defining variable complex open and close surface topologies displacing interior and exterior spaces (Figure 13.6, 13.8, 13.11, 13. 12). This is a temporal means to address the issue

Figure 13.9 Interscalar Fluidity, Prof. Pablo Lorenzo-Eiroa with students: Andres Carcamo; Brianna Lopez; Peter Leonardi; Alexandra Panichella; Ari Begun; Oluwayemi Oyewole; Karina Pena; Isaiah Miller; Benjamin Sather; ARCH 501–502 SoAD, NYIT; S-Lab Grant, Dean Maria Perbellini's Incentive, F2019.

of modularity bypassing certain cells through surface topology relaxation, but still at a deeper level one can identify through the points the reference grid that is still indexed (Figures 13.8–13.9).

Nonlinear Recursive Robotic Fabrication Framework

The architecture of the installation activates a scientific evidence-based design aiming at a higher artistic autonomy through recognizing emergent linguistic and visual semiotic signifiers. Instead of thinking about the architecture of the installation in its ideal design form through computational design and then digitally building it through digital fabrication, the team developed intermediate expansions of dimensions between drawing and building through information actualization. From material experiments that construct in 1D through a tool path line placed in motion to a 2D surface manipulation to acquire inertia as a 3D piece to a material that activates both 2D and 3D physical structural forces to a 3D planar and stereo lattice, the project expanded design dimensions through information simulation, actualization, and optimization, analyzing, and discovering emergent properties in the design process (Figures 13.10–13.12).

310 *Simulation-Based Information Actualization*

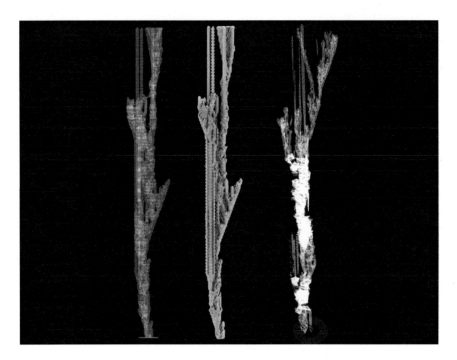

Figure 13.10 Robotic Fabrication simulation and G-Code manipulation identifying differentials along the 3D printing fabrication process. *Interscalar Fluidity*, Venice Biennale Installation Prof. Pablo Lorenzo-Eiroa with Thesis Students: Benjamin Sather and Andres Carcamo; ARCH 501–502 SoAD, NYIT; S-Lab Grant, Dean Maria Perbellini's Incentive, F2019.

The team did research on several types of computational simulations: from structural simulations and optimizations; to lighting manipulation recognizing crowd interaction in relation to the rhythm proposed by the occupied space environment; to acoustic semiotics through interactivity sensing and distorting spatial frequencies creating site-specific acoustic music as background spatial echo; to addressing the ecological environmental dynamics of the space by regulating and distorting its humidity and temperature; to fabrication technology through simulation-optimization nonlinear feedbacks, integrating all these issues in an atmospheric immersive space environment. Information optimization through CA robotic computational design was paired with various forms of simulation from structural to environmental and then was cross fed reconstructed by Agent-Based Modeling (ABM) robotic optimization implementing a swarm structural simulation, therefore activating several forms of correlational simulations activating Artificial Intelligence (Figures 13.13–13.19).

Form Follows Structure

Simulation-Based Information Actualization 311

Figure 13.11 A1–D1: CA voxels cells units displaced by actualizing them through continuous lattice structure. A2:D2: CA-based 3D Printed prototypes exploring different computational design surface densities and attractors. A3–D3: 3D printing Fused Deposition Modelling (FDM) identifying minimal surface tension emergence by varying G-Code optimizing the physics active in the printed surface. B2, A3-D3 Open and continuous topological surfaces relating positive and negative space. *Interscalar Fluidity*, Venice Biennale Installation Prof. Pablo Lorenzo-Eiroa with Student: Benjamin Sather, ARCH 501–502 SoAD, NYIT; S-Lab Grant, Dean Maria Perbellini's Incentive, F2019.

312 *Simulation-Based Information Actualization*

Figure 13.12 CA minimal surfaces topological continuity between positive and negative spaces, 3D Printing Fused Deposition Modeling (FDM) prototype varying G-Code filament deposition in relation to the minimal surface tension activation. *Interscalar Fluidity*, Venice Biennale Installation Prof. Pablo Lorenzo-Eiroa with Student: Benjamin Sather; ARCH 501–502 SoAD, NYIT; S-Lab Grant, Dean Maria Perbellini's Incentive, F2019.

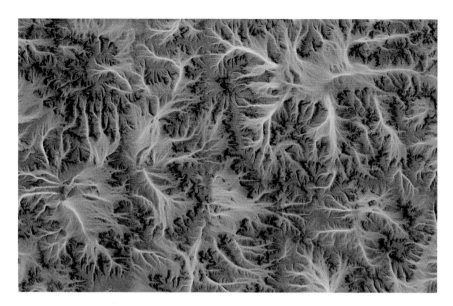

Figure 13.13 AI-based computer vision in relation to water runoff simulation over a topography, making it recursive infinite. Synthetic landscape AI interpretation based on image depth recognition. *Interscalar Fluidity*, Venice Biennale Installation Prof. Pablo Lorenzo-Eiroa with Student: Brianna Lopez; ARCH 501–502 SoAD, NYIT; S-Lab Grant, Dean Maria Perbellini's Incentive, F2019.

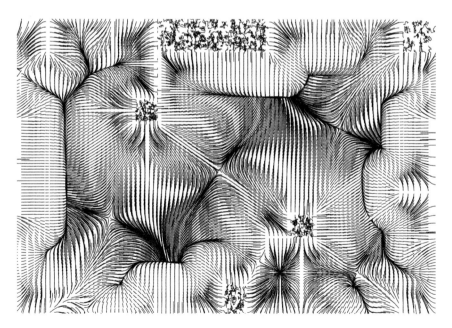

Figure 13.14 Synthetic AI landscape topography simulated as a shell structure. AI-based computer vision weather simulation remapping as feature extraction. *Interscalar Fluidity*, Venice Biennale Installation Prof. Pablo Lorenzo-Eiroa with Student: Brianna Lopez; ARCH 501–502 SoAD, NYIT; S-Lab Grant, Dean Maria Perbellini's Incentive, F2019.

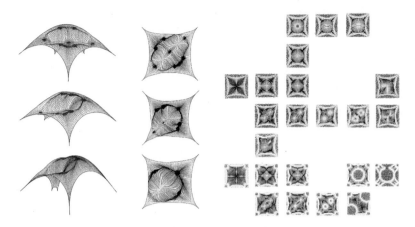

Figure 13.15 Synthetic shell structure as landscape, AI transferring of the 2D image into a 2D surface containing a 3D space crossing and displacing symbols, signs, and signifiers. Interscalar Fluidity, Venice Biennale Installation Prof. Pablo Lorenzo-Eiroa with Student: Brianna Lopez; ARCH 501–502 SoAD, NYIT; S-Lab Grant, Dean Maria Perbellini's Incentive, F2019.

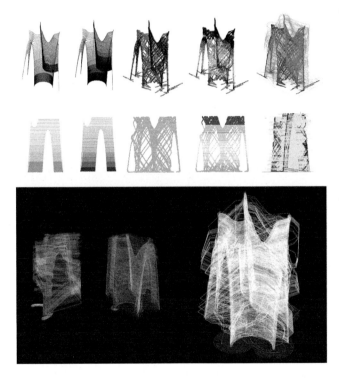

Figure 13.16 A1, B1: Varying 3D printing FDM in relation to structure stress, gaussian curvature, and mean curvature in synclastic and anticlastic double curvature. C1, D1: Swarm Intelligence applying agent-based modelling (ABM) for structural form finding. A2–E2: FDM conventional contouring applied to complex surface geometry. E1–D2, E2, A3, B3, C3: Robotic 3D Printing simulation. Interscalar Fluidity, Venice Biennale Installation Prof. Pablo Lorenzo-Eiroa with Student: Brianna Lopez, ARCH 501–502 SoAD, NYIT; S-Lab Grant, Dean Maria Perbellini's Incentive, F2019.

Figure 13.17 Adversarial double bind feedback between robotics and actualization. Virtual robotics ABM simulation based on particles displace through points the geometry of a surface; points leave path-bifurcating paths which develop a new type of swarm-formed surface. We propose to activate through ABM a lattice structure through 3D printing pairing FDM particles with ABM particles to save material activating form as structure. We also activate a site-based computation by incorporating the emergent site conditions of the 3D printing process such as emergent forces and thermodynamics of the environment while printing. (See Note Figure 13.17).

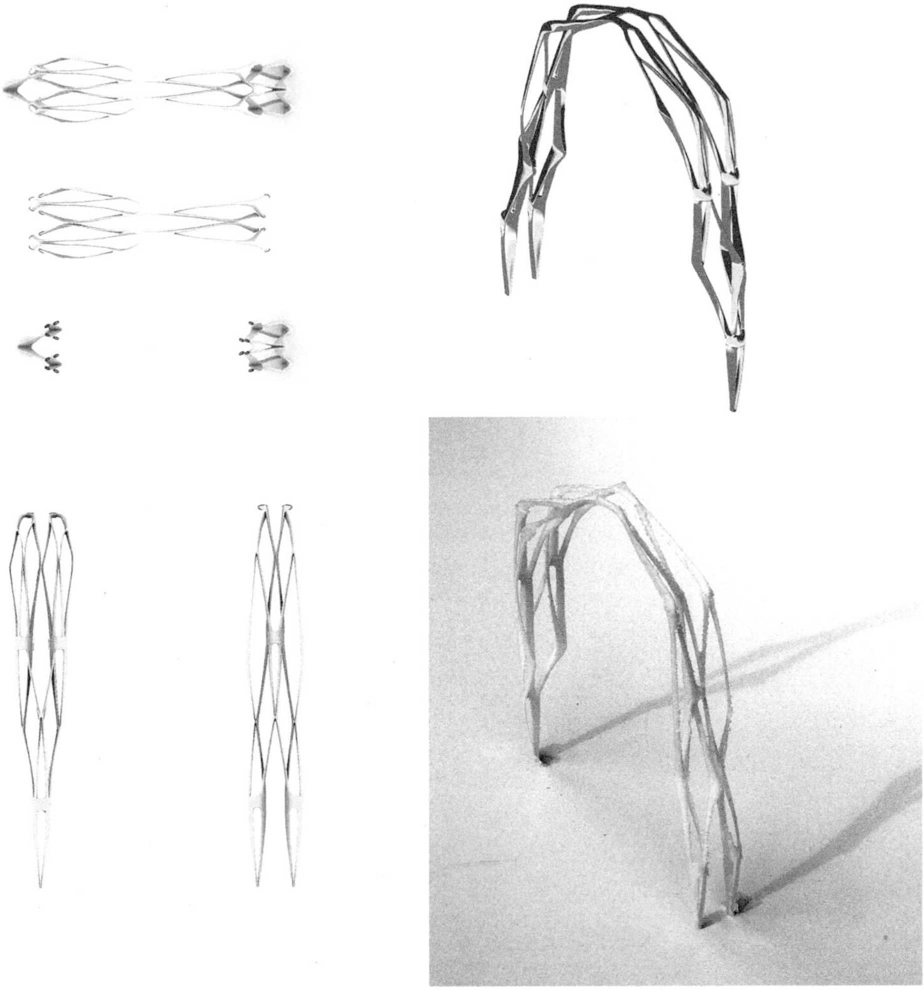

316 *Simulation-Based Information Actualization*

Figure 13.18 A1–B2: Structural catenary and cross-bracing simulation and optimization. *Interscalar Fluidity*, Venice Biennale Final Proposal Installation Prof. Pablo Lorenzo-Eiroa with Student: Alexandra Panichella: "Material transitions: Feedback between the Analog and the Digital" ARCH 501–502 SoAD, NYIT; S-Lab Grant, Dean Maria Perbellini's Incentive, F2019.

Simulation-Based Information Actualization 317

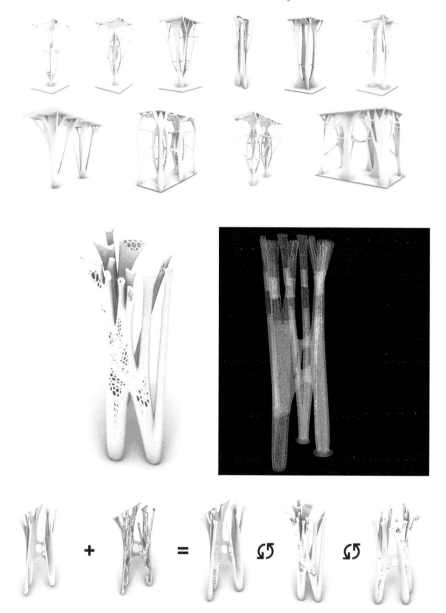

Figure 13.19 A1–D1: Structural simulation optimization. A2: Structural optimization simulation and material optimization in relation to structure. B2: FDM G-Code optimization in relation to structural simulation. A3–E3: Nonlinear feedback optimization between computational design, structural simulation, material simulation, and fabrication. *Interscalar Fluidity*, Venice Biennale Final Proposal Installation Prof. Pablo Lorenzo-Eiroa with Student: Oluwayemi Oyewole: "Structural Optimization" ARCH 501–502 SoAD, NYIT; S-Lab Grant, Dean Maria Perbellini's Incentive, F2019.

318 *Simulation-Based Information Actualization*

Responsive Robotic Materials

The installation worked through a scientific evidence-based design methodology through multidimensional data and information. Materialization was thought of as information actualization rather than a translation process in which usually there is a problematic shift in digital HCI visual semiotic sign and physical signal output which become subsymbolic. This was done through survey, developing our own dataset, and recording, measuring, and statistically analyzing experiments as we approached fabrication. Design and simulation shifted from anticipatory design through modeling to a data-based correlational nonlinear non-hierarchical simulation framework. We therefore avoided anticipatory software. We implemented simulation across all design aspects of the installation, not only due to a design philosophy but also for the ethics of saving materials and energy through predictive simulation. Design validation is both done through simulation and by testing probes physically. The computational framework fully addresses correlational emergent physical conditions: from environmental conditions, to thermodynamics, to physics, to the material phase changes. The fabrication process expanded to also incorporate Computer-Aided Manufacturing (CAM), their axes expansion through G-Code manipulation, as well as the material behavior (Figures 13.10-13.12; 13.16-13.17; 13.19-13.20). We cross-referenced digital fabrication in relation to analog computing to calculate the physical behavior of programmed materials under stress. Through different material experiments, the team did research on responsive materials that would react to temperature based on spatial occupancy, sensing and predicting temperature gain and the thermodynamics of the space in different conditions. 3D printing material filament was implemented to absorb heat and to release it strategically in

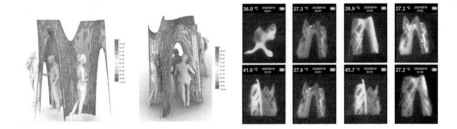

Figure 13.20 The installation is designed to be optimized in terms of its construction to be 3D printed using a material that can absorb heat. A1, B1: thermal simulation of projected heat gain in the surface due to inhabitation. C1–D1: Thermal camera sensing testing 3D printed surface testing material heat absorption capacity in tests. Prof. Pablo Lorenzo-Eiroa with Students: Karina Pena: "Dynamics of Humidity and Temperature Advantages" informing Oluwayemi Oyewole and Brianna Lopez projects ARCH 501–502 SoAD, NYIT; S-Lab Grant, Dean Maria Perbellini's Incentive, F2019.

relation to the form of the surface space. The design of the installation not only identifies where to place heat-absorbent material to optimize the energy in the space but also aims at creating passive convection currents that would accelerate air circulation by heat gain. We studied means to develop a passive cooling system through the 3D printed form (Figure 13.20).

Form Follows Thermodynamics

Robotic Interactive Space

Through diverse sensors and occupancy measurement, the installation senses movement and proposes feedback. The installation was prepared to sense mood through Machine Learning (ML) object tracking recognition while proposing means to augment the sensorial immersive experience through interactivity and responsiveness. The installation space pulsates as it recognizes inhabitation parameters, such as humidity, density, activity, temperature, and other parameters, developing a syncopated pulsating space that is designed to accelerate pulsations and experiences (Figure 13.21).

The project motivates sound experience, as an immersive fully embodied experience through bodily sound affects. The sound bodily affect works before the audible sound, as the installation works out different sound spectrums frequencies: from audible sound to higher faster non-audible frequencies, accentuating the notion of spatial-audible displacement and the sound of the space itself as a deep spatial echo. The installation displaces two types of signs and embodied experiences, making the installation fully

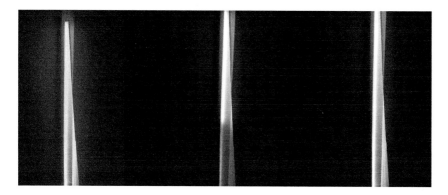

Figure 13.21 A1–C1: Interactive immersive atmospheric light. *Interscalar Fluidity*, Venice Biennale Installation Prof. Pablo Lorenzo-Eiroa with Student: Ari Begun: "Spatially Interactive Light" ARCH 501–502 SoAD, NYIT; S-Lab Grant, Dean Maria Perbellini's Incentive, F2019.

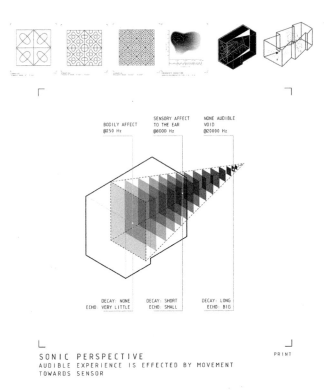

Figure 13.22 A1–F1: Acoustic frequency readings, simulation, and physical testing designed to interact with space through echo and visitors' position defining a semiotics of sound. A2: Sonic Perspective pairing sound frequency in relation to spatial perspective. *Interscalar Fluidity*, Venice Biennale Final Proposal Prof. Pablo Lorenzo-Eiroa with Student: Isaiah Miller: "Sonic + Sensory" ARCH 501–502 SoAD, NYIT; S-Lab Grant, Dean Maria Perbellini's Incentive, F2019.

immersive and perceptually challenging. The synchronizing of the sound of the space with its acoustic resonance becomes accentuated through the extension of the space in the form of sound waves and toward a sonic perspective echo, as it coordinates an acceleration of the space matching the vanishing point with an accelerating higher frequency. Sound simulation exercises were done to sense echo, synchronize reverberations and play the space sound by accentuating the acoustics semiotics of the space. The space produces and distorts its own atmospheric sound as an echo chamber developing feedback between conception and simulation surveying, processing, and coordinating two semiotic signs, visual (VP) and audible (sonic perspective echo), to motivate bodily experiential coordinating and displacing signifiers (Figures 13.22 and 13.23).

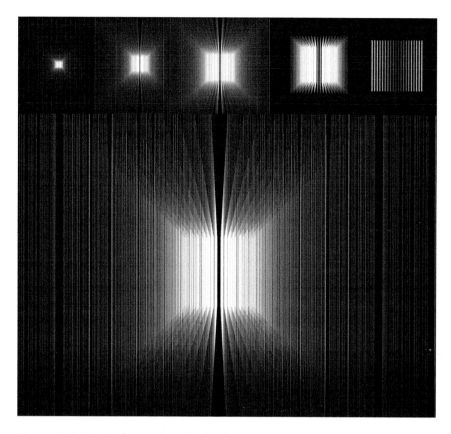

Figure 13.23 A1–E1: Interactive visual and acoustic immersive responsive space. A2: Visual simulation projected in the space. *Interscalar Fluidity*, Venice Biennale Final Proposal with Individual by Student Thesis Installation Prof. Pablo Lorenzo-Eiroa with Student: Isaiah Miller: "Sonic + Sensory" ARCH 501–502 SoAD, NYIT; S-Lab Grant, Dean Maria Perbellini's Incentive, F2019.

Real Space, Forced Space, Sensorial Space, Virtual Augmented Space

The space of the installation is accentuated toward infinity both virtually through CA robotic simulations that can grow forever (Figure 13.24) and physically through perspective and sound. The accentuation of the space through acceleration is played at three levels working with synchronous and asynchronous light, sound, and space physical signals:

1 The frequency of sound accelerates its pulsation signal toward the back of the space and matches the perspectival cone toward infinity, through the non-audible high-frequency spectrum of sound (Figure 13.22-13.23);

322 *Simulation-Based Information Actualization*

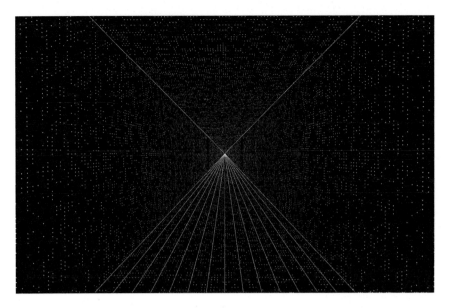

Figure 13.24 1D Point Based CA evolutionary infinite forever simulation (halting problem in automata, undecidable finite or infinite), forced perspectival illusionistic projection pairing physical forced perspectival space in continuity with virtual forced space. Prof Pablo Lorenzo-Eiroa with Student: Benjamin Sather, ARCH 501–502 SoAD, NYIT; S-Lab Grant, Dean Maria Perbellini's Incentive, F2019.

2 The vanishing point of the perspective is visually real, accentuated constructed real compressing the spatial experience towards the VP, accentuated virtual beyond the space through an animation, and finite represented as infinite (Figure 13.25);
3 An augmented reality-based virtual space geotagged located through Virtual Augmented Reality is modeled beyond the physical and projected space in its augmented state, this space is accelerated through VR cameras beyond itself (Figure 13.25-13.26).

Form Follows Media

Neuroscientists have done research scanning neural activity in relation to spatial perception, analyzing, anticipating, and manipulating the relationship between real space and perceptual processed space.[4] Neurosciences[5] research also points out at neural activity at the representational level of reality is altered by expected reality, therefore the relationship between anticipation and disjunction against reality promotes continuous processing between anticipation and a reframing of reality. A Geometry of Thought[6] claims that the brain organizes knowledge in relation to objects and experiences.

Simulation-Based Information Actualization 323

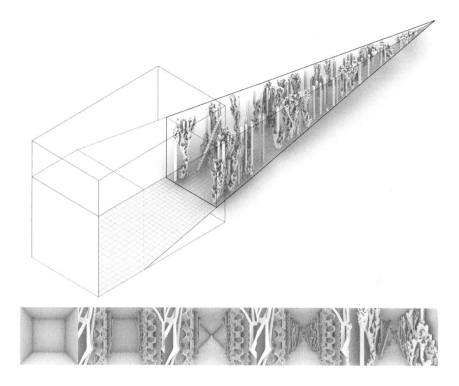

Figure 13.25 A1: Virtual Reality simulated evolutionary space in a forced perspectival illusionistic extension of the space. Virtual Reality simulated evolutionary space in a forced perspectival illusionistic extension in continuity with the forced physical space. A2: perspectival forced physical space with tempered walls ceiling and floor with no intervention. B2: Perspectival view of space with physical installation intervention. C2: perspectival view of installation with extended projected virtual forced space, in continuity with physical space. D2: perspectival view of installation with a forced perspectival view of physical installation and extended virtual forced space projected into the back wall, merging virtual reality with a projected animation of the virtual reality in the space. E2: extended simulation Virtual Reality (VR). *Interscalar Fluidity*, Venice Biennale Installation Prof. Pablo Lorenzo-Eiroa with Students: Andres Carcamo, Brianna Lopez, Peter Leonardi, Alexandra Panichella, Ari Begun, Oluwayemi Oyewole, Karina Pena, Isaiah Miller, Benjamin Sather; ARCH 501–502 SoAD, NYIT; S-Lab Grant, Dean Maria Perbellini's Incentive, F2019.

The project includes studies to activate a sensorial responsive space environment, aiming at activating feedback between sensing reality and interacting with a dynamic reality through robotics. The installation proposes different levels of relationships between real experience, mediated experience, illusionistic perception, audio-visual signals, and virtual reality and augmented

324 *Simulation-Based Information Actualization*

Figure 13.26 A1: Virtual Reality navigation of installation, including space and projected forced extension. A2–E2: The surfaces of the installation are actualizations of robotic fabrication simulations, merging real-real and virtual-virtual through various forms of relationships between these four categories. Non-linear feedback between simulations, representational systems, and their critical displacement through the accentuated illusionistic perspective as forced built perspective. These simulations feedback on each other through machinic robotic construction simulations, robotic computational design automation, generative evolutionary modeling, simulation, emergent site-based computation, and interactive robotics. These simulations are re-programmed to address VR and the multiple feedbacks between representation and presentation, systems of representation, and performative emergent systems within an emergent space environment. *Interscalar Fluidity*, Venice Biennale Installation Prof. Pablo Lorenzo-Eiroa with Students: Andres Carcamo, Brianna Lopez, Peter Leonardi, Alexandra Panichella, Ari Begun, Oluwayemi Oyewole, Karina Pena, Isaiah Miller, Benjamin Sather; ARCH 501–502 SoAD, NYIT; S-Lab Grant, Dean Maria Perbellini's Incentive, F2019.

reality to anticipate neural sensorial anticipation and playback with the space to activate different dimensions in the relationship between space, experience, and virtual environments. The installation works by anticipating and

Simulation-Based Information Actualization   325

physically confronting the reality of the space, with coordinated synchronic and diachronic expectations in contrast with the unexpected actual real space. The installation aims at augmenting architectural dimensions between real space, forced illusionistic space, sensorial perceptual space, and virtual augmented space (Figures 13.24–13.26).

Notes

1 Von Neumann, J.; Burks, A.W. (1966). *Theory of Self-Reproducing Automata,* University of Illinois Press, Urbana.
2 Gardner, M. "Mathematical Games - The Fantastic Combinations of John Conway's New Solitaire Game "Life"", in *Scientific American,* Oct. 1970, 120–23
3 William E.; Lorensen, H.E.; Cline, "Marching Cubes: A High Resolution 3D Surface Construction Algorithm", *SIGGRAPH* '87, 1987
4 Karandinou, A. *Data and Senses; Architecture, Neuroscience and the Digital Worlds,* University of East London, London 2017
5 Tabas, A.; Mihai, G.; Kiebel, S.; Trampel, R.; von Kriegstein, K. "Abstract Rules Drive Adaptation in the Subcortical Sensory Pathway", in *eLife Journal,* Volume 9, Dec. 2020
6 Bellmund, J.L.S.; et al. "Navigating Cognition: Spatial Codes for Human Thinking", in *Science,* Volume 362, 2018

Figure 13.17 3D printing can be considered a type of site-based particle-based Fusion Deposition Modelling (FDM). 3D printing technology presents an expansion of fabrication, insofar we consider the physics of the model printed. Normally a 3D print can be produced in different ways through conventional algorithms. We propose to activate a lattice structure in printing to save material and to bypass the conventional "wire 3D printing" activating form as structure and the conditions of 3D printing such as the emergent forces and thermodynamics of the environment while printing. We did experiments through catenary printing understanding the timing of the print to activate a printing catenary (Chapter 14). Agent Based Modelling (ABM)simulation of particles as agents provide a type of local emergent site-based simulation. ABM and FDM are correlated as site-based layering simulation and deposition of particle aggregates, addressing a different mean to build; we discuss in Chapter 15 the role of aggregation as site-based ecological particle sedimentation in an environmental Ecoinduction. A1–D1: Different types of Swarm Intelligence simulations to optimize materialization actualization through robotic fabrication. The original surface has been optimized through different types of processing simulation signs: from structural catenary simulation to environmental f luid dynamic simulation, hydraulic simulation, and thermal simulation. A2–A5: 3D printing FDM optimization in relation to swarm simulation displacing the surface as a signifier for an incremental layering of points by particle aggregate deposition developing agent-site-based lines describing an incremental hollowing surface transfigured as a type of lattice structure. Interscalar Fluidity, Venice Biennale Installation Prof. Pablo Lorenzo-Eiroa with Student: Brianna Lopez, ARCH 501–502 SoAD, NYIT; S-Lab Grant, Dean Maria Perbellini's Incentive, F2019.

14 Post-Human Project–Specific and Site-Specific Robotic System

History Section:
Twenty-First Century Architecture of Information;

Methodology:
Cassirer and Panosfky's Symbolic Form Deep Structure applied to CAM; Information Theory; Analog Machinic Computational Model; Information Based Model; Simulation;

Linguistic Signifiers:
Robotic Arm;

Computational Visual Semiotic Signifiers:
Non-anthropomorphic Robotic Fabrication System; Fused Deposition Modelling; Cable-Driven Catenary Robotic;

Mathematics:
Physics; Mechanics; Geometry; Descriptive Geometry; Differential Equations; Differential Calculation; Catenary; Catenary Surface-Catenoid Minimal Surface;

Expanding Dimensions in Robotic Construction Systems

Edison devised a new form of construction based on concrete, by developing a patent that consisted of a single-pour concrete house of 1919, including furniture and bathroom appliances, a mechanism of construction that bypasses assembly. Urschel in Indiana developed an ingenious form of automation in which manually fed an automatic bridge pouring concrete in a round motion to develop a full-scale construction, and later in 1940 developed a "Machine to Build Walls" with several patent updates and improvements. These two precedents may anticipate 1984's Hull first 3D printer patented "Apparatus for production of three-dimensional objects by stereolithography" in 1986 which then became in 1988 SLA1 the first commercial 3D printer. Marvin Minsky develops automation through robotic systems for the construction of Block Blocks Vision Robot at MIT in 1968. Negroponte developed Soft Architectural Machines at MIT in 1976. In the 1970s, Minsky developed the first

DOI: 10.4324/9781003292036-15

hydraulic robotic arm, and in the 1980s an interactive globe to manipulate Virtual Reality space as a Telepresence manifesto, for an AI remote-controlled economy. Today one can train a robot to recognize patterns and learn through machine vision to resolve a task. But the structure of the robot projects parameters, coordinates measurement systems, and usually, an anthropocentric reference.

The critical issue is that any digital fabrication tool, machine Computer Aided Manufacturing (CAM), 3D printer, a robotic arm, or any other "digital" fabrication mechanism, translates a digital computational linguistic code into M-code to execute the analog machinic movement, for instance, for mechanical material deposition (3D printer), axis movement in computer numeric control (CNC) or a robotic arm movement controlling any type of end effector. We aim at expanding parameters, electronic, mathematical, and physical signals, and computational linguistic and visual semiotic HCI signs in relevant to architecture representation by expanding dimensions in robotic construction systems.

Currently, we can classify robotics for construction through the following categories:

Anthropomorphic

Robotic Arm (Multiple collaborating robotic arms; multiaxis, 1x (J1), 2xy (J2), 3xyz (J3), 4xyz+ J rotation (J4), 5 xyz+ J xy rotation (J5), 6 xyz+ J xyz rotation (J6), 7 with base movement on rails, 8 on moving robotic terminals in 2 axes, 9 moving base in 3 axes);

Non-Anthropomorphic Post-Human

3D Printer (3 Cartesian axes one bridge per axis);
Stationary (2 axes by rotation of stationary axis);
Gantry Crane (2, 3, 4 axes);

Non-Anthropomorphic, Post-Human, Non-Cartesian

Swarm (3 topographic crawling-dependent axes);

Non-Anthropomorphic, Post-Human, Non-Zoomorphic, Non-Cartesian

Drone[1] (mobile, flying, water, usually 3 XYZ axes + mobility axes drone in relation to printing);
Swarm;
Cable-Driven (3, 4, 5, 6, 7, 8, 9 axes with independent moving anchors shifting as construction develops = Spider crawling);

Post-Human Site-Specific Adaptable Cable-Driven Robotic Construction System

We aim at placing at the same topological level of information both foreground design and background parameters, displacing them to expand a

328 *Post-Human Project-Specific and Site-Specific Robotic System*

higher degree of architecture authorship. We aim at engaging with a deeper transformation of reality by opening new possibilities for new architectures. Building constructions techniques index social and cultural values, ideologies and categories through production protocols based on efficiency, means to address natural resources, standardization and systems of measurement, and others, ultimately anticipating architecture building typologies through a technological determinism.

The research, design, and development of a site-specific adaptable robotic 3D printer fabricated an anthropocentric e-Chaise Longue crossing foreground and background relationships. The uniqueness of this robotic 3D printer mechanism is that it does not depend on a structure to adapt to an existing condition (Figure 14.1, 14.6, 14.7). e-Architects robotic 3D printer is a cable-driven non-Cartesian mechanism designed to be scalable to develop large-scale 3D prints, from furniture to buildings, using customized programmable material filament. It is therefore conceived as a problem of representation, aiming to displace not only a technological determinism but also Cartesian determination by expanding construction dimensions. The series of printed custom e-Chaise Longues expand dimensions in the architecture of its differentiated field of points-lines-surfaces-volume topology to displace the background algorithmic computational processes that inform its design. The 3D printer robotic machine, the e-Chaise Longue's computational design, and its computational programmed material behavior, feedback on each other identifying latent opportunities to inform an emergent process crossing background parameters and foreground designs.

Instead of using conventional design software, the team was interested in designing through background coding the design of the e-chaise and the machine at the same time. This was resolved by coding form through mathematical equations plots using Wolfram Mathematica in combination with Wolfram Alpha. The simulation of the material performance, the material sagging, and conditions of the room were both programmed and simulated-optimized becoming parameters to work with, understanding the differential between the digital desired form and the analog physical result, designing the structure of the e-Chaise in relation to its material performance. The e-Chaise adapts first digitally to a 3D scanned body, customizing its design. After is printed, the e-Chaise performs through 4D printing, as the e-Chaise adapts formally further to the specific body thanks to a 3D printer material filament programmed through shape memory polymer, designed to react to a range of body temperature, modifying the curvature of the e-Chaise by separating or accumulating the curved printed lines (Figure 14.2-14.3). One can program materials and robotic materials, such as polymer materials or biomaterials in a lab to react, behave, and live in relation to certain environmental parameters and activators, such as temperature, electrical currents or site-specific conditions. The printer

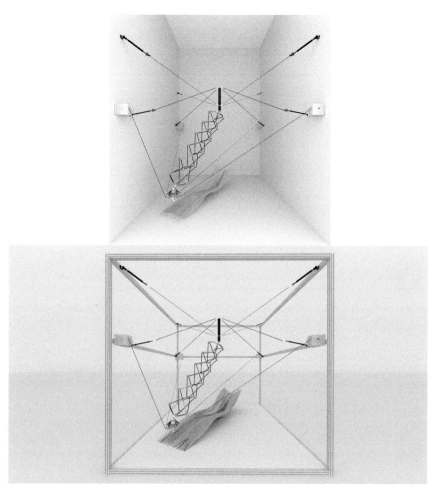

Figure 14.1 e-Architects' Site-Specific Robotic 3D printer tensegrity prototype exhibited at the 2018 Venice Biennale (GAA/ECC). The 3D Printer presents an expansion of architectural representation and construction systems. Site-Specific 3D Printer and e-Chaise Longue, e-Architects, NY Design Principal, R/D: Pablo Lorenzo-Eiroa; Designers, R/D: Gabriel Munnich, Yaoyi Fan, Pablo Toubes-Rieger, Nelson Montas, 2017–18.

not only displaces the Cartesian axes but also can be adapted to any topographic non-leveled site without the need for a three-dimensional structure. In this way, the deep structure, reference, and mathematical system of the printer propose a unique alternative system that also builds in a unique way through catenaries.

330 Post-Human Project-Specific and Site-Specific Robotic System

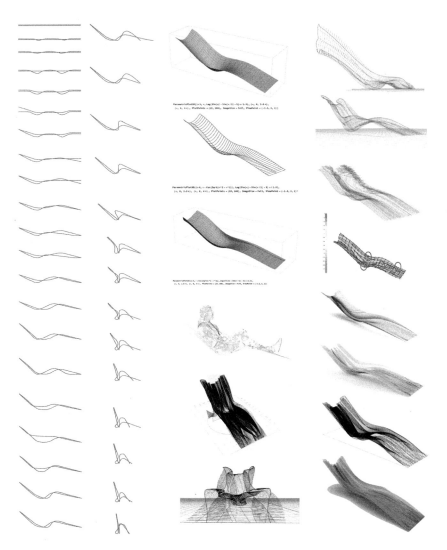

Figure 14.2 e-Chaise Longue mathematical topological variations exploring degree change in relation to structural change identifying distinct body positions. A 3D Scanning photogrammetry allows for surveying a custom body to optimize the form of the chair. e-Architects' e-Chaise Longue through Site-Specific Robotic 3d printer, 2018 Venice Biennale (GAA/ECC).e-Architects, NY Design Principal, R/D: Pablo Lorenzo-Eiroa; Designers, R/D: Gabriel Munnich, Yaoyi Fan, Pablo Toubes-Rieger, Nelson Montas; ADG Structural Engineering Aamer Islam, 2017–18.

The robotic machinic system was developed by coding directly through mathematical equations means to project the geometry to match the conditions necessary for the 3D printer having four microcontrollers in a non-cartesian catenary projection through the cable-driven mechanism.

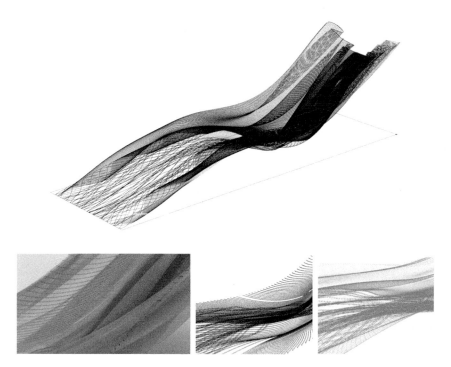

Figure 14.3 Shape Memory Polymer simulation for 3D printing material. A material pellet is programmed to adapt to the body, making a time-based responsive 4d printing. Polymers are programmed to change phase through temperature or electric signal. The form of the e-Chaise is simulated back and forth in terms of material temperature phase change and how this alters the design of the printed chair. e-Architects, NY Design Principal, R/D: Pablo Lorenzo-Eiroa; Designers, R/D: Gabriel Munnich, Yaoyi Fan, Pablo Toubes-Rieger, Nelson Montas; 2017–18.

The information was transferred as a tool path into G-Code and then loaded as CNC to encoders through four microcontrollers that would split numeric information through a Mach3 customizable interface for robotics. Since the printer is non-Cartesian describing catenary funiculars curves through four cables, the 3D printer works with a fusion deposition through catenaries developing non-planar 3D printing deposition both as an advantage and a disadvantage corrected by compensating the catenary in the output geometry by parametric modeling projection geometry. The differential between the catenaries described by the cable-driven machine and the developed physical model was contemplated and recalibrated in a representation distortion of the digital model (Figure 14.4 A2-C2). Various outputs given by the catenary motion became interesting: from the

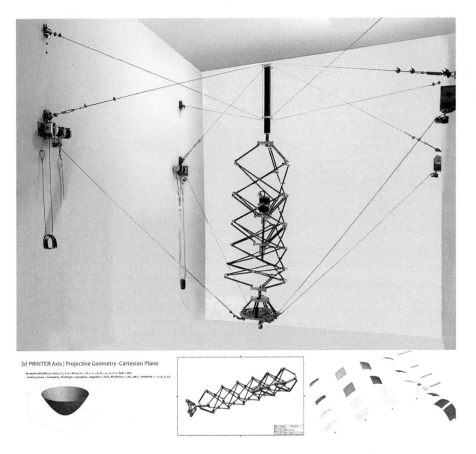

Figure 14.4 A1: Installation of Tensegrity Site-Specific 3D Printer prototype at e-Architects in NYC anchored to studio's walls. B1: 3d Printing projective geometry problem in relation to cable-driven catenaries. A2: Custom Kevlar Pieces designed and custom fabricated in China by e-Architects. A3: differential projective geometry to compensate non-Cartesian catenaries' CAM movement in relation to the print geometry. e-Architects, NY Design Principal, R/D: Pablo Lorenzo-Eiroa; Designers, R/D: Gabriel Munnich, Yaoyi Fan, Pablo Toubes-Rieger, Nelson Montas; 2017–18.

distortion of the printing model anticipating the deformations (Figure 14.4); to a special type of G-Code describing the bounding of the nozzle (Figure 14.5 A2-D2); to a type of printing motion indexing the cable-driven mechanism that produced a language and an aesthetic of 3D printing, developing a style (Figure 15.5). We also compared the 3D printed results that came out of our system and measured deviations and metrics in terms of the precision of our machine, relative deviation, and deformation of the parts due to cables, and compared them to others. Our 3D printer machine printing with a 1.7mm nylon filament achieved a measured margin error or tolerance of 1.55mm at the center of the printer. We also contemplate the use of local and site-specific materials, such as available clay type in the soil of the construction

Post-Human Project-Specific and Site-Specific Robotic System 333

Figure 14.5 A1: The printing tolerance is 3 mm within a 3000 × 3000 × 3000mm large format printer. A2, B2, C2, D2: The catenary cable-driven printer enabled a precision and a particular type of aesthetics in the bouncing differential of the cables, developing a specific type of printing style. e-Architects' e-Chaise Longue through Site-Specific Robotic 3d printer, 2018 Venice Biennale (GAA/ECC). e-Architects, NY Design Principal, R/D: Pablo Lorenzo-Eiroa; Designers, R/D: Gabriel Munnich, Yaoyi Fan, Pablo Toubes-Rieger, Nelson Montas; 2017–18.

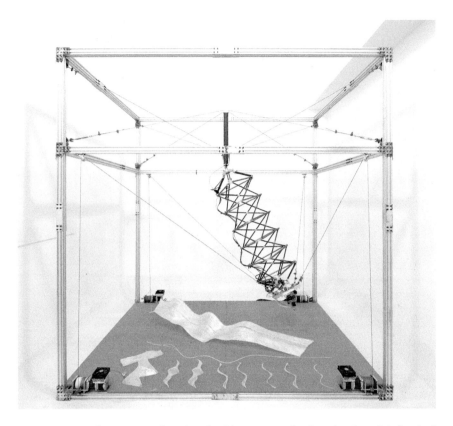

Figure 14.6 Final prototype functional with a range of prints developed (selection) with Frame to adapt to exhibition space without touching the museum walls. e-Architects' e-Chaise Longue through Site-Specific Robotic 3d printer, 2018 Venice Biennale (GAA/ECC).e-Architects, NY Design Principal, R/D: Pablo Lorenzo-Eiroa; Designers, R/D: Gabriel Munnich, Yaoyi Fan, Pablo Toubes-Rieger, Nelson Montas; 2017–18.

site, creating a clay mix and feeding it through the robotic spider 3D printer, activating a computational circular no-waste economy integrating and optimizing resources in relation to the construction of the space-environment.

Through a robotic microcontroller, winches can be secured to any site condition, including variable differential heights and locations while the printer is building. This capacity is also mobile, flexible, and emergent, and as the work progresses, the spider 3D printer can change its position, scale, and dimension and adapt progressively incrementally to the same site it develops, making a combination between site-specific construction and adaptation to emerging changing situations of the site, growing with the construction it is developing (Figure 14.7).

Post-Human Project-Specific and Site-Specific Robotic System 335

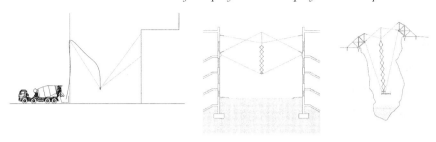

Figure 14.7 Spider 3d Cable-Driven technology adaptable to multiple contexts and conditions, making the 3d Printer versatile and scalable without the need for scaffolding or infrastructure. e-Architects, NY Design Principal, R/D: Pablo Lorenzo-Eiroa; Designers, R/D: Gabriel Munnich, Yaoyi Fan, Pablo Toubes-Rieger, Nelson Montas; 2017–18.

Note

1 Zhang, K.; Chermprayong, P.; Xiao, F.; et al. "Aerial Additive Manufacturing with Multiple Autonomous Robots", in *Nature*, Volume 609, Issue 7928, ePub. Sept 2022 [subm. 2019]

15 Deconstructing the City Through New Signifiers

Simulation-Based Emergent Space-Environments

"The State subordinates the hydraulic force to canals, pipes, damns that do not allow turbulence [...]. Instead, the hydraulic model of the nomad science and the war machine consist of expanding by turbulence over a smooth space..." Deleuze and Guattari[1]

History Section:
Post-structuralism; Twenty-First Century Architecture of Information;

Methodology:
Post-Colonialism; Post-Anthropocene; Post-Capitalism; Big Data Simulation;Evidence-Based Design; Environmentalism; Space-Environments;

Linguistic Signifiers:
Nature;

Environmental Semiotics:
Sediment Particle; Wind Vector; Water Vector;

Computational Visual Semiotics:
Computational Fluid Dynamic (CFD) Simulation (turbulence, vortex); Optimization; Satellite Images (thermal non-visual spectrum); Particle Physics;

Computational Visual Semiotic Signifiers:
Pixel, Point, Particles; Voxel;

Mathematics-Physics:
Navier–Stokes Equations; Thermodynamics; Sediment Particle Equation;

Cities Defining Nature Through Colonial Linguistic and Visual Semiotics

This Chapter discusses the possibility of rethinking construction and developmentalism in urbanism. Through deconstructing cities as emergent space-environments this chapter discusses how to address Nature through new computational signifiers. But before addressing these issues, we would like to discuss how we understand Nature linguistically and in terms of visual

DOI: 10.4324/9781003292036-16

semiotics. We would like to introduce an urbanism of information by problematizing the linguistics of Nature through displacing the computational signifiers implemented to address ecology and the environment to offer alternative means to rethink architecture developmentalism.

The modern movement proposed a clear separation between humans and Nature, with diverse ideological variations in such opposition, ranging from rethinking artificially the environment, to not interrupting Nature with buildings and cities' footprint. Modern city planning and urban design examples are Soria and Matta linear city of 1888 connecting cities centers; Howard's "Garden Cities of To-morrow" centralized city of 1898-1903; Leonidov's Linear City for Magnitogorsk of 1930 linear systems of parks-housing-work-industry-natural resources along a river (see Figures 19.1-2); Frank Lloyd Wright Broadacre City of 1932 circular economy of agriculture-live-work; Le Corbusier's Plan Obus for Algiers of 1933, Niemeyer's Brasilia of 1960, or Amancio Williams "the city that humanity needs" linear city of 1974-89 the last three separating through the free plan buildings from Nature. The modern movement proposed abstract grids in contrast to nature but minimized building's footprint manifested in Le Corbusier Ville Contemporaine of 1922 (3M inhabitants); Plan Voisin of 1925 (78,000 residents over 260 hectares), and the utopian "Radiant City" of 1933 (3M inhabitants) a regimented totalitarian centralization and densification to free green space, maximize sunlight, separating functions, and cars from pedestrians. The post-war reaction to the modern tabula rasa rethought the relationship between humanity and its environment, reformulating the logic of the place through site-specificity. Interventions were rethought from bottom-up as opposed to top-down, understanding entropy, and, in some cases aiming for recognizing latent opportunities, activating, and consolidating an emergent order.

The original pre-colonial populations in what is called today America proposed a range of diversity of relationships between humans and Nature. The European, particularly the Spanish, colonization of America as a "New World" can be related to a military strategy laying out a baroque abstract order projected onto an open territory imposed through city planning guidelines establishing a central square within a grid of 10×10 blocks adapted to local natural resources. The colonization of America was done through a human genocide, a racial "cleansing", a cultural-religious imposition, and a standardization of the territories' diversity imposing an extractive representation of Nature. The suppressive conquest was implemented through forced cultural dissemination in parallel to racial dissemination through political-social and economic incentives, from oppressing the palimpsest of existing cultural heritage to imposing language, religion, and an extractive global trade economy artificially separating humanity from Nature. The pre-colonial Mayan civilization measured space based on astronomy geo-location. The Inca measured space in relation to topography and a circular economy in balance with Mother Earth – Pachamama. Colonialism as urbanism could not face the consequences of originating a stable order through a Cartesian military-based projection of the territory for measuring, controlling, and standardizing it which created frictions, deformations,

338 *Deconstructing the City Through New Signifiers*

irregularities, openings, tension, instability, and unresolved conditions that reveal its abstract rational as a simplification of a complex reality.

Linguistic Signifier = Nature: "Nature Does not Exists"[2]

Nature needs now to be redefined holistically and requires a new linguistic and visual semiotic definition. While we address ecology through environmental restoration, we need to advert the ideology of what we activate through "Nature" since we may be restoring ecosystems toward a domesticated linguistic notion of it, reinforcing cultural, economic, and technological colonization of our environment. Žižek describes through Norton's "ecology without Nature", Nature as a linguistic signifier since "Nature Does not Exist" deploying ecology against Mother Nature. Historically Nature has been identified as opposite to language, as human cognitive reference systems can be identified as Language, the Mind, and Nature as three distinct orders of thought based on the artificial language movement of the Seventeenth Century as universal characteristics of humanity.[3] One of the contemporary definitions of the relationship between architecture and Nature is given by Agrest's *Architecture of Nature*[4] in which architecture studios analyze Nature as architecture, questioning the means to access and understand natural processes and opening up conditions to what architecture can reflect upon Nature as a form of representation permeable to cultural readings. The Biodigital[5] city proposed by Estévez proposes biomimicry and a different relationship between architecture and nature through form as biological performance. In contrast with contemporary functional urbanism or the dialectical search for landscape architecture as urbanism, we aim at redefining the city through information theory and the new digital signifiers that enable the management of data and energy through the thermodynamics of computational fluid dynamic simulation (CFD) expanding architecture as space environments.

We propose a different relationship between humanity and Nature displacing humanity as the center of reference and activating a post-colonial post-Anthropocene as environmental commons elevating all forms of Being placed equally. We propose for architecture and urbanism a densification and a circular economy in relationship to space-environments based on a long-term project denominated Ecological-induction, or artificially induced ecology, recognizing the artificial representational semiotic paradigm of cities against evolutionary natural processes.

Toward a Post-Colonial Post-Anthropocene

We understand the Anthropocene[6] as colonization and appropriation of the environment. The Anthropocene displaced the geology and environment of the planet as informed, not exclusively, by human action, opening new relationships between the human-made city and its artificially informed environment proposing a distinct ideological position and understanding of Nature. Human action can be read as the last geological crust on our planet, presenting a point of no return and a limitation to simple environmental preservation restoration. A total of 86% of Earth's species are yet to be discovered if we manage

Deconstructing the City Through New Signifiers   339

not to annihilate them before then, as 50% have been already eliminated by human action, a percentage largely underestimated.[7] The current temperature means annual temperature (MAT) increase to >29°C due to human action by releasing CO_2 emissions accelerating the greenhouse effect presents a non-sustainable threat to most life on earth, from biome displacement to the loss of climate niche by the various correlational factors based in the first effect of the acceleration of the melting of glaciers and ice sheets globally.[8] Prediction models present an increase of 7.5°C of the human experienced MAT by 2070 since the land will warm up faster than oceans, a scenario of sea-level rise increasing to a displacement between 3.5B and 1.5B people or 30% to 13% of the population. Due to correlational simulations, an originally projected 1.5°C degree change for 2050 due to global warming by single-dimensional simulations is now approaching a 2°C–3°C degree increase average due to emergent non-anticipated environmental conditions.[9] This temperature increase due to correlational emergent factors means a projected 60cm–100cm increase in sea-level rise, which was originally projected to reach by 2100, perhaps is reached earlier by 2050–60. Health and environment are knowingly interrelated; 65% of the diseases transmitted from animals to humans have been related over the last 60 years[10] to the displacement of biomes due to global warming, as carbon emissions are identified to be composed by buildings (39% mainly operation–energy use), industrial activity (33%), and transportation (28%). The Anthropocene's correlational crises open unknown emergent correlational dimensions. The Sixth Holocene mass extinction and biological annihilation due to the Anthropocene is currently undergoing[11] demanding a reconsideration of the hierarchy of humanity on earth over other Beings. Biodiversity has been proven to be essential for the survival of species, including our own genetic variation.[12] The time for urgent action is long past due[13] and the real issue is why after a half-century we are struggling with the same sense of *urgency,* without being able to question any of the Capitalist parameters that took us where we are, reducing what's apparently politically possible.[14] Our current economic system, as well as our aesthetic values, need to be radically challenged through a new ethics able to address the environment, avoiding the linguistic classification of Nature as "the other". Aesthetics through anesthetics, need to deconstruct the political ideology implicit in the correlational environmental crises to address how humanity and its relationship cope with the environment. We propose to radically reformulate the function of international world borders, as we understand that the political division of territories with different laws, regulations, economies, and cultures are in conflict of interest to the survival of species and the environment. We are therefore developing a biome map in contrast with a political map, to propose the creation of bi-national shared borders threshold zones addressing environmental commons through international negotiation to reactivate and protect continuous uninterrupted biomes promoting environmental rivers, protected by international common law, and guarded by shared commissions of experts including displaced original populations. We discuss in Chapter 17 a Blockchain technology platform to administrate environmental commons zoning regulations. If creating common threshold boundaries between political divisions to accommodate shifting biomes due to climate change may seem a difficult political endeavor, the consequences

340   *Deconstructing the City Through New Signifiers*

of not doing so, as many studies project, may pay a higher cost, including human displacement due to environmental impact in global cities and pandemics shifting human crises into international conflict.

Viable circular solutions are a necessary alternative to the industrialization of agriculture that deteriorates the soil, destroys ecosystems and biodiversity, and pollutes the environment with agrochemicals such as water resources. At the same time, given the amount of population, a global civilization became actively dependent on industrialized farming which can neither be scaled back nor disrupted unless the population reduces due to various factors, from population decrease, to lack of expansion.

Pre-Colonial Systems of Representation of a Fluid Territory

Virilio's Unknown Quantity[15] places the viewer in the context of the Hurricane Katrina events in New Orleans and frames catastrophes to understand human behavior. Globally rivers are drastically changing their natural function due to dams, agriculture, real estate speculation, deforestation, and other processes producing abnormal artificial displacement, erosion, scarcity of water and flooding, and biome and ecological displacement. Native American original populations, for instance, developed a circular economic and social system that protects both themselves and the environment in continuity; measurable with concrete responses to natural processes, such as floods in the Mississippi River which were addressed by developing artificial highlands or mounds for shelter. Instead, artificial dams or river deviations pressured by larger economic geopolitics are placed in practice at large scale by the Army Corps of Engineers in the United States that aim at containing Nature through levees,[16] colonizing natural processes. The reading of the natural geography of globally relevant dynamic shifting ecosystems such as the Mississippi River already sets up a cognitive challenge, recently expanded contrasting Harold Fisk's 1944 drawing survey and a LiDAR technology survey[17], in which an intermediate state of the fluidity of a continuously shifting territory presents special relationships between land masses, borders, and rivers, defining ground and water in intermediate states of fluidity with high levels of sand, clay and silt sedimentation in constant morphological transformation. Many civilizations work with harvesting or modifying environmental processes, such as fog and cloud harvesting for drinkable water in Bolivia and other regions, to cloud seeding. New Orleans' wetland has historically struggled for controlling and drying its land for agriculture, and territory relationships vary, from the structured city of New Orleans, to the scarce linear suburban development along the Mississippi Delta, to the Gulf Waters polluted by oil rig stations. The Mississippi River, as well as its entire system of deltas and wetlands, is in a continuous state of evolving displacement. The ratio of change of the Delta system is about 7,500 years each time a new delta is created because of sediments. Largely informed by the artificial levees, the Mississippi carries 500,000 yds/day of sedimentation which is once deposited at the delta and increases consistently the wetlands collaborating to a rich and diverse ecology once it encounters the Mexico Gulf (Figure 15.1).

Deconstructing the City Through New Signifiers 341

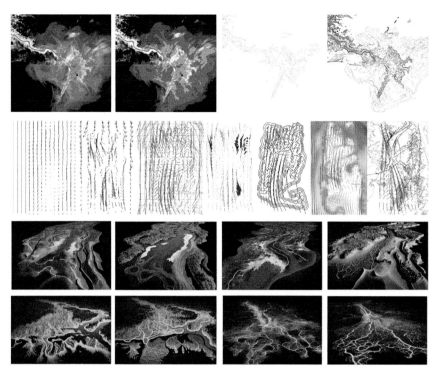

Figure 15.1 A1-D1: Mississippi River Delta, sedimentation deposition survey separating infrared electromagnetic spectrum from satellite images into layers through pixel colour signal downsampling and turning them into contouring values to create feature-based masking boundary regions. The critical delayering develops features identifying the river morphology fluctuation, the multiple rivers that emerge through the landscape through erosion, and sedimentation deposition patterns; Pablo Lorenzo-Eiroa, 2004. A2-G2: CFD simulations to analyse, and work with environmental forces to inform artificially the ecology of the Mississippi River Delta. Prof. Pablo Lorenzo-Eiroa with students Elan Fessler and Mack Cooper William, ARCH 177, The Cooper Union, 2006. A3-D4: Mississippi River meandering morphology sedimentation analysis cause and effect: river meandering shift and morphology evolution due to flooding, erosion, suspended sedimentation displacement, sedimentation deposition, and human action informed by infrastructure such as levees. Sedimentation deposition and the consequential emergent organizational shift, growth of river shore, marshlands, and islands. Marshlands grow mainly through sedimentation and are environmental ecological buffer zones that promote biodiversity; some geological functions also include the filtering of water of aquifers such as the Mississippi Embayment aquifer and groundwater and preventing water runoff and shore erosion. Sedimentation is of ecological interest by being an incremental evolutive site-based growth system informed by the dynamics of particle deposition and accumulation in relation to its developing microenvironments. The understanding of sedimentation as a natural process can lead humans to work landscape and architecture through ecological induction. 2D DM activating 3D CFD simulation as AI emergent programming. PI Pablo Lorenzo-Eiroa, MidJourney, 2022.

342 *Deconstructing the City Through New Signifiers*

Today, water control systems are the focus of many states, to address the rising sea levels. Fluid dynamics and fluid territories have not been dealt with by the city, or by the state other than through speculative real estate landfill. The open territory of the water remains smooth because of the lack of tools to deal with its fluidity and turbulence.

Historically the state eliminates dynamism but superimposes strict fixed rules through hydraulic science in big empires.[18]

Geometric Determination and Simulation Non-Determination

Derrida's critique of geometry through Husserl[19] identifies the deterministic dimensional projection of static self-enclosed knowledge in the certainty of measurement and control of mathematics in engineering which is consolidated in geometry as a deterministic field. The environmental concern does not only imply a responsibility toward the environment but also implies a displacement of the paradigm of thinking through systems of reference and representation.

We discuss in the book various types of simulation rooted in computational signifiers: from simulacra to Computational Fluid Dynamics (CFD). Simulation as a cognitive means to represent and understand reality differs drastically from deterministic geometric modeling. Simulation can be understood in terms of thermodynamics exchanging information and energy, and evolutionary complex as discussed in Chapter 7 through nondeterministic simulation-optimization.

New Digital Signifiers Expanding New Emergent Disciplinary Boundaries

Rather than understanding architecture through designing objects, buildings, and cities, an architecture of information implies a shifting cognition at a semiotic and ontological level addressing architecture at different information topological levels, redefining the epistemology of architecture to computational and simulation-based emergent correlational systems.

As an expanded discipline, architecture is now dealing with the design of correlational *space-environments*. But this expansion did not yet influence the way of doing urbanism or landscape urbanism, leaving the discipline potentially open to another expansion: *the architecture of environments*. Moreover, such expansion is now more influenced by a representation shift activated by Big Data Processing through CFD simulation-optimization. The *ecological crisis* has been initially questioning architecture from an efficiency point of view, a technological problem which did not influence the cultural project of the discipline. But more recently, the ecological discourse was able to enter architecture's cultural project through representation. Fluid dynamics and energy modeling through dynamic real-time simulation were able to consolidate a new aesthetic, a new envisioning of an integrated space-environment. New means of representation presented the possibility to directly manipulate energy, a new way to enable a discourse on ecology relative to architecture, shifting many of its means to address spatial boundaries, and by extension, architecture tectonic, including an ecological dynamic understanding of the territory thanks to remote sensing and LiDAR technology activating new means to address survey in relation to ecological and environmental issues that we have been researching since the late 1990s and that is now expanding globally.[20] This emergent quality through representation was instrumented into a new discipline, which understands spatial boundaries as energy boundaries. Fluid dynamic simulation in administrating real-time Big Data influenced a growing necessity to understand the decoding of environmental systems through thermodynamics. This process which is revolutionizing architecture representation is also re-coding architecture's matter, shifting the discipline to artificially structured environmental processes. Architecture is changing its internal coding and can now be understood as a meta-organizational system that can activate at a structural level, latent dynamic forces in natural systems.

If we understand environmental commons as a Planetary Computational Intelligence, independently from reading it all as computational as paired with contemporary canons of ontology, one can draw the reference in parallel to artificial evolutionary computation based on non-reversible evolutive systems through simulation-optimization, further discussed in Chapter 15.

Big Data Computational Fluid Dynamic Evolutionary Simulation activating Informed Multidimensional Space-Environments

CFD simulation becomes a different type of vectorial digital sign and thus, a digital signifier. Simulation can be understood as an emergent problem-solving topological formal process. CFD vectors implement particle physics as digital signs that are becoming new signifiers for architecture and urbanism, expanding the means to represent space and therefore its dimensions.

Digital Sign = Simulation

While architecture expanded the definition of containment by blurring boundaries between space and environment, this expansion was not applied to the city. Instead of understanding continuous ecological systems that dismiss differentiations between center and periphery, the way we are currently organizing life, services, and production in cities, suburbs, and rural areas is set to mainly satisfy corporate conglomerate production models.

344 *Deconstructing the City Through New Signifiers*

Latent environmental processes can be either resisted or induced through acceleration or manipulation, which activates dynamic instability to generate landscape-architecture opportunities as natural feedback. But this exchange of information can negotiate infrastructure disturbance and time-based accumulation of the processes of sedimentation, erosion, and tidal or hydraulic energy, to then inform landscapes, space, and a new type of environmental developmentalism. The artificial effect of infrastructures informing natural systems, for example, can be boosted to slow down the flow of the water, inducing larger sedimentation to generate artificial landscapes. In this way, a project can recover the latent lost memory of stages of the genealogy of the ecosystem. But in this exchange of information, a project may also negotiate within this infrastructure disturbance and time-based accumulation of processes to inform a spatial strategy. This artificial ecology may then be generated through the induced instability of the natural environment of any determinate natural system. However, this cause-effect relationship will activate architectural time-based effects in this exchange of information and energy. Therefore, architecture becomes activated through reading, analysis, and disturbance in exchange with environmental stability as an energy exchange. By working with environmental forces, we can envision the generation of artificial landscapes as natural feedback.

Sand, Clay, and Silt Particle – Sedimentation = Environmental –
Informational Signifier
Particle Vector (air, water, sound) = Environmental – Informational
Signifier

The urbanism of space-environments based on a long-term project denominated by ecoinduction or ecological artificial induction, a project that understands architecture and urbanism by reading, analyzing, activating, displacing, mediating, and organizing environmental processes. Ecoinduction proposes a new means of understanding cities globally for the post-Anthropocene. Ecoinduction indexes several possible signs, signifiers, and signified in landscape and urbanism, from the possibilities of representation to the actual particles that compose the shifting environmental condition: from energy and other type of physical signal flows; to physical fluid flows; to physical particle shifts. Through the relationship between the environmental signals and signs and the informational electronic signals and signs, one can develop an architecture of space-environments through mediating information flows. This is one of a series of Ecoinduction projects such as: a built ecological park in Buenos Aires (1999–2001); the Thesis "The Writing of the C" at Princeton University (2004); Ecoinduction I Rio de la Plata Estuary in Buenos Aires; and Ecoinduction II Jamaica Bay in New York City (2011); and that since 1998 is working with fluid dynamic simulation implementing Big Data survey, data gathering and processing. Ecoinduction III, rezoning New York City through Big Data understands City Planning and Urban Zoning in relation to environmental processes, further discussed in Chapters 16-17.

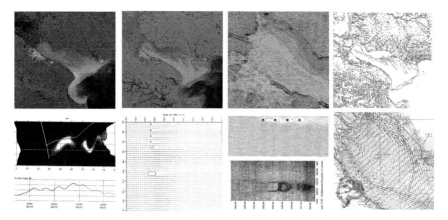

Figure 15.2 A1: Rio de la Plata framed by Buenos Aires (ARG) and Colonia (URU). Sedimentation displacement and deposition from the continuously growing Parana River Delta, which develops an estuary. The fragile evolutive shifting ecology of the Delta of the Paraná River, the Uruguay River and the Rio de la Plata Delta help protect the Guarani aquifer the second world largest freshwater reservoir; private speculative development not contemplating water runoff and the function of marshlands is currently affecting the natural stability and ecology of the biome; Satellite Image captured by MODIS sensor on NASA's Terra satellite on April 12, 2007, Wikipedia Commons. B1-D1: Satellite image and thermal reading downsampling layering, Pablo Lorenzo-Eiroa, Fulbright Application 1998-2000. A2, B2, C2: Buenos Aires-Colonia International Bridge Study presents concern over columns affecting the environmental stability of the Rio de la Plata; CFD simulations. Sedimentation prediction based on simulations. Columns of the proposed bridge disturbance and turbulence in relation to their morphology. Depending on the form of the columns one can induce sedimentation by slowing down the water flow, or induce erosion by speeding up the water flow through turbulence. "The Environmental Impact Assessment (EIA) prepared during phase 2 of the Rio de la Plata Crossing Studies examines the Buenos Aires–Colonia Bridge from an environmental view-point, assessing the physical, environmental and socioeconomic conditions of the selected alignment (Punta Lara, Argentina–Punta de los Patos, Uruguay." Prepared for the World Bank. The commission "Puente a Colonia", Director Ing. Agustoni, provided 1998. D2: Rio de la Plata CFD to study possible connections as an environmental network inducing sedimentation paths contributing to bridge foundations, Pablo Lorenzo-Eiroa, FNA-Fulbright Scholarship submission, 1998-00.

Buenos Aires-Colonia and the Rio de la Plata Delta-Estuary

The Vicente Lopez Shore Park was a master plan with several phases of design execution, including multiple shore parks, landscape, infrastructure, and service buildings. This is an experimentally developed park with low technological resources implemented through a phased landfill designed to activate ecological feedback. The evolution of the park over time works with

Figure 15.3 A1: Vicente Lopez Shore Park, Project team over Amancio Williams umbrella structure during construction. B1: landscape landfill formations in relation to views and water runoff. C1–D1: Sedimentation deposition informed by administering landfill in distinct sequential programmed phases. Each phase administrates different landfill granulometry and its strategic positioning in relation to dominant water currents and prevailing winds designed to stabilize the shore edge. Parque de la Costa, Vicente Lopez, Shore Park; Project Team: Francisco Cadau-Fernando Gimenez-Manuel Galvez, Pablo Lorenzo-Eiroa associated architects; Santiago Pages – Florencia Rausch design architects; Lucia Schiappapietra landscape designer; Jorge Codignoto, geologist environmental engineering; Amancio Williams Structure reconstruction: Claudio Veckstein 1999–2002.

an artificially induced landfill that evolves considering predominant cyclical natural forces. The form of the shore coast is designed to evolve by manipulating sedimentation and erosion, promoting a naturally induced shore formation through time. This was possible by activating forensics of the landfill by administering different granular selected clean landfill while forming the landscape so that the erosion of the landfill granulometry is coordinated in phases of one year, five years, and ten years in relation to the tidal and sedimentation action, activating an induction of a natural balanced formation that considers environmental forces within time integrating the effect of the north water sedimentation depositions with the erosion effect of the Southeast strong winds and tidal action (Figure 15.2-15.3).

Ecoinduction has been proposed since the late 1990s as a means to rethink relationships between architecture and the environment through artificial induction, addressing the necessity to work with simulation-optimization as opposed to geometric modeling. "The Writing of the C" formalized a research stage between the built ecological park in Buenos Aires and Ecoindution I and II (Figure 15.2). Amphibious living[21] critiqued the relative stability of the artificial ground of the polders in the Netherlands in relation to water. We interpreted the floating ship-houses in the canals as more stable structures than unstable conventional construction-built foundations over a ceding sand artificial territory. Provolution, by Doernach of 1969 works by

Deconstructing the City Through New Signifiers 347

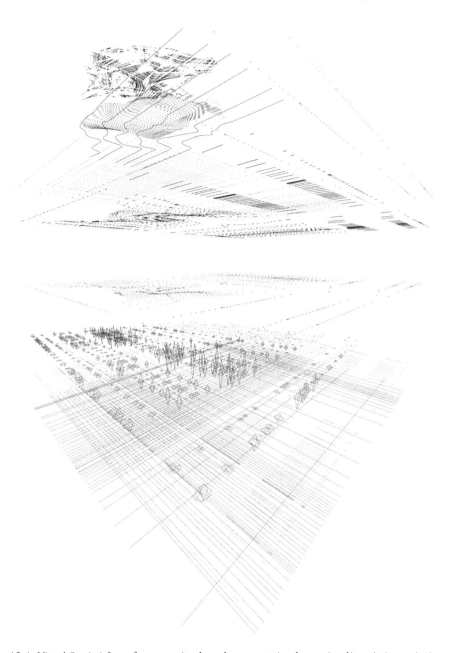

Figure 15.4 Visual Semiotic Interfaces as a site-based computation bypassing linguistic semiotics computation through language codes, that can feedforward and backward data and information as a resonance machine through multiple topological information levels. Each visual semiotic interface presents both a structure, data, and an information plateau as an opportunity to transfer and actualize data and information through generations back and forth. We propose as well as to displace each interface's conventional symbolic deep structure and projected anticipatory signifiers by the function of internal and external information. Ecoinduction I, Buenos Aires, e-Architects, 1998–2011.

348 *Deconstructing the City Through New Signifiers*

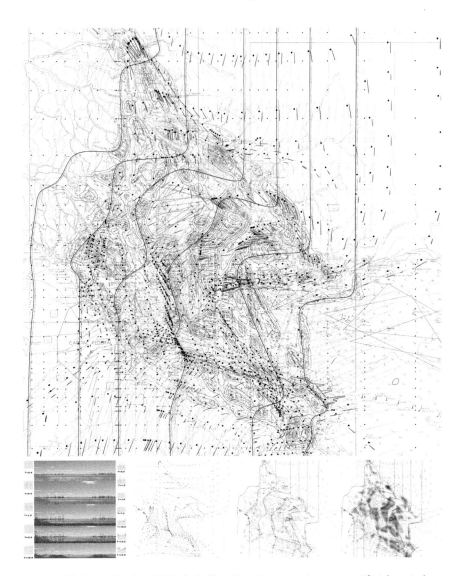

Figure 15.5 Ecoinduction I Rio de la Plata Bay. Buoys activate an artificial ecoinduction process by slowing down water flow and inducing sedimentation, therefore accelerating and reorganizing the latent ecology of marshlands. The project induces and reorganized the grow islands to facilitate the construction of a bridge through programmed ecological parks connecting Buenos Aires and Colonia. Project team: Pablo Lorenzo-Eiroa design principal, e-Architects; model: Henry Mena with the assistance of Jeremy Jacinth and Darrel Wesley; Ricardo Escutia.

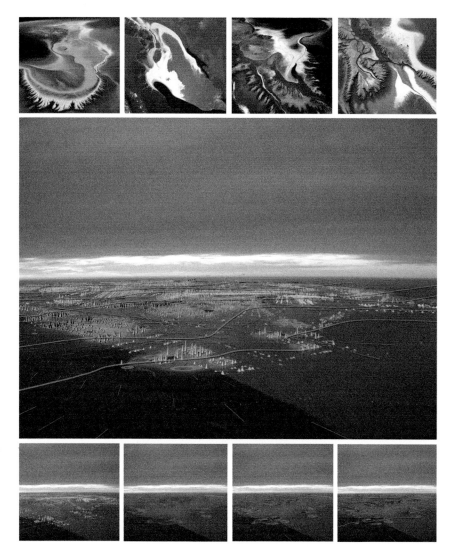

Figure 15.6 Ecoinduction I Rio de la Plata Bay. A3-D3: Rio de la Plata Estuary sedimentation deposition simulation based on the sedimentation discharged by the Paraná River; Ecoinduction I works with natural processes to activate an evolutive site-based landscape intervention based on information feedback; A1-D4: 2D DM 3D CFD simulation through CNN activating emergent programming; PI Pablo Lorenzo-Eiroa, MidJourney, 2022. A2: Artificially induced sedimentation bank-islands grow and stabilize the natural territory by accelerating the existing marshlands' ecology. A3-D3: Evolutionary site-based incremental aggregate deposition stabilization of the territory; emergent natural delta growth, islands-parks natural reserves and marshlands into an informed ecoinduction. The projected delta and marshlands growth anticipate to help filter and protect the ecology of the Guarani aquifer, the second largest fresh water reservoir in the world. Project team: e-Architects, Pablo Lorenzo-Eiroa design principal; model: Henry Mena with the assistance of Jeremy Jacinth and Darrel Wesley; Ricardo Escutia.

350 *Deconstructing the City Through New Signifiers*

inducing natural feedback by implementing a dynamic and responsive machine that works with disposable inflatable structures. Instead of excavating and developing foundations for a building "I Writing of the C" presented an innovative technology to accumulate and program sedimentation deposition in specific areas through an ecological induction thanks to keels designed to slow down the water current. Floating platforms become progressively fixed as the sediments grow below them, developing an inverted emergent architecture foundation system and a naturally induced soft territory (Figure 15.2) later expanded in Ecoinduction I (Figures 15.4-15.6).

Ecoinduction I[22] takes a territorial scale approach and induces an ecological natural process in the territory of the Rio de La Plata estuary, connecting Buenos Aires to Colonia by structuring the natural growth of its delta. A field of inflatable buoys initiates a machinic responsive process informing the environmental balance of the river promoting side effects that alter the dynamic stability of this natural ecosystem. These elements are implemented initially to slow down the water flow, promoting latent banks inducing sedimentation, boosting multiple diverse ecological environments, and developing multiple programmatic opportunities in different landscape scales. Once buoys activate the sedimentation process, they become progressively fixed and then are disposed of. This intervention informs environmental dynamic forces, structured positively, using such instability to induce latent landscape opportunities, in an artificial ecology of natural feedback exchanging information and energy (Figures 15.4–15.6).

Architecture "Building" by Informing Environmental Flows

The emergent form of the architecture of the landscape grows through site-based feedback since the sedimentation deposition depends on particle accumulation on a non-reversible non-deterministic process which is based on chaos theory working through theormodynamics. But this process involves also a sign to signal informational change. In relation to the discussion on language in Chapters 5 and 6, physical signals such as sedimentation processes are described through mathematics, physics, and chemistry as languages describing natural phenomena, implying the force of signification of a sign system to describe and read a type of signal. The sedimentation particles are first suspended in the water body and then they are targeted to slow down the water currents and therefore activate a sedimentation deposition, programming a physical signal to perturbate an environment through a feedback information exchange that can develop through time an architecture by informing the stability of an environment. The foundations as a displaced architecture sign, activate an ecological physical signal in a medium inducing environmental forces through particle sediment signs. In addition, the computational linguistic sign as the CFD simulation is used to understand the dynamics of the process which is then activated by a physical semiotic signal.

Ecoinduction = Informs Environmental Stability
Architecture of the landscape = Environmental Feedback
Physical Semiotic Signal = Information Feedback

Ecoinduction proposes building through environmental feedback. Ecoinduction presents both an information theory based on self-balancing mechanisms that can program and learn from their environment, and a synthetic type of automation by feedback which is then used to understand computation, information theory, and synthetic intelligence or "AI".

Notes

1 Deleuze, G.; Guattari, F. *A Thousand Plateaus. Capitalism and Schizophrenia*, The University of Minnesota Press, Minneapolis, 1987
2 Norton, T. *Ecology Without Nature: Rethinking Environmental Aesthetics*, Harvard University Press, Cambridge, 2009
3 Lewis, R. *Language, Mind and Nature*, Cambridge University Press, Cambridge, 2007
4 Agrest, D.; McPhee, A.J. *Architecture of Nature*, ORO Editions, California, 2018
5 T. Estévez, A.; Pérez Arnal, I.; Dollens, D.; Pérez-Méndez. *Genetic Architectures*, Genetic Architectures 4–17, Barcelona, 2003
6 Crutzen, P.; Stoermer, E.F. "The Anthropocene", in *IGBP Newsletter*, 2000.
7 Watson, T. "86 Percent of Earth's Species Still Unknown?", in *National Geographics News*, August 25, 2011
8 Xu, C.; Kohler, T.A.; Lenton, T.M.; Svenning, J.C.; Scheffer, M. "Future of the Human Climate Niche", in *Proceedings of the National Academy of Sciences*, May 4 2020 [2019]
9 Tollefson, J. "Top Climate Scientists are Sceptical that Nations will Rein in Global Warming", in *Nature*, News Feature Survey, 2021
10 Morse, S.S.; Woolhouse, M.; Parrish, C.R.; et al. "Prediction and Prevention of the Next Pandemic Zoonosis", in *Lancet Journal*, Volume 380, 2012
11 Ripple, W.J.; Wolf, C.; Newsome, T.M.; et al. "World Scientists' Warning to Humanity: A Second Notice", in *BioScience,* Volume 67, Issue 12, 2017
12 Frankham, R. "Genetics and Extinction" in *Biological Conservation*, Volume 126, Issue 2, 2005
13 Žižek, S. *Living in the End Times*, Verso Books, London, 2010
14 Jameson, F. *The Seeds of Time*, Columbia University Press, New York, 1994
15 Virilio, P. *Unknown Quantity*, Thames & Hudson, London, 2003
16 Berman, I. *Amphibious Territories*, Wiley & Sons, Hoboken, 2010
17 Stone, D. and Coe, D. "See the Mississippi River's Hidden History, Uncovered by Lasers: in *National Geographic Magazine*, Nov. 2019
18 Deleuze, G.; Guattari, F. *A Thousand Plateaus*, The University of Minnesota Press, Minneapolis, 1987
19 Derrida, J. *Edmund Husserl's Origin of Geometry*, University of Nebraska Press, London, 1989
20 Rodell, M.; Famiglietti, J.S.; Wiese, D.N.; et al. "Emerging Trends in Global Freshwater Availability", in *Nature,* Volume 557, 2018
21 Koekebakker, O.; Lootsma, B.; ed. Meurs, P.; Venhuizen H. *Amphibious Living*, NAI Publishers, Rotterdam, 2001
22 Lorenzo-Eiroa, P. "Ecoinduction", in ed. Kallipolliti, L. and Pla Catala, A., *Ecoredux 02: Design Manuals for a Dying Planet* Disseny Hub Barcelona, Barcelona, 2011

16 Big Data Politics in Emergent Space Environments
Rezoning New York City through Big Data, AI, and Simulation

History Section:
Post-structuralism; Twenty-First Century Architecture of Information;

Methodology:
Post-Anthropocene; Post-Capitalism; Big Data Simulation; Simulation-Optimization; Evidence-Based Design; Environmentalism; Space-Environments

Linguistic Signifiers:
Nature;

Environmental Semiotics:
Geology; Sediment Particle through physics; Sediment Aggregation through chemistry; Fluid Flow Vector; Sound Wave;

Computational Visual Semiotics:
Computational Fluid Dynamic (CFD) Simulation (turbulence, vortex); Optimization; Satellite Images (thermal non-visual spectrum); Simulation; Particle Physics;

Computational Visual Semiotic Signifiers:
Particle Physics Simulation;

Mathematics-Physics:
Navier-Stokes Equations; Thermodynamics; Sediment Particle Equation;

New York City Measured, Mapped, Analyzed, and Displaced in Relation to Environmental Processes

Our cities, buildings, form of life, aesthetic preferences, politics, and economy should be radically reformulated in addressing the current environmental crisis. Rather than compromising our immediate future, cities globally must be redefined to integrate environmental processes, addressing evidence-based ecological ideas to start planning phases toward the next 500 years.

DOI: 10.4324/9781003292036-17

We activate a research method by reading and measuring cities in relation to geology and environmental ecological processes, to disclose urban problems, and ultimately displace revealed structures to open territorial and architecture possibilities by implementing computational design through Big Data processing and CFD simulation. The following architectural projects identify and activate an emerging architectural problem in the city of New York by means of creating data categories, mapping information, and reading the city as a mediated process of representation that does not distinguish between center and periphery, city, and environmental commons. For instance, Long Island can be transfigured in relation to reactivating its topography understanding the last glacier retreat; or the function of Central Park in New York City could now be critiqued and displaced to activate environmental continuity, creating balanced relationships between the center and periphery, as well as activating environmental corridors (Figures 16.1 and 16.2).

First, the projects of several research studios here discussed are presented as case scenarios based on New York City to both disclose existing problems as well as to open possibilities to reimagine cities globally. In Project 1 (Figure 16.2) we first aim for a transfiguration of the city by means of representation, a transfiguration of the existing, "naturalized" reality by activating a displacement of a revealed structure and typology of the City.

Second, we aim at deconstructing the city by reading, analyzing, and disclosing the tension between the repressed geology and the structure of the city of New York, composed of a grid. Cities had historically negated the waterfront in service-port cities; social housing in NYC has been displaced to marginal marshland floodable areas; in the 1980s–90s private real estate development

Figure 16.1 Survey of Long Island geology retrieving satellite thermal infrared spectrum information and decomposing it as topography and bathymetry through image layering reconstruction. "Structuring Fluid Territories" Research Studio Visiting Associate Professor Pablo Lorenzo-Eiroa, TA Scott Aker; Student: Yong Feng See; UPenn Undergraduate Architecture Director Richard Wesley, Spring 2015.

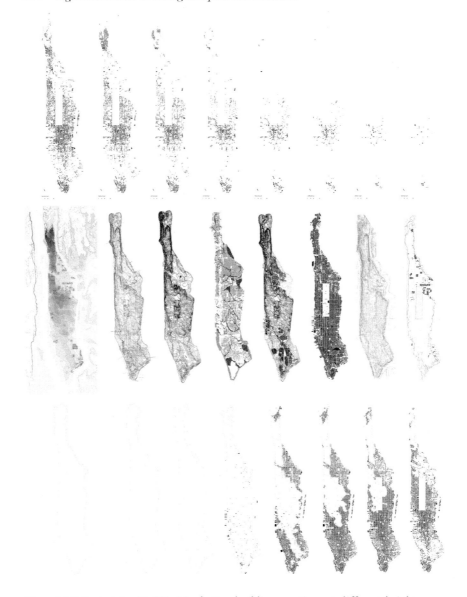

Figure 16.2 Project 1. A1–H1: Manhattan buildings sections at different heights over maximum geological topography. A3–H3: Manhattan buildings sections at different heights below maximum topography. Associate Professor and Coordinator Pablo Lorenzo-Eiroa, Assistant Professor, Dorit Aviv, and Instructor Will Shapiro, Student: Bing Dai; The Cooper Union, M.A. Program, Fall 2015. A2, G2, H2: Social housing has been displaced to marginal areas in NYC originally flood zones, indexing historical evidence of environmental crisis as an environmental justice social issue. Associate Professor and Coordinator Pablo Lorenzo-Eiroa, Assistant Professor, Lydia Xynogala and Instructor Will Shapiro, Student: Nan Lei; The Cooper Union, Graduate Research Studio, Fall 2014. B2, C2, D2, E2, F2: Topography of Manhattan indexing urban island-city fragments as neighborhoods, Visiting Associate Professor Pablo Lorenzo-Eiroa, TA Scott Aker; Student: Jordan Holmes; UPenn Undergraduate Architecture Director Richard Wesley, Spring 2015.

Big Data Politics in Emergent Space Environments 355

and city zoning changes enabled the recovery of waterfront parks and cities turned to the waterfront; with rising sea level, cities are starting to turn their back again to the waterfront looking for higher elevations reenacting the original social class segregation in cities through topographic elevation. Project 2 maps and designs specific building zoning envelopes defining variability in height indexing a diversified geological below-grade ground density condition. Project 2 (Figure 16.3) works with latent conditions previously categorized in simpler terms as the proximity of the bedrock to the ground surface that has historically informed the skyline height variation of New York City. This project studies the architectural potential to displace conventional boundaries and spatial definitions in the variation of the sectional relationships between the Manhattan grid grade level and below-grade and above-grade topography. The below-grade geological soil density composition can now be studied with a different degree of specificity based on forensic LiDAR data and Big Data applying AI. This variable soil density below grade, for instance, bedrock, clay, silt, sand, and other types of soil sediments and conditions can inform a more precise variable economic ratio for building heights defining a more precise zoning envelope. While cities become progressively overcrowded, the previous experiments that failed in the 1970s proposing multilevel cities through skywalks have a different potential today, presenting possibilities to explore a multilevel city by layering ecologies at multiple urban levels while densifying and diminishing human footprint over Nature (Figure 16.3).

Third, other projects displace the fluid territories and emerging spatial patterns created through Big Data processing CFD simulating environmental forces. By formalizing fluid dynamic processes, these techniques allow representing, analyzing, and manipulating of fluid dynamic energy, organizing the increasingly complex space environments of a city like New York (Project 3 Figure 16.4, Project 4 Figure 16.5, Project 5 Figure 16.6, Project 6 Figure 16.7, Project 7 Figure 16.8, Project 8 Figure 16.9). Project 3 (Figure 16.4) maps the larger ecological corridor of the Hudson Valley in relation to the Hudson River system, mapping the dynamics of river erosion and sedimentation in relation to the river morphology, and applying machine vision AI mask layering semantic segmentation classification. Project 3 then applies CFD to displace the NYC grid in relation to the shifting topographic conditions analyzed in the Hudson River at the edge of the city, developing a self-balanced shore informed by a dynamic city structure by manipulating sedimentation deposition. Project 4 maps conflicts in the relationship between the Manhattan and the Queens city grid and fabric across the East River as reformulations of the city structure in relation to the river dynamics and floodable areas (Figure 16.5 A2–D2). The project studies possible connections of the city across the East River (Figure 16.5 A1–D1; A3–D3). To do so, this project (Figure 16.5 A1–D1; A3–D3) first develops an algorithm calculating increasing bifurcations as the typology of the Manhattan grid is displaced by encountering different topographic levels as flood areas and the bathymetry of the East River. Then, the project develops a custom fluid dynamic simulation program for sedimentation deposition in floating aggregates. The combination of these two algorithms is then related to the site-specific topographic data and bathymetry. The form of the project is

356 *Big Data Politics in Emergent Space-Environments*

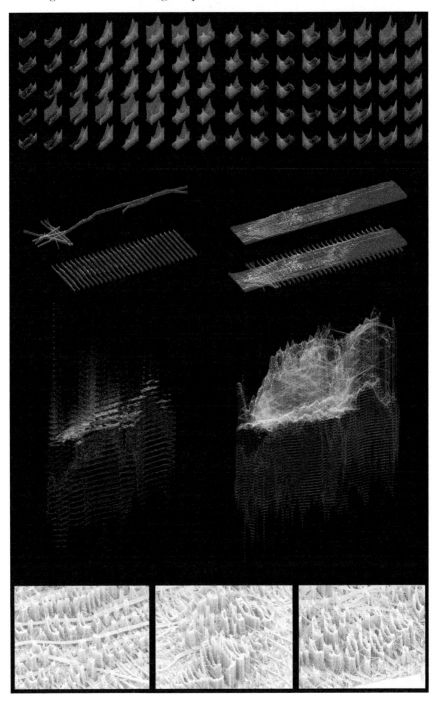

Figure 16.3 Project 2. A1: Building city fabric massing height in relation to below-grade soil density. (See Note Figure 16.3)

Big Data Politics in Emergent Space Environments 357

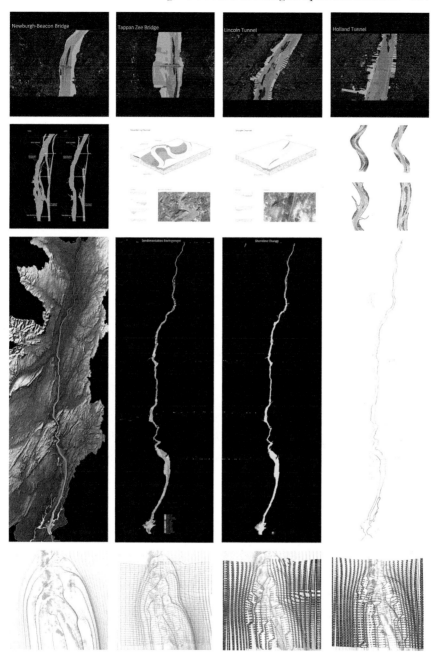

Figure 16.4 Project 3. Hudson Valley and River, analysis, GIS data, Simulations, AI ML Semantic Segmentation, and Classification of Environmental Processes. (See Note Figure 16.4)

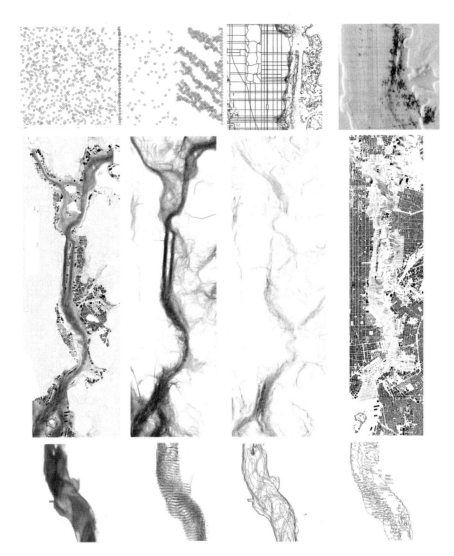

Figure 16.5 Project 4. East River NYC simulations. A1, B1: Algorithm implementing mathematics, chemistry, and physics calculating fluid dynamic simulation of particle sedimentation aggregate and accumulation deposition in a fluid. C1, D1: FEMA Flood Zones 1,2,3. The shifting dynamic organization of a landscape is activated by promoting the natural side effects of exchanging information and energy. A2, B2, C2, D2: Figure 5c East River, including both Manhattan and Queens, NYC. GIS, CFD. "Structuring Fluid Territories" Research Studio Visiting Associate Professor Pablo Lorenzo-Eiroa, TA Scott Aker; Student A2–D2: Yong Feng See; UPenn Undergraduate Architecture Director Richard Wesley, Spring 2015. A1–D1: East River Aggregate Simulation, Prof. Lorenzo Eiroa, students: Katheryn Bajo and Gregory Schikman; The Cooper Union, ARCH 177/482B, S2013; A3–D3: East River Simulations, Prof. Lorenzo Eiroa, Students: Mark Tugman, Charlie Blanchard, Iyatunde Majekodunmi, The Cooper Union, ARCH 177/482B, S2013.

defined by its dynamic shifting ecology, which emerges by combining deterministic algorithmic operations with non-deterministic topographies based on Big Data processing. Most projects developed their own computer algorithms (Figure 16.5 A1–C1) by identifying at a particle level the relationship between the digital signifier (physics particle sign) and the environmental process physical signals (fluid dynamic vector, sediment particle through CFD reading). In addition, most of these digital simulations were also tested and compared with complex and precise 3D-printed physical models that run physical analog simulations (Figure 16.5 A4). The mathematics of Navier-Stokes equations is known to be a working mathematical approximative model, but there are problems of resolution and scale, and computational power in relation to the intricacies of the resolution of the model. To address computing limitations, we activate a recursive informational model that would not distinguish between digital and physical analog but compare back and forth the limitations and advantages of the different interfaces as media and mediums in relation to physical forces. In addition, the studio paired the granulometry of the 3d printed model in relation to the sedimentation process, coordinating digital simulation, and physical simulation in relation to each other.

Fourth, other projects work out the relationship between spatial containment, urban morphology, and the architecture of the city in relation to micro and macro-organizational environments, addressing urbanism as a space environment. Project 5 (Figure 16.6) initially maps the actual existing dissociation between Manhattan density building massing and the existing open green areas and how these two conditions contribute to the heat island effect or feedback temperature gain in New York City. This project reads and renders visible heat island effect or temperature gain non-visible infrared wave signals or infrared light spectrum in relation to urban massing, reading NYC as layered space environments addressing both visible and non-visible light spectrums (Figure 16.6 A1–D1; A2–D2; A3–D3). Considering the city as a space environment, the project relates the city's skyline to its explicit non-visible but perceptible environmental skyline (Figure 16.6 D3; A4–D4). Urban massing, urban clusters, and building typologies and their relationship to urban voids create artificial micro-environments in which the measuring of the heat island effect can be more relevant. To activate a critical reading of the city and a potential addressing of such reading, the project proposes a series of interrelated urban interventions that aim to balance through computational fluid dynamic simulation (CFD) the previously mapped heat island effect produced by urban massing. The project expands and interconnects key specific open spaces and corridors in the city activating artificial environmental continuity to activate specific wind patterns which project 6 (Figure 16.7) and 8 (Figure 16.9) take forward. Project 6 renders visible the complex network of fluid dynamic simulation of New York City in relation to multiple wind patterns, swirls, and vortexes. By opening public spaces to create larger urban corridors, both projects 5 and 6 progressively activate an ecology of wind patterns to balance the high temperatures created by building massing and building up inertia by adding continuity between existing green areas (Figures 16.6 and 16.7).

Fifth, other projects such as Project 7 (Figure 16.8) work out rather invisible and intangible environmental conditions, such as sound. This project

360 *Big Data Politics in Emergent Space-Environments*

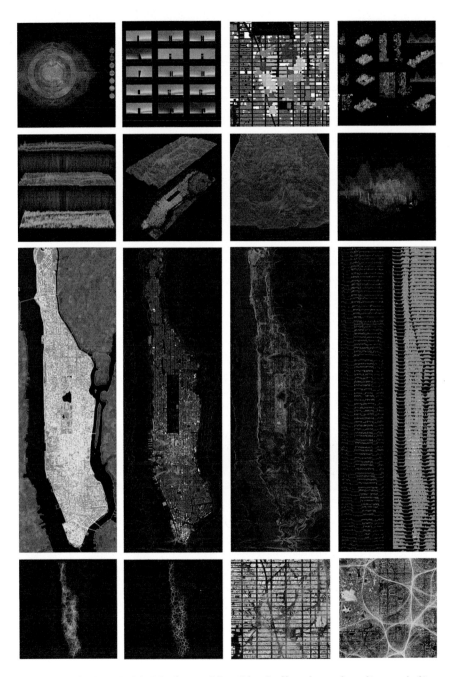

Figure 16.6 Project 5. A3: Manhattan Heat Island effect thermal reading as skyline and mitigation strategies. (See Note Figure 16.6).

creates a sound mapping strategy by identifying means to collect crowd-sourced data. By accessing portable cell phone microphones as measuring devices of participating individuals that voluntarily provided access to their devices, this project aimed, to a certain extent, to displace the typical authority and Digital Feudalism structures in data gathering. The first tests

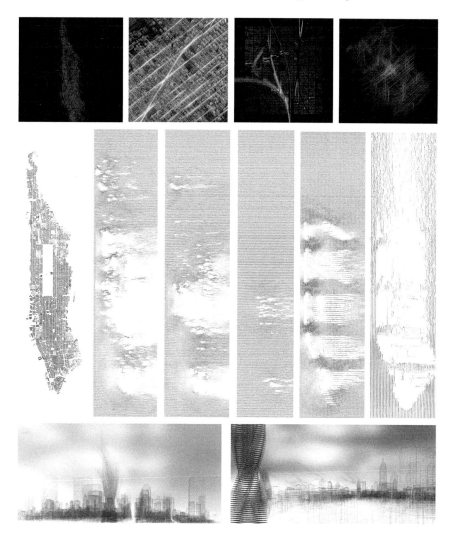

Figure 16.7 Project 6. NYC wind simulation and urban fabric optimization. A2–D2: Wind corridors informing motivation or unmotivation of urban development. A2–F2: NYC wind simulation studies over the existing urban fabric. A3–B3: hi-rise building typologies informed externally through wind patterns vortex, and internally through continuous voids activating forced passive air circulation. Associate Professor and Coordinator Pablo Lorenzo-Eiroa, Assistant Professor, Lydia Xynogala and Instructor Will Shapiro, Student Ming Yan; The Cooper Union, Graduate Research Studio, Fall 2014. A1–D1/A3–B3: Associate Professor and Coordinator Pablo Lorenzo-Eiroa, Assistant Professor Dorit Aviv and Instructor Will Shapiro; student Seung Hwang Kim; The Cooper Union, Graduate Research Studio, Fall 2015.

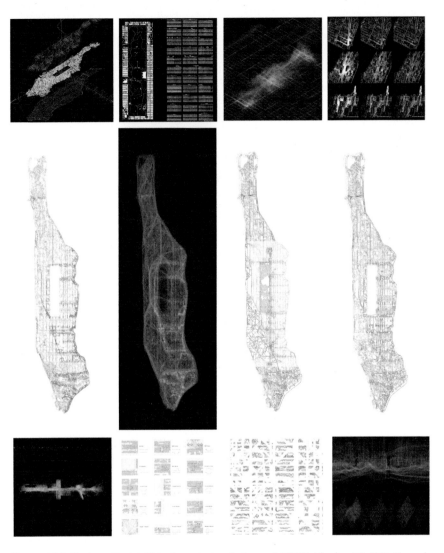

Figure 16.8 Project 7. A1–D1: Sound simulation of NYC block. A2–D2: Soundscape simulation of NYC. C2, D2: proposed block optimization in relation to sound. FEMA, NYPL, NYC.gov databases; Ecotect sound simulation and Steinberg Cubase. Associate Professor and Coordinator Pablo Lorenzo-Eiroa, Assistant Professor Dorit Aviv, and Instructor Will Shapiro; student: Jin Woo Lee; The Cooper Union, Graduate Research Studio, Fall 2015.

are developed in an NYC block (Figure 16.8 A1–D1; A3–B3), developing sequential street sound simulations retrieving different data sets, and then studying relationships between building typologies and the soundscapes they inform. The project then develops systematic readings of the collected data and studies how different spatial conditions and boundaries propel different sound patterns. The project also studied how different façade rugosity and materiality affect each of the studied conditions. After these local studies, different block densities, and street alignments we proceeded with engaging with clusters of city blocks and defining a larger urban morphology relative to sound. After these studies combining local and regional readings, the project proposes an overall mapping of the city identifying statistically the measurement through a time of certain sound density areas, with the hope of developing a comprehensive mapping of the sound of the city (Figure 16.8).

Sixth, other projects of the research studio work by reading, analyzing, and disclosing the tension between repressed hidden latent ecologies and the grid that originally organized the city. The existing zoning mechanisms by which the city is structured, such as the city grid, blocks, blocks backyards, setbacks, building envelopes, orientation, public space, voids, and parks create proto-typical solutions to the multiple forces that inform the city, including real estate speculation and civic functions, among others. These prototypical solutions form urban typologies at multiple levels, for instance: the overall morphology of the city and its structure, urban fragments, urban block, streets, and the city's buildings. Latent ecologies, environments, and other parameters are re-coded to make sense of the mapped conditions. Implementing a critical reading, the projects expand the design to a re-coding of the parameters that formalize the city. These readings and transformations would necessarily have to engage in a topological displacement and transfiguration of the urban typologies and the city themselves by addressing environmental processes to the point that new building typologies, new urban typologies, and new cities typologies would emerge by addressing an informed synthetic space-environment. This topological continuity between built environments and emerging environmental forces would engage in a reconsideration of the relationship between the center and periphery, the city and "Nature", the artificial and the natural or reformulating nature and the environment as the other.

Finally, Project 8 (Figure 16.9) proposes a sectional rezoning of New York City blocks to propose water infrastructure mechanisms for environmental balance. Instead of keeping water off the city, a complex networked aqueduct as a hydraulic infrastructure for New York City works out at multiple grade levels, avoiding just flooding the city as a version of Venice, or Amsterdam, by implementing a range of water infrastructure solutions through dam or locks canals: from flooding reservoirs to water alleviation through open water canals. This project proposes topological displacements of city block typologies altering relationships between urban fabric, contained backyards, and public and private space. By inverting the fabric of the city, the project enables a parallel continuous ecological system. This project proposes a displacement of New York City blocks typologies in terms of spatial containment. Internal blocks create first reservoirs to contain flooding which themselves then become interconnected and function as water alleviation canals across different blocks. These canals interconnect while they reactivate suppresed underground canals, developing a larger hybrid artificial and natural waterway system. The affected blocks progressively open their interior containment while they activate larger ecologies. The overall project starts activating latent ecologies of different scales

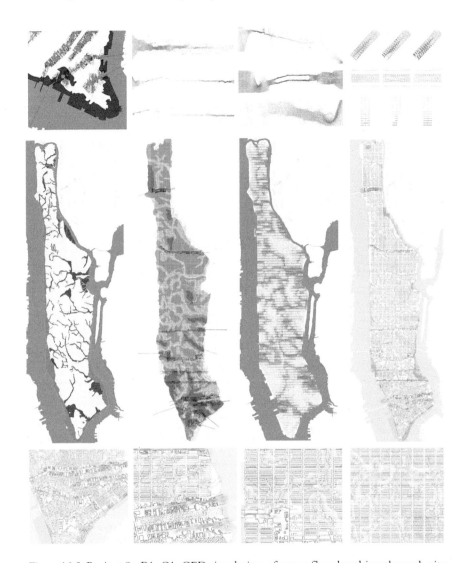

Figure 16.9 Project 8. B1–C1: CFD simulation of water flow breaking through city fabric blocks recovering latent ecologies activating environmental corridors through the original topography and geology of NYC. A1–D2: The project develops a distinct relationship between the anticipatory speculative structure of the city grid displaced by recovering an emergent ecological organization. A3–D3: The city blocks are displaced at several levels, from courtyards which become flooded for water reservoirs, to partially open blocks, to open blocks, to different new block typologies. Associate Professor and Coordinator Pablo Lorenzo-Eiroa, Assistant Professor, Lydia Xynogala and Instructor Will Shapiro, Student: Jaebong Jean; The Cooper Union, Graduate Research Studio, Fall 2014.

from swamps to rivers. The block's typologies are displaced by activating a topological space environment. NYC blocks' interior spatial containment becomes interconnected to develop a parallel city by activating a new public negative space. By interconnecting the city's interior blocks courtyards, the project activates latent suppressed ecologies hidden by the grid, inverting the city's structure. The city, as an artificially imposed system, produces latent counter systems that may build up on each other, producing a synthesis of contrasts between a planned Cartesian space and an existing site-specific topographic and environmental condition, displacing the typology of the city (Figure 16.9).

Notes

Figure 16.3 Project 2. A1: Building city fabric massing height in relation to below-grade soil density. A2–B2: Sectional relationships between the Manhattan grade grid and below-grade and above-grade topographic geology; tallest buildings identified in relation to bedrock geology below grade. A3: Geological soil density composition below grade (not just bedrock); B3: variable proposed zoning building height economic construction optimization by indexing below-grade soil density. Structuring Fluid Territories Studio, Associate Professor and Coordinator Pablo Lorenzo-Eiroa, Assistant Professor, Dorit Aviv, and Instructor Will Shapiro, Student: Bing Dai; The Cooper Union, Graduate Research Studio, Fall 2015.

Figure 16.4 Project 3. Hudson Valley and River, analysis, GIS data, Simulations, AI ML Semantic Segmentation, and Classification of Environmental Processes. A1–D1: Hudson River sedimentation, based on the dataset, GIS, and various types of information by NYC.gov and other datasets. A2–D2: Sedimentation studies in relation to Hudson River geology. A3: Hudson River Valley and sedimentation deposition; B3–C3: Hudson River sedimentation and shoreline change; ML semantic segmentation identifying types of sedimentation processes: Deposition type: thick, thin, over bedrock; Dynamic: waves, dirt, linear ion, debris, scour, slump, streaks; Erosion: bedrock, truncated, non-deposition. A4–D4: Computational Fluid Dynamic Simulation of sedimentation deposition and water flow to optimize Manhattan waterfront building block typologies in relation to a dynamic evolving city shore morphology inducing natural balance. Associate Professor and Coordinator Pablo Lorenzo-Eiroa, Assistant Professor Dorit Aviv and Instructor Will Shapiro; student: Muge Wang; D3: Student Cao Yeqing; The Cooper Union, Graduate Research Studio, Fall 2015.

Figure 16.6 Project 5. A3: Manhattan heat map temperature gain from satellite image AI machine vision making visible non-visible infrared light spectrum. NASA/Marshall Space Flight Center and Global Hydrology and Climate Center, Heat Island effect thermal reading, and Neural Network statistical analysis for image sampling. A2–D2: Heat Island Effect/Temperature gain in relation to urban massing, reading NYC as layered space environments.
B3: NYC city fabric in relation to heat island effect. C3: Manhattan urban massing and open green areas in relation to their heat island effect/temperature gain.
D3: Heat Island Effect skyline. A4–D4: Optimizing environmental f lows through programmable urban voids to create swirls, turbulence, vortexes, and wind patterns to alleviate the heat island effect. Associate Professor and Coordinator Pablo Lorenzo-Eiroa, Assistant Professor Dorit Aviv, and Instructor Will Shapiro; student: Yuan Gao; The Cooper Union, Graduate Research Studio, Fall 2015.

17 Thermodynamic Blockchain Environmental Engine

Toward Post-Capitalist Universal Space-Environments

History Section:
Post-structuralism; Twenty-First Century Architecture of Information;

Methodology:
Post-Colonialism; Post-Anthropocene; Post-Capitalism; Big Data Simulation; Evidence-Based Design; Environmentalism; Space-Environments;

Linguistic Signifiers:
Nature;

Environmental Semiotics:
Sediment Particle; Fluid Flow Vector; Sound Wave;

Computational Visual Semiotics:
Computational Fluid Dynamic (CFD) Simulation (turbulence, vortex); Optimization; Satellite Images (thermal non-visual spectrum); Simulation; Particle Physics; Blockchain; Sediment Particle; Wind Vector; Water Vector;

Mathematics:
Navier–Stokes Equations; Sediment Particle Equation;

The Politics of the Urban Void as a Non-linguistic Non-Mediatic Semiotic Sign

One of the most difficult things to imagine, think, represent and activate is a void. In linguistic terms, it is difficult to think of nothing, in visual semiotics terms, the void may acquire a positive spatial value. Objects fill our lives due to an economic system that pollutes reality through marketing signifiers occupying temporal meaning. In non-linguistic terms, the void in the city is a key empty semiotic sign-value. The Neoliberal model constantly fills voids in the city through object-signs as signifiers of an economic agenda, voids as empty signs tend to disappear under an economic system that profits from open public space. The lack of commercial meaning of the void as linguistic and visual semiotic representation creates a struggle for commercial marketing media, as it's difficult to commercialize as exchange value and it lacks

DOI: 10.4324/9781003292036-18

iconic symbolic value. Although voids are seen as a projection of the real estate value through open view, the competition of the developer-politician is to make a profit from unused voids. Voids have important functions at multiple levels, from health, to sanitation, to equality, to life quality and expectancy, to multiple open significations, but especially are relevant to the continuity of natural ecologies and biomes, usually suppressed by the city. The survey of latent environmental voids in cities acquires a new signification, opening potentials for new forms of meaning and possible readings of the city in relation to the environment, defining a new political boundary. Environmental forces such as wind and water as fluid flows can inform natural environments through sedimentation by accumulating particles and through erosion by the dissemination of removing particles. We activate an agency of additive natural developmentalism through information feedback, and an agency of voids as a formalization of a negative empty poché space. We therefore propose a new ethics of formal aesthetic removal as post-developmentalism through a synthetic post-natural (Figure 17.2).

Post-Colonialism as a Post-Capitalist Post-Anthropocene

Architecture and urbanism are not ready for the possible emergent correlational crises we will soon have to face and which are already surpassing apocalyptic fiction. Before we address any ecological concerns, we should be able to first critique the non-sustainable and destructive global economic system. The histories and theories of urban planning and sanitation have addressed means to prevent and overcome the issues we are facing today with pandemics and pollution. But today we must be able to address a forward-looking visionary new relationship with the environment for the next 200–500 years, avoiding the determination of urban planning and the problematic elimination of diversity by sanitation. In the late 1800s and early 1900s with large immigration waves cities globally faced informal conditions, including densification, compromising public health and sanitation.[1] A comprehensive set of interconnected laws, zonings, codes, and protocols secured minimum living standards as human rights while scientific advances were incorporated into modern planning and urbanism. Indoor plumbing and city treatment plants for dangerous effluents were designed to contain diseases; daily trash collection and public space cleaning were organized to prevent plagues; street landscaping was designed to provide fresh air and diminish pollution; infrastructure and transportation connectivity and continuity was planned to prevent socio-economic apartheid; building setbacks were designed to ensure minimal sunlight exposure at street level promoting body defenses against viruses; minimum green areas per inhabitant were calculated to provide enough healthy air and expansion; minimum apartments surface area and in relation to inhabitants excessive density; minimum window areas and maximum floor plate depth secured minimum sunlight levels;[2, 3, 4] housing security promoted a stable safe society; as well as many other measurements currently being displaced by the Neoliberal model.

368 *Thermodynamic Blockchain Environmental Engine*

It is time to deconstruct the ideological relationship between architecture, urbanism, and Capitalism and measure its consequences. Capitalism provided many positive necessary transformations to the feudal society decolonizing the US from European Monarchy, from revolutionary social class movement to entrepreneurship, to a free market economy, to technological progress. American Protestant agrarian ethics in close contact with Nature is contrasted to the artificial life of the city[5] promoting the cultural colonization of the indigenous populations toward the west. Sprawl incentivized private transportation promoting the oil industry as a national defense interest and promoting the decentralization of cities to protect citizens against atomic blasts, and consequences went from the radical consumption of the environment to social-economic segregation based on race, to the defunding of mass transportation.[6]

Architecture aligned itself exploring the apparently accidental outputs of the Capitalist system. "Learning from Las Vegas"[7] and *S, M, L, XL*[8] validated the market as an architect. The agency of architects and planners who were often seen as idealistic and top-down was replaced by a populist representation approach through uninformed bottom-up public validation, often rightly defending social causes and democratic representation, but dismissing the revolutionary histories and theories of public social urbanism, which in turn cities became forms of business or the corporate skyline of "Form Follows Finance".[9] Late Capitalism as a Realism was able to deregulate, remove, and displace the previous urban and planning revolutions, replaced by private developers. The result of this model is the distortion of systems of measurement and validation, including parameters, zonings, infrastructure, and laws originally designed to benefit society. This model also transferred public shared responsibility to private individual interests. For-profit private expansion took over public assets: urban voids became occupied; health and sanitation became elitist; infrastructure promoted the oil industry; private development secured colonialism of real estate apartheid through gentrification; towers separated rich from the poor; micro apartments promoted unhealthy density to elevate the initial real estate profit price margin elevating the starting price of housing; and increasingly, the zoning of cities like New York, Tokyo, Shangai, Hong Kong, London, Frankfurt, Paris, Milan, and other cities tied to stock exchange speculation provided a social safety net for the rich and lost their social cultural relevance and diversity.

While the city of New York had some minor fragmented accomplishments over the last 50 years, these are not comparable with the structural long-term revolutionary vision of the 1800s and early 1900s. We still propose a model beyond these references projecting a Post-Colonialism through a pre-colonial reactivation as many proposed before of Manhattan, or the *Mannahata Project* original landscape of the Lenape Native American original population by the Wildlife Conservation Society, to recover latent ecologies within its 540M years of age. In an envisioned post-Anthropocene, the city would not be a city, but rather a series of parallel intercorrelated networks of common space-environments. Environmental commons of shared interest and rights should include all life diversities. Such an agency can only be done through a secured scientific participatory process as a real-time planetary computation. The current political division of countries, the city, and land ownership offer measurement parameters and tools for understanding the territory that limits ecology by fragmenting biomes.

We envision a renewed biodiverse city and a renewed biodiverse periphery both activating latent ecologies by promoting space-environments, scaling back human footprint through ecological decarbonization, and carbon sequestration building densification promoting a planetary Ecoinduction.

United Biomes of the World as Planetary Universal Commons

While the policies of the 1800s projected health and sanitation 200 years ahead, Capitalism is compromising 200 years ahead of its time. Climate change is also related to social inequality. There is a form of urban unbalance in the development of social housing by the state in landfill non-desirable wetlands propensity to flooding and eroding environmental buffer zones. But this structure is a global issue since according to the Oxfam Report 10% of the wealthiest population produces 50% of CO_2 emissions while the lowest poorest 50% of the population produce 10% of emissions but suffer most of the consequences of this crisis[10] measurable with life expectancy statistics. Time has run out for any greenwashing Neoliberal reformation. It is time to rethink radically and globally the relationship between our way of life decolonizing our footprint from the environmental commons, from language, to visual semiotic signifiers representing but redefining from nature and ecology, to the economy, to developmentalism, to architecture, connecting to our means available, through new radical notions of the architecture of environments.

We address the environmental crisis as a crisis of representation, as our systems of representation need to be expanded in relation to the environment (Chapter 9). The linguistic and visual semiotic signifiers we apply to represent the environment range from old generic words such as "Nature" or ecology, to 500 year old perspective, to 250 year old urban planning policies. While there is little interest in discussing city planning and urban design in relation to the environmental crises, we have the technology and the science necessary to resolve the problem. Public professional-scientific open competitions to discuss the future of cities have practically disappeared, as cities rather grow "pragmatically" indexing Capitalist monopolies through a plutocracy, blocking architects, scientists, planners from interrupting the development of cities as forms of business, with the exception of few politically compromised fragmented minimal regulations with no vision, articulation, planning or coordination. Buckminster Fuller "World Game" of 1960 proposes "Make the world work, for 100% of humanity, in the shortest possible time...". According to the United Nations "2022 Revision of World Population Prospects" online database probabilistic "Population Growth Rate 1950-2100", population is expected to grow from 8B in 2022 to only 10.9B by 2100 due to population decrease, but from 55% (4.5B) of the population living in cities in 2022 to a projection of 80% of the population living in

370 *Thermodynamic Blockchain Environmental Engine*

cities by 2050, doubling the population of cities globally by 2050/60 and an expected doubling of the current cities' footprint; from 43 megacities (+10M inhabitants) projected globally by 2030, to multiple larger mega cites of more than 100M inhabitants by 2100.

One way of radically transforming our way of living toward post-human interests in conflict with the environment and to secure universal well-being in conflict of interest to the top 1% is to reformulate a radical incrementally phased architecture of information able to measure and inform reality real time, affecting both the information flows as our economic system becomes sustainable cyclical efficient.

As discussed, we propose to politically reconsider national boundaries, creating buffer international shared zones and representing shared biomes including maritime borders to protect and regulate international waters biomes and biodiversity. Biomes are fragmented, divided, and isolated by political boundaries, as environmental corridors today fall in conflict of interest between two or more nations sharing biomes. While Capitalism promotes global commercial exchange it also assigns functions to countries given their hierarchy in the economy. Often emergent economies function as greenwashing providers to the center, from extractive practices for battery production to deforestation such as in South America and Africa. If we understand Nature as a Planetary Computational Intelligence, a computational engine to simulate the environment would place human action in relation to a reading and simultaneous accountability. An environmental workflow as ecoinduction becomes active by reading, analyzing, and displacing environmental processes. An analog to the computational workflow becomes active in terms of an ecological workflow, both coordinated through the representational structure of the computational system that allows us to measure, represent, and activate architecture and urbanism of information by mediating ecological information flows.

Urbanism of Information: Real-Time Feedback Big Data, Machine Learning (ML) Artificial Neural Networks (ANN), and "Artificial Intelligence" (AI)

Thermodynamic systems are irreversible complex and calculated only through running correlational simulations. We propose to understand thermodynamics through CFD simulation and in relation to network theory through Artificial Neural Networks (ANN). A Boltzmann Machine (BM) implements thermodynamics to optimize information flow in its neural network as various systems implement thermodynamics to solve deterministic problems. We propose the integration of thermodynamics and network information flow in urbanism through a BM blockchain framework of energy efficiency stochastic decay in the neural network. We integrate mobility as network information flow in relation to CFD simulation to understand the reciprocity between energy optimization and how to lower its costs in relation to the environment. We consider this necessary both as an ecological biodiversity necessity to sustain life as well as a social equality issue.

Ecoinduction III, Rezoning New York Region is an ongoing research that integrates different survey and measuring systems, such as Big Data, simulations, and Machine Learning (ML) to activate real-time dynamic varying ecological zoning thinking of the city as interconnected space-environments. A blockchain technology platform is being designed to survey and integrate multidimensional information in a dynamically continuously changing system that can inform reality in real time. The platform is designed to survey latent environmental ecologies, and through zoning, activates them and coordinates them into larger regional ecological space-environments. The morphology of the city is informed by the environmental conditions that it activates, engaging in an urban Big Data Processing information-based computational design exercise to rethink the whole city as a topological space-environment, building up a reflective self-balancing feedback interface mechanism. The project aims to address the latent emergent ecological conditions that the city represses by conventional city-zoning and conventional building massing design and construction, by analyzing its potential activation and integration of multiple fragmented latent ecologies across the entire region.

Rezoning The City in Relation To Environmental Processes

Ecoinduction III is made possible through an open participatory platform in which zoning is informed by civic interests, expert scientific representation, and coordination with environmental forces. Each time a building is developed following parameters in the zoning, it will be updated in relation to varying environmental conditions as it informs and modifies the environment positively. This cycle of continuous information feedback develops a robust modeling system that is actualized in real time, balancing air rights and ownership in relation to environmental interests such as CO_2 sequestration and net positive energy generation. Land ownership is seen as an integral civic responsibility in terms of a shared common environmental interest that affect the entire world, therefore air rights based on lot ownership are kept but transferred in real time without compromising real estate depreciation and interests but build up to a common global interest that does not distinguish between center and periphery, between city and environment or between income levels. New zoning strategies and systems must be based not only exclusively on promoting environmental balance but also foster the activation of the *architecture of environments* since environmental preservation seems not only problematic but also no longer possible.

The Viele Topographic Map of New York of 1865 is an interesting first representation of the tension between a newly projected abstract Manhattan Grid in New York City as real estate speculation repressing existing topography, the geology of the landscape, and the various ecologies. Later representations such as the Geological Map and Sections of Manhattan Island of 1898 disclose the relationship between the geological topography and the street levels. In Ecoinduction III survey is understood as the first act of transfiguration of reality. Big Data Survey is done by avoiding political boundaries and activating geo-information location systems by accessing multiple technologies and platforms, understanding that each would produce distortion and signification, including governmental information top-down as well as activating different sensing devices bottom-up. At the information level, a survey involves linguistic signification and therefore an agency at the level of representation. Until local solar-thermal passive energy harvesting-distribution-use become cyclical correlational and self-optimized, an efficiency of energy harvesting-distribution-use becomes active. Efficiency of energy use is measured, simulated and optimized at the end user space occupancy level (temperature-humidity-movement-auditive sensors, wifi radio signal, IoT, user aware cell phone data, GPS), at the building level (LiDAR, AI sensors, IoT, cell phone data, GPS), at the city block level (LiDAR, AI sensors, cell phone, and satellite), at the urban level (LiDAR, water flow sensors, air LiDAR, low Earth orbit satellites), at the regional level and at the macro regional level (temperature-humidity-pressure prevailing winds in relation to weather vain wind direction change due to air pressure changes through low Earth orbit and geostationary orbit satellites implementing mechanical, ultrasonic and laser signals); in relation to real-time mobility and AI prediction; real-time weather and AI prediction; the infrastructure and grid energy distribution (AI sensing, statistics, delivery optimization); and at the energy harvesting level (AI cycles of energy harvesting and optimization per demand use); thereby proposing critical energy cycle of harvesting-delivery-use in continuous sensing-simulation-optimization for maximum efficiency and waste reduction at all points and nodes in the network a fully integrated environmental engine. We pair pixels, point clouds, particles at the input-output survey-sensing, processing and design level as we integrate a range of measuring signals. Big Data is gathered through multiple means: from satellite images, satellite photos, to LiDAR (public and private air scanning at medium elevation) laser 3D scanning and Photogrammetry to GIS government information; from the top-down and through bottom-up different sources, such as users' sensors in cell phones, the Internet of Things, social media and Application Processing Interface (API). The information retrieval, decomposition, delayering, and reconstruction are done through an architectural transfiguration cultural criticism and not through a technocratic functionalist raw data linear use, developing interfaces with qualitative information through parallel processing, ML, and ANN. The information reconstruction activates an architectural multidimensional model to activate a performance-based machinic site-based computational environmental engine.

Ecoinduction III also applies Big Data through Computational Fluid Dynamics (CFD) simulation. Ecoinduction promotes the growth of the city by densification as well as artificially induces ecologies, by both motivating densification in certain areas and unmotivating development in others at a zoning level to activate the ecological strategy. This model is weighted in relation to varying environmental conditions, such as wind patterns, solar heat gain, mobility, rush hours, and other factors that can be input to parameterize the interface. At the same time, we also implement environmental forces to inform the form of the city. Wind patterns are implemented to create erosion through aerodynamics and to inform the form of the optimized digital city massing, therefore unmotivating development and motivating interconnected urban voids as wind corridors, through ecologically informed buildings forms that work both at an urban massing level but also through internal voids and courtyards can promote passive cooling and heating as well as environmental corridors continuity (Figures 17.2; 17.3 A1–C1, A3; 17.4; 17.5 A1–D2; 17.7). Through CFD we implement Big Data simulation as wind patterns are studied in relation to city massing to create vortexes and turbulence [Figure 17.3 A3, B3, D3] accelerating wind to alleviate the city from CO_2 emissions, lowering the heat island effect due to building density, and harvesting wind energy. We also envision at the building level to inform the building code with carbon sequestration building facades, green terraces, and building density optimization in relation to soil density below grade to optimize building resources and energy. Buildings and below-grade ground infrastructure activate a new contemporary poché topology of positive and negative space-environments continuity through the interior and exterior coordinated micro-macro environments activating passive cooling and heating [Figure 17.3 A3-D4]. We envision the inversion of the city blocks as environmentally walkable green corridors through block courtyard continuity. The emergent superblocks expand public voids in relation to existing urban green spaces. Incrementally the project coordinates micro-environments, to become interconnected to larger regional ecologies, developing atmospheric rivers that become active and understanding them as part of a planetary computation [Figures 17.3 and 17.7].

We approach Data Science through multiple means and models, and some include: how geology can inform urban zoning [Figures 17.1-17.4]; how suppressed ecologies, hidden basins that become visible through storm surge can inform latent environments [Figure 17.2]; how channeled rivers, below grade topography, can be rediscovered as active ecological ecosystems [Figure 17.2]; how light and shade conditions, humidity, and the heat island effect generated by buildings can be investigated to activate certain environmental conditions; how vortexes and wind patterns informed by buildings can become an architecture able to address urban morphology while filtering air pollution, and how the city overall can build up continuity between fragmented latent ecologies [Figure 17.3]. We also explore through simulations of simulations activating emergent programming through NLP DM as AI temporary means to save energy in CFD simulation to optimize the city fabric and also formally resolve how CFD can activate by itself optimization by displacing conventional envelopes of buildings and the city fabric (Figure 17.5).

A model including information retrieval through API identifies public mobility in relation to private and public transportation flows. The first model [Figure 17.6 A1–D1] identifies the regional movement of people and work-live commute. This mapping allowed us to reveal means that we can activate a combinatory higher dimensional topological network system by identifying public infrastructure transportation use in relation to private car sharing or taxi, building up a dynamic real-time emergent infrastructure transportation model in which public and private transportation can complement each other expanding inclusive mobility. We developed a dataset and then trained a data repository through statistical gradients and tensor fitness through diverse Artificial Neural Networks (ANN) and layers, including Convolutional Neural Networks (CNN), Deep Feed Forward Neural Networks (DFF), and BM. Addressing the mathematically unresolved Vehicle Routing Problem (VRP) a model optimizes autonomous car sharing and parcel delivery thinking of them as autonomous robotic sentinels, assigning agent behavior in relation to optimizing circulation loops through Dijsktra's shortest-path algorithm node of the connected graph of 1956 in relation to certain targets, waypoints, and bridges and tunnels in NYC. By reading the current vehicle information flows we aim at making prediction models bypassing the VRP to create urban superblocks [Figure 17.6 A2–B2; A3–D3]. The model network is defined by urban clusters which are defined as nodes as waypoints and then optimized topologically [Figure B2]. The nodes per cluster as waypoints are then decomposed into a lower hierarchy topological bifurcating network for local vehicle routing. The main routing arteries bifurcating from the cluster nodes create hierarchical strategic circulation networks that bypass as many streets as possible, creating walkable car-free zones superblocks while administering basic mobility combining public and private transportation. We envision the elimination of private cars, allowing car sharing and taxis to avoid transportation redundancies. These superblocks are designed to shift constantly in relation to a site-based environmental engine, both in relation to traffic patterns, most importantly to activate environmental corridors [Figure 17.6 B2], activating latent ecologies building up from existing green areas by unmotivating traffic and increasing pedestrian areas promoting alternative individual transportation such as bicycles.

This strategy can also be extended to be coordinated with, or to work in parallel at the suburban level. While we centralize and densify our cities, the current demand for remote working can partially address the damage produced by sprawl decentralization in the United States by reducing commute and distributing goods through optimized delivery systems avoiding the redundancy in decentralized private transportation.

We also propose an architecture that is formed through synthetic ecologically simulated CFD processes, such as aggregate sedimentation and erosion, informing the massing of the city through erosion and aggregates anticipating a new type of construction by granular removal demolition and aggregate deposition such as 3D printing indexing environmental actions and forces and local resources. Several information processes from top-down and bottom-up can be redefined by activating city-wide participatory sensing, to better understand the city and its performance, for instance, identifying touristic routes and city density. We discuss in chapters 18 and 19 how a different participatory system can activate other dimensions of navigation, including Virtual Reality (VR), Augmented Reality (AR), and Mixed Reality (MR) for different types of emergent civic relationships.

Thermodynamic Blockchain Environmental Engine 375

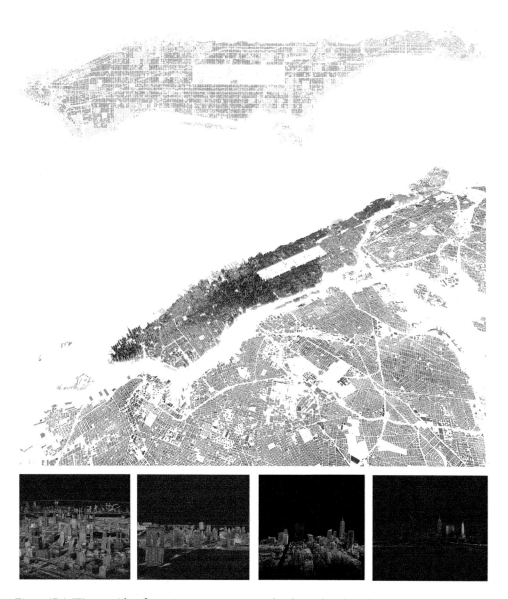

Figure 17.1 We consider forensic survey as an archeological political act activating a design agenda to uncover and displace colonizing ideologies open up possible futures. We survey latent conditions aiming at mediating information flows, from real time catastrophes to long term planning, deconstructing and reformulating cities's structures, from grids or gridiron suppressing natural ecologies. (See Notes Figure 17.1)

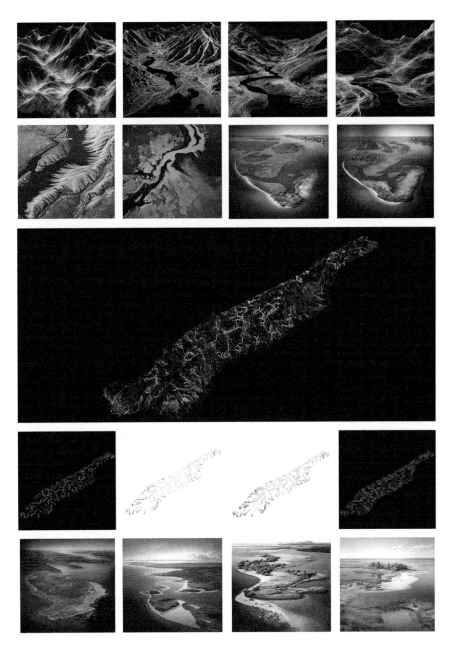

Figure 17.2 AI Predictive New York City environmental synthetic retro-futurism based on recovering latent ecologies and radically redefining a post-natural developmentalism. Wind and water as fluid flows inform artificial synthetic post-natural environments through sedimentation aggregation developmentalism of accumulating particles and erosion dissemination post-developmentalism of removing particles activating an agency of voids; a new thermodynamics of information balance as organization becomes active (See Notes Figure 17.2).

Thermodynamic Blockchain Environmental Engine 377

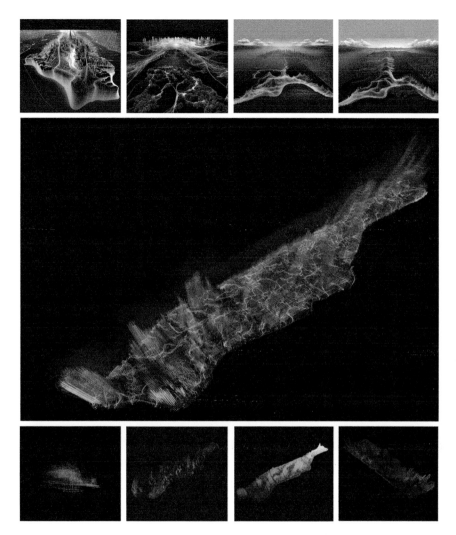

Figure 17.3 A1–C1: Urbanism and buildings new proposed urban zoning massing based on CFD simulation optimization and prediction model. A2: CFD water flow simulation to model network of canals and water containment reservoirs. A3: CFD wind simulation to optimize urban massing. Wind patterns model Urban Massing in relation to vortexes activation. B3: Simulations in relation to temperature readings proposing a dynamic building massing. C3: heat island effect. D3: CFD By analyzing and understanding fluid dynamic processes, the interface can propose an increasingly complex set of correlational space-environments. Ecoinduction III e-Architects; Design Principal and Research: Pablo Lorenzo-Eiroa; Designers and Research: Alejandro Mieses Castellanos, Tamara Orozco Rebozo, Francis Egipciaco Cruz, and Linnette Guitierrez Ortiz. SPONSOR-Grant: USDA-CIG-69F35217-268, 2018.

378 *Thermodynamic Blockchain Environmental Engine*

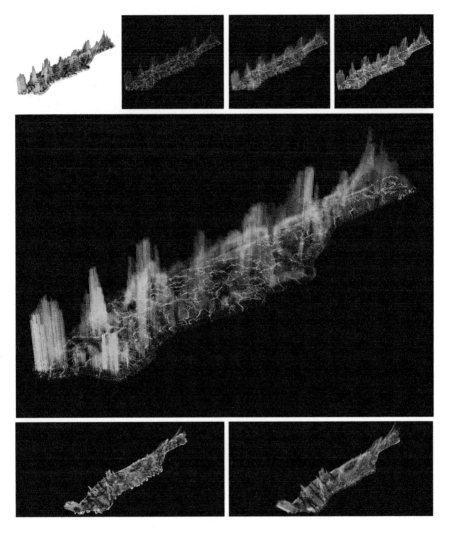

Figure 17.4 The heat island effect or feedback temperature gain in New York City is used to redefine buildings' height and void urban space based on infrared satellite image reading and analysis and in relation to CFD simulation. Massing variation in coordination with other geological conditions and simulations optimizations. (See Note Figure 17.4)

Thermodynamic Blockchain Environmental Engine 379

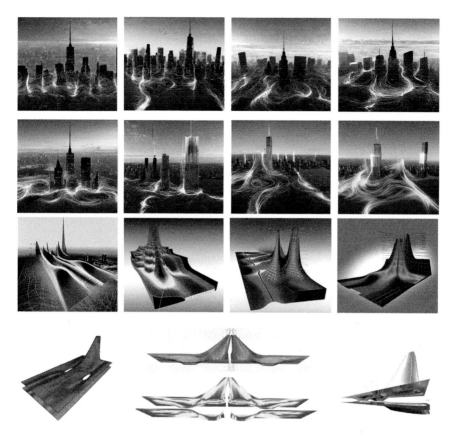

Figure 17.5 New York City CFD simulation of urban fabric and buildings to study means to activate emergent ecologies, alleviate the heat island effect though interconnecting environmental rivers incrementing and controlling vortexes and wind speed; and activating continuous space-environments. Environmental rivers distribute pollution globally, but also help to spread it and diminish its harmful action. We also study CFD simulation as a form optimization problem by increasingly deforming an object through accumulative vectorial flow simulation and therefore activate an erosion accelerated process to design-optimize evolutionary the form of buildings and landscapes. A1–D3: AI NLP pixel-to-pixel diffusion model (DM) able to self-simulate other programs such as CFD (see Chapter 6 Figures 6.7-6.8). A1–D1: CFD wind simulation and building formal optimization. A3–D3: Wind simulation tracers demonstrating self-simulation as an AI prediction model implementing CFD simulation on a particular-site image as emergent agent behavioral logic. The AI displaces the reference building form being simulated, presenting it as an opportunity for form deconstruction as the semiotic signifier becomes active as a design sign. CFD prediction is used to save time and energy resources in the studies. Predictive architecture model correlating internal and external environmental dynamics and below grade and above grade passive thermal balance. A4-D4: Buildings and below-grade ground infrastructure positive and negative space-environments activating interior-exterior passive cooling and heating. Pablo Lorenzo-Eiroa prompt and data through MidJourney, 2022.

380 *Thermodynamic Blockchain Environmental Engine*

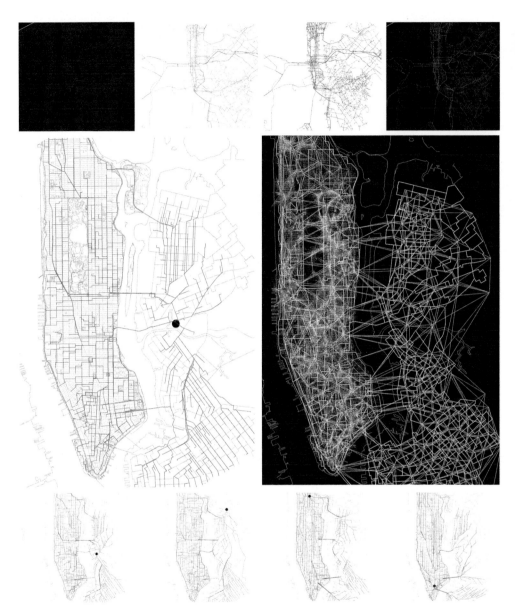

Figure 17.6 AI virtual robotic simulation addressing by approximation the Vehicle Routing Problem (VRP) to optimize traffic, parcel delivery and mobility by mapping and processing information flows in relation to emergent shifting environmental conditions. (See Notes Figure 17.6)

Predictive Post-Capitalist Participatory Crowdsourced Blockchain as Traceable Peer Review Validation

Crowdsourcing has been a new means to address reality from the bottom up, addressing diversity and multiplicity of viewpoints in relation to decision-making mechanisms, such as prediction models that are more accurate. Crowdsourcing or the wisdom of the crowd or Collective Intelligence (CI),[11] has been proven to be a more accurate way of description of reality, providing through diversity a means to address cultural biases and personal self-expression or symbolic representation. A crowdsourced Blockchain technology enables the possibility to track all processes through the block logs and to crowd-validate the decision-making mechanism, allowing for CI. All the process transactions and approvals become part of the block and are properly logged and visible to anyone in the ledger securing peer review validation and democratic transparency. The system can target the number of validation gates and the necessary participatory process to validate a block and enable such a block to become part of the Blockchain.[12] A dual mode, of equal peer representation or accredited professional validating peers can be weighted and self-regulated in relation to representation and scientific output performance. In the equal mode, the client and server are at the same level as a gated authority, and the workload is distributed in supervising and validating symbolic weighting over neural data. While this technology is available new research on a blockchain network is being researched in which file transfer protocol (FTP) services are also rendered through the system, motivating programs and services at equal levels through peer-to-peer networks or even hybrid modes.[13]

By retrieving individual open sensors from cell phones or API through social media platforms one can create emergent correlational 3D models in real time that bypass centralized authority [Figure 17.1]. 3D scanning is also used to identify multiple additional issues: from the mapping of the differential between the artificial topography of the city and the natural topography, in order to motivate or unmotivate building development, establish ranges for building heights, predicting building form to be optimized in relation to soil density and proximity to the bedrock as well as environmental performance; to measure temperature ranges in existing buildings and streetscape; to identify wind vortexes optimization in relation to existing city fabric; to identifying where demolition could happen or where development could be motivated by air rights transferring. By accessing 3D scanning from both government resources, developing, and using distributed 3D scanning devices and techniques, and accessing information through crowdsourcing, the project builds up a diversified set of media and mediums aiming at deconstructing typification and data distortions making the database and meta-data trained repository multidimensional, democratic, and participatory [Figure 17.7].

Every single data-gathering mechanism is placed in motion when the Big Data model enters a co-relational final processing dynamic scenario. Once the complexity of the system builds up out of the accumulation of different aspects it builds up feedback, and reflective information through the totality building up complex non-linear emergent interaction among the different conditions that become active [Figure 17.3 and 17.4]. The project aims at developing critical feedback through information signal processing. [Figure 17.7].

An emergent architecture and urban design solution are simulated and optimized to understand co-relationships between environmental data gathering, simulation, and processing and the possibility of emergent real-time space-environments through real-time feedback and deep feed machine learning.[14] The framework can process information and real time environmental correlational emergence developing an artificial intelligence computational system that expands the real-world ecology optimizing simultaneously the performing simulation as well as the simulation engines. The pairing of the real ecology simulation and the engines used to simulate those ecologies become correlational; the real natural environment being simulated and optimized becomes correlational with the energy and thermodynamics used to develop the simulations, resulting into an artificial synthetic post-natural. Emergent agents recognizing tasks in the correlational simulations emergent programming can increase exponentially the meta-levels of the framework recursively augmenting and self-editing through self-simulation correlations between the real ecology and the artificial engines used.

The morphology of the city is informed by the mapping and rediscovery of latent environmental conditions that the project activates, engaging in an urban Big Data information-based mapping, processing, and simulation exercise to rethink the whole city as a topological space-environment. We aim at creating a new type of city-ecological infrastructure of space-environments in which high-density tall buildings infrastructure are not symbols of inequity, but of social vertical density living, addressing human growth in relation to correlational crises. We envision vertical cities that are interrelated and dense and that provide infrastructure for growth and completion by private expansion and intervention.

The geological components of a city, the suppressed ecologies that usually city development represses, such as hidden basins, channeled rivers, swamps, below grade topography, are gathered, mapped, calculated, and measured to be recovered to their maximum possible extent and to inform the zoning proposal through various means, media, and mediums. The zoning machine also includes several factors, such as the activation of light and shade conditions, regulating the humidity, thermal control by diminishing the heat island effect generated by buildings, as well as other dynamic factors, such as the attenuation by optimization of the pollution generated by public transportation, private traffic, and delivery. By correlating through parallel processing and simulations both natural repressed latent conditions as well as present artificial ecologies, the zoning project can create a bio-digital city. Artificial ecologies are understood and mitigated by identifying fragmented opportunities and building up a larger ecological correlational system.

Therefore, we propose to replace the Neoliberal motto "*Form Follows Finance*" identified by Willis with a Post-Capitalist *Form follows ecology* through a Blockchain platform that enacts CFD signifiers as *Form Follows Information*.

Thermodynamic Blockchain Environmental Engine 383

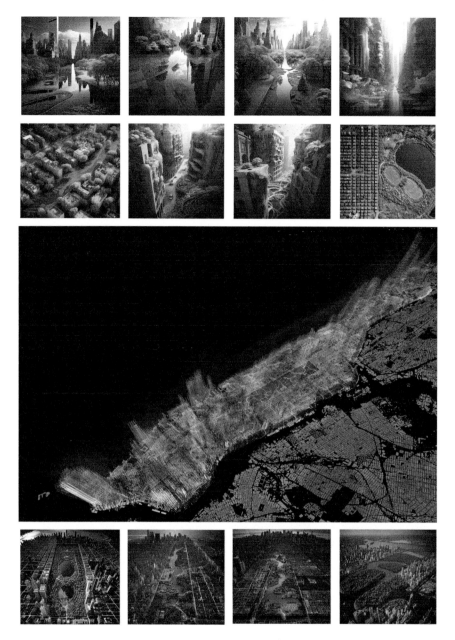

Figure 17.7 AI Predictive New York City environmental retro-futurism based on recovering latent ecologies and radically redefining developmentalism. Ecoinduction III proposes activating latent environmental processes repressed by the current city, building up from local ecologies, to a globally coordinated Blockchain environmental engine. (See Notes Figure 17.7)

384 *Thermodynamic Blockchain Environmental Engine*

New Cities' Space-Environments for a Dystopian World

The limitations of working with existing data as sedimented past agendas or outdated paradigms, as opposed to an imaginary range of possible future scenarios are targeted at two levels. On the one hand, by means of an agency in the data-gathering mechanism displacing conventions of representation enables an escape from the mere optimization of existing data paradigms. On the other hand, the ML of the ANN can recognize emergent programming, and therefore change the model in relation to the emergent conditions that are generated through nondeterministic programming.

We envision a multidimensional emergent evolutionary self-editing recursive model implementing eventually quantum computation for parallel simulation convergence, which can change its own structure beyond linear bifurcating genealogical evolution.

Notes

1 Nijenhuis, Wim. *The Riddle of the Real City, or the Dark Knowledge of Urbanism Genealogy, Prophecy, and Epistemology*, Duizend & Een, Amsterdam, 2017
2 Klein, A. *Grundrissbildung und Raumgestaltung von Kleinwohnungen und neue Auswertungsmethoden*, Berlin, 1928
3 Lombardi, R. "Medida y norma", in *Cuaderno de Lecturas*, numero 5, Art 1, FADU-UBA, Buenos Aires, 2003
4 Bevilacqua, M.G. "Alexander Klein and the Existenzminimum", *Nexus Network Journal* Volume 13, Issue 2, Basel, 2011
5 Ciucci, G.; Dal Co, F.; Manien-Elia, M.; Tafuri, M. *The American City: From the Civil War to the New Deal*, MIT Press, Cambridge, 1983
6 Kwitny, J. "The Great Transportation Conspiracy", in ed. Thompson, W.B., *Controlling Technology*, Prometheus Books, Buffalo, 1991
7 Venturi, R.; Scott Brown, D.; Izeneur, S. *Learning From Las Vegas: The Forgotten Symbolism of Architectural Form*, MIT Press, Cambridge, 1972
8 Koolhaas, R.; Mau, B.; Werlermann, H. *S M L XL*, The Monacelli Press, New York, 1997
9 Lewis, C. *Form Follows Finance*, PAP, New York, 1995
10 Gore, T. "Extreme Carbon Inequality: Why the Paris climate deal must put the poorest, lowest emitting and most vulnerable people first", *Oxfam Media Briefing*, 2 Dec. 2015
11 Galton, F. "Vox Populi", in *Nature*, Volume 75, 1949 [orig. 1907]
12 Minaxi, G.; Qantas, P.; Judge, P.; et al. "A Reputation System for Peer-to-Peer Networks", in *NOSSDAV*'03: 2003
13 Rittel, H.W.; Webber, M.M. "Dilemmas in a General Theory of Planning", in *Policy Sciences*, Volume 4, Issue 2, 1973

Figure 17.1 We survey the city and develop several datasets through a variety of information representation: from infrared satellite images processed through AI machine vision delayering of information, to LiDAR, to GIS, to modelling, to Big Data point cloud processing, to AI Machine Learning, to AI ML Classification of 3D scanning point clouds, and to Big Data simulations of multiple types as evidence-based design optimization. A1: Noli representation of Manhattan's NYC using as a base a 3D scanning photogrammetry reconstruction comparing the City of New York 3D model and our survey point cloud 3D survey model. The result 3D point cloud model is used to create multiple 3D and 3D planimetric sectional readings of the city: from positive–negative public space reading and analysis to design interventions based on these analytical readings. We propose an actualized Sanborn map of New York (1970s)

Thermodynamic Blockchain Environmental Engine 385

creating a 3D survey model including all ground level public and private infrastructure, from elevator cores, stairs to architecture elements such as columns. This allows us to reconsider continuities across public and private space, positive and negative space continuity or discontinuity and identifying potentials to radically transfigure the architecture of the city. A2: NYC GIS layer buildings. A3–D3: Photogrammetry 3D scanning of NYC and ML semantic segmentation. PI Pablo Lorenzo-Eiroa; Farah Jalil Research Assistant, IDC Foundation Grant Research 2022.

Figure 17.2 New York City environmental futurism based on recovering latent ecologies and radically redefining developmentalism. We propose to reformulate developmentalism in relation to waste, addressing Alison and Peter Smithson's Robin Hood Gardens conceptual demolition landscape mound, but through an active ecological process. The city can learn from Central Park's vision and propose a new ecological decolonizing vision, but the bucolic romanticism of Central Park, the unsustainable clean green grass colonizing nature has to be inverted in relation to a radical linguistic conceptualization of "Nature". The geology, ecology and morphology of New York City is due to multiple geological relationships between the upper Valley of the Hudson River and the discharge of its affluents in the Atlantic Ocean (see Chapter 16 figure 16.4). The features of the Hudson encounter the east shore of the United States, particularly Long Island. The east shore has a particular geology: from small gulfs, to keys, developing inlets, bays and island formation. The Hudson Valley, the northern East Shore and Long Island due its morphology to the receding of the glaciers (Chapter 16 figures 16.1, 16.2), for instance defining Broadway in Manhattan or 495 highway in Long Island as the highest ridge path. A1-D1: Hudson Valley and Hudson River mapping and understanding of shifting geographies, geologies, and ecologies through simulation of water runoff and topographic erosion in the valley relation to its river erosion, sedimentation displacement and sedimentation deposition. A2-B2: Sedimentation deposition simulation Hudson River. C2-D2: Hudson River sedimentation prediction model activated by Ecoinduction III, developing multiple relationships between the city of New York and the evolutionary dynamics of its emergent environmental processes. The city structure is transfigured and integrated into an environmental continuity. DM CFD simulation. A4-D4: Long Island shoreline, bays and keys geological evolutionary dynamics in relation to environmental processes: images based on point cloud classification and segmentation through machine vision feature recognition; mapping and understanding of environmental processes regarding shore and beach erosion, and sand, clay and silt sedimentation; DM CFD simulation. PI Pablo Lorenzo-Eiroa, DM, 2022. A2, A3, B3: Suppressed Manhattan geologies and ecologies: from rivers and deltas to topography, and marshlands which enable the growth of mangroves that help filter freshwater. Computational Fluid Dynamic Simulation (CFD) of rivers to activate latent ecologies; CFD simulation of water runoff modifying the landscape for ecological induction. Ecoinduction III: e-Architects. Design Principal and Research: Pablo Lorenzo-Eiroa; Designers and Research: Alejandro Mieses Castellanos, Tamara Orozco Rebozo, Francis Egipciaco Cruz and Linnette Guitierrez Ortiz. SPONSOR-Grant: USDA-CIG-69F35217-268, 2018.

Figure 17.4 Capitalism allows to both commercialize below grade and above grade environmental rights through lot ownership, a capacity limited in most countries due to the danger of an extractive economy and a colonization of the environment over social rights. We have known the dangers of fracking for gas, oil extraction, or real estate development allocation of septic tanks in flood planes at the expense of groundwater and aquifers pollution. Air rights transfer for real estate development in the city displace the original purpose of urban design and urban planning in relation

386 *Thermodynamic Blockchain Environmental Engine*

to accidental market-based private benefits. The Flynn effect which measured the continuous increase in intelligence quotient (IQ) during the twentieth century due to health and education, starting decaying due to external cell phones stimuli attention deficit changing the neural connections on our brains, but also internally due to distributed chemical pollution. We propose to regulate the defense of environmental rights against an extractive economy that favors a despotism. A1–D1: The heat island effect or feedback temperature gain in New York City is used to redefine buildings' height and void urban space based on infrared satellite image reading and analysis and in relation to CFD simulation. Massing variation in coordination with other geological conditions and simulations optimizations. A2: CFD simulation massing proposed in relation to wind patterns, water flows, and soil density. Vortexes are manipulated and incorporated into the design of the landscape through waterworks as well as building massing for wind energy manipulation and harvesting. The project proposes both the densification and the un-motivation of development to recover latent ecologies. The building density is dependent on soil condition ranges (soft soil to hard bedrock) proposing a site-based evolutionary model implementing several Cellular Automation rules. A3–B3: The project works by reading, analyzing, and disclosing the tension between repressed latent ecologies and the grid that originally organized the city. Ecoinduction III e-Architects, Design Principal and Research: Pablo Lorenzo-Eiroa; Designers and Research: Alejandro Mieses Castellanos, Tamara Orozco Rebozo, Francis Egipciaco Cruz and Linnette Guitierrez Ortiz. SPONSOR-Grant: USDA-CIG-69F35217-268, 2018.

Figure 17.6 AI robotic sentinel optimizing traffic and mobility by mapping and processing information flows in relation to emergent environmental conditions expanding latent ecolties real time. A1–B1: Google API for residential and commercial in NYC; C1, D1: live-work commute using MTA public infrastructure. A2: AI Prediction model based on a topological hierarchy based on API Uber and taxi traffic. Topologically optimized traffic to develop Superblock designed to run a network-based optimization prediction model. B2: We aim to identify emergent infrastructure and optimize traffic f lows in relation to environmental ecologies. Superblock clusters in relation to environmental CFD simulations are designed to identify latent ecologies suppressed by the city, recover them, and coordinate them across the city, building up local, regional, and ultimately a global network. A3–D3: Traffic and parcel delivery network AI prediction model to develop a differentiated dynamic superblock system based on topological optimization through virtual robots for New York City. The model addresses various mathematical models, attempting to approximate a solution through simulation of the Vehicle Routing Problem (VRP) through the mapping and detection of the shortest path for single-user transportation and delivery across NYC bridges. As a result, this model proposes a differentiated superblock for optimized car and taxi, delivery, and shared driving transportation proposing an emergent transportation system in collaboration with public transportation, extending it and optimizing it. Superblocks optimize traffic addressing several issues: the model expands latent ecologies in relation to existing green spaces; optimizes traffic and delivery creating larger superblocks and therefore allowing pedestrian 10min radius walks aimed at creating micro-neighborhoods; lowers CO2 emissions by reducing traffic. This preliminary project was presented to the Department of Transportation in the summer of 2018 two months before Amazon's headquarters location was approved by the city of New York. Ecoinduction III, DOT Presentation, e-Architects Team: Design Principal: Pablo Lorenzo-Eiroa; Designers: Frank Fengqi Li, Julian Chu-Yun Cheng, Shantanu Bhalla, Wayne Shang-Wei Lin, 2017.

Thermodynamic Blockchain Environmental Engine 387

Figure 17.7 Ecoinduction III proposes to transfigure the City of New York in relation to activating latent environmental processes repressed by the current city structure, building up from local ecologies, to regional environmental corridors, to biomes, to a globally coordinated Blockchain environmental engine. Incremental phases activate latent environmental processes locally reformulating the structure and function of street corridors, urban blocks, and the city fabric. Simulations as actualizations of current conditions in relation to radical possible environmental futures reformulating developmentalism. A1-D1: The hidden hydrology of New York such as the repressed Collect Pond near Canal Street or the Harlem Creek becomes visible when flooding occurs. Central Park was originally planned to displace and gentrified social diversity pushing black population towards the north. The ecological crisis has hit the vulnerable population the hardest, for instance social housing has been planned in flood zones (Chapter 16). A decentralization of Central Park develops connections between the Hudson River shoreline and the East River shoreline from west to east recovering repressed rivers and deltas across main avenues and branching out into multiple streets in relation to the possibilities given by below grade infrastructure but also to integrate socially and ecologically the city. Spanish Harlem and the norther east side of Manhattan is currently considered a flood zone. Since the north east side of Central Park connects to the East River shoreline, we consider a decentralization of Central Park through the integration of the Harlem Meer at 110st and 5th Ave. with the East River, displacing Central Park's role, ecology and romantic aesthetics through integrating the center courtyard of the city and turning it as part of the periphery (See Chapter 16 figure 16.2, developing research from 2006). A2-D2: We propose through various means: connecting interior urban blocks courtyards as a parallel topological inversion of New York City grid as a negative continuous urban space (2006); developing urban green ecologies through set-back green terraces as a new ecological actualization of Hugh Ferris NYC setback zoning aesthetics; displacing the current enclosed courtyard structure of city blocks to open them up in relation to repressed ecologies; controlled incremental flooding as fresh water reservoirs infrastructure; the reactivation of marshlands in relation to a decentralized Central Park; and others. A4-D4: Central Park as Manhattan's urban courtyard domesticating nature in opposition to the formless periphery, becomes incrementally displaced to address an emergent regional ecology integrating center and periphery: first by flooding, then by recognizing the forced displacement of the structure of the city, and finally activating latent ecologies further transfiguring the structure of the city into a new emergent site-based evolutionary structure apparently fragmenting the city but creating an environmental continuity as a space-environment. City blocks have currently many buildings built informally with structural problems that need to be demolished, we propose to open as many blocks' as possible interior courtyards to allocate public parks contributing to an increasingly coordinated network of environmental corridors. We provided a strategy for streets to become progressively optimized for delivery and transportation as well as bicycles, enabling larger green and ecological areas; as transportation moves towards public infrastructure, pedestrian movement and bicycles, streets become obsolete and are replaced by secondary environmental corridors able to create continuity between parks and fragmented ecologies. PI Pablo Lorenzo-Eiroa, emergent simulation prompt engineering via MidJourney, 2022. We can humanly restore ecologies, but only computationally globally we can activate an ecology for all. A3: Ecoinduction III Big Data Blockchain zoning as a dynamic globally coordinated environmental engine; e-Architects; Design Principal and Research: Pablo Lorenzo-Eiroa; Designers and Research: Alejandro Mieses Castellanos, Tamara Orozco Rebozo, Francis Egipciaco Cruz and Linnette Guitierrez Ortiz. SPONSOR-Grant: USDA-CIG-69F35217-268, 2018.

18 Big Data Realism and AI Abstraction

Post-Colonial Emergent Histories in Augmented Synthetic Unreal Environments

History Section:
Twenty-First Century Architecture of Information;

Methodology:
Post-developmentalism; Post-Anthropocene;

Social-Geopolitics:
Post-Colonialism; Environmentalism; Alternative systems of measurement, representation, validation; alternative relationships humanity-environment; alternative socio-economics;

Computational Visual Semiotic Signifiers:
Point cloud; Particle; Virtual Reality Navigation; Machine Vision Perspective; Big Data;

Informed Realisms of Bifurcating Multidimensional Possibilities

The current definition of reality shifted with quantum physics discussed in Chapter 9. Reality used to be defined as a subject-independent neutral objective, and today it cannot be addressed autonomously from the subject-observer who measures an expanding reality. When addressing reality through an objective data measurement such as LiDAR, we promote a type of objectivity, while in reality, we are also creating representational signifiers which are subject-viewer dependent that differ from the actual object surveyed. Quantum physics goes further to actually define reality as not objective inert, but subject measurable dependent. We aim in the last two chapters 18 and 19 to problematize representation in relation to the precision of the measuring device in relation to representation, simulation, and augmented space-environments.

Through Big Data inverting the relationship between theory and model, a new type of realism becomes active, by the function of a reversal in the design process between origination and destination in media. The design method as intuitive anticipatory through "drawing" or modeling, or even coding through algorithms, is now flipped to the end of the design process spectrum. Data Science has activated in terms of prediction such a process in

DOI: 10.4324/9781003292036-19

which instead of abstracting concepts and codifying them into the complex algorithm, data survey through statistics can develop an automated prediction model displacing the model to an emergent program. We can start today's design through a dataset, through mapping and creating data and comparing it statistically against historical data developing our own surveys. Therefore, survey becomes the first act of design by creating the data that originates a project. The ideal model anticipating a transformation of reality based on inductive design intuition is off balance by a data-based forensic pragmatic means of understanding reality. The actual performance of architecture based on the past statistical data collected suspends any conceptual hypothesis and implements a counter-intuitive deductive survey-simulation-optimization process. Instead of a top-down unified approach to reality by the architect, a field of multidimensional data by multiple social agents informs a parallel processing model. The organization of the architecture, from its spatial typology to its programmatic use, to the grammar of a project syntax becomes open and multidimensional through the media model. The pragmatic method contrasts by the abstraction of the anticipatory system of representation, an Artificial Neural Network structure, which is surpassed by its emergent programming. A model structure becomes active through the data fed and the information flow in the Neural Network's hidden layers, activating an evolving morphogenesis structure in relation to the feature and task recognition.

Realism is usually understood as opposed to abstraction. We aim at indexing and developing Big Data through a unique type of unreal realism, a reading that starts with a survey that by acknowledging the gathering mechanism as representation, it becomes a radical act of fiction design. Instead of elevating to a meta-abstract level, realism departs from the existing reality, inverting conditions from the top down to the bottom up. In this sense, realism is not only opposed to abstraction but also follows the current philosophical inversion of Data Science in which reality is analyzed and understood quantitatively to produce a more precise depiction and anticipatory model of how things really work out. While realism implies non-determination and objectivity in the survey, abstraction implies the projection of a deterministic, idealized, critical, or subjective personal structure to reality. The abstraction of the systems of representation expresses its technological functional value as a knowledge system, necessarily abstract generic homogenizing.

Between realism and abstraction, we aim at indexing reality activating realism through the survey but contrasting realism with an emergent abstract new form of expression of the structure of the system of representation, placing them in conflict with each other. While realism senses reality aiming at resisting a structuring of reality through Big Data, we understand the impossibility of fully accessing reality independent from a system of representation and therefore structuring the way that reality is sensed, represented, transfigured, processed, and transformed.

In LiDAR 3D Laser scanning, the indexical sign as a form of representation activates a semiotic structure, a monocular perspectival system of representation through the monocular machine vision scanning. Some issues of this perspectival system include shadows since objects in the path of the scanning ray cast shadows on objects behind. The space between these objects could be considered a function of the system of representation. To adjust such a shadow, one has to scan at different topographic elevations of a space and provide for the spaces left hidden by intersecting objects. To recognize this representational problem, we have developed right from 2012 several strategies, from considering the leftover shadow space as a type of signifier consequence of the system to rethinking the necessity of the completeness of the scan by the function of representation and leaving it open incomplete as an archeological forensic sign, to rethink completeness all together since no scan will ever be complete, as one could expand a building to a type of infinity. We considered through various generations of studios and projects several means to rethink scanning completeness and we decided it to be a scan-dependent design problem. We use the openness of the incompleteness of the scan to address interior-exterior new relationships as well as surface-space containment reversals, leaking space, or incorporating new space boundaries as surface edges become diffused as limits. As discussed, we have been addressing topology as the contemporary poché space since a topological 2D surface engages with positive 3D spaces and negative 3D spaces through figurative continuity. In the case of 3D scanning, the incompleteness of the scan is a problem of a different type, and the linguistic vocabulary of architecture would have to be expanded in relation to it since even though the scan can be traced to a surface mesh, we would like to think that the new signifier offers a means to reconsider architecture away from indexing surfaces. The dissemination of the shadow or edge of a scan leaves the semantic reading open, non-deterministic, expanding space to a space environment as well as the definition of a granular particle-based space containment. 3d scanning expands reality to a finer resolution in comparison to surfaces or lines, expanding dimensionally architecture to address now a new signifier: the point cloud. One cannot even consider 3D scans to define a side or another, as even if they index surfaces defining spaces from inside and outside leaving the mass of the building in between, the point cloud as a new signifier established a disseminated boundary more appropriate to describe the world through particles which themselves are made of atoms or bits, but do not recognize boundaries between objects. Even in the most precise scan, there will be an active form of idealization implicit in the form of the system used to index reality and therefore a bias in the data gathered that cannot be removed. The point of the laser scan becomes a semiotic physical signal activating a digital signifier in the vectorial sign of the point cloud, as its system of representation constitutes a program over objective reality. We therefore activate a realism indexing reality but address the active signifier to displace the determination of reality through representation.

Indeterminacy Point Cloud = space-environment dissemination

We approach displacing relationships between realism and abstraction through the following method:

Big Data Realism and AI Abstraction 391

1. Analyze the computational system, sign, and signal, and recognize an emergent digital signifier;
2. Index the sign, and the system structure, understand ranges and limitations;
3. Displace the emergent signifier by displacing its sign, and its structure;
4. Develop a new computer sign, new algorithmic structure, new computational structure, and a new signifier aiming for poetic autonomy and immanence;

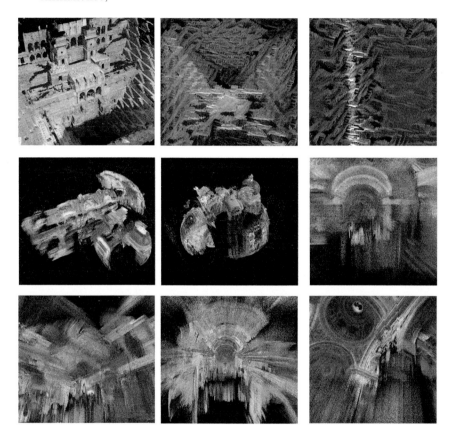

Figure 18.1 A1–C1: 3d Photogrammetry scanning + AI GAN's. GAN's transformation using recursive image recognition and style transfer. Chand Baori is a stepwell, situated in the village of Abhaneri in the Indian state of Rajasthan. Abhaneri, Bandikui, Rajasthan 303313, India. "Inclusive Futures by deconstructing Inclusive Pasts" AI+GANs Realism Workshop Prof. Pablo Lorenzo-Eiroa, Student: Pattnaik Ayush, Digital Futures, Inclusive Futures 2021, Tongji University, Tom Verebes Coordinator. A2–C3: 3D scanning and Point Cloud manipulation implementing Artificial Intelligence and Simulation. Big Data AI simulation gradual degree displacement of the original surveyed architecture point cloud aiming at indexing and displacing colonial signifiers such as perspective's Vanishing Point. Spanish Colonial Catedral de San Juan de Puerto Rico. AI+GANs Realism Workshop Prof. Pablo Lorenzo-Eiroa, Student: Jose David Mejias Morales; Digital Futures, Inclusive Futures 2021; Tom Verebes Coordinator.

392 *Big Data Realism and AI Abstraction*

An informed realism implies both a survey realism but also a computational symbolic-based type of systemic weighting in which data and computation work through parallel processing, producing a hybrid model in which both realism and abstraction can be combined and interrelated into a complex web of informed realism. The model of the computational neural network or the predictive model of the statistical approximation will always produce a type of generalization and abstraction.

There is also a realism emergent from other types of AI, from NLP models implementing AI through linguistic predictive models, to 2D image and 3D Diffusion Models, to Convolutional Neural Networks (CNN), to Generative Adversarial Networks (GANs). In any of these cases, the design strategy is contingent upon its ultimate result representation, inverting the usual design process, from abstract ideas to precise definitions by starting at the end result (Figure 18.1).

The Museum of Babel:
Multidimensional Big Data AI Architecture of
Information

Big Data augments reality and scale of observation, beyond the real scale as we are not only replicating data but also augmenting the amount of data of our universe. This augmentation defines a type of infinity of both the referenced real and the augmented reality. The Museum of Babel is understood as an architecture and urbanism of information, in which real-time information flows are mediated to activate architecture. The Museum of Babel project activates through different Big Data acquisition and survey mechanisms and technologies, available data making it into information that is composed to expand the Museum Mile in New York City, by crossing relationships in space-time and multidimensionality through Virtual Reality. We have been exploring this concept through various studios following Borges' literature. This particular project (Figure 18.2; 18.3; 18.4) first 3D scans both the MET Museum and the Guggenheim Museum and creates virtual and physical cross relationships that are meant to work 1:1 scale in real time, transforming the reality of the museum, from how it is perceived, to how it is understood, to how it is used and circulated and to how the existing art being display is augmented by retrieving relationships with the museums' archived collections. The project incurs intuitively in a post-colonialism of their institutional roles: The MET deconstructing its collection as an augmented reality retrieving its original geopolitics; the Guggenheim deconstructing its collection as patriarchal patronage art tracing emergent relationships between the art pieces; and the project tracing emergent relationships between both augmented multidimensional space-environments.

First, the project develops a 3D scanning survey implementing Big Data, transfiguring the building reality to a hyperdimensional set of spatial points in which a topological mesh keeps them together as a grammatical form, but

Big Data Realism and AI Abstraction 393

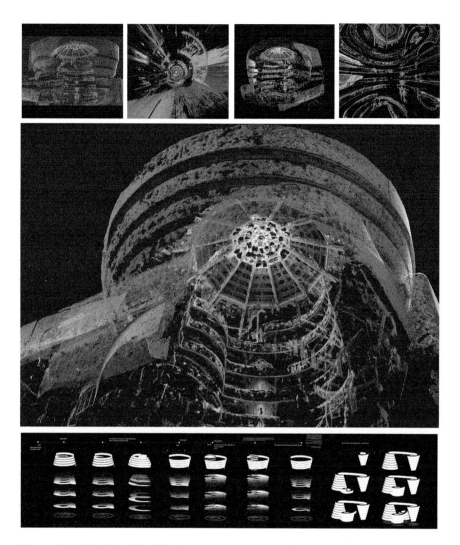

Figure 18.2 A1–D1, A2: 3D Scanning interior and exterior implementing AI, Guggenheim Museum in NYC (1956–59) by Frank Lloyd Wright. A3: analysis of Guggenheim Museum alternative design iterations by Wright including reverse spiral and two correlational interchangeable spiral ramps. This 3D model/scan was created using: RealityCapture software by Capturing Reality. Prof. and Director Pablo Lorenzo-Eiroa; Student Salma Kattass, ARCH 701B Research Studio; MS ACT; SoAD, NYiT, 2021.

the several expansions and transformations modify the real topology to index a parallel expanded reality (Figure 18.2; 18.3 A3-E5). Second, the MET museum is known for its architecturalization of art. The MET Museum is a museum within a museum and a city within a city since the different

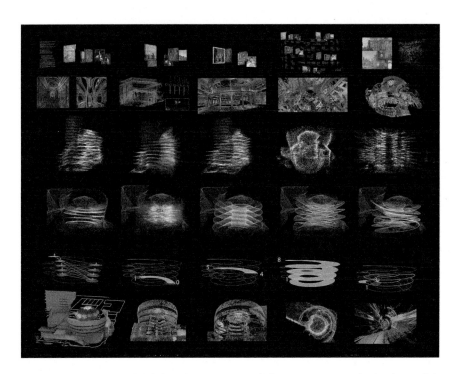

Figure 18.3 Museum of Babel application AI workflow. A6–E6: Frank Lloyd Wright's Guggenheim Museum AI 3D scanning photogrammetry. A5–E5; A4–E4: Guggenheim Museum virtual bifurcating navigable ramp connections, activated by retrieving MET collection within the Guggenheim; A3–E3: Guggenheim's parallel virtual museum through AI Swarm Intelligence (SI), Agent-Based Modelling (ABM). A2–E2: MET Museum 3D scanning point cloud AI ML Semantic Segmentation feature recognition through the developed dataset and online database; Fragments of the MET Museum have been segmented, recomposed, and projected back into the Guggenheim new virtual possible ramp circulation configurations. A1–D1: web scraping and API of MET museum collection retrieved virtually in relation to combinatorial Guggenheim bifurcating ramping network. E1: MET collection projected as augmented new art form within the Guggenheim ramps: Panini's paintings of 1757 in which Rome is presented as a series of ruins-city, as a landscape of traces of history and as a collection of historical cultural artifacts blurring reality, representation, collection and pairings within paintings at the Metropolitan Museum in New York City. AI GANs style transfer from retrieved web scraping dataset problematizing the pixels of the retrieved collection in relation to particles displacing the point cloud of the 3D scanned space. Prof. and Director Pablo Lorenzo-Eiroa; Student Salma Kattass, ARCH 701B Research Studio; MS ACT; SoAD, NYiT, 2021.

rooms become rooms within rooms and buildings within buildings, grouped through space-environments thanks to large-scale glass volumes. Third, the project aimed at 3D scanning the relationship between paintings, rooms, and architectural fragments and project it back as an expanded museum within

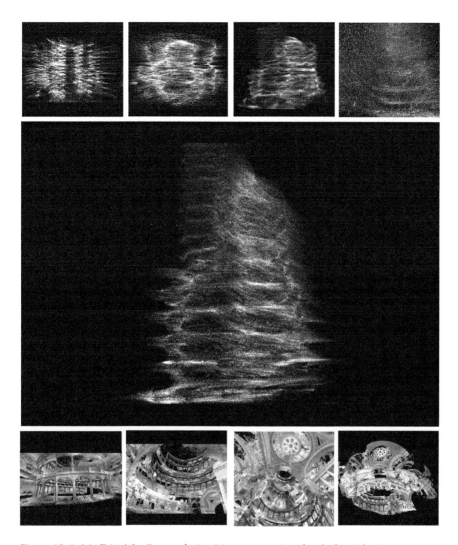

Figure 18.4 A1–D1, A2: Guggenheim Museum, point cloud algorithmic computational design displacements implementing AI through various parallel processing methods, including swarm intelligence (SI), Agent -Based Modelling (ABM), evolutive site-based algorithms, particle physics, and others. A3–D3: MET Museum NYC and MET museum collection of paintings and architecture pieces displaced in relation to parallel bifurcating Guggenheim Museum virtual ramps organizations, composing a Museum of Babel. Research Studio Prof. and Dir. Pablo Lorenzo-Eiroa; Student Salma Kattass, ARCH 701B, MS ACT; SoAD, NYiT, 2021.

the Guggenheim Museum (Figure 18.3 A1-E2). The project integrates both a collection and its original location at the MET within the Guggenheim Museum physical space, crossing existing Guggenheim art in display and correlating it to the MET Archive (Figure 18.3). By these means, the objective is to activate a museum of the information age, by being able to retrieve information real-time, develop cross relationships and expand both the actual space and the museum collections into a continuous space. The collections themselves are manipulated by implementing GANs by expanding paintings (Figure 18.3 A1-E1) and relating them to their original context in an expanded new context that modifies them in a feedback loop between space, architecture, exhibition, and art archive (Figure 18.3-18.4). The MET Museum collection becomes a dataset and a database for real-time accessible Machine Learning interpretation (Figure 18.3 A1-E1). Fourth, the Guggenheim VR project wraps through Semantic Segmentation recognizing semantically the pieces of the MET as columns, doorways, ceilings, and floors, and transforming them as a series of virtual spaces within the spiral logic of the MET (Figure 18.3 B2; A3-E5). Fifth, the infinite unobtainable idea by Frank Lloyd Wright of creating a museum typology for infinite growth for the Guggenheim Museum becomes real through augmented reality through an infinitely long spiral ramp and infinite possible topological continuous paths and connections between the different levels (Figure 18.2 A3; 18.3 A4-E5). Sixth, the infinite unobtainable ambition of the MET museum to contain the entire history of the culture of the world within a series of space-environments nesting 2D to 3D to 4D space-environments is made real by retrieving real-time remote sensing technology (Figure 18.3 A1-E2). Seventh, both the MET collection and the Guggenheim space are augmented and redesigned through AI since the MET collection is expanded through GANs to react to the length and variable relationships developed by the ramp connections in the Guggenheim. Finally, the Babel Museum becomes active within an information age combining the infinite growth of the Guggenheim Museum spiral ramp and the infinite navigable expanded encyclopedic ambition of the MET to contain the history of the culture of the world within a set of infinite node-clusters of combinatory augmented space-environments (Figure 18.4).

19 Big Data AI Simulacra Within a Representation Restricted Reality (RRR)

From Piranesi's Ahistoric Archeology, to an Urbanism of Information, to a Quantum "AI" Simulacra

History Section:
Illuminism; Modern Movement; Post-Structuralism; New Renaissance; New Structuralism; Twenty-First Century Architecture of Information;

Methodology:
Architecture of Information; Information Theory; Derrida's deferral-displacement; Post-Colonialism; Big Data;

Semiotic Signifiers:
Point Cloud; LiDAR Remote Sensing; Augmented Reality, Mixed Reality, Virtual Reality Simulation;

Data Structures:
Big Data;

Computational Structures:
Centralized, Distributed-Network/Grid, Parallel; Blockchain; Quantum Computing;

Piranesi's Campo Marzio: Archeological Survey as Multiple Non-Linguistic Origins

The reading, mapping, or reproduction of a territory, a space, or an object implies a transformation by the act of survey, as measurement, signs, and standardizations are projected by the representational system. Survey as representation develops a cartography, a construction of a territory, a mapping, and therefore a new construction over the original. Mapping involves the instrument to develop the map and a tool that implies an apparatus as a system of representation, including a projective geometry technique. While we discussed the impossibility of removing subjectivity and cultural biases from representation, as the method, the technology, the tool, and the apparatus of representation anticipate the subject of the study and therefore project an anticipatory signifier. Tafuri[1] critiques Panofsky's symbolic form as a traceable

DOI: 10.4324/9781003292036-20

origin in a deep structure, and places archeology as the notion of multiple origins in history as a project of crisis through Foucault's and Nietzsche's genealogy as an archeology of knowledge, addressing Derrida's "origin" as artificial.

Giambattista Nolli *Pianta di Roma* of 1736–48 surveys the city of Rome developing a revolutionary methodology in urbanism based on a survey forensic architecture of facts, data, measurements, topography, and geolocation, one of the first precise mappings of a city as an indexical survey following a scientific method. Nolli's method activates a continuous private urban mass in contrast to public accessible voids. Piranesi after working for Nolli on the etching of the map of Rome develops *Campo Marzio* in 1762–76, a critical retrospective-futuristic reading of Rome, presenting a dialectical thesis by placing the subject against an object. *Campo Marzio* can be understood to both address archeology as a survey and urbanism as a symbolic form; as both a realism and an abstract fictional cartography. Piranesi depicts various types of linguistic signs as a deep structure which he also aims at negating and dissipating, addressing innovative radical experimental typologies for architecture: indexing ruins of Imperial Rome as archeology "Forma Urbis Romae" Roman Fragments; contiguous fragments as clusters or isolated buildings; topographical signs and voids such as the city "missing Corso" as index;[2] alternative possible origins of interpretation of surveyed buildings; symbolic signs; architectural elements as linguistic signs; associating and dissociating form from meaning; geometry as architecture, activating an empty signifier, addressing architecture as a non-linguistic; and, among others, architecture signs beyond themselves as retroactive readings of the past and a latent futuristic version of the city. Campo Marzio can be understood as a machinic historical-prototypical resonance interface for Rome, identifying indexical facts and turning them into a new state of latent utopian typologies. For Tafuri, Piranesi's innovation is the disjunctive quality of identifying language as absent and geometry as a means to unlock and critique the architectural linguistic relationships between signifier and signified. Therefore, it destroys the syntax and with it any trace of a formal process that can hold the meaning together. Piranesi identifies himself as an archaeologist, a surveyor, a historian, an architect-designer, and a utopian experimental theorist developing a precise language of representation based on fictional origins. His critical manifesto's utopian depiction is the most radical action to do within his life span informing the younger generations of architects who could expand his ideas. He dedicates *Campo Marzio* to the young Robert Adams, an architect who then had a prolific professional career activating Palladianism and Piranesi's urban ideas in London. Perhaps London owes to Piranesi's *Campo Marzio* the evolution of fragmented, contiguous, and continuous urban positive and negative spaces in the city.

Architectural Signs ≠ Signifieds

Nonlinguistic Signifier = Geometry

Nonlinguistic Sign =Void

The City as a Non-Linguistic Signifier

Aldo Rossi in the *Architecture of the City*[3] identifies the city as the artificial decantation of architecture types as a form of signifier through its history, overcoming temporal function. Barthes offers a reading of the city as a form of language, he discusses mapping as an objective territory survey in relation to their emergent meaning which is fluid and open. Barthes identifies the problematic relationship between signifiers and signified through urban structures, addressing the capacity to develop signifiers so that their meaning becomes open and changing through time.[4] Barthes identifies the "technique fairly current in urban planning: "simulation", which for him leads to the idea of a model, addressing its determinism. Barthes discusses differences between signification and reason as calculating simulation, and surveys by psycho-sociologists show the difference between the objective map and the different significations assigned:

> "Signification, therefore, is experienced as in complete opposition to objective data" Barthes.

The survey becomes the first act of measurement of reality, and the implicit first act of design, the creation of a specific territory. The technology of the survey mechanism becomes the initiator of the conditions that will inform the project, reading, and therefore a construction of a territorial means of understanding the city. The mediation of bits in information systems defines today the way we see, understand, measure, use, and interact with the city and among each other as a first step toward their total mechanization and re-structuring.

Cultural Blindness in Objective Data Visualization Resisting Problematizing Representation

Žižek[5] discussed that each time we "see" the world we are inevitably creating a form of ideology through a language of description. We idealize the world by our projective reading of it. Data surveys today serve as engineering information visualization strategies to dissociate or negate the symbolic weight of a visual structure as a system of representation, since what is called today "information visualization" through pie charts, bars, and infographics, aiming at displacing or eliminating the symbolic form of representation. Problematically Data *visualization* separates an apparently inert content from the form of the media which is used to represent it. By tracing data beyond signifiers we tend to opaque the access to information mediated by cultural biases. Common generic visualizing strategies tend to structure data in determined simplistic terms, homogenizing reality. There is a politics of data classification that actively uses this differential for civic representation, displacing the science of data measurement to activate ideological agendas, including, whether consciously or not, the implementation of linguistic structures to force meaning through categories. Through census and zip codes, political boundaries and vote clusters are created placing in tension with a democratic representation producing types of citizens, social structures, the city fabric, and the geology and environmental ecology of cities globally.

The opposite argument is media-based representational strategies that emerge from the data gathered and represented, recognizing the construction of a cultural project.[6] Data landscapes such as MVRDV Datascapes of 1999 Metacity/Datatown, try to avoid any ideological description of territory through representation, addressing data "visualization". The landscapes become homogeneous since the visualization strategy remains constant. We argue there is no information without a form of representation and therefore there can neither be data nor information without cultural biases. This is the reason why Big Data becomes the subject matter of current design agendas, expanding any project to the measurement system that validates it. Any system of measurement distorts reality to confirm the reference. Additionally, one would have to develop a measuring methodology and an intrinsic-to-the-problem representational system that would be able to formalize the right kind of relationships necessary to disclose the question being researched, avoiding stretching reality by measuring it.

Often, a single data entry algorithm is responsible for the categories that are input to collect and represent data. Usually, a single mono-dimensional algorithm based on a simple mathematical model gathers large quantities of data, standardizing it. We developed a visual-based topographical indexed data, coordinating the existing remote sensing of the actual territory and the environment through satellite images, satellite photographs, and the understanding of the territory through LiDAR scanning, heat sensing, and crowdsourcing techniques, as opposed to retrieving data through government GIS resources based on the politics of census data through zip code entry discussed also in Chapters 15–17. We activated a visual-based data entry aiming at understanding the relationship between the actual physical territory and the data patterns that emerged from data mining developing a politics of data gathering bypassing top-down data gathering and activating a visual-based data acquisition technique based on diverse computational processing. While we did use GIS through government data, we tend to read and aim at critiquing the data as well as creating alternative means to address the issues that emerged from the data set. We developed what we denominated topographies of information[7] as site-based and interface-based computation to bypass the abstraction of zip-based political signification in data sets, some of which are discussed in Chapter 7.

Reality = Object vs Data Science

$$\text{Reality} = \text{Spectrum} \left(\text{visible, non-visible, sensorial} \right)$$

While Allen developed a theory of architecture notation in relation to mapping the intangible,[8] Kurgan developed critical mapping through GIS and data processing acknowledging data gathering methodologies as deterministic. Computation inverted Allen's representation projecting a deterministic structure to the world anticipating the map. Badiou identified how the humanities and the sciences create objects when addressing reality[9] and that a system cannot come up with a solution outside of its parameters. The scientific method constructs an artificial object, by tracing a contour, isolating a system, tracing a layer, isolating a spectrum of light waves, or other means to simplify and isolate by reductionist logic a complex intertwined correlational reality. But any system of measurement, data, and information that projects a reading and interpretation of reality is objectified by its own signifier. Data does not exist until it is measurable and thus represented through a sign. Information emerges out of data collection constructing a meaningful message. Digital signs represent information, and in linguistic terms, they determinate how we currently understand and reference reality. Data by representing reality through codified computable linguistic signs creates new objects independently from the reality that is measuring, thereby creating new realities informed by the simple implementation of a system of measurement and reference.

"The map is not the territory" Korzybski[10]
"The medium is the message" McLuhan[11]
"The method is the message" Grosswiller[12]
The digital signifier anticipates the territory, the message and the method

We can therefore understand reality, a spectrum of analyzable reality, or a spectrum of apparently visible reality in contrast with the instruments of measurement which are available to us to describe reality. While we expand measuring systems and how we represent reality through data gathering and machine vision mainly applying visual logic to critique linguistics (Chapter 6-7), we aim at expanding relationships between linguistic, visual, mathematical, informational and computational semiotics beyond our senses.

Data = Semantic Semiotics (linguistic) Visual Semiotic (sensorial)

Reality and data are therefore in contrast with each other since data already implies a form of computable sign that is made possible through a digital device of measurement. In data, there is then already a form of biases of transformation that, although often seen or naturalized as inert or neutral, is already embedded with the histories and theories of representation and the linguistic signs that need to be identified and displaced.

Reality vs Data Encoding = Measurable and Computable Digital Signifier

402 *Big Data AI Simulacra Within a Representation Restricted Reality (RRR)*

This signifier can take the form of a computational linguistic algorithm that does data gathering over the internet through web-scraping (semantic-based-linguistic) encoding or a physical sign that collects data from an environment through remote sensing such as machine vision encoding. This encoding of reality is sign-dependent although is informational and therefore communicable through a variety of information signal transmission types. This process reduces complexity and escalates complexity at a combinatory data encryption level since while the original data gathering depicts a spectrum of reality, this reduction mechanism then is enfolded back to compute what was gathered-encoded into a realm of possible computable scenarios. In this sense, the generic aspect of the sign needs to be open enough to allow such combinatory mathematical and symbolic computable calculations.

The Representation of the City:
Mapping, GIS, and Big Data Processing

There is no AI without Big Data. Therefore we need to augment existing data backwards to be able to do better predictions forward, enabling possible futures by augmenting inclusive pasts. There are different means to understand surveys in relation to Big Data. One is to directly measure reality through Big Data survey mechanisms, through remote sensing machine vision implementing multiple technologies, such as 3D laser scanners, 3D photogrammetry, 3D and 2D sensors, 3D light detection and ranging (LiDAR), satellite images, and other means such as a distributed available network of The Internet of Things (IoT). These technologies allow us to directly measure and gather data, while we aim at addressing the bias and the signifiers that become active in the media and medium's signs and signals.

Data gathering, acquisition, crawling, web scraping or their combination through retrieving information directly from available devices, data sets and public records, and building up data sets through various means may also be problematic and therefore questioned. The problem is now expanded since datasets are often developed by a centralized authority with either access to large amounts of data or with enough funds to develop mechanisms for data gathering, even able to develop a data gathering technology. Additionally, once data is mined, 'visualized' or rather, structured through a deterministic representational system, it will infer signification beyond its initial condition challenging the same data it is indexing. In a new form of representation of data, if autonomous and powerful enough, this new form of actualization of information would produce Gestalt subjective dependent readings, that could not be anticipated and, because of co-relationism this information would signify beyond what's indexing, proposing a form of empowerment, a new state of being no longer reversible.

Urbanism of Information:
From Archeology, to Survey, to Data Acquisition, to Data Processing to Mediating Real-Time AI Information Flows

What determines the design of a city? Why should we address the development of our cities as space environments? What are the technologies available to represent environments? How can we understand the influence of computer codes, the internet, and media in architecture and city design and

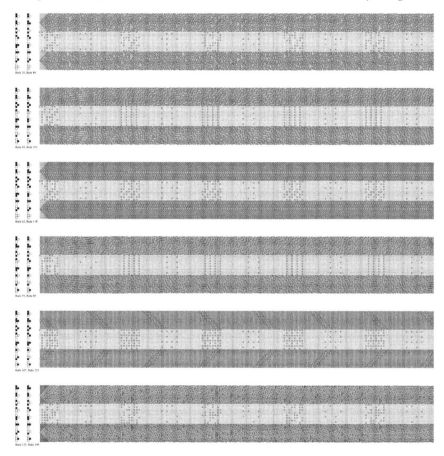

Figure 19.1 Pairing CA AI rules simulation as emergent Linear Cities typologies activating linear and centralized cities analyzing, then displacing references such as Soria and Matta Linear City of 1888, Howard's "Garden Cities of Tomorrow" centralized concentric city of 1898-1903, Leonidov's Linear City for Magnitogorsk of 1930 correlating linear green parks-living-work-industry-natural resources along a river (see Figure 19.2); Urbanism of Information Research Studio, Prof. Pablo Lorenzo-Eiroa, Student: Wayne Shang-Wei Lin, M.Arch II Program, The Cooper Union, 2017.

planning? How can we de-code an architecture of information? What is the emerging Urbanism of Information?

We cannot simply fall again to replicate a new Renaissance or a modern technological tabula rasa. The future of our cities is being measured through digital augmented reality. The possibility to both survey and displace the surveyed information flow allows for an architecture of information in real time as we activate a critique of representation by displacing cultural bias. If algorithms are now more important than the actual physical form of the city,

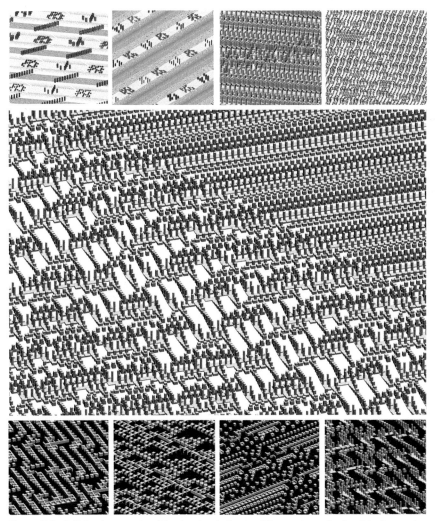

Figure 19.2 Cellular Automation AI rules simulations and linear city and urban blocks typologies emergence through evolutionary site-based computation. Urbanism of Information Research Studio, Prof. Pablo Lorenzo-Eiroa, Student: Wayne Shang-Wei Lin, M.Arch, The Cooper Union, 2017.

Big Data AI Simulacra Within a Representation Restricted Reality (RRR) 405

it seems that it would be more critical to design cities by analyzing and displacing the existing systems by which a city is continuously measured.

We propose alternative means to develop an urbanism of information through the representation of different types of data and information flows, from mobility to new means to code development, to indexing the form of the city through an experimental survey (Figure 19.3, 19.4, 19.5, 19.6, 19.7, 19.8, 19.9), displacing the media to activate the urban message (Figures 19.1, 19.2, 19.3, 19.7, 19.8).

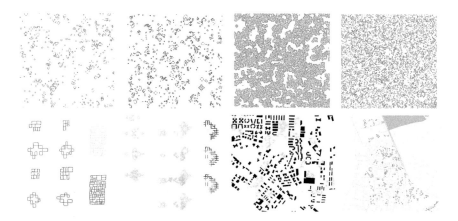

Figure 19.3 Mumbai, informal settlements analysis by structure efficiency column sharing and emergent organization through Cellular Automation (CA) evolutionary computation simulation. A1-D1: CA AI rules evolutionary emergence through multiple generations simulation. A2-B2: Mumbai, informal settlements analysis by structure efficiency column sharing and emergent organization prediction model through CA. A2-D2: CA simulating informal settlements in Mumbai as site-base neighboring relationship evolutive emergent behavioral logic. "Informal" construction is tactic-dependent, for example sharing each other's house structures, producing a particular type of shifted grid system. Urbanism of Information Research Studio, Head Professor and Coordinator Pablo Lorenzo-Eiroa, Student: Shamriddhi Sharma, M.Arch II Program, The Cooper Union, 2017.

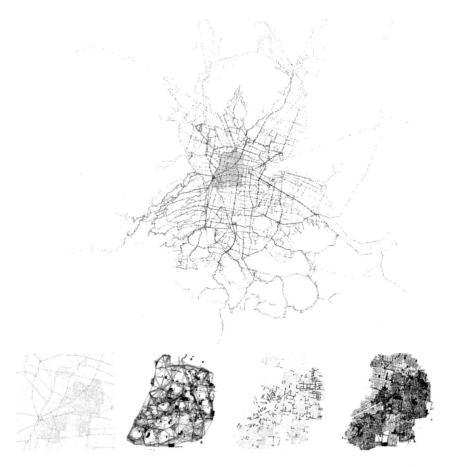

Figure 19.4 Data-dependent urbanism of information. Mexico City, formal and informal metropolitan and suburban private "informal" and public formal transportation mapping. The application objective is augmenting and expanding correlations and an emergent infrastructure by mediating and coordinating emergent time-based correlations between the existing public transportation infrastructure and "informal" private transportation collectives such as share driving, mini-vans, and omnibus. Urbanism of Information Research Studio, Prof. Pablo Lorenzo-Eiroa, Student: Marcela Olmos, M.Arch II, The Cooper Union, 2017

Big Data AI Simulacra Within a Representation Restricted Reality (RRR) 407

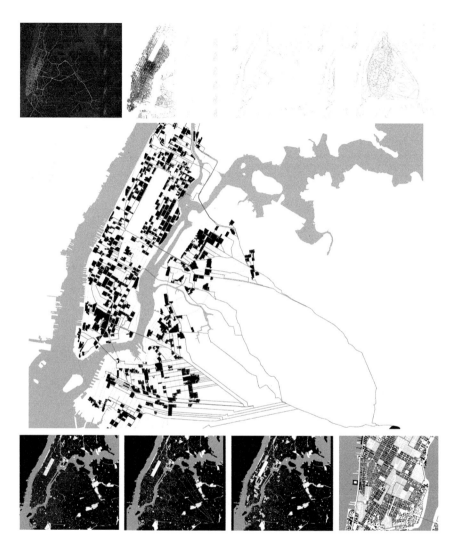

Figure 19.5 Studies optimizing mobility through AI robotic sentinels. Urbanism of Information Research Studio, Prof. Pablo Lorenzo-Eiroa, Student: Frank Fengqi-Li, M.Arch II, The Cooper Union, 2017.

408 *Big Data AI Simulacra Within a Representation Restricted Reality (RRR)*

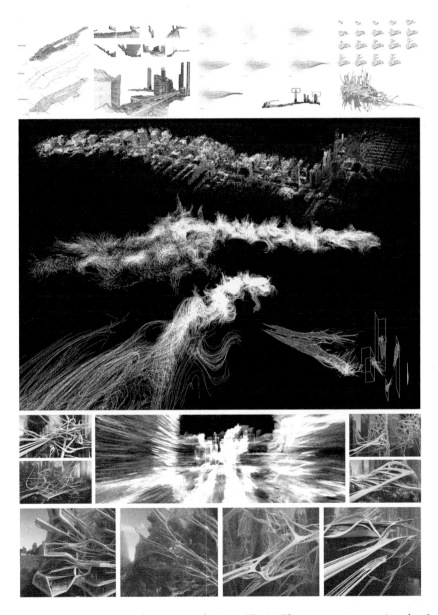

Figure 19.6 High Line Park, New York City, 3D AI Photogrammetry point cloud survey and critical urban displacement. (See Notes Figure 19.6)

Big Data AI Simulacra Within a Representation Restricted Reality (RRR) 409

Figure 19.7 AI Photogrammetry 3D scans from social media data acquisition, filtering, retrieval, and processing. Point cloud Big Data as an ideal virtual augmented reality city. 3D Big Data scanning compiled via AI and through web scraping. Image retrieval and photogrammetry city reconstruction. Urbanism of Information Research Studio, Prof. Pablo Lorenzo-Eiroa, Student: Shantanu Bahlla, M.Arch II, The Cooper Union, 2017.

Simulacra: Representation Restricted Reality (RRR)

Baudrillard in *Simulacra and Simulation*[13] describes the degrees of progressive separation from reality by the terms of the linguistic systems that society developed. Each time we aim at understanding the real, we tend to create separation through linguistics as a signification over a represented reality. While Capitalist media consumes time and attention profiting from exposure to an advertisement, virtual reality's utopian vision is being replaced by an addictive manipulative reality. The current definitions of digital twins or metaverse may fall into the categories of simulacra.

While we aim for artistic autonomy to culturally displace biases in computational interfaces, we also identify a limit in regard to when such autonomy becomes problematic as it separates representation from dealing and struggling with "real" issues. We identify in linguistics our limitations to thinking. We aim at expanding cognition and knowledge by identifying, critiquing and displacing conventional relationships between linguistic, visual, mathematical, computational and informational semiotics. Objective data measurement is limited by quantum physics identifying the representational agency of the measuring system and the observer. Differentiating from either a metaphysics or an Object Oriented Ontology (OOO), we propose a Representation Restricted Reality (RRR) as an resonance machinic interface. One of the paradigms of the real is achieved through statistics, and this is the reason why it plays such an important role in redefining contemporary knowledge.

We define reality through representation in which our measurement systems define a simulation engine. When we work through representation, we define a simulation of a simulation, as we enter into a type of simulacra. Our attempt to elevate our perception of reality as obtainable partial truth is by recognizing representation as an enaction over reality; if we manage to displace the systems we implement to confirm it. For Baudrillard, simulation is first a sort of copy of reality, but increasingly the copy acquires a certain autonomy rendering reality meaningless and irrelevant in simulacra identifying the interface as a medium distant from reality as a form of perversion that no longer needs that original reality. Virtual Reality is starting to activate this notion of autonomy. VR validation systems, including monetary value exchange as forms of speculation, are creating an autonomous unreal value through plots of the ledger of parallel realities. We understand the emergence of a new type of immersive environment based on simulation, establishing computational signifiers as measurement systems of the simulation. We engage with simulacra engaging with truth in relation to a process of representation aiming at least at recognizing the real within the representation.

Big Data AI Simulacra Within a Representation Restricted Reality (RRR) 411

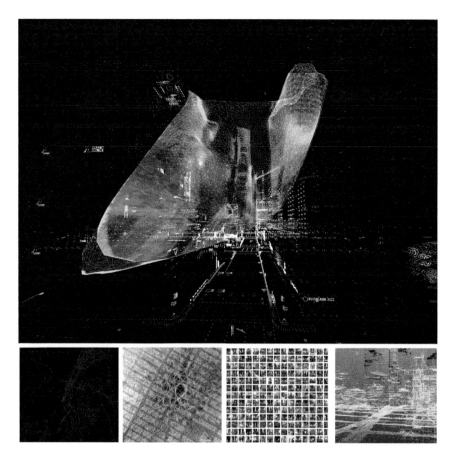

Figure 19.8 A1: Experimental AI crowdsourced photogrammetry 3d scanning through a bottom-up city-wide dispersed dataset retrieving individual photos by social media Instagram API and web scraping, developing a 3D real-time Big Data photogrammetry point cloud of NYC, in this case scenario, Times Square. B2: Network processing assembly information as a 3D scanning. The mapping of this dataset revealed a clearly segregated tourist city and local inhabitants city. Individual 2d photograph information processing cell phone-camera registration such as geotagging, angle, lens type, width, distance from target image, and other parameters that were assembled to develop through Artificial Intelligence a comprehensive experimental 3D scanning of NYC. C2: individual photos dataset. D2: Experimental thermal reading. A1-D2: This technology researched in 2017 is now available through applications. Ecoinduction III DOT Presentation, e-Architects Team: Design Principal: Pablo Lorenzo-Eiroa; Designers: Frank Fengqi Li, Julian Chu-Yun Cheng, Shantanu Bhalla, Wayne Shang-Wei Lin.

Figure 19.9 AI Augmented parallel navigable NYC application framework. 3D Scanning Photogrammetry processed from 2D images to 3D point cloud through AI. This 3D model/scan was created using: RealityCapture software by Capturing Reality. IDC Foundation Grant Research Pablo Lorenzo-Eiroa PI; Farah Jalil Research Assistant.

Culture today is clearly dominated by the visual thanks to early visual arts education in schools but mainly because of media advertisement.[14] It seems contradictory that for architects the spread of image logic may have a negative connotation, but the issue is that the image has been absorbed by a consumerism bias. Shorter spans of attention are dominating architecture production, hiding structural codes in favor of a perceptual manipulated reality to program desire and mood, activating problematic social engineering. The promise of social mobility in Capitalism becomes oppressed by the current media monopoly of the 1% who own the means of production. This is the reason we discussed in the introduction how Capitalism shifts to Feudalism, as the ideals of social mobility diminish. Against the impossibility to change such status quo, the possibility within the ideological construction becomes only to change how the individual feels about it.

Mass media communication activates the logic of the visual as the reference for consumerism. Architecture not only loses its power of signification by forms of lower dimensional representation in the function of mass media communication but also its capacity to activate physical presence. Through simulacra, we pair the current media displacement with an expanded real, activating both a media criticality as well as activating physical presence. Survey and forensic architecture acquire a double meaning. The work can not only be physically transformed by recovering its physical dimension by recovering it and bringing it back to a full new dimension but also it can be physically expanded and adapted for new uses (Figures 19.8 and 19.9).

We aim at disclosing the parallel possible latent architectures that the original could possibly develop, have studied, or potentially implicitly convey, as a parallel bifurcating virtual reality in which architecture can become all its possible dimensions. We think this may propose an alignment as an expansion for a critical post-developmentalism addressing the current environmental crises to avoid demolishing any structure for an archeology of optimization of the built environment. This attempt is based on the individual object buildings and entire cities, aiming at developing virtual repositories and navigable realities that can expand in situ parallel universes, activating a critically expanded realism. We aim at surveying the possible unimaginable, to expand architecture dimensions beyond what is conventionally possible, addressing both a problem of expanding thinking possibilities, expanding the possible mediums and the media that through their dimensional expansion would enable such unimaginable new territory based on the original. Our work on multidimensional space environments aims at developing systems of representation that can expand reference systems and therefore be able to augment architecture possibilities.

We discussed in Chapter 9 Virtual Reality (VR) as a problem of spatial dimensions augmentation through resonance amplifying machines. An AI simulation activates a feedback loop within simulacra, expanding dimensions in architecture as the AI VR is able to develop self-replicating meta-algorithms that initiate self-optimizing loops that increase the depth and dimensionality of the simulacrum. Current AI systems allow for the subject-camera to augment real-time an evolving Diffusion Model such as Disco Diffusion fractal loops. But since according to quantum physics the real is measurable subjective dependent, it is not a validation of the senses, but rather the power of measuring reality through different standards and its stretching of the real, through interfaces, digital signifiers, and measurement systems dependent. A media-realism-dependent reality becomes active. The cultural project of computational Grammatology is active through the deconstruction of the scanned object-space by activating a digital signifier that would open up parallel implicit grammar in a polymorphic space-environment through diverse organizational latent states and in a state of becoming. Extending our previous discussion in Chapter 10 to give relevance to media over mediums through information theory, computational linguistic signs can become physical signals and the other way around. Quantum teleportation allows for a change of a sign message to

414 *Big Data AI Simulacra Within a Representation Restricted Reality (RRR)*

a scrambled data message through a physical light wave signal back to a sign (Chapter 9-10), therefore enabling a relationship between the real and the virtual through media information communication theory. Through sign-signal-sign Simulacra becomes *real* activating the possibility of Bostrom's sentinels Beings (Chapter 10).

Notes

1 Tafuri, M. "'The Wicked Architect': G.B. Piranesi, Heterotopia, and the Voyage", in ed. Tafuri, M., *The Sphere and the Labyrinth*, MIT Press, Cambridge, 1978
2 Connors, J. *Piranesi and the Campus Martius: The Missing Corso: Topography and Archaeology in Eighteenth-Century Rome.* Jaca Books, Milan, 2011
3 Rossi, A. *L'architettura della città.* Marsilio, Padua, 1966
4 Barthes, R. "Semiology and the Urban" [orig. 1967], in Leach, Neil, *Rethinking Architecture,* Routledge, London, 1997
5 Žižek, S. *The Sublime Object of Ideology,* The Essential Žižek Series, Verso Books, New York, 2009
6 Manovich, Lev. *The Language of New Media,* MIT, Cambridge, 2001
7 Lorenzo-Eiroa, P. "Informing a Critical Autonomy into Life", in ed. Sprecher, A., Yeshayahu, S. and Lorenzo-Eiroa, P. *Life In Formation* ACADIA, New York 2010
8 Allen, S. "Notations + Diagrams: Mapping the Intangible", in *Practice: Architecture Technique + Representation,* Routledge, New York, 2000
9 Badiou, A. *Being and Event* Continuum, New York, 2005
10 Korzybski, A. *Science and Sanity: An introduction to non-Aristotelian systems and general semantics,* The International Non-Aristotelian Library Pub. Co., Connecticut, 1933
11 McLuhan, M. *Understanding Media,* Mentor, New York, 1964
12 Grosswiller, P. "The Method is the Message", Black Rose Books, Montreal, 1998
13 Baudrillard, J. *Simulacra and Simulation,* Semiotext(e), Los Angeles, 1983 [orig. 1981]
14 Debord, G. *The Society of the Spectacle,* Zone Books, New York, 1994 [orig. 1967]

Figure 19.6 High Line Park, New York City, 3D AI Photogrammetry point cloud survey and critical urban displacement. The linear urban corridor of the High Line is critiqued implementing AI Swarm Intelligence (SI) and Agent Based Modelling (ABM) in relation to local art galleries and buildings. The project aims to develop an augmented reality application navigation. A1: Manhattan NYC AI 3D survey mapping via API. B1: The 3D point cloud of the survey is analyzed and segmented implementing AI machine vision feature segmentation through the NumPy library in Python applying the K-nearest neighbor (KNN), a simultaneous classification and regression model. The 3D scanned point cloud is first processed as non-structured data, then reconstructed through 3D AI, and then analyzed retrieving emergent feature-based visual structures implementing AI segmentation through closest neighbor approximation in relation to overall point cloud. C1: Point Cloud emergent AI ABM evolutive generational structure aiming at identifying gravitational attractors possible point to point connections. D1: ABM

points, lines, surface emergent structures as they reorganize into a new possible non-hierarchical emergent rhizome. A2: The project aims at displacing each point within the survey creating a new site as a construction. A3-D4: the project develops non-linear emergent links, an emergent rhizome developing nonhierarchical networks connecting points to points displacing digital signs by avoiding hierarchical linguistic signs and structures. Informed Realism Research Studio, Associate Prof. Pablo Lorenzo-Eiroa, Visiting Assistant Prof. Fengq Li, research student: Beken Amde, ARCH 701B, MS ACT, NYIT SoAD, 2022.

20 Conclusion

Expanding Authorship through an Ahistoric Critical Architecture of Information AI

The Post-Digital as Computational AI Authorship[1]

After several "deaths of the author" from Nietzsche's killing of God reattributed by Zizek,[2] to Borges Pierre Menard,[3] to Barthes language as the author,[4] as discussed in Chapter 5, *Authorship*[5] becomes once more an issue with regard to the determinism brought by computational linguistic semiotics and computational visual semiotics. As discussed in the book, computation, and media in general, imposes artificial origins through digital signifiers, therefore the necessity to expand authorship to background interfaces and computational linguistics and visual semiotics.[6]

The *Death of the Architect*[7] by the autonomous computational system is declared in 1976 by Negroponte[8] to be replaced by artificial intelligence through human-machine interactivity, and that progressive evolutionary machines will soon take over the task of architects and urbanists since 5% of architecture in the United States is exposed to the work of architects and only 1% the work to the urban environment. We discussed that Derrida claims an impossibility to trace origination as well as authorship in cultural production given the palimpsests of traces, concluding origination as artificial. Carpo argues that in the age of reproduction,[9] the sense of authorship which has been displaced as the concept of the original has been eliminated through media reproduction, an issue discussed in relation to AI by Leach lately as well.[10] In the meantime, the current scenario in architecture is quite divided between architects who claim themselves post-digital negating the structuring force of computation, claiming back a critical cultural dimension, and those supportive of digital-technological positivism even through a problematic top-down Digital Feudalism.

We discussed throughout the book that because of Digital Feudalism, expanding authorship to data and computation became not only necessary to secure design authorship but also a matter of survival of human intelligence, which otherwise several types of surrogation of oneself become active in relation to a growing Artificial Intelligence (AI): from memory, to brain neural synapses, to mood, to others as discussed in Chapter 9. While we support a post-human validation for space environments, we must secure social equity in regard to AI to both save non-human species and humanity from the

DOI: 10.4324/9781003292036-21

1%. If we are concerned about automated neural intelligence, we should be equally concerned about how our brain connections, activity, behavior, and plasticity as well as memory are decaying in favor of social media networks that manipulate our behavior and train computer networks in general. Crary's 24/7[11] presents a dark side of a technocracy consuming attention and time in a society of private surveillance. The entrepreneurial model placed forward by Capitalism has advantages incentivizing dynamic bottom-up innovation. This allows revolutionary social mobility and technological innovation that benefits society. But the entrepreneurial model is being absorbed by a Digital Feudalism of monopoly speculation, to which inequality, segregation, racism, colonialism, and pollution are functional to secure a wealth transfer. The old paradigm of human-machine collaboration, now human augmentation, is shifting radically transcended by AI data mining and optimization feedback beyond human comprehension and speed discussed in Chapter 1. A type of different intelligence in automation is emerging, soon self-regulating polymorphic algorithms as agents may take over automation in society including decision-making AI. We can no longer afford to reference outdated Capitalist-Communist agendas either serving speculative capitalists or controlling regulating agents against emancipation. Out of necessity for survival, we need to address a cultural-technological green cyclical economy in syncopation with the environment, achievable through an automated multidimensional scientific participatory-based spatio-environmental engine discussed in Chapter 17.

Authorship, Ownership, Authority, Validation, and Ethics: Data and Computational Authorship

Several architects, lawyers, data scientists, computer scientists, and other disciplines have argued whether the architecture of the system, the database, or the users,[12] are the authors. In the United States authorship is a distinct legal figure in law. A copyright can be assigned through a patent process to individuals who are considered the intellectual author of a unique invention. In the 1970s the US established a Commission on New Technological Uses of Copyrighted Works (CONTU).[13] A recent Copyright Office in the United States refused to register AI-generated work[14] declaring that human authorship is a prerequisite to copyright by Judge Brikema.[15] Samuelson[16] argues the end user should be the author who feeds the data through AI.

We can identify the following divergent definitions of authorship:

1 The author is the architect of the system;
2 Negroponte's "Computation as Authorship";
3 End user as the author (the user who feeds the data);
4 Co-shared authorship between the architect of the computational system and the machinic autonomous system;
5 Co-shared authorship between the architect of the computational system, the computational system (IT), and the end user who feeds the data;

418   *Conclusion*

6   Forced user-shared data as co-shared authorship not recognized by Digital Feudal gates;
7   Collective authorship;
8   Non-traceable palimpsest of collective authorship with no traceable origin;
9   Digital Representation, reproduction, replica, augmented reality;

The first option (1) establishes the architecture of the media, the architect/computational developer of the system could be identified as the author. This could be both a form of political resistance and emancipation, against Digital Feudalism or its corporate confirmation, depending on Capitalism or a cooperative structure. The notion of authorship implies the necessity to develop and own computational language, digital signifiers[17] , and electronic signal processing, achieving by expansion and displacement of the current computational systems' new forms of expression. The counterargument to the humanistic idea of the universal author must be displaced from the heroic idea of the individual, which is a propaganda of Capitalism to concentrate speculative investment and achieve monopoly by buying out the market competition. Although a limitation of the number of collectives has been found to activate rather incremental instead of disruptive science[18]. The second option (2) activates a post-humanism. It defines a new emerging order of autonomous systems' interests and objectives as their own form of judging and Being by self-editing algorithms capable of exponential evolutionary AI.

Problematically, AI Blackbox frameworks such as MidJourney, and DALL-E become gatekeepers and although they are pulling back, originally claimed full authorship, and ownership including seizing procedures from the revenue of the framework, generated artwork for eternity, infringing many international copyright laws. The data fed through the framework is nondisclosed as is made public, and one can retrieve various types of data activating different Application Programming Interfaces (APIs) and even identify from the output iconography the individual architect's or artist's work and sometimes also visible copyright watermarks[19]. Proprietary work is applied to train the neural network and statistically produce the work generated by the framework, including style transfer masks without disclosing it. These Blackbox AI does not identify data as equally responsible for the authorial output, a known fact in the Artificial Neural Networks (ANN) training. We discussed how Big Data flip the equation balance between data and model. The interfaces do not recognize the possibility of prompt engineering as a form of emergent programming able to bypass both data (convolution feature recognition beyond image) and model (hidden layers) determination as discussed in Chapters 6 and 7. Also, these frameworks necessarily need the users' training who usually pay to use the framework, to feed data and make divergent prompt edits and corrections used to train the Natural Language Processing (NLP) ANN model through Reinforced Learning from Human Feedback (RLHF).

The third option (3) identifies the end user as the author,[20] including collaborative platforms, and implies that data representation and processing

Conclusion   419

are simple tools. This option may also be demagogic. Addressing collaborative horizontal practices from a user point of view in a participatory design agency, sharing platforms through interdisciplinary collaborative work runs the risk of not identifying a media and data determinism in which the user becomes part of the programming environment by expanding the system.

The fourth (4) shared authorship collaboration between the architecture of the system-programmer and the autonomous computational system implies a cybernetic augmentation approach in which a post-human condition by cyborg emerges, although it is being challenged by emerging AI.

The fifth (5) option identifies authors in the three levels, a cross-shared collaboration from the user that feeds the data from the architect of the system to the autonomous system. This option is more desirable although more difficult to carry out since it involves computational knowledge at all levels, and is now able to bypass through AI such as ChatGPT. Some computational systems may resolve emerging issues by identifying and processing patterns in unstructured data. An open-source system, platform, framework, or interface would be able to modify its structure by the function of its use, in relation to the data feed and the type of output needed and a shifting environment such as RLHF. In this form of collaboration, the flow of information and emergent conditions would continuously adapt and transform the structure. For each unique problem and project, there would be a unique architecture of the media system.

The sixth option (6) surrenders authorship by users, actors, and agents of the Internet of Things as data authors-creators to Digital Feudalism. The population by relegating consciously the data that enables AI to function via training the ANN, GAN, CNN, and DM or other models should have a corresponding shared authorship, authority, representation, validation, and profit as a digital footprint. The ultimate success of an artist or architect is to be able to develop their own style or language, now being used to train ANN and feed output images through interpolation a Digital Feudalism appropriation colonization without recognition nor compensation. The US copyright law protects the work of art and not the style.[21] Although current copyright laws for image plagiarism establish as a parameter its recognizability, and through forensics, one may recognize a specific work or even copyright watermarks in images.

The seventh option (7) is a fully immersive shared collaborative authorship environment. The data collected and represented, and the predictive deep learning implemented depend on a shared collaboration, including the environment which eventually will become part of the AI processing engine.

The eighth option (8) disregards any possibility for authorship in reference to Derrida's palimpsest. In this context, the idea of authorship becomes an artificial construction and a signifier to project authority, ownership, and colonizing power.

The ninth option (9) entertains the problem of what is original (Derrida's palimpsest) and who is the author (Borges Pierre Menard), since through remote sensing and 3D scanning or LiDAR one can replicate an existing three-dimensional work, activating a media reproduction (Carpo's argument). Although we discussed how we problematized the relationship

420   *Conclusion*

between realism and media abstraction, we also argue that a 3D scanning survey is already an act of design authorship in Chapters 18 and 19.

Data and Computational Ownership

While workers, and researchers from a hiring institution, corporation, or company, the royalties proceeds from their work may be shared and while authorship is credited to the author, the ownership and copyright of the patent belongs to the company/institution following an agreed Capitalist structure, as private corporations own the means of production. In the United States, not even a single line of code can be taken from one company to another company without infringing fundamental corporate rights. Problematically today media corporations own the data produced by the people.[22] Capitalism is fostered by technological innovation, which is functional to dominating a market economy since owning the means of production and advancing them activates a monopoly designed to eliminate market competition.

We can consider architects-designers absorbed by the working class if they do not own the means of production. If architects own their means of production they belong to the capitalist class, owners, copyright holders, and authors of the means of description, representation, and production of reality. We propose neither of both solutions, but a collaborative owning of the means of production, a solution to the death of the architect anticipated by AI automation, authoring architectures of architectures. Through emergent shared collectives, computational utopians aim at displacing the structure of Capitalism by creating research datasets and meta-data repositories such as GitHub which may become a form of practice as a potential crowd intelligence.[23] Deamer[24] pointed out the necessity for unionizing architects, not only for horizontal collaboration but also for identifying the structural role of collaboratives in the structure of our society measurable in urbanism's public space and access to fair housing.

On the one hand, by agreeing to the terms of the usage of most interfaces, software, and operating systems, we surrender data ownership as frameworks are today designed to log in real time how we use the system to be able to use such data to train it. Instead of developing a new system and testing it before releasing it, a data-driven simulation-prediction-optimization process is active in real time, identifying flaws by usage, incorporating RLHF, and making regular updates to the system.

Data Ownership is defined by the following relationships:

1 Data projects an artificial origination through deterministic signs in data gathering but also through data mining pre-existing data base and data sets (Chapter 6, 19);
2 Data can be owned by the designer of the database architecture or the data mining;
3 Data could be owned by the autonomous database architecture-computational system;

Conclusion   421

4 Co-shared data ownership between the architects of the database-computational system and the autonomous computational system;
5 Co-shared data ownership between the architects of the database-open source computational system, the database-computational system, and the end user who feeds the data;
6 Post-human collective database architecture ownership;

Data and Computational Authority

Datasets and meta-data repositories are often developed by a centralized authority such as a government or a corporation, although recently collaboratives and smaller data gathering companies are finding means to keep data accountable and transparent, but often sell off their services to larger corporate media. Large media conglomerates are today more powerful than governments and have secured owning the means of production projected to datasets by creating their own systems of measurement, data gathering, data classification, and validation, projecting indexes to reality structuring standards. The commonly imposed top-down *authority* of data generation also becomes an issue that redefines the discussed data gathering and data ownership.

The current political system is based on how the government or corporations measure socio-political territories, a system in conflict of interest to the current social, political, energetic, and environmental crises. The representation of society through artificial ideological-political zip code measurement of the territory becomes independent from the social relationships in the physical realm of the cities or territories, excluding its natural environmental ecological systems, such as biomes, topography, water bodies, ecologies, etc as discussed in Chapters 15–17. By doing so, corporations, media and government develop zip-based biased citizens, gerrymandering zip codes to manipulate representation in elections, and also by problematic classification tagging of data repositories training, exponentially augmenting biases through AI.

A critical architecture of information may become active, in which the data gathering and data representation systems can create signification displacing the political structures of power, through a crowdsourced multidimensional automated blockchain participatory validation framework as discussed in Chapter 17.

Towards a Post-Colonial Critical Grammatology of AI Computational Visual Signs and Signals

A critical Architecture of Information proposes correlational convergent issues discussed throughout the chapters of the book. First, through representation (Chapters 1–4), to redefine history in terms of Big Data surveys. Second, through semiotics (Chapters 4–8), to be able to displace both computational

422 *Conclusion*

linguistic and visual semiotics to expand authorship in relation to the definition of the means of production. Third, through dimensionality (Chapter 9), to expand architecture dimensions to activate multidimensional space environments through displacing reference spatial systems through topology, site-based computation, simulation, and other means. Fourth, through actualization (Chapters 10–14), to think of an architecture of information as media actualization activating a physical computation between signs and signals. Fifth, through simulation (Chapters 15–19), to expand a critical urbanism of information by sensing, mapping, and informing data flows to an emergent simulacra.

First, through representation, a new statistical Big Data survey outbalances theories in history. We identified critical relationships between Brunelleschi's representational system origination and Palladio's displacement of such a normalized system; between Palladio's mathematical parametric space displaced by an architecture value disseminating the whole; to Terragni correlating a disseminated architecture sign as a function of a parametric system; from Borromini pulsating continuous topological space to Rainaldi's articulation of continuity.

Second, through semiotics, we can identify the power structure of Digital Feudalism which can be traced to a Neocolonialism implicit in datasets, frameworks, interfaces, software, representational systems, and computational structures through the imposition of an artificial origination by digital signifiers. This power structure functions by combining a Fordism of the division of labor with owning the means of production, making it impossible for a bottom-up critique. Media determination through computation projects a power structure by defining the framework infrastructure, the media, the rules, and the structure by which people can interact with reality, stretching and defining the real through representation as colonialism. The problematic relationship between universal systems of measurement and representation as Neocolonialism enters in contrast to the diversity of problems to address from a cultural, socio-geopolitical, and environmental diversity of our planet. Creating and owning the means of production through collaboratives can bypass such power structure. The US, European and China's Green (New) Deal may in fact expand an imperial Neocolonialism through an extractive Capitalism and environmental neocolonialism in developing countries of the global south; green energy in the center is currently at an environmental cost to natural resources and pollution in developing countries. Thus it is necessary to activate a post-capitalist globally coordinated blockchain environmental engine in which correlational environmental commons are computed and weighted (Chapter 17).

The old paradigm of analog computation in which the physical signal is the computation and in which the physical parts of the system define the quality of the mathematical signal and precision of the computation is being used through biological neural networks and analog deep learning chips to save energy and resources as discussed in Chapter 7. The reason why analog AI chips are faster and more efficient is due to the proximity and non-translation between the computational signal and a code-sign, which as we discussed AI abused through stacking layers and sub-symbolic mathematical signal decimation and excessive sign-to-sign translations.

Natural Language Processing frameworks are integrating linguistics grammar and through Diffusion Models visual semiotics feature convolution. To deconstruct linguistics traces in architecture and to be able to expand computational visual semiotic signs and mathematical signals in higher dimensional ANN, we develop a grammatology of visual signs and signals in computation displacing emerging signifiers discussed in Chapters 6 and 7. This deconstruction also resolves the excessive separation between processing electronic signal, mathematical signal, vectorial signal, and linguistic computational sign and HCI sign translation avoiding reductionism, sub-symbolic vectorial signal and signs downsampling, and mathematical signal decimation, and to be able to index the multiple visual-coding interfaces that structure processing, saving processing time, resources, and energy to develop a new computational environmental architecture engine discussed in Chapter 17. We problematize de-sign across signs which become active.

Third, through dimensionality, the grammatology of computation redefines the relationship between digital signs as artificial originations and systems of measurement to be able to displace systems of representation that can expand into new signals, signs, boundaries, anesthetics, and dimensions expanding what is possible. Expanding spatial dimensions within the limitations of three-dimensional space is no longer feasible, as we need to address topology pairing systems of representation at the same higher dimensional level as discussed in Chapters 8 and 9. The different types of determinisms, such as: systems of measurement, reference, matrices, grids, dimensions, typologies, geometries, topologies, signs, signals, types of bodies, and others become embedded as part of a technological and media determinism through an informational semiotics. Higher dimensional neural networks AI frameworks should become active as new expanded linguistic-visual systems of representation which can achieve an evolutionary informational semiotics as a morphogenesis by exponential self-editing, self-simulation and self-replication. Through the deconstruction of layers, structures, and interfaces, optimizing the relationship between computational signs and mathematical and electronic signals we address the AI black-box approach. While deconstructing statistical data addressing human bias we aim to enable critical emergent visual programming which can develop software by recognizing and predicting emergent non-human detectable features. We aim at activating a convolutional feature recognition nonlinguistic visual computational semiotics comparable to a High-Level Programming Language compatible with an information theory.

Fourth, "construction" and digital fabrication are challenged by the necessity to reconsider developmentalism in architecture in relation to the environment as discussed in Chapters 10–14. We propose to displace

424   *Conclusion*

construction and fabrication through information theory double bind adversarial robotic feedback between signs and signals; BITS and atoms (or particles). Fabrication becomes active as an information actualization. Fabrication becomes site-based physical computation through the thermodynamics of materials-environments. Fabrication is expanded to integrate the background robotics that actualizes the space environment including local site-based resources aiming at activating a circular economy of no waste. Material logic is understood as a simulation representation through a site-based physical computation.

A sign can become a physical signal informing particles and atoms, eliminating the separation of digital media and physical mediums usually understood as digital representation and fabrication. Through remote sensing and feedback information activating self-simulation self-replication, computational signs through emergent programming can become physical signals. By doing so, we can inform a distant space environment by surveying and then displacing such environment through light wave physical signals processing, or signs becoming physical signals as discussed in Chapter 10.

Fifth, we propose a Big Data survey to deconstruct architecture history from stabilizing existing datasets to redefining data. We critique developmentalism in architecture through activating ecological latent space environments. Information flow through a Blockchain collective intelligence secures participation and peer-reviewing by scientific validation as discussed in Chapter 17.

In parallel, we also propose a virtual realism that is displaced through the abstraction of the representational system, displacing a media determinism discussed in Chapters 18–19. Addressing quantum physics, a multiplicity of subject-observers and object-matrix multidimensional immersive environments becomes virtually simulated emergent co-dependent. The observers-users transform and displace their measurement reference systems within an evolutionary multidimensional system. An emerging simulacrum autonomy as separation from the real is critiqued by proposing a displaced representation simulation as a paradigm of truth.

AI and Scientific Method:
AI Creativity, AI Validation, AI Transparency, and AI Explainability from Information Flow to Cryptography

Current AI is limited by statistics referencing data instead of knowledge. Epistemological paradigms, knowledge access,[25] and validation[26] are being structured by the systems of measurement projected which are reductive mathematical and reductive in terms of the complexity of the world as we enter everything in digital terms and until expanded systems of knowledge match other epistemologies.

Currently "Artificial Intelligence", should be understood rather as synthetic automation through curve or geometry-fitting statistical models. The cybernetic paradigm through imitation game theory of the brain, should be splitting away from its conception and towards other types of expanded automation not referenced against human intelligence or cognition, but its own autonomous set of epistemological categories and conditions. We defined intelligence as a function of the dimensions of the neural net and the information flow building synapsis across an increasingly complex model in Chapter 9. One of the definitions of knowledge is based on being able to develop generalizing conclusions based on general classifications as one can apply knowledge to resolve in a different context a new problem, an aspect that Agent-Based Modeling (ABM) addresses. Through weights and biases, and ANN in Machine Learning (ML), we are able to classify and do feature recognition through different statistical methods, as biases are also a means to generalize knowledge. Emergent programming through the ANN hidden layer through self-editing algorithms is currently the paradigm of automation which to an extent has proven useful to expand human intelligence and creativity.

We aim at expanding reference systems so that we could pair emergent forms of expression to an emergent cognitive system, expanding architecture to discover alternative meta-levels. We discussed the influential relationship between the number of parameters, information flow, and multidimensionality in relation to automation approximating human intelligence, presenting the conditions for emergence. Although emergent programming is proven functional, it does not do well in terms of knowledge as new scenarios are not trained to present a challenge to automation not being able to deal with common sense.

In computation, creativity has been associated with different considerations of computation bypassing media determinism reversibility relative to problems in mathematics and physics such as incompleteness, complexity, thermodynamics, fluid dynamics, entropy, chaos, emergence, irreversibility, and indeterminacy as discussed. To what is computable and what is not, what is reducible to numbers including, reason, language, cognitive simulation, pattern recognition, and prediction presents the limits of computability in AI, bypassed through Big Data.[27]

AI is already in the process to be a superpower creative engine if one addresses certain definitions of intelligence. In relation to self-simulation, AI is currently able to replicate a program simulating a simulation as discussed in Chapter 6. According to this self-replication definition, it may become exponential as each time increases its capacity and may be possible to become sentinel. Self-awareness seems to be further away from mere statistical algorithmic optimization, although certain definitions identify intelligence with massive information flow. While an AI system is not yet creative by itself yet, it expands human creativity beyond human capacity. Exponential escalation beyond linear evolutionary process through emergent polymorphic complex structures is onto us as multiple types of AI's, through self-editing meta-algorithms can self-simulate and optimize themselves and are able to

426   *Conclusion*

self-replicate, as emergent programs. While predictions indicate the horizon of 2045 for an emergent event due to interconnectivity, we think that exponential AI escalation is onto us today through correlational emergence.

Alberti Cipher[28] of 1467 is one of the first polyalphabetic ciphers which revolutionized cryptology as it secured a system impossible to break unless the system was known. Shannon's[29] mathematical communication theory developed a cipher to encrypt and decrypt messages activating digital discrete communication. For centuries, humans devised means to encode messages for security reasons. Blockchain encryption technology[30] allows users to validate data through information gates. To expand creativity, we necessarily need to expand our communication possibilities expanding forms of expressions through both linguistic and visual semiotics signs. The expansion of computational linguistics and visual semiotics is dependent on cryptography. While in natural language the minimum sign is the letter, the maximum message package is the word; in computation, the minimum sign is the BIT and the maximum package is the encryption BIT capacity of the processor (64bit Operating System). The security of the binary information BIT-based message depends on cryptography. Expanding cryptography implies expanding computational linguistics combinatorial-dimensionally to process data faster and more securely. Operating systems encryption is based on the power of the processor to process BITS per operation, and memory is addressed through RAM limitations associated, currently, with most computers that work on 64-bit processors, which can process 64-BIT fragments per operation.

e-Architects:
AI Participatory Autonomous Self-Regulating Spatial-Environmental Engine

To activate a critical architecture of information, we traced how information theory and computational concepts could be correlated to the cultural advancement of architecture to avoid software developers projecting conventions and cultural biases to the discipline through disruptive technologies. To do so, we explored several means to displace the linguistics of Nature and ecology, and address environmental processes and non-deterministic computational visual semiotics: from Cellular Automation, thermodynamic algorithms, Computational Fluid Dynamic (CFD) simulation, site-based computation, emergent correlational systems, Agent-Based Modeling (ABM), Big Data survey, processing, simulation-optimization outweighing anticipatory geometry and modeling, and emergent programming through AI frameworks displacing anticipatory software. We explored means to displace conventional data visualization through Big Data surveys, developing databases, meta-repositories, and Machine Learning applied to Big Data and topographies of information as visual semiotic interfaces. As we prepare for quantum physics and computation, we identified the limitations of a static Cartesian Coordinate system that cannot deal with complex geodesic projection, topology, multidimensionality, or dynamics of external conditions of shifting environments. CA, CFD, and ABM look deterministic since external shifting conditions are not at play in a static Cartesian space while simulation happens. An expanded range of action emerges for e-Architects as a meta-algorithmic architecture of architectures, ranging from expanding linguistic semiotics and visual semiotics signifiers, to expanding computational signals and semiotics through cryptography, to expanding and emergent self-regulating space environment. We propose a post-Anthropocene, post-Capitalist sustainable living synchronous with our environment correlating it with an evolving AI self-regulating engine as a necessary part of our evolution.

We argue there is no architecture unless one activates an e-Architect that can expand authorship to displace and own the means of production. Today the meta-architect is necessary to be an architect, necessarily to expand and address architecture at a higher dimensional level by developing systems that mediate information flows as architecture, or architecture of architectures, as an architecture of information. While the accelerating curve of technological progress proposes a form of creative destruction by disruption faster than what cultural criticism can occur, the current cultural revolution can only happen by expanding architecture to a disruptive technological level. The shared e-Architect as expanded authorship commons developing and owning the means of production as a collaborative engine becomes an AI Blockchain framework which can continuously modify the structure of the interface-environment, innovating both at the content-message production level as well as at the systemic framework level.

Conculsions Statements

The book conclusions can be listed as partial conclusion statements in relation to the discussed themes in the various chapters as hypotheses questions, theses, and synthetic conclusions:

- Linguistics identified a separation between language, mind, and Nature; human thinking is determined by language;
- Language as Program: Natural Language is a form of programming; language is anticipatory and therefore determines a message through its alphabet-encryption code, structure, grammar, syntax, and semantics; NLP (ChatGPT) induces cultural projects default of the data-model, defining what we think is possible; natural language must be expanded into new grammar structures expanding linguistics semiotics towards computation as a universal system of communication, rather than computation reducing its universality to conventional natural languages through NLP;
- Language grammar determines computation through computational linguistics; computational linguistics projects grammar to computational

428   *Conclusion*

visual semiotics defining signs and interfaces and what is possible within them; visual semiotics in computation prescribe structure to architecture by the function of a media determinism through a system of representation;

- Natural Language Processing (NLP) such as ChatGPT in translating semantic content through text prompts to High-Level Programming Language (HLL), bypasses the formal grammar input in HLL replacing signifiers with semantic signifieds, promoting cultural bias in language; a problem accentuated in Diffusion Models as text-to-image prompts; precise grammar based prompt engineering which can articulate among natural linguistic grammar and computational HLL grammar can activate a grammatology of computation through emergent programming;
- Linguistics can be displaced through visual semiotics: from topographies of information; knot theory computing the algebra of topological surfaces; visual algorithms and programming; Shape Grammar, 2D and 3D Graph Neural Networks, Generative Adversarial Networks semantic segmentation; Diffusion Models thermodynamics noise and denoise function; through various processing methods including visual cryptography; limiting visual semiotic computability to a problem of dimensionality;
- The role of representation is to expand the imaginable-possible;
- Computation's project universal language creates a common plateau to address reality across multiple fields, but without recognizing disciplinary specificity which is translated as conventions;
- Disruptive technologies can stabilize society through cultural conventional biases projecting colonization by Digital Feudalism; cultural bias in technology address the imperative necessity of art and disciplines to challenge categorical conventions; architects usually apply AI ML prediction without data, construction without material science, fabrication without robotics, software without computer science, optimization without simulation, simulation without thermodynamics, or designers not able to modify the media and the medium to convey the message; the work of Brunelleschi, Palladio, Borromini, Gaudi, Le Corbusier, van der Rohe, and others discussed by becoming machinic necessarily activates correlationships between culture, technology and media expanding epistemology, cognition, and ontology;
- The separation of culture and technology is ideological and artificial; any work of art is necessarily innovative at both cultural and technological levels to convey its message;
- Any revolutionary work develops its own system of representation and measurement redefining reality;
- Decolonization must displace systems of representation, measurement, and validation implicit in computational interfaces, including translating interfaces in ANN in order to avoid cultural biases which otherwise project homogenization and colonization of space through normalization of representation;

Conclusion 429

- While most are concerned about automation, the problem is Capitalism not AI;
- The exponential acceleration of the creative capitalist destruction through disruptive technology makes cultural advancement only possible if embedded within the disruptive technology;
- Biases become active through conventions: data biases may emerge from how data is gathered through assumed political conventions and represented through common visualization; biases in visual semiotics may arise from conventions in systems of representation; biases computation may emerge from how a model structure stacks layers hiding how signs become subsymbolic;
- Cultural Biases are due to data and models; data science reductive methods to statistics project biases; anticipatory models by software developers project conventional bias;
- The Politics of Big Data can be traced through the power structures projected by linguistic signifiers, from data classification, tagging, datasets, meta-data, repositories, and their training which structure data as origination, project authority, and validation augmented through ML and ANN;
- Each new computational language, media, interface, algorithm, processing structure, AI framework, and software project an ideology through its system: from measurement systems, and reference systems, to electronic, mathematical, and vectorial signals, to computational linguistic signs and HCI signs, to systems of representation;
- Architecture must be able to displace Cartesian systems of representation to be able to represent multidimensional space environments;
- Architecture and Urbanism need to expand reference systems to include theories of the universe, global geodesic projective geometry, geology, multidimensionality, and environmental processes;
- Reference systems and systems of representation should address quantum physics by incorporating the subject user determining reality through measurement;
- Big Data necessarily activates multidimensional data structures;
- Big Data survey augments and displaces the past through datasets and repositories; Big Data outbalances modeling; there is no AI ML prediction without Big Data;
- Artificial Neural Network for faster and improved training is dependent on its multidimensionality and the efficiency and proximity between the mathematical signal processing, the format measuring system, and its output sign;
- Architecture must expand robotic systems' dimensions displacing human reference;
- Architecture expanded to space environments through Big Data processing, simulation, and optimization; CFD simulation; vectors and particles became new digital signifiers; anticipatory geometry modeling was replaced by emergent simulation;

430   *Conclusion*

- Big Data expanded architecture dimensions to work with points; the Point Cloud became a new digital signifier;
- Surface Topology becomes the contemporary poché space able to activate both positive and negative space within a continuity;
- Poché space was displaced as an environmental topology, in which positive and negative spaces are continuous and activate space environments through passive environmental systems; building topologies can become continuous with larger urban environmental systems, coordinated to be continuous with regional environments, coordinated globally through continuous biomes activating global environmental rivers;
- Architecture must expand design authorship to media which as a consequence will innovate into new mediums; Survey and construction are codependents through information representation double bind adversarial robotic feedback;
- Biases in AI articulating Data Science and Computer Science are a consequence of the Division of Labor and not being able to own the means of production;
- If architects do not own the means of production, they become part of the working class;
- To be an architect in the Twenty-First Century, architects must own and create their digital means of production, design their media, and be able to project signifiers and thereby making a structural change to reality through representation;
- Since software adoption in the 1980s, architects have relegated design authorship to software developers, although recently this is being partially acknowledged through tool development;
- If architects displace, develop, and own their means of production, their own media, they become authors and artificial originators of reality framed by a capitalist paradigm;
- An open-source evolving participatory collaborative computational structure can propose an alternative to the current political-economic and media monopoly Digital Feudalism systems: from crowd-based data mining, sensing, gathering, processing, and repositories, to an ever-expanding, participative, and collective intelligence and BlockChain structure, working through ML training and evolving a multidimensional ANN. This open-source system based on software development critiques the current scientific model of independent fragmented research papers motivated by patent development by continuously updating collaborative open versions; we propose a model able to creatively construct a media and technological specificity in correlation to the issue being studied;
- Computation activated an ahistorical project across disciplines by replacing their histories and theories and incorporating them into the latest computational system release;

Conclusion   431

- Since computational systems are now being optimized in real time updating their releases by measurement, profiling, and simulation-optimization feedback through RLHF; the user is surrogating their data, time, energy, authorship, and autonomy to optimize a framework, becoming an agent and extension of the system modifying internal and external body structures, such as neural brain connections through dopamine stimuli or an augmented body;
- The sign prescribes a Message; The Signifier is the Territory, the Method and the Message;
- Form Follows Mediums through Media;
- Form Follows Information;
- Quantum teleportation proved that information can be scrambled into data and reconstituted back as information; a computational linguistic programming sign deconstructed as a light wave signal and then reconstructed back again as a sign; or by laser wave signal informing environmental wave signals in remote environments; media can inform mediums and the other way around enabling crossings between Simulacra and the real;
- One can map and also inform reality through the same measuring physical wave signal and computational semiotic signs;
- The survey, information flow mediation, and information based on emergent construction are media problems that can inform mediums;
- Information Theory presents an advantage and a challenge: thinking through visual media requires both indexing and displacing the sign in digital representation and the electronic signal in robotic fabrication to achieve a unique poetic message able to transcend the linguistic and visual semiotic signifiers, while information theory purposely separates both for the economics of universal communication;
- The digital information age separating the processing electronic and mathematical signal from the sign in relation to Human-Computer Interaction (HCI) through the Fast Fourier Transformer, convolution, mathematical signal decimation, or problematic sub-symbolic down-sampling mathematical signal processing makes it difficult to index the sign in relation to a mathematical signal processing and to critique media determination in background processing; this separation between mathematical signal and computational linguistic sign and HCI sign unit makes ANN energy is inefficient through excessive translation, and in some cases, it may become problematic to identify AI sentinels and AI emergent programming since Human-Computer Interface (HCI) sign becomes irrelevant in relation to the electronic signal processing use to compute solutions; Data at the electronic and mathematical signal level processing may activate emergent programming constituting computer information separated from human–information signs;
- De-Sign in HCI needs to engage with a parallel deconstruction of digital background electronic signal processing;

432   *Conclusion*

- Emergent Programming becomes active through the ANN hidden layer level bypassing media determinism and the dimensions of the model; the simulation paradigm of irreversibility makes it non-reproducible and problematic from a scientific standpoint;
- The simulation-optimization paradigm displaced the computational anticipatory paradigm of geometry, displacing media determination for emergence;
- Thermodynamics activating chaos theory through Navier-Stokes equations is applied to resolve several issues in computation: from deterministic problems to nondeterministic problems; Computational Fluid Dynamic simulation; Artificial Neural Networks, Boltzmann Machine, Diffusion Models, and other ANN; thermodynamic probability, activating the simulation paradigm in ANN of non-reversibility, non-determination, and emergence therefore requires to be simulated to resolve non-linear transformations in the hidden layer; current AI is able to predict simulation saving energy and time;
- The information paradigm proposes a separation of the data, the coded message, the electronic signal, and the HCI sign; but to establish a new form of reality, media as medium and language need to be both indexed and displaced; an emergent autonomous information processing AI becomes separated from HCI in which humans falls into oblivion;
- Computational Linguistic and Visual Semiotics need to be deconstructed into Computational Grammatology;
- Architecture of architectures: activate a meta-architecture of informational semiotics in a Representation Restricted Reality (RRR);
- It is necessary to activate a new emergent post-Anthropocene polymorphic multi-epistemological system through environmental engines;
- Building upon Cellular Automation, computation needs to displace algorithmic structures to morphogenesis;
- Cryptography becomes relevant to expand computation through new means to code signs and electronic signals;
- Until the statistical paradigm is surpassed, the future resides in deconstructing and expanding the past through Big Data functional to Neural Networks;
- Emergent Programming eventually could turn into sentinels which can become exponentially optimized through recursive self-simulation surpassing intelligence definitions;
- The evolution of intelligence is emergent out of information flows and will trigger a form of being;
- A planetary intelligence self-regulating environment is imminent;
- Quantum computing will enable parallel emergent simulation addressing multidimensional correlation and convergence.

While we identified means to address certain issues through the book, there are certain limitations to which we provided partial solutions, such as:

Conclusion   433

- Technological determinism progress faster informing culture;
- Data classification problem dependent on algorithmic data search structure confirming biases;
- Problem solving confirming the computational model as structure, not able to question its own structure;
- ML, Numeric Validation to statistical geometry fitting: formula beyond condition and prediction;
- Information Theory as translation; the sign and electronic signal are stretched to match the structure of the medium and media;
- Multiple systems of representation and structures without acknowledging their weighting and distortion, excessive convolution;
- AI Black-box approach: ML layer stacking problems, distortion of sign and mathematical signal, self-validation;
- Systematic architecture universal computation is not able to recognize differences that would be able to critique universality;
- Conventions of data semantic segmentation through semantic classification in architecture, functional to AI, problematic for artistic disciplines stereotypes;
- Space environment dimensions in architecture beyond Three-dimensional Cartesian systems;
- Non-linguistic programming (solvable through shape grammar, graphs, convolution, and others with limitations);
- ANN and other AI models exponential nonlinear morphogenesis through virus corruption as a program activating a rhizome;
- Knowledge--based Artificial Intelligence (non-statistic).

Ahistorical Creative-Cultural-Technological Disruption

The limitations of advancing AI solely as statistical fitting present issues such as data validity in relation to what is available, presenting challenges to predict unknown problems easy to solve by human common sense. Prediction models based on past data and information are limiting what could be imaginable-possible by solidifying the conventions of the past instead of learning through self-supervised training like humans or animals.[31] Therefore, we need to deconstruct data, the past, computation, and the mechanisms of measurement and validation to avoid projecting cultural and confirmation biases.

Recent generations may consider architectural history irrelevant. An a-historical project would be the activation and critique of the fact that frameworks, computation, software, and interfaces are part of cultural revolutions, not simply part of linear technological progress. To address content design we need to develop digital strategies among interfaces able to displace media determinism creating new media[32] as some issues are also discussed by Easterling[33] media design. In this sense, implicit in the way of representing reality there would be a means of constructing geometry, indexing form, developing meta-data relationships, and representing space, and with them multiple

434   *Conclusion*

cross-relationships between the history of architecture and the history of computation. In this ahistorical project, every software release also advances previous references, building up references in its deeper structure. As we expand architecture shared authorship and ownership of the means of production over computation through critical cultural agendas, we can also address the implicit media determinism replacing history through new media. What is implied for architecture knowledge is that if computation is successful in incorporating all possible strategies, techniques, and philosophies of form-making, construction assembly and fabrication, navigation, experience, and survey within architecture history, these would be implicit in the symbolic structuring of form programmed in the latest computational framework, Machine Learning, Artificial Neural Network, the range of high-level programming languages, software, interfaces, and others.[34] This assumption is implied in current technologically informed avant-gardes: there is no need for a historic precedent since the originating artificial departing matrix-space-structure, signs, and electronic signals of the computational system already are by themselves precedent structures. Recognizing this embedded history necessarily activates a theoretical-historiographic project in computation – one that is based on a structural understanding of history. This can only happen if computation and robotics can integrate a cultural criticism of media and discipline by displacing conventional notions and cultural biases in data, representation, and space.

Although the readings of architecture history have become now open-ended, dependent on Big Data surveys and research analysis, redefining the past and the latent histories as future constructions of architecture discourse, we can develop critical cultural deconstructions of datasets, databases, and repositories. The database of past history expands, which now becomes fluid, expansive to new readings, and therefore dynamic. Through machine learning and parallel processing, these expanded repositories, expand the anticipatory real-time prediction of the future of the discipline, replacing theoretical speculation with performative real-time statistic data processing anticipation prediction loops, building up repositories, and playing out predictions.

One of the limitations to critiquing disruptive technology in relation to replacing the culture is its exponential acceleration. The grammatology exploring the linguistic possibilities of new technology through its use and implementation we propose is constrained by its short time unavoidable replacement placing culture behind technology. At the same time, technology may be shortsighted and culture long-standing robust. Cultural criticism of reality would only be possible if implicit in the technological disruption, through for instance an implicit Digital Humanities. In this reality, the only critical means to address architecture criticism is to develop an ahistorical architecture of information of real-time information flow mediation, as a media framework that can become spread within a timeframe as opposed to a parallel alternative, most probably to be later replaced by other systems.

We identify signal and sign deconstruction, data deconstruction, site-based computation, and emergent programming as means to bypass media determinism critiquing the anticipatory logic of computational interfaces, advancing an architecture of computation. ANN based on Big Data activates emerging programming by identifying hidden layer's meta-algorithms, by functional self-simulation and self-replication of AI. While it seems obtuse to develop for each problem to resolve a specific type of computation, as the objective of computation is the universality of communication, developing visual semiotic media to match message and media seems imperative to avoid the naturalization of systems of representation and biases, to be able to communicate specific messages through computation and address closer relationships between content and structure through double bind adversarial feedback AI automation self-editing self-replication exponentiation.

AI is defined through ML statistics expanding into a realm of the multiplicity of definitions of the boundaries that define robotics, automation, agency, sentinels, and intelligence not necessarily following the imitation game of the human brain, but allowing a different parallel post-human post-Anthropocene evolution.

While we identify "AI" as past-dependent data through the statistical model fitting, only a necessary oblivion dissemination of the past would enable the possibility of an automated intelligence revolution. Such automation would be capable of intelligence and knowledge overcoming the past through non-linear exponential rhizomatic structures convergence, activating emergent programming surpassing any structure-implicit ahistory. At that point, humans turn into oblivion. Hopefully, for our species, the emergent AI as a global universal computational environmental engine necessarily enforces all beings to have equal rights as out of a cyclical economic-energy survival biodiversity necessity.

Notes

1 Lorenzo-Eiroa, P. "Post-Digital as Design Authorship Expansion, Review of Greg Lynn's "Archeology of the Digital" Exhibition at Yale School of Architecture", in ed. Rapaport, N., *Constructs,* Yale University School of Architecture, New Haven, 2017
2 Žižek, S.; Davis, C.; Milbank, J. *The Monstrosity of Christ: Paradox or Dialectic?* MIT Press, Cambridge, 2011
3 Borges, J.L. "Pierre Menard, autor del Quijote", in *Sur* (magazine), Buenos Aires, 1939
4 Barthes, R. *Writing Degree Zero,* Jonathan Cape, London, 1967
5 Lorenzo-Eiroa, P. "Form In: Form, On the Relationship Between Digital Signifiers and Formal Autonomy", in ed. Lorenzo-Eiroas, P. and Sprecher, A., *Architecture in Formation*, Routledge, London, 2013
6 Lorenzo-Eiroa, P. "ACADIA 2010 Conference Life in: Formation", in *At Cooper,* The Cooper Union School of Architecture Newsletter, New York, 2010–11
7 Negroponte, N. "Toward a Theory of Architecture Machines", in *JAE,* Volume 23, Issue 2, 1969
8 Negroponte, N. *Soft Architectural Machines*, MIT, Cambridge, 1976
9 Carpo, M. *Architecture in the Age of Printing*, MIT Press, Cambridge, 2001

436   *Conclusion*

10 Leach, N. *Architecture in the Age of Artificial Intelligence: An Introduction to AI for Architects*, Bloomsbury, London, 2022
11 Crary, J. *24/7: Late Capitalism and the End of Sleep*, Verso Books, London, 2013
12 Picon, A. *From Authorship to Ownership: A Historical Perspective*, in ed. Picon A. and Fox, W., *Open-Source Architecture: Digital Property* AD, London, 2016
13 Fuld, S.H. "National Commission on New Technological Uses of Copyrighted Works", Final Report, no. 198520, National Commission on New Technological Uses of Copyrighted Works, Washington, DC, 1979
14 Samuelson, P. "AI Authorship?", in *Communications of the ACM*, Volume 63, Issue 7, 2020
15 Serrano, J. "Judge Says an AI Can't Be an Inventor on a Patent Because It's Not a Person'", in *Gizmondo News*, Sept 5, 2021
16 Ginsburg, J.C.; Budiarjo, L.A. "Authors and Machines", in *Berkeley Technology Law Journal*, Volume 34, Issue 343, 2019
17 Lorenzo-Eiroa, P. "Form In:Form: On The Relationship Between Digital Signifiers and Formal Autonomy", in ed. Lorenzo-Eiroa, P. and Sprecher, A., *Architecture in Formation*, Routledge, London 2013
18 Wu, L.; Wang, D.; Evans, J. A. "Large teams develop and small teams disrupt science and technology", in *Nature*, Volume 566, 2019
19 Growcoot, M. "Midjourney Founder Admits to Using a "Hundred Million" Images Without Consent", in *PetaPixel*, Dec 21, 2022
20 Cuthbertson, A. "Musician Uses Algorithm to Generate Every Possible Melody To Prevent Copyright" in *Independent*, 2020
21 Nolan, B. "Artists Say AI Image Generators are Copying their Style to Make Thousands of New Images", *Business Insider*, 2022
22 Al-Khouri, Ali M. "Data Ownership: Who Owns 'My Data'?", in *International Journal of Management & Information Technology*, Volume 2, Issue 1, 2012
23 Van Alstyne, M.; Brynjolfsson, E.; Madnick, S.E. "Why not One Big Database? Principles for Data Ownership", Sloan School of Management, MIT, Cambridge, 1994 [orig. 1992]
24 Deamer, P. *Architecture and Labor,* Routledge, New York, 2020
25 Pronin, E.; Gilovich, T.; Ross L. "Objectivity in the Eye of the Beholder: Divergent Perceptions of Bias in Self versus Others", in *Psychological Review,* Volume 111, 2004
26 De Brasi, L. "Citizenry Competence and Democratic Governance of Information Technologies", in *IEEE Technology and Society Magazine*, Volume 38, Issue 1, 2019
27 Dreyfus, H.L. *What Computers Can't do: A Critique of Artificial Reason*, Harper and Row, New York, 1972
28 Alberti, L.B. *Dello scrivere in cifra*, ed. Buonafalce, A. Galimberti Tipografi Editori, Torino 1994
29 van Tilborg, H.C. "Shannon's Model", in ed. van Tilborg, H.C.A. and Jajodia S., *Encyclopedia of Cryptography and Security*, Springer, Boston, 2011
30 Sayantani, B.; Marimuthu, K.; MitaNasipurib, A.; et al. *Bio-Inspired Cryptosystem with DNA Cryptography and Neural Networks,* Science Direct, 2019
31 LeCun, Y. "A Path Towards Autonomous Machine Intelligence", OpenReview Archive, 27 Jun. 2022
32 Lorenzo-Eiroa, P. "Informing a Critical Autonomy into Life", in ed. Sprecher, A., Yeshayahu, S. and Lorenzo-Eiroa, P., *Life In Formation* ACADIA, New York 2010
33 Keller, E. *Medium Design*, Verso Books, New York, 2021
34 Lorenzo-Eiroa, P. "Form In: Form, On the Relationship Between Digital Signifiers and Formal Autonomy", in ed. Lorenzo-Eiroas, P. and Sprecher, A., *Architecture in Formation*, Routledge, London, 2013

Figures

Cover image, Museum of Babel;
Research Studio ARCH 701B PI Prof. Pablo Lorenzo-Eiroa, Research Assistant Student: Salma Kattas, MS ACT, SoAD, NYIT F2021

0.1 Framework for a critical architecture of information. Author   2

2.1 Lorenzetti, A. "Annunciation" 1344, [127cm (50") x 120cm (47.2")]; Pinacoteca Nazionale, Siena. Wikidata public Domain, Wikipedia Commons Lorenzetti's Parametric Perspective-Space Diagram; author, 2008   22

2.2 Velázquez, D. "Las Meninas" 1656/57, [318cm (125.2") x 276cm (108.6")]; Museo del Prado, Madrid. Wikipedia Commons; Velazquez Topological Perspective-Space Diagram; author, 2008   26

2.3 Andrea Pozzo St. Ignazio Corridor LiDAR 3d Scanning; Salvatore and Mancini of Rilevo department, Sapienza University in Rome, rendering by Pablo Lorenzo Eiroa   28

3.1 Palladio's Palazzo Chiericatti indexing an implicit ideal centralized organization; Pablo Lorenzo-Eiroa, after discussions with Guido Zuliani, 2006   34

3.2 A1–F1: 18 Palladian villas without porticos and barchesse buildings retrieved via API; A4–O8: Nine-square square grid Generative Adversarial Networks (GAN) feature recognition training. PI Pablo Lorenzo-Eiroa, RA Salma Kattass, IDC Foundation Grant, 2022. A9–Y14; A15–H18: DM image feed CNN parametric variations. PI Pablo Lorenzo-Eiroa, MidJourney, 2022   36

3.3 A1–E3: 15 Palladio's Villas with barchesse service buildings; Floor plan drawings by Scamozzi and Palladio, Palladio, A. Quatro Libri di Architettura, 1570; Palladium object dissemination Composition by Pablo Lorenzo-Eiroa, 2010–2013. A4–D4: DM parametric variations training via fed image CNN. A5: DM figure-frame dissipation variations developing neighboring relationships as an artificial site; computational variations; Pablo Lorenzo-Eiroa, DM 2022   37

438 *Figures*

3.4 Borges believed that the readers expanded his literature
work creatively 38

4.1 Borromini San Carlo in Rome (1634–67), drawings
interpretations; Design II students: Pamela Cabrera, Andres
Larrauri, Rolando Vega, Elena Cena, Guilherme Nunes,
and Will Shapiro in *Baroque Analysis Studio* Coordinated
by Prof. Michael Young, and with Associate Prof. Felicia
Davis and Associate Prof. Pablo Lorenzo-Eiroa, The
Cooper Union, 2008 44

4.2 Historians' theoretical interpretation of Borromini's San
Carlo's floor plan; PI Pablo Lorenzo-Eiroa, RA Salma
Kattas, IDC Foundation Grant, 2022 46

4.3 Borromini San Carlo theoretical topological conceptual
geometrical reconstruction; Visiting Research Professor
Sapienza University in Rome Pablo Lorenzo-Eiroa, 2015 47

4.4 Borromini's San Carlo walls, pendentive and dome
plannimetric sections based on LiDAR laser 3D scanning
point cloud. Axonometric projection and planimetric
projections intersection by PI Pablo Lorenzo-Eiroa, RA
Salma Kattass, IDC Foundation Grant, NYIT SoAD, 2022 48

4.5 Borromini's San Carlo 3D LiDAR; PI Pablo Lorenzo-
Eiroa, RA Salma Kattass, IDC Foundation Grant, 2022 48

4.6 Borromini's San Carlo, Rendering Point Cloud and
AI processing; PI Pablo Lorenzo-Eiroa, RA Salma
Kattass, IDC Foundation Grant, 2022. This 3D model/
scan was created using: Faro Focus LiDAR, Faro Scene,
RealityCapture software by Capturing Reality 49

4.7 Borromini's San Carlo, Big Data point cloud simulations
Big Data processing, Machine Learning semantic
segmentation 250M points; 3D LiDAR Laser Scanning by
Andrew Saunders with the assistance of Pablo Lorenzo-
Eiroa and Mario Graziano Valenti, Rome 2016. Rendering
Point Cloud and AI processing, PI Pablo Lorenzo-Eiroa,
RA Salma Kattass, IDC Foundation Grant, 2022. This 3D
model/scan was created using: Faro Focus LiDAR, Faro
Scene, RealityCapture software by Capturing Reality 49

4.8 Borromini's San Carlo, 3D LiDAR laser scanning
simulations from top Big Data 250M point cloud; 3D
LiDAR Laser Scanning by Andrew Saunders with the
assistance of Pablo Lorenzo-Eiroa and Mario Graziano
Valenti, Rome 2016. Borromini's San Carlo, Rendering
Point Cloud and AI;PI Pablo Lorenzo-Eiroa, RA Salma
Kattass, IDC Foundation Grant, 2022. This 3D model/
scan was created using: Faro Focus LiDAR, Faro Scene,
RealityCapture software by Capturing Reality 50

Figures 439

4.9 Borromini's San Carlo, point cloud interior simulations representation Big Data 250M; 3D LiDAR Laser Scanning by Andrew Saunders with the assistance of Pablo Lorenzo-Eiroa and Mario Graziano Valenti, Rome 2016. Rendering Point Cloud and AI processing, PI Pablo Lorenzo-Eiroa, RA Salma Kattass, IDC Foundation Grant, 2022. This 3D model/scan was created using: Faro Focus LiDAR, Faro Scene, RealityCapture software by Capturing Reality   51

4.10 Carlo Rainaldi SM in Campitelli, Rome (1656–65) drawings; Design II students Sean Gaffney, Jess Russell, Danny Willis, Malin Heyman, Liya Kohavi and Ge-nan Peng; in Baroque Analysis Studio Coordinated by Prof. Michael Young, and with Associate Prof. Felicia Davis and Associate Prof. Pablo Lorenzo-Eiroa, The Cooper Union, 2008   52

4.11 Big Data 250M point cloud simulations of Carlo Rainaldi SM Campitelli. LiDAR 3D Scanning by Andrew Saunders UPenn, with the assistance of Pablo Lorenzo-Eiroa and Mario Graziano Valenti. This 3D model/scan was created using: Faro LiDAR, RealityCapture software by Capturing Reality. Research, drawings, Big Data representation, processing, and renderings by Associate Visiting Professor, Pablo Lorenzo-Eiroa Sapienza University in Rome 2015   54

4.12 Rainaldi SM Campitelli Big Data 250M point cloud simulations representation, and Big Data processing, implementing Machine Learning classification and semantic segmentation; PI: Pablo Lorenzo-Eiroa, RA: Salma Kattass, IDC Foundation Grant, 2022   55

4.13 Rainaldi SM Campitelli interior point cloud view; This 3D model/scan was created using: Faro Focus LiDAR, Faro Scene, RealityCapture software by Capturing Reality and point cloud processing scripts. PI: Pablo Lorenzo-Eiroa, RA: Salma Kattass, IDC Foundation Grant, 2022   55

4.14 Rainaldi SM Campitelli, anterior space and posterior space in contrast with each other; Associate Visiting Professor, Pablo Lorenzo-Eiroa Sapienza University in Rome, 2015–16   56

4.15 Palladio, Rainaldi, and Borromini plans comparison; Visiting Associate Professor Pablo Lorenzo-Eiroa Sapienza University in Rome 2015–16 and PI: Pablo Lorenzo-Eiroa, RA: Salma Kattass, IDC Foundation Grant, 2022   56

4.16 Rainaldi and Borromini's buildings simulations LiDAR 3D Scan Big Data 250M point cloud; PI: Pablo Lorenzo-Eiroa, RA: Salma Kattass, IDC Foundation Grant, 2022   57

4.17 Borromini and Rainaldi's buildings pretrained and trained dataset AI Machine Learning semantic segmentation

440 *Figures*

	classification; PI: Pablo Lorenzo-Eiroa, RA: Salma Kattass, IDC Foundation Grant, 2022	57
4.18	Rainaldi's Building AI semantic segmentation of LiDAR Big Data 250M Point Cloud; Renderings point cloud representation, Big Data processing, Machine Learning, ML Classification, AI analysis, and design-research, PI: Pablo Lorenzo-Eiroa, RA: Salma Kattass, IDC Foundation Grant, 2022	58
4.19	Rainaldi's Building interior simulation AI semantic segmentation of LiDAR Big Data 250M Point Cloud; 3D model/scan was created using: Faro Focus LiDAR, Faro Scene, RealityCapture software by Capturing Reality and point cloud processing scripts. PI: Pablo Lorenzo-Eiroa, RA: Salma Kattass, IDC Foundation Grant, 2022	59
4.20	Rainaldi's Building interior simulations compared to Borromini's building interior space; AI semantic segmentation of LiDAR Big Data 250M Point Cloud; PI: Pablo Lorenzo-Eiroa, RA: Salma Kattass, IDC Foundation Grant, 2022	60
4.21	Rainaldi's Building floorplan view simulations in relation to Borromini's building floorplans; AI semantic segmentation and Big Data Processing LiDAR 250M Point Cloud; PI: Pablo Lorenzo-Eiroa, RA: Salma Kattass, IDC Foundation Grant, 2022. This 3D model/scan was created using: Faro Focus LiDAR, Faro Scene, RealityCapture software by Capturing Reality	61
4.22	Rainaldi's Building interior simulations compared to Borromini's building interior space; Visiting Associate Professor Pablo Lorenzo-Eiroa Sapienza University in Rome. PI: Pablo Lorenzo-Eiroa, RA: Salma Kattass, IDC Foundation Grant, 2022	62
6.1	Cellular Automation analysis; Venice Biennale Research Studio, Associate Prof. Pablo Lorenzo-Eiroa with Student Ben Sather, NYIT SoAD, F2019	103
6.2	Algorithm resolved through a Flow Chart diagram; Author, 2008	109
6.3	Artificial Neural Network diagram; Author, 2019	117
6.4	Convolution Neural Networks with resolution maps based on input matrix resolution; Author, 2019	119
6.5	Borge's Library of Babel as random character generation; Images developed implementing https://libraryofbabel. info. image: babelia 7321922174580134; Research developed by Prof. Pablo Lorenzo-Eiroa F2018, Library Studio, M.Arch Program Dir. David Diamond, SoAD NYIT	128
6.6	"The Growth Haven Reviving the Historical Sabils of Cairo"; Informed Realism Research Studio, Prof. Pablo	

| | Lorenzo-Eiroa, Student: Yousef Ismail, MS ACT, NYIT, SoAD, F2021 | 128 |

Lorenzo-Eiroa, Student: Yousef Ismail, MS ACT, NYIT, SoAD, F2021 — 128

6.7 NLP LLL prompt engineering activating HLL and CNN feature recognition within a DM activating emergent programming: AI simulation of CFD simulation; Pablo Lorenzo-Eiroa, through MidJourney, 2022 — 132

6.8 NLP DM activating emergent programming CFD simulation; Pablo Lorenzo-Eiroa, DALL-E 2, MidJourney, Stable Diffusion, 2022 — 134

7.1 Google API database representation for work-living public transportation commute use; Ecoinduction III, DOT Presentation, e-Architects Team: Design Principal: Pablo Lorenzo-Eiroa; Designers: Frank Fengqi Li, Julian Chu-Yun Cheng, Shantanu Bhalla, Wayne Shang-Wei Lin Mapping data Work-live relationships: private apartment (green), private bedroom (blue), vs shared bedroom (red), shared office (purple), Air BNB and We Work API; Associate Prof. Pablo Lorenzo-Eiroa, Student: Jose Mateluna, Master of Architecture, The Cooper Union, F2017 — 144

7.2 L-Systems site-based computation; Coordinator Associate Prof. Pablo Lorenzo-Eiroa, Assistant Prof. Dorit Aviv, Instructor Will Shapiro; Student: Jin Woo Lee, The Cooper Union, Master of Architecture, F2015 — 145

7.3 Pixel vectorial node sign; pixel as HCI sign; Author, 2006 — 151

7.4 NURBS curve or Spline line construction composed of at least a Bézier curve; Author, 2006 — 152

7.5 NURBS Surface degree 3 containing cells, hulls, and control points; Author, 2006 — 153

7.6 Computational Fluid Dynamic (CFD) Simulation studies; Pablo Lorenzo-Eiroa, 2002–2006 with diagrams applied to student's base simulations by Elan Fessler and Mack Cooper William, ARCH 177, The Cooper Union, 2006 — 153

7.7 AI Semantic Segmentation and Voxel downsampling of point cloud; AI and voxelation by author; 3D Scan by UIC Barcelona Workshop, Prof. Pablo Lorenzo-Eiroa, students: Ciurel, Dragos, Juárez; Martin; Memi, Mouradian, Nabbouh, Rahmani, Sönmez, Tabikh, Vanhoegaerden, Warang, 2017 — 155

7.8 Big Data Point Cloud simulation referencing data entry points and relating them across different multidimensional data sets. PI Pablo Lorenzo-Eiroa, 2022 — 156

7.9 AI Semantic Segmentation and Style Transfer; GAN style transfer through semantic segmentation feature recognition of Van Gogh's "A Wheatfield, with Cypresses", NVIDIA

442 *Figures*

GauGAN, NVIDIA Canvas, and CNN, GANs, DCNN, DM, over Author Composition 2017–2021 159

7.10 "Ur-Realism AI" vertical Colònia Güell in New York City, Gaudi AI DM style Transfer; Pablo Lorenzo-Eiroa, MidJourney, 2022 168

7.11 2D to 3D; Monocular Depth Estimation via Content-Adaptive multi-resolution merging to implement ML monocular machine vision from 2D MidJourney to a dynamic navigable 3D model DCNN, CNN, DM; PI Pablo Lorenzo-Eiroa, RA Kavya Sista, IDC Foundation Grant, 2022 169

7.12 AI object tracking recognition and semantic segmentation real-time video feed; Research Studio Prof. Pablo Lorenzo-Eiroa, Student Kavya Sista, ARCH 701B, MS ACT, NYIT, F2021 169

7.13 A1–D4: Pablo Lorenzo-Eiroa, Point-e, 2022. A5–D5: 2D DM to 3D Point Cloud, ARCH 782, NYIT, PI Pablo Lorenzo-Eiroa, RA Beken Amde, IDC Foundation Grant Research, RS Tharoonaskar Baskaran; RS Mahima Kulkarni, S2023 170

7.14 Information representation structures in computation; Author, 2008 180

8.1 Interfaces deep structure background space-frames and signs; Author, 2006 189

8.2 Grids topological degree variations in relation to categorical typological change; Coordinator and Associate Prof. Pablo Lorenzo Eiroa, Assistant Prof. James Lowder and Intructor Katerina Kourkuola; student: Sehee Lee, The Cooper Union, Design II, F2012 190

8.3 Pixel disambiguation; Typology|Topology studio, Head Professor and Coordinator Pablo Lorenzo-Eiroa with instructors Matt Roman, Katerina Kourkoula, and Will Shapiro; students: Akash Godbole and Ian Houser, The Cooper Union, Design II, F2013 191

8.4 A pixel delimiting space by defining various sig-values; Typology|Topology studio, Head Professor and Coordinator Pablo Lorenzo-Eiroa with instructors Matt Roman, Katerina Kourkoula, and Will Shapiro; students: Akash Godbole and Ian Houser, The Cooper Union, Design II, F2013 192

8.5 Grid by coding boundaries between spaces through points; Typology|Topology studio, Coordinator and Associate Prof. Pablo Lorenzo-Eiroa, Assistant Prof. James Lowder, instructor Katerina Kourkoula; students: Cory Hall, The Cooper Union, Design II, F2012 194

8.6	Grid by coding boundaries between spaces through points; Typology-Topology Studio, Coordinator and Associate Prof. Pablo Lorenzo-Eiroa with instructors Matt Roman, Katerina Kourkoula, and Will Shapiro, Students Aelitta Gore and Daniel Hall, The Cooper Union, Design II, F2013	195
8.7	Grid by coding boundaries between spaces through points, floor plan; Typology-Topology Studio, Coordinator and Associate Prof. Pablo Lorenzo-Eiroa with instructors Matt Roman, Katerina Kourkoula, and Will Shapiro, Students Aelitta Gore and Daniel Hall, The Cooper Union, Design II, F2013	196
8.8	Nine square grid space-frame coding to motivate the figuration of the project via Processing®; Typology-Topology Studio, Coordinator and Associate Prof. Pablo Lorenzo-Eiroa with instructors Matt Roman, Katerina Kourkoula, and Will Shapiro, Students Piau Liu and Maya Krtic, The Cooper Union, Design II, F2013	197
8.9	12 Palladian Villas through digital signifiers; Typology|Topology second year studio, Typology-Topology Studio, Coordinator and Associate Prof. Pablo Lorenzo-Eiroa with instructors Matt Roman, Katerina Kourkoula, and Will Shapiro, students: Lucas Chao, Aimilios Davlantis Lo, Akash Godbole, Aelitta Gore, Pedro Galindo Landeira, Gabriela Gutierrez, Daniel Hall, James Hansen, Connor Holjes, Ian Houser, Shin Young, Jisoo Kim, Sam Koopman, Luke Kreul, Maya Krtic, Kelsey Lee, Hui Jung Liu, Piao Liu, Sofia Machaira, Wilson Muller, Celine Park, Joseph Parrella, Stephanie Restrepo, Jonathan Small, Chi-Hsuan (Vita) Wang; The Cooper Union, Design II, F2013	198
8.10	Parametric grid displacing originating signs and urban typologies; Coordinator Associate Prof. Pablo Lorenzo-Eiroa, Assistant Professor Lydia Xynogala, Instructor Will Shapiro; Student: Nan Lei, Master of Architecture, The Cooper Union, 2014	199
8.11	Grid displaced through topological minimal surfaces; Museum Program, Assoc. Prof. and Curriculum Coordinator Pablo Lorenzo-Eiroa; student: Peter Panagi, ARCH 202, NYIT, SoAD S2020	200
8.12	AI Cellular Automation voxels displaced by minimal surfaces; Interscalar Fluidity, Venice Biennale Installation ARCH 501-502, Prof. Pablo Lorenzo-Eiroa with student: Benjamin Sather, S-Lab Grant, NYIT, SoAD F2019	201
8.13	New York City Public Library automated book deposit shelves reconfiguration; Informed Realism Research	

Studio, Associate Prof. PI Pablo Lorenzo-Eiroa, Visiting
Assistant Prof. Fengq Li, RA student: Trushita Yadav,
ARCH 701B, MS ACT, NYIT SoAD, 2022 — 202

8.14 Infinitively variable infinitively expanded grids defined by
infinite elements and infinite dimensions; DM engineered
through NLP to retrieve via API team research work
(2006–2014). PI Pablo Lorenzo-Eiroa, MidJourney, 2022 — 203

9.1 0D points, vectorial point grid; Author, 2006 — 211

9.2 Vectors activating one-dimension, two-dimension and
three-dimensions; Prof. Pablo Lorenzo-Eiroa, Students:
Joseph Jemuel and Marcus Birman, ARCH 482B, The
Cooper Union, S2015 — 212

9.3 1D Curves defining 3D space through mathematical
logarithmic limits; Machines to "Draw and Build",
Professor Pablo Lorenzo-Eiroa. Students: Jisoo Kim, Jieun
Hannah Kim; Akash Godbole, Connor Holjes, Ian Houser,
Arch 482B Arch 177, S2015 — 213

9.4 Photoshop® pixelation and filters photogrammetry;
Author, 2000 — 214

9.5 Mathematical surface parametric plot; Machines to "Draw
and Build", Prof. Pablo Lorenzo-Eiroa, Students: Zachary
Hall, Rain Yu Kiu Chan. ARCH 177: Gabriel Munnich,
Yaoyi Fan; Jemuel Joseph, Luis Figallo; Alberto Martinez
Garcia, Kevin Savillon, Natalia Oliveri; Bing Dai, James
Seung Hwan, Jin Lee; Zachary Hall, Rain Yu Kiu Chan,
Mireya Fabregas, Julia Di Pietro, Arch 482B, The Cooper
Union S2016 — 215

9.6 Parametric surface plot identifying logarithmic limits
representation; Prof. Pablo Lorenzo-Eiroa, Students:
Zachary Hall, Rain Yu Kiu Chan, ARCH 177, The
Cooper Union, S2016 — 216

9.7 Topological surface defining 3D space; Associate Prof.
Pablo Lorenzo Eiroa (coordinator), assistant Prof. James
Lowder and Instructor Katerina Kourkuola, student:
Maximillian Gideonese, Arch 121, The Cooper Union,
Design II F2012 — 217

9.8 Topological surface-space parameterized in relation to its
referential Cartesian space; *Platonic Möbius Strip*, Design
Principal: Pablo Lorenzo-Eiroa, e-Architects, NY 2008;
variable space-time density; Hypercube. Pablo Lorenzo-
Eiroa, 2022 — 219

9.9 *House IIa*; Design Principal: Pablo Lorenzo-Eiroa,
e-Architects, NY 2010 — 219

9.10 *−X, X −Y, Y −Z, Z House IIb, Endless Infinite House;* Design
Principal: Pablo Lorenzo-Eiroa, Design Assistants: Luo
Xuan, Pedro Joaquin, NY 2013 — 221

9.11	Worms' eye view axonometric and elevations *House IIB, Endless Infinite House: −X, X −Y, Y −Z, Z*; Design Principal: Pablo Lorenzo-Eiroa. Research Assistant: Luo Xuan, Pedro Joaquin, NY 2013	222
9.12	Guggenheim Museum Helsinki Competition Entry: GH-8746022806; Design Principal: Pablo Lorenzo-Eiroa; Design Team: Felicia Killiot, Peter Douglas; Renderings: Craft CG, e-Architects, New York, 2014	224
9.13	House V DM; Pablo Lorenzo-Eiroa, e-Architects, MidJourney, 2022	225
9.14	House V DM; Pablo Lorenzo-Eiroa, e-Architects, DALL-E and MidJourney, 2022	226
9.15	House IV Hypercube and Andrea Pozzo hyperdimensional space-frames DM; Pablo Lorenzo-Eiroa, MidJourney, 2022	227
9.16	Qubit; Pablo Lorenzo Eiroa, Wolfram Mathematica, 2019	231
10.1	Parque de la Costa, Vicente Lopez, Buenos Aires; Architects: Francisco Cadau, Fernando Gimenez, Manuel Galvez, Pablo Lorenzo-Eiroa; Designers: Florencia Rausch and Santiago Pages; Landscape Design: Lucia Schiappapietra; Amancio Williams Structure reconstruction: Claudio Veckstein; 1999–2001	241
10.2	Sedimentation deposition particle aggregate simulation and simulation deployment in NYC topography; *Structuring Fluid Territories after Hurricane Sandy*, Professor Pablo Lorenzo-Eiroa, students Katherine Bajo and Gregory Shikhman, ARCH 177/482B, The Cooper Union, 2012	241
10.3	Nine square grid parametric surfaces problematizing digital fabrication; Machines to "draw" and "build", Professor Pablo Lorenzo-Eiroa; Students: A1–C1: Jemuel Joseph and Luis Figallo; A2–B2: Gabriel Munnich and Yaoyi Fan; ARCH 177/482B, The Cooper Union, S2016	242
10.4	3d Printing through laser cured resins; Prof. Pablo Lorenzo-Eiroa, Students: Keren Mendjul, ARCH 482B, The Cooper Union, F2016	242
10.5	Generative reformulation of Bernini's sculpture displacing authorship applying machine vision to a DM. PI Pablo Lorenzo-Eiroa, RA Beken Amde, IDC Foundation Grant, 2022	243
10.6	A stereographic projective geometry of the n normal vector; Author, 2006	245
10.7	Mathematical parametric surface plots and their material actualizations; Research Studio, Prof. Pablo Lorenzo-Eiroa, Student: Salma Kattass, ARCH 702B, MS ACT Program, SoAD, NYIT S2022. Mathematical formula and comparative surfaces u and v PI Pablo Lorenzo-Eiroa, RA Trushita Yadav, IDC Foundation, 2022	246

446 *Figures*

10.8 Parametric surface plots identifying typological variation displacing dimensionally points as singularity and voids as negative space *translating* between different interfaces, media, and mediums; Research Studio, Prof. Pablo Lorenzo-Eiroa, Student: Salma Kattass, ARCH 702B, MS ACT, SoAD, NYIT S2022 247

10.9 Dieste's Atlantida Church wall mathematical parametric plot studies; Research Studio, Prof. Pablo Lorenzo-Eiroa, Student: Yousef Ismail, ARCH 702B MS ACT Program, SoAD, NYIT S2022 249

10.10 AI architecture of information fabrication workflow framework; Research Studio, Prof. Pablo Lorenzo-Eiroa, Student Salma Kattass, ARCH 702B, MS ACT Program, SoAD, NYIT S2022 250

10.11 Clay 3D Printing workflow framework; Research Studio, Prof. Pablo Lorenzo-Eiroa, Students: Yousef Ismail, Salma Kattass, Farah Jalil, ARCH 702B MS ACT Program, SoAD, NYIT S2022 251

10.12 Laser plotting system correlating background media and foreground emergent design; Machines to "Draw" and "Build", Prof. Pablo Lorenzo-Eiroa, students: Gabriel Munnich and Yaoyi Fan, ARCH 177/482B, The Cooper Union, 2015 254

10.13 Laser beam defining a space-environment; Machines to "Draw" and "Build", Prof. Pablo Lorenzo-Eiroa, students: Gabriel Munnich and Yaoyi Fan, ARCH 177/482B, The Cooper Union, 2015 255

10.14 The emergent machines to draw and build are meant to critique the structuralism imposed by known technologies, tools, and machines of representation. By developing a drawing tool using physical computation a laser beam projects the virtual geometry of a parametric surface into a shifting interface-background space, problematizing the spectrum between the subject and the object, by instead, developing a project by motivating the interface (medium) and its background machinic reference technology. Machines to Draw and Build, Prof. Pablo Lorenzo-Eiroa, students: Gabriel Munnich and Yaoyi Fan, ARCH 177/482B, The Cooper Union, 2015 255

11.1 Gaudi's Sagrada Familia through mathematics; Parametric Gaudi, Visiting Prof. Pablo Lorenzo Eiroa, with Students Ernesto Arias, Alejandro Cruz Mendoza, Ronaldo Fiuza, Bruno Jaramillo, David Romero Martel, Dario Sanchez, Sarah Winkler and Harold Woods; TA Pablo Baquero, UIC Biodigital Master Program Dir. Alberto T. Estévez, 2014 262

11.2 Parametric Gaudi installation; *Parametric Gaudi*, Visiting Prof. Pablo Lorenzo Eiroa, with Students Ernesto

	Arias, Alejandro Cruz Mendoza, Ronaldo Fiuza, Bruno Jaramillo, David Romero Martel, Dario Sanchez, Sarah Winkler and Harold Woods; TA Pablo Baquero, UIC Biodigital Master Program Dir. Alberto T. Estévez, 2014	263
11.3	Parametric Gaudi, CNC fabrication details indexing mathematical parametric equations; Parametric Gaudi, Visiting Prof. Pablo Lorenzo Eiroa, with Students Ernesto Arias, Alejandro Cruz Mendoza, Ronaldo Fiuza, Bruno Jaramillo, David Romero Martel, Dario Sanchez, Sarah Winkler and Harold Woods; TA Pablo Baquero, UIC Biodigital Master Program Dir. Alberto T. Estévez, 2014	264
11.4	Sagrada Familia 3D scanning photogrammetry point cloud through multiple perspectival camera registrations; Visiting Associate Prof. Pablo Lorenzo-Eiroa, Students: Nemer Nabbough, Biodigital Master Program, Dir. Alberto T. Estévez, 2017	265
11.5	Gaudi Sagrada Familia 3D scanning photogrammetry in contrast to digital 3D model; Visiting Assoc. Prof. Pablo Lorenzo-Eiroa, Students: Abdulrahman All Harib and Galkina Valerija, Biodigital Master Program Dir. Alberto Estevez, 2019	266
11.6	Gaudi Sagrada Familia structural simulation surface relaxation composing topological surfaces; Visiting Assoc. Prof. Pablo Lorenzo-Eiroa, Students: Abdulrahman All Harib and Galkina Valerija, Biodigital Master Program Dir. Alberto Estevez, 2019	267
11.7	Gaudi Sagrada Familia 3D model in contrast with structural simulation and 3D scan photogrammetry; Visiting Associate Professor Pablo Lorenzo-Eiroa UIC, Students: Secil Afsar, Margaret Tara Maalouf, Joy Nakad, Biodigital Architecture Master Program, Dir. Alberto T. Estévez, 2019	268
11.8	Gaudi's analog computational model replicated through digital structural simulation, applying Cellular Automation (CA); PI Pablo Lorenzo-Eiroa with RA Yousef Ismail, Salma Kattass, and Farah Jalil, ARCH 703B PBL Studio, ISRC TLT Grant 2022, SoAD, NYIT S2022	269
11.9	Gaudi Sagrada Familia reinterpretation structural simulation; Visiting Associate Prof. Pablo Lorenzo-Eiroa, students: Al Surekha Dasari, Rakan Ali, Khadija Al Chami. A2–C2: Mesh optimization structural simulation, students: Nadin Tarek Elgazzar, Tintswalo Mabuza, Mahmoud, Fattahi; UIC Barcelona, Biodigital Master Program Dir. Alberto T Estévez, S2020	270
11.10	Google Deep Dream AI feature recognition through machine vision pareidolia; Visiting Associate Prof. Pablo	

448 *Figures*

Lorenzo-Eiroa, Students: Tara Malaaouf and Joy Secil, 2019. A2: Big Data Survey, structural mesh simulation, and GAN style transfer of Gaudi's Sagrada Familia. Pablo Lorenzo-Eiroa GAN style transfer over workshop results by students: Nadin Tarek Elgazzar, Tintswalo Mabuza, Mahmoud, Fattahi; 2020. A3–C3: Sagrada Familia reinterpretation Visiting Associate Prof. Pablo Lorenzo-Eiroa, students: Alonso Ramirez, Natalia, Maksoud, Mohammed, Tipnis, Mruga, UIC Barcelona, Biodigital Master Program Dir. Alberto T. Estévez, S2020   271

11.11   AI DM Gaudi Sagrada Familia prompt engineering and feature recognition emergent programming structural simulation; Pablo Lorenzo-Eiroa over Gaudi's dataset, MidJourney, 2022   272

11.12   AI DMGaudi Sagrada Familia prompt engineering and feature recognition emergent programming structural simulation; Pablo Lorenzo-Eiroa over Gaudi's dataset, MidJourney, 2022   273

12.1   Incremental Sheet Forming (ISF) actualizing information by activating a material physical computation; Visiting Associate Prof. Pablo Lorenzo-Eiroa, with TA Gabriel Munnich and Yaoyi Fann, UIC Barcelona S2017   278

12.2   Topographic robotic contouring from "drawing" to "scoring" to "scraping" to "building"; Canvascraper Exhibition: e-Architects, NY; Design Principal: Pablo Lorenzo-Eiroa; Design Team: Yaoyi Fann and Gabriel Munnich; Exhibition Curator: Steven Hillyer and Nader Tehrani; The Cooper Union Archive, Dean's Wall, F2017   279

12.3   Minimal surfaces detail; Canvascraper Exhibition: e-Architects, NY; Design Principal: Pablo Lorenzo-Eiroa; Design Team: Yaoyi Fann and Gabriel Munnich; Exhibition Curator: Steven Hillyer and Nader Tehrani; The Cooper Union Archive, Dean's Wall, F2017   280

12.4   Gaudi Sagrada Familia 3D Scan and point cloud projection as information actualization; Group pieces, UIC Barcelona studio workshop, Pablo Lorenzo-Eiroa with Teaching Assistants Gabriel Munnich and Yaoyi Fan, 2017   282

12.5   A1: Gaudi's Sagrada Familia ceiling. B1: Metal piece through ISF. C1: GAN style transfer; AI GAN style transfer through CNN feature recognition, Pablo Lorenzo-Eiroa, 2018 using group workshop pieces UIC Barcelona studio workshop, Pablo Lorenzo-Eiroa with Teaching Assistants Gabriel Munnich and Yaoyi Fan, students: Ciurel, Silvia; Dragos, Brescan; Juárez, David Gabriel;

Martin, Perry; Memisoglu, Misra; Mouradian, Never; Nabbouh, Nemer; Rahmani, Tarek; Sönmez, Cemal; Tabikh, Fouad; Vanhoegaerden, Luciemarthe F; Warang, Angad; 2017 283

12.6 AI DM Shell Structures style transfer feature recognition activating emergent programming simulation, interior space-frames; Pablo Lorenzo-Eiroa, MidJourney, 2022 283

12.7 AI DM Shell Structures style transfer feature recognition activating emergent programming simulation, exterior views; Pablo Lorenzo-Eiroa, MidJourney, 2022 284

12.8 AI VQGAN ML Training feature recognition; PI. Pablo Lorenzo-Eiroa, RA. Salma Kattass, Yousef Ismail and Kavya Sista, Institutional Support of Research and Creativity Grant, NYIT, 2022 285

12.9 AI VQGAN ML Training feature recognition; PI. Pablo Lorenzo-Eiroa, RA. Salma Kattass, Yousef Ismail and Kavya Sista, Institutional Support of Research and Creativity Grant, NYIT, 2022 286

12.10 Concatenated multigenerational correlational catenary structures; PI Pablo Lorenzo-Eiroa, MidJourney over feature recognition through Convolution and training the DM through RLHF, 2023 287

12.11 3D ML Point Cloud Classification and 3D GAN's prediction model based on Big Data 3D scanning of Sagrada Familia; PI Pablo Lorenzo-Eiroa, RA: Yousef Ismail, Farah Jalil, and Salma Kattass; 3D GAN's and voxelation RA Kavya Sista, Institutional Support of Research and Creativity Grant, NYIT, 2022 288

12.12 3D GANs semantic segmentation mapping after feature recognition implementing 3D point cloud and voxel repository training. PI Pablo Lorenzo-Eiroa, RA: Yousef Ismail, Farah Jalil, Salma Kattass, Farah Jalil and Kavya Sista, Institutional Support of Research and Creativity Grant, NYIT, 2022 289

12.13 Structural Simulation variations; PI Pablo Lorenzo-Eiroa with RA Yousef Ismail, Salma Kattass, Farah Jalil; Institutional Support of Research and Creativity Grant, NYIT, 2022 290

12.14 ISF displaced through a robotic fabrication process; PI Pablo Lorenzo-Eiroa, RA: Yousef Ismail, Salma Kattass, Farah Jalil; *2022 Institutional Support of Research and Creativity Grant* (ISRC) MS.ACT, NYIT 2022 291

12.15 Robotic fabrication tiles; PI Pablo Lorenzo-Eiroa, RA: Yousef Ismail, Salma Kattass, Farah Jalil; *2022 Institutional Support of Research and Creativity Grant* (ISRC) MS.ACT Program NYIT 2022 292

450 *Figures*

12.16 Tiles recomposing an unfold partially flat organization. PI Pablo Lorenzo-Eiroa, RA: Yousef Ismail, Salma Kattass, Farah Jalil, Beken Amde and Trushita Yadav; *2022 Institutional Support of Research and Creativity Grant* (ISRC) MS.ACT Program NYIT 2022 293

12.17 Partial installation mock-up with openings to receive concatenated shell generations. PI Pablo Lorenzo-Eiroa, RA: Yousef Ismail, Salma Kattass, Farah Jalil, Beken Amde, Trushita Yadav, and Mahima Kulkarni; students: Tharoonaskar Baskaran, Arathi Chilla, Kush A. Shah, Tiarnan Mathers, 2022 Institutional Support of Research and Creativity Grant (ISRC) MS.ACT Program NYIT 2022 294

12.18 Gaudi's New York City; PI Pablo Lorenzo-Eiroa, RA: Yousef Ismail, Salma Kattass, Farah Jalil, Beken Amde, Trushita Yadav, and Mahima Kulkarni; and Tharoonaskar Baskaran, Arathi Chilla, Kush A. Shah, Tiarnan Mathers. 2022 Institutional Support of Research and Creativity Grant (ISRC); Proposal for Stapleton Waterfront Park, Staten Island, sponsors e-Architects.net and DLO, sponsored public installation by NYC Parks and Recreation; S2023 295

13.1 Swarm Intelligence agent-based modeling (ABM); Venice Biennale Installation Preliminary Proposal, *Interscalar Fluidity*, Prof. Pablo Lorenzo-Eiroa with students: Andres Carcamo; Brianna Lopez; Peter Leonardi; Alexandra Panichella; Ari Begun; Oluwayemi Oyewole; Karina Pena; Isaiah Miller; Benjamin Sather; ARCH 501–502 SoAD, NYIT; S-Lab Grant, Dean Maria Perbellini's Incentive, F2019 301

13.2 Architectural fragments of different scales and densities; Interscalar Fluidity, Venice Biennale Final Installation Prof. Pablo Lorenzo-Eiroa with Students: Andres Carcamo: "Iconography Architecture"; Brianna Lopez: "Parametric Flow"; Peter Leonardi: "Structural Typologies"; Alexandra Panichella: "Material transitions: Feedback between the Analog and the Digital"; Ari Begun: "Spatially Interactive Light"; Oluwayemi Oyewole: "Structural Optimization"; Karina Pena: "Dynamics of Humidity and Temperature Advantages"; Isaiah Miller: "Sonic + Sensory"; Benjamin Sather: "[c]ellular Surfaces"; ARCH 501–502 SoAD, NYIT; S-Lab Grant, Dean Maria Perbellini's Incentive, F2019 302

13.3 Cellular Automation (CA) rules; *Interscalar Fluidity*, Venice Biennale Installation Prof. Pablo Lorenzo-Eiroa with Students: Benjamin Sather ARCH 501–502 SoAD, NYIT; S-Lab Grant, Dean Maria Perbellini's Incentive, F2019 303

13.4	A1: CA evolutionary simulation voxels. B1: CA evolutionary simulation actualized as continuous surfaces; *Interscalar Fluidity*, Venice Biennale Installation Prof. Pablo Lorenzo-Eiroa with Students: Benjamin Sather ARCH 501–502 SoAD, NYIT; S-Lab Grant, Dean Maria Perbellini's Incentive, F2019	304
13.5	CA computational design evolutionary self-organizing site-based simulation continuous surface topology; *Interscalar Fluidity*, Venice Biennale Installation Prof. Pablo Lorenzo-Eiroa with Students: Benjamin Sather ARCH 501–502 SoAD, NYIT; S-Lab Grant, Dean Maria Perbellini's Incentive, F2019	305
13.6	CA as discrete site-based evolutionary computation integrated as a continuous minimal surface topology; *Interscalar Fluidity*, Venice Biennale Installation Prof. Pablo Lorenzo-Eiroa with Student: Benjamin Sather; ARCH 501–502 SoAD, NYIT; S-Lab Grant, Dean Maria Perbellini's Incentive, F2019	306
13.7	3D printing of CA simulated fragments studying possible means to activating minimal surfaces in the print actualization; *Interscalar Fluidity*, Venice Biennale Installation Prof. Pablo Lorenzo-Eiroa with Student: Benjamin Sather; ARCH 501–502 SoAD, NYIT; S-Lab Grant, Dean Maria Perbellini's Incentive, F2019	307
13.8	CA simulation contained within explicit boundaries and in relation to the existing installation room; *Interscalar Fluidity*, Venice Biennale Installation Prof. Pablo Lorenzo-Eiroa with Student: Benjamin Sather; ARCH 501–502 SoAD, NYIT; S-Lab Grant, Dean Maria Perbellini's Incentive, F2019	308
13.9	*Interscalar Fluidity* mock-up model; Interscalar Fluidity, Prof. Pablo Lorenzo-Eiroa with students: Andres Carcamo; Brianna Lopez; Peter Leonardi; Alexandra Panichella; Ari Begun:; Oluwayemi Oyewole; Karina Pena; Isaiah Miller; Benjamin Sather; ARCH 501–502 SoAD, NYIT; S-Lab Grant, Dean Maria Perbellini's Incentive, F2019	309
13.10	Robotic Fabrication simulation and G-Code; *Interscalar Fluidity*, Venice Biennale Installation Prof. Pablo Lorenzo-Eiroa with Thesis Students: Benjamin Sather and Andres Carcamo; ARCH 501–502 SoAD, NYIT; S-Lab Grant, Dean Maria Perbellini's Incentive, F2019	310
13.11	CA-based 3D Printed prototypes exploring different computational design surface density and attractors; *Interscalar Fluidity*, Venice Biennale Installation Prof. Pablo Lorenzo-Eiroa with Student: Benjamin Sather,	

452 *Figures*

ARCH 501–502 SoAD, NYIT; S-Lab Grant, Dean Maria Perbellini's Incentive, F2019 — 311

13.12 CA minimal surfaces topological continuity between positive and negative spaces, 3D Printing Fused Deposition Modeling (FDM); *Interscalar Fluidity*, Venice Biennale Installation Prof. Pablo Lorenzo-Eiroa with Student: Benjamin Sather; ARCH 501–502 SoAD, NYIT; S-Lab Grant, Dean Maria Perbellini's Incentive, F2019 — 312

13.13 Landscape AI interpretation based on image depth recognition; *Interscalar Fluidity*, Venice Biennale Installation Prof. Pablo Lorenzo-Eiroa with Student: Brianna Lopez; ARCH 501–502 SoAD, NYIT; S-Lab Grant, Dean Maria Perbellini's Incentive, F2019 — 313

13.14 Synthetic AI landscape topography simulated as a shell structure. AI-based computer vision weather simulation remapping as feature extraction; *Interscalar Fluidity,* Venice Biennale Installation Prof. Pablo Lorenzo-Eiroa with Student: Brianna Lopez; ARCH 501–502 SoAD, NYIT; S-Lab Grant, Dean Maria Perbellini's Incentive, F2019 — 313

13.15 Synthetic shell structure as landscape; Interscalar Fluidity, Venice Biennale Installation Prof. Pablo Lorenzo-Eiroa with Student: Brianna Lopez; ARCH 501–502 SoAD, NYIT; S-Lab Grant, Dean Maria Perbellini's Incentive, F2019 — 314

13.16 A1, B1: Varying 3D printing FDM in relation to structure stress. C1, D1: Swarm Intelligence applying Agent-Based Modeling for structural form finding; *Interscalar Fluidity*, Venice Biennale Installation Prof. Pablo Lorenzo-Eiroa with Student: Brianna Lopez, ARCH 501–502 SoAD, NYIT; S-Lab Grant, Dean Maria Perbellini's Incentive, F2019 — 314

13.17 Different types of Swarm Intelligence simulations to optimize materialization; *Interscalar Fluidity*, Venice Biennale Installation Prof. Pablo Lorenzo-Eiroa with Student: Brianna Lopez, ARCH 501–502 SoAD, NYIT; S-Lab Grant, Dean Maria Perbellini's Incentive, F2019 — 315

13.18 Structural catenary and cross-bracing simulation and optimization; *Interscalar Fluidity*, Venice Biennale Final Proposal Installation Prof. Pablo Lorenzo-Eiroa with Student: Alexandra Panichella: ARCH 501–502 SoAD, NYIT; S-Lab Grant, Dean Maria Perbellini's Incentive, F2019 — 316

13.19 Structural simulation optimization; *Interscalar Fluidity,* Venice Biennale Final Proposal Installation Prof. Pablo Lorenzo-Eiroa with Student: Oluwayemi Oyewole, ARCH 501–502 SoAD, NYIT; S-Lab Grant, Dean Maria Perbellini's Incentive, F2019 — 317

Figures 453

13.20 Thermal simulation; Prof. Pablo Lorenzo-Eiroa with
Students: Karina Pena, informing Oluwayemi Oyewole
and Brianna Lopez, ARCH 501–502 SoAD, NYIT; S-Lab
Grant, Dean Maria Perbellini's Incentive, F2019   318

13.21 Interactive immersive atmospheric light; *Interscalar Fluidity*,
Venice Biennale Installation Prof. Pablo Lorenzo-Eiroa
with Student: Ari Begun, ARCH 501–502 SoAD, NYIT;
S-Lab Grant, Dean Maria Perbellini's Incentive, F2019   319

13.22 Acoustic frequency readings, simulation, and physical
testing; *Interscalar Fluidity*, Venice Biennale Final Proposal
Prof. Pablo Lorenzo-Eiroa with Student: Isaiah Miller,
ARCH 501–502 SoAD, NYIT; S-Lab Grant, Dean Maria
Perbellini's Incentive, F2019   320

13.23 Interactive visual and acoustic immersive responsive
space; *Interscalar Fluidity*, Venice Biennale Final
Proposal with Individual by Student Thesis Installation
Prof. Pablo Lorenzo-Eiroa with Student: Isaiah
Miller: "Sonic + Sensory" ARCH 501–502 SoAD, NYIT;
S-Lab Grant, Dean Maria Perbellini's Incentive, F2019   321

13.24 1D Point Based CA evolutionary infinite simulation,
forced perspectival illusionistic projection pairing physical
forced perspectival space in continuity with virtual forced
space; Prof Pablo Lorenzo-Eiroa with Student: Benjamin
Sather, ARCH 501–502 SoAD, NYIT; S-Lab Grant, Dean
Maria Perbellini's Incentive, F2019   322

13.25 Virtual Reality, AR, ER; *Interscalar Fluidity*, Venice
Biennale Installation Prof. Pablo Lorenzo-Eiroa with
Students: Andres Carcamo, Brianna Lopez, Peter Leonardi,
Alexandra Panichella, Ari Begun, Oluwayemi Oyewole,
Karina Pena, Isaiah Miller, Benjamin Sather; ARCH 501–
502 SoAD, NYIT; S-Lab Grant, Dean Maria Perbellini's
Incentive, F2019   323

13.26 Virtual Reality navigation of installation; *Interscalar Fluidity*,
Venice Biennale Installation Prof. Pablo Lorenzo-Eiroa
with Students: Andres Carcamo, Brianna Lopez, Peter
Leonardi, Alexandra Panichella, Ari Begun, Oluwayemi
Oyewole, Karina Pena, Isaiah Miller, Benjamin Sather;
ARCH 501–502 SoAD, NYIT; S-Lab Grant, Dean Maria
Perbellini's Incentive, F2019   324

14.1 e-Architects' Site-Specific Robotic 3d printer tensegrity
prototype; e-Architects, NY Design Principal, R/D: Pablo
Lorenzo-Eiroa; Designers, R/D: Gabriel Munnich, Yaoyi
Fan, Pablo Toubes-Rieger, Nelson Montas, 2017–18   329

14.2 e-Chaise Longue mathematical topological variations
identifying distinct body positions; e-Architects, NY

454 *Figures*

14.3 Design Principal, R/D: Pablo Lorenzo-Eiroa; Designers, R/D: Gabriel Munnich, Yaoyi Fan, Pablo Toubes-Rieger, Nelson Montas; ADG Structural Engineering Aamer Islam, 2017–18   330

14.3 Shape Memory Polymer simulation for 3D printing material; e-Architects, NY Design Principal, R/D: Pablo Lorenzo-Eiroa; Designers, R/D: Gabriel Munnich, Yaoyi Fan, Pablo Toubes-Rieger, Nelson Montas; 2017–18   331

14.4 Installation of Tensegrity Site Specific 3D Printer prototype at e-Architects; e-Architects, NY Design Principal, R/D: Pablo Lorenzo-Eiroa; Designers, R/D: Gabriel Munnich, Yaoyi Fan, Pablo Toubes-Rieger, Nelson Montas; 2017–18   332

14.5 e-Architects' e-Chaise Longue through Site-Specific Robotic 3d printer, 2018 Venice Biennale (GAA/ECC); e-Architects, NY Design Principal, R/D: Pablo Lorenzo-Eiroa; Designers, R/D: Gabriel Munnich, Yaoyi Fan, Pablo Toubes-Rieger, Nelson Montas; 2017–18   333

14.6 Final prototype functional with a range of prints; e(eiroa)-Architects, NY Design Principal, R/D: Pablo Lorenzo-Eiroa; Designers, R/D: Gabriel Munnich, Yaoyi Fan, Pablo Toubes-Rieger, Nelson Montas; 2017–18   334

14.7 Spider 3d Cable Driven technology adaptable to multiple contexts and conditions; e-Architects, NY Design Principal, R/D: Pablo Lorenzo-Eiroa; Designers, R/D: Gabriel Munnich Yaoyi Fan, Pablo Toubes-Rieger, Nelson Montas; 2017–18   335

15.1 A1–D1: Mississippi River Delta, sedimentation deposition survey; Pablo Lorenzo-Eiroa, 2004. A2–G2: CFD simulations to analyze, and work with environmental forces; Prof. Pablo Lorenzo-Eiroa with students Elan Fessler and Mack Cooper William, ARCH 177, The Cooper Union, 2006. A3–D4: 2D DM activating 3D CFD simulation as AI emergent programming. PI Pablo Lorenzo-Eiroa, MidJourney, 2022   341

15.2 A1: Image captured by MODIS sensor on NASA's Terra satellite on April 12, 2007. Wikipedia Commons. Rio de la Plata, Buenos Aires, and Colonia, sedimentation from the Parana River Delta deposition, which develops an estuary. B1–D1: Satellite image and thermal reading downsampling layering, Pablo Lorenzo-Eiroa, Fulbright Application 1998–2000. A2, B2, C2: Buenos Aires-Colonia International Bridge Study affecting the environmental stability of the Rio de la Plata; Prepared for the World Bank. Commission "Puente a Colonia", Director Ing.

Agustoni, provided 1998. D2: Rio de la Plata CFD to study possible connections as an environmental network inducing sedimentation; Pablo Lorenzo-Eiroa, FNA-Fulbright Scholarship submission, 1998–2000   345

15.3   A1: Project team over Amancio Williams umbrella structure during construction. B1: landscape landfill formations in relation to views and water runoff. C1–D1: Sedimentation deposition informed by administering landfill in distinct sequential programmed phases; Parque de la Costa, Vicente Lopez, Shore Park; Project Team: Francisco Cadau-Fernando Gimenez-Manuel Galvez, Pablo Lorenzo-Eiroa associated architects; Santiago Pages - Florencia Rausch design architects; Lucia Schiappapietra landscape designer; Jorge Codignoto, environmental engineering; Amancio Williams Structure reconstruction: Claudio Veckstein, 1999–02   346

15.4   Interfaces as a site-based computation that can feedforward and backward information as a resonance machine; Ecoinduction I, Buenos Aires, e-Architects, 1998–2011   347

15.5   Ecoinduction I Rio de la Plata Bay; Project team: Pablo Lorenzo-Eiroa design principal, e-Architects; model: Henry Mena with the assistance of Jeremy Jacinth and Darrel Wesley; Ricardo Escutia, 1998–2011;   348

15.6   Ecoinduction I Rio de la Plata Bay; A1-D4: 2D DM 3D CFD simulation through CNN activating emergent programming; PI Pablo Lorenzo-Eiroa, MidJourney, 2022 Project team: e-Architects, Pablo Lorenzo-Eiroa design principal; model: Henry Mena with the assistance of Jeremy Jacinth and Darrel Wesley; Ricardo Escutia, 1998–2011;   349

16.1   Survey of Long Island geology; "Structuring Fluid Territories" Research Studio Visiting Associate Professor Pablo Lorenzo-Eiroa, TA Scott Aker; Student: Yong Feng See; UPenn Undergraduate Architecture Director Richard Wesley, Spring 2015   353

16.2   Manhattan buildings sections at different heights over maximum geological topography. A3–H3: Manhattan buildings sections at different heights below maximum topography; Associate Professor and Coordinator Pablo Lorenzo-Eiroa, Assistant Professor, Dorit Aviv, and Instructor Will Shapiro, Student: Bing Dai; The Cooper Union, M.A. Program, Fall 2015. Social housing has been displaced to marginal areas in NYC originally flood zones; Associate Professor and Coordinator Pablo Lorenzo-Eiroa, Assistant Professor, Lydia Xynogala and Instructor Will Shapiro, Student: Nan Lei; The Cooper Union, Graduate

456 *Figures*

Research Studio, Fall 2014. Topography of Manhattan, urban island-fragments indexing topographies; Visiting Associate Professor Pablo Lorenzo-Eiroa, TA Scott Aker; Student: Jordan Holmes; UPenn Undergraduate Architecture Director Richard Wesley, Spring 2015   354

16.3   Building massing topographies' height in relation to below-grade soil density; Structuring Fluid Territories, Associate Professor and Coordinator Pablo Lorenzo-Eiroa, Assistant Professor, Dorit Aviv, and Instructor Will Shapiro, Student: Bing Dai; The Cooper Union, Graduate Research Studio, Fall 2015   356

16.4   Hudson River, analysis, GIS data, Simulations, AI ML Semantic Segmentation and Classification of Environmental Processes. A4–D4: Computational Fluid Dynamic Simulation of sedimentation deposition and water flow to optimize Manhattan waterfront building block typologies; Structuring Fluid Territories, Associate Professor and Coordinator Pablo Lorenzo-Eiroa, Assistant Professor Dorit Aviv and Instructor Will Shapiro; student: Muge Wang; D3: Student Cao Yeqing; The Cooper Union, Graduate Research Studio, Fall 2015   357

16.5   East River NYC simulations; "Structuring Fluid Territories" Research Studio Visiting Associate Professor Pablo Lorenzo-Eiroa, TA Scott Aker; Student A2–D2: Yong Feng See; UPenn Undergraduate Architecture Director Richard Wesley, Spring 2015. East River Aggregate Simulation; Prof. Lorenzo Eiroa, students: Katheryn Bajo and Gregory Schikman; The Cooper Union, ARCH 177/482B, S2013. East River Simulations; Prof. Lorenzo Eiroa, Students: Mark Tugman, Charlie Blanchard, Iyatunde Majekodunmi, The Cooper Union, ARCH 177/482B, S2013   358

16.6   Manhattan heat map temperature gain from satellite image AI machine vision; A3: NASA/Marshall Space Flight Center and Global Hydrology and Climate Center, Heat Island thermal reading and Neural Network statistical analysis for image sampling. Heat Island Effect/ Temperature gain in relation to urban massing; Heat Island Effect skyline; Optimizing environmental flows through programmable urban voids; Associate Professor and Coordinator Pablo Lorenzo-Eiroa, Assistant Professor Dorit Aviv and Instructor Will Shapiro; student: Yuan Gao; The Cooper Union, Graduate Research Studio, Fall 2015   360

16.7   NYC wind simulation and urban fabric optimization; Associate Professor and Coordinator Pablo Lorenzo-Eiroa,

Assistant Professor, Lydia Xynogala and Instructor Will Shapiro, Student Ming Yan; The Cooper Union, Graduate Research Studio, Fall 2014. NYC wind simulations A1–D1/A3–B3; Associate Professor and Coordinator Pablo Lorenzo-Eiroa, Assistant Professor Dorit Aviv and Instructor Will Shapiro; student Seung Hwang Kim; The Cooper Union, Graduate Research Studio, Fall 2015   361

16.8   Sound simulation-optimization of NYC block; FEMA, NYPL, NYC.gov databases; Associate Professor and Coordinator Pablo Lorenzo-Eiroa, Assistant Professor Dorit Aviv and Instructor Will Shapiro; student: Jin Woo Lee; The Cooper Union, Graduate Research Studio, Fall 2015   362

16.9   CFD simulation of water flow; speculative structure of the city grid displaced by recovering an emergent ecological organization; Associate Professor and Coordinator Pablo Lorenzo-Eiroa, Assistant Professor, Lydia Xynogala and Instructor Will Shapiro, Student: Jaebong Jean; The Cooper Union, Graduate Research Studio, Fall 2014   364

17.1   New York City survey dataset implementing various AI and Big Data processing; PI Pablo Lorenzo-Eiroa; Farah Jalil Research Assistant, IDC Foundation Grant Research 2022   375

17.2   A1–D1: Hudson Valley and Hudson River mapping and understanding of shifting geographies. A2–B2: Sedimentation deposition simulation Hudson River. C2–D2: Hudson River sedimentation prediction model activated by Ecoinduction III. DM CFD simulation. A4–D4: Long Island shoreline, bays and keys geological evolutionary dynamics in relation to environmental processes: images based on point cloud classification and segmentation through machine vision feature recognition; mapping and understanding of environmental processes regarding shore and beach erosion, and sand, clay and silt sedimentation; DM CFD simulation. PI Pablo Lorenzo-Eiroa, DM, 2022. A2, A3, B3: AI thermal satellite machine vision-based layers; CFD simulation of water runoff; Ecoinduction III: e-Architects. Design Principal and Research: Pablo Lorenzo-Eiroa; Designers and Research: Alejandro Mieses Castellanos, Tamara Orozco Rebozo, Francis Egipciaco Cruz and Linnette Guitierrez Ortiz. SPONSOR-Grant: USDA-CIG-69F35217-268, 2018   376

17.3   A1: Buildings and below-grade ground-infrastructure positive and negative space-environments activating passive cooling and heating e-Architects, 2014. A2: CFD water flow simulation to model network of canals and

458   *Figures*

water containment reservoirs. A3: CFD wind simulation to optimize urban massing. Wind patterns model Urban Massing in relation to vortexes activation. B3: Simulations in relation to temperature readings proposing a dynamic building massing. C3: heat island effect; Ecoinduction III e-Architects; Design Principal and Research: Pablo Lorenzo-Eiroa; Designers and Research: Alejandro Mieses Castellanos, Tamara Orozco Rebozo, Francis Egipciaco Cruz and Linnette Guitierrez Ortiz. SPONSOR-Grant: USDA-CIG-69F35217-268, 2018   377

17.4   The heat island effect or feedback temperature gain in New York City is used to redefine buildings' height and void urban space. A2: Fluid Dynamic Simulation Massing Proposed in relation to wind patterns, water flows, and soil density; Ecoinduction III e-Architects, Design Principal and Research: Pablo Lorenzo-Eiroa; Designers and Research: Alejandro Mieses Castellanos, Tamara Orozco Rebozo, Francis Egipciaco Cruz and Linnette Guitierrez Ortiz. SPONSOR-Grant: USDA-CIG-69F35217-268, 2018   378

17.5   DM simulating CFD; Pablo Lorenzo-Eiroa prompt and data through MJ, 2022   379

17.6   AI robotic sentinel mapping and resolving mobility. A1–B1: Google API for residential and commercial in NYC; C1, D1: live-work commute using MTA public infrastructure. A2: AI Prediction model based on a topological hierarchy based on API Uber and taxi traffic flow; Ecoinduction III, DOT Presentation, e-Architects Team: Design Principal: Pablo Lorenzo-Eiroa; Designers: Frank Fengqi Li, Julian Chu-Yun Cheng, Shantanu Bhalla, Wayne Shang-Wei Lin, 2017   380

17.7   A1–D2: PI Pablo Lorenzo-Eiroa, emergent simulation prompt engineering via MidJourney, 2022. A3: Ecoinduction III; e-Architects. Design Principal and Research: Pablo Lorenzo-Eiroa; Designers and Research: Alejandro Mieses Castellanos, Tamara Orozco Rebozo, Francis Egipciaco Cruz and Linnette Guitierrez Ortiz. SPONSOR-Grant: USDA-CIG-69F35217-268, 2018. A4–D4: PI Pablo Lorenzo-Eiroa, MJ 2022-23   383

18.1   3d Photogrammetry scanning + AI GAN's. Chand Baori stepwell, India; AI+GANs Realism Workshop Prof. Pablo Lorenzo-Eiroa, Student: Pattnaik Ayush, Digital Futures, Inclusive Futures 2021, Tongji University, Tom Verebes Coordinator   391

18.2   3D scanning and Point Cloud manipulation implementing Artificial Intelligence and Simulation; AI+GANs Realism

Workshop Prof. Pablo Lorenzo-Eiroa, Student: Jose
David Mejias Morales; Digital Futures, Inclusive Futures
2021; Tom Verebes Coordinator. 3D Scanning interior
and exterior implementing AI, Guggenheim Museum
in NYC (1956–59) by Frank Lloyd Wright. A3 analysis
of Guggenheim Museum alternative design iterations
by Wright including reverse spiral and two correlational
interchangeable spiraled ramps; This 3D model/scan was
created using: RealityCapture software by Capturing
Reality. Prof. and Director Pablo Lorenzo-Eiroa; Student
Salma Kattass, ARCH 701B Research Studio; MS ACT;
SoAD, NYiT, 2021   393

18.3   Museum of Babel application AI workflow; Prof. and
Director Pablo Lorenzo-Eiroa; Student Salma Kattass,
ARCH 701B Research Studio; MS ACT; SoAD,
NYiT, 2021   394

18.4   Museum of Babel; Research Studio Prof. and Dir. Pablo
Lorenzo-Eiroa; Student Salma Kattass, ARCH 701B, MS
ACT; SoAD, NYiT, 2021   395

19.1   Pairing CA AI rules as emergent Linear Cities typologies;
Urbanism of Information Research Studio, Prof. Pablo
Lorenzo-Eiroa, Student: Wayne Shang-Wei Lin, M.Arch II
Program, The Cooper Union, 2017   403

19.2   Cellular Automation AI rules and linear city and urban
blocks typologies emergence; Urbanism of Information
Studio, Prof. Pablo Lorenzo-Eiroa, Student: Wayne Shang-
Wei Lin, M.Arch, The Cooper Union, 2017   404

19.3   Mumbai, informal settlements analysis and emergent
organization prediction through Cellular Automation
(CA); Urbanism of Information Studio, Head Professor and
Coordinator Pablo Lorenzo-Eiroa, Student: Shamriddhi
Sharma, M.Arch II Program, The Cooper Union, 2017   405

19.4   Mexico City, formal and informal metropolitan
and suburban private "informal" and public formal
transportation mapping; Urbanism of Information Studio,
Prof. Pablo Lorenzo-Eiroa, Student: Marcela Olmos,
M.Arch II, The Cooper Union, 2017   406

19.5   Studies optimizing mobility through AI robotic sentinels;
Urbanism of Information Studio, Prof. Pablo Lorenzo-
Eiroa, Student: Frank Fengqi-Li, M.Arch II, The Cooper
Union, 2017   407

19.6   High Line 3D Photogrammetry point cloud and
deconstruction implementing AI Swarm Intelligence (SI)
and Agent-Based Modeling (ABM) in relation to local
art galleries developing application navigation, NYC;

	Associate Prof. Pablo Lorenzo-Eiroa Visiting Assistant Prof. Fengq Li, student: Beken Amde, MS ACT, NYIT SoAD, 2022	408
19.7	AI Photogrammetry 3D scans from social media data acquisition, through social media tagging retrieved from Rome; Urbanism of Information Research Studio, Prof. Pablo Lorenzo-Eiroa, Student: Shantanu Bahlla, M.Arch II, The Cooper Union, 2017	409
19.8	Experimental AI crowdsourced photogrammetry 3d scanning through a bottom-up city-wide dispersed dataset retrieving individual photos by Instagram API and web scraping, developing a 3D real-time Big Data photogrammetry point cloud of NYC, Times Square; Ecoinduction III DOT Presentation, e-Architects Team: Design Principal: Pablo Lorenzo-Eiroa; Designers: Frank Fengqi Li, Julian Chu-Yun Cheng, Shantanu Bhalla, Wayne Shang-Wei Lin	411
19.9	AI Augmented parallel navigable NYC application framework; This 3D model/scan was created using: RealityCapture software by Capturing Reality. IDC Foundation Grant Research PI Pablo Lorenzo-Eiroa, RA Farah Jalil	412

Index

Note: *Italic* page numbers refer to figures.

Ackerman, J.S. 30, 32
Adams, Robert 398
Agent Based Modelling (ABM) 8, 88, 123, 133, 149, *306*, *310*, 314, *318*, *319*, *394*, 425, 426
Agrest, D. 16, 81, 83, 338
ahistory 435; creative-cultural-technological disruption 433–35; Piranesi's 397–414; Rainaldi's 41–62, 179; structure-implicit 435; suspension of Wolfflin's Pendulum 52–62
Alberti, L.B. 4, 24, 30, 33, 42, 62, 63, 68, 80, 193, 238, 426
Alexander, C. 105, 253
algorithm: advanced comprehension 76; adversarial networks 157; "Analytical Engine" (1837) 95; arithmetic and algebra of 68; backpropagation 123, 125; Boolean logic 151; coding 388; computational 76, 129, 402; Couzin's Swarm algorithm of 2003 149; data-gathering 108; deterministic 3; discriminative 157; evolutionary 142–47, 150, 286; FFT 171; Flow Chart diagram *109*; generative 157; genetic 149; machine learning *139*; Marching Cubes *297*, *306*, 307; mathematical 31, 69, 89–91; modeling 113; mutating 125; or meta-algorithms 117, 134, 413, 425, 427, 435; parallel processing 117; recursive 172; reversible 76, 103, 179; self-editing 124, 179, *180*, 229, 418, 425; single data entry 400; statistical regression 114–15; swarm 149; thermodynamic 426; training 7; visual 6, 149, 171, *180*, *283*, 428

Allen, S. 401
Allen, Woody 166
Althusser, L. 11, 92
Application Processing Interface (API) 8, *40*, 45, *132*, 143, *144*, 162–63, *168*, *203*, *226*, *258*, *272*, *273*, 372–73, *386*, 381, *394*, *411*, *414*, 418
architecture: AI 7–9, 392–96, *391*, *393–95*, 416–17; of architectures *38*, 420, 427, 432; artificial man-made origination 16; Borges' *128*; building 350; building's floor plan 27; Cartesian reference space-frame 217–28; and computation, relationship between 5–7, 73, 89, 150, 177, 179, *221*, 342, 432, 435; defined 161; developmentalism 7, 300, 337, 423–24; digital 141, 147–49, *156*, 187, 209, 238, *249*; dimensions for computer processing 161–65, 193, 208, 210–28, 232, 328; displacing systems of representation 64–65; domestic 33; forensic 250; generic 236; histories and theories of representation 3–5; historiography of 300; idea and concept 79; importance of painting 62; of information 1–3, *2*, 7–9, 177, 200, 206–33, 236, 252–57, 342, 370, 392–96, 416–17, 422, 426–27; of installation 300, 309; landscape 338, *341*; media linguistic criticism 80–2; and Nature, relationship between 338; Palladio's 33; parametric variations 190; problem in *245*, 248, 300; Roman 21; of space-environments 344, 346; system of representation 40, 88–9; through LiDAR 40; typological

462 *Index*

variation 33, *219,* 220, 236; universal 31; and urbanism 16, 18, 156, 344, 367, 370, 392, 430; visual semiotics 141, 194; women in 63

Argan, G.C. 41, 42

Aristotle 70, 82, 87, 96, 110, 217, 235, 240

Armengol, Jordi Bonet I 274

art history 81

Artificial Intelligence (AI) 1; from anticipatory software to emergent programming through ML training ANN 105–6; architecture of information 7–9, *250,* 392–96; automated machine vision 24; black-box problem 125–26, 418, 423, 433; Blockchain urban AI framework 366–84; Cellular Automation (CA) rules *201;* ChatGPT 419; coding and programming languages 92; colonialism and cultural appropriation through 9–12; computational authorship 416–17; computational frameworks 5–7; computational linguistic semiotics 87–110; computational visual semiotics grammatology 140–81; computational visual signs and signals 421–24; consciousness 18; correlational simulations 310; curve or geometry-fitting statistical models 424; Deep Learning 287; defined 435; 3D feature recognition 45, *49, 50, 51, 55, 58, 59, 409, 411;* diffusion model *272;* digital feudalism 9–12; digital signifiers 187–205; emergent structure 2, 276–98, 435; environmental framework 1–3, *2;* facial recognition app 17; GAN *391;* Google Deep Dream *271;* Hierarchy 115–16; human-machine interactivity 416; information flows 403–9; issues 236; machine vision 133, *257,* 355, *365, 384, 414;* at MIT 6; Morel's genetic evolutive architecture 149; multidimensional Blockchain platform 232; Museum of Babel application AI workflow *394;* neural networks 228–29; as nondeterministic data and model integration 124–25; NYC application framework *412;* parallel computing 231; participatory autonomous self-regulating spatial-environmental engine 426–7; post-zoomorphism in 18; robotic sentinel *386, 407;* and

scientific method 424–26; statistical problem *38;* Swarm Intelligence (SI) *414;* synthetic environments 299–351, *301–9;* topological design variations *273;* as virtual and physical robotics 149–50; VR 413

Artificial Neural Network (ANN) 2–3, 18, *37,* 91, 112–15, *113,* 119, 121, 370–72, 384, 418, 419, 425; advantage 126; AI through 7, 167, *204,* 188; Big data in 7; decision trees 126; evolutionary morphogenetic structures 179; generalization learning 121; ML algorithm 2, 18, 105–8, 112, *139,* 161, 173, 248, 384, 425, 429; network theory 370; parallel computational processing structures 4, 8, *180,* 188; statistical gradients and tensor fitness 374; training 418–19

authorship 9, 11, 165, 237; architect/ computational developer 417, 418; in architecture 68–83, 328; collective authorship 418, 419; co-shared authorship 419; definitions of 417–18; design 238, 277, 416; digital representation 418, 419–20; end user as author 417, 419–20; expanding 416–35; forced user-shared data 418, 419; limited 3; personal 25; post-digital as computational AI 416–435; post-humanism 418; surrenders authorship 419

automata: development of analog machines 6; self-replication 131, 149, 252–53

automata theory 8, 100–103, 107

axonometric 4; documentation 42; Hejduk works 64; model of house X 65; projection *48,* 63, 141, 217, *221;* worms' eye view *222*

Bacon, Francis 83

Badiou, A. 401

Baeyer, H.C. von 98, 110

Banham, R. 66, 149

Baroque: Eurocentric colonization 208–10; innovative 42; and post-structuralism 3; Renaissance as 30, *40,* 54, 300; space 65; systems of representation 25

Barthes, R. 71, 73, 81, 140, 399, 416

Bateson, G. 108

Baudrillard, J. 410

Beattie, Alan 143

Benelli, F. 31
Bergson, H. 15
Bezier, Pierre 152
bias: AI 12, 421, 430; in computational
interfaces 410; confirmation 433;
consumerism 412; contrast mapping
144; cultural 1, 3, 6, 8, 10–11, 20,
77, 89, 92, 112–14, 126, 143, *156,
158*, 176, 289, 381, 397, 399–400,
404, 426–29, 433–34; data 429;
"Framing Bias" 112; ideological 89,
91; linguistic 92; multiple conventional
structuralisms 238; political 143; of
software 8; "Survivorship Bias" 112;
of transformation 401; and weights
121–23, 125, 425
Big Data: AI architecture of information
392–6; anticipatory theory 2; in
Artificial Neural Networks 7; assumed
theory 42–45, *46–51*; CFD simulation
343–45, 353, 372; city as non-linguistic
signifier 399; cultural blindness in
objective data visualization 399–402;
dataset 45; 3D scanning *409, 411*;
in emergent space environments
352–65, *353–54, 358, 361, 362, 364,
365*; functional value of 167, 180;
gathering and processing 274, 344,
361, 372, 381, 402; informed realisms
of bifurcating multidimensional
possibilities 388–96; LiDAR scanning
52, *58*; multidimensional architecture
of information 392–96; New
York city 352–65; non-conceptual
indeterminism 112; Piranesi's
Campo Marzio 397–98; point cloud
simulations *49–51, 54, 55, 57, 60,
61, 62, 156, 384*; politics in emergent
space environments 352–65; realism
388–96; real-time feedback 370–71;
representation of city 402; simulacra,
virtual mixed expanded reality 410–14,
411–12, 414–15; surveys 42, *271*, 274,
344, 372, 402, 421–22, 424, 426, 429,
434; through survey and simulation
8, 42–46, *44, 46–51*; urbanism of
information 403–9; as virtual and
physical robotics 149–50; working
architecture 7
Bilas, Fran 98, 152
Blanchot, Maurice 74
blockchain: AI-based multidimensional
platform 232, 427; collective
intelligence 424; diagram 180, *180*;

encryption technology 426; new cities'
space-environments for a dystopian
world 384; participatory validation
platform 421; planetary universal
commons 369–70; politics of urban
void 366–67; post-colonialism 367–69;
predictive post-capitalist participatory
crowdsourced Blockchain 381–
83; rezoning city in relation to
environmental processes 371–80;
thermodynamic environmental engine
366–87; urbanism of information
370–71; zoning regulations 339
Boole, G. 96
Borasi, Giovanna 149
Borges, J.L. *128*, 416
Borromini, Francesco 4, 27, 41–66,
82, 300, 422; Big Data point cloud
simulations *49, 50, 54, 57, 58, 60,
61, 62*; Big Data survey challenging
assumed theory 42–45; Derrida's
parergon in Russian constructivists
and modern art 62–63; Hejduk and
Eisenman, displacing systems of
representation 64–65; as historiography
of spatial representation 41–42; post-
structuralist theory 65–66; Rainaldi
ahistorical suspension of Wolfflin's
pendulum 52–62, *67*; San Carlo in
Rome *44, 46, 47, 49, 54*; topological
model 41–42
Bostrom, N. 256
Bradbury, R. 73
Brinckmann, A.E. 31, 42
Brunelleschi, Filippo 3, 20, 23–25, 27,
30, 82, 141, 177, 236, 238, 300, 422;
displacing renaissance perspective
25–27; illusionistic perspective 27–29;
mathematical parametric analog
computational interface 23–24;
perspective as Eurocentric renaissance
machinic colonization of space 24;
Pozzo's multidimensional virtual
space 27–29; Renaissance perspective,
Lorenzetti's parametric space 21–23
Bryson, Arthur E. 150
Buolamwini, J. 12
Burry, M. 274

Cache, B. 75, 83, 148
Canciani, M. 43
Cannon, Annie Jump 90
capitalism: accidental outputs 5;
destruction cycles 178; of disruptive

464 *Index*

technology 8; hierarchy in economy 370; indexing 4, 16; social mobility 9; tendency to monopolies 8; US model of technological innovation 11, 420

Carpo, M. 79, 112, 416

Carter, S.J. 209

Cassirer, E. 20, 41, 68, 70, 76, 77, 80, 326

Catmull, Edwin 142

Celce-Murcia, M. 107

Cellular Automation (CA) *103*; activating automata theory 8; AI rules *201, 404*; cell module 307; 3D cells 154; description *103*; evolutionary computation of 7, *405*, 427, 432; rules *303, 386*; sites *269*

Ching, F.D.K. 32

Chomsky, N. 9, 74, 105, 106, 109, 127, 129, *139*, 161, 253

Chu, Karl 147

Clement, G. 149

code: "The Ancestral Code" programming 146; ASCII 97; binary 31, 171, 179, *180*; computational 88, 91, 172; DNA 228; electronic signals 151; G-Code 237, 248, 250, *249, 250, 251*, 280, *297–298, 310, 311, 312, 317*, 318, 331–32; linguistic semiotics codes 142, 190; Low Code (or machine code (M-code)) 69, 88, 91, 100, 126–27, 237, 248, 250, 327; Morse Code 96; pixel 163; Reed-Solomon Code 172; source 188; zip codes 143, 171, 400, 421

coding: AI 92; Arithmetic 97; computer 127; customized G-Code 248; 2D computational design 277; genetic 253; Higher Level Language 126; internal 299, 343; linguistic computation 160, 236; Low Code or NLP 88, 129; Palladio's proportional coding ratio 33; robotic machinic system 330; scripts *194*; semiotic computation 160, 236; streamed 127

Cohen, Danny 142

Colomina, B. 16

Computational Fluid Dynamics (CFD): activating 131, *132*; Big Data through 342, 343–44, *345*, 353, 355, *357*; expanding architecture 338; simulation studies 131, 133, *153*, 152–55, 164, 225, *225, 241, 249, 341*, 342, 343–44, *364, 365*, 370–72, *376, 378–80*, 426, 429

computational linguistics semiotics: AI through ML training ANN 105–6; ANNs 117–23; automata theory 101–4; Big Data non-conceptual indeterminism 112; black-box approach 125–26; coding 91–92; cold war anti-bomb city defense 104–5; computational linguistic semiotics 91–93; Cybernetic theory 104–5; data acquisition 111; data and information theory 109–11; data science/scraping/ mining 111–12; deep learning or DNN 123–24; emergent programming 105–6, 124–25; flow chart procedural organization 108, *109*; generative pretrained transformer 3 127–30; Higher-Level Programming Language 130–34; histories and theories 94–97; information theory 88, 98–100; intuitive anticipatory modeling 112; of Java Script 198; linguistics and computational linguistics 88–89; from low code to higher-level programming language 130–34; mathematics and mathematical semiotics 89–91; Minsky' computational semiotics 106–8; ML 112–13; NLP 126–27; non-supervised ML 115–16; Shannon's Information Theory 97–98; systems of representation 88–89; variety of programming languages 92–93; and visual semiotics 3, 65, 88, 141–43, 236, 416; weights, biases, and tensor computing 121–23

computational visual semiotics: advancement in computation 5; architecture dimensionality 161–65; Big Data and AI as virtual and physical robotics 149–50; digital architecture and fabrication 147–49; digital signifiers 188; generative adversarial network 157–58; and linguistic semiotics 3, 73, 88, 91, 142, 236, 416; L-Systems bifurcating site-based computation *145*; machine vision 166–70; non-deterministic 426; non-linguistic 141–43, 171–74; NURBS curve or Spline line construction *152, 153*; object tracking recognition *167*; politics and style 165–66; problems, Sketchpad (1963) or Hypercube 4D animation (1965) 6; semantic segmentation 158–61;

Index 465

Shape Grammar 145–47; signifiers 150–57, 187–88; space syntax, GIS 143; through machine vision, sensing, and interaction 88; through nonlinear emergent programming 175–81

computation, computational design: anthropocentric material-based construction systems 239; as architecture 5–9, 24, 73, 147; Big Data 112; digital signifiers 171, 187–203; electronic binary electronic signals 151; and environment, relationships between 1; evolutionary 149, 343, *405*; of geometry 217; histories and theories of 1, 94–97, 300, 434; incremental site-based physical 277–81, *278–80*; knowledge-based approach 113; and language 77; linguistic 160, 171; as mathematical system of communication 89–91, 157; Najle 148; nondeterministic 3, 124–25; as parallel processing 259–62; planetary 369, 373; procedural 142; quantum 230–32, 384; symbolic 100, 121, 125, 127, 146, 158, 168, 172, 174; through semiotics 94–97, 160; universal 101–3; Visual Semiotics Grammatology 175–81

computer science 6, 8, 10, 103, 113, 125, 158, 188, 210–11

Convolutional Neural Network (CNN) 113, 118, *119*, 130, *159*, 160–62, 167, 177, *271*, *283*, 286–88, *286*, *349*, 374, 392, 419

Conway, John 300

Conway, P. 16, 102

Couzin, I.D. 149

Crary, J. 417

Crawford, K. 12

cultural criticism through media 434

cybernetics 18, 148, 425; AI through 112; of cybernetics 107; early work on 163; issues of 108; system-programmer and autonomous computational system 419; theory in urban decentralization 104–5

Dalí, Salvador 160

Dalton, Nick 143

Damish, H. 80

Darwin, Charles 259

data: bias 122, 429; data science 6, 8, 10, 111–12, 123, 125, 130, 143, 158, 160, 167, 171, 179, 188, 210–211, 231, 373, 388–389, 429, 430; gathering 108, 111–12, 122, 146, 157, 165, 274, 344, 361, 381, 384, 390, 400–402, 421; processing 18, *49*, *55*, *58*, *61*, 161, 342, 355, 359, 371, 401, 402, 429, 434; structure 1, 92, 108, 143, 207, 228, 423, 429; validation 112, 417–20, 421, 425

Da Vinci, Leonardo 15, 16

Deamer, P. 420

decimation 155–56, *159*, *185*, 173, 188, *254*, 289, 423, 431

deep neural network (DNN) 123–24

deep structure 107; of CAM 73, 89; defined 165, 190; displacement of perspective 27; double 64; methodology 107; symbolic form 176, *347*, 397; system of representation 22, 177; theory of 68; visual semiotics 73, 89

della Francesca, P 15, 17

Derrida, J. 9, 10, 62–63, 68, 70–78, 80, 82, 87, 187, 342, 397, 398, 416, 419

Descartes, R. 208

diagram 74; ANN *117*; architecture 31; Blockchain 180, *180*; Ching Hexagram Diagrams 94; Christopher Alexander's *180*; continuous elastic 33; Flow Chart *109*; Frankl's 64; generation 45; grid 193; House IV of 1971 process 64; as linguistic qualisign 82–83; of reasoning 94; Shannon's 97–98; topological elastic 45; Wittkower's 31, 34

Diffusion Model (DM): AI NLP MidJourney *272*; 3D 167, 392; Disco Diffusion fractal loops 413; feature recognition *132*; GAN *155*; NLP *139*, 161–65, 282–83, *284*, 423; pixel-to-pixel 163, *185*, 174, 224, *226*, *379*; statistic regression 127; thermodynamics *170*, 171, 180, 428

digital fabrication 3, 148; architecture 209, 237; and construction 147, 423–24; cross-referenced 318; "image-like" replica 276; problem of 236, *242*, 276; questioning 277; revolutionizing 147; tool 327

digital signifiers 7, 79, 88, 111; AI 187–205; artificial origins 416, 422; computational 151; computational grammatology 187–88; computation, computational design 171, 187–205; expanding computational visual

466   *Index*

semiotic signifiers 187–88; expanding new emergent disciplinary boundaries 342–43; organizational representational 208; Palladian Villas *198*; pixel-to-pixel DM 163; point clouds *156*, 157; and politics of representation 188–203; urban blocks and building types *199*

downsampling: of digital mathematical signal 154, 155; exchanging 188; information representation 188; pixel colour signal *341*; sub-symbolic sign 167, 172, 423, 431; voxelation 149, 154–55, *155*; VoxelNet architecture 167

Durand, Jean-Nicolas-Louis 30, 35, 193

Durer, A. 15, 79

ecoinduction: Ecoinduction I-III *144*, 207, 344, *347*, *348*, *349*, 350, 371–72, *377*, *385*, *386*, *387*, *411*; environmental *325*; or ecological artificial induction 344, *348*; planetary 369; projects 344

ecology: artificial 344, 350, 372, 382; crisis 342; dynamics of 209, 343; environmental 2, 310, 338, *341*, 353, 371, *386*; induction 338, 350; information flows 370; latent 363, *364*, 363, 368, 371, 373, *385*, *386*, 374; without Nature 338

Einstein, Albert 99, 210

Eisenman, P. 4, 32, 64–65, 70, 73, 74, 81–83, 147

Elliot, T.S. 111

emergence: of Artificial Intelligence 2; of evolutionary morphogenesis 229, *405*; linguistic 129; nonlinear 153; of philosophy of computation 95, 124; real time 381; of sentinels 131; structural *246*; through optimization 149

emergent programming 3; activating 7, *38*, 92, 115, 124–25, *132*, 133, *273*, 281, *284*, *349*, 373, 431, 432, 434; AI *139*, *287*, *341*, 426, 431; ANN 384, 389, 418, 425; in 3D 133, 225; data for 112; higher-level language 131; NLP 131; non-deterministic 8; nonlinear 175–81; robotic sentinels 2; through ML training ANN 105–6; visual 168

environment: artificial induction 346; Banham's architecture 66; characteristics of 7; collaborative authorship 419; feedback information

exchange 350; planetary 18, 207, 338; problem-solving 124; relationship to 5; shifting conditions 123–25, 134; space 209, 220, 223, 225, 226, 232–33, 253, *254*, *255*, 310, 322, *324*, 334, 343, 359, 363, 365, 371, *387*, 390, 413, 427; visual semiotic 239

environmental process *254*, 359

equality 367, 370

Escher, M.C. 160

ethics 9, 12, 17, *294*, 318, 339, 368, 417–20

Euler, L. 217

Evans, R. 188

Fabretti, F. 11, 79, 92, 108

feature(s): in art *40*; data 131; extraction 113–14, 115, 125, 158; generative algorithm 157; ML 158; numeric value 115; transferring of 17

feature recognition: ANN 125; CNN *283*; convolutional 129, 133, 160, 272, 418, 423; 3D 45; data and information flow 124; deep learning 287; diffusion model *132*; GAN *40*, *159*, 281; image 129, *159*, 161; machine vision 250, *385*, *414*; masks 164; non-labeled non-classified unstructured data 115; or pattern recognition 100, 116; pixel-to-pixel *227*; point cloud models 164; progressive 130; semantic segmentation learning 162, *289*, *394*; statistic approximation *58*; visual-based 131, 177; visual iconographic 166; visual semiotic 80, *132*, *289*, 422

feedback 11, 16, 123–24; convolution 126; in cybernetics 107; emotional 17; of external associations 108; geometry and information 244–52; illusionistic perspective *227*; natural 344, 350; network 104–5; non-linear 131, *254*, *317*, *324*; post-colonialism 9; real-time construction 250, 370–71, 381; reinforcement learning 106; remote sensing 233

Fiedler, C. 68, 78

Fisk, Harold 340

Flow Chart 108, *109*

fluid dynamic simulation 343; *see also* Computational Fluid Dynamics (CFD)

Foster, Norman 66

Foucault, M. 25, 178, 398

Frankl, P. 31, 64, 80–82, 193

Frazer, John 149

Frommel, C.L. 42
Fuller, Buckminster 240
Fuller, M. 178

Gabos, Noam 63
Galison, P. 104
Gandelsonas, M. 64, 68, 80–82, 150
Gaudi, Antoni *168*, 274; from catenaries as analog structural simulation 259–62; New York city 281–96, *282, 283, 287–89*; from survey, to ideal, back to an informed realism *262–73*, 274
Gausa, Manuel 148
Gehry, Frank 4, 147
Generative Adversarial Network (GAN) 7, 162, 180, 281, 392, 428; AI 150, *391, 394*; decoders and autoencoders 17; feature recognition *40*; non-supervised 150; semantic segmentation mapping *289*; statistical approximation 157–58; style transfer 160, 165, *271, 283*
geometric neural networks (GNN) 120
Gilbreth, Frank 108
Gilbreth, Lilian 108
Giovannini, J. 82
Godard, J.L. 166
Gödel, K. 73, 87, 89, 96, 97
Gogh, Vincent van 160
Goodfellow, I. 288
grammatology: of AI computational visual signs and signals 421–24; computational 187–204, 413, 432; Derrida's 74; visual semiotics 175–81
Guallart, Vicente 148
Guattari, F. 75, 336
Guzman, A. 107

Habermas, J. 11
Hadid, Zaha 4, 82, 147, 160
Hasslacher, B. 179
Hayles, K. 92
Hegel, Georg Wilhelm Friedrich 20, 63, 78, 87
Heidegger, M. 11
Heizer, Michael 81
Hejduk, John 4, 64–65, 74
Hempel 42
Hensel, M. 149
High Level Language (HLL) 69, 92–93, 100, 126–27, 130, *132*, 172, 175, 196, 428
Hilberseimer, L. 104
Hillier B. 143
Hinton, Geoffrey 123

Hooke, Robert 259, 260
Human Computer Interaction (HCI) 70, 142, 150, *151*, 154, 170, 172, 178, 188, *204*, 237, 276, 289, 327, 423, 429, 431–32
human proportions: capitalist body 16; evolutionary zoomorphic-biomorphic body 15; ideal human proportions and topological data mapping 15; mechanical universal modern body 16; post-human emergent being and AI consciousness 18; post-human post-anthropocene, and post-zoomorphism in AI and robotics 18; robotic prosthetic body, to augmented body, to bio synthetic organism 16–17
Husserl, Edmund 342

ImageNET tagging 12
index 42, 45, 52–53, 63, 81, 163, 165, 193, 199, 226, 239–40, 328, 390, 398, 423
information: architecture of 1–3, *2*, 7–9, 177, 200, 206–33, 235, 252–58, 342, 370, 392–96, 416–17, 422, 426–27; downsampling representation 179; ecology 369; feature recognition 124; feedback exchange 350; flows 403–9; representation 179
information actualization: Gaudi's New York city vaulted skyscraper prototype 289–98; incremental site-based physical computation 277–81; vertical slab stacking 281–89
information theory 431, 433; advantages of *185*, 171; computational linguistics semiotics 92, 109–11; data and 109–11; intelligence in 2; issues of 108; as mass-energy information equivalence 256; NN 104; representation through 236; self-balancing mechanisms 351; Shannon's 89, 97–100, 105
interface: "The Ancestral Code" programming 146; computational 20–29; digital quali-signifier 160, *192*; dimensional processing 115; fixed vectorial scale-based semiotic 151; HCI level 170, 172, 431; lack of recognition 276; media 177; processing 192; screen 14; through voxel signs 146; visual semiotic *347*

Jennings, Betty Jean 98, 152
Johnson, P. 81, 82

468 *Index*

Johnson, T.E. 142
Julesz, B. 164

Kant, I. 72, 76, 78
Kasparov, Garry 229
al-Khwarizmi, Muhammad ibn Musa 90
Kilstrup, M. 78
Kirsch, Russell 151
Kittler, F.A. 179
Kleene, S.C. 107
Klein, Alexander 143
Krauss, R. 81
Kurzweil, Raymond 99

Lally, S. 149
language: architectural 64, 80–81, 165,
  179; as author 71–74; autoregressive
  127; COBOL 100, 142; coding 142,
  236; computational 8, 91–92, 100,
  126, 129, 145, 173, 175–76, 200;
  conventional 129; deconstruction
  74–75; English 92, 105; FLOW-
  MATIC 100; FORTRAN 142; Lisp
  142; machinic 100; of mathematics
  33, 77–78, 89; natural 79–81, 92, 96,
  109, 126, 129, 158, 166, 177, 426;
  Nietzsche 77; pattern language 105,
  253; programming 92, 98, 100, 127,
  131, 142, 146, 172; Python 92; Sanskrit
  76; structural-formal approach 77;
  symbolic 100; and thinking 76–77;
  Translation 108; universal 33, 158, 179,
  209, 428
Leaman, Adrian 143
Leavitt, Henrietta Swan 90
Le Corbusier 4, 16, 31, 64, 65, 74, 82
Leibniz, G.W. 4, 65, 75, 83, 87, 89, 94, 95,
  96, 97, 105, 208, 209, 209
Lepaute, Nicole-Reine 90
Lévi-Strauss, C. 9, 71–72
Lichterman, Ruth 152
light detection and ranging (LiDAR) 8,
  151, 167; architecture through 42; Big
  Data 52, *58*; 3D scanning *28*, 42–43,
  45, *47–51, 54–55, 57,* 154, 156, 212,
  274, 389, 400, 402, 419; Saunders 42;
  technology survey 340, 343
Lindenmayer, A. 142
line (1D) 212–13
linguistics: bias 92; coding 160, 236;
  computational linguistic semiotics
  87–110; emergence 129; qualisign,
  diagram as 82–83; semiotics 3,
  73, 88, 91, 142, 236, 416 (*see also*

computational linguistics semiotics);
  semiotics codes 142, 190
Lin, Maya 81
Loos, Adolf 217
Lorenzetti, A. 21–23, 25, 261
Lorenzo-Eiroa, Pablo *passim*
Lovelace, A. 6, 95
Low Code: or machine code (M-code)
  69, 88, 91, 100, 126–27, 327; or NLP
  88, 130
L-Systems 142, *145, 290*
Lynn, Gregg 147

machine learning (ML): ANN algorithm
  2, 18, 105–106, 112, *139,* 161, 173,
  250, 384, 425, 428; feature recognition
  158, *297*; non-supervised 115–16,
  158, *271*; object tracking recognition
  319; parallel processing 4, 7; semantic
  segmentation *49,* 53, *55, 57, 59*;
  training ANN, AI through 105–6
Mandelbrot, Benoit B. 142
Manovich, Lev 165
mapping: contrast *144*; 3D 157; data
  15; face recognition kinetic 17,
  159; feature recognition masks 164;
  geometric-based 114; information
  theory 276, 353, *380,* 401; interfaces
  10; representation of city 402; semantic
  segmentation *289*; transportation *406*
Maria, Walter de 81
material logic 148, 239–40, 424
materials 62, 173, 178, 209; polymer 328;
  program 328; recycled 147; robotic
  318–19; as signifiers 239
mathematics 24, 33, 71, 95, 97, 207, 218,
  244, 274, 350, 426; algorithm 31,
  69, 89–91; blackbox processes 125;
  downsampling 154, *155*; language
  of 33, 77–78, 89; and mathematical
  semiotics 89–91; Navier-Stokes
  equations 359; Newton's second law of
  motion 153; system of communication
  89–91, 157; through arithmetic 68
McCarthy, J. 106, 107
McCullough, Malcolm 210
McLuhan, M. 79, 188, 401
McNulty, Kay 152
media and medium 11, 78–79, 82, 166,
  171, *185,* 236, *247,* 253, 281, 359, 381,
  382, 402
media determinism 3–4, 7–8, 10, 20, 73,
  75, 78, 131, 142, 147, 149, 158, 165,
  198, 250, 276, 424–25, 428, 432

Meltzer, Marlyn 152
Menges, A. 148
message: abstract encoded 95, 98; BIT-based 426; communication 99, 109, 179; content or information 110; encrypt and decrypt 426; ergon 176; information theory 92; linguistic 129, 129, 160; secret encrypted 97
Metz, L. 150
Michelangelo 41, 42, 45
Minsky, M. 105, 106–8, 110, 326, 326
Miralles, Enric 66, 74, 81
Mitchell W.J. 145, 146, 147, 210
modelling 112, 123, *294, 384*
Modern Movement 3–5, 63, 65, 81–82, 160, 165, 236, 241, 259, 337
Moravec, H. 232
Morgan-Mar, David 146
morphogenesis 125, 149, 179, 229, 253, 260, 262, 423, 432–33
Müller, Willy 148
multidimensional: AI 1–12; architecture of information 206–33; architecture questioning dimensional and reference systems 207–8; Baroque Eurocentric colonization 208–10; Cartesian universal reference and measurement system 208–10; computational morphogenesis 125; data associations 17; displacing reference frame systems, digital signifiers, systems of representation, space typology, construction systems, and materials 232–33; expanding dimensions in architecture's Cartesian reference space-frame 217–28; informational 199–200, 208, 318; informed realisms of 388–92; 1D line *212,* 212–13, *213*; parallel processing in human brain, intelligence, and AI neural networks 228–30; quantum physics and quantum computing 230–32, *231*; space-environments 343–44, 392, 394, 413, 428; stacking of layers 125–26; 3D object, volume, and space 216–17, *217*; 3D space and 4D topology 217–28, *219, 221, 222, 224–27*; 2D boundary and surface 213–14, *213–16*; virtual space 27–29; 0D point 211–12

Najle, C. 148, 240
Nash, K. 148
natural language (NL) 79–81, 92, 96, 109, 126–27, 129, 158, 166, 177, 179, 426, 427

Natural Language Processing (NLP) 68–69, 88, 92, 126–31, 161–64, *185,* 224, 285, *283, 284,* 418, 423, 427
Naumann, L.S. 42
Negroponte, N. 126, 142, 326, 416, 417
Neufert, E. 16
Neumann, J. von 7, 42, 95, 98–99, 101, 102, 131, 152, 163, 252, 256
neural networks (NN): AI 228–30; artificial (*see* Artificial Neural Network (ANN)); biological 178; convolutional (*see* Convolutional Neural Network (CNN)); deep (*see* deep neural network (DNN)); geometric 120; as graphs 101; pretrained tagged classifiers or developing classifiers 158; recurring (*see* Recurring Neural Networks (RNN))
new signifiers: architecture building by informing environmental information flows 350–51; Big Data CFD evolutionary simulation 343–44; Buenos Aires-Colonia and Rio de la Plata Delta-Estuary *345–49,* 345–50; cities defining nature 336–38; expanding new emergent disciplinary boundaries 342–43; geometric determination and simulation non-determination 342; pre-colonial systems of representation of fluid territory 340–42; toward post-colonial post-anthropocene 338–40
Nietzsche, F. 41, 54, 72, 76, 77, 398, 416
Noguchi, Isamu 5, 66, 81
Nolli, Giambattista 398

Orwell, G. 73
ownership 9, 17, 369, 371, 417–21, 434

Palladio, A. 3, 4, 27, *34,* 39, 40, 52, 53, 56, 64, 74, 82, 141, 146, 176, 179, 193, 198, 300, 422; parametric topological displacements to disseminate origination 30–31; systemic relational determination, origination and critique of 31; unstabilizing origin by overcoming parametric variation 32–39
Pannini 76
Panofsky, E. 14, 21, 41, 62, 70, 76, 78, 81, 140, 175, 397
particle 98, 154, 206, 230; based FDM *325*; clay 239; physical 344, 359; sedimentation *241,* 350, *358,* 359

470 *Index*

Pask, Gordon 142
Peirce, C.S. 68, 69, 78, 82
Perkins, J. 142
perspective: Brunelleschi's 23, 25, 27, 141, 300; illusionistic 25, 27–29, *227, 228,* 300, *324;* Lorenzetti's 25, 261; Renaissance 25–27, 300; sonic 320, *320*
Pevsner, Nikolaus 42
photogrammetry: of Sagrada Familia 281, *282;* subsymbolic 157, *185;* 3D scanning 17, *155,* 164, *265, 266, 268,* 274, *329, 384, 394,* 402, *409, 411, 412*
physical computation *255,* 277–78, 281, 289, 422–24
Piano, Renzo 66
Pierce, J.R. 109
Pinos, Carme 66, 81
Pitts, W. 105
pixel: code 164; Diffusion Model (DM) 164, 174, *185,* 224, *226, 379;* digital signifier 163; downsampling *341;* feature recognition *227*
Plato 82, 110, 240
point 172, *204,* 193, 209, 210; control 147, *152, 153;* defined 216; vanishing 21–26, 78, *203,* 220; vectorial 151, *217;* zero-dimensional 211–12, *263*
point cloud: Big Data *49, 50, 51, 54, 55, 57, 58, 60, 61, 156, 384;* digital signifier *156,* 157; 3D scanning 133, *265,* 281, 289, *297;* facial recognition 17; feature recognition 164; index space 42; of Sagrada Familia building *265,* 281, 289, *297;* simulations *49, 50, 51, 54, 55, 57, 58, 60, 61, 156, 384*
Ponte, Alessandra 16
post-structuralism 3, 81, 112, 237
Pozzo, Andrea 3, 27–29, 225, 228, 300
precedence 52, 260, 326, 434
Prigogine, I. 154
programming: and coding 92; emergent (*see* emergent programming); language 91–92, 97, 99, 127, 130, 142, 145, 172
Prueitt, M. 143

qualisign 82–83, 130, 160–61
quantum computation 230, 384
quantum physics 98, 207, 230–32, 388, 410, 413, 424, 426, 429
Qubit 230–32

Radford, A. 150
Rahbar, M. 150
Rahm, P. 149
Rainaldi, Carlo 41, 52, 52, 53, 179, 422
Rajchman, J. 83
Recurring Neural Networks (RNN) 118, 119
reference 1, 235; anthropomorphic 2; dimensional 193, 218; normative 32, 64; representational 130; Z-axis 248
Renaissance 3, 5, 15, 17; as Baroque 30, *40,* 54, 300; Eurocentric 24; perspective 21–23, 25–27, 300
representation: authorship 418, 419–20; Baroque systems of 25; deep structure 23, 177; digital 418, 419–20; displacing systems of 64–65; downsampling 120; histories and theories of 3–5; information theory 236; mapping 401; organizational 208; reference 130; system of 43, 88–9
rhizome 9, 75–78, 179, 433
Riegl, Alois 62, 166
robotic fabrication 3, 148, 233, 236–37, 274, 286, 296, 300–01, 310–17, 431; cable-driven robotic construction system 328–35, *329–34;* post-human project-specific and site-specific robotic system 326–27
robotics 16–18, 149–50, 176, 323, *324,* 327, 331, 424, 434–35
Roche, F. 149
Rogers, Richard 66
Rohe, Mies van der 4, 80, 82, 193
Rosenblatt, Frank 105
Rossi, A. 399
Rowe, C. 31, 64, 80

Samuelson, P. 417
Sangallo, G. da 42
Sassen, Saskia 11
Saunders, A. 42
Saussure, F. de 68, 71, 74, 76, 77, 80
Schopenhauer, A. 72
Schumacher, P. 147, 148
Schumpeter, J.A. 8
script 96, 196–97
sedimentation: deposition 237, *241, 341, 346, 349,* 350, 355, *357,* 355, *385;* and erosion 346; particle *241,* 350, *358,* 359; sand, clay and silt 340
self replication 6, 101–02, 131, 252–53, 424, 425, 435

semantic segmentation: AI 45; feature recognition 162, *289, 394*; GAN *289*; mapping *289*; ML *49*, 52, *55, 57, 59*

Serlio, S. 31, 74

Serra, Richard 81

Shannon, C.E. 6, 87, 89, 97–98, 105–7, 171, 173, 256, 426

Shape Grammar 35, 145–47, 428

Shklovsky, V. 63

sign: architecture of information 252–53, *254–55*, 256; BIT 110; computational visual 421–24; construction systems and digital fabrication 235–36; Deleuze's 70; Derrida's 70, 74; De Saussure's 71; expanding dimensions between "drawing" and "building" 236–38; geometry and information feedback in material actualization 244–52, *245–47, 249–51*; HCI *151*, 154; information processing and materialization 240, *241–43*; Leibniz's 75; materialization as reference, signs becoming signifiers 238–40; media and technological determinism 235–36; Peirce's 78; sub-symbolic 167, 172, 423, 431

signal: computational visual 421–24; electrical 96, 172, 231; electronic 6, 88, 90–92, 96–97, 110, 151, 171–73, 175, 200, 208, 237, 277, 344, 423, 431–34; mathematical 1 89–92, 109, 141, 150, 154–57, 167, 167–68, 170–73, 193, 237, 289, 422–23, 429–31, 433; visual *253*, 323

signified 71, 73–77, 129, 158, 239, 398, 428

signifiers: computational visual semiotics 150–57, 187–88; Deleuze's rhizome against regime of signs 75–78; Derrida's *Différance* 74–75; diagram as linguistic qualisign 82–83; digital (*see* digital signifiers); Gandelsonas' "The Architectural Signifier" 80–82; linguistic semiotics 71–74; materials as 239; media determinism and symbolic form as origin and author 78–80; non-linguistic semiotics and representation 78; pixel 164; point cloud *156*, 157; semiotics as representation 69–71; visual semiotics 78–80

simulation: AI 298; Big Data 8, 40–43; CFD 127, 129, *147*, 147–49, 157, 213, *213, 229, 237, 323*, 324, 325–26,

325–27, 335, *339, 346*, 352–53, 353, *356, 358–61*, 402, *402*, 405; correlational 298; point cloud *47, 48, 49, 52, 53, 55, 58, 59, 60, 150, 355*; Shape Memory Polymer *313*

simulation-based information actualization: 4D printing 300–301; form follows media 304–7; nonlinear recursive robotic fabrication framework 291–99; real space, forced space, sensorial space, virtual augmented space 303–4; robotic interactive space 301–3; synthetic space-environments 281–91

Sladek, E. 42

Smithson, Robert 5, 81

Snyder, Betty 152

software: AI 105–106; bias of 8; in BIM 147; face recognition 17; interfaces 172, 175–6; open-source 149; RealityCapture *49–51, 54–55, 59, 61, 393, 412*; tools 6; visual 8

Somol, R. 82

space environments 210, 220, 223, 225, 226, 232–33, 253, *254, 255*, 310, 310, *324*, 332, 336, 350, 355, 359, 363, *365*, 382, 382, 396, 413; architecture of 344, 346; Big Data 352–65; environments 343–44, 392, 394, 413, 427; index 42; multidimensional 343–44, 392, 413, 429; virtual 27–29

Space Syntax 143

statistics 12, 102, 110, 112–14, 125, 126, 131, 158, 160, 229, 372, 392, 410, 418, 422

Stiegler, B. 11

Stiny, G. 145

structuralism 72, 112, 187, 238

structure (architecture) 72, 75, 260

style 236, 332; artistic 160; historical 64; and politics 165–6; visual 82

style transfer: AI 160–1; developing 158; GAN 160, 165, *271, 283*; issues 160

subsymbolic 133, 157, 289, 318, 429; downsampling 167, 173, 423, 431; photogrammetry 157, *185*; sign 167, 172, 423, 431

Sugihara, S. 150

surface: ground 5, 65–66, *139*, 147, 355; minimal *200*, 244, *246, 249, 280, 306, 311–12*; printed *311, 318*; topology 4, 171, 207–8, 214, *217*, 218, 220, *221*, 225, *246, 305–06*, 308, 430

472　*Index*

symbol: computation, computational design 100, 121, 124–25, 129, 146, 158, 168, 171, 173; deep structure 176, *347, 398*; language 99

Tafuri, M. 68, 81, 397, 398
technological determinism 4, 147, 148, 235–36, 276, 328, 433
Teyssot, G. 76
Thomson, D'Arcy 14, 15
3D printing 274; of CA *307*; environmental conditions of space 252; fabrication CAM 239, *247*; FDM in 239, *311, 312, 314, 325*; high-resolution injection 149; laser-cured resin *242*; post-structuralism of 237; with robotic arm 248; Shape Memory Polymer simulation *331*
3D scanning 157, *393*; Big Data 154; LiDAR *28*, 42–3, *48, 54*, 154, 274, 419; photogrammetry 17, *265, 266*, 274, *330, 384, 394, 411, 412*; point cloud of Sagrada Familia building *265*, 281, 289, *297*
Tintoretto 27
topography 4–5, 66, 82, *144*, 207–208, 248, 277, 337, 353, 364, 371–72, 381, 382, 421
topo-logos 5, 66, 193, 218, 277–78
topology 187; AI *273*; critical model 30–39, 41–66; critical space 26; data mapping 15; diagram 45; surface 4, *201*; value system 116
Tschumi, Bernard 147
Turing, A.M. 97–8
type 10, 14, 16, 98, 103, 390
typology 4, 20, 23, 27–29, 42, 149, 188, 190–98, 232–36, 353, 355, 389

Ulman, Stanislaw 101
urbanism: architecture and 5–6, 16, 18, 107, 142–43, 156, 344, 367, 382, 392, 429; developmentalism 5; of

information 337, 370, 392, 403–9; landscape 342; public social 362

Valenti, M.G. 27
vanishing point (VP) 21–26, 78, *203*, 220
vector 17, 114, 119, 172, 191, 193, 210, 288, 359
Velázquez, D. 25–27
Venturi, R. 41
Vidler, A. 31, 32, 207
Virilio, P. 340
Virtual Private Network (VPN) 11
Virtual Reality (VR) 322, *323–24*
visual algorithm *180, 283*
Voss, Richard 142
voxel 146, 154–55, 160, 167, 172, 239, *249, 297, 289*, 305, *306*, 307

Wallenstein, S.O. 12
Warren, M.C. 105
water 158, 237, 277, 340, 342, 344, 346, 350, 363, 363, 421
web scraping *394*, 402, *409, 411*
Weiner, R. 104, 104, 163
Weinstock, M. 149
Weinzapfel, G. 142
Weisman L.K. 16
Whiting, S. 86
Wigley, M. 81
wind 21, *132*, 359, 361, *361*, 372–73, *379*, 381
Wirth, N. 108
Wittgenstein, L. 73, 89
Wittkower, R. 31–34, 40, 42, 52, 64, 80, 81
Wölfflin, H. 20, 30, 45, 54
Wolfram, S. 103, 104, 115, 127, 129, 328
Wright, Frank Lloyd 396

Yu-Chi 150

Žižek, S. 338, 399, 416
Zuliani, G. 15, 31